CCNP™ Cisco® Certified Network Professional Test Yourself Practice Exams

CCNP™ Cisco® Certified Network Professional Test Yourself Practice Exams

Syngress Media, Inc.

Osborne McGraw-Hill

Berkeley New York St. Louis San Francisco Auckland Bogotá Hamburg London Madrid Mexico City
Milan Montreal New Delhi Panama City Paris São Paulo Singapore Sydney Tokyo Toronto

Osborne McGraw-Hill
2600 Tenth Street
Berkeley, California 94710
U.S.A.

For information on translations or book distributors outside the U.S.A., or to arrange bulk purchase discounts for sales promotions, premiums, or fund-raisers, please contact Osborne/**McGraw-Hill** at the above address.

CCNP Cisco Certified Network Professional Test Yourself Practice Exams

1234567890 DOC DOC 019876543210

ISBN 0-07-212109-2

Publisher
Brandon A. Nordin

Associate Publisher and Editor-in-Chief
Scott Rogers

Acquisitions Editor
Gareth Hancock

Editorial Management
Syngress Media, Inc.

Project Editor
Jennifer Wenzel

Editorial Assistant
Tara Davis

Series Editor
Mark Buchmann

Technical Editor
Richard Hornbaker

Copy Editor
Nancy Faughnan

Proofreader
Rhonda Holmes

Computer Designers
Jani Beckwith
Dick Schwartz
Gary Corrigan

Illustrators
Brian Wells
Beth Young
Robert Hansen

Series Design
Roberta Steele

Cover Design
Regan Honda

This book was published with Corel VENTURA.

From Global Knowledge

At Global Knowledge we strive to support the multiplicity of learning styles required by our students to achieve success as technical professionals. In this series of books, it is our intention to offer the reader a valuable tool for successful completion of the CCNP Certification Exams.

As the world's largest IT training company, Global Knowledge is uniquely positioned to offer these books. The expertise gained each year from providing instructor-led training to hundreds of thousands of students worldwide has been captured in book form to enhance your learning experience. We hope that the quality of these books demonstrates our commitment to your lifelong learning success. Whether you choose to learn through the written word, computer-based training, Web delivery, or instructor-led training, Global Knowledge is committed to providing you the very best in each of those categories. For those of you who know Global Knowledge, or those of you who have just found us for the first time, our goal is to be your lifelong competency partner.

Thank you for the opportunity to serve you. We look forward to serving your needs again in the future.

Warmest regards,

Duncan Anderson
President and Chief Executive Officer, Global Knowledge

The Global Knowledge Advantage

Global Knowledge has a global delivery system for its products and services. The company has 28 subsidiaries, and offers its programs through a total of 60+ locations. No other vendor can provide consistent services across a geographic area this large. Global Knowledge is the largest independent information technology education provider, offering programs on a variety of platforms. This enables our multi-platform and multi-national customers to obtain all of their programs from a single vendor. The company has developed the unique CompetusTM Framework software tool and methodology which can quickly reconfigure courseware to the proficiency level of a student on an interactive basis. Combined with self-paced and on-line programs, this technology can reduce the time required for training by prescribing content in only the deficient skills areas. The company has fully automated every aspect of the education process, from registration and follow-up, to "just-in-time" production of courseware. Global Knowledge, through its Enterprise Services Consultancy, can customize programs and products to suit the needs of an individual customer.

Global Knowledge Classroom Education Programs

The backbone of our delivery options is classroom-based education. Our modern, well-equipped facilities staffed with the finest instructors offer programs in a wide variety of information technology topics, many of which lead to professional certifications.

Custom Learning Solutions

This delivery option has been created for companies and governments that value customized learning solutions. For them, our consultancy-based approach of developing targeted education solutions is most effective at helping them meet specific objectives.

Self-Paced and Multimedia Products

This delivery option offers self-paced program titles in interactive CD-ROM, videotape and audio tape programs. In addition, we offer custom development of interactive multimedia courseware to customers and partners. Call us at 1 (888) 427-4228.

Electronic Delivery of Training

Our network-based training service delivers efficient competency-based, interactive training via the World Wide Web and organizational intranets. This leading-edge delivery option provides a custom learning path and "just-in-time" training for maximum convenience to students.

ARG

American Research Group (ARG), a wholly-owned subsidiary of Global Knowledge, one of the largest worldwide training partners of Cisco Systems, offers a wide range of internetworking, LAN/WAN, Bay Networks, FORE Systems, IBM, and UNIX courses. ARG offers hands on network training in both instructor-led classes and self-paced PC-based training.

Global Knowledge Courses Available

Network Fundamentals

- Understanding Computer Networks
- Telecommunications Fundamentals I
- Telecommunications Fundamentals II
- Understanding Networking Fundamentals
- Implementing Computer Telephony Integration
- Introduction to Voice Over IP
- Introduction to Wide Area Networking
- Cabling Voice and Data Networks
- Introduction to LAN/WAN protocols
- Virtual Private Networks
- ATM Essentials

Network Security & Management

- Troubleshooting TCP/IP Networks
- Network Management
- Network Troubleshooting
- IP Address Management
- Network Security Administration
- Web Security
- Implementing UNIX Security
- Managing Cisco Network Security
- Windows NT 4.0 Security

IT Professional Skills

- Project Management for IT Professionals
- Advanced Project Management for IT Professionals
- Survival Skills for the New IT Manager
- Making IT Teams Work

LAN/WAN Internetworking

- Frame Relay Internetworking
- Implementing T1/T3 Services
- Understanding Digital Subscriber Line (xDSL)
- Internetworking with Routers and Switches
- Advanced Routing and Switching
- Multi-Layer Switching and Wire-Speed Routing
- Internetworking with TCP/IP
- ATM Internetworking
- OSPF Design and Configuration
- Border Gateway Protocol (BGP) Configuration

Authorized Vendor Training

Cisco Systems

- Introduction to Cisco Router Configuration
- Advanced Cisco Router Configuration
- Installation and Maintenance of Cisco Routers
- Cisco Internetwork Troubleshooting
- Cisco Internetwork Design
- Cisco Routers and LAN Switches
- Catalyst 5000 Series Configuration
- Cisco LAN Switch Configuration
- Managing Cisco Switched Internetworks
- Configuring, Monitoring, and Troubleshooting Dial-Up Services
- Cisco AS5200 Installation and Configuration
- Cisco Campus ATM Solutions

Bay Networks

- Bay Networks Accelerated Router Configuration
- Bay Networks Advanced IP Routing
- Bay Networks Hub Connectivity
- Bay Networks Accelar 1xxx Installation and Basic Configuration
- Bay Networks Centillion Switching

FORE Systems

- FORE ATM Enterprise Core Products
- FORE ATM Enterprise Edge Products
- FORE ATM Theory
- FORE LAN Certification

Operating Systems & Programming

Microsoft

- Introduction to Windows NT
- Microsoft Networking Essentials
- Windows NT 4.0 Workstation
- Windows NT 4.0 Server
- Advanced Windows NT 4.0 Server
- Windows NT Networking with TCP/IP
- Introduction to Microsoft Web Tools
- Windows NT Troubleshooting
- Windows Registry Configuration

UNIX

- UNIX Level I
- UNIX Level II
- Essentials of UNIX and NT Integration

Programming

- Introduction to JavaScript
- Java Programming
- PERL Programming
- Advanced PERL with CGI for the Web

Web Site Management & Development

- Building a Web Site
- Web Site Management and Performance
- Web Development Fundamentals

High Speed Networking

- Essentials of Wide Area Networking
- Integrating ISDN
- Fiber Optic Network Design
- Fiber Optic Network Installation
- Migrating to High Performance Ethernet

DIGITAL UNIX

- UNIX Utilities and Commands
- DIGITAL UNIX v4.0 System Administration
- DIGITAL UNIX v4.0 (TCP/IP) Network Management
- AdvFS, LSM, and RAID Configuration and Management
- DIGITAL UNIX TruCluster Software Configuration and Management
- UNIX Shell Programming Featuring Kornshell
- DIGITAL UNIX v4.0 Security Management
- DIGITAL UNIX v4.0 Performance Management
- DIGITAL UNIX v4.0 Intervals Overview

DIGITAL OpenVMS

- OpenVMS Skills for Users
- OpenVMS System and Network Node Management I
- OpenVMS System and Network Node Management II
- OpenVMS System and Network Node Management III
- OpenVMS System and Network Node Operations
- OpenVMS for Programmers
- OpenVMS System Troubleshooting for Systems Managers
- Configuring and Managing Complex VMScluster Systems
- Utilizing OpenVMS Features from C
- OpenVMS Performance Management
- Managing DEC TCP/IP Services for OpenVMS
- Programming in C

Hardware Courses

- AlphaServer 1000/1000A Installation, Configuration and Maintenance
- AlphaServer 2100 Server Maintenance
- AlphaServer 4100, Troubleshooting Techniques and Problem Solving

About Syngress Media

Syngress Media creates books and software for Information Technology professionals seeking skill enhancement and career advancement. Its products are designed to comply with vendor and industry standard course curricula, and are optimized for certification exam preparation. You can contact Syngress via the Web at www.syngress.com.

About the Contributors

Alex Goldstein (CCDA, CCNA, ACRC, CLSC) is a technical analyst at Sprint Paranet. Alex has over 13 years in the information industry with the last four years being dedicated to infrastructure. Alex has chosen to further his career by focusing on achieving the coveted CCIE certification.

Martin Walshaw is a network consultant based in South Africa. He holds several certifications including CCNA,CCDA,CCNP,CCDP, and NNCSS (Routers, Switches & Network Management). He specializes in Cisco product design and installations, and over the last few years has been involved in several large Cisco implementations. During his 12 years plus experience, he has dabbled with many aspects of the computer industry, from PC sales to programming. Martin would like to thank his wife Val, and his son Joshua for all those nights when he should have been at home, but wasn't. Without their support and understanding, this project and many others would not be possible.

Chuck Gibson (CCSI, CCNA) is a senior partner and co-founder of ICM, Inc., a network training company in Redmond, WA. He has over 20 years of experience in network consulting, design, implementation, and training. He has developed and taught a full range of courses involving both network hardware and software at the high-end technical level. These include classes on LANS, WANs, and MANs, including Ethernet, Token Ring, OSI, TCP/IP, Novell SPX/IPX, SNA/VTAM, Advanced Voice and

Data, X.25, ATM, Frame Relay and related protocols, Executive Management Overviews, hands-on labs, and more. He has led network training seminars in Canada, China, India, and Europe. In addition, he is the author of several articles on telecommunications and teleprocessing.

Robert Shields (CCNA, CCDA) is the Director of Architecture Services for Network Architecture Implementation & Support, L.L.C. (NAIS), a network consulting corporation offering services throughout all phases of a data network's lifetime. Mr. Shields' internetworking experience includes enterprise WAN design and implementation of large-scale multiprotocol networks. Mr. Shields is a Cisco Certified Network Associate, a Cisco Certified Design Associate, and has passed the CCIE written exam with his lab scheduled for the fall of 1999. Mr. Shields has a Bachelor of Science degree in Electrical Engineering from George Mason University, Fairfax, VA.

David Wolsefer (CCNA, MCSE) is an Internetworking Engineer with Dimension Enterprises. His experience includes system migration, Web design and implementation, and software, hardware, and quality assurance acceptance testing. He has also executed projects involving WAN security and penetration methods. Mr. Wolsefer is a Cisco Certified Network Associate and a Microsoft Certified Systems Engineer. In addition, he holds a bachelor's degree in Engineering Sciences from the University of Florida.

Dana Lee is an Associate Network Consultant with Infonetic. Dana's most recent consulting project was the integration of two large Cisco networks as part of the merger of two large financial institutions. Dana has seven years experience as a Cisco router expert, working with the entire Cisco product line—from the access servers to familiarization training on the new GSR-12000s. Dana's interests include OSPF optimizations, troubleshooting BGP peering issues, ISDN access configuration, and network security implementation. Prior to working at Infonetic, Dana worked as a Senior Network Engineer with a global ISP, after receiving a MS EE from MIT. Just for fun, Dana likes to hack the Linux kernel and collect airline emergency exit instruction cards.

Series Editor

Mark Buchmann (CCIE #3556, CCSI #95062) is a Cisco Certified Internetworking Expert and has been a Certified Cisco Systems Instructor since 1995. He is the owner of MAB Enterprises, Inc., a company providing consulting, network support, training, and various other services. Mark is also a co-owner of www.CertaNet.com, a company providing online certification assistance for a variety of network career paths including all the various Cisco certifications. In his free time he enjoys spending time with his family and boating. He currently lives in Raleigh, North Carolina. Mark is Series Editor for Syngress Cisco books.

Technical Reviewer

Richard D. Hornbaker (CCIE #3355, CNX, MCSE, MCNE) is a consultant with the Forté Consulting Group, based in Phoenix, Arizona. He specializes in large-scale routing and switching projects for Fortune 500 companies. Recent projects include a 12,000-node campus network using a combination of routing, switching, and ATM. Richard is currently designing the network for a major corporate merger.

Richard has more than 10 years of internetworking experience and holds several certifications. His skills are diverse, ranging from operating systems and software to telephony systems and data networks. Protocol analysis and troubleshooting are among his strong suits.

ACKNOWLEDGMENTS

We would like to thank the following people:

- Richard Kristof of Global Knowledge for championing the series and providing us access to some great people and information.

- To all the incredibly hard-working folks at Osborne/McGraw-Hill: Brandon Nordin, Scott Rogers, and Gareth Hancock for their help in launching a great series and being solid team players. In addition, Tara Davis, Jennifer Wenzel, and Carolyn Welch for their help in fine-tuning the book.

CONTENTS AT A GLANCE

CONTENTS

Part I
ACRC Objectives (Exam 640-403)

Part 2
CIT 4.0 (Exam 640-440)

Part 3
CLSC (Exam 640-404)

Part 4
BCRAN (Exam 640-505)

Part 5
Test Yourself: ACRC Practice Exams (Exam 640-403)

Part 6
Test Yourself: CIT Practice Exams (Exam 640-406)

We built this book for a specific reason. Every time we asked Cisco certified technicians and CCNP candidates what they wanted in their study materials, they answered "More questions!" Based on that request, we built a book full of over 750 new questions on the CCNP exams so you can test yourself to your heart's content. Osborne's *CCNP Cisco Certified Network Professional Test Yourself Practice Exams* covers concepts that are necessary for the CCNP designation. This book is not sponsored or endorsed by Cisco.

In this book, you'll find coverage of three CCNP exams: Advanced Cisco Router Configuration (ACRC), Cisco Internetwork Troubleshooting 4.0 (CIT), and Cisco LAN Switch Configuration (CLSC). Also featured is full coverage of Cisco's Building Cisco Remote Access Networks (BCRAN) curriculum. As of this writing the final BCRAN exam is under development, but we cover Cisco's BCRAN course objectives so you'll be prepared when the exam goes live!

In This Book

This book is organized in parts or modules, around the topics covered within the Cisco exam administered at Sylvan Testing Centers. We cover each of the exams in a separate section and we also have a separate "Test Yourself" module. Cisco has specific objectives for the CCNP exams: we've followed their list carefully, so you can be assured you're not missing anything.

The Q & A Modules

You will find a Q & A module for each of the four exams—ACRC, CIT, CLSC and BCRAN. Each module has original questions, followed by an answer section that has full explanations of both the correct and incorrect choices.

Each module is divided into categories, so you will cover every topic tested by Cisco. Each topic is a heading within the chapter, so you can study by topic if you like. Should you find you need further review on any particular topic, you will find that the topic headings correspond to the chapters of Osborne/McGraw-Hill's CCNP Study Guides. Want to simulate an actual exam? The section "The Test Yourself Modules" explains how.

In addition, throughout the Q & A modules, we have sprinkled helpful notes in the form of Exam Watches and Q & A scenarios:

exam
ⓦatch

- **Exam Watch** notes call attention to information about, and potential pitfalls in, the exam. These helpful hints are written by authors who have taken the exams and received their certification—who better to tell you what to worry about? They know what you're about to go through!

- **Q & A** sections lay out problems and solutions in a quick-read format:

QUESTIONS AND ANSWERS

My network consists of various discontigous subnets...	Use EIGRP, disable auto summarization, and manually summarize when possible on the appropriate outbound interfaces.
Most of my remote sites have dual serial lines, but for financial considerations, the link speeds are not always identical...	Use the VARIANCE command in either IGPR or EIGRP to allow for unequal load balancing, but do not exceed a variance value of 2.

The Test Yourself Modules

If you have had your fill of exam questions, answers, and explanations, the time has come to test your knowledge. Or maybe, you want to start with a practice exam in the Test Yourself module to see where your strengths and weaknesses are, and then review only certain topics. Either way, turn to Parts 5 through 8 of the book, the Test yourself Practice Exams. In this section we actually simulate the exams. We have given you two practice test per exam, with the number of questions corresponding to the actual exam.

Lock yourself in your office or clear the kitchen table, set a timer, and jump in.

The Global Knowledge Web Site

Check out the Web site. Global Knowledge invites you to become an active member of the Access Global Web site. This site is an online mall and an information repository that you'll find invaluable. You can access many types of products to assist you in your preparation for the exams, and you'll be able to participate in forums, on-line discussions, and threaded discussions. No other book brings you unlimited access to such a resource. You'll find more information about this site in Appendix A.

How to Take a Cisco Certification Examination

by Richard D. Hornbaker (CCIE #3355, CNX, MCSE, MCNE), Forté Consulting Group

This chapter covers the importance of your CCNP certification and prepares you for taking the actual examination. It gives you a few pointers on methods of preparing for the exam, including how to study register, what to expect, and what to do on exam day.

Catch the Wave!

Congratulations on your pursuit of Cisco certification! In this fast-paced world of networking, few certifications compare to the value of Cisco's program.

The networking industry has virtually exploded in recent years, accelerated by non-stop innovation and the Internet's popularity. Cisco has stayed at the forefront of this tidal wave, maintaining a dominant role in the industry.

Since the networking industry is highly competitive, and evolving technology only increases in its complexity, the rapid growth of the networking industry has created a vacuum of qualified people. There simply aren't enough skilled networking people to meet the demand. Even the most experienced professionals must keep current with the latest technology in order to provide the skills that the industry demands. That's where Cisco certification programs can help networking professionals succeed as they pursue their careers.

Cisco started its certification program many years ago, offering only the designation of Cisco Certified Internetwork Expert, or CCIE. Through the CCIE program, Cisco provided a means to meet the growing demand for experts in the field of networking. However, the CCIE tests are brutal, with a failure rate over 80 percent. (Fewer than five percent of candidates pass on their first attempt.) As you might imagine, very few people ever attain CCIE status.

In early 1998, Cisco recognized the need for intermediate certifications, and several new programs were created. Four intermediate certifications were added: CCNA (Cisco Certified Network Associate), CCNP (Cisco Certified Network Professional), CCDA (Cisco Certified Design Associate), and CCDP (Cisco Certified Design Professional). Two specialties were also created for the CCIE program: WAN Switching and ISP Dial-up.

I would encourage you to take beta tests when they are available. Not only are the beta exams less than the cost of the final exams (some are even free!), but also, if you pass the beta, you will receive credit for passing the exam. If you don't pass the beta, you will have seen every question in the pool of available questions, and can use this information when preparing to take the exam for the second time. Remember to jot down important information immediately after the exam, if you didn't pass. You will have to do this after leaving the exam area, since materials written during the exam are retained by the testing center. This information can be helpful when you need to determine which areas of the exam were most challenging for you as you study for the subsequent test.

Why Vendor Certification?

Over the years, vendors have created their own certification programs because of industry demand. This demand arises when the marketplace needs skilled professionals and an easy way to identify them. Vendors benefit because it promotes people skilled in their product. Professionals benefit because it boosts their career. Employers benefit because it helps them identify qualified people.

In the networking industry, technology changes too often and too quickly to rely on traditional means of certification, such as universities and trade associations. Because of the investment and effort required to keep network certification programs current, vendors are the only organizations suited to keep pace with the changes. In general, such vendor certification programs are excellent, with most of them requiring a solid foundation in the essentials, as well as their particular product line.

Corporate America has come to appreciate these vendor certification programs and the value they provide. Employers recognize that certifications, like university degrees, do not guarantee a level of knowledge, experience or performance; rather, they establish a baseline for comparison. By seeking to hire vendor-certified employees, a company can assure itself that, not only has it found a person skilled in networking, but it has also hired a person skilled in the specific products the company uses.

Technical professionals have also begun to realize the value of certification and the impact it can have on their careers. By completing a certification program, professionals gain an endorsement of their skills from a major industry source. This endorsement can boost their current position, and it makes finding the next job even easier. Often, a certification determines whether a first interview is even granted.

Today, a certification may place you ahead of the pack. Tomorrow, it will be a necessity to keep from being left in the dust.

Signing up for an exam has become more effortless with the new Web-based test registration system. To sign up for any of CCNP exams, access http://www.2test.com, and register for the Cisco Career Certification path. You will need to get an Internet account and password, if you do not already have one for 2test.com. Just select the option for first time registration, and the Web site will walk you through that process. The registration wizard even provides maps to the testing centers, something that is not available when calling Sylvan Prometric on the telephone.

Cisco's Certification Program

As previously mentioned, Cisco now has six certifications for the Routing and Switching career track, and four certifications for the WAN Switching career track. While Cisco recommends a series of courses for each of these certifications, they are not required. Ultimately, certification is dependent upon a candidate passing a series of exams. With the right experience and study materials, each of these exams can be passed without taking the associated class. Table i-1 shows the various Cisco certifications and tracks.

TABLE i-1   Cisco Certifications

Track	Certification	Acronym
Routing and Switching: Network Support	Cisco Certified Network Associate	CCNA
Routing and Switching: Network Support	Cisco Certified Network Professional	CCNP
Routing and Switching: Network Support	Cisco Certified Internetwork Expert (Routing and Switching)	CCIE-R/S
Routing and Switching: Network Support	Cisco Certified Internetwork Expert (ISP Dial Technology)	CCIE-ISP Dial
Routing and Switching: Network Design	Cisco Certified Design Associate	CCDA
Routing and Switching: Network Design	Cisco Certified Design Professional	CCDP
WAN Switching: Network Support	Cisco Certified Network Associate—WAN switching	CCNA-WAN Switching
WAN Switching: Network Support	Cisco Certified Network Professional—WAN switching	CCNP-WAN Switching
WAN Switching: Network Support	Cisco Certified Internetwork Expert—WAN Switching	CCIE-WAN Switching
WAN Switching: Network Design	Cisco Certified Design Professional—WAN Switching	CCDP-WAN Switching

Figure i-1 shows Cisco's Routing and Switching track, with both the Network Design and Network Support paths. The CCNA is the foundation of the Routing and Switching track, after which candidates can pursue either the Network Design path to CCDA and CCDP, or the Network Support path to CCNP and CCIE.

In addition to finding the technical objectives that are being tested for each exam, you will find much more useful information on Cisco's Web site at http://www.cisco.com/warp/public/10/wwtraining/certprog. You will find information on becoming certified, exam-specific information, sample test questions, and the latest news on Cisco certification. This is the most important site you will find on your journey to becoming Cisco certified.

FIGURE i-1

Figure Cisco's Routing and Switching certification track

Network Support

ISP Dial Technology — CCIE
Cisco Certified Internetwork Expert

Network Support

Routing & Switching — CCIE
Cisco Certified Internetwork Expert

Network Design

CCDP
Cisco Certified Design Professional

CCDA
Cisco Certified Design Associate

CCNP
Cisco Certified Network Professional

CCNA
Cisco Certified Network Associate

Table i-2 shows a matrix of the exams required for each Cisco certification. Note that candidates have the choice of taking either the single Foundation R/S exam, or the set of three ACRC, CLSC, and CMTD exams—all four exams are not required.

You may hear veterans refer to this CCIE R/S Qualifying Exam as the "Cisco Drake test." This is a carryover from the early days, when Sylvan Prometric's name was Drake Testing Centers and Cisco only had the one exam.

| TABLE i-2 | Examinations Required for Cisco Certifications |

Exam Name	Exam #	CCNA	CCDA	CCNP	CCDP	CCIE
CCNA 1.0	640-407	x	x	X	x	
CDS 1.0	9E0-004		x		x	
Foundation Routing and Switching	640-409			X	x	
ACRC	640-403			X	x	
BCRAN	640-505					
CLSC	640-404			X	x	
CMTD	640-405			x	x	
CIT 4.0	640-440			x		
CID	640-025				x	
CCIE R/S Qualifying						x
CCIE Lab						x

When I find myself stumped answering multiple-choice questions, I use my scratch paper to write down the two or three answers I consider the strongest, and then underlining the answer I feel is most likely correct. Here is an example of what my scratch paper looks like when I've gone through the test once:

21. B or C
33. A or C

This is extremely helpful when you mark the question and continue on. You can then return to the question and immediately pick up your thought process where you left off. Use this technique to avoid having to re-read and re-think questions.

You will also need to use your scratch paper during complex, text-based scenario questions to create visual images to better understand the question. For example, during the CCNP exam you will need to draw multiple networks and the connections between them. By drawing the layout while you are interpreting the answer, you may find a hint that you would not have found without your own visual aid. This technique is especially helpful if you are a visual learner.

Computer-Based Testing

In a perfect world, you would be assessed for your true knowledge of a subject, not simply how you respond to a series of test questions. But life isn't perfect, and it just isn't practical to evaluate everyone's knowledge on a one-to-one basis. (Cisco actually does have a one-to-one evaluation, but it's reserved for the CCIE Laboratory exam, and the waiting list is quite long.)

For the majority of its certifications, Cisco evaluates candidates using a computer-based testing service operated by Sylvan Prometric. This service is quite popular in the industry, and it is used for a number of vendor certification programs, including Novell's CNE and Microsoft's MCSE. Thanks to Sylvan Prometric's large number of facilities, exams can be administered worldwide, generally in the same town as a prospective candidate.

For the most part, Sylvan Prometric exams work similarly from vendor to vendor. However, there is an important fact to know about Cisco's exams: they use the traditional Sylvan Prometric test format, not the newer adaptive format. This gives the candidate an advantage, since the traditional format allows answers to be reviewed and revised during the test. (The adaptive format does not.)

Many experienced test takers do not go back and change answers unless they have a good reason to do so. Only change an answer when you feel you may have misread or misinterpreted the question the first time. Nervousness may make you second-guess every answer and talk yourself out of a correct one.

To discourage simple memorization, Cisco exams present a different set of questions every time the exam is administered. In the development of the exam, hundreds of questions are compiled and refined using beta testers. From this large collection, a random sampling is drawn for each test.

Each Cisco exam has a specific number of questions and test duration. Testing time is typically generous, and the time remaining is always displayed in the corner of the testing screen, along with the number of remaining questions. If time expires during an exam, the test terminates, and incomplete answers are counted as incorrect.

I have found it extremely helpful to put a check next to each objective as I find it is satisfied by the proposed solution. If the proposed solution does not satisfy an objective, you do not need to continue with the rest of the objectives. Once you have determined which objectives are fulfilled you can count your check marks and answer the question appropriately. This is a very effective testing technique!

At the end of the exam, your test is immediately graded, and the results are displayed on the screen. Scores for each subject area are also provided, but the system will not indicate which specific questions were missed. A report is automatically printed at the proctor's desk for your files. The test score is electronically transmitted back to Cisco.

In the end, this computer-based system of evaluation is reasonably fair. You might feel that one or two questions were poorly worded; this can certainly happen, but you shouldn't worry too much. Ultimately, it's all factored into the required passing score.

Question Types

Cisco exams pose questions in a variety of formats, most of which are discussed here. As candidates progress toward the more advanced certifications, the difficulty of the exams is intensified, both through the subject matter as well as the question formats.

In order to pass these challenging exams, you may want to talk with other test takers to determine what is being tested, and what to expect in terms of difficulty. The most helpful way to communicate with other CCNP hopefuls is the Cisco mailing list. With this mailing list, you will receive e-mail every day from other members discussing everything imaginable concerning Cisco networking equipment and certification. Access http://www.cisco.com/warp/public/84/1.html to learn how to subscribe to this wealth of information.

True/False

The classic true/false question format is not used in the Cisco exams, for the obvious reason that a simple guess has a 50 percent chance of being correct. Instead, true/false questions are posed in multiple-choice format, requiring the candidate to identify the true or false statement from a group of selections.

Multiple Choice

Multiple choice is the primary format for questions in Cisco exams. These questions may be posed in a variety of ways.

"SELECT THE CORRECT ANSWER."   This is the classic multiple-choice question, where the candidate selects a single answer from a list of about four choices. In addition to the question's wording, the choices are presented in a Windows "radio button" format, where only one answer can be selected at a time.

"SELECT THE 3 CORRECT ANSWERS."   The multiple-answer version is similar to the single-choice version, but multiple answers must be provided. This is an "all-or-nothing" format; all the correct answers must be selected, or the entire question is incorrect. In this format, the question specifies exactly how many answers must be selected. Choices are presented in a check box format, allowing more than one answer to be selected. In addition, the testing software prevents too many answers from being selected.

"SELECT ALL THAT APPLY."   The open-ended version is the most difficult multiple-choice format, since the candidate does not know how many answers should be selected. As with the multiple-answer version, all the correct answers must be selected to gain credit for the question. If too many answers are selected, no credit is given. This format presents choices in check box format, but the testing software does not advise the candidates whether they've selected the correct number of answers.

Make it easy on yourself and find some "braindumps." These are notes about the exam from test takers, which indicate the most difficult concepts tested, what to look out for, and sometimes even what not to bother studying. Several of these can be found at http://www.dejanews.com. Simply do a search for CCNP and browse the recent postings. Another good resource is at http://www.groupstudy.com.

Freeform Response

Freeform responses are prevalent in Cisco's advanced exams, particularly where the subject focuses on router configuration and commands. In the freeform format, no choices are provided. Instead, the test prompts for user input and the candidate must type the correct answer. This format is similar to an essay question, except the response must be very specific, allowing the computer to evaluate the answer.

For example, the question
Type the command for viewing routes learned via the EIGRP protocol.
requires the answer

```
show ip route eigrp
```

For safety's sake, you should completely spell out router commands, rather than using abbreviations. In the above example, the abbreviated command SH IP ROU EI works on a real router, but might be counted wrong by the testing software. The freeform response questions are almost always commands used in the Cisco IOS.

Fill in the Blank

Fill-in-the-blank questions are less common in Cisco exams. They may be presented in multiple-choice or freeform response format.

Exhibits

Exhibits accompany many exam questions, usually showing a network diagram or a router configuration. These exhibits are displayed in a separate window, which is opened by clicking the Exhibit button at the bottom of the screen. In some cases, the testing center may provide exhibits in printed format at the start of the exam.

Scenarios

While the normal line of questioning tests a candidate's "book knowledge," scenarios add a level of complexity. Rather than just ask technical questions, they apply the candidate's knowledge to real-world situations.

Scenarios generally consist of one or two paragraphs and an exhibit that describe a company's needs or network configuration. This description is followed by a series of questions and problems that challenge the candidate's ability to address the situation. Scenario-based questions are commonly found in exams relating to network design, but they appear to some degree in each of the Cisco exams.

You will know you are coming up on a series of scenario questions, because they are preceded with a blue screen, indicating that the following questions will have the same scenario, but different solutions. You must remember the scenario will be the same during the series of questions, which means you do not have to spend time reading the scenario again.

Study Techniques

First and foremost, give yourself plenty of time to study. Networking is a complex field, and you can't expect to cram what you need to know into a single study session. It is a field best learned over time, by studying a subject and then applying your knowledge. Build yourself a study schedule and stick to it, but be reasonable about the pressure you put on yourself, especially if you're studying in addition to your regular duties at work..

One easy technique to use in studying for certification exams is the 15-minutes per day effort. Simply study for a minimum of 15 minutes every day. It is a small, but significant commitment. If you have a day where you just can't focus, then give up at 15 minutes. If you have a day where it flows completely for you, study longer. As long as you have more of the "flow days," your chances of succeeding are extremely high.

Second, practice and experiment. In networking, you need more than knowledge; you need understanding, too. You can't just memorize facts to be effective; you need to understand why events happen, how things work, and (most importantly) how they break.

The best way to gain deep understanding is to take your book knowledge to the lab. Try it out. Make it work. Change it a little. Break it. Fix it. Snoop around "under the hood." If you have access to a network analyzer, like Network Associate's Sniffer, put it to use. You can gain amazing insight to the inner workings of a network by watching devices communicate with each other.

Unless you have a very understanding boss, don't experiment with router commands on a production router. A seemingly innocuous command can have a nasty side effect. If you don't have a lab, your local Cisco office or Cisco users group may be able to help. Many training centers also allow students access to their lab equipment during off-hours.

Another excellent way to study is through case studies. Case studies are articles or interactive discussions that offer real-world examples of how technology is applied to meet a need. These examples can serve to cement your understanding of a technique or technology by seeing it put to use. Interactive discussions offer added value because you can also pose questions of your own. User groups are an excellent source of examples, since the purpose of these groups is to share information and learn from each other's experiences.

And not to be missed is the Cisco Networkers conference. Although renowned for its wild party and crazy antics, this conference offers a wealth of information. Held every year in cities around the world, it includes three days of technical seminars and presentations on a variety of subjects. As you might imagine, it's very popular. You have to register early to get the classes you want.

Then, of course, there is the Cisco Web site. This little gem is loaded with collections of technical documents and white papers. As you progress to more advanced subjects, you will find great value in the large number of examples and reference materials available. But be warned: You need to do a lot of digging to find the really good stuff. Often, your only option is to browse every document returned by the search engine to find exactly the one you need. This effort pays off. Most CCIEs I know have compiled six to ten binders of reference material from Cisco's site alone.

Scheduling Your Exam

The Cisco exams are scheduled by calling Sylvan Prometric directly at (800) 204-3926. For locations outside the United States, your local number can be found on Sylvan's Web site at http://www.prometric.com. Sylvan representatives can schedule your exam, but they don't have information about the certification programs. Questions about certifications should be directed to Cisco's training department.

The aforementioned Sylvan telephone number is specific to Cisco exams, and it goes directly to the Cisco representatives inside Sylvan. These representatives are familiar enough with the exams to find them by name, but it's best if you have the specific exam number handy when you call. After all, you wouldn't want to be scheduled and charged for the wrong exam (for example, the instructor's version, which is significantly harder).

Exams can be scheduled up to a year in advance, although it's really not necessary. Generally, scheduling a week or two ahead is sufficient to reserve the day and time you prefer. When scheduling, operators will search for testing centers in your area. For convenience, they can also tell which testing centers you've used before.

Sylvan accepts a variety of payment methods, with credit cards being the most convenient. When paying by credit card, you can even take tests the same day you call—provided, of course, that the testing center has room. (Quick scheduling can be handy, especially if you want to re-take an exam immediately.) Sylvan will mail you a receipt and confirmation of your testing date, although this generally arrives after the test has been taken. If you need to cancel or reschedule an exam, remember to call at least one day before your exam, or you'll lose your test fee.

When registering for the exam, you will be asked for your ID number. This number is used to track your exam results back to Cisco. It's important that you use the same ID number each time you register, so that Cisco can follow your progress. Address information provided when you first register is also used by Cisco to ship certificates and other related material. In the United States, your Social Security Number is commonly used as your ID number. However, Sylvan can assign you a unique ID number if you prefer not to use your Social Security Number.

Table i-3 shows the available Cisco exams and the number of questions and duration of each. This information is subject to change as Cisco revises the exams, so it's a good idea to verify the details when registering for an exam.

In addition to the regular Sylvan Prometric testing sites, Cisco also offers facilities for taking exams free of charge at each Networkers conference in the USA. As you might imagine, this option is quite popular, so reserve your exam time as soon as you arrive at the conference.

| TABLE i-3 | Cisco Exam Lengths and Question Counts |

Exam Title	Exam Number	Number of Questions	Duration (minutes)	Exam Fee (US$)
Cisco Design Specialist (CDS)	9E0-004	80	180	$100
Cisco Internetwork Design (CID)	640-025	100	120	$100
Advanced Cisco Router Configuration (ACRC)	640-403	72	90	$100
Building Cisco Remote Access Networks (BCRAN)	640-505			
Cisco LAN Switch Configuration (CLSC)	640-404	70	60	$100

TABLE i-3	Cisco Exam Lengths and Question Counts *(continued)*			
Exam Title	**Exam Number**	**Number of Questions**	**Duration (minutes)**	**Exam Fee (US$)**
Configuring, Monitoring, and Troubleshooting Dialup Services (CMTD)	640-405	64	90	$100
Cisco Internetwork Troubleshooting 4.0 (CIT)	640-440	77	105	$100
Cisco Certified Network Associate (CCNA)	640-407	70	90	$100
Foundation Routing & Switching	640-409	132	165	$100
CCIE Routing & Switching Qualification	350-001	100	120	$200
CCIE Certification Laboratory	N/A	N/A	2 days	$1000

Arriving at the Exam

As with any test, you'll be tempted to cram the night before. Resist that temptation. You should know the material by this point, and if you're too groggy in the morning, you won't remember what you studied anyway. Instead, get a good night's sleep.

Arrive early for your exam; it gives you time to relax and review key facts. Take the opportunity to review your notes. If you get burned out on studying, you can usually start your exam a few minutes early. On the other hand, I don't recommend arriving late. Your test could be cancelled, or you may not be left with enough time to complete the exam.

When you arrive at the testing center, you'll need to sign in with the exam administrator. In order to sign in, you need to provide two forms of identification. Acceptable forms include government-issued IDs (for example, passport or driver's license), credit cards, and company ID badge. One form of ID must include a photograph.

Aside from a brain full of facts, you don't need to bring anything else to the exam. In fact, your brain is about all you're allowed to take into the exam. All the tests are "closed book", meaning you don't get to bring any reference materials with you. You're also not allowed to take any notes out of the exam room. The test administrator will provide you with paper and a pencil. Some testing centers may provide a small marker board instead.

Calculators are not allowed, so be prepared to do any necessary math (such as hex-binary-decimal conversions or subnet masks) in your head or on paper. Additional paper is available if you need it.

Leave your pager and telephone in the car, or turn them off. They only add stress to the situation, since they are not allowed in the exam room, and can sometimes still be heard if they ring outside of the room. Purses, books, and other materials must be left with the administrator before entering the exam. While in the exam room, it's important that you don't disturb other candidates; talking is not allowed during the exam.

Once in the testing room, the exam administrator logs onto your exam, and you have to verify that your ID number and the exam number are correct. If this is the first time you've taken a Cisco test, you can select a brief tutorial for the exam software. Before the test begins, you will be provided with facts about the exam, including the duration, the number of questions, and the score required for passing. Then the clock starts ticking and the fun begins.

The testing software is Windows-based, but you won't have access to the main desktop or any of the accessories. The exam is presented in full screen, with a single question per screen. Navigation buttons allow you to move forward and backward between questions. In the upper-right corner of the screen, counters show the number of questions and time remaining. Most importantly, there is a 'Mark' checkbox in the upper-left corner of the screen—this will prove to be a critical tool in your testing technique.

Test-Taking Techniques

One of the most frequent excuses I hear for failing a Cisco exam is "poor time management." Without a plan of attack, candidates are overwhelmed by the exam or become sidetracked and run out of time. For the most part, if you are comfortable with the material, the allotted time is more than enough to complete the exam. The trick is to keep the time from slipping away during any one particular problem.

The obvious goal of an exam is to answer the questions effectively, although other aspects of the exam can distract from this goal. After taking a fair number of computer-based exams, I've naturally developed a technique for tackling the problem, which I share with you here. Of course, you still need to learn the material. These steps just help you take the exam more efficiently.

Size Up the Challenge

First, take a quick pass through all the questions in the exam. "Cherry-pick" the easy questions, answering them on the spot. Briefly read each question, noticing the type of question and the subject. As a guideline, try to spend less than 25 percent of your testing time in this pass.

This step lets you assess the scope and complexity of the exam, and it helps you determine how to pace your time. It also gives you an idea of where to find potential answers to some of the questions. Often, the answer to one question is shown in the exhibit of another. Sometimes the wording of one question might lend clues or jog your thoughts for another question.

Imagine that the following questions are posed in this order:

Question 1: "Review the router configurations and network diagram in exhibit XYZ (not shown here). Which devices should be able to ping each other?"

Question 2: "If RIP routing were added to exhibit XYZ, which devices would be able to ping each other?"

The first question seems straightforward. Exhibit XYZ probably includes a diagram and a couple of router configurations. Everything looks normal, so you decide that all devices can ping each other.

Now, consider the hint left by the Question 2. When you answered Question 1, did you notice that the configurations were missing the routing protocol? Oops! Being alert to such clues can help you catch your own mistakes.

If you're not entirely confident with your answer to a question, answer it anyway, but check the Mark box to flag it for later review. In the event that you run out of time, at least you've provided a "first guess" answer, rather than leaving it blank.

Take on the Scenario Questions

Second, go back through the entire test, using the insight you gained from the first go-through. For example, if the entire test looks difficult, you'll know better than to spend more than a minute or so on each question. Break down the pacing into small milestones; for example, "I need to answer 10 questions every 15 minutes."

At this stage, it's probably a good idea to skip past the time-consuming questions, marking them for the next pass. Try to finish this phase before you're 50 – 60 percent through the testing time.

By now, you probably have a good idea where the scenario questions are found. A single scenario tends to have several questions associated with it, but they aren't necessarily grouped together in the exam. Rather than re-reading the scenario every time you encounter a related question, save some time and answer the questions as a group.

Tackle the Complex Problems

Third, go back through all the questions you marked for review, using the Review Marked button in the question review screen. This step includes taking a second look at all the questions you were unsure of in previous passes, as well as tackling the time-consuming ones you deferred until now. Chisel away at this group of questions until you've answered them all.

If you're more comfortable with a previously marked question, unmark it now. Otherwise, leave it marked. Work your way through the time-consuming questions now, especially those requiring manual calculations. Unmark them when you're satisfied with the answer.

By the end of this step, you've answered every question in the test, despite having reservations about some of your answers. If you run out of time in the next step, at least you won't lose points for lack of an answer. You're in great shape if you still have 10 – 20 percent of your time remaining.

Review Your Answers

Now you're cruising! You've answered all the questions, and you're ready to do a quality check. Take yet another pass (yes, one more) through the entire test, briefly re-reading each question and your answer. Be cautious about revising answers at this point unless you're sure a change is warranted. If there's a doubt about changing the answer, I always trust my first instinct and leave the original answer intact.

Rarely are "trick" questions asked, so don't read too much into the questions. Again, if the wording of the question confuses you, leave the answer intact. Your first impression was probably right.

Be alert for last-minute clues. You're pretty familiar with nearly every question at this point, and you may find a few clues that you missed before.

The Grand Finale

When you're confident with all your answers, finish the exam by submitting it for grading. After what will seem like the longest 10 seconds in of your life, the testing software will respond with your score. This is usually displayed as a bar graph, showing the minimum passing score, your score, and a PASS/FAIL indicator.

If you're curious, you can review the statistics of your score at this time. Answers to specific questions are not presented; rather, questions are lumped into categories, and results are tallied for each category. This detail is also printed on a report that has been automatically printed at the exam administrator's desk.

As you leave the exam, you'll need to leave your scratch paper behind or return it to the administrator. (Some testing centers track the number of sheets you've been given, so be sure to return them all.) In exchange, you'll receive a copy of the test report.

This report will be embossed with the testing center's seal, and you should keep it in a safe place. Normally, the results are automatically transmitted to Cisco, but occasionally you might need the paper report to prove that you passed the exam. Your personnel file is probably a good place to keep this report; the file tends to follow you everywhere, and it doesn't hurt to have favorable exam results turn up during a performance review.

Re-Testing

If you don't pass the exam, don't be discouraged—networking is complex stuff. Try to have a good attitude about the experience, and get ready to try again. Consider yourself a little more educated. You know the format of the test a little better, and the report shows which areas you need to strengthen.

If you bounce back quickly, you'll probably remember several of the questions you might have missed. This will help you focus your study efforts in the right area. Serious go-getters will re-schedule the exam for a couple days after the previous attempt, while the study material is still fresh in their mind.

Ultimately, remember that Cisco certifications are valuable because they're hard to get. After all, if anyone could get one, what value would it have? In the end, it takes a good attitude and a lot of studying, but you can do it!

Part I

ACRC Objectives (Exam 640-403)

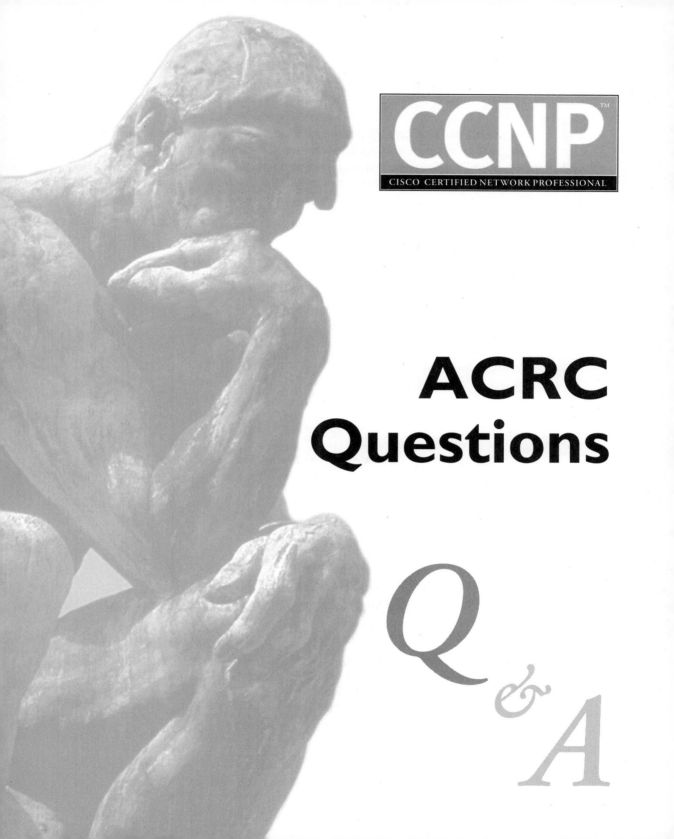

ACRC
Questions

Q & A

T his section is designed to help you prepare for the Advanced Cisco Router Configuration exam so you can begin to reap the career benefits of CCNP certification. The following questions are structured in a format similar to what you'll find on the ACRC exam. Read all the choices carefully, as there may be more than one correct answer. Choose all correct answers for each question.

Scaleable Internetworks

1. What is the default switching type for all Access and distribution-layer router types manufactured by Cisco?

   A. Process switching
   B. Fast switching
   C. Optimum switching
   D. Distributed switching

2. What are the two types of load balancing?

   A. Per packet and per destination
   B. Symmetrical and asymmetrical
   C. NO IP ROUTE-CACHE and IP ROUTE-CACHE
   D. Per packet and per interface

QUESTIONS AND ANSWERS

Just how many routers can an internetwork scale to?	Cisco claims that, using good design principles, over 10,000 is possible.
How many routers can be connected together in series? What is the maximum recommended?	Using the three-tiered topology model, more than six routers in series will never be required.
Do I always need all three layers for a good network design?	No. One- and two-layer designs are fine for smaller networks, but as your network grows, so can the number of layers.
How do I reduce convergence time in my routers?	First, choose a fast-converging protocol like EIGRP or OSPF. Next, tune the components that make up convergence time. They include Keepalive timers, Hello timers, SPF timers, and Update timers.
Are there different choices for tunnel encapsulation?	Yes, but GRE is the most commonly used.
What kind of serial interfaces can use DDR?	Any serial interface (synchronous or asynchronous) that has a dial-up modem attached. ISDN interfaces also require DDR configuration.
When should I not use any form of high-speed switching?	Sometimes high-speed switching can cause packet drops on an interface's output queue. This is usually only a problem with low-speed serial interfaces. Turning all switching off will slow down packets from entering the output queue of an interface.
Is there really a performance difference using fast switching techniques?	Absolutely—a difference of tens of thousands of PPS, or even hundreds of thousands of PPS.

3. What is the exchange of route information between routing protocols called?

   A. Redistribution
   B. Network-address translation
   C. Route summarization
   D. Distributed switching

There are two kinds of load balancing: packet by packet, and per destination. Remember that load balancing is defaulted to On for IP routing.

4. On what type of interface is compression typically configured?

    A. High-speed serial interfaces
    B. Slow-speed serial interface
    C. Ethernet interfaces
    D. ATM interfaces

Redistribution is a configurable feature that translates one routing protocol into another.

DDR is an acronym for dial-on-demand routing, Cisco's configuration command set that allows for ISDN and other dial-up services.

5. Which tools can be used on a Cisco router to define routing policies at the distribution layer of a hierarchical network model?

    A. Standard and extended access lists
    B. Routing protocols and redistribution
    C. Encryption and Network Address Translation
    D. All the above

Weighted fair queuing (WFQ) is the default for slow-speed serial interfaces. WFQ separates transaction-oriented packets from other application types and puts these packets in a high-priority output queue.

exam
Ⓦatch   *Make sure you know the basic difference between process, fast, optimum, and distributed switching. Remember that fast switching is usually the default for all router interfaces. The exception is 7500 series router interfaces, which default to optimum.*

exam
Ⓦatch   *Remember the basic rule of access lists: one access list per protocol, per direction (inbound/outbound), per interface. Also know the difference between standard and extended access lists.*

exam
Ⓦatch   *PPP is commonly used on dial-up links because it is an open standard that all vendors support. Moreover, it has many negotiable features such as authentication, IP addresses, compression, and encryption.*

IP Traffic Management

1. Which of the following is false in regard to access lists?

   A. Follow top-down processing
   B. Defined access lists cannot be applied to more than one interface
   C. Can be applied to interfaces as either incoming or outgoing
   D. Once a match is found, no further processing of the access list is performed

exam
Ⓦatch   *IP standard and extended access lists in Cisco routers use the wildcard mask to specify one IP address or a range of addresses. The wildcard mask is exactly the opposite of the subnet mask, and is attained by subtracting the subnet mask from all 255s.*

2. Helper-address interface configuration commands are used for what purpose?

A. To help forward specific UDP broadcast traffic to an appropriate destination address

B. To help forward all broadcast traffic to an appropriate destination address

C. To help forward specific UDP broadcast traffic as a UDP broadcast address

D. To help forward all UDP broadcasts to all interfaces

---

exam
Ⓦatch

The access list by itself, whether standard or extended, does nothing. Only when you apply it to an interface does it have meaning. The interface is also where you decide if the list is incoming or outgoing.

---

exam
Ⓦatch

With IP extended access lists, you must always specify both a source and destination IP address and wildcard mask. The source wildcard mask is optional (default 0.0.0.0) only with IP standard access lists.

---

3. Which Cisco IOS command allows a user to view the contents of only access list 110?

A. SHOW ACCESS-L 110

B. SHOW ACCESS-LIST

C. SHOW ACCESS-GROUP 110

D. None of the above

---

exam
Ⓦatch

Although it is possible to filter entire routing protocols with IP extended access lists, you have greater filtering control with IP standard access lists within distribution filters.

QUESTIONS AND ANSWERS

I configured an access list in my router, but now nobody can get anywhere...	You probably did not create any specific PERMIT lines within the access list. By default, the access list denies everything.
I created an access list to deny Telnet from one subnet and permit everything else, but nothing is being blocked...	Take a look at whether the access list is applied as an incoming or outgoing list. If pointed in the wrong direction, it will have no effect.
I configured an access list to permit only the applications that I need, but after a few minutes of use, I could not get anywhere in my network...	You probably forgot to include a PERMIT statement for the routing protocol in your network.
While I was configuring an access list at a remote site, my Telnet session locked up and eventually dropped...	You apparently applied an access list on the interface you used to reach the remote router. Try to Telnet to a different interface. You might have to use the console of the remote router to correct the problem.
I tried to deny a particular network from the routing protocol we are using, but it seems that every network is being blocked...	Access lists only block entire packets. Distribution filters (which use access lists) allow you to selectively remove items from packets (such as particular routes from a routing update).
Our security policy individually lists machines that are permitted and denied through our network. But this creates a monster-size access list...	Use the wildcard mask to cover broad ranges of IP addresses instead of listing them one by one.
We implemented our security policy to the letter, but now our administrators and network management platforms do not seem to work...	Sometimes a network security policy considers only the operation of the network and forgets about the maintenance. You must determine the appropriate modifications to the access lists to allow for such maintenance packets.

exam
ⓦatch   *Although you can filter on both a source and destination port, the source port is often a random number, and thus an unreliable value to compare against.*

Novell IPX/SPX Traffic Management

1. What is the full name for SAP (which has protocol characteristics that are similar to RIP-IPX except that it advertises services instead of routes)?

    A. Service access point

    B. Service advertising protocol

    C. Server adjacency protocol

    D. Server access protocol

Refer to the Following Illustration for Questions 2–5

If a specification is not listed for a router, assume it is the default.

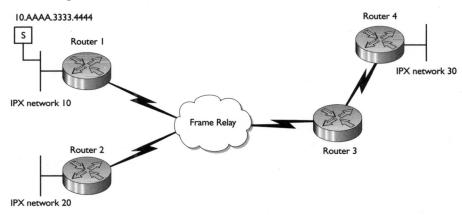

2. Which interface configuration command will apply the following extended access list as a generic filter to the serial interface on Router 1?

```
access-list access-list-number {deny | permit}
protocol [source-network][[[.source-node]
source-node-mask] | [.source-node
source-network-mask.source-node-mask]] [source-socket]
[destination-network][[[.destination-node]
destination-node-mask] | [.destination-node
destination-network-mask.destination-nodemask]]
[destination-socket] [log]
```

A. IPX ACCESS-LIST 901 IN
B. IPX ACCESS-GROUP 901 IN
C. IPX ACCESS-LIST 801 IN
D. IPX ACCESS-GROUP 901

---

e x a m
 ⓦa t c h   *As you study IPX access lists, be sure to focus on all the ways the lists can be applied, and which lists can be used for each purpose. Be prepared to type the commands into a text box from memory.*

---

3. Router 1's Ethernet segment has several IPX servers; however, services to be offered to remote sites must come from the server IPX address, 10.AAAA.3333.4444. Which of the following commands would appropriately filter other services from being advertised by Router 1? The interface configuration is being performed on the serial interface.

A. ROUTER_1(config)# ACCESS-LIST 1001 PERMIT
    10.AAAA.3333.4444
    ROUTER_1(config-if)# IPX OUTPUT-SAP-FILTER 1001
B. ROUTER_1(config)# ACCESS-LIST 1001 DENY -1
    ROUTER_1(config-if)# IPX OUTPUT-SAP-FILTER 1001
C. ROUTER_1(config)# ACCESS-LIST 1001 PERMIT
    10.AAAA.3333.4444
    ROUTER_1(config-if)# IPX OUTPUT-SAP-FILTER 1011
D. ROUTER_1(config)# ACCESS-LIST 1001 PERMIT
    10.AAAA.3333.4444
    ROUTER_1(config-if)# IPX INPUT-SAP-FILTER 1001

QUESTIONS AND ANSWERS

How can I filter several networks that all begin with the same numbers, with only one access list statement?	You need to use a network mask with the IPX extended access list. The mask is available for host bits in both standard and extended IPX access lists, but extends into the network number bits only with the IPX extended access list.
I had defined packet filters, route filters, and SAP filters to limit traffic within my IPX network, but when I migrated from RIP to NLSP they all stopped working. What happened?	NLSP is a link-state routing protocol, and all the routers within an area need to share the same information; therefore, no filters are allowed within NLSP areas. You need to define NLSP areas with the area boundaries located where you want the filtering to take place, then filter on the area boundaries.
I built an access list to filter SAP entries for the Novell servers on network number 1234ABCD, but the entries still appear in the router's SAP table.	All services for Novell servers have the server's internal IPX network number as their address. Be sure to use this number, not the physical network number the server is on, in your SAP filter statement. If in doubt, consult the output of SHOW IPX SERVERS on your router for the correct network numbers to use in SAP filtering.
I am using NLSP as my IPX routing protocol, but I want to be sure no RIP routing updates go over my low-bandwidth WAN links.	Use the IPXWAN protocol for WAN links. When the link comes up, the IPXWAN protocol will negotiate a routing protocol to use on the link, and NLSP will be chosen by default.

4. If Routers 1, 2, and 3, connected via the Frame Relay network, are only supporting IP, what configuration technique can be used to provide connectivity among the IPX networks?

   A. Redistribution

   B. Protocol translation

   C. IP tunneling

   D. All of the above

5. If the WAN circuit between Router 3 and 4 is slow, which technique can be used to conserve bandwidth?

A. Adjust SAP timers

B. Filter unnecessary services being advertised by SAP

C. Use NLSP or EIGRP routing protocols over the link

D. All of the above

---

e x a m
ⓦa t c h   *Don't neglect the verification commands in your studying! These are considered very important. Be sure you know exactly what information is available from the output of each of the commands, and don't be surprised if you're asked to type the correct command in a text box on the exam!*

AppleTalk Traffic Management

1. Which of the following does NOT describe Phase II or AppleTalk extended-network topologies?

A. Segments can contain a range of network numbers

B. Zones may span multiple extended networks

C. Nodes belong to one zone

D. Segments can contain multiple, noncontiguous networks

Refer to the Following Illustration for Questions 2–4

If a specification is not listed for a router, assume it is the default.

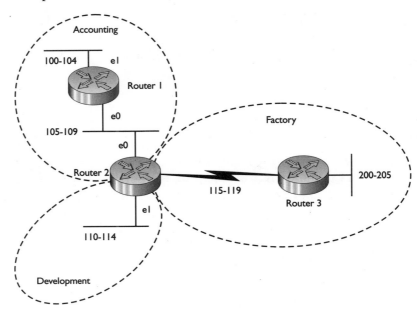

2. What type of AppleTalk network implementation does the illustration demonstrate?

   A. Phase I

   B. Non-extended network

   C. Phase II

   D. None of the above

exam
ⓦatch   *Extended networks can contain multiple contiguous network numbers and zones can span multiple extended networks.*

3. It has been decided that Appletalk networks within the Factory and Development zones will not require communication with network 100–104. Which of the following commands, once applied to Router 2, will configure an access list to filter this network?

A. ACCESS-LIST 610 DENY CABLE-RANGE 100-104

B. ACCESS-LIST 610 DENY NETWORK 100-104
ACCESS-LIST 610 PERMIT OTHER-ACCESS

C. ACCESS-LIST 610 DENY NETWORK 100-104

D. ACCESS-LIST 610 DENY CABLE-RANGE 100-104

E. ACCESS-LIST 610 PERMIT OTHER-ACCESS

---

exam
ⓦatch   *RTMP updates are sent every 10 seconds. They contain full routing table updates.*

---

4. If you have already filtered as many networks and zones as possible over the WAN link, what type of filter will allow you to further filter selected components within a network?

A. NCP

B. Zone

C. NBP

D. RTMP

---

exam
ⓦatch   *If you forget the PERMIT OTHER ACCESS statement at the end of your NBP filter, you will probably end up blocking more traffic than you anticipated.*

QUESTIONS AND ANSWERS

I need to block AppleTalk routing updates between whole regions of my network...	RTMP filters are the easiest way to block network updates between regions, since they restrict the advertisement or acceptance of network route updates.
What do I do if I am losing zone information for zones that extend across multiple networks?	Make sure that your routers have the global command APPLETALK PERMIT-PARTIAL-ZONES if you want to see zones with some of their networks denied.
I am getting inconsistent zone lists on my client Macintoshes when I use GZL filters...	If you have more than one router on your network, make sure the same GZL filter is applied to each of them.
How do I know which AppleTalk filters I have applied to my interfaces?	The command SHOW APPLETALK INTERFACE shows almost everything you want to know about how AppleTalk is configured on your router's interfaces.
I want to set up filters, but I want to be very selective about which items on my network I filter. What kind of filter should I use?	The NBP filter is the most selective type of filter available. Use it to hide single devices or types of devices.
What is a ZIP storm, and how do I avoid this situation?	A ZIP storm is a network "traffic jam" caused by the propagation of AppleTalk routes whose zone can't be determined. The rule to remember is to never filter out the only zone on a network.

Configuring Queuing

1. The following describes a queuing technique: Allows for four queue types, high, medium, normal, and low, for which specific data protocols can be directed. Packets in the high queue will be sent first until the queue is exhausted, then the medium queue will be permitted to transmit and so forth down to the low queue, permitting that higher-prioritized queues do not accumulate packets during this time. After a packet has been transmitted out of a queue other than the high queue, the higher-prioritized

queues will be checked to see if any packets have accumulated. If so, the higher queue will be allowed to transmit. What is this queuing technique called?

A. WFQ

B. FIFO

C. Priority queuing

D. Custom

---

exam
ⓦatch *Weighted fair queuing is the default queuing service configured on serial interfaces that have less than two Mbps of bandwidth.*

---

2. Which global configuration command is used to set the priority within priority queuing on inbound traffic through an interface to a specific queue type?

A. PRIORITY-LIST DEFAULT

B. PRIORITY-LIST PROTOCOL

C. PRIORITY-LIST INTERFACE

D. PRIORITY-GROUP LIST

---

exam
ⓦatch *When priority queuing is implemented, and the first packet has been transmitted from the normal queue, the high queue will be checked again before the normal queue is allowed to send another packet.*

---

3. Which custom queuing command will set the byte count to 1000 for queue number 3 and queue number 7?

A. QUEUE-LIST 7 QUEUE 3 BYTE 1000

B. QUEUE-LIST 3 QUEUE 7 BYTE-COUNT 1000

C. QUEUE-LIST 7 QUEUE 3 BYTE-COUNT 1000

D. QUEUE-GROUP 3 QUEUE 7 BYTE-COUNT 1000

QUESTIONS AND ANSWERS

What is the default queuing method for interfaces above the E3/T3 level?	FIFO
What is the default queuing method for interfaces below the E3/T3 level?	WFQ
I have an X.25 link. What kind of queuing can I use?	Priority queuing
I need to prioritize video transmissions over the network. What kind of queuing should I use?	Priority queuing should be used for any traffic needing prioritization.

exam
ⓦatch

When custom queuing is implemented, the default byte count is 1500 bytes.

Routing Protocols

1. Hierarchical network designs enable what capability that can greatly reduce the number of routes that each router has to maintain within an Internetwork?

   A. Route filtering
   B. Border routers
   C. Network-address translation
   D. Route summarization

exam
ⓦatch

Distance vector protocols use the Bellman-Ford algorithm to calculate the best route paths. Link-state protocols use the SPF algorithm to calculate the best route paths.

exam
ⓦatch   *The metric used by link-state algorithms is a numerical value*
called cost. Cost is based on bandwidth, which is a relative indication
of line speed.

2. What concept was created to allow subnetting of previously subnetted
   networks in order to better allocate IPv4 network addressing?

   A. VLAN
   B. VLSM
   C. CIDR
   D. NAT

exam
ⓦatch   *A router running a link-state algorithm uses a hello packet to*
establish a formal connection with each directly connected
neighbor.

exam
ⓦatch   *When a router using a link-state algorithm learns about a change*
in the network topology, it updates its link-state table and then sends
an LSU containing information only about the change.

3. What OSPF occurrence determines that a neighbor is down?

   A. Hello packets have not been received within 40 seconds
   B. The dead interval has expired
   C. The port has gone down on the neighboring router
   D. It has been notified by a link-state update packet

Interior Gateway Routing Protocol (IGRP) Configuration

Refer to the Following Illustration in Answering Questions 1–2

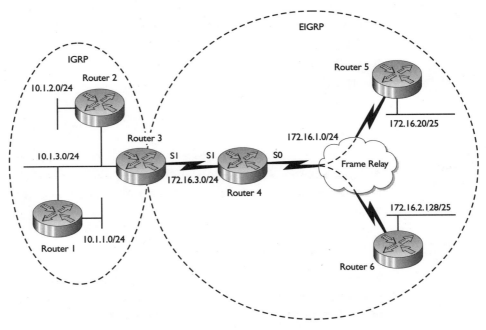

1. What would be the correct configuration for EIGRP on Router 3 if it should automatically redistribute with the IGRP routing domain?

   A. ROUTER EIGRP 5
      NETWORK 172.16.0.0
   B. ROUTER EIGRP
      NETWORK 172.16.1.0

C. ROUTER EIGRP 5
      NETWORK 172.16.1.0
D. ROUTER EIGRP 10
      NETWORK 172.16.0.0

---

e x a m
  Ⓦa t c h   *Remember that although EIGRP can handle discontiguous subnets, it must be configured manually, because by default, EIGRP summarizes subnets at the classful network boundary when the update crosses another network.*

---

2. Although automatic redistribution is being used in this example between the IGRP and EIGRP routing domains, what additional commands are necessary on Router 4 to ensure that all EIGRP routes will be redistributed within IGRP?

A. INTERFACE SERIAL0
      IP HOLD-TIME EIGRP 5 300
B. ROUTER EIGRP 10
      PASSIVE-INTERFACE SERIAL1
C. ROUTER EIGRP 5
      REDISTRIBUTE IGRP 5
D. INTERFACE SERIAL1
      IP SUMMARY-ADDRESS EIGRP 5 172.16.2.0 255.255.255.0

---

e x a m
  Ⓦa t c h   *Although both IGRP and EIGRP can use five different metrics to calculate the best path to any network, only bandwidth and delay are enabled by default.*

QUESTIONS AND ANSWERS

My network consists of various discontigous subnets...	Use EIGRP, disable auto summarization, and manually summarize when possible on the appropriate outbound interfaces.
Most of my remote sites have dual serial lines, but for financial considerations, the link speeds are not always identical...	Use the VARIANCE command in either IGRP or EIGRP to allow for unequal load balancing, but do not exceed a variance value of 2.
I need to migrate my network from IGRP to a routing protocol that supports VLSM, yet is simple to configure and administer...	Select EIGRP, and use the same AS that you have configured for IGRP. During the migration, IGRP routes are automatically redistributed into EIGRP.
I am building a small, Cisco-based network, and desire a simple DVRP for IP...	IGRP is an obvious selection over RIP, due to the much faster convergence time. However, EIGRP is the best choice, since it is a classless protocol and allows for VLSM.
My client has both IP and AppleTalk running in their network and they complain of occasional network slowdowns and routing loops...	Change from the current routing protocols for IP and AppleTalk to EIGRP. Although you must configure a separate process for each (since there are distinct routing tables), both IP and AppleTalk will benefit from the better path selection and phenomenal convergence time.
A network consultant that we hired said that we should set the bandwidth to be equal on the dual serial links that we have between sites so that EIGRP can load-balance, even though we have dissimilar link speeds on the lines...	A better solution is to enable unequal load balancing. By setting the bandwidth to be equal, the router will attempt equal load balancing. Since the links are not the same, unequal load balancing will perform load balancing based on the ratio of the metrics of the interfaces involved.
We just merged two separate IGRP networks together, and each uses a unique AS number, but routing updates are not travelling between the two...	Since there are unique AS numbers involved, routing updates will not travel between them. You must either perform route redistribution from one AS to the other (and vise-versa), or configure static routes from each AS to reach the other.

ACRC
QUESTIONS

exam
Ⓦatch   *IGRP automatically disables split-horizon on multipoint serial*
interfaces. This allows for complete network connectivity in a
partially meshed network. EIGRP does not behave this way.

3. What is the administrative distance assigned to an EIGRP summary route?

A. 20

B. 5

C. 90

D. 100

exam
Ⓦatch   *IGRP and EIGRP are the only routing protocols that allow for load*
balancing across unequal paths. However, this is not an automatic
feature of either protocol.

OSPF Configuration

I. Which OSPF router configuration command would accurately enable
OSPF on interfaces that contained IP addresses within the range
172.16.64.1–172.16.79.254 and assign them to area 5?

A. AREA 5 RANGE 172.16.64.0 255.255.240.0

B. NETWORK 172.16.64.0 0.0.15.255 AREA 5

C. AREA 5 NETWORK 172.16.64.0 255.255.240.0

D. NETWORK 172.16.64.0 0.0.240.255 AREA 5

exam
Ⓦatch   *Be sure you understand the roles of the DR and BDR and how they*
get elected. Remember that there is no DR or BDR on a
point-to-point link.

Refer to the Following Illustration in Answering Questions 2–3

If a specification is not listed for a router, assume it is the default.

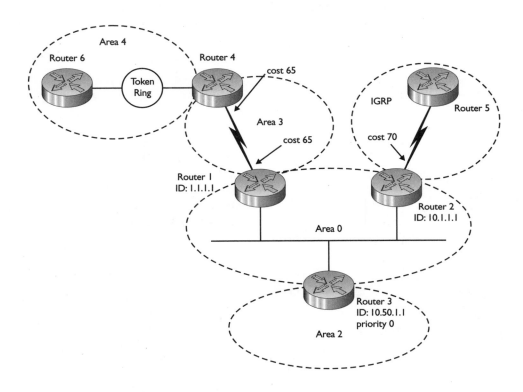

2. What additional router configuration would be necessary to ensure that hosts on Router 4's Token Ring segment will have full connectivity to all other nodes on the network, without propagating default routes?

A. Configure Area 4 as a stubby area

B. Configure a virtual-link between Router 2 and Router 4

C. Configure Area 4 as a totally stubby area

D. Configure a virtual link between Router 1 and Router 4

QUESTIONS AND ANSWERS

I've configured OSPF on my network, but my routers aren't passing any routing information. What could be wrong?	Check your OSPF neighbor table. If you don't see any neighbors, or you don't see the ones you are expecting, verify that your routers are configured for the same IP subnets on that link, and that their hello/dead intervals, authentication, and area identifiers are the same.
We are merging two companies' networks, and cannot configure the two backbone areas with a direct physical link between them. How can we merge the networks without causing a major disruption of service?	A virtual link can connect two backbone areas together.
Our network has more than 200 routers, and calculation of the SPF algorithm takes up significant CPU cycles in our routers when links go down.	Redesign your network to take advantage of OSPF areas. This will enable you to hide the topology of the individual areas from the rest of the network, and only the routers within the area will have to recalculate the SPF algorithm.
Many of the routers at remote branch offices in my network are older and don't have as much processing power and memory as it takes to run OSPF with a full routing table. I still want to run OSPF throughout my network.	Use the summarization and stub area features of OSPF to reduce the memory and processing requirements for internal routers.
I cannot get routes redistributed from my IGRP network to my OSPF network.	Be sure you are running both routing processes on the ASBR. If routes in your IGRP network are subnetted, be sure to use the SUBNETS keyword in the REDISTRIBUTE command.

exam
Ⓦatch   *A good rule for any certification exam is: whenever there's information that lends itself to presentation in a table, there's bound to be important test information in there! Know the LSA types and the routers that source them, and what they describe.*

It is very important that you be able to use the inverse mask in the NETWORK statement to place interfaces in the correct areas. Be certain that you can look at an OSPF configuration and recognize the effect of each NETWORK statement if you are given a list of interfaces and their IP addresses.

3. Within OSPF terminology, what is another name for the area that connects Routers 1, 2, and 3?

   A. Backbone area
   B. Core area
   C. Distribution area
   D. None of the above

Be sure you understand the binary behind summarization. This is a really important topic, not only for the ACRC exam but for the CCIE exam as well. Go through the previous examples and make up some of your own. Work through them bit by bit, and make sure you understand the powers of two. It's the only way to become fluent.

Don't ignore the SHOW commands! Cisco accords these commands every bit as much importance as the configuration commands. Be sure you know the key information that is available from the output of each SHOW command presented here, and take note of how these commands were used in the preceding examples to verify that our OSPF routers were configured correctly.

IPX NLSP Configuration

I. Of what does NLSP's cost metric consist?

A. 1–63

B. cost = 100,000,000/BW

C. 1–6300

D. None of the above

---

exam
ⓦatch   *Designated routers manage the topological view of the network, along with the entire database synchronization process.*

Refer to the Following Illustration in Answering Questions 2–4

If a specification is not listed for a router, assume it is the default.

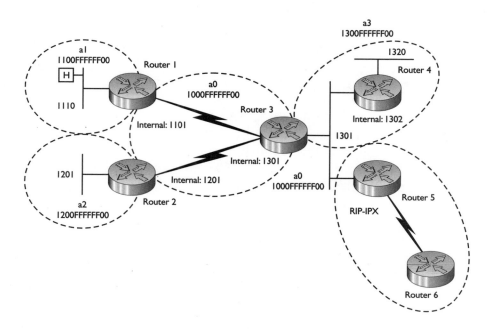

2. Which of the following commands on Router 4 enables it for NLSP operation and not RIP-IPX?

A. HOSTNAME ROUTER4
   IPX ROUTING 0000.0C34.84E2
   !
   INTERFACE ETHERNET0
    IPX NETWORK 1320
    IPX NLSP A3 ENABLE
   INTERFACE ETHERNET1
    IPX NETWORK 1310
    IPX NLSP A3 ENABLE
   !
   IPX ROUTER NLSP A3
    AREA-ADDRESS 1300 FFFFFF00

B. HOSTNAME ROUTER4
   IPX ROUTING 0000.0C34.84E2
   IPX INTERNAL-NETWORK 1302
   !
   INTERFACE ETHERNET0
    IPX NETWORK 1320
    IPX NLSP A3 ENABLE
   INTERFACE ETHERNET1
    IPX NETWORK 1310
    IPX NLSP A3 ENABLE
   !
   IPX ROUTER NLSP A3
    AREA-ADDRESS 1300 FFFFFF00
   IPX ROUTER RIP
    NO NETWORK 1320
    NO NETWORK 1310

C. HOSTNAME ROUTER4
   IPX ROUTING 0000.0C34.84E2
   IPX INTERNAL-NETWORK 1302
   !
   INTERFACE ETHERNET0
    IPX NETWORK 1320
    IPX NLSP A3 ENABLE

```
        INTERFACE ETHERNET1
         IPX NETWORK 1310
         IPX NLSP A3 ENABLE
         !
         IPX ROUTER NLSP A3
          NETWORK 1320
          NETWORK 1310
         IPX ROUTER RIP
          NO NETWORK 1320
          NO NETWORK 1310
   D. HOSTNAME ROUTER4
         IPX ROUTING 0000.0C34.84E2
         IPX INTERNAL-NETWORK 1302
         !
         INTERFACE ETHERNET0
          IPX NETWORK 1320
          IPX NLSP ENABLE
         INTERFACE ETHERNET1
          IPX NETWORK 1310
          IPX NLSP ENABLE
         !
         IPX ROUTER NLSP A3
          AREA-ADDRESS 1300 FFFFFF00
```

---

exam
ⓦatch   *NLSP only sends out routing updates once every two hours, or when a change in the network topology is recognized.*

---

3. What command would Router 3 use to display whether or not it has created adjacencies with its NLSP neighbors?

  A. SHOW IPX NLSP NEIGHBORS DETAIL

  B. SHOW IPX NLSP

  C. SHOW IPX NLSP DATABASE

  D. SHOW IPX ROUTE

QUESTIONS AND ANSWERS

I want to deploy a large-scale internetwork utilizing Novell protocols, but need to keep overhead to a minimum...	Use the Netware Link Services Protocol to minimize required overhead, since it employs route aggregation, and less processor-intensive route calculations.
My current IPX network is being saturated by routing table updates...	When properly configured, NLSP only sends out routing table updates every two hours, or when a change in the network is noticed.
We have departments still using both Novell SAP and RIP, so I need to provide backward compatibility for them...	NLSP supports backward compatibility for both RIP and SAP.
Our network is already over-utilized, so we can't afford additional network saturation from link-state packets ...	Once NLSP is configured, a designated router is automatically chosen within a network, unless it is specifically configured within a router's configuration to act as the DR. It controls the database synchronization process, and sends out the LSPs, instead of all the routers sending them out.
My client is planning a large-scale expansion of their network. Should we use NLSP?	Yes, your client could probably use NLSP to their advantage. NSLP employs a cost metric, similar to OSPF, which has a maximum value of 128. This allows a larger network topology, without exceeding the routing protocols' limitations.

4. Which command would you execute on Router 1 to test if the aggregate route feature is working correctly on Router3?

   A. SHOW IPX NLSP NEIGHBOR DETAIL
   B. SHOW IPX ROUTE-AGGREGATION
   C. SHOW IPX ROUTE
   D. SHOW IPX NLSP DATABASE

exam
ⓦatch

Not many commands are used to verify correct operation of NLSP, so indications that it is functioning correctly may be found within information gathered from other commands within the IOS.

Enhanced IGRP (EIGRP) Configuration

Refer to the Following Scenario and Illustration in Answering Questions 1–2

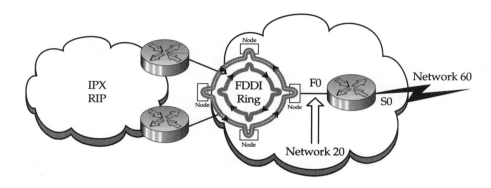

Network 50 is another IPX RIP network. The EIGRP autonomous system number is 1. Here is a part of the configuration on Router A

```
ipx routing
!
ipx router eigrp 1
network 20
network 50
!
ipx router rip
no network 20
no network 50
!
interface fddi0
ipx network 20
ipx sap-incremental eigrp 1
!
interface serial 0
ipx network 50
```

I. In this example, which command assigns EIGRP for IPX updates to Network 50?

A. NETWORK 50

B. IPX NETWORK 50

C. NO NETWORK 50

D. IPX ROUTER EIGRP 1

2. How is a new successor chosen when the current successor fails?

A. The router immediately sends out a query packet to all its neighbors to learn if they have a path to the given destination

B. The router flags the failed route in an active state

C. The router selects the next route based upon feasible successor

D. The router removes the route from the route table and sends out an all-routes explorer packet

Border Gateway Protocol (BGP)

1. Which one of the following commands correctly implements a static route for the situation depicted in the following illustration?

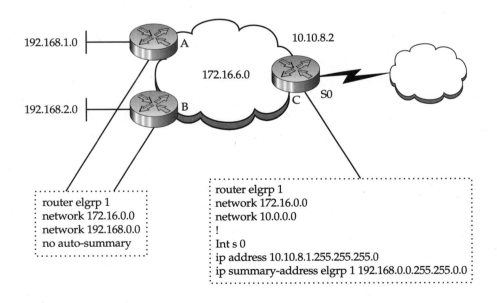

```
192.168.1.0 ———| A

172.16.6.0

10.10.8.2

C   S0
```

```
router elgrp 1
network 172.16.0.0
network 192.168.0.0
no auto-summary
```

```
router elgrp 1
network 172.16.0.0
network 10.0.0.0
!
Int s 0
ip address 10.10.8.1.255.255.255.0
ip summary-address elgrp 1 192.168.0.0.255.255.0.0
```

QUESTIONS AND ANSWERS

I have only one link to my ISP, and I want to run BGP over that link. How should I begin?	There is no need for you to run BGP if you have a single link to your provider and if your routing policy is the same. Use a default route pointing to the link to your ISP.
When I use SHOW IP BGP SUMMARY, I can see that my connection is "Active," but no routing information is being passed.	A connection in "Active" state is one that is not established. "Active" means only that BGP is trying to start a TCP connection with that peer. No routing information will be passed until the session is established.
I made a change to my BGP configuration, but I don't see it reflected in my BGP table.	Use CLEAR IP BGP to reset the particular BGP session to which you made changes.

A. IP ROUTE 0.0.0.0 255.255.255.255 S0

B. IP ROUTE 10.0.0.0 0.0.0.0 S0

C. IP ROUTE 10.0.0.0 255.255.255.255 S0

D. IP ROUTE 0.0.0.0 0.0.0.0 S0

exam
Ⓦatch   *Static and default routes are often a preferable way to connect your enterprise to the Internet. BGP4 is not always better just because it's complicated!*

exam
Ⓦatch   *A route must either exist in the IP routing table, or be defined by the network statement in BGP for the route to be advertised.*

2. With what is a BGP session established between two routers?

A. Hello packets

B. A connection-oriented session in the form of TCP

C. A connectionless session in the form of UDP

D. ICMP

Configuring **WAN** Connectivity

1. Which packet-switched technology uses 53-byte cells?

   A. Frame Relay
   B. ISDN
   C. SMDS
   D. ATM

Remember that HDLC encapsulation is the default setting for Cisco routers' synchronous interfaces. This input is needed only if the default has been changed and you want to go back to HDLC encapsulation.

---

2. What command enables Multilink PPP?

   A. ENCAPSULATION PPP MULTILINK
   B. PPP MULTILINK
   C. PPP LINK MULTI
   D. DIALER MULTILINK PPP

QUESTIONS AND ANSWERS

I want to use HDLC encapsulation on my Cisco product network...	HDLC is the default encapsulation for Cisco to Cisco products on synchronous interfaces.
Does HDLC have a major advantage over other protocols?	Yes. It has low overhead, windowing for network lag.
I am told that HDLC and LAPB are the same protocols and only have different names because of vendor difference...	HDLC and LAPB are both standards. LAPB was derived from changing HDLC to conform to X.25. They are not the same protocol.
We are opening a new office in another part of the United States. Can we use the same WAN service wherever we go?	Part of your planning should include considerations of availability of services. You should check the services available in the new region before making a final selection.

QUESTIONS AND ANSWERS

Our company has a multirouter WAN. Should we use per-interface compression?	No. Due to the total link compression, the data would have to be decompressed and then compressed again at each IS. This introduces unneeded latency.
Do we even need data compression on our WAN?	Planning is the key to avoiding bandwidth-related problems. Do you constantly exceed your CIR? Is your connection constantly slow? Is an increase in bandwidth out of the question? If the answer to these questions is Yes, your WAN could benefit from compression.

exam
ⓦatch

SLIP is not an Internet standard. It is, however, the default encapsulation method for asynchronous interfaces on Cisco routers.

exam
ⓦatch

Point-to-Point Protocol is an Internet standard and is the most widely used standard for transmission of IP packets over a serial line.

exam
ⓦatch

It is important to remember that, with specialized hardware and software, the B channels can be combined to provide larger throughput.

exam
ⓦatch

PAP provides no security from trial-and-error attacks due to its clear text transmittal.

Configuring ISDN connectivity

1. Which of the following are allowable line codes when configuring a PRI using a T1/E1 controller? Choose three.

   A. B8ZS
   B. ESF
   C. AMI
   D. HDB3
   E. CRC4

---

exam
Watch *ISDN Primary Rate Interface uses an entire D channel exclusively for signaling, while channelized T1s and E1s borrow 8 kbps of the available 64 kpbs per channel.*

---

exam
Watch *DDR is very useful as a backup or fail-over type of configuration because it allows an affordable redundancy.*

---

2. ISDN protocols that begin with *E* do which of the following?

   A. Deal with concepts, terminology, and general methods
   B. Cover how switching and signaling should operate
   C. Recommend telephone network standards for ISDN
   D. Recommend a network layer between the terminal end point and the local ISDN switch

---

exam
Watch *CHAP and PAP are both PPP authentication protocols. TACACS was developed by Cisco.*

Frame Relay

1. Which of the following protocols can be used on an NBMA network? Choose three.

A. AppleTalk

B. IP

C. IPX

D. SNA

---

exam
ⓌatchThe NNI is a switch-to-switch interface. It is used between the Frame Relay networks. Be aware that UNI will not work in this situation.

---

exam
ⓌatchDLCIs are local. This means that for a PVC between Router A and Router B, Router A can identify the PVC with a DLCI of 500, and Router B can identify the same PVC with a DLCI of 600.

---

2. What is the difference between point-to-point interfaces and multipoint interfaces in a Frame Relay network? Choose two.

A. A point-to-point subinterface can only have one DLCI associated with it

B. A multipoint subinterface can have multiple DLCIs assigned to it

C. Both point-to-point and multipoint subinterfaces can have only one DLCI assigned to them

D. A multipoint subinterface can have more DLCIs assigned to it than a point-to-point subinterface can

---

exam
ⓌatchThe DLCI is a local identifier for a PVC. The switch knows how to forward a packet based on the DLCI.

ACRC
QUESTIONS

QUESTIONS AND ANSWERS

Jeff is configuring a branch-office router for a single PVC to a central router at HQ. He enters the FRAME-RELAY MAP IP 160.100.48.2 303 BROADCAST command at the router after entering the FRAME-RELAY INTERFACE-DLCI 303 command. The router does not bring up the connection. Why?

Jeff used two commands to describe the same connection. The FRAME-RELAY MAP IP command cannot be used after the FRAME-RELAY INTERFACE-DLCI command.

Configuring Bandwidth-on-Demand

1. Joe wants to use access list 101 to specify interesting traffic. Which of the following commands would Joe use to do this?

   A. DIALER-LIST 1 PROTOCOL IPX LIST 101
   B. DIALER-LIST 1 PROTOCOL IP LIST 101
   C. DIALER-LIST 1 IPX PROTOCOL LIST 101
   D. DIALER-LIST 1 IP PROTOCOL LIST 101

---

e x a m
ⓦa t c h   *The dialer list number must match the dialer group number in the configuration.*

---

2. Joe decides that he also wants to configure dial backup to connect if the Serial 0 link exceeds 80 percent utilization and disconnect when utilization drops below 25 percent. Which commands should Joe use?

   A. BACKUP INTERFACE SERIAL 1
      BACKUP-LOAD 80 25
   B. BACKUP INTERFACE SERIAL 1
      BACKUP LOAD 80 25

QUESTIONS AND ANSWERS

How can I limit the DDR link to specific traffic only?	Use a dialer list with an access list to filter for specific traffic.
We need to configure DDR over Frame Relay...	Be sure to use a legacy DDR configuration that supports Frame Relay.
What command can I use to check the dialer interface?	SHOW DIALER
Can dialer profiles be used on a router running Cisco IOS 11.1?	No. Dialer profiles are only supported on Cisco IOS 11.2 and higher.
Our WAN link is fairly reliable, but we'd like to have near 100 percent coverage...	Configure a dial backup solution for your network using DDR.

      C. BACKUP-INTERFACE SERIAL 1
         BACKUP LOAD 80 25
      D. BACKUP INTERFACE SERIAL 1
         BACKUP LOAD 25 80

Integrating Nonrouted Services and IRB

1. Which commands can be used to verify IRB operation? Choose two.

    A. SHOW INTERFACES *interface* IRB
    B. SHOW IRB INTERFACES
    C. SHOW INTERFACE *interface-name*
    D. SHOW INTERFACE *interface* IRB

exam
ⓦatch   *With standard bridging, a given protocol can be either routed or bridged on all interfaces.*

Refer to the Following Illustration in Answering Questions 2–3

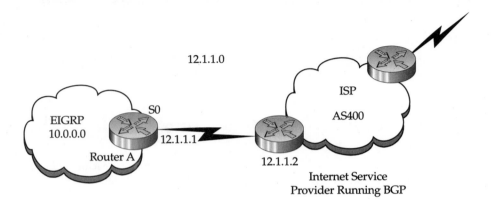

12.1.1.0

EIGRP
10.0.0.0

S0

12.1.1.1

Router A

ISP

AS400

12.1.1.2

Internet Service
Provider Running BGP

2. What is the proper command sequence for routing IPX over the bridge group interfaces?

A. BRIDGE IRB
   BRIDGE 20 ROUTE IPX
   NO BRIDGE 10 BRIDGE IP

B. BRIDGE 20 IRB
   BRIDGE 20 ROUTE IPX
   NO BRIDGE 10 BRIDGE IP

C. BRIDGE IRB
   BRIDGE 20 ROUTE IPX
   NO BRIDGE IP

D. BRIDGE 20 IRB
   BRIDGE 20 ROUTE IP
   NO BRIDGE 10 BRIDGE IP

---

exam
ⓦatch   *With CRB, a given protocol can be either routed or bridged on a given interface. Groups of routed and bridged interfaces are isolated.*

QUESTIONS AND ANSWERS

To enable IRB...	Use the BRIDGE IRB command
To configure the spanning tree...	Use the BRIDGE PROTOCOL command
To configure interfaces...	Use *protocol enablers* or the BRIDGE-GROUP command
To configure the BVI...	Use the INTERFACE BVI command
To configure protocols for routing and/or bridging...	Use the BRIDGE ROUTE and/or BRIDGE BRIDGE commands
To check the configuration...	Use the SHOW INTERFACES IRB command

exam
ⓦatch

With IRB, a given protocol can be either routed or bridged on a given interface. The BVI is a virtual link between groups of routed and bridged interfaces.

3. With both CRB and IRB enabled, each routable protocol can be:

    A. Bridged on all interfaces

    B. Routed on all interfaces

    C. Simultaneously routed and bridged on all interfaces

    D. None of the above

exam
ⓦatch

The BVI is a routed interface representing a given bridge group to the routed world. All necessary network layer attributes, and no bridge-group attributes, should be configured on the BVI. The BVI number is the number of the bridge group it represents. The BVI borrows its MAC address from the first interface in the bridge group.

Transparent Bridging

I. The statement Port 2 (Ethernet0) of bridge group 1 is forwarding in the tenth line of the output below says that Port 2 is forwarding. What are the other possible values for the state of the interface? Choose four.

```
R2#show span
Bridge Group 1 is executing the IEEE compatible Spanning Tree protocol
  Bridge Identifier has priority 32768, address 0000.0c5d.9e23
  Configured hello time 2, max age 20, forward delay 15
  We are the root of the spanning tree
  Topology change flag set, detected flag set
  Times:  hold 1, topology change 30, notification 30
          hello 2, max age 20, forward delay 15, aging 300
  Timers: hello 1, topology change 21, notification 0
Port 2 (Ethernet0) of bridge group 1 is forwarding
  Port path cost 100, Port priority 128
  Designated root has priority 32768, address 0000.0c5d.9e23
  Designated bridge has priority 32768, address 0000.0c5d.9e23
  Designated port is 2, path cost 0
  Timers: message age 0, forward delay 0, hold 0
```

A. Down

B. Listening

C. Disabled

D. Blocking

E. Learning

F. Flooding

exam
Ⓦatch *Remember that a repeater operates at Layer 1, a bridge at Layer 2, and a router at Layer 3.*

exam
ⓦatch   *It's important to realize that the spanning-tree algorithm was developed as a way to control bridging loops in a complex bridged topology.*

2. If we bridge all ports in the following illustration, we would expect that one port would have to be shut down to avoid a loop. The diagram below is followed by the results of the SHOW SPAN command for each. Which interface is shut down as a result of the spanning-tree algorithm?

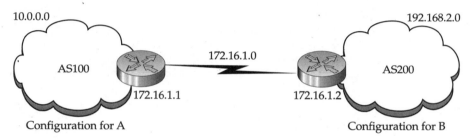

10.0.0.0

192.168.2.0

AS100

172.16.1.0

AS200

172.16.1.1

172.16.1.2

Configuration for A

Configuration for B

router bgp 100
network 10.0.0.0
neighbor 172.16.1.2 remote-as 200

Router A

```
Router A# show span
Bridge Group 1 is executing the IEEE compatible Spanning
Tree protocol
   Bridge Identifier has priority 100, address
0000.0c5d.9e23
   Configured hello time 2, max age 20, forward delay 15
   We are the root of the spanning tree
   Topology change flag not set, detected flag not set
   Times:  hold 1, topology change 30, notification 30
           hello 2, max age 20, forward delay 15, aging
300
   Timers: hello 2, topology change 0, notification 0
Port 2 (Ethernet0) of bridge group 1 is forwarding
   Port path cost 32000, Port priority 128
   Designated root has priority 100, address
0000.0c5d.9e23
```

```
    Designated bridge has priority 100, address
0000.0c5d.9e23
    Designated port is 2, path cost 0
    Timers: message age 0, forward delay 0, hold 0
Port 5 (Serial1) of bridge group 1 is forwarding
    Port path cost 1, Port priority 128
    Designated root has priority 100, address
0000.0c5d.9e23
    Designated bridge has priority 100, address
0000.0c5d.9e23
    Designated port is 5, path cost 0
    Timers: message age 0, forward delay 0, hold 0
```

Router B

```
Router B#show span
Bridge Group 1 is executing the IEEE compatible Spanning
Tree protocol
  Bridge Identifier has priority 32768, address
0060.7015.aa55
  Configured hello time 2, max age 20, forward delay 15
  Current root has priority 100, address 0000.0c5d.9e23
  Root port is 5 (Serial1), cost of root path is 1
  Topology change flag not set, detected flag not set
  Times:  hold 1, topology change 30, notification 30
          hello 2, max age 20, forward delay 15, aging 300
Timers: hello 0, topology change 0, notification 0
Port 3 (Ethernet1) of bridge group 1 is blocking
    Port path cost 1000, Port priority 128
    Designated root has priority 100, address
0000.0c5d.9e23
    Designated bridge has priority 100, address
0000.0c5d.9e23
    Designated port is 2, path cost 0
    Timers: message age 2, forward delay 0, hold 0
Port 5 (Serial1) of bridge group 1 is forwarding
    Port path cost 1, Port priority 128
    Designated root has priority 100, address
0000.0c5d.9e23
    Designated bridge has priority 100, address
0000.0c5d.9e23
    Designated port is 5, path cost 0
    Timers: message age 1, forward delay 0, hold 0
```

A. Router A interface S 0
B. Router A interface E 0
C. Router B interface S 1
D. Router B interface E 1

---

exam
ⓦatch

Remember that Spanning-Tree Protocol packets are called BPDUs.

---

exam
ⓦatch

Keep in mind that there are two Spanning-Tree Protocols used with transparent bridging: the DEC Spanning-Tree Protocol (used for compatibility with older DEC bridges), and the newer IEEE 802.1d Spanning-Tree Protocol.

---

exam
ⓦatch

Be sure to know the parameters that are used in determining which bridge will become the root bridge. Also, remember that one of these parameters, bridge priority, can be set by the network administrator to a low number (high priority), on any given bridge, in order to ensure that it will become the root bridge.

---

exam
ⓦatch

Remember that circuit groups allow you to utilize the full bandwidth of multiple, parallel, bridged serial links while still having them participate in the Spanning-Tree Protocol.

---

exam
ⓦatch

Be sure to know the exact syntax of the commands used in configuring transparent bridging on a Cisco router, as well as what type of command it is (global configuration command, interface configuration command, or other).

QUESTIONS AND ANSWERS

You suspect physical layer problems including bad cabling, collisions, resets, and carrier transitions…	SHOW INTERFACES
You want to see if multiple spanning trees are running on the network…	SHOW SPAN (look for multiple root bridges)
You want to check if hello packets are being seen at a given bridge as would be expected…	DEBUG SPANNING TREE
You want to see what bridge groups are assigned to the interfaces on a bridge…	SHOW STARTUP-CONFIG SHOW RUNNING-CONFIG
You want to see the contents of the access lists…	SHOW ACCESS-LISTS

exam
Watch

Remember that the SHOW SPAN command is a good way to check if you have multiple spanning trees running on your network, since it will show you any bridge that's configured as a root bridge.

Source-Route Bridging

I. Which bridging scheme would be most appropriate in a Token Ring network where some hosts do not support source routing?

A. SRB

B. SRT

C. Transparent Bridging

D. SR/TLB

exam
ⓦatch

IEEE 802.5 and Token Ring can coexist in an internetwork. When designing a mixed IEEE 802.5 and IBM Token Ring internetwork, each specification's limits for the numbers of bridges and routers should be taken into account. IEEE 802.5 allows 13 bridges and 14 rings. IBM Token Ring allows 7 bridges and 8 rings.

Use the Following Illustration for Questions 2–3

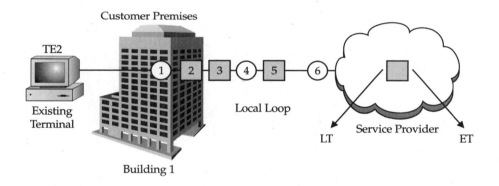

2. In the illustration, Host X wants to send data to host Y. What is the first step?

   A. Host X transmits an all-routes explorer frame

   B. Host X transmits a single-route explorer frame

   C. Host X transmits a local-ring explorer frame

   D. Host X transmits an all-routes broadcast

e x a m
ⓦatch

Virtual rings are created from specifying SOURCE-ROUTE REMOTE-PEER commands on routers, which then become peers. This command has three parameters: the local ring number, the bridge number, and the target ring. The target ring parameter is the number assigned to the virtual ring. Make sure that the virtual ring number is unique on the internetwork, and utilized by each of the peers.

3. What is the correct command sequence for the Token Ring interface 0 using Bridge number 1 on this dual-port bridge in the illustration?

   A. INTERFACE TOKENRING 0
      SOURCE-BRIDGE 401 1 400
      SOURCE-BRIDGE SPANNING
   B. INTERFACE TOKENRING 0
      SOURCE-BRIDGE 400 401 1
      SOURCE-BRIDGE SPANNING
   C. INTERFACE TOKENRING 1
      SOURCE-BRIDGE 400 1 401
      SOURCE-BRIDGE SPANNING
   D. INTERFACE TOKENRING 0
      SOURCE-BRIDGE 400 1 401
      SOURCE-BRIDGE SPANNING

e x a m
ⓦatch

The use of SRT increases overhead on the processor of the router, since each frame must be examined for the presence or absence of a Routing Information Field. Presence of the RIF prompts the use of source-route bridging. Absence of a RIF prompts for the use of transparent bridging.

exam
ⓦatch   *The global command syntax to lower explorer max rate is*
SOURCE-BRIDGE EXPLORER-MAXRATE X, where X is rated
in bytes per ring. The default is 38400.

Data-Link Switching Plus (DLSw+)

1. DLSw uses only a single encapsulation type, TCP/IP. DLSw+ supports
   which of the following encapsulation types?

   A. TCP/IP
   B. FST/IP
   C. LLC2
   D. All the above

2. Which of the following makes up an end-to-end DLSw+ circuit? Choose all
   that apply.

   A. Source MAC address
   B. Destination MAC address
   C. Source-link Service Access Point (SAP)
   D. Data-link control port ID
   E. A, B, D only
   F. All the above

QUESTIONS AND ANSWERS

I would like to use DLSw+ to tunnel my SNA traffic over the IP infrastructure, but how can I keep unwanted explorers off interfaces, on routers running DLSw+, which are not part of the SNA network?	You can contain broadcasts from being flooded out of specific interfaces by using port lists.
How can I limit the number of peer connections within a fully meshed topology?	You can limit the number of peer connections within a fully meshed topology by using peer groups.
How can I ensure redundancy without the overhead of multiple peer connections being active at one time?	You can have redundancy without the overhead of multiple active connections by using backup peers instead of alternate peers.
When using alternate peer connections, how can I ensure that data will take the path I choose?	The cost parameter allows you to specify which peer connection passes data and which will act as the alternate. Remember that the lowest number is the preferred connection.
How can I ensure that my Cisco router will communicate with other DLSw switches not using the advanced features supplied by DLSw+?	Cisco routers can be placed in different modes of operation that allow them to learn about the DLSw switch on the other end of the connection. For DLSw switches based on RFC 1795 and the standard produced by AIW, you can place the Cisco router into standards compliance mode. When this is done, the Cisco router will learn and adapt to the standards-based switch during the capabilities exchange.

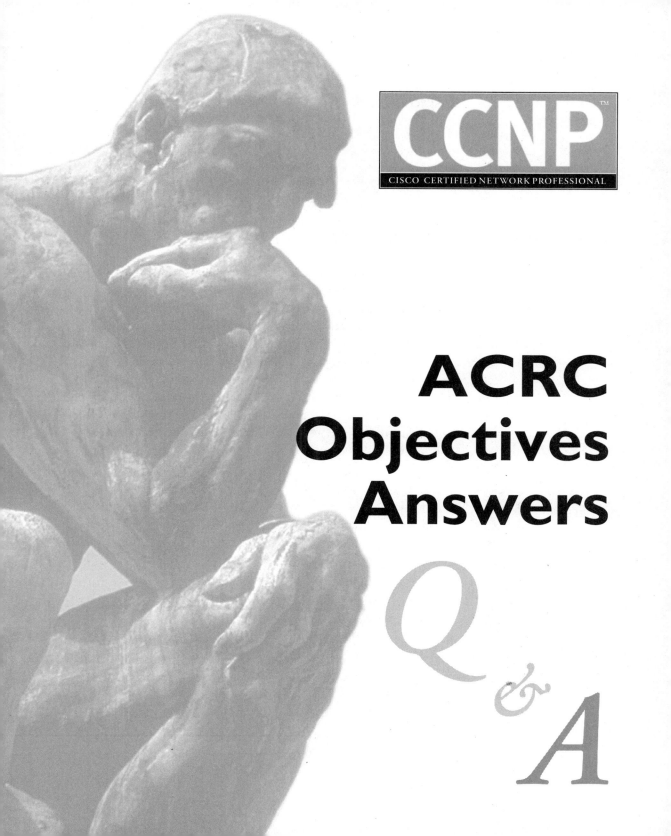

CCNP™
CISCO CERTIFIED NETWORK PROFESSIONAL

ACRC
Objectives
Answers

Q & A

Threbe answers to the questions are in boldface, followed by a brief explanation. Some of the explanations detail the logic you should use to choose the correct answer, while others give factual reasons why the answer is correct. If you miss several questions on a similar topic, you should review the corresponding section in the *CCNP ACRC Advanced Cisco Router Configuration Study Guide* before taking the ACRC test.

Scaleable Internetworks

1. ☑ **B.** Fast switching is the correct answer because it is the default switching type for all router interfaces except for the Cisco 7500 series router, which is considered a core router. Fast switching works by creating a route cache in memory after the first route table lookup is performed for a particular destination. This is faster than process switching because process switching requires that each individual packet refer to the routing table for forwarding.

   Optimum switching is an option only available on the 7500 and 7200 series routers and is actually the default for the 7500 series. It is even faster than fast switching due to the improved switching fabric logic of these core routers. VIP cards of a 7500 series router use distributed switching.

   ☒ **A.** Process switching is incorrect because it is slower and requires more CPU utilization than fast switching. To enable process switching, type NO IP ROUTE-CACHE from within interface configuration mode. **C.** Optimum switching is incorrect because it is not supported on Access and distribution-layer routers. **D.** Distributed switching is incorrect because it is also not supported on Access and distribution-layer routers.

2. ☑ **A.** Per packet and per destination are the two types of load balancing provided by Cisco. Per destination is the default and is used when fast switching is enabled. Per-destination load balancing means that once a packet is sent to a remote location for which there are redundant paths, the path selected by the first packet (depending on link utilization at that time) will determine the path that all subsequent packets will follow for that destination address. The destination address is cached in memory, so if the router is power cycled or links go up and down, the cached entry could be deleted. Also, the routing protocol you are using must support load balancing, such as OSPF or EIGRP. Per-packet is enable when fast

switching is disabled with the NO IP ROUTE-CACHE interface
configuration command. The load-balancing technique forwards packets
alternately between redundant links.

☒ **B.** Symmetrical and asymmetrical is incorrect because the terms have
nothing to do with load balancing. **C.** NO IP ROUTE-CACHE and IP
ROUTE-CACHE are incorrect because these interface commands are how
per-packet and per-destination load balancing, respectively, are enabled on
the router. **D.** Per packet and per interface is incorrect because per interface
is not a load balancing technique; however, different types of load balancing
can be performed on different interfaces.

3. ☑ **A.** Redistribution exchanges information between routing-protocols.
Cisco routers allow for redistribution between all of its routing protocols.
The results of redistribution between routing protocols are not always what
one might expect, due to differences within the routing protocols
themselves, such as path metrics or support for VLSM.

☒ **B.** Network-address translation (NAT) is incorrect because NAT is a
router process that translates IP packet addressing so that an internal
network can appear to external networks as having a different network
address. **C.** Route summarization is incorrect because it is a feature of
sophisticated routing protocols to advertise one route entry as opposed to
several continuous network addresses. **D.** Distributed switching is incorrect
because it is a high-speed route caching technique used by VIP cards in
forwarding data packets.

4. ☑ **B.** Slow-speed serial interfaces is correct because of the overhead that
compression imposes on a router. The interface would have to constitute a
bottleneck in order for this technique to increase efficiency in the overall
packet-per-second (PPS) performance of the router. All of the other options
represent high-speed interfaces for which the process routines that
compression would impose may actually reduce overall data throughput.

☒ **A.** High-speed serial interfaces (HSSI), is incorrect because typically the
high-speed links that these interfaces support are less likely to constitute a
bottleneck, since sheer bandwidth is unlikely. **C.** Ethernet interfaces is
incorrect because it is a high-speed LAN interface. **D.** ATM interfaces is
incorrect because this is also a high-speed interface.

5. ☑ **D.** All the above Cisco configuration features can construct a routing policy. Standard and extended access-list can be used to create traffic or routing filters. Routing protocols and redistribution can be configured to dynamically handle routing and can be manipulated for desired performance. Encryption and NAT can also define security policies when connecting to the Internet or other public networks.

IP Traffic Management

1. ☑ **B.** Defined access lists cannot be applied to more than one interface. If an access list defines the same routing policy that is required for more than one interface, it can be applied to all the interfaces that require it. The following sequence applies to access lists:
   Access list commands are order specific, with the first command entered being placed at the top of the list. Processing of the access list then starts at the top and continues with each sequential command until a match is found. The packet is then either permitted or denied and no further commands are evaluated for that packet. When access lists are applied to interfaces as data filters, they are required to be defined as either an incoming or outgoing filter.
   ☒ **A.** Access lists follow top-down processing is incorrect because this is a true statement. **C.** Access lists can be applied to interfaces as either incoming or outgoing is incorrect because this is also a true statement. **D.** Once a match is found, no further processing of the access list is performed is incorrect because this is also a true statement.

2. ☑ **A.** To help forward specific UDP broadcast traffic to an appropriate destination address. Helper address commands are a support feature to help forward specific UDP broadcasts, such as BOOTP, that a router would otherwise suppress. When where a workstation's BOOTP server is located on a remote segment, the router will forward the workstation's request for boot information to the remote segment. When configuring a helper-address command, an appropriate destination address must be specified. Appropriate helper addresses are defined as being either a node address or a directed-broadcast address.
   ☒ **B.** To help forward all broadcast traffic to an appropriate destination address, is incorrect because only specific UDP broadcasts are forwarded by

default. **C.** To help forward specific UDP broadcast traffic as a UDP broadcast address is also incorrect because a UDP broadcast address can be the all-networks broadcast address, 255.255.255.255, such as an initial BOOTP request. The helper address specifies the forwarding address as either a node or directed broadcast. **D.** To help forward all UDP broadcasts to all interfaces, is incorrect because forwarded packets will be sent out the one interface that reflects the forwarding address.

3. ☑ **A.** SHOW ACCESS-L 110 is the best answer since it is not indicated whether or not there are other access lists configured on the router. The command, with the optional access list number specified, will display the filtering policies that exist for the specified numbered list only. Remember that Cisco IOS commands can be abbreviated as long as they are not ambiguous.

☒ **B.** SHOW ACCESS-LIST is not the best answer because this command will display the filtering policies of all the access lists that exist on a router. **C.** SHOW ACCESS-GROUP 110 is incorrect because the keyword *access-group* makes this an illegal command. **D.** None of the above is incorrect.

Novell IPX/SPX Traffic Management

1. ☑ **B.** Service advertising protocol is the correct meaning of the acronym for SAP in this case. Within an IPX environment, SAP is the protocol that enables servers to offer or advertise its services, such as file sharing and printer services, to its IPX clients. On a Cisco router, services can be displayed, filtered, or enabled to answer Get Nearest Server (GNS) queries from clients when there is not an IPX server on that segment. This is the default. Of course, like RIP-IPX, SAP broadcasts every 60 seconds the services it has learned about from one interface to the others, once IPX has been configured on that interface.

☒ **A.** Service access point is incorrect because this acronym for SAP represents the IPX encapsulation type that includes the IEEE 802.2 header within the IEEE 802.3 header. **C.** Server adjacency protocol is incorrect because there is no such protocol within networking. **D.** Server access protocol is incorrect for the same reason.

2. ☑ **B.** IPX ACCESS-GROUP 901 IN applies an access list as an incoming filter on an interface. IPX access lists, when applied as generic data filters, are applied similarly to the manner in which IP filters are applied. Filters can be applied per interface and per direction, although only one access list can be specified per any one interface/direction pair. If the default direction that a filter is applied to an interface is not stated, it is outgoing. Access lists are applied to IPX routing protocols very differently than for data filters. They are also applied differently depending on which IPX routing protocol is being used.

☒ **A.** IPX ACCESS-LIST 901 IN is incorrect and illegal due to the use of the keyword ACCESS-LIST instead of ACCESS-GROUP. **C.** IPX ACCESS-LIST 801 IN is incorrect because it uses the incorrect access-list number. **D.** The configuration command IPX ACCESS-LIST 901 is incorrect because without stating the keyword IN, the filter will be applied as an outgoing filter, since this is the default.

3. ☑ **A.** ACCESS-LIST 1001 PERMIT 10.AAAA.3333.4444 and IPX OUTPUT-SAP-FILTER 1001 together will limit SAP advertisement to only those services which are provided by the IPX server who's address is 10.AAAA.3333.4444. In order to conserve bandwidth on WAN links, it is recommended that filters be applied to the outgoing interface that would have otherwise advertised the routes or services. Router WAN ports are still recommended to have incoming filters to serve as a backup for filtering unnecessary information in the event that another WAN-connected router's outgoing filter is temporarily disabled.

☒ **B.** Both ACCESS-LIST 1001 DENY –1 and IPX OUTPUT-SAP-FILTER 1001 are incorrect because the access list would deny all SAP advertisements. **C.** Both ACCESS-LIST 1001 PERMIT 10.AAAA.3333.4444 and IPX OUTPUT-SAP-FILTER 1011 are incorrect because the access-list number in the OUTPUT-SAP-FILTER command does not match 1001. **D.** Both ACCESS-LIST 1001 PERMIT 10.AAAA.3333.4444 and IPX INPUT-SAP-FILTER 1001 are incorrect due to the filter being applied as an incoming, rather than outgoing, filter.

4. ☑ **C.** IP tunneling will allow communication between discontiguous, routed-protocol networks that are interconnected via an IP network. In this

case our discontiguous networks are IPX networks, connected by an IP
network running over a Frame Relay cloud. Once IP tunnels are configured
between the edge routers of the cloud, IPX packets will be encapsulated
within an IP header and forwarded to the appropriate IP interfaces where
they will be de-encapsulated and put on the IPX network segment.
☒   **A.** Redistribution is incorrect because it is the terminology used to
describe the exchanging of routing information between routing protocols.
B. Protocol translation is incorrect because it only translates between
different virtual terminal protocols, not routed protocols.

5. ☑   **D.** All the above configuration techniques can help to minimize
unnecessary traffic over WAN links. Adjusting SAP timers on both sides of a
WAN link reduces the number of retransmissions of service advertisements;
however, setting the interval too high can result in inconsistent service
tables. Filtering unnecessary service advertisements is a very effective tool in
conserving bandwidth. Finally, using EIGRP or NLSP as the primary routing
protocol ensures that only updated packets are exchanged between routers
once changes have been observed from the initial topology. This is in contrast
to using the default protocols to handle the exchanging of routes and services,
RIP-IPX and SAP respectively, due to their bandwidth-intensive characteristic
of periodically broadcasting entire tables of information.

AppleTalk Traffic Management

1. ☑   **D.** Segments can contain multiple noncontiguous networks does not
describe an AppleTalk extended network. Phase II network implementations
can contain multiple, contiguous networks that make up a range. Zones
for these networks can then be configured so that they contain multiple
networks. The Cisco IOS command to assign a Phase II network address is
the APPLETALK CABLE-RANGE command, which includes a network
address range followed by the actual node address.
☒   **A.** Segments can contain a range of network numbers is incorrect
because this does describe an AppleTalk extended network. **B.** Zones may
span multiple extended networks is incorrect for the same reason that **A.** is
incorrect. **C.** Nodes belong to one zone is incorrect for the same reason that
A. and **B.** are incorrect.

2. ☑ **C.** Phase II. As we can tell from the network diagram, cable ranges have been used to assign network numbering. This is not a feature that was allowable within Phase I or non-extended networks. Phase 1 only allowed for single 8-bit network ID, allowing 254 network addresses (two are reserved). The assigned zones span multiple segments, which is also a characteristic of extended networking.

☒ **A.** Phase I is incorrect because this type of network implementation is only for a single network address, which the diagram does not constitute. **B.** Non-extended network is also incorrect because this is simply another name for AppleTalk Phase I.

3. ☑ **D.** ACCESS-LIST 610 DENY CABLE-RANGE 100-104 and ACCESS-LIST 610 PERMIT OTHER-ACCESS are correct because, for Phase II RTMP filtering, they will successfully filter routing updates to include the network 100–104. For Phase I RTMP filtering, the global configuration command ACCESS-LIST NETWORK should be used to specify a network address.
The command syntax for filter Phase II network addresses is:

```
access-list access-list-number {deny | permit} cable-range cable-range
```

The command syntax to explicitly permit or deny all other networks within AppleTalk is:

```
access-list access-list-number {deny | permit} other-access
```

☒ **A.** The configuration command ACCESS-LIST 610 DENY NETWORK 100-104 is incorrect because it would deny all network advertisements, since it does not contain an explicit PERMIT ALL at the end. **B.** The configuration command ACCESS-LIST 610 DENY NETWORK 100-104 is incorrect because the keyword NETWORK is used for Phase I network addressing. **C.** The configuration commands ACCESS-LIST 610 DENY NETWORK 100-104 and ACCESS-LIST 610 PERMIT OTHER-ACCESS are incorrect for the same reasons.

4. ☑ **C.** NBP. The filtering of NBP replies in large networks can greatly improve performance throughout the network. When an AppleTalk client opens their Chooser application and selects a service type and zone, NBP multicasts are transmitted by the router attached to that zone. Each device within the zone will then replay to that originating node if they provide that service. It is probably easy to see why, within a big network, filtering specific NBP replies can be critical to the performance of the network.

☒   **A.** NCP is incorrect because this is an IPX protocol. **B.** Zone is incorrect because the question stated that all applicable zone filters were already applied. **D.** RTMP is incorrect for the same reason.

Configuring Queuing

1. ☑   **C.** Priority queuing is the correct queuing technique as described by the question. A network administrator needs to be very careful when using this type of queuing algorithm because of its discriminatory nature. Packets allocated to lower-priority queues may timeout because they are sitting in the queue. On the other hand, for critical data types or applications, this feature can be a lifesaver if other bandwidth-intensive traffic periodically attempts to consume a slow WAN link.

   ☒   **A.** WFQ is incorrect because it does not meet the description. **C.** FIFO, and **D.** Custom are also incorrect for this reason.

2. ☑   **C.** PRIORITY-LIST INTERFACE is the correct answer because this command, once forwarded to an outbound interface, will allow incoming traffic for a particular interface to be set to a specific priority level. Since the queue type was specified as medium, it should be obvious that we are using priority queuing.

   ☒   **A.** PRIORITY-LIST DEFAULT is incorrect because this command is used to change the default queue to be used for unspecified traffic. **B.** PRIORITY-LIST PROTOCOL is incorrect since it is used to establish queuing priorities based on protocol types. **D.** PRIORITY-GROUP LIST is incorrect because this command assigns a priority list to an interface for outbound packets.

3. ☑ **B.** The configuration command QUEUE-LIST 3 QUEUE 7 BYTE-COUNT 1000 is the correct answer since it appropriately uses the correct command syntax for setting the byte count for a custom queue. The command syntax for setting the byte count for a custom queue is the following:

```
queue-list list-number queue queue-number byte-count byte-count-number
```

☒ **A.** The command QUEUE-LIST 7 QUEUE 3 BYTE 1000 IS ILLEGAL because the keyword BYTE should read BYTE-COUNT. It also has the queue list and queue number reversed. **C.** The command QUEUE-LIST 7 QUEUE 3 BYTE-COUNT 1000 is incorrect because it, too, has the queue list and the queue number reversed. **D.** The command QUEUE-GROUP 3 QUEUE 7 BYTE-COUNT 1000 is incorrect because the keyword QUEUE-GROUP is incorrect.

Routing Protocols

I. ☑ **D.** Route summarization is the correct answer because when hierarchical network design and contiguous network addressing are allocated to each separate region or area within the network, route summarization can be successfully implemented. Within flat networks, all routers learn explicit routers to one another because their is not a mechanism designated to maintain routers in there own separate regions. ☒ **A.** Route filtering is incorrect because this is not enabled by hierarchical design. Route filtering can be performed on routers in flat or hierarchical networks. **B.** Border routers is incorrect because this is simply a term used to describe routers in more than one area within an OSPF network. **C.** Network address translation is incorrect because this feature is also not dependent on the architecture of the network hierarchy.

2. ☑ **B.** Variable-length subnet masking (VLSM) allows subnetted networks to be further subnetted on different segments. This technique, along with classless interdomain routing (CIDR), have greatly enable the Internet to survive by prolonging available IP network addresses and reducing routing tables, respectively.

☒ **A.** VLAN is incorrect because it is a Layer 2 technique that provides flexible association to virtual LANs among physical segments. **C.** CIDR is incorrect because classless interdomain routing is concerned with aggregate routing and enabling classful subnets to be shortened. **D.** NAT is incorrect because this feature will allow for the translation of private network addresses into publicly routable addresses, for Internet support.

3. ☑ **B.** The dead interval has expired is correct because when OSPF routers have formed an adjacency, they must have agreed on a hello and dead interval time. Hello intervals are sent to initially exchange information to form the adjacency; however, once up, they serve as a mechanism to inform the neighbor that they are still up and operational. Each time a hello packet is received, a router resets its dead interval counter to zero. If a neighbor does go down and so stops sending hello packets, the adjacent router's dead-interval timer (usually set to four times the interval of the hello interval) will eventually expire, resulting in a topology change and link-state updates being sent to all remaining neighbors.

☒ **A.** Hello packets have not been received within 40 seconds is incorrect because although 40 seconds is the default value for the dead interval, it is able to be configured. **C.** The port has gone down on the neighboring router is also incorrect because this will eventually cause OSPF to recognize that the neighbor is down, but not until the dead interval has expired. **D.** When it has been notified by a link-state update packet is not the best answer, though, in rare instances, a router could be notified through an alternate path from convergence before the dead interval expires.

Interior Gateway Routing Protocol (IGRP) Configuration

1. ☑ **A.** ROUTER EIGRP 5 and NETWORK 172.16.0.0 is the correct answer for this question because in order for EIGRP to automatically redistribute with IGRP, the same autonomous system number must be used for each routing domain. Also, this configuration uses the correct command syntax to the successful enabling of EIGRP on Router 3. The command syntax for enabling the EIGRP routing protocol is:

```
router eigrp autonomous-system-number
```

The router configuration command to specify a network for EIGRP operation is:

```
network network-number
```

☒ **B.** ROUTER EIGRP and NETWORK 172.16.1.0 is incorrect because the autonomous system number is not specified and because the network address should be specified in its classful notation, 172.16.0.0.
C. ROUTER EIGRP 5 and NETWORK 172.16.1.0 is incorrect because the network address should be specified in its classful notation, 172.16.0.0.
D. ROUTER EIGRP 10 and NETWORK 172.16.0.0 is incorrect because the autonomous system number is not 5.

2. ☑ **D.** INTERFACE SERIAL1 and IP SUMMARY-ADDRESS EIGRP 5 172.16.2.0 255.255.255.0 is correct because it is necessary to summarize the network addresses 172.16.2.0/25 and 172.16.2.128/25 into the above address since IGRP does not support VLSM and therefore can only

maintain one subnet mask. Router 4's Serial 1 port is a logical place to make this aggregation because it is before the router performing redistribution and all paths reaching the summarized destinations must transverse this interface. The interface configuration command to summarized an aggregate address is:

```
ip summary-address eigrp autonomous-system-number address mask
```

⊠ **A.** INTERFACE SERIAL0 and IP HOLD-TIME EIGRP 5 300 is incorrect because these commands will change the holddown timer on Serial 0 to five minutes. **B.** ROUTER EIGRP 10 and PASSIVE-INTERFACE SERIAL1 is incorrect because this tells summary addresses are not defined within router configuration mode, much less within AS 10, for this example, and the passive-interface command tells a router not to advertise out that interface. **C.** The commands ROUTER EIGRP 5 and REDISTRIBUTE IGRP 5 is incorrect because these commands have nothing to do with route summarization, nor would they ever be necessary since redistribution between EIGRP and IGRP with the same AS number is automatically performed.

3. ☑ **B.** 5 is the administrative distance assigned to an EIGRP summary route. Summary addresses, such as the one in this example, are automatically assigned an administrative distance of 5 on the router that learns of these routes. This specific type of route is not subject to being changed by manual configuration.

⊠ **A.** 20 is incorrect because this is the default administrative distance for External BGP. **C.** 90 is incorrect because this is the default administrative distance for EIGRP. **D.** 100 is incorrect because this is the default administrative distance for External IGRP.

OSPF Configuration

1. ☑ **B.** NETWORK 172.16.64.0 0.0.15.255 AREA 5 is the correct command to successfully enable OSPF for interfaces within the specified range of IP address and assign them to OSPF area 5. There are probably several ways to decipher this problem, one of which would be to first identify which network address and subnet mask that the range of host addresses is specifying. This would be 172.16.64.0 255.255.240.0, since the third octet of the IP address range is 64–79 and we can determine that there must be four additional host bits within the third octet (2 exp. 4 = 16). Other than correct command syntax, the remaining task is to convert the subnet mask to the inverse, or wildcard, mask. This is done by looking at the subnet mask in 32-bit form and inverting every bit (0s to 1s and 1s to 0s, in effect). This results in the following network address and wildcard mask, 172.16.64.0 0.0.15.255. Remember that 0s in a wildcard mask explicate a match with the network address, while the 1s are *don't care* bits.
☒ **A.** AREA 5 RANGE 172.16.64.0 255.255.240.0 is incorrect because this command summarizes the specified range and, if this router is configured as an ABR, it will propagate this route to all other areas. **C.** AREA 5 NETWORK 172.16.64.0 255.255.240.0 is incorrect because its command syntax is invalid. **D.** 172.16.64.0 0.0.240.255 AREA 5 is incorrect because its wildcard mask is invalid.

2. ☑ **D.** Configure a virtual link between Router 1 and Router 4 is the correct answer because this will provide Area 4 with virtual connectivity to the backbone area, ensuring that it receives appropriate routing updates, including external routes. Remember that the OSPF protocol requires that all areas be either directly attached to the backbone area or virtually attached via a virtual link.
☒ **A.** Configure Area 4 as a stubby area is incorrect because stubby areas rely on default routes for connectivity to external networks. Also, this does

not elevate the requirement for connecting all areas to the backbone.
B. Configure a virtual link between Router 2 and Router 4 is incorrect
because a virtual link is configured to the closest ABR that is connect to the
backbone, thus crossing only one transit area which, for this example, is
Area 3. **C.** Configure Area 4 as a totally stubby area is incorrect because
totally stubby areas require default routes for connectivity to both external
routes and inter-area routes.

3. ☑ **A.** Backbone area is correct, since within OSPF, Area 0 is often referred
to as the backbone area. This is the area to which all other areas are required
to connect to update routing information, thus making it an aggregate area
for inter-area communications. The backbone area is the most critical
within an OSPF design, which is why its design characteristics stress
redundancy, throughput, and configuration simplicity.
☒ **B.** Core area is incorrect within OSPF terminology, although Area 0
does represent the core layer within the hierarchical network design
model. **C.** Distribution area is incorrect because this term has no meaning
within OSPF.

IPX NLSP Configuration

1. ☑ **A.** 1–63 is the range of NLSP's cost metrics. The actual default cost
depends on the bandwidth of the interface's media. Some typical media
default costs include Ethernet (default cost is 20), FDDI (default cost is 14),
and Token Ring (16Mbps default cost is 19; 4Mbps default cost is 25). The
default cost can be changed, however, on a per interface basis by using the
IPX NLSP METRIC interface configuration command.
☒ **B.** Cost = 100,000,000/BW is incorrect because this describes the
default cost for the OSPF routing protocol. **C.** 1–6300 is incorrect because
this range does not exist for this topic.

2. ☑ **B.** is the configuration that successfully enables NLSP on both its interfaces, including using the required IPXWAN on the serial interface. This example also manually disables RIP-IPX, which runs by default whenever IPX routing is turned on. Finally, it uses the IPX ROUTER NLSP and AREA-ADDRESS commands to fulfill the NLSP configuration requirements. The configuration command syntax for enabling an IPX routing protocol is:

```
ipx router {nlsp [tag]|rip|eigrp autonomous-system-number}
```

The router configuration command for defining network numbers for an NLSP area is:

```
area-address address mask
```

☒ **A.** This configuration is incorrect because it does not specify an internal network number, which is required by NLSP, nor does it disable RIP-IPX, as specified. **C.** The router configuration command for NLSP makes this answer incorrect. NLSP uses the AREA-ADDRESS command to define a set of network numbers to an area, then enable the interface for NLSP operation on the interface itself. **D.** The interface configuration commands to enable NLSP are missing the A3 tag, which associates it to the network ranges created within the NLPS router configuration. This configuration also fails to disable RIP-IPX.

3. ☑ **A.** The command SHOW IPX NLSP NEIGHBORS DETAIL displays all the neighbors with whom NLSP has formed adjacencies. If a router you anticipated is not displayed, check for connectivity and that both routers contain the same AREA-ADDRESS command within their NLSP router configurations.

☒ **B.** SHOW IPX NLSP is incorrect because it is an ambiguous command. **C.** SHOW IPX NLSP DATABASE is incorrect because this command displays entries with the link-state database, which does not include adjacency status. **D.** SHOW IPX ROUTE is incorrect because this command displays IPX routing information only—not adjacency status.

4. ☑ **C.** SHOW IPX ROUTE displays routing information. The network and mask, 1300 FFFFFF00, should be displayed if everything is configured correctly. This route should also have an NA in the far left column, indicating that it is an NLSP aggregate route.
☒ **A.** SHOW IPX NLSP NEIGHBOR DETAIL is incorrect because it displays neighbor information. **B.** SHOW IPX ROUTE-AGGREGATION is not a valid NLSP command. **D.** SHOW IPX NLSP DATABASE is incorrect because it displays a summary of the list-state database.

Enhanced IGRP (EIGRP) Configuration

1. ☑ **A.** is correct because the command IPX ROUTER EIGRP 1 starts EIGRP for IPX as Autonomous System 1 and the next two statements, NETWORK 20 and NETWORK 50, assign EIGRP for IPX updates to these networks.
☒ **B.** is incorrect because this command assigns Network 50 to the S0 port of Router A. **C.** is incorrect because the NO NETWORK 50 command turns off RIP updates on Network 50. **D.** is incorrect because the IPX ROUTER EIGRP 1 command starts an EIGRP for IPX process as Autonomous System 1.

2. ☑ **C.** is the correct answer because if a route fails, the router looks for a feasible successor in its topology table. If a feasible successor exists, it is promoted to successor and added to the routing table and used.
☒ **A.** is incorrect because the router only sends out a query packet if there is no feasible successor in the topology table. **B.** is incorrect because the router only flags the route as in an active state if no feasible successor is available. **D.** is incorrect because of the key words *all-routes explorer packets*. This term comes from Token Ring source-route bridging and does not apply to the successor process in EIGRP.

Border Gateway Protocol (BGP)

1. ☑ **D.** The route 0.0.0.0 is the default route in the routing table. If there is no matching route for a destination IP address in the routing table, then 0.0.0.0 will match the address and cause the packet to be routed out the S0 interface to the ISP.

   ☒ **A.** is incorrect because the 255.255.255.255 mask is incorrect. **B.** is incorrect because you want a default route that will match any unknown packet and send it out the S0 interface. 10.0.0.0 will not do that. If a packet were destined for, say, the 5.0.0.0 network, then it would never leave the internal system. **C.** is incorrect for the same reasons. It is an incorrect mask and does not provide a default for all routes.

2. ☑ **B.** A connection-oriented session in the form of TCP. Since the question asks about establishing a session, you should immediately think of a connection-oriented session. Since TCP is connection oriented and UDP is not, it is the only logical choice.

   ☒ **A.** is incorrect because hello packets are used by link-state protocols to maintain neighbor relationships. BGP uses hello's to maintain connectivity, but only after a TCP connection is established. **C.** is incorrect because a BGP session requires a connection-oriented protocol and UDP is connectionless. **D.** is incorrect because ICMP is a protocol for generating error messages and is irrelevant to the problem.

Configuring WAN Connectivity

1. ☑ **D.** ATM uses 53-byte cells with 5 bytes of header and 48 bytes of data. It would be more correct to say that ATM is cell switched.

   ☒ **A.** is incorrect because Frame Relay switches packets, not cells. Frame Relay packets are also considerably larger than 53 bytes, and are more likely to be 476 or 1500 bytes. **B.** is incorrect because ISDN is circuit switched, not packet switched. **C.** is incorrect because, while SMDS is a packet-switched service, it does not use 53-byte cells.

2. ☑ **B.** PPP MULTILINK enables Multilink on a rotary group.
☒ **A.** is incorrect because, while ENCAPSULATION PPP is a proper command, there are no additional optional settings. **D.** is incorrect because the DIALER command has no option for Multilink, so is incorrect syntax. **C.** is also incorrect syntax.

Configuring ISDN Connectivity

1. ☑ **A, C, D.** Both T1 and E1 can use Alternate Mark Inversion (AMI) as the default line-code type, but T1 can also use Binary 8-Zero Substitution (B8ZS) for PRI configuration. E1 can use High-Density Bipolar 3 (HDB3) for PRI configurations. Linecoding and frame type are determined by the service provider and are usually based upon the service requested.
☒ **B.** is incorrect because ESF is the Extended Super Frame type for a T1 configuration. **E.** is incorrect because CRC4 is the default frame type for E1 configuration.

2. ☑ **C.** Protocols beginning with E recommend telephone network standards for ISDN such as the E.164 protocol, which describes international addressing for ISDN.
☒ **A.** is incorrect because protocols that begin with I deal with concepts, terminology, and general methods. An example of this is I.400, which describes how the User Network Interface (UNI) is provided. **B.** is incorrect because protocols that begin with Q cover how switching and signaling should operate. **D.** is incorrect because Q.193 recommends a network layer between the terminal end point and the local ISDN switch.

Frame Relay

1. ☑ **A, B, C.** are correct because they are all routable protocols. Note that IPX and AppleTalk are configured in much the same way as IP, but there are some special considerations, namely broadcasts.
☒ **D.** is incorrect because although DLSW+ and IP tunneling allow one to use SNA in an NBMA network, SNA is a nonroutable protocol.

2. ☑ **A, B.** A point-to-point subinterface can have one and only one DLCI associated with it, while a multipoint subinterface can have multiple DLCIs assigned to it.

☒ **C.** is incorrect because a multipoint can have multiple DLCIs assigned to it. **D.** is incorrect because, although it is certainly true that a multipoint subinterface can have more DLCIs assigned to it than a point-to-point, which can only have only one, **A, B.** are better choices.

Configuring Bandwidth-on-Demand

1. ☑ **B.** is the correct command because the correct syntax for this command is:

```
dialer-list dialer-group protocol protocol-name [permit|deny|list]
access-list-number
```

Since the access-list number is 101, we know this access list is an IP extended access list. If the number had been 1–99 it would have been an IP standard access list. If the number were 800–899, then it would have been an IPX standard access list. If the number had been 900–999, then it would have been an IPX extended access list.

☒ **A.** is incorrect because the access-list number indicated that this is an IP access list. **C.** is incorrect for the exact same reason. **D.** is incorrect because although it specifies the IP protocol, the syntax is incorrect. The command should read PROTOCOL IP, not IP PROTOCOL.

2. ☑ **B.** The syntax is to first indicate which interface to backup in case the primary link traffic load is too much. The command syntax for this is BACKUP INTERFACE *interface-name*. The next task is to set the traffic load thresholds for dial backup service using the command BACKUP LOAD {*enable-threshold* | **never**} {*disable-load* | **never**}

☒ **A.** is incorrect because of the hyphen between BACKUP and LOAD in the second command. **C.** is incorrect because of the hyphen between BACKUP and INTERFACE in the first command. **D.** is incorrect because the ENABLE-THRESHOLD and the disable threshold are backwards in the BACKUP LOAD command.

Integrating Nonrouted Services and IRB

1. ☑ **A, C.** SHOW INTERFACES *interface* IRB allows you to view the protocols this bridged interface can route, the protocols this bridged interface bridges, and the entries in the software MAC-address filter. SHOW INTERFACE *interface-name* allows you to view information about the BVI including the BVI MAC address and processing statistics.
☒ **B.** is incorrect because of incorrect syntax. **D.** is incorrect because of the incorrect keyword INTERFACE. The correct word is INTERFACES.

2. ☑ **A.** You first have to enable IRB, which is accomplished with the BRIDGE IRB command. Next, you have to enable the BVI to accept and route routable packets received from its corresponding bridge group using the BRIDGE *bridge-group* ROUTE *protocol.* Finally, you need to disable bridging over a defined bridge group for those protocols that you want to route only over the bridge group interfaces. Use the NO BRIDGE *bridge-group* ROUTE *protocol.* Note that you cannot disable bridging for nonroutable protocols such as SNA.
☒ **B.** is incorrect because the first command to enable IRB is incorrect. There is no need to specify a bridge group to enable IRB. **C.** is incorrect because of incorrect syntax in the command to disable bridging for IP. **D.** is incorrect because IRB is not enabled correctly. There is again no need to specify a ring group to enable IRB.

3. ☑ **D.** is the correct answer because CRB and IRB cannot both be enabled at the same time.
☒ **A.** is incorrect because with CRB packets entering a bridged interface, they can only exit another bridged interface. **B.** is incorrect because CRB packets entering a routed interface can only exit another routed interface. In both cases, no mixing of bridged and routed interfaces is allowed. **C.** is incorrect because CRB and IRB cannot be configured simultaneously on the same router.

Transparent Bridging

1. ☑ **A, B, D, E.** IOS documentation states that the allowable values for the state of the interface are forwarding, down, listening, blocking and learning.
☒ **C.** is incorrect because, if an interface is disabled, then it is down. Disabled is not the correct word to describe a down interface. **F.** is incorrect because even though a flood may be occurring, flooding is not an allowable interface state. In the event of a flood, the most likely interface state would be forwarding.

2. ☑ **D.** Router B interface E 1, as seen in the SHOW SPAN output for Router B line 10 where it says: Port 3 (Ethernet1) of bridge group 1 is blocking. The key word is BLOCKING. Since the status of the interface is blocking, spanning-tree has shut down this interface to avoid a loop.
☒ **A, B, C.** are incorrect because if we examine the results of the SHOW SPAN command for each of these interfaces, we see that each interface is forwarding.

Source-Route Bridging

1. ☑ **B.** In an environment in which some hosts support source routing and some do not, you must use source-route transparent bridging (SRT). Source-route transparent bridging combines implementations of transparent bridging and SRB algorithms.
☒ **A.** is incorrect because the problem specifically states that some hosts do not support source routing. **C.** is incorrect because transparent bridging does not support those hosts that use source routing. Transparent bridging is more frequently associated with Ethernet networks. **D.** is incorrect because no translational bridging is necessary since this is a pure Token Ring environment.

2. ☑ **C.** The source-end terminal will first transmit a local test frame to determine if the destination is on the local ring.

☒ **A.** is the incorrect answer because the source-end terminal doesn't transmit an all-routes explorer frame unless the destination address is not on the local ring. Note that, although this is the way SNA acts, NetBIOS transmits a single-route explorer instead. This is the reason **B.** is incorrect. **D.** is incorrect for the same reason as **A.** The all-routes explorer is a broadcast frame.

3. ☑ **D.** Proper configuration requires one to identify the interface to be bridged, so one needs to specify the correct local-bridge connection using the syntax SOURCE-BRIDGE *local-ring bridge-number target-ring*. You can then activate either manual spanning by using the command SOURCE-BRIDGE SPANNING or automatic spanning by using the command SOURCE-BRIDGE SPANNING *bridge-group* [path-cost *path-cost*]. The SOURCE-BRIDGE SPANNING command enables the forwarding of spanning-tree explorers on all ring interfaces. A spanning-tree explorer packet is an explorer packet sent to a defined group of hosts configured as part of a spanning tree in the network.

☒ **A.** is incorrect because the order in the second line is backwards. The correct syntax requires you to specify the local ring first rather than the target ring. **B.** is incorrect because the order of the bridge number and target ring is backwards. The bridge number should come before the target ring. **C.** is incorrect because it identifies the incorrect interface. The interface should be TOKENRING 0 instead of TOKENRING 1.

Data-Link Switching Plus (DLSw+)

1. ☑ **D.** DLSw+ supports four types of encapsulation: TCP/IP, FST/IP, direct encapsulation for point-to-point connections, and LLC2 encapsulation for Frame Relay connections.

2. ☑ F. A circuit ID consists of the source and destination MAC addresses, SAP, and data-link control port ID.

☒ All the other answers are incorrect because, although they are part of a circuit ID, it takes all four parts for a complete circuit.

Part 2

CIT 4.0
(Exam 640-440)

EXAM TOPICS

Troubleshooting Methodology

LAN Troubleshooting Problem Areas

WAN Troubleshooting Problem Areas

The Internet Protocol (IP)

Novell's Internetwork Packet Exchange (IPX) Protocol

AppleTalk Protocol

Common Routing Protocols

Troubleshooting Tools

Cisco's Diagnostic Tools

Advanced Diagnostic Tools

Campus Switches and VLANs

Hands-on Troubleshooting

Troubleshooting the ISDN Basic Rate Interface (BRI)

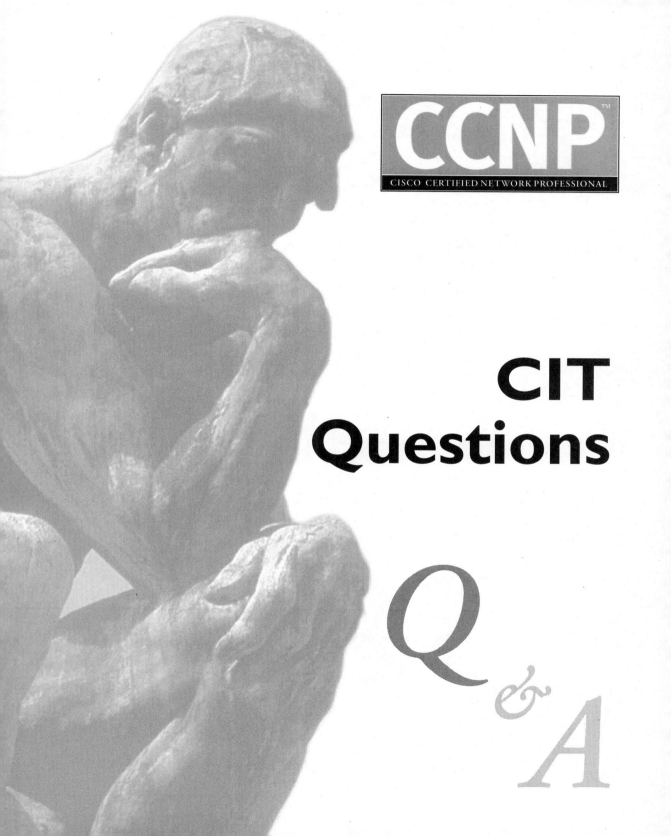

This section is designed to help you prepare for the Cisco Internetwork Troubleshooting 4.0 (CIT) exam, so you can begin to reap the career benefits of CCNP certification. The following questions are structured in a format similar to what you'll find on the CIT exam. Read all the choices carefully, as there may be more than one correct answer. Choose all correct answers for each question.

Troubleshooting Methodology

1. What is the 80/20 rule?

   A. 80 percent of the traffic for 20 percent of the users

   B. 80 percent of the traffic for local users and 20 percent for remote users

   C. 80 percent of the traffic for local use and 20 percent for internetworking

   D. 80 percent of the traffic for internetworking and 20 percent for local use

2. When are short-term collision rates considered unacceptable?

   A. When rates are below 20 percent of available bandwidth

   B. When rates are as high as 20–25 percent of available bandwidth

   C. When anything exceeds 30 percent of available bandwidth

   D. You can ignore collision statistics as long as users are satisfied with response times

3. You are a new Network Engineer for Major International Bank, and the finance department is having problems communicating with the remainder of the network. Which document should you look at to define and state the problem?

   A. Employee phone listing

   B. Diagram of the network topology

   C. Diagram of the office floor plan

   D. None of the above

4. Utilization levels, frame transmission per second, frame size, collision rates jabbers, runts and fragment totals, and CRC errors that are collected on a regular basis are items that you would be checking on your network to determine what?

A. Network utilization

B. Analyzing problems

C. Baselining

D. Network performance

5. Which type of protocol provides a virtual link between devices, sequenced packet delivery, and guaranteed data delivery?

A. Connection-oriented protocol

B. Connectionless protocol

C. Private virtual circuit (PVC)

D. SNMP

exam
ⓦatch

For every short-term period, network utilization may be peaking toward 100 percent—without noticeable network delays or performance degradation. This is possible during a large FTP file transfer between two high-performance end stations. One thing to keep in mind is that each application environment behaves differently, depending on variables such as bandwidth, routing protocols, and so on.

6. Which of the following are indicators that CSMA/CD increases the amount of transmission time it takes to send packets and frames?

A. If two stations transmit simultaneously, the information transmitted will collide at some point

B. A station will only receive information that has been sent in order of transmission

C. A station will send a jam signal to stop all other stations from sending in order to send its own information

D. Once a station sends information, no other devices on an Ethernet LAN can transfer data until that station has completed its transmission

7. What typed of media does FDDI communicate on?

   A. Coaxial cable

   B. Twisted-pair phone cable (Category 3)

   C. Twisted-pair phone cable (Category 5)

   D. Fiber optic cable

8. Which TCP/IP Internet address format class(s) are used for Multicasting?

   A. Class B

   B. Class C

   C. Class D

   D. Class E

---

exam
Ⓦatch

After monitoring network traffic, you can use a ping test to actively test your network. These tests will provide you with detailed statistical information (depending on command options used) about network traffic and particular devices.

---

9. A non-extended AppleTalk network allows which of the following?

   A. 127 hosts

   B. 127 servers

   C. 253 hosts/servers

   D. Both A and B

LAN Troubleshooting Problem Areas

1. What layer of the OSI can perform both error and flow control?

A. Physical

B. Data link

C. Network

D. Transport

2. Which of the following statements is true?

A. LLC type 1 does not require data links or link stations to be established

B. Once an LLC type 2 connection is established, link state information is centrally managed

C. Since LLC is a subset of HDLC, link stations must operate in a connection-oriented hierarchy

D. SNA traffic must be encapsulated in LLC2 frames in order to traverse a network

3. What is the minimum frame size of an Ethernet frame?

A. 32 bits

B. 512 bits

C. 1024 bits

D. 1518 bits

exam
ⓦatch
Remember to track and monitor excessive collision rates. Keep in mind the utilization rate must be high before collisions present serious problems on the network.

QUESTIONS AND ANSWERS

I'm getting calls from the solution center regarding slow response times.	Rule of thumb: First find the network segment where users are located, and what resources they are contending for. Check that particular LAN segment (say, Ethernet interface E2/2). Look for errors, collision rates, and so on, to isolate the problem. Track the problem and convert the data into a statistical analysis for problem isolation and root cause. Check logs and utilization rates for that particular interface. This is a good starting point.
Our Token Ring isn't functioning at all. Where do I start?	Start by using the SHOW INTERFACE TOKEN command to look at a particular token interface. The output will help you determine the status of the interface. If the token interface and line protocol aren't active, try a NO SHUTDOWN command. This will attempt to re-initialize (restart) the interface. Secondly, check cabling to make sure it's physically connected and in good condition. Check configuration, as well, to make sure the interface is configured properly.
I'm getting alarms that indicate duplicate hardware addresses. Why?	This can happen if routers' MAC addresses are administered locally. A good starting point would be to test the duplicate address from a booting device using a network analyzer. If the device gets a response, there is a high probability that another station has the identical MAC address. Correct the problem by changing the MAC address of one of the devices, and re-initialize.
What are some helpful general troubleshooting tools?	Ping is the most useful general-help tool. It will tell you whether a device is reachable by sending ICMP echo request and waiting for a reply. If no reply comes back, you know there's a problem with that device. A protocol analyzer is also a good troubleshooting tool. Traceroute is also a helpful tool.

QUESTIONS AND ANSWERS

What is the difference between routed protocols and routing protocols?	Routed protocols direct user traffic. Routing protocols work *between* routers to maintain routing tables and paths.
I just received 10 new employees in my existing workgroup. There is no available space to connect additional users to our LAN. What do I do?	You'll probably have to get some type of hub to provide additional ports to accommodate new users. Depending on your current LAN infrastructure, this approach may not be feasible.
How can I connect two dissimilar LANs?	You can achieve this by way of encapsulation. *Translational encapsulation* is a method of connecting LANs that have dissimilar Physical and Data Link architecture (MAC sublayer protocols), such as Token Ring to Ethernet.

4. What is the correct sequence for a new station to enter a Token Ring network?

   A. Station runs a NIC card self diagnostic, then station searches for the active monitor station. If there is no active monitor the station initiates a claim process.
   B. Station conducts a media check. Station then transmits a duplicate address test frame.
   C. Station conducts a check of the existing lobe connections. Station then transmits a neighbor notification frame signaling that the station is preparing to enter the ring.
   D. Station searches the ring for an active monitor. Station then requests a unique station address from the ring active monitor.

5. In an ATM network the LEC MAC address in an ELAN is assigned by?

   A. LEC
   B. LES
   C. BUS
   D. LECS

WAN Troubleshooting Problem Areas

1. What are the three primary parts of a PPP frame?

    A. Header, address, data

    B. Header, data-control field, trailer

    C. Address, data, trailer

    D. Header, payload, trailer

2. Which of the following statements is NOT true?

    A. SDLC differs from HDLC in that it is not used for peer-to-peer communications

    B. SDLC uses a framing format similar to that of the HDLC frame

    C. SDLC is a proven standard and is known for its great error recovery method

    D. SDLC typically supports two types of line encoding, NRZi and non-NRZi

3. How many octets are in the LMI header?

    A. Four

    B. Five

    C. Six

    D. Seven

4. The X.121 standards used in an X.25 network dictates that a Network User Address (NUA) can have up to how many digits?

    A. Eight

    B. 10

    C. 12

    D. 14

5. What is the total number of bytes in an SMDS and ATM cell structure?

A. 48 bytes

B. 53 bytes

C. 128 bytes

D. 256 bytes

6. Which ATM adaptation layer (AAL) supports both connectionless and connection-oriented protocols?

A. AAL1

B. AAL2

C. AAL3/4

D. AAL5

7. Which test is run intrusively to identify basic logic errors on a data circuit?

A. Bipolar violation

B. Bit errors

C. CRC errors

D. Frame errors

exam
ⓦatch

In order to provide Frame Relay users with access to SMDS, a Bellcore standard called the SMDS Interface Protocol Relay Service (a.k.a. SIP Relay) was released. This standard enables SMDS to be encapsulated and transported within Frame Relay, as well.

The Internet Protocol (IP)

1. Once a request-for-comments (RFC) document is given an RFC number, what does it represent?

    A. It has been accepted as a comment and will be awaiting further review to determine if the standard it is proposing is complete and accurate
    B. It has been reviewed and it is awaiting a proposal to determine if it is complete and accurate
    C. It has been reviewed and the proposal has been completed and is deemed to be the final specification for whatever it is documenting
    D. None of the above

2. IP Version 6 has how many categories of addresses?

    A. Two
    B. Three
    C. Four
    D. Five

3. What happens when a TCP packet is received and the checksum and sequencing are correct?

    A. Nothing
    B. The receiving station sends an acknowledgement packet back to the transmitter of the sent packet
    C. The receiving station sends a message asking for the frame or packet to be retransmitted.
    D. The receiving station waits for the transmitter to send an acknowledgment packet to the receiver stating that the transmission is complete.

4. A port on a server represents which of the following?

    A. HyperText Transfer Protocol (HTTP)
    B. File Transport Protocol (FTP)
    C. Services offered by the server
    D. Simple Mail Transport Protocol (SMTP)

5. You are capturing packets on your network. Listed below is a packet you have captured. What is the source port number of this packet?

```
TCP: ----- TCP Header -----
TCP:
TCP: Source port = 25
TCP: Destination port = 65445
TCP: Sequence number = 1094177019
TCP: Acknowledgement number = 16927231
TCP: Data offset = 24 bytes
TCP: Flags = 0X12
TCP:        . . 0 . . . . . = No urgent pointer
TCP:        . . . 1  . . . . = Acknowledgement
TCP:        . . . . 0 . . . = No push
TCP:        . . . . . 0 . . = No reset
TCP:        . . . . . . 1 . = Syn
TCP:        . . . . . . . 0 = No Fin
TCP: Window = 8760
TCP: Checksum = 0x1f7d
TCP: Urgent pointer = 0
TCP: Options:  (4 bytes)
TCP:    - Maximum segment size = 1460 bytes
TCP:
```

A. 25

B. 65445

C. 8760

D. 0x1f7d

exam **Watch**

Try to get comfortable with examining packet captures. You'll find that a number of questions on the exam will be presented in the form of a packet capture, and you'll be asked to identify individual parts of the capture or identify the purpose of the packet overall. These won't be limited to IP, and the question may involve topics that are covered in other sections of the CCNP CIT 4.0 Study Guide, such as Token Ring and IP together.

6. UDP packets perform which of the following?

A. Checksum

B. Three-Way Handshake

C. Sequence numbers

D. Sliding Window

---

exam
ⓦatch

Another way to think of the sliding window is by looking at how many bytes the receiving host has set aside to receive packets. Be prepared to identify window sizes in a packet capture, and to answer questions that call it the "sliding window" or "receive buffer."

---

7. When a host or client makes a request for a DNS name resolution, what type of protocol would it use?

A. TCP

B. UDP

C. SNMP

D. None of the above

---

exam
ⓦatch

Be aware of the advantages and disadvantages of connection-oriented and connectionless protocols. Also, be aware that UDP isn't the only connectionless protocol. The exam may mix IP connectionless vs. connection-oriented characteristics with the characteristics of other protocols, such as IPX and SPX.

QUESTIONS AND ANSWERS

I want to be able to add or move hosts without having to change their IP addresses.	You can't avoid changing their IP addresses if they move to a different subnet, but you can make the process automatic with DHCP.
One host doesn't seem to communicate with any other hosts on any subnets.	This is most likely a Layer 1 or 2 problem. If the ARP table is empty, check the cables, check link lights, etc.
I can ping hosts on the same subnet as my host, but not on other subnets.	There are two likely causes: Either bad routing information (missing or wrong default gateway), or the subnet mask is wrong (trying to ARP directly instead of using default gateway).
I have two routers on my subnet. Which do I pick as the default gateway?	It doesn't really matter. If they both have complete routing tables, your packets will always get where they are supposed to go. Consider checking to see if your host can run a routing protocol, or be configured to accept ICMP redirects to improve its routing information.
My host can't get an address via DHCP.	There are many things that might be broken in this scenario. First, check to see if other hosts on that same subnet can get DHCP addresses. If not, check the router forwarding or DHCP server. If other hosts can get the DHCP addresses, check the cables, the NIC, etc. If possible, swap cables with a working host to see if the problem follows the host or the cable.
I can't retrieve a web page from a remote web server.	Ping it. If it doesn't respond, troubleshoot it as a Layer 3 problem, possibly using TRACEROUTE. If the ping works, TELNET to port 80 and issue a GET command. If you get HTML back, check the settings on your browser software.
When I TELNET to a TCP port to test if the server is listening on that port, I get "connection refused."	The server isn't listening on that port, or it's configured to refuse connections from your IP address. If you get back a refusal right away instead of having to wait a few minutes for a timeout, it is almost certainly a server problem and not a network problem. The exception would be some sort of firewalling.

CIT
QUESTIONS

Novell's Internetwork Packet Exchange (IPX) Protocol

1. What would be the correct IPX addressing format for a workstation on network 123 with Media Access Control (MAC) address of 0080C712202D?

   A. 0080C712202D:00000123

   B. 00000123; 0080C712202D

   C. 00000123:0080C712202D

   D. 0080C712202D;00000123

---

2. Which of the following is an accurate statement about Service Advertising Protocol (SAP)?

   A. SAP broadcasts are generated every 30 seconds

   B. SAP is a routable protocol

   C. SAP uses a split-horizon broadcast scheme

   D. SAP stores information about how to reach its remote networks

exam
ⓦatch

NLSP is the default routing protocol for newer versions of NetWare, but it can be changed to RIP/SAP through the INETCFG server utility. RIP/SAP is automatically enabled on Cisco routers when IPX is configured, but NLSP is not. To enable NLSP, the administrator must first assign an IPX internal address to the router, enable NLSP, then assign an area address and mask. Once this is done, the administrator can enable NLSP on individual router interfaces.

3. What is the standard number of the checksum field in an IPX packet?

A. FFFF

B. AAAA

C. 00FF

D. 0FFF

exam
ⓦatch

If you wish to configure a NetWare server to not automatically answer all NCP Get Nearest Server requests, type the following command at the server console prompt: set reply to get nearest server = off. This command can be added to AUTOEXEC.NCF if you want to make this setting automatically upon server startup.

AppleTalk Protocol

1. The Routing Table Maintenance Protocol (RTMP) routing is turned on by issuing which of the following Cisco IOS commands?

A. APPLE TALK ROUTING

B. APPLETALK ROUTING

C. APPLE TALK ROUTE

D. APPLETALK ROUTE

exam

ⓦ **a t c h** *Try to get used to identifying the various parts of AppleTalk packets. You may be asked to identify the protocol of a packet, its purpose, and so forth.*

2. Which of the following statements is true about the Datagram Delivery Protocol (DDP)?

A. DDP is an unreliable, connectionless protocol

B. DDP is an unreliable, connection-oriented protocol

C. DDP is a reliable, connection-oriented protocol

D. DDP is a reliable, connectionless protocol

3. If there is no router present, the AppleTalk device will keep its startup address and use it to communicate. For which of the following is this useful?

A. Simple file sharing and printing

B. Simple file sharing only

C. Simple printing only

D. Zone lists

exam

ⓦ **a t c h** *A Macintosh stores the previous network address and zone name on its hard drive, but it keeps other kinds of information in a special, small section of memory called Parameter RAM (PRAM). PRAM stores special settings about the Mac, mostly hardware information (about the hard drive, video card, and so on). If you're familiar with PC hardware, think of PRAM as similar to the CMOS. PRAM also stores information about the network card. On occasion, PRAM becomes corrupt or miss-set and needs to be cleared. You may need to perform the following procedure if a Mac doesn't seem to be recognizing its network card properly.*

To clear the PRAM on a Mac, restart it; and while it's restarting (before the "happy Mac" picture appears), press and hold down COMMAND-OPTION-P-R. *Yes, indeed, that's four keys, all pressed at the same time. When the PRAM has been cleared, the boot process may be different while the Mac rediscovers its hardware.*

4. If two seed routers are on the same network segment, what must match?

   A. Cable range

   B. Zone lists

   C. Cable range and zone lists

   D. None of the above

---

e x a m
ⓦa t c h

There may be one shortcut available to you while doing a manual TRACEROUTE, and the next router is a Cisco router. Cisco has written a proprietary protocol called the Cisco Discovery Protocol (CDP). CDP's purpose in life is to help various pieces of Cisco equipment find one another, for network management purposes. We can take advantage of this as well, since one item of information passed via CDP is the AppleTalk address. Here is the command to use, followed by its output list of neighboring Cisco devices:

```
Router>show cdp neighbor detail
Device ID: Router2
Entry address(es):
 IP address: 10.0.0.12
 Appletalk address: 9000.127
Platform: cisco 7000,  Capabilities: Router
Interface: Fddi4/0,  Port ID (outgoing port):
Fddi3/0
Holdtime : 129 sec
Version :
Cisco Internetwork Operating System Software
IOS (tm) GS Software (GS7-K-M), Version 10.3(12),
RELEASE SOFTWARE (fc1)
Copyright (c) 1986-1996 by cisco Systems, Inc.
Compiled Mon 03-Jun-96 12:59 by dschwart
```

As you can see, CDP provides a handy map of IP address to AppleTalk address. Be prepared to answer questions about CDP on the exams.

QUESTIONS AND ANSWERS

I want to be able to use my old LocalTalk devices with my EtherTalk devices.	You have two choices: Buy a converter for each of the LocalTalk devices, or get some LocalTalk-to-EtherTalk routers.
I need to be able to use more than 253 devices on the same network number. How do I arrange this?	You can't. You can, however, achieve the same effect by creating a cable range that consists of multiple, contiguous network numbers. This is, for all intents and purposes, just like having a larger network with a single network number.
I want to document my AppleTalk network so I'm prepared when trouble arises.	Good. Pick a time when your network is operating properly, log in to a router, and copy the output from the SHOW APPLETALK ZONE and SHOW APPLETALK ROUTE commands. Save a backup copy of all of your router configuration files. Create a file to track usage of your network numbers, so you can allocate new ones without conflict. Create a list of network numbers and the router they are on, so you can track them down if they fall out of the routing table.
Should I use RTMP or EIGRP for my AppleTalk routing?	It depends on your environment. If you have a small network with mostly LAN connections, RTMP will probably be simpler. If you have a large network with lots of WAN links, EIGRP is probably better.
One of my users doesn't have any zones in their Chooser. Why?	Go through your normal Layer 1 and 2 troubleshooting sequence (link light, etc.). If there are other protocols on the Mac, try those as well. Do you have enough addresses in your cable range? Is the right protocol selected (for instance, EtherTalk and not LocalTalk)? Have you tried rebooting? Do the drivers need updating?
My user's printer isn't showing up in the zone where it's supposed to be. Why?	Is the printer turned on and otherwise ready to print? Is the printer in the right zone? If it's a printer that prints a "test page" on startup, power it off and back on, and look at the test page to see if it shows which zone it's in. Can anyone else print to the printer? Is all of the networking cabling in place?
I don't have enough addresses for all of my AppleTalk devices. How do I deal with this?	Expand or replace the cable range on that network segment. Try to allocate about twice as much address space as is needed for all the devices. Remember to change the cable range on all seed routers if more than one exists on that network segment.

Common Routing Protocols

I. Which of the following statements is true?

  A. BGP and OSPF are link-state, event-driven routing protocols

  B. RIP and IGRP are distance-vector, periodic-broadcast routing protocols

  C. Link-state protocols maintain the entire network topology and centrally determine the best path to each destination network

  D. Distance-vector routing protocols only maintain a database of the destination routes

e x a m
ⓦatch   *Always include the keyword "subnets" when redistributing routes.*

2. Which of the following is the correct list of routing protocols, sorted by highest to lowest administrative distance:

  A. RIP, IS-IS, IGRP, OSPF

  B. External BGP, OSPF, static route, connected interface

  C. RIP, IGRP, Connected interface, Static route

  D. RIP, OSPF, IGRP, static route

e x a m
ⓦatch   *Running RIP with an instance of another periodic broadcast routing protocol, such as IGRP, can result in routing issues. This is because the asynchronous updates and administrative distances compete to insert routes into the forwarding table.*

3. Which of the following statements is NOT true?

A. AppleTalk phase 1 allows for only one zone per network

B. AppleTalk phase 2 allows for 254 node devices per network

C. An AppleTalk network can be a member of multiple zones

D. An AppleTalk node can only be a member of one zone

---

exam
ⓦatch

When redistributing routing protocols with classless VLSM networks into IGRP, be sure that there are classful static routes with a Null next hop redistributed as well.

---

4. What are the timers associated with RIP? Choose all that apply.

A. Update

B. Invalid

C. Flush

D. Destination

---

exam
ⓦatch

Understand how to use OSPF on point-to-point, point-to-multipoint, and broadcast media.

---

exam
ⓦatch

Be sure to design an OSPF network and assign IP addresses so that they summarize. In addition, beware of summarizing routes and then redistributing them into classful routing protocols.

---

5. When a ZIP broadcast storm occurs what is the best method for detecting many ZIP requests in succession?

A. Enabling DEBUG APPLETALK EVENTS

B. Enabling APPLETALK EVENTS

C. Enabling DEBUG EVENTS APPLETALK

D. Enabling DEBUG EVENTS–APPLETALK

exam
Watch

When redistributing OSPF routes, be sure to include external1, external 2, and subnets keywords.

exam
Watch

Know how and where to use virtual links for extending a backbone area.

6. Which of the following is considered an IGP protocol?

A. OSPF

B. IS-IS

C. EBGP

D. EIGRP

exam
Watch

Synchronization should almost always be disabled for BGP.

exam
Watch

*When generating an EBGP route using the **NETWORK** command, make sure that the route is already in the IGP routing table.*

Troubleshooting Tools

1. Which of the following is a Cisco IOS client utility?

    A. Telnet

    B. Ping

    C. Traceroute

    D. All of the above

exam
ⓦatch

Most UNIX operating systems and the Cisco IOS use UDP packets as the packets that are intended to expire along the way. The destination port number is usually somewhere in the 33,000 range. These port numbers don't mean anything in particular because they're intended to expire. The tracert program that comes with Microsoft Windows does something a little different, however: It uses ICMP packets instead of UDP. Specifically, it sends ICMP echo requests, essentially ping packets. The protocol used isn't really important, since it's the side effect that's desired. In practice, though, it may make a difference when a firewall is being used; one type of traceroute will work across the firewall, while another won't. If you have a Windows desktop computer, it may be useful to be able to execute UDP-style traceroutes from your router. On the Cisco exam, be prepared to recognize which type of traceroute is sent by a particular operating system, and how traceroute works in general.

QUESTIONS AND ANSWERS

Which tool will help me build a visual map of my network?	One of the easiest ways to do this is with an SNMP management package that has an autodiscovery feature, such as CiscoWorks.
I want to build a set of Web pages to report various things about my network. How do I do this?	There are a few ways to do this. If you already have a network-management package, see what kind of Web reporting capabilities it has. You can also obtain a scriptable SNMP package such as CMU SNMP and write your own scripts; or use something like the MRTG package designed for just that purpose. You may also be able to make use of the web server feature in newer IOS versions.
How can I tell if a cable is working?	You can either try it to see if it works, and watch the error counters; or you can use a specialized testing device. A tester will perform a better test faster, but may be expensive to purchase. Don't forget that cables which work fine at 10 Mbps may not work well at all at 100 Mbps, even if they're supposed to. If the cables will be used for 100 Mbps operation, test them at 100 Mbps.
I have a remote user complaining about not being able to communicate with a particular host, but I can reach it just fine. What's happening?	Symptoms experienced by remote users will reflect the state of their subnet, their equipment, and so on—not yours. You may need to do your troubleshooting from a device closer to the remote user, such as a router, switch, or UNIX host on their subnet. In some cases, you may have to talk the user through the steps of the tests you'd perform if you were there, and have them read the results to you.
How do I tell if a host is using all the bandwidth on a particular network, and which host is doing it?	Many packet analyzer programs include a "top talker" feature that can be used to determine exactly this information. Also, if the traffic is crossing a router, you can turn on the accounting router feature to get similar information.
How do I tell which switch port a particular host is connected to?	You can script your own tool to pull a list of port-to-MAC-address maps for each switch. Or, if you have CiscoWorks, UserManager will do it for you.

2. When a router passes a packet, the router subtracts 1 from the TTL value. If a loop occurs, the packet will loop for a maximum of how many hops?

    A. 255

    B. 254

    C. 16

    D. 15

---

exam
  Ⓦatch

Be prepared to answer somewhat imprecise questions about CiscoWorks. For example, you may be asked which CiscoWorks application is used to manage VLANs across multiple switches (the answer is VLANDirector). In previous CIT exams, the questions haven't been much more specific than that. It's possible that Cisco wants its certified professionals to be aware of CiscoWorks, without requiring detailed knowledge. Be familiar with the various CiscoWorks application names and their basic functions.

---

3. Which of the following is NOT a CiscoWorks application?

    A. ATMDirector

    B. CiscoDirector

    C. TrafficDirector

    D. UserTracker

exam
ⓦatch

Cisco routers provide a way for you to load a configuration file into them, via SNMP and TFTP. This configuration file need not be a complete file, so this also represents a way to execute arbitrary commands. This is very useful if you've lost the Telnet password or enable password, but you have an SNMP password for the router that is allowed to write. Here's an example of this technique:

```
# snmpset router private .1.3.6.1.4.1.9.2.1.53.10.1.99.34 string
router-confg
Received GET RESPONSE from 10.1.250.12
requestid 0x5d5b errstat 0x0 errindex 0x0
Name:
.iso.org.dod.internet.private.enterprises.cisco.local.1.53.10.1.99.34 -
> OCTET STRING- (ascii):        router-confg
#
# cat router-confg
line vty 0 4
password test

# telnet router
Trying 10.1.250.12...
Connected to router.
Escape character is '^]'.


User Access Verification

Password:
Router>
```

You'll substitute your router name or IP address for the word router in the snmpset command, and use the IP address of your TFTP server at the end of the OID (where the example has "10.1.99.34"). The example shown above sets the VTY password to "test." Be prepared to identify this as a password recovery technique on an exam.

  This example was prepared using the CMU snmpset program. For further examples (using HP OpenView) see: http://www. cisco.com/warp/public/490/11.html. Again, for this to work, SNMP must already be configured and you must have an SNMP write password. And watch out—this means anyone who has the SNMP write passwords to your router can have full control of it.

4. Which of the following is not a hardware troubleshooting tool?

   A. Sniffer Pro

   B. Continuity tester

   C. TDR

   D. Signal-quality tester

5. You are a Cisco Engineer for a major telecom company. Part of your job is to monitor router error messages. What command would you use to configure a router to log errors to a remote Syslog server?

   A. LOGGING BUFFERED

   B. LOGGING HOST

   C. LOGGING REMOTE

   D. LOGGING TO SERVER

Cisco's Diagnostic Tools

1. Of the following choices, which does the SHOW IP INTERFACE BRIEF command NOT display?

   A. Encapsulation

   B. IP address

   C. Administrative and physical status on each interface

   D. Protocol signaling on the interface

Watch out for "no keepalives" during troubleshooting.

2. Which of the following is the LAN interface IPX encapsulation for a Cisco router?

   A. HDLC

   B. Frame Relay

   C. Novell-Ether

   D. ATM

exam
Watch   *Verify netmasks during troubleshooting.*

3. Which of the following is NOT an output from SHOW ATM
INTERFACE command?

A. Verifying framing encapsulation, whether PLCP or direct map
B. Verifying whether the clock source is being obtained internally or from
the line
C. Viewing packet loss
D. Viewing PVC status change for instability

exam
Watch   *Be aware of the LMI type used for Frame Relay.*

4. To view each PID with dead processes retaining memory, what Cisco IOS
command is used?

A. SHOW MEMORY SUMMARY
B. SHOW SUMMARY MEMORY
C. SHOW PROCESSES MEMORY
D. SHOW MEMORY PROCESSES

exam
Watch   *Be familiar with both subinterfaces and protocol mapping on a
common interface.*

exam
Watch   *If your'e using Frame Relay subinterfaces, then split-horizon is on by
default. On non-subinterfaces, it is disabled by default.*

5. Choose all of the protocols that are supported by the PING command in Cisco IOS.

A. IP

B. IPX

C. AppleTalk

D. All of the above

---

e x a m
ⓦatch   *Know which IOS version is loaded on the router.*

Advanced Diagnostic Tools

I. Which of the following is NOT a benefit of performing advanced diagnostics on Cisco hardware?

A. Gathering valuable information

B. Performing important monitoring of the network and hardware

C. Gaining insight into future trends of Cisco technology

D. Gaining insight into fundamental operations of network protocol

---

e x a m
ⓦatch   *Be sure to understand ISDN DDR in terms of both configuration and troubleshooting.*

---

2. Which of the following commands is NOT a valid logging command?

A. LOGGING BUFFERED

B. LOGGING 10.1.1.2

C. LOGGING CONSOLE

D. LOGGING AUXILIARY

exam
ⓦatch   *Become intimately familiar with using a Cisco 2511 or 2611 as a multiconsole access device, and with switching between multiple reverse-Telnet sessions.*

3. Which command will execute the core dump file to its destination?

A. DUMP CORE
B. WRITE CORE
C. LOGIN CORE
D. READ CORE

exam
ⓦatch   *Be prepared to recover a lost password.*

4. Which of the following SHOW statements cannot be found in the SHOW TECH command?

A. SHOW VERSION
B. SHOW RUNNING-CONFIG
C. SHOW IP ROUTE
D. SHOW PROCESS MEMORY

Refer to the Following Scenario to Answer Question 5

Consider the following SHOW INTERFACE ETHERNET 0 output:

```
Router>show interface Ethernet 0

Ethernet0 is up, line protocol is up
    Hardware is Lance, address is 00e0.1e5d.f5d2 (bia 00e0.1e5d.f5d2)
    Internet address is 192.168.75.193/30
    MTU 1500 bytes, BW 10000 Kbit, DLY 1000 usec, rely 128/255, load
24/255
    Encapsulation ARPA, loopback not set, keepalive set (10 sec)
    ARP type: ARPA, ARP Timeout 04:00:00
    Last input never, output 00:00:02, output hang never
    Last clearing of show interface" counters never
    Queueing strategy: fifo
```

```
        Output queue 0/40, 0 drops; input queue 0/75, 0 drops

5 minute input rate 5600 bits/sec, 270 packets/sec
    5 minute output rate 1550 bits/sec, 650 packets/sec
        2298990 packets input, 305539870 bytes, 0 no buffer
        Received 876780 broadcasts, 13200 runts, 0 giants, 0 throttles
        3 input errors, 4 CRC, 0 frame, 0 overrun, 0 ignored, 0 abort
        0 input packets with dribble condition detected
        3595770 packets output, 436550980 bytes, 89890 underruns
        70 output errors, 990 collisions, 0 interface resets
        0 babbles, 0 late collision, 0 deferred
        10 lost carrier, 0 no carrier
        0 output buffer failures, 0 output buffers swapped out
```

5. Which of the following statements is NOT true?

A. The counters have never been cleared since it was up

B. There have been some packets smaller than 64 bytes discarded

C. Based on the current Ethernet interface load, this is a busy network

D. There are sufficient buffers to handle the current traffic load

---

Command level expertise with the Cisco 2511 in moving from session to session can save considerable time when concurrently configuring and monitoring many routers.

Be prepared to change configuration register settings to recover passwords or a hung router.

Campus Switches and VLANs

1. Which command is used to set up a VLAN as a logical broadcast domain?

A. VLAN 1 SET 2/5

B. SET VLAN 3/4

C. SET VLAN 0 2/5

D. VLAN SET 3/4

2. Which of the following commands set an Ethernet port speed on a Catalyst 5000?

A. SET PORT-SPEED 2/8 FULL

B. SET PORT 2/8 SPEED AUTO

C. SET PORT SPEED 1/4 100

D. SET PORT SPEED 3/12 10

3. Implementing security on a Catalyst means locking the secured port to a particular MAC address. What will happen when a passive hub that contains multiple connections to stations is plugged into a security-enabled port of a Catalyst?

A. The secured port will be locked with the MAC address of the hub and no station can connect

B. The secured port will be locked with the MAC address of the hub and all of the stations work

C. Only one of the stations will have a connection

D. None of the above

4. With version 3.1(1), CISCO introduced Virtual Trunking Protocol 2(VTP2). What new enhancements does this version provide?

A. Token Ring features, a transparency option, and consistency checks

B. SDSL features, a transparency option, and consistency checks

C. Fast Ethernet features, a transparency option, and consistency checks

D. ATM features, a transparency option, and consistency checks

5. When the network manager knows for sure that only end-stations are directly attached to ports, such as file servers or application servers, he can speed up the establishment of traffic by enabling PortFast. Which of the following is the correct command?

A. SET PORT 2/12 PORTFAST ENABLE

B. SET PORTFAST 3/1-4 ENABLE

C. SET PORT 3/1 SPANTREE FAST ENABLE

D. SET SPANTREE PORTFAST 3/1-10 ENABLE

CIT
QUESTIONS

6. What happens to ports in a VLAN if the VLAN is deleted?

A. The ports will be reset to default settings

B. The ports will send out broadcast frames to start a Spanning Tree recalculation

C. The ports become inactive, while retaining the old VLAN number

D. The ports will revert to normal bridging mode, while negotiating speed and duplex mode

QUESTIONS AND ANSWERS

What is the short list of steps to take to add a new Catalyst to an existing Catalyst network?	Install the hardware. Connect a terminal to the console. Assign a VTP domain and other VTP information to match the rest of the network. Assign an IP address to the switch. Assign a trunk port if needed. Assign ports to VLANs.
What do I do if the ports say they're inactive?	Check that the VLAN to which they're assigned is defined on that switch. If it's a new card, make sure your software version is new enough to support the card.
How do I track down a node on my switch network?	Get the MAC address, possibly via an ARP table. Do a SHOW CAM DYNAMIC on each switch that has the appropriate VLAN, and look for the MAC address.
I want to use a SPAN port to monitor traffic.	Set a destination port *before* you do a SET SPAN ENABLE. Also make sure that you're monitoring the right port or VLAN (default is all of VLAN 1 in that switch).
I plugged my running laptop into the switch, but I can't get a DHCP address.	With the default settings, it will take 30 to 60 seconds for a port on a switch to become "live." This is to avoid loops. If just waiting a minute is a problem in your situation, carefully read this chapter's section on PortFast.
Is there any way to reduce the amount of time it takes for the network to reroute to a redundant path when a link goes down?	With careful design, UplinkFast can be used in conjunction with normal Spanning Tree features to reduce convergence time for specific redundant links.
Some of my servers aren't running at 100 Mbps, even though they have 100 Mbps cards and I've got them patched into 100 Mbps-capable switch ports. Why?	Various NIC cards don't always properly auto-sense 100 Mbps and/or full duplex. The solution may include forcing the switch to 100/full, rebooting the servers, or manually configuring the server software.

Hands-on Troubleshooting

CIT
QUESTIONS

1. Which of the following commands is NOT correct on a Cisco 7507?

A. SHOW INTERFACES ETHERNET 0/0/1 ACCOUNTING

B. SHOW INTERFACE ETHERNET 0/0/1

C. SHOW INTERFACES ALL

D. SHOW INTER TOKENRING

2. What are the three wiring standards for 10-megabit Ethernet?

A. 10Base2, 10Base5, 100Base2

B. 10BaseT, 100Base2, 10Base2

C. 10BaseT, 10Base2, 10Base5

D. 10Base2, 100Base2, 10Base5

3. When troubleshooting a Token Ring network, which of the following commands is used?

A. SHOW TOKENRING INTERFACE

B. SHOW TOKENRING PACKETS

C. SHOW TOKENRING ERRORS

D. SHOW INTERFACE TOKENRING

exam
ⓦatch

*Be sure to familiarize yourself with the SHOW CONTROLLERS
commands. Pay particular attention to the cable type
(DCE or DTE). The syntax is
SHOW CONTROLLERS {bri|e1|ethernet|fddi|lex|mci|pcbus|serial|token}.*

exam
ⓦatch

*Remember to review IP addressing and binary conversion before
the exam. You may be asked to segment a network or apply a subnet
mask. You need to be able to do the binary calculations by hand. Also,
in troubleshooting, you sometimes will have to determine an incorrect
mask to identify a problem.*

QUESTIONS AND ANSWERS

My router is seeing duplicate routing updates.	A bridge is being used in conjunction with the router.
Some of my protocols are being routed, while others are not.	Incorrect access lists. Use traceroute to pinpoint the router that has the incorrect access list. This is usually the point where the tracert will stop. Telnet to the router and check the route table by using show ip route. To test the access list, try disabling them all, and then bring them back up one at a time while pinging the remote node. When the pings start to time out, you will know which access list had the undesirable effect. Correct the list and retest.
I lose my connection as the load of my serial link gets greater.	Overutilized serial line or dirty serial line.
My serial line goes down at a certain time every day.	Congested serial line, overused at a particular time of the day. Pay attention to the time of day your link is going down and try to determine what is causing the increase in traffic. It may be that backups are being run that can be done during off-hours instead, thus solving your problem. Or the problem may be a symptom of a larger issue. Be sure to investigate to determine the root cause.
My Novell NetBIOS packets cannot get past the router.	Input the ipx type-20-propagation command into your router configuration. You must enter into configuration mode before you can add this command to your configuration.
I can't talk to my local IPX server.	Workstation is configured with wrong encapsulation frame type. Check the configuration files on the workstation to see if it is using the correct frame type.
I can't talk to my remote IPX server.	Workstation or router is configured with wrong encapsulation frame type. Check the configuration files on the workstation to see if it is using the correct frame type. Also, check the router by using the show run command; this will show you the current running router configuration. Check out what frame encapsulation is being used. Be careful not to use show config, because this will only show you the configuration that was last saved.
In my AppleTalk network, sometimes my services are dropped unexpectedly.	Check your routes, looking for an unstable route. Also check for a ZIP storm.
In my AppleTalk network, I can see the services but I can't connect to them.	Incorrect access list.

4. Which of the following is NOT a Cisco command?

   A. SHOW IP ACCESS-LIST

   B. SHOW IP ROUTE

   C. SHOW ETHERNET INTERFACE

   D. SHOW IP OSPF DATABASE

5. When a workstation cannot connect to a server on a Novell LAN, what is mismatched?

   A. NIC makes and brands

   B. CPU speeds on the workstation and the server

   C. Protocols and frame types used by the server and the workstation

   D. All of the above

6. A corporate network is subdivided into several segments interconnected by multiple CISCO routers. IP and IPX are the main protocols with Novell servers located at different locations throughout the campus. Some users on one subnet complain that after booting up their PCs, connection is made to a remote server instead of the local server. What could you do on the router to solve this problem?

   A. Decrease IPX OUTPUT-SAP-DELAY <# of milliseconds> on the local interface

   B. Increase IPX GNS-RESPONSE-DELAY <# of milliseconds> on the local interface

   C. Decrease IPX OUTPUT-RIP-DELAY <# of milliseconds> on the local interface

   D. Increase IPX NLSP PRIORITY <priority-number> on the local interface

e x a m
ⓦ a t c h *If you see the words "Novell" or "NetWare" in responses to debug commands, immediately look for answers regarding IPX or any components of IPX (such as SAP advertisements).*

7. What is NOT a cause for a user to find that network services are sometimes unavailable?

A. Duplicate network number

B. Incorrect cable range

C. Same cable ranges on overlapping networks

D. Incorrect wiring

---

exam
ⓦatch

The two of the most common problems in an AppleTalk network are duplicate network numbers and unmatched configurations. So when you're presented with a problem, check to see if the routers all have the correct cable-range setting and list of zones. Then verify that the overlapping networks do not have the same cable ranges.

---

exam
ⓦatch

If you're given a problem with a Macintosh in your network, you must be running AppleTalk as a network protocol. This is usually in addition to running IP or IPX.

---

exam
ⓦatch

Check out the Cisco Web site before taking any exam, because things are often changing. New developments may have occurred since the publishing of this book.

Troubleshooting the ISDN Basic Rate Interface (BRI)

1. If the ISDN SWITCH-TYPE is configured as DMS-100 then what else typically must be configured for a North American BRI service?

A. The ISDN NT1 interface if it is internal to the BRI interface

B. The Q.921 SAPI=16 for connecting via X.25 over the D channel

C. The initial response TEI of 64 or 65 for normal BRI operation in North America

D. The ISDN SPID

---

exam
ⓦatch   *One of the reasons for the widespread confusion over SPIDs is the fact that they are sometimes necessary and sometimes not. If the ISDN switch type is a Nortel DMS-100 or National ISDN (ni), SPIDs are required. If the switch is a 5ESS, SPIDs may or may not be required.*

---

2. What is the ISDN's physical layer encoding scheme?

A. B8ZS

B. ESF

C. 2B1Q

D. AMI

exam
ⓦatch

By far the most informative of the Q.931 messages, the Setup message is the first place to look once you've verified the Physical layer, the Data Link layer (Q.921), and DDR. All of the Q.931 message-type packets mentioned above contain fields called Information Elements (IEs). In the Setup message, these IEs contain information vital to the call establishment procedure. The most important IEs in the Setup packet are the Bearer Capability, Called Party Number, Calling Party Number, and the Call Reference Value.

3. You want to setup a dial-on-demand connection with a BRI ISDN circuit using a method of traffic filtering. What commands are used to bring the ISDN link up for IP traffic?

   A. ROUTER# CONFIGURE TERMINAL
      ROUTER(config)# INTERFACE BRI 0
      ROUTER(config-if)# DIALER-LIST 7
      ROUTER(config-if)# PERMIT IP PROTOCOL DIALER-LIST 7
   B. ROUTER# CONFIGURE TERMINAL
      ROUTER(config)# DIALER-LIST 10 PROTOCOL IP PERMIT
      ROUTER(config)# INTERFACE BRI 0
      ROUTER(config-if)# DIALER-GROUP 10
   C. ROUTER# CONFIGURE TERMINAL
      ROUTER(config)# INTERFACE BRI 1
      ROUTER(config-if)# DIALER-GROUP 10 PROTOCOL TCP PERMIT
      ROUTER(config-if)# DIALER-LIST 10
   D. ROUTER# DIALER-GROUP ISDN PROTOCOL IP PERMIT

CHAP, the Challenge Handshake Authentication Protocol, is the successor to PAP. The CHAP password is never sent over the link in cleartext. Instead, the called party responds to the calling party by sending its hostname and a random "challenge" string. The calling party encrypts the password (an identical password that was preconfigured on both sides) with this challenge string and then sends it back to the called party, along with the calling party's hostname. The called party then encrypts its password, configured for the calling party, with the same challenge. If the result is the same, the called party accepts the connection; otherwise, it rejects the connection. If a Cisco router calls another Cisco router, this CHAP process occurs in both directions. If a PC PPP client (such as Windows Dial-Up Networking) dials into the router, only the PC is challenged.

4. While debugging an outbound dialer problem for an analog dial modem in the United States, you turn on DEBUG ISDN Q.931 and see the channel assigned bearer capability is 0x8890. What is most likely the problem?

A. A clear voice-grade channel of 64 Kbps is required and this bearer capability is only offering 56 Kbps

B. The Cisco router needs to negotiate a bearer capability of 0x8890218F. Consequently, the switch is dropping the second byte of the Q.931 and the telephone company needs to help troubleshoot.

C. The Cisco router needs to negotiate a bearer capability of 0x8890218F in order to communicate with the modem

D. There is insufficient information to determine what the problem is from the information provided.

QUESTIONS AND ANSWERS

Symptom from a Ping with DEBUG DIALER Enabled	Likely Cause
Unrecognized host, or protocol not running	No IP address configured on the BRI interface.
No output	"Interesting" packets are not being identified. Check your dialer-list and dialer-group for accuracy.
Dialing cause is identified, but you receive no dialer string and dialing cannot occur	The dialer map statement is not mapping the IP address—you are pinging to a telephone number.
Wait for carrier timeout	ISDN Q.931 issues, such as "User Busy"

5. As a LAN administrator you have started receiving complaints from users that they often get busy signals when dialing into the department. You have asked your manager for new equipment and additional inbound BRI circuits, and your manager has rejected your request. Instead, your manager has told you to tune your equipment so that more incoming calls can be handled by the existing equipment. Which of the following actions will least disruptively meet the requirements provided to you by your manager?

A. HEADQUARTERS# CONFIGURE TERMINAL
   HEADQUARTERS(config)# INTERFACE BRI 0/0
   HEADQUARTERS(config-if)# DIALER IDLE-TIMEOUT 60

B. HEADQUARTERS# CONFIGURE TERMINAL
   HEADQUARTERS(config)# INTERFACE BRI 0/0
   HEADQUARTERS(config-if)# DIALER FAST-IDLE 30
   HEADQUARTERS(config-if)# DIALER IDLE-TIMEOUT 120

C. HEADQUARTERS# CONFIGURE TERMINAL
   HEADQUARTERS(config)# INTERFACE BRI 0/0
   HEADQUARTERS(config-if)# DIALER FAST-IDLE 120
   HEADQUARTERS(config-if)# DIALER IDLE-TIMEOUT 30

D. None of the above

The answers to the questions are in boldface, followed by a brief explanation. Some of the explanations detail the logic you should use to choose the correct answer, while others give factual reasons why the answer is correct. If you miss several questions on a similar topic, you should review the corresponding section in Osborne's *CCNP Cisco Internetwork Troubleshooting 4.0 Study Guide* before taking the test.

Troubleshooting Methodology

1. ☑ **C. 80 percent of the traffic for local use and 20 percent for internetworking.** In most of today's enterprise networks, many components are connected and attached to existing backbone infrastructures to support the evolving strategies of a corporation. The 80/20 rule simply states that 80 percent of the traffic on a given network is local and not more than 20 percent of traffic requires internetworking. So, 80 percent of the traffic is destined for local resources within your network and 20 percent of the traffic is destined for the Internet or has Internet-related functions, such as e-mail.
☒ **A.** 80 percent of the traffic for 20 percent of the users, is incorrect because the use of the network is not sectioned off for only 20 percent of the users. **B.** 80 percent of the traffic for local users and 20 percent for remote users, is incorrect because the percentage of traffic is not sectioned off for only remote users. **D.** 80 percent of the traffic for internetworking and 20 percent for local use, is incorrect because the inverse is correct.

2. ☑ **D. You can ignore collision statistics as long as users are satisfied with response times.** On a functional Ethernet segment, you can have what is considered short-term collision rates as high as 20–25 percent. Anything exceeding 30 percent, however, would be studied and administered carefully.
☒ **A.** Rates below 20 percent of available bandwidth, is incorrect because it

is not a statistic that you should be concerned with. **B.** Rates as high as 20–25 percent of available bandwidth, is incorrect. It could be a statistic that you may want to look at and evaluate if it appears that you are having consistent complaints of slowness, but for the most part is not necessarily something that will cause your network performance to be degraded. **C.** Anything exceeding 30 percent of available bandwidth is incorrect. It should alert you that something is wrong. For a short-term situation it may be nothing to worry about. If you see collisions that consume 30 percent or more bandwidth, you may want to monitor this Ethernet segment closely for a short time to determine if this will turn into a problem which will require action to be taken.

3. ☑ **B.** Diagram of the network topology. Any network that you are supporting should have a copy of the network topology. This document should have a diagram of the physical layout of the network with a description of all links and segments that are contained in your network. This documentation will allow you to determine the packet flow, which will give you the ability to rule out specific areas of your network. This is an invaluable resource when you have a large enterprise. A network topology document will allow you to track the information from its origination to its destination.

☒ **A.** Employee phone listing, is incorrect. It will not allow you to determine the physical layout of the network. **C.** Diagram of the office floor plan, is incorrect. This will only give you the layout of the office space. Although this may be a good thing to know, it does not tell you where your wiring closets are or where all of your network equipment is. **D.** None of the above, is incorrect because knowing where all of your equipment is will allow you to rule out a possible hub or a backbone link when looking to see the areas that can and cannot be seen by the finance department.

4. ☑ **C.** Baselining. Baselining is the act of collecting information about your network that will let you know what is normal for your network. Baselining will alert you to areas of your network that may need your attention. Once you know how your network performs, you can take steps to be proactive in the maintenance of the network and head off minor problems before they become major problems.

☒ **A.** Network utilization, is incorrect. The statistics are related to network health, not just utilization. **B.** Analyzing problems, is incorrect. This is what you would do once you notice that there is a problem with your network. You would not analyze your network if everything is normal. **D.** Network performance, is incorrect. This shows the performance of your network. This does not tell you what is normal for your network. You could end up working to fix an assumed problem when that is normal for your network or network segment.

5. ☑ **A.** Connection-oriented protocol. Connection-oriented protocols do several things: they provide a virtual link between devices, sequenced packet delivery, and guaranteed data delivery. Connection-oriented protocols also require end nodes to acknowledge each frame or packet of data received. If the frame or packet is not acknowledged it will be retransmitted.

☒ **B.** Connectionless protocol, is incorrect. It does not provide for any virtual circuits of any type. It does provide for the dynamic flow of information that will use alternate paths to reach the destination device. **C.** Private virtual circuit, is incorrect. It doesn't allow for a dedicated connection between two or more locations. It is not a protocol that has characteristics of a virtual circuit, switched virtual circuit, or even a single path through the network for all packets and frames. **D.** SNMP, is incorrect. It is not a protocol that has characteristics of a virtual circuit, switched virtual circuit, or even a single path through the network for all packets and frames.

6. ☑ **A, D.** If two stations transmit simultaneously, the information transmitted will collide at some point and once a station sends information, no other devices on an Ethernet LAN can transfer data until that station has completed its transmission. The increase in transmission time is related to the delays and retransmission attempts made by the sending station. If two stations transmit simultaneously, the information transmitted will collide at some point; therefore, each station must stop its transmission and wait for a random period of time, then retransmit.

☒ **B.** A station will only receive information that has been sent in order of transmission, is incorrect. This describes characteristics of a connection-oriented protocol and not characteristics of CSMA/CD. **C.** A station will send a jam signal to stop all other stations from sending in order to send its own information, is incorrect. This describes an altered situation for a jam signal that doesn't have the same characteristics of CSMA/CD.

7. ☑ **D.** Fiber-optic cable. Fiber Distributed Data Interface (FDDI) is a standard for data transmission on fiber-optic lines within a LAN. Fiber optic LANs use fiber optic cabling as their media for transmission.

☒ **A.** Coaxial cable, is incorrect. **B.** Twisted-pair phone cable (Category 3), is incorrect. **C.** Twisted-pair phone cable (Category 5) is incorrect. They are not valid media for FDDI to communicate on. FDDI uses only fiber optic media.

8. ☑ **C.** Class D. Multicasting and Experimental address ranges are not used frequently. Although they have special uses it is important to understand that they do exist and have their purposes. Class D addresses are reserved for Multicasting purposes.

☒ **A.** Class B, is incorrect. **B.** Class C, is incorrect. These are due to these classes being reserved for personal and business Internet addressing purposes. **D.** Class E, is incorrect since these addresses have been reserved for experimental purposes

9. ☑ **D.** Both **A** and **B.** A non-extended AppleTalk network allows 127 hosts and 127 servers per network. Only a single network number is allowed per wire and only a single zone is allowed per wire.

☒ **A.** 127 hosts, and **B.** 127 servers, are incorrect independently. Using a non-extended AppleTalk network, your network will be split to a maximum of 127 hosts and 127 servers per network. **C.** 253 hosts/servers, is incorrect, as it is an extended AppleTalk network specification.

LAN Troubleshooting Problem Areas

1. ☑ **B.** Data link. The data-link layer provides control functionality for synchronization, error control, and flow control.

☒ **A.** Physical, is incorrect since the physical layer does not perform error control or flow control. **C.** Network, is incorrect since the network layer does not perform flow control. **D.** Transport, is incorrect since the transport layer does not provide frame-oriented error control.

2. ☑ **A.** LLC type 1 does not require data links or link stations to be established. LLC 1 traffic is connectionless. Since it is connectionless, data links do not need to be established.

☒ **B.** Once an LLC type 2 connection is established, link state information is centrally managed, is incorrect since once a connection has been established, a mode setting command is required, thus requiring each link station to manage its own link-state information. **C.** Since LLC is a subset of HDLC, link stations must operate in a connection-oriented hierarchy, is incorrect. Although LLC is a subset of HDLC, link stations can usually operate as peers. **D.** SNA traffic must be encapsulated in LLC2 frames in order to traverse a network, is incorrect since SNA can be directly encapsulated in Frame Relay.

3. ☑ **B.** 512 bits. It takes 512 bit times for a frame to propagate from one end of an Ethernet collision domain to the other. 512 bits equates to 64 bytes, which is the minimum frame size of an Ethernet frame.
☒ **A.** 32 bits, is incorrect. 32–43 bits is the pattern length for the jam pattern. **C.** 1024 bits, is incorrect, since 1024 bits equals 128 bytes. 128 bytes is not a valid Ethernet frame. **D.** 1518 bits, is incorrect since 1518 bits does not equal a full byte pattern.

4. ☑ **B.** Station conducts a media check. Station then transmits a duplicate address test frame. A new station activation first conducts a media check. This is followed by an active monitor check. Finally a duplicate address check is performed.
☒ **A.** Station runs a NIC card self diagnostic, then station searches for the active monitor station. If there is no active monitor, the station initiates a claim process, is incorrect since a NIC self diagnostic is not required. **C.** Station conducts a check of the existing lobe connections, station then transmits a neighbor notification frame signaling that the station is preparing to enter the ring, is incorrect since Token Ring does not transmit a neighbor notification frame to enter the ring. **D.** Station searches the ring for an active monitor. Station then requests a unique station address from the ring active monitor, is incorrect since Token Ring stations do not request a unique station address from the ring active monitor.

5. ☑ **A.** LEC. The LEC provides a MAC-level emulated Ethernet IEEE 802.3 or IEEE 802.5 service interface.
☒ **B.** LES, is incorrect since the LES resolves conflicts with MAC addresses, but does not perform address assignment. **C.** BUS, is incorrect since the BUS mediates multicast and broadcast traffic. **D.** LECS, is incorrect since the LECS provides the LEC the LES ATM address.

WAN Troubleshooting Problem Areas

1. ☑ **D.** Header, payload, trailer. The PPP frame consists of three primary parts. It contains a header, which is subdivided into an eight-bit address field, a nine-bit control field, and a 16-bit protocol field. The payload or body of the packet contains a variable length (up to 1500 bytes) of reserved bandwidth for user data. Finally, there is a trailer that contains a 16-bit frame-check sequence (FCS).

   ☒ **A.** Header, address, data, is incorrect because the address is part of a header, therefore missing the payload or body of the frame. **B.** Header, data-control field, trailer, is incorrect because the data-control field is again part of the header, thus missing the payload or body of the frame. **C.** Address, data, trailer, is incorrect because the header of a PPP frame contains more than just the address field.

2. ☑ **C.** SDLC is a proven standard and is known for its great error recovery method. One of the most typical problems associated with SDLC is its error recovery. In situations where problems exist, for example when noisy lines create disturbances, the error-recovery mechanism causes many frames to be continually retransmitted and causes latency.

   ☒ **A.** SDLC differs from HDLC in that it is not used for peer-to-peer communications, is incorrect because it is true that SDLC can be used for peer-to-peer communications. **B.** SDLC uses a framing format similar to that of the HDLC frame, is incorrect because it is true that SDLC uses a framing format similar to that of the HDLC frame. It is used primarily for multi-point networking. An address control field is added to distinguish conversations between the primary and each of its secondary, with each secondary having a different address. **D.** SDLC typically supports two types of line encoding, NRZi and non-NRZi, is incorrect. SDLC typically supports two types of line encoding, NRZI and NRZ, either Non-Return to Zero Inverted (NRZi) or Non-Return to Zero (NRZ). More commonly used, NRZi encoding ensures that one zero is transmitted out of every five bit times at a minimum to aide synchronization.

3. ☑ **C.** Six octets. The exchange consists of a requesting frame comprising a six-octet header and a list of information elements (IE) that carry the status information. The first two octets contain the necessary identifiers. The third octet identifies all (LMI) frames as being informational. The fourth octet contains a protocol discriminator. The fifth octet contains a dummy field that is always set to 0. Finally, the sixth octet identifies the message type (either from the subscriber or provider). Behind the header information is the IE. LMI recognizes three types of IE: report type, keepalive, and PVC status.

☒ **A.** Four octets, is incorrect because octet 5 is a required octet that is always set to 0 and octet 6 identifies the message type. **B.** Five octets, is incorrect because octet 6 is needed to identify the message type. **D.** Seven octets, is incorrect because LMI header by definition only has a maximum of six octets.

4. ☑ **D.** 14 digits. The X.25 networks have unique addresses that use the X.121 standard, commonly referred to as Network User Addresses (NUAs). This addressing scheme dictates that an up to 14-digit address can be assigned. However, addresses may be as small as 1 digit.

☒ **A.** Eight digits, is incorrect. **B.** 10 digits, is incorrect. **C.** 12 digits, is incorrect. The X.121 standard allows up to 14 digits for an X.25 NUA. Although the last two digits are sub-addressing, it is still part of the 14-digit NUA format.

5. ☑ **B.** 53 bytes. SMDS and ATM both have similar 53 bytes cell-relay packets with 48 bytes for data and a five-byte address header. The 48 bytes of data are sometime referred to as the *payload*. The five-byte address header is made up in one of two formats, either User-to-Network Interface (UNI) or Network Node Interface (NNI). The 53-byte cell is used in order to divide data into smaller and more manageable packets. This allows quicker cell relay across a better range of high performance communications networks.

☒ **A.** 48 bytes, is incorrect because the cell structure needs an additional five bytes for the address header. **C.** 128 bytes, and **D.** 256 bytes, are incorrect because SMDS and ATM use a 53-byte structure.

6. ☑ **C. AAL3/4** supports both connectionless and connection-oriented protocols by using a variable bit rate such as SMDS. The actual encapsulation type is aal34smds.

    ☒ **A. AAL1**, is incorrect because it's used for connection-oriented, delay-sensitive services such as DS-1 or DS-3. **B. AAL2**, is incorrect because it supports connection-oriented services that do not require a constant bit rate. This is currently an incomplete standard. **D. AAL5**, is incorrect because it's used for connection-orientated services, such as LANE and classic IP over ATM. The actual encapsulation types are AAL5SNAP (sub-network access protocol), aal5mux (MUX type) and AAL5NLPID (network-layer protocol identifier).

7. ☑ **B. Bit errors.** Bit error is the basic performance evaluator and can only be tested intrusively by taking the circuit down. By sending predetermined and stressing test patterns through the circuit, these errors are basically logic errors, meaning 1s that should have been 0s, and vice versa.

    ☒ **A. Bipolar violation**, is incorrect because bipolar violation is a transmission error that occurs every time consecutive pulses of the same polarity are transmitted in violation of the bipolar signal format. This type of signal violation can be monitored without taking the circuit down, or during pattern testing. **C. CRC errors**, is incorrect because Cyclic Redundancy Check (CRC) error is an error detection incorporated in blocks of live data. CRC works by building a mathematical equation and transmitting it across the control bits in an ESF frame. The result of the calculation is then transmitted in the next frame. The distant end performs the calculation and compares answers. If the resulting answers do not match, a CRC is incremented. **D. Frame errors**, is incorrect because frame error is measured by the number of times an incorrect value appears in the framing bit position. The circuit can be monitored (not affecting live traffic) to identify these errors, but they are usually difficult to uncover. This is generally because the framing bit is only the 193rd bit in each frame and therefore appears less than one percent of the time.

The Internet Protocol (IP)

1. ☑   **C.** It has been reviewed and the proposal has been completed and is deemed to be the final specification for whatever it is documenting. All of the Internet-related protocols are documented in RFC documents. Once a document is assigned an RFC number, it represents the final specification for whatever it is documenting, until it is supplanted by a later RFC.
   ☒   **A.** It has been accepted as a comment and will be awaiting further review to determine if the standard it is proposing is complete and accurate, is incorrect. It does not allow for the RFC to have completed the technical design, review and validation prior to assigning it a number. **B.** It has been reviewed and it is pending a proposal to determine if it is complete and accurate, is incorrect. This allows the RFC to have completed the technical design and assigns it a number pending the review and validation. **D.** None of the above, is incorrect.

2. ☑   **B.** Three. There are three categories of IPV6 addresses: unicast, multicast and anycast. Unicast is defined as an identifier for a single interface. Multicast is defined as an identifier for a set of interfaces. A packet sent to a multicast address will be sent to all addresses identified by that address. Anycast is also defined as an identifier of a set of interfaces, except that a packet sent to an Anycast address will be received by the nearest device that is identified by that address.
   ☒   **A.** Two, is incorrect; **C.** Four, is incorrect; and **D.** Five, is incorrect. There are three categories of addresses: unicast, multicast and anycast.

3. ☑ **B.** The receiving station sends an acknowledgement packet back to the transmitter of the sent packet. When the sequence number and checksum are correct, the sending host at the far end will then send back a response that essentially acknowledges it. If the sending host at the far end doesn't get a packet at all, or if something doesn't match, it does nothing. After a certain amount of time, if the sending host has not received an acknowledgement message, it resends the packet.

☒ **A.** Nothing, is incorrect. It would be correct if the packet were received without checksum and sequencing. This would be considered a UDP packet which doesn't require an acknowledgement. **C.** The receiving station sends a message asking for the frame or packet to be retransmitted, is incorrect. It would be the action a receiving station would take if it had not received a packet. **D.** The receiving station waits for the transmitter to send an acknowledgment packet to the receiver stating that the transmission is complete, is incorrect. This has the explanation in reverse. It is the sending station that waits for the receiving station to send an acknowledgement packet to the sender.

4. ☑ **C.** Services offered by the server. The port on the server usually represents a service, and this is how the client requests a particular service that it thinks the server is offering. If you are an Internet user, you may be familiar with some port numbers already, such as port 80 (HTTP service) or port 23 (Telnet service). The ports are there and listening for the appropriate communication, but that does not mean that the service is being provided by the server.

☒ **A.** HyperText Transfer Protocol (HTTP), **B.** File Transport Protocol (FTP), and **D.** Simple Mail Transport Protocol (SMTP), are incorrect. They are the protocols that are used to communicate through their respective ports to access the service that their respective ports provide. Although, these ports all have a default port number, these services can be configured to listen on a separate port.

5. ☑   **A.** 25. Don't get confused with the source and destination ports. The source port in this example is 25. The source port designates the port from which the server or client is communicating. The destination port is the port on which the server or client is going to listen for a response. If the server or client does not receive any communications from the other on the destination port that it is listening on, the communications session will time out after a period of time.

☒   **B.** 65,445, is incorrect. It is the destination port on which the server or client will be listening for a response. **C.** 8760, is incorrect. This is the window size. **D.** 0x1f7d, is incorrect. This is the checksum total.

6. ☑   **A.** Checksum. UDP packets use a checksum. Like TCP, UDP has port numbers, and they are assigned in the same way by the operating system. Like TCP, UDP uses a checksum. But the similarities pretty much end there.

☒   **B.** Three-Way Handshake; **C.** Sequence numbers; and **D.** Sliding Window, are incorrect. They are not used by a UDP packet. There are no three-way handshakes, no sequence numbers, no system-imposed retransmissions, and no automatic sliding window protocol.

7. ☑   **B.** UDP. DNS uses UDP packets to request information from a DNS server. DNS clients typically need only a short answer to a short question, so UDP is ideal.

☒   **A.** TCP, is incorrect. It would not be efficient for the amount of information that is being requested. **C.** SNMP, is incorrect. It is used to collect information about the network and to perform some network management functions. **D.** None of the above is incorrect.

Novell's Internetwork Packet Exchange (IPX) Protocol

1. ☑ **C.** 00000123:0080C712202D. The correct addressing format in an IPX network begins with the network number followed by the MAC address. A colon separates the two fields.

   ☒ **A.** 0080C712202D:00000123, is incorrect because the field sequence is reversed. **B.** 00000123; 0080C712202D, is incorrect because a semi-colon separates the fields. A colon should separate the two fields. **D.** 0080C712202D;00000123, is incorrect. It has two errors. The field sequence is reversed and a semi-colon separates the fields.

2. ☑ **C.** SAP uses a split-horizon broadcast scheme. The split horizon broadcast scheme dictates that a router will not broadcast information received from a given route back through that same route. This prevents the retransmission of information to its point of origin. SAP sends and receives broadcasts according to this scheme.

   ☒ **A.** SAP broadcasts are generated every 30 seconds, is incorrect. By default, SAP broadcasts are generated every 60 seconds. **B.** SAP is a routable protocol, is incorrect. SAP is not a routable protocol. **D.** SAP stores information about how to reach its remote networks, is incorrect. SAP does not store information about how to reach remote networks. It depends on routers to determine the appropriate route for its destination.

3. ☑ **A.** FFFF. The checksum field in an IPX packet is always set to FFFF.

   ☒ **B.** AAAA; **C.** 00FF; and **D.** 0FFF are all incorrect numbers.

AppleTalk Protocol

1. ☑ **B.** APPLETALK ROUTING. This is the correct command for turning on RTMP routing.

   ☒ **A.** Apple Talk routing, **C.** Apple Talk route, and **D.** AppleTalk route, are incorrect because they do not use the proper command format. Therefore, they are not valid Cisco IOS commands.

2. ☑ **A.** DDP is an unreliable, connectionless protocol. By definition, DDP is an unreliable, connectionless protocol.
☒ **B.** DDP is an unreliable, connection-oriented protocol, is incorrect. Although DDP is unreliable, it is not a connection-oriented protocol.
C. DDP is a reliable, connection-oriented protocol, is incorrect. DDP is neither reliable nor connection-oriented. **D.** DDP is a reliable, connectionless protocol, is incorrect because DDP is not a reliable protocol, although it is connectionless.

3. ☑ **A.** Simple file sharing and printing. A startup address without a router is sufficient for simple file sharing and printing functions.
☒ **B.** Simple file sharing only, is incorrect. Simple file sharing only is a partially correct but incomplete answer. **C.** Simple printing only, is incorrect. Simple printing only is a partially correct but incomplete answer. **D.** Zone lists, is incorrect. Zone lists come from the AppleTalk router. There is no router present in this scenario; answer **D** is not relevant.

4. ☑ **C.** Cable range and zone lists. The cable range and zone lists must match if two seed routers are on the same network segment.
☒ **A.** Cable range, is incorrect. It is a partially correct, but incomplete answer. **B.** zone lists, is incorrect. Zone lists is a partially correct, but incomplete answer. **D.** None of the above, is incorrect by the presence of the correct answer.

Common Routing Protocols

1. ☑ **B.** RIP and IGRP are distance-vector, periodic-broadcast routing protocols. RIP and IGRP are also legacy routing protocols.
☒ **A.** is incorrect because, although both BGP and OSPF are event-driven protocols and OSPF is a link-state protocol, BGP is a distance-vector protocol. **C.** is incorrect because, although link-state protocols maintain the entire network topology, they locally determine the best path to each destination network. **D.** is incorrect since distance vector protocols not only maintain a database of the destination routes, but they maintain the metrics required to reach the network.

2. ☑ **D.** RIP, OSPF, IGRP, static route. The administrative distance for RIP is 120. The administrative distance for OSPF is 110. The administrative distance for IGRP is 100. The administrative distance for a static route is 1.
☒ **A.** RIP, IS-IS, IGRP, OSPF, is incorrect since IGRP has an administrative cost of 100, which is lower than the administrative cost for OSPF of 110. **B.** External BGP, OSPF, static route, connected interface is incorrect since external BGP has an administrative cost of 20, which is lower than the administrative cost of 110 for OSPF. **C.** RIP, IGRP, connected interface, static route, is incorrect since connected interfaces have an administrative distance of 0, which is less than the administrative cost of 1 for a static route.

3. ☑ **B.** AppleTalk phase 2 allows for 254 node devices per network. In AppleTalk phase 2 there can be 253 node devices per network. It is in AppleTalk phase 1 that there can be 254 devices per network.
☒ **A** is incorrect since it is true that AppleTalk phase 1 only allows for one zone. **C** is incorrect since an AppleTalk network can, in fact, be a member of multiple zones. **D** is incorrect since it is true that an AppleTalk node can only be a member of one zone.

4. ☑ **A, B, C.** Update timers is the frequency at which the entire routing table is broadcast. The default time for this counter is 30 seconds. Invalid timers is the interval after which a route is determined to be no longer valid and will no longer be advertised. The default time for this counter is 90 seconds. Flush timers is the interval after which a route is removed from the RIP table. RIP defaults to 270 seconds for the flush timer.
☒ **D.** destination timers, is incorrect since this is not a valid timer for the RIP protocol.

5. ☑ **A.** By enabling DEBUG APPLETALK EVENTS. You can detect a ZIP storm by looking for many ZIP requests in succession while enabling DEBUG APPLETALK EVENTS.
☒ **B, C, D,** by enabling APPLETALK EVENTS, DEBUG EVENTS

APPLETALK, and DEBUG EVENTS–APPLETALK, are incorrect since they are not correct IOS commands.

6. ☑ **A, B, D.** OSPF, IS-IS, and EIGRP. All three are considered IGP protocols.
   ☒ **C.** EBGP, is not.

Troubleshooting Tools

1. ☑ **D.** All of the above. Telnet, Ping and Traceroute are all Cisco IOS client utilities. Telnet is used to verify connectivity to most TCP services. Ping is used to test connectivity to a remote site. Traceroute is used for remote diagnosis of TCP/IP network problems.
   ☒ **A, B, C.** All of these are correct, so **D.** All of the above is the only correct answer choice.

2. ☑ **B.** The packet will loop for a maximum of 254 hops and then it will be discarded.
   ☒ **A.** 255, is incorrect because this is the initial TTL value chosen by the sending host. The routers, not the host, will use this initial value in the manner described in the question to determine whether or not the packet has reached the maximum number of hops. **C.** 16, and **D.** 15, are invalid values.

3. ☑ **B.** CiscoDirector is not a valid CiscoWorks application.
   ☒ **A.** ATMDirector, is incorrect. It is used for various ATM switch management and discovery functions. **C.** TrafficDirector, is incorrect, as it is used for gathering statistics via SNMP and RMON. **D.** UserTracker, is incorrect because it displays end-station information retrieved from switches and routers.

4. ☑ **A.** Sniffer Pro is a network troubleshooting software tool used to capture and analyze packets. It is designed to analyze the data itself, not hardware devices on the network.

☒ **B.** continuity tester, is incorrect. It is a simple, inexpensive type of cable tester and is used to verify that voltage does or does not pass successfully through the wires in a network cable. **C.** the time-domain reflectometer (TDR), is another type of cable tester and is incorrect here. It measures the length of cable or the distance to a break within the cable. It does this by sending a signal through the wire and measuring the length of time elapsed before the signal's echo returns or bounces back. **D.** signal-quality tester, is incorrect. It is another type of cable tester that performs several tests in succession, such as continuity, cable length, and attenuation tests. It provides you with a report card, giving a pass/fail rating for each test conducted. This gives you a detailed picture of the performance of the cable in question. As you may have guessed by now, cable testers are available with a wide range of features and price tags. The tester that you choose will be a function of both your networking needs and your budget.

5. ☑ **B.** The LOGGING HOST command configures the router to log error messages to a remote Syslog host.

☒ **A.** LOGGING BUFFERED, is incorrect, since this command configures the router to log error messages locally. **C.** LOGGING REMOTE, and **D.** LOGGING TO SERVER, are incorrect. These are invalid commands.

Cisco's Diagnostic Tools

1. ☑ **A.** Encapsulation is displayed under SHOW IPX INTERFACE BRIEF, not under SHOW IP INTERFACE BRIEF.

☒ **B, C,** and **D** are incorrect. They are all displayed under SHOW IP INTERFACE BRIEF.

2. ☑ **C.** Novell-ether is the default IPX encapsulation for Ethernet LAN interface on a Cisco router.

☒ **A.** HDLC, is incorrect. It is the Cisco default encapsulation over serial link. **B.** Frame Relay, is incorrect. Frame Relay is the encapsulation for Frame Relay network over serial link. **D.** ATM, is incorrect. ATM is the encapsulation for ATM network over serial link.

3. ☑ **D.** Viewing PVC status change for instability is the output of the SHOW FRAME-RELAY PVC.

☒ **A.** verifying framing encapsulation, whether PLCP or direct map, is incorrect, as it is the partial output from SHOW ATM INTERFACE. **B.** verifying whether the clock source is being obtained internally or from the line, comes from the command SHOW ATM INTERFACE. **C.** viewing packet loss, is the output from the command SHOW ATM INTERFACE.

4. ☑ **C.** SHOW PROCESSES MEMORY will display each PID, dead processes retaining memory, total memory, used memory, and free memory.

☒ **A.** SHOW MEMORY SUMMARY, is incorrect. This command will display total, used, free, lowest, and largest memory. **B.** SHOW SUMMARY MEMORY, is incorrect. It is not a Cisco IOS command. **D.** SHOW MEMORY PROCESSES, is incorrect. It is also not a Cisco IOS command.

5. ☑ **D.** All of the above protocols are supported by PING.

☒ **A, B,** and **C,** IP, IPX, and AppleTalk, are supported by PING and must all be included in answering the question correctly.

Advanced Diagnostic Tools

1. ☑ **C.** Gaining insight into future trends of Cisco technology. Performing advanced diagnostics on Cisco hardware is a tool for real-time troubleshooting and viewing the current state of network and Cisco hardware health. It does not provide any information for future trends of Cisco technology.

   ☒ **A.** gathering valuable information, is incorrect. **B.** performing important monitoring of the network and hardware, is also incorrect. **D.** gaining insight into fundamental operations of network protocols, is also incorrect. The benefits of performing advanced diagnostics on Cisco hardware include gathering valuable information when working with Cisco TAC or advanced-support mailing lists, performing important monitoring of the network and hardware, and gaining considerable insight into the fundamental operations of network protocol or hardware functionality.

2. ☑ **D.** LOGGING AUXILIARY is not a valid Cisco logging command.

   ☒ **A.** LOGGING BUFFERED, is incorrect, as it instead copies logging messages to an internal Cisco hardware buffer. **B.** LOGGING 10.1.1.2, is incorrect. It sends the logging information to a Syslog server, identified by the IP address 10.1.1.2. **C.** LOGGING CONSOLE, is incorrect, as it allows the logging messages to be viewed on the Cisco hardware console screen.

3. ☑ **B.** WRITE CORE is the correct command to write the core file to its destination.

   ☒ **A.** Dump Core, **C.** Login Core, and **D.** Read Core, are incorrect, since they are not valid commands.

4. ☑ **C.** SHOW IP ROUTE cannot be found in the SHOW TECH command. There is no SHOW IP ROUTE statement in the SHOW TECH command.

   ☒ **A.** SHOW VERSION, **B.** SHOW RUNNING-CONFIG, and **D.** SHOW PROCESS MEMORY, are incorrect. All three statements can be found in the SHOW TECH command.

5. ☑ **C.** Based on the current Ethernet interface load, this is a busy network. The information above shows the interface is experiencing about nine percent of load. This is considered a normal traffic load. Note: If the load reaches more than 30 percent, it is considered a busy network.

☒ **A.** the counters have never been cleared since it was up, is incorrect. Last clearing of SHOW INTERFACE counters shows that the interface counters have never been reset. **B.** there have been some packets smaller than 64 bytes being discarded, is incorrect. Any Ethernet packet that is less than 64 bytes is considered a runt. There are 13,200 packets being discarded because they are the runt packets. **D.** there are sufficient buffers to handle current traffic load, is incorrect. "There are no output failures" is the statement that indicates that current system buffers are sufficient.

Campus Switches and VLANs

1. ☑ **B.** SET VLAN 3/4. The VLAN number setting is assigned by the command SET VLAN <vlan #> <mod#/port#>. VLAN 1 is assigned by default.

☒ **A.** VLAN 1 SET 2/5, is incorrect because it is an invalid IOS command. **C.** Set VLAN 0 2/5, is incorrect because VLAN 0 is invalid. **D.** VLAN SET 3/4, is incorrect because it is an invalid command.

2. ☑ **D.** SET PORT SPEED 3/12 10. The correct syntax to set the port speed on Ethernet LAN is SET PORT SPEED <mod#/port#> <10|100|auto>.

☒ **A.** SET PORT-SPEED 2/8 FULL, is incorrect because the FULL option is not part of the SET PORT SPEED command, but refers to the duplex method of the port. **B.** SET PORT 2/8 SPEED AUTO, is incorrect because it places the SLOT/PORT prior to the SPEED command and this is incorrect command syntax. **C.** SET PORT SPEED 1/4 100, is incorrect because slot 1 is reserved for supervisor modules, which have only two Ethernet ports.

3. ☑ **C.** Only one of the stations that is connected to the passive hub will make the connection to the Catalyst. The first MAC address that transmits will be locked to the secured port. Passive hubs cannot be assigned an IP address and do not have a MAC address.

☒ **A.** the secured port will be locked with the MAC address of the hub and no station can connect, and **B.** the secured port will be locked with the MAC address of the hub and all of the stations works, are incorrect. Passive hubs do not have MAC addresses issued to them. The first station to initialize on the passive hub will pass the MAC address to the secured port on the Catalyst. **D.** none of the above, is incorrect.

4. ☑ **A.** Token Ring features, a transparency option, and consistency check are enhancements introduced with VTP2.

☒ **B.** Catalyst switches, do not have SDSL features in VTP2. **C.** Fast Ethernet features, are not new because they were introduced in VTP1, not VTP2. **D.** ATM features are in routers, not on the switch.

5. ☑ **D.** SET SPANTREE PORTFAST <mod#/port#> <enable | disable>. This command should only be used on ports that are known to be connected directly to a server or workstation.

☒ **A, B,** and **C** are wrong answers because they do not follow the command syntax.

6. ☑ **C.** All ports assigned to a particular VLAN will become inactive when that VLAN is deleted.

☒ **A, B,** and **D** are incorrect. The VLAN assignment to the port still remains until removed.

Hands-on Troubleshooting

1. ☑ **C.** SHOW INTERFACES ALL. SHOW INTERFACES without option will list the information of all available interfaces of the router. IOS commands are not case sensitive and you can abbreviate keywords.

☒   **A.** SHOW INTERFACES ETHERNET 0/0/1 ACCOUNTING, **B.** SHOW INTERFACE ETHERNET 0/0/1, and **D.** SHOW INTER TOKENRING, are all corrected on a Cisco 7507.

2. ☑   **C.** 10BaseT, 10Base2, 10Base5. Ethernet operates at a baseband signaling rate of 10 Mbps, hence the 10Base notation in the wiring standards.
☒   **A.** 10Base2, 10Base5, and 100Base2, and **B.** 10BaseT, 100Base2, and 10Base2, are incorrect because there is no 100Base2 standard. **D.** 10Base2, 100Base2, and 10Base5, is incorrect because there is no 100Base5 standard.

3. ☑   **D.** The correct command to troubleshoot Token Ring network is SHOW INTERFACE TOKENRING. To use the SHOW INTERFACE command, you must be in privileged mode.
☒   **A.** SHOW TOKENRING INTERFACE, **B.** SHOW TOKENRING PACKETS, and **C.** SHOW TOKENRING ERRORS, are incorrect because they are incorrect syntax on Cisco routers.

4. ☑   **C.** SHOW ETHERNET INTERFACE. There is no such command.
☒   **A.** SHOW IP ACCESS-LIST, **B.** SHOW IP ROUTE, and **D.** SHOW IP OSPF DATABASE, are incorrect because they all are valid Cisco commands.

5. ☑   **C.** Protocols and frame types used by the server and the workstation. All Network Interface Cards, regardless of make or brand, should adhere to IEEE standards and are interoperable. CPU speed does not affect its capability to connect to the LAN.
☒   **A.** NIC makes and brand, is incorrect. Due to standardization efforts, most media-type NIC cards inter-operate. **B.** CPU speeds on the workstation and the server, is incorrect. CPU-related issues do not normally cause connectivity problems since CPU clock speed does not directly relate to network communications rates. **D.** All of the above, is incorrect.

6. ☑ **B.** Increase IPX GNS-RESPONSE-DELAY <# of milliseconds> on the local interface. The local server might have a slow processor or NIC and may be slow to respond to GNS requests.

☒ **A.** Decrease IPX OUTPUT-SAP-DELAY, is incorrect. This increases the advertisement of services of remote servers. **C.** Decrease IPX OUTPUT-RIP-DELAY <# of milliseconds> on the local interface is incorrect. This changes the timing of routing-table updates. **D.** Increase IPX NLSP PRIORITY <priority-number> on the local interface, is incorrect. This modifies the election of designated router.

7. ☑ **D.** Incorrect wiring. Two of the most common problems in an AppleTalk network are duplicate network numbers and unmatched configurations. Incorrect wiring in this scenario would probably not cause an intermittent problem.

☒ **A.** Duplicate network number, **B.** incorrect cable range, and **C.** same cable ranges on overlapping networks, are incorrect. They are all possible causes for network services disappearing intermittently.

Troubleshooting the ISDN Basic Rate Interface (BRI)

1. ☑ **D.** The ISDN SPID. Typically in North America the ISDN signaling requires a SPID field to be configured. If the ISDN switch type is a Nortel DMS-100 or National ISDN (ni), then SPIDs may be required.

☒ **A.** the ISDN NT1 interface, if it is internal to the BRI interface, is incorrect since most Cisco equipment does not even have a configurable NT1 interface. **B.** the Q.921 SAPI=16 for connecting via X.25 over the D channel, is incorrect since this is only applicable if the D channel will be connected to an X.25 interface. **C.** the initial response TEI of 64 or 65 for normal BRI operation in North America, is incorrect. TEI 64 and 65 are optional, but may be configured for use in North America. Consequently this optional field usually does not need to be configured.

2. ☑ **C.** 2B1Q. ISDN uses 2B1Q as physical layer encoding scheme.
☒ **A.** B8ZS, **B.** ESF, and **D.** AMI, are incorrect. They are not valid answers.

3. ☑ **B.** ROUTER# CONFIGURE TERMINAL/ROUTER (CONFIG)# DIALER-LIST 10 PROTOCOL IP PERMIT/ROUTER(CONFIG)# INTERFACE BRI 0/ROUTER(CONFIG-IF)# DIALER-GROUP 10. You first use the command DIALER-LIST <dialer-list> PROTOCOL <protocol-type> <permit|deny> to select the protocol of the traffic. Then the DIALER-GROUP command ties the <dialer-list#> to the BRI interface number.
☒ **A.** ROUTER# CONFIGURE TERMINAL/ROUTER(CONFIG)# INTERFACE BRI0/ROUTER(CONFIG-IF)# DIALER-LIST 7/ROUTER(CONFIG-IF)# PERMIT IP PROTOCOL DIALER-LIST 7, is incorrect. It has an invalid command assigning a dialer-list to an interface. **C.** ROUTER# CONFIGURE TERMINAL/ROUTER(CONFIG)# INTERFACE BRI 1/ROUTER(CONFIG-IF)# DIALER-GROUP 10 PROTOCOL TCP PERMIT/ROUTER(CONFIG-IF)# DIALER-LIST 10, is incorrect. It has a wrong protocol specified and also assigns a dialer-list to an interface. **D.** ROUTER# DIALER-GROUP ISDN PROTOCOL IP PERMIT, is an invalid command.

4. ☑ **C.** The Cisco router needs to negotiate a bearer capability of 0x8890218F in order to communicate with the modem. The router needs to have a bearer capability of 0x8890218F in order to communicate with the modem. In the United States, the analog modem voice data calls need a bearer capability of 56 Kbps.
☒ **A.** A clear-voice grade channel of 64 Kbps is required and this bearer capability is only offering 56 Kbps, is incorrect since the required channel needs to be 56 Kbps. **B.** The Cisco router needs to negotiate a bearer capability of 0x8890218F. Consequently, the switch dropping the second byte of the Q.931 and the telephone company needs to help troubleshoot. This is incorrect. If the equipment is working correctly, all the fields of the bearer capability will be transferred. **D.** There is insufficient information to

determine the nature of the problem, is incorrect since the DEBUG provides you with a problem symptom at the Q.931 layer that needs to be resolved.

5. ☑ **D.** None of the above. All of the configurations shown deal with outbound calls, not inbound calls.

☒ **A.** HEADQUARTERS# CONFIGURE TERMINAL/HEADQUARTERS(config)# INTERFACE BRI 0/0/HEADQUARTERS(config-if)# DIALER IDLE-TIMEOUT 60, is incorrect since this just reduces the idle timer to one minute for users who are currently dialed in. Although this will reduce traffic to some extent, some users will probably dial back in and possibly not be able to finish their session. **B.** HEADQUARTERS# CONFIGURE TERMINAL/HEADQUARTERS(CONFIG)# INTERFACE BRI 0/0/HEADQUARTERS(config-if)# DIALER FAST-IDLE 30/HEADQUARTERS(config-if)# DIALER IDLE-TIMEOUT 120, is incorrect since this only sets the fast-idle time to 30 seconds for users who are not busy on their dial-in line while leaving the normal idle timeout at two minutes, thus addressing only outbound, not inbound calls. **C.** HEADQUARTERS# CONFIGURE TERMINAL/HEADQUARTERS(config)# INTERFACE BRI 0/0/HEADQUARTERS(config-if)# DIALER FAST-IDLE 120/HEADQUARTERS(config-if)# DIALER IDLE-TIMEOUT 30, is incorrect since this sets the fast idle timer to a value higher than the idle timer. In this case, the fast-idle timer will probably never be invoked in the normal course of operation.

Part 3

CLSC
(Exam 640-404)

INTRODUCTION TO SWITCHING CONCEPTS

T he following questions are to help you, the network professional, achieve the Cisco LAN switching requirement for the CCNP. These questions will provide a basis for passing the Cisco Exam 64-404. The questions are designed to provide you with more information than required, since, although passing the exam is the goal, a thorough understanding of Cisco switches in a network environment will provide you with better knowledge in the work place, and as you continue your certification process, you'll be better prepared to go on to the coveted CCIE certification.

This chapter is designed to expand your understanding of networking in switched environments at the fundamental level of networking. Its specific focus is on Cisco's switch platforms.

Studying the material so that you have a firm understanding, rather than studying only to pass the exam, will help you achieve your desired certification goals, and help you perform better in the work place.

Introduction to Switching Concepts

1. Switches forward packets based on which of the following? (Choose all that apply.)
    A. VLAN number
    B. IP address
    C. MAC address
    D. None of the above

---

exam
Watch   *It is important to remember the different results that routers, bridges, and switches present when used to segment local-area networks.*

---

2. What is a translational bridge?
    A. A device that forwards dissimilar IP addresses
    B. A device that can connect two networks
    C. A device that enables communication between dissimilar LAN topologies
    D. A device that functions as a transparent bridge

QUESTIONS AND ANSWERS

The performance on my LAN is slowing to a crawl due to the amount of broadcasts traversing the wire...	Segment the network using a router. Using a router reduces the size of your broadcast domains.
My network is growing rapidly and I would like to segment the network at Layer 2 of the OSI model...	Segment the network using a bridge. Bridges function at Layer 2 of the OSI model.
My network uses Ethernet and I would like to increase the bandwidth available to each of my end users...	Replace the hubs with switches. Plug the Ethernet cable of each end user's system into one of the available ports on the switches. This will give each user his or her own 10/100 Mbps of bandwidth.

exam
ⓦatch   *Cisco uses two varieties of the cut-through method, FastForward and FragmentFree. FastForward immediately forwards a frame after receiving the destination address. FragmentFree determines that the frame is not a collision fragment before it is forwarded. Collision fragments are normally less than 64 bytes. If the frame is over 64 bytes, then the FragmentFree mode considers the frame valid.*

3. In source-route bridging, what is the name of the field that contains a list of bridges that a packet should traverse to reach its destination?

A. CAM

B. RIF

C. RIP

D. SRB

exam
ⓦatch   *The Catalyst 5000 and Catalyst 5500 switches use the store and forward method of switching.*

VLANs

1. Why do VLANs provide a form of security when a router is not implemented?

   A. The switch will not know where to forward packets at the data-link layer

   B. Packets will not be forwarded outside the VLAN

   C. Allowing packets to traverse the VLAN will greatly hinder performance

   D. Without a router, you cannot get valid sniffer traces

---

exam
ⓌⒶⓣⒸⒽ

There are many acronyms associated with ATM. You will need to memorize what they stand for and what functions they represent.

---

2. What does Token Ring BRF and CRF provide a Token Ring Switched Network?

   A. It enables spanning tree

   B. It provides for redundant paths

   C. It provides for a hierarchical design

   D. It enables Token Ring to effectively work with Ethernet

---

exam
ⓌⒶⓣⒸⒽ

You will probably see questions on the test involving Token Ring bridging functions. It's likely that you will only be given the abbreviations (TrCRF, TrBRF) and be expected to answer based on their meanings. Be sure that you know what they stand for and how they interrelate. If you are clear on what a concentrator is and what a bridge is, you should be able to distinguish the two, but you must memorize what the acronyms stand for. Be especially aware of how many of something can be used (one TrBRF per TrCRF).

QUESTIONS AND ANSWERS

How do I decide which trunking protocol to use?	This will depend on your needs and your infrastructure. If you need to interoperate with another switch vendor, you'll have to find a common protocol. If you have an ATM backbone, you'll have to use LANE. If you have a Cisco FDDI backbone, you'll want to use 802.10. If you're building from scratch using all Cisco gear and Fast Ethernet links, ISL is easy to use.
How do I start using LANE?	This chapter only covers ATM lightly. To get started, a good place to look is Chapter 11, which covers LANE in detail.
Which is better, frame tagging or frame filtering?	It's a bit of a moot point unless you're using LANE. It seems pretty clear that frame tagging is the preferred method.

Placing Catalyst 5000 Series Switches in Your Network

1. What needs to be considered when placing local and global resources?

A. Bandwidth to the resource

B. The local resource cannot be on a shared segment, because it is local

C. A global resource should have a dedicated segment

D. None of the above

exam
ⓦatch   *Be aware of the differences between demand nodes and resource nodes. Demand nodes are basically workstations that are requesting (demanding) information from a resource. An example would be a workstation requesting a file from a file server. A resource node is a device that provides the information requested from a demand node. An example of a resource node is a file server or router.*

The difference between local resources and remote resources is the location of the resource with respect to the node that is demanding the information. A local resource is a device that is located on the same physical wire as the demand node. A remote resource is a device that is not located on the same physical wire as the demand node.

Bottlenecks and buffer overflow are the usual suspects when a problem occurs for which there is no obvious cause. To prevent problems, planning where to place the Catalyst 5000 switch is very important. Be able to identify the places in a network topology where bottlenecks are likely to occur. Understand how buffer overflow can affect network performance and how to make changes to correct this.

Catalyst 5000 Series Switch Architecture

I. What is the catalyst supervisor II console port?

A. A DB-9 DTE receptacle

B. A DB-25 DTE receptacle

C. A DB-9 DCE receptacle

D. A DB-25 DCE receptacle

Useful or not, you'll need to know a few things about the SLIP capabilities of the Catalyst for the test. You'll need to know, for example, that the Catalyst supports SLIP, and not PPP.

QUESTIONS AND ANSWERS

What's the best way to achieve a high-availability LAN environment?	Take a good look at the 5500, with dual supervisors and dual power supplies. If you need to do better than that, and your budget allows for it, you can run dual 5500 chassis with cross-links.
I have a number of Catalyst 5000s. Can these be upgraded in some way?	The Supervisor II and Supervisor III let you take advantage of the NetFlow features, if the NFFC is installed. You can also install an RSM module. However, due to the 5000's limited backplane speed (compared to the 5500) and the limited number of slots, you might consider upgrading to a 5500.
What's the best way to set up a large LAN installation using Catalyst switches?	In terms of how to interconnect switches and routers, probably the best topology (budget allowing) is to have a master LAN router Catalyst with an RSM (or bigger model with equivalent feature built in), or even a pair. From those, connect all other Catalysts back to that central point.
What's the best way to monitor traffic passing through a Catalyst switch?	It depends on what type of monitoring equipment you have. Do you already own a sniffer or RMON probe? If you have to purchase new monitoring gear, you might consider the NAM.
What am I going to be tested on?	Make certain you know the meaning of all the acronyms, and what each item does. For example, know what EARL stands for, and what the EARL does.

Catalyst 5000 Series Switch Hardware

1. AP Manufacturing has three campus-like facilities across the country. If the backbone switches at each campus were Catalyst 5500, what supervisory engine module would the switch accept? Choose all that apply.

A. Supervisor Engine I

B. Supervisor Engine II

C. Either A or B

D. None

e x a m

ⓦatch

Cisco's Catalyst 5000 series switches have been widely accepted by the information technology industry. Large enterprise networks have demanded cost-effective, stabilized intranets. You should be aware of the practical difference between the various models of Catalyst 5000 series switches. As a part of the certification process, or for network administration, it is essential to understand the design implications involved in these switches. The major differences among the models are the support for redundant supervisor engine operation and support for a large number of modules of different types. In the certification exam, you will be tested on selecting the best switch model for a particular networking requirement.

2. When installing redundant modules, what slots must the supervisory modules be installed in?

   A. Slot 1, and any other
   B. Slot 1, 13
   C. Slot 13, 5
   D. Slot 1,2

3. Which command is used to verify port speed?

   A. SHOW PORT [mod_num[/port_num]]
   B. SHOW PORT SPEED [mod_num[/port_num]]
   C. SHOW RUNNING-CONFIGURATION
   D. SHOW VLAN

4. What command do you use to enable a LES/BUS for the ELAN?

   A. LANE DATABASE ELAN-NAME
   B. LANE CLIENT ETHERNET VLAN_ID ELAN-NAME
   C. LANE SERVER-BUS ETHERNET ELAN-NAME
   D. LANE ELAN NAME

QUESTIONS AND ANSWERS

Can I achieve redundant supervisor engine operation with Catalyst 5002?	No. You have to use Catalyst 5505, Catalyst 5509, or Catalyst 5500.
I need to swap a supervisor engine module from the switch when the switch is online. Can I do this?	Yes. You can swap the supervisor engine module if it is in standby mode or not active. If it is the only module in the switch, then removing the module will halt the functioning of the switch.
When the standby supervisor engine module is swapped with a new supervisor engine module, do I need to restart the switch for the standby module to get the configuration information?	No. When the new supervisor engine module is connected, it automatically goes into standby mode. The active module will interact with the standby module and transfer the configuration file.
How do I know whether the supervisor engine module has failed?	There are two ways. The front panel Status LED gives information about the status of the module. The other method is to use the SNMP Management software, which collects the traps generated by the module and represents them in a visual format.
Is it always necessary to have two supervisor engine modules in a switch?	The switch is capable of operating effectively with a single supervisor engine. But you have to make the decision based on the criticality of the network. If the network applications demand zero down time, then obviously you have to go in for a redundant supervisor engine configuration.
Which is better, Supervisor Engine II or Supervisor Engine III?	Both modules have their own specific features suitable for specific applications. If Supervisor Engine II is used, then it will utilize the 1.2-Gbps backplane in the switch. If Supervisor Engine III is used, it will be capable of utilizing all three 1.2-Gbps backplanes in a Catalyst 5500 switch, enabling 3.6 Gbps operation.

You have to understand the entire concept of routing within a switch. The RSM module is capable of doing this, but the most important application has to be the RSM with a VIP2 module in it. On the exam, you will be tested about the RSM module types and their features. You have to know the LEDs on the front panel and their functions. We can use the CiscoView software to look into the status of the unit from a remote location. You have to be aware of the application of SNMP-based management in a real networking environment.

5. What is the result of the FDDI-to-Ethernet translation when IP fragmentation in FDDI is disabled?

   A. Only frames larger than 1514 are dropped
   B. Set VLAN
   C. Holds the MTU minimum to 1514
   D. Nothing happens

Configuring the Catalyst 5000 Series Switches

1. What commands need to be input to configure a new Ethernet module for default settings on Catalyst switches?

   A. Set default
   B. Set VLAN
   C. Set Ethernet *slot/port*
   D. No configuration is required

Remember, in a Catalyst 5000, the running config is always the same as the saved config file with the exception of commands that require hardware resets to become active.

2. Which command shows Cisco equipment that is directly attached?

A. SHOW ATTACHED

B. SHOW CDP NEIGHBORS

C. DISPLAY NEIGHBORS

D. WHO

---

exam
ⓦatch   *To configure a BOOTP server, you use the first MAC address listed for the active Supervisor by the SHOW MODULE command. This MAC address will be assigned the IP address you configure in the BOOTP server.*

---

3. What is the command to set priority on a port?

A. SET PRIORITY {normal | high} PORT/MOD_NUM

B. SET PORT LEVEL MOD_NUM/PORT_NUM {normal | high}

C. PRIORITY-QUEUE PRIORITY {normal | high} PORT/MOD_NUM

D. PRIORITY-LIST {normal | high} PORT/MOD_NUM LIST#

4. What are the three components that make up an SNMP system?

A. SNMP manager, SNMP agent, and management information base (MIB)

B. MIB manager, MIB agent, and management information base (MIB)

C. Managed devices, agents, network-management system (NMS)

D. Stats, alarm, history

QUESTIONS AND ANSWERS

I can't PING my Catalyst from a PC that is directly connected to it. What should I do?	Approach this problem from the point of view of the OSI layered model. PING is a program that tests connectivity at Layer 3 of the model. To troubleshoot Layer 3 problems, first make sure that the PC and the Catalyst have IP addresses in the same network number. Use the SET INTERFACE SC0 command on the Catalyst NMP Image CLI and the Network Neighborhood | Properties control panel on MS Windows PCs to set the IP address of both devices.
	If this doesn't resolve the problem, examine Layer 2 of the model. At the data-link layer we are concerned with the VLAN configuration of the Catalyst. Use the SHOW PORT and SHOW INTERFACE commands to ensure that the port with which your PC connects and the sc0 interface both belong to the same VLAN. If they are configured in separate VLANs, the Catalyst IP stack can't hear your PC sending an ARP request. Use the SET INTERFACE SC0 command and the SET PORT commands to reconfigure VLANs.
	If Layer 2 appears to be correctly configured, move on to Layer 1. In order to test connectivity at the physical layer, look at the SHOW PORT command again to see if the port state is Connected and that the port speed and duplex mode match the settings of our PCs NIC. Use the SET PORT commands to modify any of these settings on the Catalyst, but keep in mind that you may have to reset the port after reconfiguration with the SET PORT DISABLE and SET PORT ENABLE commands.
I'm worried about security for my Catalyst. What options do I have?	You have the ability to filter Telnet and SNMP access to the Catalyst NMP Image IP stack based on the source IP address. Recall the SET IP PERMIT LIST command. You can also prevent all access to your Catalyst IP stack by disabling the sc0 interface. Use the SET INTERFACE SC0 DISABLE command to prevent all IP access to the Catalyst NMP Image.
Help! I disregarded your advice about configuring the SLIP ATTACH command from a Telnet session. Now I can't communicate with the switch. Is there any hope of redemption for me?	If you have messed up a Supervisor II and you have a Catalyst 5500, you are in luck. The Catalyst 5500 supports dual Supervisor II modules. When you place a functional Supervisor II in the second slot of the 5500, both the configuration file and the IOS are copied from the primary supervisor to the secondary supervisor. Lacking this hardware combination, you will need to obtain either a replacement bootflash SIMM or replace the entire Supervisor.

5. What is the command for loading an image from a TFTP server for a single Supervisor II Engine? Choose all that apply.

A. COPY TFTP FLASH
B. CONFIGURE NETWORK
C. DOWNLOAD HOST FILE [mod_num]
D. CONFIGURE TFTP FLASH

6. Which of the following commands is used to write a configuration to a host?

A. COPY TFTP FLASH
B. WRITE TERMINAL
C. WRITE NETWORK
D. CONFIGURE NETWORK

7. How do you set the port speed on an Ethernet port?

A. SET PORT SPEED SLOT/PORT {10 | 100 | auto}
B. SET SPEED SLOT/PORT {10 | 100 | auto}
C. SET SLOT/PORT SPEED {10 | 100 | auto}
D. None of the above

Catalyst 5000 Series Switch Software

1. Which of the following two commands can be used to configure a switch for CGMP?

A. SET ROUTER CGMP ENABLE
B. SET CGMP ENABLE
C. SET MULTICAST ROUTER CGMP ENABLE
D. SET MULTICAST ROUTER 3/1
E. SET IGMP ENABLE

Since TACACS+ is carried in a TCP session, your Catalyst must have a valid IP address. You can manually configure an IP address using the CLI or an NMS. You can also automatically configure an address with a BOOTP or RARP server.

2. From the information given in the output below, which one of the following statements is true?

```
C5k> (enable) show trunk
Port      Mode          Encapsulation  Status        Native VLAN
--------  -----------   -------------  -----------   -----------
1/1       nonegotiate   dot1q          trunking      1
Port      Vlans allowed on trunk
--------  ----------------------------------------------------------
1/1       1,7,11,100,102-103,301,303-304,400-402
Port      Vlans allowed and active in management domain
--------  ----------------------------------------------------------
1/1       1,7,11,100,102-103,301,303-304,400-402
Port      Vlans in spanning tree forwarding state and not pruned
--------  ----------------------------------------------------------
1/1       1,7,11,100,301,400-401
```

A. Port 1/1 will use only dot1q trunking

B. VTP pruning has been used

C. ISL is the secondary trunking protocol

D. The link 1/1 is not working correctly

The Catalyst 5000 family does not implement frame filtering, an early mechanism for multiplexing the traffic of several VLANs over a single connection. In frame filtering, the MAC database of each switch is transmitted to the other switches on a periodic basis in much the same manner as a distance vector routing protocol periodically sending its routing table.

3. What is NTP used for in network environments?

A. To broadcast proper time of day

B. To synchronize network device clocks for error reporting and network management

C. To provide a means of distributing network transfer protocols

D. To distribute all kinds of Token Ring traffic

exam
Ⓦatch

When one IP station wishes to send unicast traffic to another one on the same subnet, it must map the known destination IP address of the station to a possibly unknown MAC address. The mechanism for accomplishing this mapping, when the media involved is one of the IEEE 802 LANs, is an Address Resolution Protocol (ARP) request. The mapping learned through ARP is cached by most IP stacks for a period of from one minute to possibly several days. A small delay in communication may be noticed when sending IP traffic to a station whose MAC address is not cached in the local ARP table.

QUESTIONS AND ANSWERS

When I configure my RSM with a new subinterface, I often find that I can't ping it right away. The #SHOW INTERFACE display says that it is up and up. What's up?	You are experiencing an interaction between the Catalyst CAM table learning function and the RSM software. The fastest way to clear this condition is to ping the Catalyst SC0 IP client address from the RSM. This forces the RSM's MAC address into the CAM table, resolving the problem.
I think a PC with a jabbering NIC is attached to my switch. When I configure SPAN on the suspect port, I don't see any bad frames. What's going on?	Since the Catalyst uses store and forward switching, only frames that pass the FCS test are carried to the Synergy switching bus. In order to diagnose this problem with your Catalyst, you will need the Catalyst Management module, which implements a switch probe on the blade.

4. What is a reason for creating VLANs?

   A. To limit broadcast traffic

   B. To disallow specific unicast traffic

   C. To limit traffic from one network to the next

   D. To limit broadcast flooding

5. On a Catalyst switch, what are the two trunking protocols used for Fast Ethernet and Gigabit Ethernet VLAN-trunk configuration?

   A. VTP

   B. ISL

   C. 802.1D

   D. 802.1Q

6. Which one of the following features is available on software release 2.3?

   A. MAC address-based port security

   B. CGMP/IGMP support

   C. VTP pruning

   D. Trunking

Managing the C5k Series Switch

1. Which of the following answers are true about CDP?

   A. CDP works on all equipment

   B. CDP is a Layer 3 protocol

   C. Cisco devices never forward CDP packets

   D. The CDP database is flushed every four hours

QUESTIONS AND ANSWERS

How do I use RMON to track network traffic?	You'll need a network management application to take advantage of RMON information. You can use a commercial application like CiscoWorks, or find a free package like the Multi Router Traffic Grapher (MRTG). Do a Web search to track down MRTG. In general, CiscoWorks will have better support of Cisco devices than other packages. MRTG requires much more manual setup.
What's the easiest way to spot-check network health?	If you have only a few switches, it's probably easier to use Telnet and do a few SHOW commands to determine how things are going. If you have a large network, or you need to keep any kinds of trends or history, you'll probably have to take a look at an SNMP package for automatic monitoring.
Commercial SNMP packages are expensive. Is there anything cheaper?	You can get free SNMP packages, such as the CMU SNMP applications. The problem with these, however, is that they tend to have much fewer features than the commercial packages. They also require a minimum of programming experience, and a lot more manual work to get going. Still, you can't beat the price. Even if you have a commercial package, the free packages may be useful for special applications, Web page building, or something similar.
How can I manage my switches securely?	Unfortunately, almost all of the mechanisms for managing Catalyst switches have some security issues. SNMP and Telnet both send passwords as clear text, meaning that if anyone is able to monitor your management traffic, they can see your passwords. With a modem, you have to be concerned about who might dial up. If you're truly paranoid, you can always keep your Catalysts locked in the wiring closets, and manage them via the console port only.

CLSC
QUESTIONS

---

exam
Ⓦatch

Try to memorize the types of statistics that are tracked in the statistics group. Also be sure to memorize the names and functions of the four embedded RMON groups that are supported on the Catalyst 5000 Ethernet ports. Cisco tests you on which ones are supported, and what they do. For example, you may be asked to identify which group tracks statistics over time (the history group.)

A typical application of the RMON feature is utilization graphing. It's often very useful to see what a network looks like over time. A common use is to graph what a particular network port (which may be a single machine, a whole subnet, or a trunk link) looks like over a day, a week, a month, or a special time period such as year-end closing. Using such a graph, a network manager can look for peaks or low spots, which may help decide when network backups should run, for example.

---

exam
Ⓦatch

For the CLSC test, Cisco doesn't expect you to know a great deal of detail about CWSI, but they do expect you to know the names of each of the individual applications in the packages, and their major functions. Do your best to memorize the list.

Troubleshooting the Catalyst 5000

1. A new line module has been inserted into a Catalyst 5500. After several minutes, you notice that the status light is red. What could this indicate?

A. That the module is working correctly, but a specific port is disabled

B. That the module is working correctly

C. That the module has failed

D. That the module is booting up

The sl0 interface is used for the SLIP interface to log in remotely via modem through the console port. The sc0 and sl0 cannot be in the same subnet. If you configure both interfaces in the same subnet, the switch will shutdown one of the interfaces because, by default, both the interfaces are assigned the 0.0.0.0 IP address.

---

2. Which command would you use to find out if both installed power supplies are working and are within their limits?

A. SHOW PSU

B. SHOW SYSTEM

C. SHOW HARD

D. SHOW POWER

E. SHOW ROM

3. A new server is installed onto a 10/100 Ethernet port running at 100 Mbps on the existing Category 3 cable. The connection does not work. What could be the problem?

A. The server can only run at 10 Mbps

B. The network port can only run at 10 Mbps

C. Category 3 cable is only for 10 Mbps

D. The cable run is 74 meters, which is too long for Category 3 cable

Catalyst 5000 Series Switch FDDI Module

1. In the following illustration, what type of network is portrayed?

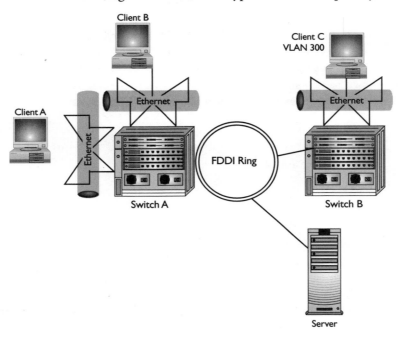

A. Star network

B. Bus network

C. Shared FDDI backbone network

D. Hybrid network

QUESTIONS AND ANSWERS

When should I use the FDDI/CDDI Card?	Whenever campus connectivity to (through) a legacy FDDI ring is required.
To which VLAN should the FDDI card belong if it is being used for trunking only?	Leave the FDDI card as part of VLAN 1 unless there are devices on the FDDI ring that need connectivity to Ethernet PCs.
Do I have to trunk all of my VLANs, or can I trunk only a subset?	You will trunk any VLANs for which you have created FDDI mappings. If you wish to only trunk a subset (corporate-wide VLANs) of your campus, then only create FDDI VLANs for the subset and use the TRANSLATION command for only that subset.
Is the FDDI card hot swappable?	The FDDI card supports online insertion and removal like all Catalyst line cards.
Can I use the FDDI card to do full-duplex FDDI switching?	No, the Catalyst FDDI card is half duplex only.

exam
ⓌatcＨ

Remember that the TRANSLATION command must go from either Ethernet or Token Ring frame types to FDDI, and vice versa. Be on the lookout for questions that try to translate Ethernet VLANs to Ethernet VLANs or Token Ring to Token Ring. There should be a FDDI VLAN on one side of the TRANSLATION parameter and either a Token Ring or an Ethernet VLAN on the other.

exam
ⓌatcＨ

Trunking has four states in Ethernet: on, off, auto, and desirable. The FDDI card does not support the auto or desirable states. Trunking must be turned on manually when it is required. Watch out for questions trying to make the FDDI card support the auto or desirable states.

ATM and LANE

1. Which of the following performs the segmentation and re-assembly of an ATM packet?

   A. AAL1
   B. AAL2
   C. AAL3/4
   D. AAL5
   E. ATMizer chip

2. On an ATM interface, you are assigned 16 addresses, starting at 1000.1000.1000 and ending at 1000.1000.100f. Which of the assigned addresses below are incorrect?

   A. Any BUS gets the address of 1000.1000.1003
   B. Any BUS gets the address of 1000.1000.1002
   C. Any LEC gets the address of 1000.1000.1000
   D. Any LEC gets the address of 1000.1000.1003
   E. Any LECS gets the address of 1000.1000.1003
   F. Any LECS gets the address of 1000.1000.1001

Catalyst 1900 and 2820 Switches

1. When using the SPAN port on the Catalyst 1900/2820 Series switch, which of the following are NOT true?

   A. STP is automatically disabled on a SPAN port
   B. You can define which ports to monitor
   C. By default port 1 is enabled for the SPAN function
   D. The SPAN port configuration is accessed by pressing *m* on the main menu screen
   E. BOOTP is automatically disabled on a SPAN port

exam
ⓦatch   *Be familiar with the components that comprise the ClearChannel architecture. Be able to describe the different components and the tasks that each component performs. Also, know how the components communicate with each other to provide wire-speed switching capability.*

exam
ⓦatch   *Be able to describe the different switching options available on the 1900/2820 series of Catalyst switches. Know the benefits that each mode provides and how each is tailored to take advantage of different network topologies. Be able to identify which mode is used, based on network use.*

exam
ⓦatch   *Note which types of changes take effect immediately or are deferred. Menu console changes and some Web console changes take effect right away. Be aware there are some changes made via the Web console that need to be "applied" before the change takes effect.*

Catalyst 3000 Switches

1. Which command is used to go back to the main menu from a subscreen on a Catalyst 3000 Series switch?

A. <CTRL> B
B. <CTRL> X
C. <CTRL> C
D. <CTRL> Q
E. <CTRL> P

exam
Ⓦatch

You should be familiar with the Catalyst 3000 series AXIS bus architecture and how the modules use the bus to communicate with each other. Know the different components that comprise the bus and how they function.

exam
Ⓦatch

You should be familiar with the various Catalyst 3000 series modules and how they communicate on the AXIS bus. Be prepared to describe each of the modules, with emphasis on the Ethernet, FDDI, and ATM modules. Be aware of how the 3011 WAN access module is installed in the chassis (using the FlexSlot) and how to communicate via the Configuration menu. The Catalyst Matrix is a specialized module that allows multiple Catalyst 3000 switches to join together to form a stack.

exam
Ⓦatch

ATM and LANE are a popular choice for campus and LAN connectivity. Catalyst switches can be configured for ATM and LANE connectivity with little difficulty. Be prepared to use your knowledge of configuring and monitoring the Catalyst 3000 series in an ATM/LANE environment.

The answers to the questions are followed by a brief explanation. Some of the explanations detail the logic you should use to choose the correct answer, while others give factual reasons why the answer is correct. If you miss several questions on a similar topic, you should review the corresponding section in the *Cisco LAN Switch Configuration Study Guide* before taking the CLSC test.

Introduction to Switching Concepts

1. ☑ **A and C.** Switches are Layer 2 or data-link devices that forward information on the MAC address. The MAC source-and-destination address, as well as the network on which the devices reside, are analyzed and a forwarding decision is made based on that information.
   In the case of broadcast or multicast frames, the packets are flooded to every port in the corresponding VLAN. If there is traffic destined to another network, it will not be forwarded unless a router is in place.
   ☒ **B.** Forwarding IP addresses requires some sort of routing mechanism because IP address analysis and forwarding decisions are done at the network layer.

2. ☑ **C.** A translational bridge provides the capability of incorporating dissimilar LAN topologies, such as from Ethernet to Token Ring, or FDDI to Ethernet. The application for this technology can be seen in the situation where two companies merge. The probability of both organizations running similar technologies is pretty remote. The industry recognized this, and so, found a market where organizations need to integrate dissimilar technologies.
   ☒ **A.** A device that forwards dissimilar IP addresses, is incorrect. This would probably mean different network addresses, and in that case would require a network-layer forwarding device, also known as a router. **B.** A device that can connect two networks, is incorrect. Translational bridges can connect two LANs, but the LANs must reside on the same network. A router is required to connect two networks, and communication occurs at the network layer.

D. A device that functions as a transparent bridge, is incorrect. A transparent bridge does not provide any translational capabilities.

3. ☑ **B.** Route Information Field (RIF). This is the database that is stored in each device for determining which path to take to a destination. If the RIF doesn't contain a path to a destination, the sending host station will send out a local explorer frame, without traversing any bridges or switches. If the sending station does not receive a reply from the desired host, then an all routes explorer frame is issued. Upon receiving a reply from the desired host, the best path is determined, and that information is stored in the RIF. ☒ **A.** CAM, is an acronym for Content Addressable Memory. This is a database that is stored in bridges and switches that correlates Mac addresses to specific bridge or switch ports. **C.** RIP, is a distance vector routing protocol and does not play a role in switching. **D.** SRB, is the acronym for source route bridging.

VLANs

1. ☑ **B.** VLANs are used to break broadcast domains into smaller groups, sometimes for security reasons. Without a router, VLANs cannot forward information beyond the VLAN boundary. This would ensure a level of security that disallows access to resources within a protected VLAN. Additionally, this level of security would disallow access to resources outside the VLAN boundary. Communicating outside a VLAN boundary requires a router, or other Layer 3 device. ☒ **A.** The switch doesn't know where to forward packets at the data-link layer, is incorrect. The VLAN doesn't know where to forward packets because the VLAN doesn't know of the existence of any other VLANs. From the perspective of the VLAN, it believes it's the only LAN in existence. **C.** Without a router, frames are not able to traverse VLANs.

D. Without a router, you cannot get valid sniffer traces, is incorrect. You can still get a sniffer trace.

2. ☑ **A.** The Catalyst 5000 series Token Ring software runs an instance of STP for each TrBRF VLAN and each TrCRF VLAN. For TrCRF VLANs, STP removes loops in the logical ring. For TrBRF VLANs, STP interacts with external bridges to remove loops from the bridge topology, similar to STP operation on Ethernet VLANs. Note that in order for TrCRF to function, TrBRF must be configured.

☒ **B.** Provide for Redundant paths, is incorrect. Redundant paths cannot not be active with spanning tree running. A path that is redundant is blocked and will become active if the primary path fails. **C.** TrBRF or TrCRF does not provide a hierarchical design. **D.** For Token-Ring and Ethernet to effectively work together, either a translational bridge, or a router would have to be implemented.

Placing Catalyst 5000 Series Switches in Your Network

1. ☑ **A and C.** Bandwidth for resources, especially global resources, is very important in order to enable that resource to provide services for the network. Global resources should be on a dedicated segment to guarantee the maximum throughput that particular topology can afford. For example, 100BaseT should be configured for full duplex 100BaseT to get a throughput of 200 Mbps.

☒ **B.** is incorrect because local resources should be placed on a segment with the users who access those resources most. **D.** None of the above, is incorrect.

Catalyst 5000 Series Switch Architecture

1. ☑ **D.** A DB-25 DCE receptacle. The console port on supervisory engines is a 25-port DCE receptacle. This port is used for out-of-band management, initial

configuration of the switch using the command line interface, and for network management SNMP tools.

☒ **A.** A DB-9 DTE receptacle, and **B.** A DB-25 DTE receptacle, are incorrect because they specify DTE, not DCE receptacles. **C.** A DB-9 DCE receptacle, is wrong because it specifies a 9-port DCE, not a 25-port receptacle.

Catalyst 5000 Series Switch Hardware

1. ☑ **B.** Supervisor Engine II. Catalyst 5500 supports two supervisor modules (Supervisor Engines II, III, III FSX, or III FLX) for redundancy.
☒ **A.** Supervisor Engine I, is incorrect. It will work in the 5000-series Catalyst switching chasses, but not the 5500 switch. **C.** either A or B, and **D.** none, are incorrect.

2. ☑ **D.** You must install redundant supervisor engine modules in slots 1 and 2 of the chassis. Redundant supervisor engine modules are not swappable. The system continues to operate with the same configuration after switching over to the redundant supervisor engine.
☒ **A, B,** and **C** are incorrect. In redundant supervisor configurations supervisor modules must be installed in slots 1 and 2.

3. ☑ **A.** The proper syntax is SHOW PORT [mod_num[/port_num]]. The following is a sample output from the SHOW command:

```
Console> (enable) show port 1
Port Name              Status     Vlan   Level   Duplex  Speed  Type
---- ----------------  ---------  -----  ------  ------  -----  ---------
1/1  Router Connection connected  trunk  high    half    100    100BaseTX
1/2  Server Link       connected  trunk  normal  half    100    100BaseTX
-------------------------
Tue Jun 16 1998, 16:25:57
Console> (enable)
```

☒ **B.** SHOW PORT SPEED [mod_num[/port_num]], is incorrect syntax, as the speed statement is not required. **C**

SHOW RUNNING- CONFIGURATION is a router command that lists the configuration of a router. **D.** SHOW VLAN, will show all the VLANs that are configured in the switch.

4. ☑ **C.** LANE SERVER-BUS ETHERNET ELAN-NAME. At least one LES/BUS must be configured for each ELAN on an ATM LANE network. The LES/BUS for each ELAN must be configured on separate subinterfaces of the major ATM interface on the ATM module. Listed below is a sample configuration for setting up the LES/BUS.

```
ATM(config)#interface atm0.1
ATM(config-subif)#lane server-bus Ethernet default
ATM(config-subif)#interface atm0.2
ATM(config-subif)#lane server-bus Ethernet MfgELAN
```

Note that the LES/BUS will not be in operation until one or more LECs are configured and the LECs database is set up.

☒ **A, B,** and **D** are incorrect syntax for the operation.

5. ☑ **A.** Only frames larger than 1514 are dropped. IP fragmentation allows the Catalyst 5000 series switches to fragment large FDDI packets (larger than 1514 bytes) into smaller packets so that the packets may be transmitted on Ethernet segments. When FDDI fragmentation is disabled, large IP packets are dropped instead of being fragmented and forwarded. FDDI frame fragmentation allows packets larger than the MTU of 1514 to be segmented and forwarded on Ethernet segments.

☒ **B.** Frames larger than 1514 are fragmented, is incorrect. When FDDI fragmentation is disabled, frames larger that 1514 bytes are NOT fragmented. Disabling the fragmentation feature stops a large frame from being fragmented and forwarded. **C.** Disabling fragmentation on FDDI actually allows the MTU on FDDI to go above the MTU for Ethernet. So, IP frames larger than 1514 bytes will attempt to be forwarded on Ethernet segments, only to be dropped. **D.** Nothing happens, is incorrect. From FDDI to FDDI nothing happens, but from FDDI to Ethernet, IP frames larger than 1514 bytes will not be forwarded.

Configuring the Catalyst 5000 Series Switches

1. ☑ **D.** The Catalyst switches are ready to go right out of the box for LANs that do not require any VLANs setup, or management. For a default, single VLAN Ethernet configuration, no configuration needs to be done. The table below contains a list of the default settings of an Ethernet module in a Catalyst switch.

   ☒ **A, B,** and **C** are all forms of configuration attempts and do not need to be input for the default Ethernet configuration.

Port enable state	All ports are enabled
Port name	None
Port priority	Normal
Duplex mode	Half duplex for 10 Mbps Ethernet ports Auto-negotiate speed and duplex for 10/100-Mbps Fast Ethernet ports Auto-negotiate duplex for 100 Mbps Fast Ethernet ports Full duplex for 1000 Mbps Gigabit Ethernet ports
Flow control (Gigabit Ethernet only)	Flow control set to *off* for receive (Rx) and *desired* for transmit (Tx)
Link negotiation protocol (Gigabit Ethernet only)	Enabled
Spanning-Tree Protocol	Enabled
Native VLAN	VLAN 1
Port VLAN cost	Port VLAN cost of 100 for 10 Mbps Ethernet ports Port VLAN cost of 19 for 10/100 Mbps Fast Ethernet ports Port VLAN cost of 19 for 100 Mbps Fast Ethernet ports Port VLAN cost of 4 for 1000 Mbps Gigabit Ethernet ports
Fast Ethernet Channel	Disabled on all Fast Ethernet ports (auto mode)

2. ☑ **B.** SHOW CDP NEIGHBORS. Cisco Discovery Protocol (CDP) is a media- and protocol-independent protocol that runs on all Cisco equipment. CDP is a Layer 2 protocol that enables you to view information on all directly connected Cisco equipment. Information such as device name, IP address, version of IOS or operating system (Catalyst 5000 series switches) is displayed. In addition, network management applications can retrieve device information.

Cisco devices never forward CDP information. When new CDP information is received, devices discard the old information. CDP is a periodic function, which takes place every 60 seconds by default. This interval can be adjusted.

☒ **A.** SHOW ATTACHED, is not a valid Cisco command. **C.** DISPLAY NEIGHBORS, is not a valid Cisco command **D.** WHO, is not a valid Cisco command.

3. ☑ **B.** SET PORT LEVEL MOD_NUM/PORT_NUM {normal | high}. Each port can be configured for priority levels. This allows a port with a higher priority to be acknowledged at higher rates. The forwarding ratio for ports configured as high priority is 5:1. Following is an example of the command syntax:

```
Console> (enable) set port level 1/1 high
```

☒ **A.** SET PRIORITY {normal | high} PORT/MOD_NUM, is wrong; the command syntax is incorrect and has no function in a Cisco environment. **C.** PRIORITY-QUEUE PRIORITY {normal | high} PORT/MOD_NUM, is incorrect. Although queuing can be an option on routers, the Catalyst switch, excluding the RSM, does not support queuing. **D.** PRIORITY-LIST {normal | high} PORT/MOD_NUM LIST#, is incorrect. Once a priority-queue is configured the queue does need to be applied to a port, but this application methodology is akin to routers, not the Catalyst-switch family.

4. ☑ **C.** An SNMP managed network consists of three components, namely, managed devices, agents, network-management system (NMS). The managed device is a node on the network which contains an SNMP agent, and resides

on the managed network. Managed devices collect and store network information, and make this information available to NMSs using SNMP. Managed devices can be switches, routers, access servers, a computer host, or printers. An agent is a network-management software application that resides in a managed device. An agent has local knowledge of management information, and forwards the management information to a network management host NMS. An NMS runs applications that monitor and control managed devices. NMS stations provide the processing and memory resources. At least one NMS station must exist on any managed network. ☒ **A.** SNMP manager, SNMP agent, and management information base (MIB), is incorrect. This is almost a correct answer, but the last selection is incorrect. **B.** MIB is the Management Information Base, is incorrect. This is a database of over 30,000 command definitions. **D.** Stats, Alarm, and History are used, but are part of the IETF-standard monitoring specifications that allow network agents and console systems to exchange information.

5. ☑ **A and C.** Downloading a software image can be done in two ways: by using the DOWNLOAD command, as outlined in the steps below; or via the commands that mirror IOS command syntax. COPY TFTP FLASH is valid syntax.

1. Copy the software image to a TFTP server that the switch will be accessing
2. Log into the Catalyst 5000 series switch the console port or Via Telnet
3. Download the image from the TFTP server
4. DOWNLOAD HOST FILE [mod_num] is the command syntax to start the process. The host IP address or host name needs to be specified, and the image name of the file, to be downloaded. Here is the syntax to start the download:

```
Console> (enable) download 172.20.52.3
cat5000-fddi.3-1-1.bin 3
```

The prompts are as follows:

```
Download image cat5000-sup.4-2-1.bin from 172.20.52.3 to
module 1 FLASH (y/n)
[n]? y
```

```
Finished network single module download. (2748504 bytes)
FLASH on Catalyst:
Type             Address              Location
Intel 28F016     20000000             NMP (P3) 8MB SIM
Erasing flash sector...done.
Programming flash sector...done.
Erasing flash sector...done.
Programming flash sector...done.
Erasing flash sector...done.
Programming flash sector...done.
```

The system needs to be reset to run the new image.

☒ **B.** Configure network is commanded to download a saved configuration file, not an image (image refers to the platform operating system). **D.** CONFIGURE TFTP FLASH is not a valid command. It mixes the COPY TFTP FLASH command with the CONFIGURE NETWORK command, and thus makes this answer an invalid choice.

6. ☑ **C.** To write a configuration to a host for backup or editing purposes the WRITE NETWORK command is used. The user must be in privileged command mode to be able to upload a current configuration to a host. It's worth noting that you cannot write network-to-upload software to the ATM module. Also remember that this command writes the CONFIGURATION and not the operating system.

☒ **A.** COPY TFTP FLASH, is incorrect. It is a method for loading an operating system image into the flash memory of the Catalyst switch. This form is considered the Alias, and the true method is DOWNLOAD *host file-name*. **B.** WRITE TERMINAL, will write the configuration to the screen of the terminal you are using. This command is like the SHOW RUN command when using IOS. **D.** This command downloads an image from a host file into the Catalyst switch.

7. ☑ **A.** SET PORT SPEED SLOT/PORT {10 | 100 | auto}. Setting the port speed allows older NICs to connect to the Catalyst 5000 Series switch. The port-speed function also helps hosts that are having trouble with the auto-negotiation process to lock into a 100 Mbps speed. You may come

across situations where both the port on the Catalyst switch and the NIC on the host are 100 Mbps capable, but either error out, or continuously connect at 10 Mbps. Setting the port speed will sometimes relieve problems, and it is often recommended to set the speed of the port when inconsistent problems arise. For example, setting the port speed on a Catalyst 5000 switch:

```
Console> (enable) set port speed 2/2 100
Port 2/2 speed set to 100 Mbps.
```

☒   **B.** SET SPEED SLOT/PORT {10 | 100 | auto}, is incorrect. This does not specify what is being set at the selected speed. The switch must be told that the port speed is being set. **C.** SET SLOT/PORT SPEED {10 | 100 | auto} is incorrect. Before choosing the slot or port, the switch must be told that port speed is going to be set. **D.** None of the above, is incorrect.

Catalyst 5000 Series Switch Software

1. ☑   **B** and **D.** The SET CGMP ENABLE command allows a switch to automatically search and find any routers capable of running CGMP. The second command, SET MULTICAST ROUTER 3/1, specifically tells the switch that there is a CGMP-compatible router at the remote end of the link.
☒   **A.** SET ROUTER CGMP ENABLE, **C.** SET MULTICAST ROUTER CGMP ENABLE, and **E.** SET IGMP ENABLE, are incorrect. They are not valid switch commands.

2. ☑   **A.** Port 1/1 will use only dot1q trunking. The port mode is set to non-negotiate, where it will not negotiate any kind of encapsulation type. The encapsulation type is set for dot1q, which means the trunk will only use dot1q trunking.
☒   **B.** VTP pruning has been used, is incorrect. Looking further down the output, you can see that only certain VLANs, which are forwarding and not pruned, are allowed to be inactive in the management domain. **C.** This is untrue as the trunk is not set up to not negotiate an encapsulation type, which means it will only use the encapsulation type specified, which in this

case is dot1q. **D.** There is no evidence from the output to say that the link is not working correctly. It is in forwarding mode, which means that it is forwarding traffic

3. ☑ **B.** NTP is the acronym for Network Time Protocol. NTP synchronizes timekeeping among a set of distributed time servers and clients. This allows events to be correlated when system logs are created and other events occur. NTP runs over UDP. NTP is documented by RFC 1305, and all NTP communications use Coordinated Universal Time (UTC), which is the same as Greenwich Mean Time. A network using NTP will usually get its time from an authoritative source like a radio clock or atomic clock. NTP is considered an extremely efficient protocol with no more that one packet per minute required to synchronize machines to within a millisecond of each other.

☒ **A** is incorrect because broadcasting time of day is a function of NTP, but a router is not really concerned with the time of day, other than for logging or management reasons. **C.** To provide a means of distributing network transfer protocols, is incorrect because NTP is a network timing protocol which synchronizes network device time keeping for the purpose of logging events and management. **D.** To distribute all kinds of Token Ring traffic, is incorrect because NTP has nothing to do with Token Ring packet distribution.

4. ☑ **A.** Setting up VLANs will limit broadcast traffic. If the whole switch is set up as VLAN 1, broadcast traffic will still be forwarded to every port, even though each port on a switch is a collision domain. VLANs are broadcast domains, so if two VLANs are set up on a switch, and a host on VLAN 1 sends broadcast traffic, the broadcast traffic will be sent out every port on that VLAN, but not on any other VLAN configured on that switch's ports.

☒ **B.** To disallow specific unicast traffic, is wrong because a switch that is configured with VLANs does allow specific unicast traffic within a VLAN. The packet must be destined for a host within the VLAN. That means the source and destination stations must reside in the VLAN. **C.** To limit traffic from one network to the next, is wrong because a switch configured with VLANs essentially designates each VLAN as an individual network. So traffic is not only limited, but will not traverse from one VLAN to the other without a router in place. **D.** To limit broadcast flooding, is wrong because broadcast flooding is an invalid term.

5. ☑ **B and D.** Inter-switch link (ISL) is a Cisco proprietary trunking protocol used for Fast Ethernet and Gigabit Ethernet. IEEE 802.1Q is an industry standard for Fast Ethernet and Gigabit Ethernet. You can configure a single port or multiple Fast or Gigabit Ethernet channel ports. ISL is usually used when connecting Cisco equipment together, although you can set the switch trunks to communicate via 802.1Q. If you are connecting dissimilar equipment, you must use 802.1Q. Non-Cisco products will not understand the ISL encapsulation and errors will occur.

☒ **A** is incorrect because VTP is the protocol that facilitates the communication between switches. VTP is a software feature on the Catalyst 5000 series switches that allows you to map trunking protocols together to create an integrated VLAN implementation across a user-defined management domain. It works in the following way: Each Catalyst 5000 Series switch advertises on its trunk ports, management domain, configuration revisions, VLANs that it knows about, and parameters for each known VLAN. These advertisements are sent through a multicast address to be received by all neighboring devices. All devices in the management domain learn about new VLANs configured in the transmitting device. Ultimately, a new VLAN need only be created or configured on only a single device in the management domain. The information is learned by all other devices in the management domain automatically. **C.** 802.1D, is incorrect. It is the IEEE spanning tree, which is not a trunking protocol, but an algorithm to detect and stop loops in a LAN.

6. ☑ **C.** VTP pruning is a feature on the software release 2.3 for the Catalyst 5000 series switches. VTP pruning restricts flooded VLAN traffic to trunks required to reach the appropriate network devices on each VLAN.

☒ **A.** MAC address-based port security, **B.** CGMP/IGMP support, and **D.** Trunking, are incorrect. They are features available on software release 2.2.

Managing the C5k Series Switch

1. ☑ **C.** CDP is a Layer 2 protocol that runs on all Cisco Switches and routers. Cisco devices NEVER forward CDP information that it receives, when a device receives a CDP packet with new information, it merely updates its neighboring table with the correct or new information, while the older information is aged out of the CDP table.

☒ **A.** CDP works on all equipment, is incorrect. CDP is Cisco specific, and will only work with Cisco equipment. **B.** CDP is a Layer 3 protocol, is incorrect. CDP is actually a data-link protocol, which is Layer 2, not Layer 3. **D.** The CDP database is not flushed every four hours.

Troubleshooting the Catalyst 5000

1. ☑ **D.** The module has failed. A line module that has a red light in the status LED is deemed to have a serious problem. The red light indicates that the module has failed for some reason. The best way to check the reason for the failure is to insert the module and see what errors come up on the screen. This can then either be fed back to Cisco, or possibly, if you are lucky, the reason can be found on CCO.

☒ **A.** If the module has been inserted correctly, then the status light should be green. **B.** The module is working correctly, but a specific port is disabled, is incorrect. On certain modules, if the status light is orange, it may indicate that there is a faulty port rather than a faulty card. **B** is incorrect because if the module has inserted correctly, the status light should be green. **D** is incorrect; if the module is booting up, the status light is usually amber.

2. ☑ **B.** The SHOW SYSTEM command will give you information about the power supplies, as shown in the following output:

```
C5k> (enable) show system
PS1-Status PS2-Status Fan-Status Temp-Alarm Sys-Status Uptime d,h:m:s Logout
---------- ---------- ---------- ---------- ---------- -------------- ------
ok         ok         ok         off        ok         80,20:30:06    none

PS1-Type  PS2-Type   Modem    Baud   Traffic  Peak  Peak-Time
--------  ----------  -------  -----  -------  ----  ---------
WS-C5508  WS-C5508   disable  9600   0%       4%    Wed Jun 23 1999, 12:01:51
System Name  System Location  System Contact
-----------  ---------------  --------------
C5k>
```

☒ **A.** SHOW PSU, is incorrect. This command is not a valid Catalyst 5000 command. **C.** SHOW HARD, is incorrect. It is short for SHOW HARDWARE. This command is a valid IOS command for showing what hardware is installed in a router, but it is not valid for the Catalyst 5000 series switch. **D.** The SHOW POWER command is not a valid Catalyst 5000 command. **E.** The SHOW ROM command is not a valid Catalyst 5000 command.

3. ☑ **C.** Category 3 cable is only supposed to be used for implementations of 10 Mbps Ethernet, and will not work on implementation of any speeds above 10 Mbps (i.e. 100 Mbps Fast Ethernet).

☒ **A.** The server can only run at 10 Mbps, is incorrect. The question stated that the server is running 100 Mbps, and Category 3 cable is not supported on 100 Mbps, only on 10 Mbps. The only options would be to change the network card in the server to 10 Mbps or to change to Category 5 cable. **B.** The network port can only run at 10 Mbps, is incorrect. The question mentions that the port is 10/100 auto-sensing. There are certain network cards which do not auto-sense properly, so this could be part of the problem. **D.** The cable run is 74 meters, which is too long for Category 3 cable, is incorrect. The cable distance is well within the limits of Category 3 UTP cabling. The maximum distance supported is 100 meters.

Catalyst 5000 Series Switch FDDI Module

1. ☑ **C.** From the looks of the network in the illustration (repeated below), most of the workstations and servers need to traverse the backbone to access each other, this type of network design is called a shared FDDI backbone network.

☒ **A.** Star network, is incorrect. This network could not be called Star, as there is only a single FDDI ring, and multiple VLANs are not really needed. **B.** Bus network, is incorrect. A bus network is, in its basic form, an Ethernet network, with every client accessing the same bus. **D.** Hybrid network, is incorrect. A hybrid network, is a collection of star and/or bus networks and, although the illustrated network has both Ethernet and FDDI, it is very basic and not really big enough to be called a hybrid network.

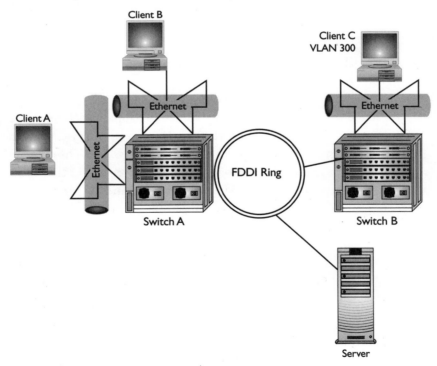

ATM LANE

1. ☑ **E.** SAR is performed by the ATMizer chips on the LANE module. The AAL has nothing to do with the actual SAR.

   ☒ **A.** AAL1, is incorrect. It uses a constant bit rate, and works with TDM protocols using circuit emulation examples of AAL1 implementation, including E1, DS1 lines. **B.** AAL2 uses a variable bit rate and is able to support packetized audio and video. **C.** AAL3/4, uses a variable bit rate, and is most commonly found in implementations of SMDS. **D.** AAL5, is currently the most-used implementation of the ATM adaptation layer, and provides the segmentation and re-assembly of ATM packets. It uses a variable bit rate.

2. ☑ **B, C,** and **E.** The BUS is assigned the third ESI (MAC address) assigned to an interface. The LEC gets assigned the third ESI (MAC address) assigned on an ATM interface. The LECS gets assigned the fourth ESI (MAC address) on an ATM interface.

   ☒ **A.** Any BUS gets the address of 1000.1000.1003, is incorrect. The BUS actually gets assigned the third ESI (MAC address) on an interface, and, according to the output in the question, the address specified is actually the LECS ESI. **D.** Any LEC gets the address of 1000.1000.1003, is incorrect as the LEC actually gets assigned the first ESI (MAC address) assigned to an interface. From the output in the question, the address specified is actually the LECS address. **F.** Any LECS gets the address of 1000.1000.1001, is incorrect as the LECS actually gets the fourth ESI (MAC address) assigned to an interface. From the output in the question, the address specified is actually the LES address.

Catalyst 1900 and 2820 Switches

1. ☑ **C.** By default, the SPAN function is disabled, not assigned to port 1.

   ☒ **A, B, D,** and **E** are all incorrect. Both STP and BOOTP are automatically disabled when a port is enabled to be a SPAN port. When you are defining ports to monitor, it is possible to monitor more than one port at a time. From the main menu, press *m* to go to the monitoring configuration menu. From the screen presented, you can make all the configuration changes to the SPAN port that are needed.

Catalyst 3000 Switches

1. ☑ E. The <CTRL> P command is used to go back to the main menu.
   ☒ A. <CTRL> B, B. <CTRL> X, C. <CTRL> C, and D. <CTRL> Q, are all incorrect commands. Only <CTRL> P will work.

Part 4

BCRAN
(Exam 640-505)

SCALING AND TROUBLESHOOTING REMOTE ACCESS NETWORKS

Introduction to Building Remote Access Networks

Identifying Cisco Solutions for Remote Access Needs

Enabling On-Demand Connections to the Central Site

Controlling Network Access with PAP or CHAP

Enhancing On-Demand Connectivity

Optimizing the Use of DDR Interfaces

Configuring a Cisco 700 Series Router

Enabling Permanent Connections to the Central Site

Queuing and Compression

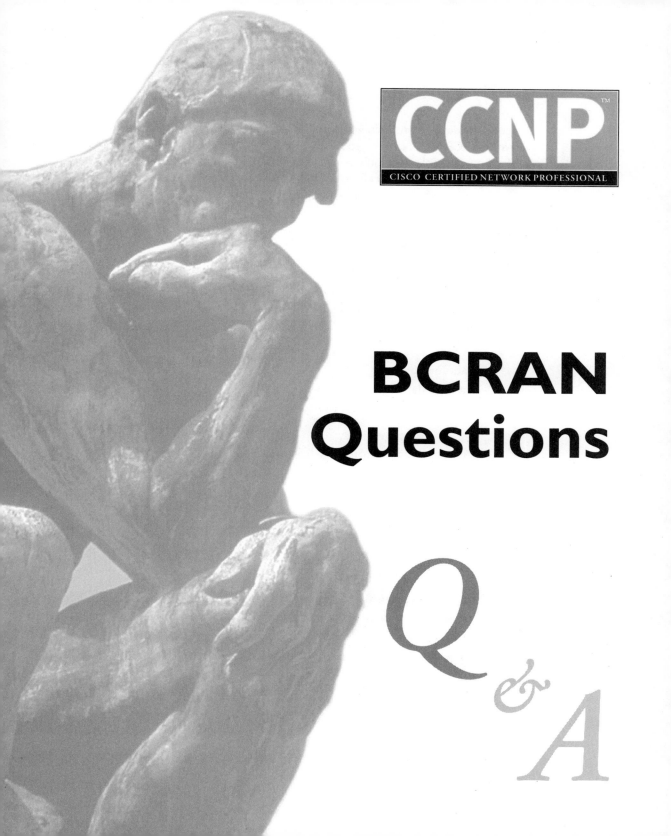

This section is designed to help you prepare for the Building Cisco Remote Access Networks (BCRAN) exam, so you can begin to reap the career benefits of CCNP certification. The following questions are structured in a format similar to the BCRAN exam. Read all the choices carefully, as there may be more than one correct answer. Choose all correct answers for each question.

Introduction to Building Remote Access Networks

1. Which layer(s) of the OSI reference model covers the functions of WAN technologies?

   A. Physical layer
   B. Data-link layer
   C. Physical, data-link, and network layers
   D. Data-link, network, and transport layers

2. Which design model creates the best managed, scaleable Internetworks?

   A. A flat model
   B. A hierarchical model
   C. A hybrid flat and hierarchical model
   D. The OSI reference model

3. Which routing protocols supported by Cisco promote increased accessibility and decreased internetwork convergence time? Choose all that apply.

   A. RIP
   B. NLSP
   C. EIGRP
   D. RTMP

4. Which Cisco IOS feature is used to reduce the size of very large routing tables?

   A. Snapshot routing

   B. Bridging

   C. Route summarization

   D. Compression over WANs

5. You have just received a new Cisco router and have been told to configure its serial 0 interface for HDLC. The router at the other end of serial 0 is also a Cisco router. Which of the following configurations is most correct?

   A. INT S0
       IP ADDRESS 192.168.200.5 255.255.255.252
       ENCAPSULATION HDLC

   B. INT S0
       IP ADDRESS 192.168.200.5 255.255.255.252

   C. INTERFACE S0
       IP ADDRESS 192.168.200.5 255.255.255.252
       ENCAPSULATION-HDLC

   D. INT S0
       IP ADDRESS 192.168.200.5 255.255.255.252
       DEFAULT-ENCAPSULATION

6. One of your colleagues has asked you to demonstrate the command used to show the network layer address and DLCI for each remotely connected router. Choose the correct command.

   A. SHOW INTERFACES SERIAL

   B. SHOW FRAME-RELAY PVC

   C. SHOW FRAME-RELAY MAP

   D. SHOW FRAME-RELAY LMI

7. Your organization has asked you for a recommendation on building a responsive, low-cost, full mesh WAN network between each of your local and remote sites. Which WAN technology would you recommend?

   A. Point-to-point lines using HDLC encapsulation
   B. X.25 network services
   C. ISDN service
   D. Frame Relay service

Identifying Cisco Solutions for Remote Access Needs

1. What is the default encapsulation for a synchronous WAN interface on a Cisco router?

   A. SDLC
   B. LAPB
   C. HDLC
   D. ISDN

2. Which WAN technologies does HSSI support? Choose all that apply.

   A. SONET
   B. T-3
   C. T-4
   D. E-3

3. How many network module slots does a Cisco 3640 chassis support?

   A. 36
   B. 40
   C. 3
   D. 4

4. You are performing password recovery on a Cisco 3640 with Flash memory intact and you are currently at the ROMMON > prompt. What should you type at this point?

A. CONFREG 0X41

B. CONFREG 0X42

C. O/R 0X2142

D. O/R 0x2141

5. You have received a Cisco 766 router that has an unknown power-up password. How will you go about recovering the power-up password?

A. Interrupt the power-up sequence to place the router in ROM monitor mode, then follow standard password recovery procedures for a Cisco router

B. Let the router boot up, then use configuration commands to change the password

C. Strap the proper jumpers on the motherboard, power up the router, then use configuration commands to change the password

D. None of the above

6. The LED on the lower-left side of your powered-up 3640s front panel is solid green in color. What information does this light indicate to you?

A. The router is operating in ROM monitor mode

B. The router is operating normally

C. The router is receiving power, but not operating properly

D. The router is going through power-on self test

7. You are observing one of your colleagues configure an interface on a Cisco 2600 series router and the command line shows INTERFACE ETHERNET 1/0. Which Ethernet interface is he configuring?

A. This interface does not exist

B. The interface is Ethernet 0, in slot 1

C. The interface is Ethernet 1, in slot 0

D. The interface is Ethernet 1, in slot 1

Enabling On-Demand Connections to the Central Site

1. What type of jack is used to connect to a WIC-1DSU-T1 card?

   A. RJ-11C

   B. RJ-45

   C. RJ-49C

   D. RJ-48C

2. Which two statements about the Cisco 2500 series routers are true?

   A. Supports 1–2 LAN interfaces

   B. Supports 8–16 asynchronous lines

   C. Supports internal digital modems on asynchronous dial-up lines

   D. Supports internal analog modems on asynchronous dial-up lines

3. A replacement Cisco 2500 series router from one of your remote locations was express mailed to you for immediate installation. You were told that it does not have a LOGIN CONSOLE password, but that it does have an ENABLE password. You booted the router and it displayed a > prompt. What mode is the router in?

   A. Normal mode

   B. Config mode

   C. Boot mode

   D. ROMMON mode

4. Which statement best defines FDM?

   A. A single digital channel separated by multiple frequencies

   B. Multiple analog channels separated by a single digital signal

   C. Parallel analog channels separated by parallel digital signals

   D. Parallel analog channels separated by different frequencies

5. You have been asked to manually change the modem command strings in six modems connected to a Cisco 2500 series access router, as shown in the following configuration. You need to access the connected modems in order to make the changes.

```
Router(config)#ip host Tacoma1 2001 10.1.1.1
Router(config)#ip host Tacoma2 2002 10.1.1.1
Router(config)#ip host Tacoma3 2003 10.1.1.1
Router(config)#ip host Tacoma4 2004 10.1.1.1
Router(config)#ip host Tacoma5 2005 10.1.1.1
Router(config)#ip host Tacoma6 2006 10.1.1.1
Router(config)# end
```

Which command would you enter to begin performing this task on the first modem attached to the first line?

   A. TACOMA1

   B. TACOMA101 2007

   C. TACOMA 2007

   D. None of the above

6. There are six asynchronous lines attached to your 2500 series access router. You want to configure the router so that each external modem is properly reset after a user logs off. You are using are Viva modems. Which command would you use to accomplish this?

A. ROUTER(CONFIG)# LINE 1 6
   ROUTER(CONFIG-LINE)# AUTOCONFIGURE MODEM TYPE VIVA
   ROUTER(CONFIG-LINE)# END

B. ROUTER(CONFIG)# LINE 1 6
   ROUTER(CONFIG-LINE)# MODEM AUTOCONFIGURE TYPE VIVA
   ROUTER(CONFIG-LINE)# END

C. ROUTER(CONFIG)# LINE 0 5
   ROUTER(CONFIG-LINE)# AUTO-CONFIGURE MODEM VIVA
   ROUTER(CONFIG-LINE)# END

D. ROUTER(CONFIG)# LINE 0 5
   ROUTER(CONFIG-LINE)#
   MODEM-AUTOCONFIGURE-TYPE VIVA
   ROUTER(CONFIG-LINE)# END

7. What types of servers are supported by default in a Windows95/98 dial-up connection configuration? Choose all that apply.

A. AppleTalk

B. IPX/SPX

C. TCP/IP

D. NetBEUI

8. How many end-user DS-0 channels can be derived from an E-1 line?

A. 24

B. 32

C. 28

D. 30

Controlling Network Access with PAP or CHAP

1. Which of the following are advantages of PPP, but not of SLIP? Choose all that apply.

A. Supports SPX/IPX and AppleTalk

B. Supports TCP/IP

C. Supports CHAP

D. Supports asynchronous dial-up connections

2. Which of the following statements regarding PPP are true? Choose all that apply.

A. PPP supports synchronous and asynchronous media

B. PPP supports dial-up asynchronous media only

C. PPP does not support Stacker compression

D. PPP supports Predictor compression

3. Which DTE-DCE interfaces are supported by PPP? Choose all that apply.

A. RS232

B. V.35

C. HSSI

D. 802.3

4. You have just begun configuring a serial interface for PPP and CHAP authentication and want to verify the CHAP configuration at this point in the configuration. Which command would you enter?

A. SHOW STARTUP-CONFIG

B. SHOW PPP INTERFACE

C. DEBUG PPP CHAP

D. DEBUG PPP LINE

Enhancing On-Demand Connectivity

1. Your users at a branch site have been complaining about the "network being slow" during large file transfers. The branch site is connected to headquarters by multiple asynchronous lines. You have decided that MLP may be a possible solution. What features does MLP provide? Choose all that apply.

   A. Bandwidth on demand
   B. MTU calculation
   C. Reduced transmission latency
   D. Designed to maximize ISDN investment

2. One of your colleagues wants to observe the PPP authentication process in action on one of the configured interfaces. She asks you which IOS command would make this possible. What is your response?

   A. DEBUG INTERFACE
   B. DEBUG PPP AUTHENTICATION
   C. SHOW INTERFACE
   D. SHOW RUN

3. What type of information is displayed with the SHOW DIALER command? Choose all that apply.

   A. Call-specific information
   B. RE-ENABLE TIMER value
   C. Information about the existing bundles in Multilink PPP
   D. Calling router name

4. Which of the following commands is used to select the Predictor compression algorithm, on Serial interface 1?

A. ROUTER(config)#INT S1
    ROUTER(config-int)#PREDICTOR COMPRESS

B. ROUTER(config)#INT S1
    ROUTER(config-int)#COMPRESS PREDICTOR

C. ROUTER(config)#INT S1
    ROUTER(config)#PREDICTOR COMPRESS

D. ROUTER(config)#INT S1
    ROUTER(config)#COMPRESS PREDICTOR

Optimizing the Use of DDR Interfaces

1. In DDR, to how many physical interfaces can a logical interface be applied?

A. One

B. No more than three

C. One on each analog line

D. As many dial interfaces as there are on the router

2. When many interfaces are configured in a dialer rotary group, which physical interface is required for the outgoing call?

A. Always the first one in the dialer rotary group

B. Always the last one in the dialer rotary group

C. Any available interface in the dialer rotary group

D. The one with the highest priority

3. Enabling DDR on an asynchronous interface defines what command string?

A. DIALER IN-BAND
B. DIALER ROTARY-GROUP group-#
C. DDR ASYNC
D. None of the above

4. Which command helps you best determine the status of a dialer connection?

A. SHOW DIALER
B. SHOW LINE
C. SHOW INTERFACE
D. SHOW RUNNING CONFIG

5. How are the logical and physical configurations bound together dialer profiles?

A. They are permanently bound together
B. They are dynamically bound together on a per-call basis
C. They are dynamically bound together
D. None of the above

6. A dialer pool can have multiple physical interfaces as members and multiple physical interfaces can be members of a single pool. Which command defines the physical interface as a member of a pool?

A. DIALER POOL-MEMBER pool-#
B. DIALER POOL pool-#
C. POOL-MEMBER pool-#
D. POOL pool-#

7. Routing protocols are not desirable when implementing a dial back-up solution. If a router is using the IGRP routing protocol and this routing protocol is not allowed to be propagated over the dial interface, which access list prevents IGRP from crossing over the link?

A. ROUTER (config) # ACCESS-LIST 10 DENY IGRP ANY ANY

B. ROUTER (config-if) # ACCESS-LIST 10 DENY IGRP ANY ANY

C. ROUTER (config) # ACCESS-LIST 101 DENY IGRP ANY ANY

D. ROUTER (config) # ACCESS-LIST 101 DENY IGRP

Configuring a Cisco 700 Series Router

1. Which protocol(s) do(es) Cisco 700 series routers NOT support?

A. SNMP

B. IP

C. IPX

D. AppleTalk

2. Which telephone services are NOT available on the Cisco 700 series routers? Choose all that apply.

A. Call waiting

B. Call hold

C. Call transfer

D. Three-way calling

E. None of the above

3. The 765 and 766 models of the Cisco 700 series routers have a feature that the 761 and 762 models of the Cisco 700 series do not have. What is the feature?

A. Token Ring support

B. Two B-channel pairs

C. Two RJ-11 interfaces

D. Call waiting

4. In which environment is the Cisco 700 series router best used?

A. Enterprise solutions

B. Occasional connection to an ISP

C. Voice, video and data solutions

D. Continuous connection to a corporation

5. After being defined by the user, where are profiles saved and stored in a Cisco 700 series router?

A. RAM

B. Flash

C. NVRAM

D. PCMCIA storage

6. What are the three required software configuration tasks?

A. Global, interface, sub-interface

B. Profile, LAN, user

C. User, LAN, system

D. Remote, local, internal

7. In the configuration line below, what does *cost 1* specify?

```
Router> set ip route destination 1.2.3.4/8 gateway
1.1.1.1 propagate on cost 1
```

A. The dollar cost associated with that connection

B. The RIP hop count

C. The static route hop count

D. None of the above

Enabling Permanent Connections to the Central Site

1. Why is the Cisco 700 series router especially designed for international use?

A. ISDN is used all over the world

B. RJ 45 connectors are a worldwide standard

C. Cisco 700 series routers are certified in 25 countries

D. The availability of RJ-11 analog ports

2. What function does Caller ID provide to the Cisco 700 series router?

A. Allows the router to identify who is calling in

B. Allows only a specific caller to call into the router

C. Matches a SPID to an IP address

D. None of the above

3. These phases are associated with a type of VC: Call setup, information transfer, and call clear. Which type of VC does this describe?

A. PVC

B. SVC

C. LCN

D. VCI

4. Which resolution process answers the question: *I know your IP. What is your MAC address?*

   A. ARP
   B. Inverse ARP
   C. RARP
   D. AARP

5. Your company's corporate office currently uses Cisco routers and communicates with its remote facilities with frame relay. Your company has also just purchased an organization that uses non-Cisco equipment to communicate with its remote facilities. In setting up the connection between your corporate office and the office of the new company, you are having trouble getting the data links to successfully communicate. After checking with the provider, verifying proper configuration on its part, and checking and re-checking your configuration, you notice a configuration mismatch. What will resolve this problem?

   A. Power cycle the routers at both ends of the link
   B. Power cycle the CSU
   C. Input the command FRAME RELAY LMI-TYPE ANSI in your corporate office router
   D. Input the command ENCAPSULATION FRAME RELAY IETF in your corporate office router

6. Referring to the scenario and problem posed in the previous question, what is the diagnostics command that would display the encapsulation mismatch?

   A. SHOW INTERFACE
   B. SHOW FRAME-RELAY MAP
   C. SHOW FRAME-RELAY PVC
   D. SHOW RUNNING-CONFIG

7. Which two methods are available to provide a more granular control of traffic being forwarded to a VC?

A. Setting a CIR

B. Queuing

C. Generalized BECN support

D. Access lists

Queuing and Compression

1. Why did the need to prioritize packets arise?

A. Different data needs to have different priorities set

B. File transfers require a high priority

C. Different types of traffic that share a data path can impact each other

D. Video conferencing demanded it

2. If, after careful analysis, the network performs poorly but the routers do not show congestion, what is the appropriate action?

A. Implement a queuing method

B. Analyze the LAN where the problem may be

C. Implement ACCESS LIST

D. None of the above

3. What is the difference between custom and priority queuing?

A. Custom queuing processes queues on a first come, first served basis, regardless of traffic type, and priority queuing provides a certain amount of bandwidth for each packet type

B. Custom queuing dispatches packets through the queue based on which packet header arrives at the queue first, while priority queuing processes packets through the queue with the highest priority

C. Custom queuing provides a specified amount of bandwidth to each defined traffic type, while priority queuing processes packets with high priority first with the possibility that traffic in the lower queues may not get processed

D. None of the above

4. Which two compression methods does the PPP link compression algorithm utilize?

A. Payload

B. STAC

C. Header

D. Predictor

5. With which protocol is header compression used?

A. TCP/IP and IPX

B. TCP only

C. IPX only

D. Header compression is not protocol specific

Scaling and Troubleshooting Remote Access Networks

1. To which problem does network address translation (NAT) help provide a solution? Choose all that apply.

A. Private networks with enough addresses for the internal networks

B. Private networks that need to connect to public networks

C. Private networks that need to connect to multiple facilities

D. Two autonomous private networks that need to connect to one anther

2. When is DUAL NAT used?

A. When networks with different addressing schemes communicate

B. When two networks have overlapping network addresses

C. If more than two routers are communicating

D. If both networks wish to do NAT

3. What's the advantage of using NAT to connect to an ISP?

A. Not being required to have registered IP addresses and saving a lot of money

B. Having a flexible Internet service that allows you to use any address you wish

C. Only having private global addresses

D. None of the above

4. What is the Cisco application that allows a Web-based Java configuration and a management tool that simplifies server administration and enables multiple system administrators to simultaneously manage security services?

A. IOS

B. ACS

C. TACACS+

D. RADIUS

5. Up to four authentication methods can be defined in AAA. What is the process of authenticating through the four methods?

A. If authentication is denied on the first method, the next method is queried, and so on

B. If an authentication method times out, the next method is queried

C. The user picks which method he/she wishes to authenticate on

D. None of the above

6. Your organization wishes to take account of all the users that access a router and make configuration changes. Which of the following AAA accounting commands will provide the proper data?

A. AAA ACCOUNTING EXEC START-STOP TACACS+

B. AAA ACCOUNTING COMMAND 15 START-STOP TACACS+

C. AAA ACCOUNTING CONNECTION START-STOP TACACS+

D. AAA ACCOUNTING SYSTEM START-STOP TACACS+

BCRAN QUESTIONS

Though answers to the questions are in boldface, followed by a brief explanation. Some of the explanations detail the logic you should use to choose the correct answer, while others give factual reasons why the answer is correct. If you miss several questions on a similar topic, you should review the corresponding section in the *Building Cisco Remote Access Networks Study Guide* (due to publish in early 2000) before taking the BCRAN test.

Introduction to Building Remote Access Networks

1. ☑ **C. Physical, data-link, and network layers.** WAN technologies cover the lowest three layers of the OSI reference model. WAN technologies cover the specifications to define the types of media and signaling over the media at the physical layer. The type of WAN technology chosen also defines the type of framing that will be used between WAN DTEs. Finally, some WAN services such as X.25 also define network-layer packet format and addressing.

   ☒ **A.** The physical layer, is incorrect. This defines the types of signaling and media and nothing else. **B.** Data-link layer, is incorrect because it only defines the type of framing used. **D.** Data-link, network, and transport layers, is incorrect because it includes the transport layer, which is supported in the end devices, not in network components.

2. ☑ **B.** A hierarchical model provides the best model for controlling growth while meeting network requirements and simplifying network management. This model also facilitates implementation and troubleshooting tasks.

   ☒ **A.** A flat model, is incorrect because it implies Layer 2 switching as a means to scale an internetwork's growth. **C.** A hybrid flat and hierarchical model, is incorrect. The hierarchical model includes switching (a flat network model) at the access layer of the model. **D.** The OSI reference model, is incorrect because it describes the functions performed by network components and not how networks should be designed.

3. ☑ **B and C.** NLSP and EIGRP are routing protocols that overcome the metric problems of distance-vector routing protocols such as RIP and RTMP. These protocols use cost as a metric rather than hop count. They keep a network topology map and quickly notify other routers of any changes in the internetwork topology. Thus, they provide better internetwork availability and reliability.

   ☒ **A.** RIP, and **D.** RTMP, are incorrect because both are distance-vector routing protocols that use hop count as a metric and exchange routing updates on a periodic basis.

4. ☑ **C.** Route summarization is used to reduce the number of entries in a routing table by advertising a number of routes with one routing table entry. Network addressing must be planned carefully in order to make use of route summarization.

   ☒ **A.** Snapshot routing, is incorrect because it is used to exchange full distance vector updates over a dialup connection. **B.** Bridging, is incorrect because there are no routing tables associated with bridges. **D.** Compression over WANs, is incorrect because it is used to reduce the traffic over a WAN, but not reduce the size of routing table entries.

5. ☑ **B.** The key word here is *new* Cisco router. There is no need to specify HDLC as the encapsulation on the interface because it is the default encapsulation type on Cisco router serial interfaces.

   ☒ **A.** would be a correct answer if you were changing from another type of encapsulation back to HDLC. **C.** is incorrect because of the encapsulation-HDLC format. **D.** is incorrect because there is no such command.

6. ☑ **C.** SHOW FRAME-RELAY MAP. The command displays the static or dynamic Frame Relay route maps. The remotely connected router's network layer address and DLCI is shown with this command.

   ☒ **A.** SHOW INTERFACES SERIAL, is incorrect. It shows information about the local router's interface. **B.** SHOW FRAME-RELAY PVC, is incorrect because it shows statistics on the local router's DLCI. **D.** SHOW FRAME-RELAY LMI, is incorrect. This command shows information about the local router's LMI.

7. ☑ **D.** Frame Relay service offers many network topology options, including a full mesh topology using PVCs rather than dedicated circuits. The service reduces the cost of router hardware (fewer physical interfaces) and carrier costs (no long-distance circuit charges). Generically it is cheaper and has less latency than X.25.

☒ **B.** X.25 network services, is not correct because it has more latency than Frame Relay networks. **C.** ISDN service, is incorrect because this is a dial-up service not suited for building mesh networks. **A.** Point-to-point lines, is not correct due to the higher tariff cost of circuits and increased hardware cost.

Identifying Cisco Solutions for Remote-Access Needs

1. ☑ **C.** HDLC is the default encapsulation on a Cisco router synchronous serial interface. This information can be displayed by the SHOW INTERFACE command. Cisco HDLC can only be used between Cisco routers.

☒ **A.** SDLC, and **B.** LAPB, are incorrect because they have to be selectively configured on the router's interface. **D.** ISDN, is incorrect because it is used as a dial-up digital interface.

2. ☑ **A, B,** and **D.** HSSI support speeds up to 52 Mbps. SONET is supported at 51.82 Mbps, T-3 at 45 Mbps, and E-3 at 34 Mbps. HSSI is a standard known as EIA612/613.

☒ **C.** T-4, which operates at 274 Mbps, is incorrect.

3. ☑ **D.** Four (4) network modules. The Cisco 3640 is a modular platform that supports multiple services in the same device. It supports LAN-to-LAN, dial access, routing, and integration of voice, data, and video.

☒ **A.** 36, **B.** 40, and **C.** 3, are incorrect because the 3640 supports four modules.

4. ☑ **B.** CONFREG 0X42. This will set the configuration-register to 0x2142 and allow the router to be rebooted from Flash and bypass the configuration file in NVRAM. The password(s0) can now be changed and the configuration register setting restored to 0x2102, for a normal boot sequence.

☒ **A.** CONFREG 0X41 would be correct if Flash is erased or not installed. However, you can erase the configuration but not change the password. **C.** O/R 0X2142, and **D.** O/R 0x2141, are not correct for this type of router.

5. ☑ **D.** None of the above. The power-up password on a 700 series router cannot be recovered. A special program must be used to erase the configuration and operating system. Then they must be loaded in again from the console port.

☒ **A, B,** and **C** are incorrect because none of these sequences will work on the 700 series routers.

6. ☑ **B.** The router is operating normally. It has booted up properly without errors.

☒ **A.** The router is operating in ROM monitor mode, is incorrect because the LED would be blinking green. **C.** The router is receiving power, but not operating properly, is incorrect because the LED would be amber colored in this case. **D.** The router is going through a power-on self-test, is incorrect, as the LED would be blinking green and amber.

7. ☑ **B.** The command ETHERNET 1/0 represents the Ethernet 0 interface on the card in slot 1. The command format is INTERFACE TYPE followed by the chassis slot number, a forward slash (/), and the interface number on the card in that slot.

☒ **A.** This interface does not exist, is incorrect because this is a valid command. **C.** The interface is Ethernet 1, in slot 0, is incorrect because the slot and interface number are reversed. **D.** The interface is Ethernet 1, in slot 1, is incorrect because it represents the wrong Ethernet interface.

Enabling On-Demand Connections to the Central Site

1. ☑ **D.** RJ-48C. This WAN interface card requires an FCC-registered jack-type 48C. This is a standard jack, used in the telephone industry to terminate certain digital-access line services such as a T1 line.

    ☒ **A, B,** and **C** are jacks used to terminate different types of WAN and LAN services such as analog lines (RJ-11C), Ethernet (RJ-45), and ISDN BRI (RJ-49C). These services do not apply for the type of card mentioned in the question.

2. ☑ **A** and **B.** Supports 1–2 LAN interfaces and supports 8–16 asynchronous lines. The Cisco 2500 series routers support 1–2 Ethernet or Token Ring LAN interfaces. This 2500 access-server series supports 8–16 asynchronous lines with integrated RJ-11 jacks.

    ☒ **C.** Supports internal digital modems on asynchronous dial-up lines, and **D.** supports internal analog modems on asynchronous dial-up lines, are incorrect because the 2500 series does not support internal modems or CSUs.

3. ☑ **D.** ROMMON mode. The router is in the ROM monitor mode. There could be a number of reasons that the router is in this mode. The boot process could have been interrupted. The boot system ROM command could be set in its configuration file. The default configuration register could have been set to boot up in this mode.

    ☒ **A.** Normal mode, is incorrect because the prompt displayed would be ROUTER>. **B.** Config mode, is wrong because the router does not boot up in Configuration mode. **C.** Boot mode, is incorrect because there is no boot mode.

4. ☑ **D.** Parallel analog channels separated by different frequencies. Frequency division multiplexing takes the available bandwidth and divides it into sub-channels, each of which is separated by a band of frequencies.

☒ **A, B,** and **C** are incorrect. They represent situations that are not electrically possible for communications channels.

5. ☑ **A.** TACOMA1 tells the router to open a reverse TELNET session with the modem on line 1. The 2001 represents the TELNET port 2000 and the line number 1 equals 2001. The router would then prompt for the line password, after which the modem should be available to accept AT commands.
☒ **B.** and **C.** are wrong because there is no entry for TACOMA or TACOMA 101 in the host table, so the 2007 would be ignored. **D.** None of the above, is incorrect.

6. ☑ **B.** ROUTER(CONFIG)# LINE 1 6
ROUTER(CONFIG-LINE)# MODEM AUTOCONFIGURE TYPE VIVA
ROUTER(CONFIG-LINE)# END
The MODEM AUTOCONFIGURE command causes the IOS to send an initialization string to the type of modem specified in the IOS command string. The initialization string is sent to modems on lines 1–6. The Cisco IOS supports seven modem initialization strings. Each string has its own unique name.
☒ **A, C,** and **D** are incorrect command syntax.

7. ☑ **B, C,** and **D.** IPX/SPX, TCP/IP, and NetBEUI are the server types that are selected by default in Windows 95/98 dialup networking configurations. You may select any of these protocols with your mouse.
☒ **A.** AppleTalk, is the wrong answer because it is not one of the defaults.

8. ☑ **D.** 30 end-user DS-0 channels can be derived from an E-1 line. Thirty-two total channels can be derived, but two of the channels are used by the provider of the E-1 service for order wire.
☒ **A.** 24, is wrong because it applies to a T-1 line. **B.** 32, is wrong because two of the 32 channels are not available to end users. **C.** 28, is wrong because no carriers provide this service.

Controlling Network Access with PAP or CHAP

1. ☑ **A** and **C.** PPP provides support for SPX/IPX, AppleTalk, and CHAP, which SLIP does not support. PPP supports all of the features mentioned, as well as others not listed, such as PAP and synchronous media.
   ☒ **B.** Supports TCP/IP, and **D.** Supports asynchronous dial-up connections, are incorrect because these are features supported by both protocols.

2. ☑ **A** and **D.** PPP supports both asynchronous and synchronous media like POTS and ISDN. PPP supports both Stacker and Predictor compression protocols for reducing the amount of bandwidth consumed by data traffic.
   ☒ **B.** PPP supports dial-up asynchronous media only, is wrong because PPP supports dial-up and dedicated lines, as well as synchronous and asynchronous media. **C.** is incorrect because PPP does support Stacker compression.

3. ☑ **A, B,** and **C.** RS232, V.35, and HSSI. All of these DTE-DCE interfaces are supported by PPP. PPP can operate over any DTE-DCE interface. PPP also does not have a bit-rate restriction except as imposed by a specific interface.
   ☒ **D.** 802.3, is wrong because it is a LAN interface not a WAN interface.

4. ☑ **C.** DEBUG PPP CHAP will display any errors that occurred during the authentication process. The display will show the time and date, as well as whether the error was caused by the local or remote system.
   ☒ **A.** SHOW STARTUP-CONFIG, is incorrect because at this point the PPP configuration information has not been saved to NVRAM. **D.** DEBUG PPP LINE, is incorrect syntax. **B.** SHOW PPP INTERFACE, is wrong because it shows the status of the PPP protocol configured on the interface, which includes information on LCP and NCP.

Enhancing On-Demand Connectivity

1. ☑ A and C. MLP (Multilink PPP) lessens the latency on WAN lines by providing bandwidth on demand. Lines can be automatically added as the load increases beyond a preset user-defined load threshold.
   ☒ B. MTU calculation, is incorrect because MLP does not calculate MTU load. It does respond to a defined traffic load. D. Designed to maximize ISDN investment, is incorrect because MLP was not designed to maximize ISDN investment. This may, however, be an added benefit to its use.

2. ☑ B. The DEBUG PPP AUTHENTICATION command displays the authentication sequence of events as they happen on the target line. This command must be issued before the PPP session is established.
   ☒ A. DEBUG INTERFACE, is the wrong command syntax. C. SHOW INTERFACE only shows static information about PPP. D. SHOW RUN, is incorrect because it shows the present running configuration file in RAM.

3. ☑ A, B and C. Call specific information, such as calls connected to phone number, timer information, call successes and failures, the value of call timers such as the RE-ENABLE timer, idle timers and others, and information on each active line in a multilink configuration is shown.
   ☒ D. Calling router name, is incorrect. The calling router's name is not shown.

4. ☑ B. COMPRESS PREDICTOR at the config-nt prompt is the correct format to start this compression algorithm on the interface.
   ☒ A, C, and D are all improper formats for activating the Predictor algorithm.

Optimizing Use of DDR Interfaces

1. ☑ **D.** A single logical interface can be applied to as many dial interfaces as there are on the router. So, if the router had eight interfaces that were capable of dialing either ISDN or analog, a single logical interface can be set up on all eight ports. This application can be used in the case where a company may need more bandwidth than a single line can provide. With threshold configuration parameters in place, additional lines could be brought to support the extra bandwidth requirements.

   ☒ **A.** One, is incorrect. More than one physical interface can be mapped to a logical interface. More bandwidth may be required and, with proper configuration, the logical interface can be used to bring up additional lines to support the bandwidth requirement. **B.** No more than three, is incorrect. The only limit to the number of physical interfaces to which a logical interface can be mapped is the number of physical interfaces on the router. **C.** One on each analog line, is incorrect. Logical interfaces can be mapped to ISDN lines as well.

2. ☑ **C.** Any of the available interfaces in the rotary group can be used for the outgoing call. So if an interface in the dialer group is busy either due to a call to the same destination or another, the dialer rotary group will go to the next interface within the group. This feature provides for great flexibility in router configuration.

   ☒ **A.** Always the first one in the dialer rotary group, and **B.** always the last one in the dialer rotary group, are incorrect because there is no specified requirement for the dialer rotary group to use the first or last physical interface in the rotary group. The interface is chosen on its status. If the physical interface is busy, or in connection tear down, the next interface in the rotary group is addressed and again status is checked. If no interface is accessible, a connection error will be returned to the user. **D.** The one with the highest priority, is incorrect because in a rotary group, no one interface in that group can be given priority.

3. ☑ **A.** The DIALER IN-BAND command enables DDR on an asynchronous interface. This command tells the router that the interface will be used for analog dialing. This command can be applied to low-speed async serial interfaces and sync/async interfaces.
☒ **B.** DIALER ROTARY-GROUP *group-#,* is incorrect because the command 'Dialer rotary-group *group-#'* maps a physical interface to the properties of the logical interface. **C.** DDR ASYNC, is incorrect because it is not a valid Cisco IOS command. **D.** None of the above, is incorrect.

4. ☑ **A.** SHOW DIALER. This command will show the status of a dialer interface, either physical in the case of ISDN, or logical if logical interfaces are configured. The following is the proper syntax for the command:

SHOW DIALER [interface type number]

For example, to view the status of ISDN interface BRI 0, the following command is typed in either user or privileged modes:

SHOW DIALER INTERFACE BRI 0

☒ **B.** SHOW LINE, is incorrect because the command shows the status of calls established by analog connections, but does not provide status of calls established via BRI. **C.** SHOW INTERFACE, is incorrect because, although you will get information regarding the interface, the status is best defined by the SHOW DIALER command. The SHOW INTERFACE command will not provide information such as the dial string, what channels are active in BRI, or how long the call has been active. **D.** SHOW RUNNING CONFIG, is incorrect because it is an invalid command for this purpose.

5. ☑ **B.** In a dialer profile the logical and physical configurations are dynamically bound to each other on a per-call basis. This allows physical interfaces to dynamically take on different characteristics based on the requirements of the inbound/outbound call. Profiles can define encapsulation, access lists, and can turn the feature on or off.
☒ **A.** They are permanently bound together, is incorrect because dialer profiles are set up on a per-call basis. The requirements of a call from a source may be be different than a call to a destination, although the calls may take place on the same physical interface. **C.** They are dynamically bound together, is incorrect because the statement is not complete. Once the call is complete and the connection is terminated, the interface will be free to take on other profiles that are configured. **D.** None of the above, is incorrect.

6. ☑ **A.** DIALER POOL-MEMBER pool-# is the command that establishes a physical interface as a member of a dialer pool. As indicated by the introduction of the question, a physical interface can be a member of multiple dialer pools, as multiple dialer pools can have a single interface as its member. If multiple physical interfaces are members of multiple pools, priorities may be set so that specific interfaces are chosen first when the demand for a dialer profile arises to activate a physical interface. This is a feature that dialer rotary groups do not have.
☒ **B.** DIALER POOL *pool-#*, is incorrect because this is the syntax applied to a dialer interface to define the pool. After the pool is defined at a logical interface, it may be applied to a physical interface. **C.** POOL-MEMBER *pool-#*, and **D.** POOL *pool-#*, are incorrect syntax for application, either on a logical or physical interface.

7. ☑ **C.** ROUTER (config) # ACCESS-LIST 101 DENY IGRP ANY ANY. The configuration syntax requires that the router be in global configuration mode. Also, to properly identify the IGRP protocol, an extended access list is required. An extended access list is defined by access list numbers 100–199.

☒ **A.** ROUTER (config) # ACCESS-LIST 10 DENY IGRP ANY ANY, is incorrect because the access list number defines a standard access list and not an extended access list. An extended access list is required to define protocols within IP. **B.** ROUTER (config-if) # ACCESS-LIST 10 DENY IGRP ANY ANY, is incorrect because the router prompt is at an interface, plus this is not an extended access list. **D.** ROUTER (config) # ACCESS-LIST 101 DENY IGRP, is incorrect because there are no source or destination addresses defined.

Configuring a Cisco 700 Series Router

1. ☑ **D.** AppleTalk is not supported on the 700 series routers.

☒ **A.** SNMP, **B.** IP, and **C.** IPX, are all incorrect. The Cisco 700 series routers all support IP, IPX and Simple Network Management Protocol (SNMP). The 700 series routers also support multiple levels of authentication and Multilink Point-to-Point Protocol (MLP).

2. ☑ **E.** None of the above. Call waiting, call hold, call transfer and three-way calling are all services that the Cisco 700 series routers may provide.

3. ☑ C. Two RJ-11 interfaces. The 765 and 766 model Cisco 700 series routers come with two RJ-11 interfaces to support analog devices such as standard telephone, fax machines, and modems. This feature eliminates the need for multiple telephone lines or expensive ISDN telephones. Using Cisco's call-priority feature, the 765 and 766 model routers can drop one or both ISDN BRI B-channels being used for data to accept calls in or out.

☒ A. Token Ring support, is incorrect because the 700 series router does not support Token Ring. B. Two B-channel pairs, is incorrect because the 700 series router does not support two B-channel pairs, but one pair to provide a combined throughput of 128 Kbps uncompressed. C. Two RJ-11 interfaces, is incorrect because all the 700 series routers support call waiting.

4. ☑ C. Voice, video and data solutions. Because of the flexibility of the Cisco 700 series router, it's well suited to function in the three environments of voice, video and data. The Cisco 700 can provide a good video solution because of the fast throughput capabilities when combining both ISDN B-channels (128 Kbps) and additionally, the application of a compression algorithm to both B-channels (512 Kbps).

☒ A. Enterprise solutions, is incorrect because they require great flexibility in the kinds of connections, the type of traffic required, and filtering capabilities. B. Occasional connection to an ISP, is incorrect because an occasional requirement for connection to an ISP makes an ISDN solution uneconomical. A better solution would be an analog solution. This would be cheaper, and although ISDN would mean higher throughput, an occasional user does not have the requirement for high throughput. D. Continuous connection to a corporation, is incorrect because if continuous connections were required, ISDN prices could become quite high.

5. ☑ **C.** After being defined by the user, profiles are saved and stored in a Cisco 700 series nonvolatile random access memory, or NVRAM. NVRAM is the memory where configurations are stored. A profile is a set of configurations customized for communications with a specific remote device.

☒ **A.** RAM, is incorrect because RAM is used to hold configurations, routes and other information, which is not, saved when the router is powered down or reset. **B.** Flash, is incorrect because Flash is the memory that stores the operating system. **D.** PCMCIA storage, is incorrect because the Cisco 700 series router does not support PCMCIA storage devices.

6. ☑ **C.** The three required configuration tasks are user, LAN, and system. These profiles must be configured to prepare the Cisco 700 series router for operation. The user profiles specify the characteristics of each user you plan to dial. A separate profile is created for all remote locations to which the user plans to connect. The parameters to be configured are user name, IP routing ON, the framing type, the ISDN phone number, the encapsulation type, and the static route. The LAN profile configuration specifies the IP address and subnet mask for the Ethernet interface and the type of traffic to be routed. The system level profile configuration has parameters that define the switch type at the central office (CO), the directory numbers, and the service profile identifiers (SPID) that define the destination details. The system-level configuration also includes defining the system name and setting the Multilink PPP.

☒ **A.** Global, interface, sub-interface; **B.** Profile, LAN, user; and **D.** Remote, local, internal; are all incorrect because they include elements other than the essential three tasks of user, LAN, and system.

7. ☑ **B.** The RIP hop count. The *cost 1* part of the command string specifies the RIP hop count. The whole command specifies a default route that points to a specific address. The address specified is the IP address of an ISDN interface at the remote site. All traffic for this user goes to the same IP address. To enable this static route, you must disable bridging and set the user profile to *active*.

☒ **A.** The dollar cost associated with that connection, is incorrect because tracking the cost of a link cannot be accomplished on the Cisco 700 series router. **C.** The static route hop count, is incorrect because it cannot be defined on the Cisco 700 series router.

Enabling Permanent Connections to the Central Site

1. ☑ **C.** Cisco 700 series routers are certified in 25 countries. The Cisco 700 series routers also support major ISDN central office switches all over the world. The 700 series routers generate local tones (425 Hz) for international analog telephone service support. The 700 series routers have met U.S. and international regulatory approval.

☒ **A.** ISDN is used all over the world, is incorrect because, though this is a true statement, it does not explain why Cisco 700 series routers are especially designed for international use. **B.** RJ 45 connectors are a worldwide standard, is incorrect because RJ-45 connectors are industry standard and are used by every manufacturer of network equipment. **D.** The availability of RJ-11 analog ports, is incorrect because all analog ports are standard for all phone, fax, and modems.

2. ☑ **B.** Caller ID on the Cisco 700 series router allows calls to be authorized, if received from the number defined in the command string that activates caller ID. For example:

```
RouterA> set callidreceive 1234567890
```

This configuration statement allows calls to be received if the source number is 1234567890. Otherwise, the call will not be allowed.
☒ **A.** Allows the router to identify who is calling in, is incorrect because when a call is made and the link becomes active, the user can see what number is calling from statistics available on the Cisco 700 series router. **C.** Allows only a specific caller to call into the router, is incorrect because caller ID does not match SPIDs with IP addresses. **D.** None of the above, is incorrect.

3. ☑ **B.** The switched virtual circuit (SVC) requires a call setup before data can begin to be transferred, and requires a call tear down after transfer is complete. The three phases of an SVC are call setup, information transfer, and call clearing, or tear down. A permanent virtual circuit (PVC) is the other option when implementing X.25. A PVC is similar to a point-to-point leased line. PVCs use no call setup or call tear down that the user knows about. The PVC is always present, even when there is no data being transferred.
☒ **A.** PVC, is incorrect because a PVC does not go through a call setup, data transfer, call tear down procedure. A PVC is permanent, as its name suggests. **C.** LCN, is a Logical Channel Identifier. This term is used interchangeably with Virtual Circuit. **D.** VCI, is a Virtual Channel Identifier, which is another term that is used interchangeably with Virtual Circuit.

4. ☑ **A.** ARP resolves a network address to a destination Mac. This function is usually performed on the LAN side of the network at the Ethernet port of a router. The router creates an IP-to-MAC table. If a destination MAC address is not known, the router will resolve the destination network address to a MAC address.

☒ **B.** Inverse ARP, is incorrect because it is a method of resolving DLCI numbers to network addresses in Frame Relay. **C.** RARP, is incorrect. Reverse Address Resolution Protocol (RARP) is a function that resolves network addresses MAC addresses to network addresses. **D.** AARP, is incorrect. AppleTalk Address Resolution Protocol (AARP) maps network node addresses to underlying data links.

5. ☑ **D.** Input the command ENCAPSULATION FRAME-RELAY IETF in your corporate office router. When communicating with non-Cisco equipment the ENCAPSULATION FRAME-RELAY IETF command must be input. Without this command, Cisco and non-Cisco devices will not be able to communicate. Frame Relay supports the encapsulation of the IP protocol in conformance with RFC 1294, allowing interoperability between multiple vendors. Use the IETF form of Frame Relay encapsulation if your communication server is connected to another vendor's equipment across a Frame Relay network. While other router manufacturers use the RFC encapsulation, Cisco created its own proprietary encapsulation.

☒ **A.** Power cycle the routers at both ends of the link, is incorrect because power cycling a Cisco router that is connected to a non-Cisco router will not change the encapsulation. The encapsulation is required for the two routers to communicate successfully. **B.** Power cycle the CSU, is incorrect because power cycling a CSU will not change the encapsulation. The encapsulation is required for the two routers to communicate successfully. **C.** Input the command FRAME RELAY LMI-TYPE ANSI in your corporate office router, is incorrect because LMI type is significant only to a router and its directly connected frame-relay switch.

6. ☑ **B.** The SHOW FRAME-RELAY MAP command provides information that will help you decipher the problem. Following is a sample output of the command. In the third line, the Frame Relay encapsulation is defined. If communicating with another manufacturer's router, this should read *IETF*.

```
Router# show frame-relay map

Serial 1 (administratively down): ip 131.108.177.177

dlci 177 (0xB1,0x2C10), static, broadcast,

CISCO

TCP/IP Header Compression (inherited), passive (inherited)
```

☒ **A.** SHOW INTERFACE, is incorrect because the information output from the show interface command shows LMI status and other statistics. This command will look as if the configuration is working properly. The interface and line protocol will show up and up because the router will be communicating fine with the Central Office Switch. **C.** SHOW FRAME-RELAY PVC, is incorrect because status and statistics about the permanent virtual circuit is displayed, with no reference to encapsulation. **D.** SHOW RUNNING-CONFIG, is incorrect because this command displays the configuration of the router, with no diagnostic information provided. However, you will use this command often to review the configuration of the router.

7. ☑ **B** and **D.** Queuing, and access lists. Setting priorities to different types of traffic with one of the queuing methods will help control the possible congestion of the VC by prioritizing traffic. Also, access lists will disallow traffic that is not necessary to cross the network span.

☒ **A.** Setting a CIR, is incorrect because the CIR is set by the circuit provider. If controlling traffic and applying queuing methods or/and ACCESS LIST is still not effective, then a higher CIR can be purchased (it does cost more to have a higher CIR). **C.** Generalized BECN support, is incorrect because generalized BECN support is already on by default. Statistics can be viewed that display BECN conditions. Setting the router to enable traffic shaping based on BECNs is a configuration task, but is not a generalized support event.

Queuing and Compression

1. ☑ **C.** Different types of traffic that share a data path can impact each other. The need to prioritize packets arose from the diverse mixture of protocols and the behavior that these protocols display. Different types of traffic that share a data path can impact each other, and in different ways.

☒ **A.** Different data needs to have different priorities set, is incorrect because different data types do not have to have priorities applied to them. Priorities are applied to protocols to improve a chosen protocol's performance. **B.** File transfers require a high priority, is incorrect because file transfers are not typically given high priority, but in fact, are given lower priority when traffic is prioritized. **D.** Video conferencing demanded it, is incorrect because the ability to prioritize traffic was not developed specifically to benefit video conferencing, although it certainly does.

2. ☑ **B.** Analyze the LAN where the problem may be. If, after careful analysis, no congestion is shown on the WAN links and the network still shows poorly, a careful analysis must be done on the LAN. Cabling, server configurations, and protocols need to be examined.

☒ **A.** Implement a queuing method, is incorrect because queuing should only be implemented when proven necessary. In this case, a careful analysis is required before a solution can be determined. **C.** Implement ACCESS LIST, is incorrect because ACCESS LIST will not provide benefits to the LAN if the WAN is not congested. **D.** None of the above, is incorrect.

3. ☑ **C.** Custom queuing provides a specified amount of bandwidth to each defined traffic type, while priority queuing processes packets with high priority first with the possibility that traffic in the lower queues may not get processed. Custom queuing is a queuing method that lets you assign a portion of the total bandwidth to particular traffic types. So, if your network is running IP, IPX, and AppleTalk and you wish to provide more bandwidth to IP, less bandwidth to IPX, and even less to AppleTalk (with the remainder set for default traffic), the percentage of the total bandwidth that you a allot to each protocol is guaranteed. A total of 16 queues can be configured with each queue being serviced sequentially by the router. A configurable amount of traffic is forwarded before the next-lower queue is serviced.

☒ **A.** Custom queuing processes queues on a first come, first served basis, regardless of traffic type, and priority queuing provides a certain amount of bandwidth for each packet type, is incorrect because custom queuing does not process queues on this basis, and priority queuing does not provide a certain amount of bandwidth for each packet type. **B.** Custom queuing dispatches packets through the queue based on which packet header arrives at the queue first, while priority queuing processes packets through the queue with the highest priority, is incorrect because custom queuing does not base packet forwarding on which packet arrives first. The description of priority queuing is correct.

BCRAN ANSWERS

4. ☑ **B and D.** STAC, Predictor. Link-compression algorithms use the STAC and Predictor methods. If data is moved across a point-to-point connection, use the link-compression algorithm. In link compression, the entire packet is compressed and the switching information in the header is not available for WAN switching networks. That makes point-to-point connections with limited hop counts most suitable for link compression. Leased line or ISDN are appropriate environments in which to use link compression. STAC works by searching for redundant strings of data, which are replaced by a token. These tokens are smaller than the data strings. Predictor works by predicting the sequence in a data stream by using an index to look up a sequence in a compression dictionary.

☒ **A.** Payload, is incorrect because payload compression is a compression algorithm just as link compression is. **C.** Header, is incorrect because header is a compression algorithm just as link compression is.

5. ☑ **B.** TCP only. Header compression lowers the overhead that is generated by the disproportionately large header that TCP/IP generates. These large headers are transmitted across the WAN regardless of the size of the data packet. Header compression is protocol specific and only compresses the TCP header.

☒ **A.** TCP/IP and IPX, is incorrect because header compression is exclusive to TCP. **C.** IPX only, is incorrect because header compression is exclusive to TCP. **D.** Header compression is not protocol specific, is incorrect because header compression is specific to TCP.

Scaling and Troubleshooting Remote Access Networks

1. ☑ **B and D.** Private networks which need to connect to public networks, such as the Internet, but have not registered IP addresses can use NAT to translate from private addresses to the public addresses. Another application of NAT is when two autonomous networks need to communicate with each other. An example of this is when companies merge. Both companies can be using legal private addresses like 10.1.2.3 and 192.168.4.5. Integrating the two companies without NAT would be very difficult. With NAT the integration can be approached methodically, and can be implemented in steps.

   ☒ **A.** Private networks with enough addresses for the internal networks, is incorrect because private networks that set themselves up with enough addresses and do not have reason to communicate with public networks do not have reason to implement NAT. **C.** Private networks that need to connect to multiple facilities, is incorrect because companies that have multiple facilities set themselves up with private addresses. Unless the remote facility is an acquisition, NAT should not be a requirement.

2. ☑ **B. When two networks have overlapping network addresses.** When two networks with network addresses that overlap need to communicate with one another, a method of preventing duplicate IP addresses must be deployed to prevent the addresses from conflicting. DUAL NAT translates the two networks' overlapping IP source addresses to addresses within a pool of two network addresses. For example, if a HostA with address 10.1.1.1 needs to communicate with HostB 10.1.1.2, the DUAL NAT would translate HostB's 10.1.1.2 address to 192.4.4.4 and also translate HostA's address to 192.5.5.5 in order to communicate without an IP address conflict.

☒ **A.** When networks with different addressing schemes communicate, is incorrect because if two networks have different addresses, the two networks do not need to employ DUAL NAT. There is no address overlap. **C.** If more than two routers are communicating, is incorrect because the two routers must be on the same network at the serial interface. The only circumstance where there would be overlapping addresses is in the case of Ethernet interfaces, which would be two networks with overlapping addresses, but on the HOST side. **D.** Both networks wish to do NAT, is incorrect because, even if both sides wish to use NAT, the addresses of the networks do not necessarily overlap, which is a precondition of using DUAL NAT.

3. ☑ **A. Not being required to have registered IP addresses and saving a lot of money.** Using NAT to connect to an ISP relieves an organization of renting blocks of IP addresses, especially when not everyone in an organization uses the Internet. With NAT, the ability for overloading will also save money, since, by not having to pay for the use of many IP addresses and then renting as few as possible to provide authorized individuals with adequate service levels. Many companies use NAT to access the Internet. Using NAT also provides an organization with the flexibility to use any private addressing scheme the company chooses.

☒ **B.** Having a flexible Internet service that allows you to use any address you wish, is incorrect because an Internet company is allocated only a certain number of public network addresses. If an ISP allowed an organization to have any address that company chose, there would be many conflicts that would affect the entire Internet. **C.** Only having private global addresses, is incorrect because private addresses may not be used on the public Internet. **D.** None of the above, is incorrect.

4. ☑ **B.** CiscoSecure Access Control Server (ACS) incorporates a multi-user, Web-based Java configuration and management tool that simplifies server administration and enables multiple system administrators to simultaneously manage security services from multiple locations. The GUI supports two of the most popular browsers, Netscape and Microsoft IE. Security cards from organizations like Security Dynamics are now fully supported.

☒ **A.** IOS, is incorrect because it has many features which support and complement AAA security, but requires some external intervention to provide security levels that organizations require. Comparatively simpler security can be implemented for communications between routers like PAP or CHAP. **C.** TACACS+, and **D.** RADIUS, are incorrect because these provide the methods for the AAA part of the package, but the complete ACS package consists of the AAA server, the Netscape FastTrack server, and the relational database management system.

5. ☑ **B.** If an authentication method times out, the next method is queried. The methods defined in an AAA command execute authentication methods in the order listed. If a method times out, Cisco IOS moves on to the next method and tries to authenticate. If authentication is attempted and fails, access is denied.

☒ **A.** is incorrect because, if authentication fails at any of the authentication methods, access is denied. **C.** The user picks which method to authenticate on, is incorrect because the user does not get to pick the method of authentication. The methods are chosen by the order in which they are written. **D.** None of the above, is incorrect.

6. ☑ **D.** AAA ACCOUNTING SYSTEM START-STOP TACACS+. This command string runs start-and-stop accounting for all system-level events not associated with users, such as configuration changes and reloads.

 ☒ **A.** AAA ACCOUNTING EXEC START-STOP TACACS+, is incorrect because the command string runs start-and-stop accounting for all character mode service requests and uses the TACACS+ server. **B.** AAA ACCOUNTING COMMAND 15 START-STOP TACACS+, is incorrect because the command string runs start-and-stop accounting for all commands at privilege level 15. **C.** AAA ACCOUNTING CONNECTION START-STOP TACACS+, is incorrect because the command string runs start-and-stop accounting for all outbound Telnet and login sessions.

Part 5

Test Yourself: ACRC Practice Exams (Exam 640-403)

Test Yourself: ACRC Practice Exam I Questions

$$Q \& A$$

Before you register for the actual exam, take the following test and see how you make out. Set a timer for 90 minutes—the time you'll have to take the live CCNP Advanced Cisco Router Configuration certification exam— and answer the following 72 questions in the time allotted. Once you've finished, turn to the ACRC Practice Exam 1 Answers section and check your score to see if you passed. Good luck!

ACRC Practice Exam 1 Questions

1. A certain Cisco queuing technique allows high, medium, normal, and low queuing categories, for which different traffic types can be configured. Their priority corresponds to the order in which they are mentioned, with *high* having the highest priority and *low*, the lowest. All packets allocated to the high queue are transmitted before the router starts processing the medium queue. After each packet in a low queue is transmitted, all higher-priority queues are checked again to see if they have accumulated packets. All higher-priority queues must be emptied before lower-priority queues are allowed to transmit. Which queuing technique does this describe?

   A. Weighted fair

   B. Priority

   C. FIFO

   D. Custom

2. What is the default queuing technique used on interfaces with less than 2Mbps of bandwidth?

   A. WFQ

   B. FIFO

   C. Priority

   D. Custom

3. Which of the following is false in regard to the differences between NLSP and RIP-IPX?

A. RIP-IPX is a distance vector routing protocol and NLSP is a link-state routing protocol

B. NLSP converges faster than RIP-IPX

C. RIP-IPX networks are flat while NLSP networks are considered hierarchical

D. RIP-IPX has a hop count limitation of 15 while NLSP has a hop count of 31

4. Joe has an IPX network and decides that the IPX watchdog service is causing too much traffic over his 56K Frame Relay network. Joe decides to configure IPX spoofing to cut down on this traffic. Which of the following steps is not necessary to configure IPX spoofing?

A. Turn off route caching

B. Turn on SPX spoofing

C. Turn on watchdog spoofing

D. Turn on route caching

5. Since the ACME Rocket Science Company decided to go with a full-time connection and chose to use Cisco routers, what have they realized major benefit of the HDLC protocol?

A. Its quick response to missing datagrams

B. Low overhead

C. Header compression

D. Compatibility with LAPB

Refer to the Following Scenario and Illustration to Answer Question 6

There are two possible paths to the destination from terminal X to terminal Y. The two routes from Host X to Y are:

```
Ring 400 to bridge 1 to ring 401 to bridge 2 to ring 402
Ring 400 to bridge 3 to ring 403 to bridge 4 to ring 402
```

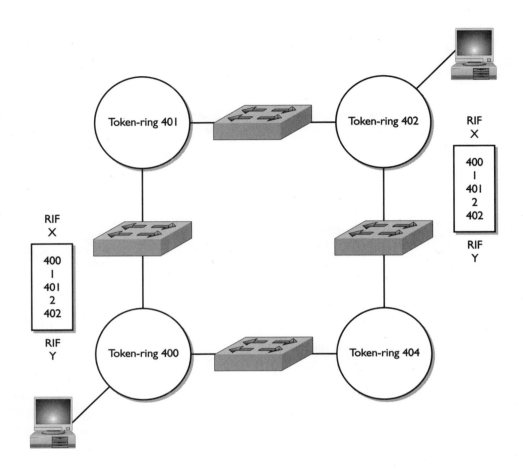

6. When the all-routes explorer packet reaches Host Y via either of these routes, how is it returned if the protocol is NetBIOS?

A. As a single-route explorer
B. As an all-routes explorer
C. As a local explorer
D. As a multicast explorer

7. Which of the following is the correct command syntax for allowing ICMP packets between network 172.16.20.0/24 and host 172.16.30.1?

A. ACCESS-LIST 110 PERMIT IP 172.16.20.0.255.255.255.0 HOST 172.16.30.1 EQ ICMP

B. ACCESS-LIST 110 PERMIT ICMP 172.16.20.0.255.255.255.0 HOST 172.16.30.1

C. ACCESS-LIST 105 PERMIT ICMP 172.16.20.0 0.0.0.255 HOST 172.16.30.1 ECHO ECHO-REPLY

D. ACCESS-LIST 105 PERMIT ICMP 172.16.20.0 0.0.0.255 HOST 172.16.30.1

8. What would be the correct interface configuration to apply the above access list against incoming traffic on an interface?

A. IP ACCESS-GROUP 110 IN

B. IP ACCESS-GROUP 110

C. IP ACCESS-GROUP 105 IN

D. IP ACCESS-LIST 105 IN

9. Which of the following queuing techniques best is described by the following?
—Allows for the use of 16 queues, which are emptied in a round-robin fashion.
—Bandwidth control is provided by allowing the byte-count threshold to be adjusted on a queue-by-queue basis.

A. FIFO

B. WFQ

C. Priority queuing

D. Custom

10. Which of the following statements is true when it comes to NLSP being interoperable with RIP-IPX and SAP?

A. NLSP is incompatible with RIP-IPX and SAP

B. NLSP can either be configured as *on* or *off* in regard to maintaining RIP-IPX and/or SAP on an interface

C. NLSP, by default, only sends RIP-IPX or SAP information on a segment if it has discovered another device that is using RIP-IPX and/or SAP on that segment

D. NLSP must be configured with redistribution commands within router configuration mode in order for NLSP and RIP-IPX to exchange information

11. Why is ATM designed to support speeds of 155Mbps and 622Mbps?

A. OC-3 Sonet is 155Mbps and an OC-12 Sonet is 622Mbps

B. T-3 is 155Mbps and T-12 is 622Mbps

C. These speeds were the fastest available serial links when ATM was developed

D. These were international standard speeds for ATM

12. Which description best fits Multilink PPP? Choose all that apply.

A. Multilink PPP bundles multiple physical interfaces into a single logical interface

B. Multilink PPP bundles multiple logical interfaces into a single physical interface

C. Multilink PPP bundles multiple subinterfaces into a single physical interface

D. Multilink PPP bundles multiple physical interfaces into a single virtual interface

13. Which of the following types of segments can DLSw+ connect over a WAN? Choose three.

A. Token Ring to Token Ring

B. Token Ring to SDLC

C. Ethernet to SDLC

D. Ethernet to QLLC

14. What is the basis for a standard IP access list to either permit or deny traffic?

A. Both the source and destination addresses

B. The source IP address

C. The destination IP network address

D. The destination IP address

15. Which parameters are configurable within WFQ?

A. Dynamic queues

B. Congestive-discard-threshold

C. Reserveable queues

D. All the above

Refer to the Following Illustration
to Answer Question 16–17

If a specification is not listed for a router, assume it is the default.

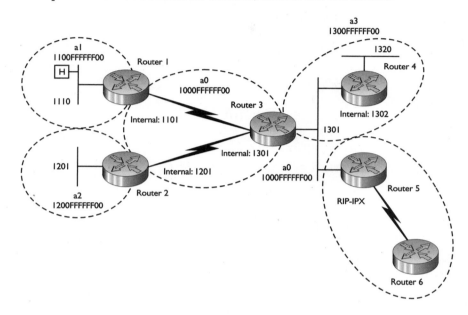

16. What is the correct configuration for Router 1's Serial0 port?

A. INTERFACE SERIAL0
   ENCAPSULATION PPP
   IPX IPXWAN 0 UNNUMBERED ROUTER3
   IPX NLSP A0 ENABLE

B. INTERFACE SERIAL0
   ENCAPSULATION PPP
   IPX IPXWAN 0 UNNUMBERED ROUTER1
   IPX NLSP ENABLE

C. INTERFACE SERIAL0
   ENCAPSULATION PPP
   IPX NLSP A0 ENABLE

D. INTERFACE SERIAL0
   ENCAPSULATION PPP
   IPX IPXWAN 0 UNNUMBERED ROUTER1
   IPX NLSP A0 ENABLE

17. If Router 5 is running RIP-IPX only, which configuration commands are necessary on Router 3 to redistribute between RIP-IPX and NLSP? Assume Router 4 is configured to disallow RIP-IPX redistribution.

A. INTERFACE ETHERNET0
 IPX NETWORK 1310
 IPX NLSP A3 ENABLE
 !
 IPX ROUTER NLSP A3
 AREA-ADDRESS 1300 FFFFFF00
 IPX ROUTER RIP
 REDISTRIBUTE NLSP A3

B. INTERFACE ETHERNET0
 IPX NETWORK 1310
 IPX NLSP A3 ENABLE
 !
 IPX ROUTER NLSP A3
 AREA-ADDRESS 1300 FFFFFF00

C. INTERFACE ETHERNET0
 IPX NETWORK 1310
 IPX NLSP A3 ENABLE
 IPX NLSP RIP OFF
 !
 IPX ROUTER NLSP A3
 AREA-ADDRESS 1300 FFFFFF00
 ROUTER RIP IPX
 NO NETWORK 1310

D. INTERFACE ETHERNET0
 IPX NETWORK 1310
 !
 IPX ROUTER RIP
 NETWORK 1310

18. You want to configure channelized T1 for a network interface module (NIM) 0 of a Cisco 4000 using ESF as the T1 frame type. Enter the appropriate command to define ESF framing at the following prompt:

```
Router(config-controller)#
```

A. FRAMING SF

B. LINECODE FRAMING ESF

C. FRAME ESF

D. FRAMING ESF

19. For what purpose is a dialer profile used?

A. It allows the creation of unique configurations for different users

B. It uses to bundle multiple physical links into a single, logical link

C. It allows dialer information to be configured on a physical interface

D. It makes a group of virtual interfaces available to a dialer interface

20. Which protocols were DLSw designed to accommodate? Choose three.

A. SNA

B. NetBIOS

C. HDLC

D. LLC2

21. What task does an IP named access list enable a network administrator to perform that could not be performed on a Cisco router prior to IOS version 11.2?

A. Filter based on Layer 4 ports

B. Create extended IP access list

C. Delete single-line entries within the access list

D. All the above

22. Which of the following connects physically separate LAN segments into one logical LAN?

A. Bridging

B. Routing

C. Source-route bridging

D. VLANs

23. What advantages does EIGRP have over IGRP? Choose all that apply.

    A. Rapid convergence

    B. Automatically redistributes routes learned from other protocols

    C. Multiple network-layer support

    D. Uses the OSPF algorithm in a hybrid manner

    E. Reduced bandwidth usage

24. What is the difference between a BRI and a PRI in terms of ISDN in North America?

    A. A BRI has two 64K-B channels and a 16K-D channel, while a PRI shas 23 64K-B channels and a 64K-D channel

    B. A BRI has two 64K-B channels and a 16K-D channel, while a PRI has 30 64K-B channels and a 64K-D channel

    C. A BRI has two 64K-B channels and a 64K-D channel, while a PRI has 23 64K-B channels and a 64K D channel

    D. A BRI has two 64K-B channels and a 16K-D channel, while a PRI has 23 64K-B channels and a 16K-D channel

    E. A BRI has 23 64K-B channels and a 16K-D channel, while a PRI has two 64K-B channels and a 16K-D channel

25. Which of the following describes how bridged interfaces and routed interfaces interact using IRB?

    A. Via a bridge group

    B. Via a router group

    C. Via a BVI

    D. Via a virtual router interface

26. Two basic types of connections exist in DLSw+, namely, a DLSw+-to-DLSw+ peer connection and an end-to-end system circuit traversing a DLSw+ peer-to-peer connection.

Which two commands can be used to view the status of these two types of connections? Choose two.

A. SHOW DLSW PEERS
B. SHOW DLSW CIRCUITS
C. SHOW DLSW INTERFACES
D. SHOW DLSW PROTOCOLS

27. Which of the following is true with regard to an IPX address? Choose all that apply.

A. An IPX address contains a 32-bit network number and a 48-bit node number
B. The node number defaults to the 48-bit MAC address for an interface on a Cisco router
C. Preceding zeros in a network number are not necessary for configuration on a Cisco router
D. All the above

28. How can the class of an IP address be determined?

A. By applying the subnet mask
B. By the number of bits that are 1s within the subnet mask
C. By looking at the highest-ordered bits within the first octet of the IP address
D. None of the above

29. Which of the following routing protocols is not considered a link-state protocol?

A. EIGRP
B. OSPF
C. NLSP
D. IS-IS

30. Which three of the following protocols does EIGRP support? Choose three.

   A. DECnet

   B. SNA

   C. AppleTalk

   D. IPX

   E. IP

   F. NetBIOS

31. What does the SHOW IP EIGRP TRAFFIC command do?

   A. It displays the IP EIGRP topology table

   B. It displays the status and parameters of the active routing protocol process

   C. It displays the number of IP EIGRP packets sent and received

   D. It displays current EIGRP entries in the routing table

Refer to the Following Illustration to Answer Question 32

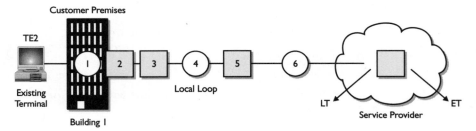

32. What is the proper location for the Network Termination 1 (NT1)?

   A. 1

   B. 2

   C. 3

   D. 4

   E. 5

Refer to the Following Illustration to Answer Question 33

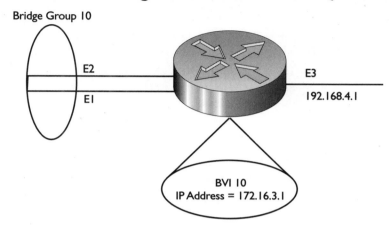

Bridge Group 10

E2

E1

E3

192.168.4.1

BVI 10
IP Address = 172.16.3.1

33. Which command enables the BVI to accept and route routable packets received from its corresponding bridge group?

   A. BRIDGE IRB

   B. INTERFACE BVI 10

   C. BRIDGE 10 ROUTE IP

   D. INTERFACE BVI 10
       IP ADDRESS 172.16.3.1 255.255.255.0

34. Which of the following routing protocols for IPX is considered a distance vector protocol that broadcasts its routing table every 60 seconds on all its configured interfaces?

   A. RIP-IPX

   B. EIGRP

   C. NLSP

   D. Static

35. Hold-down timers are used for what purpose?

A. The amount of time that routers suppress routing information on an interface to avoid learning or advertising potentially bad routes

B. The amount of time a router waits to advertise a link-state change

C. The amount of time a router holds down an interface from participating in exchanging routing updates once it has been manually shutdown and then brought back up

D. All of the above

Refer to the Following Illustration and Scenario to Answer Question 36

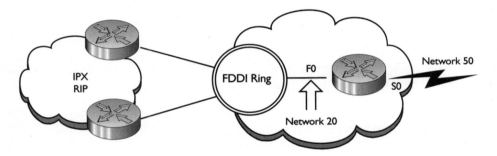

Network 50 is another IPX RIP network. The EIGRP autonomous system number is 1. Here is a part of the configuration on Router A:

```
ipx routing
!
ipx router eigrp 1
network 20
network 50
!
ipx router rip
no network 20
no network 50
!
interface fddi0
ipx network 20
ipx sap-incremental eigrp 1
!
```

```
interface serial 0
ipx network 50
```

36. What does the IPX SAP-INCREMENTAL EIGRP 1 command do in the configuration above?

A. Enables incremental SAPs on all interfaces of Router A

B. Enables incremental SAPs on interface S0 of Router A

C. Enables incremental SAPs on interface FDDI 0 of Router A

D. Enables incremental SAPs over EIGRP only

E. Enables incremental SAPS over RIP only

37. When connecting an autonomous system to an ISP, it is not always necessary to use BGP. What other methods can be used when connecting to a single ISP? Choose two.

A. Default routes

B. Static routes

C. Gateway of last resort

D. OSPF

38. Which of the following commands can be used to verify proper Multilink PPP operation? Choose two.

A. SHOW MULTILINK

B. SHOW DIALER

C. DEBUG PPP MULTILINK

D. DEBUG DIALER

39. Which of the following is true of IRB? Choose two.

A. You should configure any protocol attributes on the bridge interfaces when both routing and bridging a given protocol

B. You must configure bridging attributes on the BVI

C. You should determine whether you need to redefine the BVI's MTU size

D. By default IRB bridges all protocols so routing must be explicitly enabled for packets that need to be routed

Refer to the Following Illustration
to Answer Questions 40–41

If a specification is not listed for a router, assume it is the default.

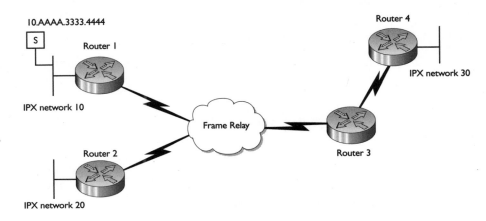

40. Which of the following configuration commands would create an IPX
standard access list on Router 1's incoming serial interface that would allow
any IPX network address to connect to only server 10.AAAA.3333.4444?

A. ACCESS-LIST 801 PERMIT –1 10

B. ACCESS-LIST 901 PERMIT FFFFFFFF 10.AAAA.3333.4444

C. ACCESS-LIST 801 PERMIT ANY 10.AAAA.3333.4444

D. ACCESS-LIST 801 PERMIT -1 10.AAAA.3333.4444

41. We now want to change the IPX filter of the previous question to allow
only IPX traffic from source IPX networks 20 or 30. The destination
host should still be10.AAAA.3333.4444. What command will change
the IPX filter?

A. ACCESS-LIST 901 PERMIT ANY 10.0000.0000.0000
    30.FFFF.FFFF.FFFF.FFFF ALL 10.AAAA.3333.4444 ALL

B. ACCESS-LIST 901 PERMIT 10.0000.0000.0000
   30.FFFF.FFFF.FFFF.FFFF ALL 10.AAAA.3333.4444 ALL

C. ACCESS-LIST 801 PERMIT 10.0000.0000.0000
   30.FFFF.FFFF.FFFF.FFFF 10.AAAA.3333.4444

D. ACCESS-LIST 801 PERMIT 10 30 10.AAAA.3333.4444

42. Which of the following is NOT a characteristic of EIGRP?

A. Support for VLSM

B. Fast convergence

C. Partial updates

D. Support for areas

43. Which type of BGP would be appropriate for connections between routers in the same autonomous system?

A. EBGP

B. IBGP

C. IGRP

D. EIGRP

44. Which LMI types does the Cisco IOS support? Choose all that apply.

A. Cisco

B. ANSI

C. q933a

D. IETF

45. Which one of the following is a routable protocol?

A. NetBIOS

B. SNA

C. AppleTalk

D. LAT

46. What is a node belonging to one organizational group within its AppleTalk network called?

   A. Phase II

   B. Zones

   C. Cable ranges

   D. Phase I

Refer to the Following Illustration to Answer Questions 47–48

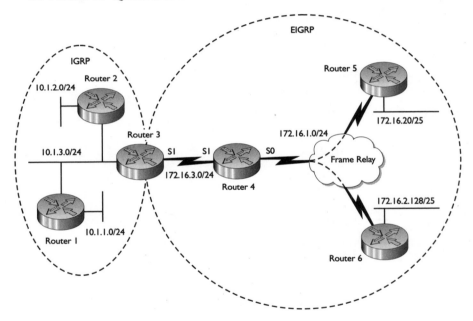

47. Which of the following commands will configure Router 1 for IGRP routing?

   A. ROUTER IGRP
      NETWORK 10.1.1.0
      NETWORK 10.1.3.0

   B. ROUTER IGRP 5
      NETWORK 10.0.0.0

   C. ROUTER IGRP
      NETWORK 10.0.0.0

D. ROUTER IGRP 5
   NETWORK 10.1.1.0
   NETWORK 10.1.3.0

48. Since the NBMA Frame Relay cloud is configured as one subnet, which of the following commands will be required on Router 4's Serial 0 interface in order to ensure connectivity between Router 5 and Router 6's sub-networks?

A. IP SUMMARY-ADDRESS EIGRP 5 172.16.2.0 255.255.0.0
B. NO AUTO-SUMMARY
C. NO IP SPLIT-HORIZONS EIGRP
D. NO DEFAULT-INFORMATION IN

49. Which configuration for Router B would be appropriate for the example shown in the following illustration?

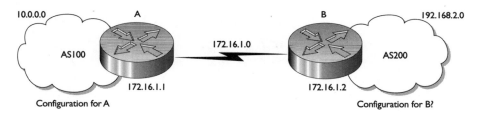

10.0.0.0   A   B   192.168.2.0

AS100   172.16.1.0   AS200

172.16.1.1   172.16.1.2

Configuration for A   Configuration for B?

```
router bgp 100
network 10.0.0.0
neighbor 172.16.1.2 remote-as 200
```

A. ROUTER BGP 100
   NETWORK 192.168.2.0
   NEIGHBOR 172.16.1.1 REMOTE-AS 200
B. ROUTER BGP 100
   NETWORK 192.168.2.0
   NEIGHBOR 172.16.1.1 REMOTE-AS 100
C. ROUTER BGP 200
   NETWORK 192.168.2.0
   NEIGHBOR 172.16.1.1 REMOTE-AS 100
D. ROUTER BGP 200
   NETWORK 192.168.2.0
   NEIGHBOR 172.16.1.1 REMOTE-AS 200

**Refer to the Following Illustration
to Answer Questions 50–51**

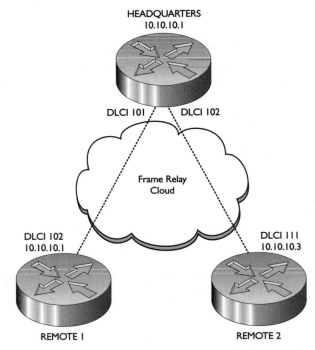

50. If Inverse ARP is used exclusively, which of the following is true? Choose all that apply.

   A. Remote 1 can ping Headquarters and Remote 2

   B. Remote 2 can ping Headquarters and Remote 1

   C. Headquarters can ping both Remote 1 and Remote 2

   D. Remote 1 can ping Headquarters, but not Remote 2

   E. Remote 2 can ping Headquarters, but not Remote 1

   F. Headquarters can ping neither Remote 1 nor Remote 2

51. There were some connectivity problems associated with using only Inverse ARP in a partially meshed Frame Relay network in the preceding question. How could they be resolved? Choose all that apply.

   A. Add an additional PVC between Remote 1 and Remote 2

   B. Configure point-to-point interfaces

    C. Configure Frame Relay map statements

    D. Configure point-to-point subinterfaces

52. What is the correct command for selecting the IEEE Spanning Tree Protocol for a transparent bridge using a bridge number of 1.

    A. BRIDGE 1 PROTOCOL IEEE

    B. BRIDGE PROTOCOL IEEE

    C. BRIDGE-GROUP 1 PROTOCOL IEEE

    D. BRIDGE-GROUP PROTOCOL IEEE 1

53. Which of the following AppleTalk traffic management information can be controlled by configuring filters on Cisco routers?

    A. Zones, RTMP, and NBP

    B. Zones, RIP, and NCP

    C. Cable ranges, RTMP, and NBP

    D. Cable ranges, RIP, and NCP

54. Out of the following four active interfaces and IP addresses that are assigned to a router participating within an OSPF routing domain, which interface's IP address would serve as this router's OSPF router ID?

    A. Ethernet0, 172.16.120.1

    B. Serial0, 172.16.122.1

    C. Loopback0, 10.1.1.1

    D. Loopback1, 10.2.2.1

55. When using route redistribution, what is the default administrative distance for BGP? Choose two.

    A. Internal BGP–200

    B. Internal BGP–110

    C. External BGP–20

    D. External BGP–110

    E. External BGP–120

56. What command would you enter to provide detailed information about the type of Spanning-Tree Protocol (IEEE or DEC) the bridge group is executing?

A. SHOW TRANSPARENT-BRIDGE

B. SHOW BRIDGE

C. SHOW BRIDGE SPAN

D. SHOW SPAN

57. What is an NBMA network?

A. A hub-and-spoke Frame Relay network

B. A nonbroadcast, Multilink PPP network

C. A nonbroadcast, multi-access network

D. A nonbroadcast, meshed-node network

Refer to the Following Illustration to Answer Questions 58–59

If a specification is not listed for a router, assume it is the default.

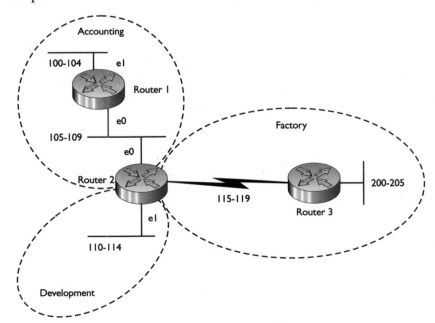

58. Which interface configuration command would apply an access-list number 605 as a ZIP reply filter on Router 2's serial 0 port?

A. ZIP-FILTER 605
B. APPLETALK ACCESS-GROUP 605 IN
C. APPLETALK GETZONELIST-FILTER 605
D. APPLETALK ZIP-REPLY-FILTER 605

59. Which of the following commands would successfully apply the route filter from the above specifications?

A. ROUTER2(config)# INTERFACE ETHERNET0
ROUTER2(config-if)# APPLETALK DISTRIBUTE-LIST 610 IN
B. ROUTER2(config)# INTERFACE ETHERNET1
ROUTER2(config-if)# APPLETALK DISTRIBUTE-LIST 610 OUT
ROUTER2(config-if)# INTERFACE SERIAL0
ROUTER2(config-if)# APPLETALK DISTRIBUTE-LIST 610 OUT
C. ROUTER3(config)# INTERFACE SERIAL0
ROUTER3(config-if)# APPLETALK DISTRIBUTE-LIST 610 IN
D. None of the above

60. What is the meaning of 110 in ROUTER OSPF 110?

A. It's the internal OSPF process identifier
B. It's the OSPF area
C. It's the autonomous system number
D. None of the above

61. Which encapsulation protocols do Frame Relay networks use? Choose two.

A. LAPB
B. LAPD
C. HDLC
D. IETF
E. CSLIP

62. What are some special considerations for using AppleTalk in an NBMA network? Choose two.

A. AppleTalk can only be configured using Inverse ARP and map statements, not using subinterfaces.

B. AppleTalk needs to add the broadcast parameter to all map statements.

C. In a hub-and-spoke NBMA topology with AppleTalk, you need to disable split-horizon on the hub router.

D. With multipoint NBMA configurations, you don't need to use the AppleTalk LOCAL ROUTING command. All interfaces on the multipoint subnet can already access each other.

63. About which two source-route characteristics does the RIF route descriptor have information in an IBM Token Ring frame? Choose two.

A. Type

B. Ring numbers

C. Bridge numbers

D. Direction

E. Length

F. Largest frame

64. When does a queuing strategy become something worth considering? Choose the best answer.

A. When you have low bandwidth or transmission capacity

B. When transmission capacity is greater than the traffic load

C. When you are configuring a serial interface

D. When the traffic load becomes greater than the transmission capacity

Refer to the Following Illustration to Answer Questions 65–67

If a specification is not listed for a router, assume it is the default.

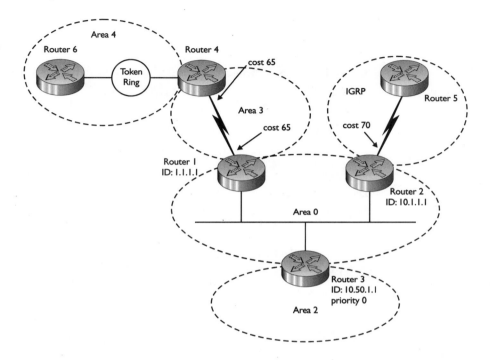

65. If Routers 1, 2, and 3 were powered up at the same time, which routers would become the designated router (DR) and which, the backup designated router (BDR), for the multi-access Ethernet segment?

A. Router 1 as DR and Router 2 as BDR

B. Router 3 as DR and Router 2 as BDR

C. Router 2 as DR and Router 1 as BDR

D. None of the above

66. If Router 3 is advertising a summarized route for Area 2 as 172.16.32.0 255.255.224.0, how will this route be displayed when Router 4 issues a SHOW IP ROUTE command?

A. 172.16.32.0/19

B. E1 172.16.32.0/19

C. E2 172.16.32.0/19

D. IA 172.16.32.0/19

67. Which of the following OSPF router configuration commands summarizes Area 2, which has a summarized route of 172.16.32.0 255.255.224.0?

   A. NETWORK 172.16.32.0 255.255.224.0 AREA 2

   B. NETWORK 172.16.32.0 0.0.31.255 AREA 2

   C. AREA 2 RANGE 172.16.32.0 255.255.224.0

   D. AREA 2 RANGE 172.16.32.0 0.0.31.255

68. After evaluating their corporate needs, the ACME Rocket Science Company has decided that they need a full-time connection. Which of the following is the most appropriate option?

   A. DDR

   B. Circuit-switched services

   C. PPP

   D. Point-to-point serial links

69. What command can you use to obtain general diagnostic information about the dialer interface?

   A. SHOW SNAPSHOT *interface*

   B. SHOW DIALER

   C. SHOW PPP MULTILINK

   D. SHOW DIALER INTERFACE

70. Which command will set up bridge 1 between local ring 500 and target ring 501 in the following illustration?

Token-ring 500   Bridge 1   Token-ring 501

   A. SOURCE-BRIDGE 501 1 500

   B. SOURCE-BRIDGE 1 500 501

C. SOURCE-BRIDGE 500 501 1

D. SOURCE-BRIDGE 500 1 501

71. Which encapsulation does DLSw Lite use?

A. HDLC

B. PPP

C. LL2

D. SDLC

72. How can you verify SRB operation? Choose three.

A. ROUTER#SHOW SOURCE-BRIDGE

B. ROUTER#SHOW RIF

C. ROUTER#SHOW INTERFACES TOKENRING

D. ROUTER#SHOW SRB

E. ROUTER#SHOW SOURCE-BRIDGE RIF

Test Yourself: ACRC Practice Exam 1 Answers

Q&A

The answers to the questions are in boldface, followed by a brief explanation. Some of the explanations detail the logic you should use to choose the correct answer, while others give factual reasons why the answer is correct. If you miss several questions on a similar topic, you should review the corresponding section in the *CCNP ACRC Advanced Cisco Router Configuration Study Guide* before taking the CCNP test.

ACRC Practice Exam I Answers

1. ☑ **B.** Priority queuing. A network engineer must be careful when using this type of queuing, because if higher-priority traffic types are enough to saturate the link, no lower-priority traffic will get through. All unspecified traffic types will default to the normal queuing type, except for keepalive traffic.

   Keepalive traffic is what is known as *system-level* traffic. This type of traffic goes into the system-level queue, which is located at a level higher than the high queue.

   ☒ **A.** Weighted-fair queuing (WFQ) is incorrect because it determines whether traffic is transaction oriented or batch oriented, giving priority to the transaction-oriented data. **C.** First-in first-out queuing (FIFO) is incorrect because this is the queuing technique used by high-speed interfaces. **D.** Custom queuing is incorrect because, although it allows traffic to be prioritized, it still processes the queues in a round-robin fashion.

2. ☑ **A.** WFQ automatically classifies data into either transaction-oriented (low-bandwidth) or batch-oriented (high-bandwidth) queues. Transaction-type packets are then given higher priority than the batch-oriented packets, which otherwise have a tendency to saturate the more time-sensitive transaction packets.

   ☒ **B.** FIFO is incorrect because, as previously discussed, this is the default for high-speed LAN interfaces. **C.** Priority is incorrect because this queuing technique requires additional configuration. **D.** Custom is incorrect for the same reason.

3. ☑ **D.** RIP-IPX has a hop count limitation of 15 while NLSP has a hop count of 31 is false in regard to NLSP. NLSP does not have a concept of hop-counts and is therefore not specifically limited in the size of the network. Other benefits to NLSP over RIP-IPX include a faster convergence time, since it is a link-state protocol in which routers notify their neighbors as soon as they become aware that a change in the topology has occurred. NLSP is also a hierarchical protocol, containing the concept of levels and areas, which allows route aggregation to reduce routing tables throughout the NLSP routing domain.
☒ **A.** RIP-IPX is a distance vector routing protocol and NLSP is a link-state routing protocol is incorrect because it is a true statement with regard to RIP-IPX and NLSP. **B.** NLSP converges faster than RIP-IPX is incorrect for the same reason. **C.** RIP-IPX networks are flat while NLSP networks are considered hierarchical is also incorrect for the same reason.

4. ☑ **D.** In order to configure IPX spoofing, route caching must be turned off and stay turned off.
☒ **A.** is incorrect because you must turn off route caching as the first step. **B.** is incorrect because once you turn off route caching, the next step is to turn on SPX spoofing. Note that SPX is the connection-oriented counterpart to IPX. **C.** is incorrect because once SPX spoofing is turned on, the next step is to turn on watchdog spoofing, followed by the final step of configuring the SPX idle timer.

5. ☑ **B.** is the correct answer because HDLC is the default Cisco encapsulation, which has a lower overhead than most other protocols.
☒ **A.** is incorrect because HDLC is a link-layer protocol and does no error correction. **C.** is incorrect because header compression actually causes greater overhead on a router's CPU. **D.** is incorrect because LAPB is an X.25 encapsulation protocol and is not at all compatible with HDLC.

6. ☑ **B.** In NetBIOS, the destination host replies to each frame individually, reverses the direction of the frame, and sends it back along the same path to the source host as an all-routes explorer frame, even though it received the frame as a single-route broadcast frame.

☒ **A.** is incorrect because only the frame sent by the source is a single-route explorer. The returned frame is an all-routes explorer. **C.** is incorrect because the source sends a local explorer frame initially to determine if the destination is on the local ring. This local explorer would not reach a destination host on a different ring. **D.** is incorrect because the all-routes explorer frame is sent out as an all-routes broadcast frame, not as a multicast frame.

7. ☑ **D.** ACCESS-LIST 105 PERMIT ICMP 172.16.20.0 0.0.0.255 HOST 172.16.30.1 is the only legal command that allows all ICMP types entry into the router interface. The correct command syntax for an extended access list is:

```
access-list access-list-number [permit|deny] protocol
source-IP-address source-wildcard-mask
destination-IP-address destination-wildcard mask
[additional options]
```

This command is entered within configuration mode.

☒ **A.** ACCESS-LIST 110 PERMIT IP 172.16.20.0.255.255.255.0 HOST 172.16.30.1 EQ ICMP is incorrect because this is an illegal command since ICMP is a Layer 3 protocol specifying a range of ports and control messages. **B.** ACCESS-LIST 110 PERMIT ICMP 172.16.20.0.255.255.255.0 HOST 172.16.30.1 is incorrect because this, too, is an illegal command. A wildcard mask, not a subnet mask, is required to specify a range of allowable addresses. **C.** ACCESS-LIST 105 PERMIT ICMP 172.16.20.0 0.0.0.255 HOST 172.16.30.1 ECHO ECHO-REPLY is incorrect because this permits only specific ICMP types.

8. ☑ **C.** IP ACCESS-GROUP 105 IN is the correct answer since it contains the correct access-list number, 105, associated with the interface and uses the correct command syntax. Cisco IOS documentation describes the command syntax as, IP ACCESS-GROUP *access-list-number* [**in**|**out**]. This command is entered within interface configuration mode.

☒ **A.** IP ACCESS-GROUP 110 IN is incorrect because 110 is not the correct access-list number associated with the previous question. **B.** The interface configuration command IP ACCESS-GROUP 110, is incorrect for the same reason and because it does not apply the list only to incoming traffic. **D.** The interface configuration command IP ACCESS-LIST 105 IN is incorrect because this is an illegal interface configuration command. *Access-list* should read *access-group*.

9. ☑ **D.** Custom queuing takes characteristics from both WFQ and priority queuing, giving a network administrator the ability to prioritize traffic in a less discriminatory way. Custom queuing can become very configuration intensive.

☒ **A.** FIFO is incorrect because it does not meet the description. **B.** WFQ is incorrect for the same reason. **D.** Priority queuing is also incorrect for this reason.

10. ☑ **C.** NLSP, by default, only sends RIP-IPX or SAP information on a segment if it has discovered another device that is using RIP-IPX and/or SAP on that segment. NLSP was created with IPX's two best-known advertisement protocols, RIP-IPX and SAP. RIP-IPX routes and SAP service advertisements are absorbed by NLSP and retained in its database. Also by default, NLSP interfaces reply to any RIP or SAP requests.

☒ **A.** NLSP is incompatible with RIP-IPX and SAP is incorrect because this statement is not true. **B.** NLSP can either be configured as *on* or *off* in regard to maintaining RIP-IPX and/or SAP on an interface is incorrect because the default setting is *auto*, as described in the answer. **D.** NLSP must be configured with redistribution commands within Router Configuration Mode in order for NLSP and RIP-IPX to exchange information is incorrect because NLSP is automatically configured to redistribute RIP and SAP into its topology database.

11. ☑ **A.** OC-3 Sonet is 155Mbps and an OC-12 Sonet is 622Mbps. Engineers wanted to match Sonet speeds so that four OC-3s could be combined into an OC-12.

    ☒ **B.** is incorrect because a T-3 is 45Mbps. **C.** is incorrect because these speeds were actually faster than serial lines. **D.** is incorrect because there were no international standards for ATM at the time of development.

12. ☑ **A, D.** Multilink PPP is the bundling of multiple physical interfaces into a single logical interface. If you look at the SHOW USER command when an MLP connection is active, you see VI2, etc. These are VIRTUAL INTERFACES. If you type in SHOW INTERFACE VI2, it will tell you that you are looking at virtual interface 2.

    ☒ **B.** is incorrect because this is the opposite of the way Multilink PPP works. Multilink PPP bundles physical into logical, not the other way around. **C.** is incorrect for the same reason. You bundle physical into logical for Multilink PPP.

13. ☑ **A, B, D.** DLSw+ evolved from Remote Source Route Bridging or RSRB, which links remotely attached Token Ring source route bridged networks. DLSw+ is also fully backwards compatible with RSRB. RFC 1795 states that DLSw+ can connect the following types of segments over the WAN:

    - Token Ring to Token Ring
    - Token Ring to Ethernet
    - Ethernet to Ethernet
    - Token Ring to SDLC
    - Token Ring to QLLC
    - Ethernet to QLLC

RFC 1795 defines an Ethernet to QLLC connection. Note that RFC 1795 defines standard DLSw.

☒　**C.** is incorrect because RFC 1795 does not define an Ethernet to SDLC connection.

14. ☑　**B.** The source IP address. When filtering policies can be defined by only specifying a source IP address or range of addresses, the standard access list is the simplest way to achieve this. Also, when filtering routing updates, which are also called distribution filters, standard access lists allow the source IP specifications to be applied against the network address information included within a routing update. Therefore, standard access lists are a network administrator's best choice for route filtering.

☒　**A.** Both the source and destination addresses is incorrect because a destination IP address or network address can only be filtered by using an extended access list. **C.** The destination IP network address is also incorrect for the same reason. **D.** The destination IP address is incorrect for the same reason.

15. ☑　**D.** All the above is correct since the command syntax for specifically configuring WFQ on an interface is the following:

```
fair-queue [congestive-discard-threshold][dynamic-queues][reservable-queues]
```

The congestive-discard threshold sets the number of messages allowed in each queue. The default is 64 and the range is 1–4096. The dynamic-queues parameter defaults to 256 (possible values are 16, 32, 64, 128, 256, 512, 1024, 2048, and 4096) and represents the number of dynamic queues used for normal, best-effort conversations. Reservable queues are the number of queues that can be used for RSVP. The default is 0 and the range is from 0–1000.

16. ☑ **D.** These configurations use the appropriate syntax and specification to implement the required IPXWAN protocol over the serial link. The command syntax to enable IPXWAN across a serial link is:

```
ipx ipxwan [local-node {network-number | unnumbered}
local-server-name retry-interval retry-limit]
```

☒ **A.** These commands are incorrect because the local-server-name is set incorrectly. **B.** These configuration commands are incorrect because the command enabling NLSP on the interface does not contain the tag A0. **C.** These commands are incorrect because the command to enable the IPXWAN protocol is missing. This configuration is not ideal because it does not allow for the correct tick calculation for a serial link using NLSP.

17. ☑ **B.** These commands are correct because RIP-IPX is enabled by default once IPX routing is enabled. NLSP and RIP-IPX redistribute information to one another by default, so no special configuration is necessary to redistribute between RIP-IPX and NLSP.
☒ **A.** These commands are incorrect because the RIP router configuration command is unnecessary and illegal. **C.** These commands are incorrect because RIP-IPX is disabled on the Ethernet segment within both RIP-IPX and NLSP, therefore disallowing Router 5 to receive RIP updates over this segment. **D.** These commands are incorrect because NLSP is not configured on the interface, therefore disallowing routing updates to be exchanged with Router 4.

18. ☑ **D.** FRAMING ESF. There are only two types of framing with a channelized T1, the default Super Frame (SF) and Extended Super Frame (ESF).
☒ **A.** is incorrect because this is the correct syntax to specify Super Frame rather than Extended Super Frame. **B.** is incorrect because ESF is a framing type rather than a linecode type. **C.** is improper syntax. The correct keyword is *framing*, rather than *frame*.

19. ☑ **A.** Dialer profiles allow us to create multiple virtual interfaces called dialer interfaces that can be customized for different circumstances. All physical interfaces are placed into a dialer pool and used by any dialer interface that has access to that pool. Note this feature did not appear until IOS release 11.2. Prior to this IOS release, only legacy DDR was available.

☒ **B.** is incorrect because this is actually a description of Multilink PPP. **C.** is incorrect because dialer profiles are used to configure virtual interfaces, not physical interfaces. **D.** is incorrect because the physical interfaces are placed into a dialer pool, which can then be used by the dialer interface. The dialer interface is the virtual interface.

20. ☑ **A, B,** and **D.** RFC 1795 states that the design objective of DLSw+ is to make "the corporate Internetwork appear as one big LLC2 LAN." RFC 1795 further states, "Data-link switching was developed to provide support for SNA and NetBIOS in multi-protocol routers." Since SNA and NetBIOS are connection-oriented protocols, they use IEEE 802.2 Logical Link Control (LLC) Type2 for data-link control.

☒ **C** is incorrect because data-link switching uses the SDLC protocol to accommodate SNA over the WAN, rather than HDLC.

21. ☑ **C.** Delete single-line entries within the access list. Prior to this feature, deleting a single-line entry meant deleting the entire access list and building it again from scratch. Access lists are order specific and newly added entries are always applied at the bottom of the list. Editing existing access list entries is not a supported option.

☒ **A.** Filter based on Layer 4 ports is incorrect because numbered, extended access lists have this capability. **B.** Create extended IP access list is also incorrect because numbered access lists have always included extended access lists. **D.** All the above is incorrect.

22. ☑ **A, C,** and **D.** Bridging is the layer-2 (OSI model) technique for making two physically distinct networks appear to hosts on the networks as local. Source-route bridging is a specific type of bridging, typically found within the Token Ring environment. VLANs is a similar concept; however, it can be more flexible within its implementation.

☒ **B.** Routing is incorrect because this is a Layer 3 technique for providing connectivity between different remote LANs.

23. ☑ **A, C,** and **E.** Because EIGRP uses the Diffusing Update Algorithm (DUAL) to converge rapidly and stores backup routes, it can quickly adapt to changes. EIGRP also provides multiple network-layer support because is supports IP, IPX, and AppleTalk. EIGRP also reduces bandwidth usage by using incremental updates rather than sending the entire routing table as you would see with RIP. In addition, EIGRP sends information about network changes only to the routers that need it, which differs from the way normal link-state protocols work. A link-state protocol sends a change to all routers within an area.

   ☒ **B.** is incorrect because EIGRP only automatically redistributes IGRP routes when the EIGRP and IGRP systems have the same autonomous number. EIGRP also automatically redistributes AppleTalk RTMP and IPX RIP, but all other protocols require manual redistribution. **D.** is incorrect because EIGRP uses the DUAL algorithm rather than the OSPF algorithm.

24. ☑ **A.** The D channel for a BRI line is only 16K while the D channel for a PRI is a full 64K. A BRI also has two 64K channels, while a PRI has 23 B channels in North America.

   ☒ **B.** is incorrect because these are the specifications for Europe and much of the rest of the world. **C.** is incorrect because a BRI only has a 16K-D channel. **D.** is incorrect because a PRI has a 64K-D channel. **E.** is incorrect because a BRI only has two B channels, while a PRI has 23 B channels.

25. ☑ **C.** IRB works by creating a logical interface called a Bridged Virtual Interface (BVI) which allows bridged traffic of a given network protocol layer to be forwarded to a routed interface of the same protocol and vice versa.

   ☒ **A.** is incorrect because the interface number of the BVI is the same number as the bridge group that this virtual interface represents. **B.** is incorrect because *router group* is a nonexistent term here. There are only bridge groups. **D.** is incorrect because IRB works using a BVI, not any sort of virtual router interface.

26. ☑ **A** and **B.** SHOW DLSW PEERS monitors a DLSw+ peer-to-peer connection and SHOW DLSW CIRCUITS can monitor DLSw+ end

system-to-end system circuits. An examination of the output of these two commands will reveal that these two types of DLSw+ connections use different address formats.

☒   **C, D.** are incorrect because they are not IOS commands, such as is shown here:

R1#SHOW DLSW ?
capabilities   Display DLSw capabilities information
circuits   Display DLSw circuit information
fastcache   Display DLSw fast cache for FST and Direct
local-circuit   Display DLSw local circuits
peers   Display DLSw peer information
reachability   Display DLSw reachability information
statistics   Display DLSw statistical information

27. ☑   **D.** All the above. All IPX addresses within an Internetwork must be unique. IPX addresses are expressed in hexadecimal format and contain a dot to separate the network and node portions of the address. Cisco also uses two dots to separate the 12-digit hexadecimal node portion of the address. An IPX address with the network number, 00005110, and node number, 000056568787, would display on a Cisco router as the following: *5110.000.5656.8787.*

☒   **A.** An IPX address contains a 32-bit network number and a 48-bit node number is incorrect. **B.** The node number defaults to the 48-bit MAC address for an interface on a Cisco router is incorrect for the same reason. **C.** Preceding zeros in a network number are not necessary for configuration on a Cisco router is correct for the same reason.

28. ☑   **C.** By looking at the two highest-ordered bits within the first octet of the IP address, is the correct answer because classful addressing was first introduced with routing protocols that did not carry subnet masks and that were calculated by deciphering the high-order bits of the first octet in the IP address. The following table lists the highest-ordered bits, the most common classful categories, and their default subnet masks:

Highest-Ordered Bit	Most Classful Category	Default Subnet Mask
0	Class A	255.0.0.0
10	Class B	255.255.0.0
110	Class C	255.255.255.0

☒ **A.** By applying the subnet mask is incorrect because this will result in deciphering the network address, not the class of the address. **B.** By the number of bits that are 1s within the subnet mask is incorrect because, with the introduction of VLSM, subnet bits cannot be relied on as an indication of the class of an address.

29. ☑ **A.** EIGRP is correct because it is the only answer that is considered a distance vector protocol. OSPF, NLSP, and IS-IS are all link-state protocols. These protocols are characterized by fast convergence times, hierarchical design, support for VLSM and summarization, optimal routing, and the ability to handle large network infrastructures. EIGRP, however, is not a typical distance vector protocol in that it also offers fast convergence, support for VLSM, optimal routing, and larger networks than are typical for distance vector protocols.
☒ **B.** OSPF is incorrect because it is a link-state protocol. **C.** NLSP is incorrect for the same reason. **D.** IS-IS is also incorrect for this reason.

30. ☑ **C, D,** and **E.** EIGRP supports IP, IPX, and AppleTalk, but it is important to note that EIGRP for AppleTalk can only be run in a clientless environment because AppleTalk clients expect RTMP information from a local source. EIGRP also supports IPX SAPs.
☒ **A.** is incorrect because, although DECnet is a routable protocol, EIGRP does not support DECnet. **B** is incorrect because SNA is not a routable protocol. **F.** is icorrect because NetBIOS is also not a routable protocol. You need to use a bridging method to handle SNA and NetBIOS.

31. ☑ **C.** This command displays the number of EIGRP packets sent and received and displays statistics on hello, updates, queries, and acknowledgements.

☒ **A.** is incorrect; the SHOW EIGRP TOPOLOGY command displays the topology table. **B.** is incorrect; the SHOW IP PROTOCOLS command displays the parameters and current state of the active routing protocol. **D.** is incorrect because the SHOW IP ROUTE EIGRP command displays the current EIGRP entries in the routing table. Note that IPX uses similar commands to display EIGRP information.

32. ☑ **E.** 5. NT1 converts BRI signals into a form used by the ISDN digital line.
☒ **A, B.** have already been discussed, but **C.** is incorrect because this is the NT2 or point at which all ISDN lines at a customer site are aggregated and switched using a customer switch. **D.** is incorrect because this is the point referenced by S/T that connects into the NT2, or customer-switching device.

33. ☑ **C.** The syntax for the command to enable the BVI to accept and route routable packets is ROUTER(config)#BRIDGE *bridge-group* ROUTE *protocol.*
☒ **A.** is not correct because the BRIDGE IRB command enables IRB. **B.** is incorrect because this command is used to configure the BVI by assigning the corresponding bridge group's number to the BVI. **D.** is incorrect because these commands enable routing on the BVI for those protocols that you want to route from the bridge group.

34. ☑ **A.** RIP-IPX is similar to RIP for IP in that they are both distance vector protocols that maintain hop counts, and broadcast every 60 seconds by default. These broadcasts contain routing information that can become very bandwidth intensive on big networks. EIGRP is also a distance vector protocol; however, it has improvements for convergence times and operating efficiency over RIP-IPX. NLSP is a link-state protocol based on the Open Systems Interconnections IS-IS protocol.
Although the latter two protocols, EIGRP and NLSP, are considered more sophisticated, they require more complex configuration. RIP-IPX is the default protocol that is immediately activated on a configured IPX interface.
☒ **B.** EIGRP is incorrect because it does not send routing updates every 60 seconds, only when the status of a destination network has changed. **C.** NLSP is incorrect because it is a link-state protocol that also uses triggered updates. **D.** Static is incorrect because it is not a dynamic-routing protocol.

35. ☑   **A.** The amount of time that router suppresses routing information on an interface to avoid learning or advertising potentially bad route. This is a technique used by distance vector protocols to avoid routing loop situations. ☒   **B.** The amount of time a router will wait to advertise a link-state change is an incorrect for this question and, since there is no such concept within link-state protocols. **C.** The amount of time a router will hold down an interface from participating in exchanging routing updates once it has been manually shutdown and then brought back up is incorrect because hold-down timers are not used on initializing interfaces.

36. ☑   **C.** is correct because the statement follows the INTERFACE FDDI 0 and IPX NETWORK 10 commands and applies only to the F0 interface. ☒   **A.** is incorrect because IPX SAP-INCREMENTAL EIGRP 1 applies only to the F0 interface. **B.** is incorrect because the command enables SAPs on just the F0 interface, not the S0 interface. **D.** is incorrect because although the command enables incremental SAPs over EIGRP only, the better choice is **C**, since it also specifies the correct interface. **E.** is an incorrect answer because the command enables incremental SAPs over EIGRP, not RIP.

37. ☑   **A, B.** In most cases, where you are connecting your autonomous system to a single ISP, the routing policy that will be implemented in your autonomous system is consistent with the policy implemented in the ISP autonomous system. In this case, it is not necessary, nor even desirable, to configure BGP in your autonomous system because of the complexity of BGP implementation. Instead, use a combination of static routes and default networks for connectivity. ☒   **C.** is incorrect because the gateway of last resort is a setting for routers on your own internal autonomous system rather than for the router connecting that system to an ISP. **D.** is incorrect because OSPF is an interior routing protocol. BGP is not really a routing protocol, but rather a "pathing" protocol. BGP affords interdomain systems a way to guarantee loop-free exchange of routing information.

38. ☑   **B, C.** SHOW DIALER displays information about existing bundles and DEBUG PPP MULTILINK displays event information.

☒ **A.** is incorrect because there is no such command. **D.** is also not correct because the syntax is improper.

39. ☑ **C, D.** The MTU of the BVI is the same as the biggest MTU among the bridged interfaces in this bridged group. This MTU is dynamically adjusted as bridge group membership changes. The problem is that increasing the MTU size does not allow fragmentation of routed packets, which can result in big packets being dropped in the bridging path when the destination interface has a smaller MTU than the BVI's MTU. Since routing must be explicitly enabled for packets that need to be routed, this is indeed the default route/bridge behavior in a bridge group when RIB is enabled. You must explicitly configure routing on the BVI for all the protocols you want routed.

☒ **A.** is incorrect because this is the opposite of the correct choice. You should NOT configure any protocol attributes on the bridge interfaces when both routing and bridging a given protocol. **B.** is incorrect because bridging attributes cannot be configured on the BVI.

40. ☑ **D.** ACCESS-LIST 801 PERMIT -1 10.AAAA.3333.4444 is correct for filtering IPX traffic to only the specified destination address 10.AAAA.3333.4444. Access-list numbers 800–899 are reserved for standard IPX access lists. Notice, however, that the characteristic of a standard IPX access list differs from that of the standard IP access list. With an IPX access list, we can specify both a source or destination address for hosts or ranges of hosts within an IPX network. We cannot, however, specify a range of IPX network addresses. This would take additional commands or would require using an extended IPX access list.

☒ **A.** ACCESS-LIST 801 PERMIT –1 10 is incorrect because this command only filters based on the destination IPX network address, not the full IPX host address. **B.** ACCESS-LIST 901 PERMIT FFFFFFFF 10.AAAA.3333.4444 is incorrect because this is an illegal command since it is using an IPX extended access-list number without appropriate parameters. **C.** ACCESS-LIST 801 PERMIT ANY 10.AAAA.3333.4444 is incorrect because the keyword for any IPX network address is *-1*, not *any*.

41. ☑ **A.** ACCESS-LIST 901 PERMIT ANY 10.0000.0000.0000
30.FFFF.FFFF.FFFF.FFFF ALL 10.AAAA.3333.4444 ALL uses
the appropriate command syntax to filter packets based on the given
specifications. IPX extended access lists are able to inspect packet headers
for list matches based on source and destination network ranges, as well as
host ranges, IPX protocols, and IPX source and destination sockets. The
command syntax for the IPX extended access list is the following:

```
access-list access-list-number
{deny | permit} protocol [source-network]
[[[.source-node] source-node-mask] | [.source-node
source-network-mask.source-node-mask]] [source-socket]
[destination-network][[[.destination-node]
destination-node-mask] | [.destination-node
destination-network-mask.destination-nodemask]]
[destination-socket] [log]
```

☒ **B.** ACCESS-LIST 901 PERMIT 10.0000.0000.0000
30.FFFF.FFFF.FFFF.FFFF ALL 10.AAAA.3333.4444 ALL is illegal
because it does not include a keyword for the IPX protocol, which
should be ANY in this example. **C.** ACCESS-LIST 801 PERMIT
10.0000.0000.0000 30.FFFF.FFFF.FFFF.FFFF 10.AAAA.3333.4444 is
illegal since it uses a standard access-list number. **D.** ACCESS-LIST 801
PERMIT 10 30 10.AAAA.3333.4444 is also an illegal command, due to
an incorrect access-list number, and missing and illegal parameters.

42. ☑ **D.** Support for areas is correct because a single EIGRP process or
autonomous system is analogous to one area of a link-state protocol. A hierarchical
architecture can be achieved through multiple EIGRP processes, which will
provide a boundary for routing information propagation. Within an EIGRP
process, any router can be configured to filter and announce aggregate routes.
☒ **A.** Support for VLSM is incorrect because VLSM is supported by EIGRP.
B. Fast convergence is incorrect because EIGRP does converge fast since it sends
appropriate partial-update packets as soon as it becomes aware of a topology
change. **C.** Partial updates is incorrect because this is a characteristic of EIGRP.

43. ☑ **B.** An Internal BGP (IBGP) session occurs between routers in the same autonomous system and is used to coordinate and synchronize routing policy within that autonomous system. Neighbors may be located anywhere in the same autonomous system.

☒ **A.** is incorrect because External BGP is used for sessions between two different autonomous systems. These routers are usually adjacent to one another and share the same subnet and media. **C, D.** are incorrect because neither is a BGP.

44. ☑ **A, B, C.** are the correct answers because the Cisco IOS supports all three standard LMI signaling formats including Cisco's own LMI as defined by the Gang of Four (which is also the default), ANSI Annex D, defined by ANSI standard T1.617, and ITU-T (q933a) Annex A, defined by Q.933.

☒ **D.** is incorrect because IETF is not an LMI type but rather a Frame Relay encapsulation type.

45. ☑ **C.** AppleTalk has a 16-bit network address and an 8-bit host address.

☒ **A, B, D.** are incorrect because none of these protocols have both Layer 2 and Layer 3 addresses. LAT was developed by DEC to transport terminal traffic to and from DEC minicomputers. IBM developed NetBIOS in the mid-80s as part of its LAN implementation strategy. IBM also developed SNA. which is the traditional protocol for communicating to a mainframe.

46. ☑ **B.** Zones. AppleTalk nodes are configured to exist within one zone. Within AppleTalk Phase II or extended network implementation, multiple network addresses can be contained within one zone. The Chooser application, which can be run from an AppleTalk client, can then select services per zones it has discovered from the network. Zones are intended to follow the organization structure of a company, thus allowing a sensible means for managing the network.

☒ **A, C, D.** The other choices are all incorrect terms for nodes.

47. ☑ **B.** ROUTER IGRP 5 and NETWORK 10.0.0.0 use the correct command syntax for enabling IGRP operation on all interfaces within the Class A address 10.0.0.0. The first command defines the autonomous system number to be 5 for the IGRP routing domain. The command syntax for enabling the IGRP routing protocol is:

    `router igrp` autonomous-system-number

    The router configuration command to specify a network for IGRP operation is:

    `network` network-number

    ☒ **A.** ROUTER IGRP, NETWORK 10.1.1.0, and NETWORK 10.1.3.0 is incorrect because the autonomous system number is not specified and because the network address should be specified in its classful notation, 10.0.0.0. **C.** ROUTER IGRP and NETWORK 10.0.0.0 is incorrect because the autonomous system number is not specified. **D.** ROUTER IGRP 5, NETWORK 10.1.1.0, and NETWORK 10.1.3.0 is incorrect because the network address should be specified in its classful notation, 10.0.0.0.

48. ☑ **C.** NO IP SPLIT-HORIZONS EIGRP is correct because, with the conditions described above, split-horizons would need to be disabled in order for the routes being advertised via Router 5 and Router 6 to be sent back out the same interface on Router 4 in order that Routers 5 and 6 each receive updates about the other's networks. The interface configuration command for disabling split-horizons within EIGRP is the following:

    `no ip split-horizon eigrp` autonomous-system-number

    ☒ **A.** IP SUMMARY-ADDRESS EIGRP 5 172.16.2.0 255.255.0.0 is incorrect because this command would define a summarized route on the interface. **B.** NO AUTO-SUMMARY is incorrect because this is a router configuration command for turning off automatic summarization between two or more different network addresses configured within EIGRP by the network command. **D.** NO DEFAULT-INFORMATION IN is incorrect because this is also a router configuration command for disabling automatic redistribution of incoming default information.

49. ☑ **C.** correctly identifies which autonomous system to route and the correct network associated with AS 200. A further requirement is to activate a BGP session with a neighbor router in the AS 100 autonomous system using the NEIGHBOR REMOTE-AS command. The correct syntax for this command is:

```
Router(config-router)#neighbor ip-address remote-as autonomous-system
```

An important command to know in conjunction with the above configurations is the CLEAR command, which can be used to reset BGP connections after changing BGP configuration. The syntax for this command is:

```
Router#clear ip bgp {* | address} where the * is a wildcard for all addresses
```

☒ **B.** is incorrect because the first statement, ROUTER BGP 100, identifies the incorrect autonomous system. AS 100 is associated with Router A. The statement should read ROUTER BGP 200. **A.** is incorrect for the same reason, but also because it identifies the incorrect autonomous system in the neighbor statement. The correct answer identifies AS 100 as the neighboring AS. **D.** is incorrect because although the first two lines are correct, the third line incorrectly identifies the neighboring AS.

50. ☑ **C, D, E.** Because this is a partially meshed Frame Relay network using only Inverse ARP, Remote 1 cannot ping Remote 2 since they are not directly connected, and vice versa. Headquarters, however, can ping both Remote 1 and Remote 2 because Headquarters is directly connected to both sites.
☒ **A, B.** are incorrect because neither Remote 1 nor Remote 2 can ping the other since they are not directly connected. **F.** is incorrect because Headquarters can ping both sites since it is directly connected to them.

51. ☑ **A, C, D.** Adding a PVC between the Remote sites will make the network fully meshed and since all sites would be directly connected, each site would be able to ping all the other sites. Frame Relay map statements statically map local DLCIs to remote network-layer addresses. An important point is that when using Frame Relay map statements for a particular protocol, Inverse ARP will be disabled for that protocol only for the DLCI referenced in the map statement. Point-to-point subinterfaces completely bypass the DLCI-to-network address-mapping issue.

☒ **B.** is incorrect because there is no provision in the Cisco IOS for configuring point-to-point interfaces in the same manner.

52. ☑ **A.** is the correct choice because the syntax used to select a specific spanning-tree protocol for a bridge group is as follows:

```
Router(config)#bridge bridge-group protocol {ieee | dec}
```

bridge-group identifies a particular set of bridged interfaces, a decimal number from 1–63, and is referred to as a bridge number. Transparent bridging only uses the IEEE and DEC Spanning-Tree Protocols.

☒ **B.** is incorrect because it does not specify which bridge number to use. **C.** is incorrect because of the key word BRIDGE-GROUP. The correct key word is simply BRIDGE. Finally, **D.** is incorrect because of the incorrect keyword, but also because the bridge number is in the incorrect location. The number 1 needs to immediately follow the key word BRIDGE to identify the correct bridge number.

53. ☑ **A.** Zones, RTMP, and NBP. Zones can be filtered on Cisco routers in two different ways—between clients and router, and between routers. A GetZoneList filter hides zone information from clients requesting this through a GETZONELIST query. Zone Information Protocol (ZIP) reply filters are used to hide zone information between routers by denying replies to routers' ZIP queries for learned network addresses. Router Table Maintenance Protocol (RTMP) is the default and more widely implemented routing protocol for AppleTalk. Applying filters for RTMP is done as an interface configuration command, similar to RIP-IPX. Finally, Name Binding Protocol (NBP) filters allow an administrator to hide more specific services being provided within an AppleTalk network by filtering replies to NBP requests.

☒   **B.** Zones, RIP, and NCP is incorrect because RIP and NCP are IPX protocols. **C.** Cable ranges, RTMP, and NBP is incorrect because cable ranges are filtered via RTMP filters. This answer also neglects Zone filters. **D.** Cable ranges, RIP, and NCP is incorrect for the same reasons.

54. ☑   **D.** Loopback1, 10.2.2.1. If these were the only four active interfaces on the router, 10.2.2.1 would be used as the OSPF router ID because it represents the highest loopback IP address. Remember that the highest physical interface's IP address is only selected if there are no loopback interfaces configured on the router. When one or more loopback interfaces is configured, OSPF will select the highest of these addresses to ensure stability, since loopback interfaces are actually virtual interfaces that are always "up".

☒   **A.** Ethernet0, 172.16.120.1 is incorrect because it is a physical interface and it has a lower IP address than Serial0. **B.** Serial0, 172.16.122.1, is incorrect because it is a physical interface and there are loopback interfaces that exist on the router. **C.** Loopback0, 10.1.1.1 is incorrect because it is the lowest loopback IP address on the router.

55. ☑   **A, C.** are correct because the default distance for External BGP is 20 and the default distance for Internal BGP is 200, as shown in the following table.

Route Source	Default Distance
Connected Interface	0
Static Route	1
Enhanced IGRP Summary Route	5
External BGP	20
Internal Enhanced IGRP	90
IGRP	100
OSPF	110

Route Source	Default Distance
IS-IS	115
RIP	120
EGP	140
External Enhanced IGRP	170
Internal BGP	200
Unknown	255

    ☒   **B, D, E.** are incorrect because their values do not match those in the table and have incorrect default distances.

56. ☑   **D.** SHOW SPAN. You can obtain a wealth of information using this command, including which protocol (IEEE or DEC) the bridge group is executing. The current operating parameters of the spanning tree, and the state of the interface. You can also learn the state of the interface as well as the path cost associated with this interface.

    ☒   **A.** is incorrect because there is no IOS command that allows you to specify the type of bridging. **B.** is incorrect because the SHOW BRIDGE command is used to verify bridging, not to verify the Spanning-Tree Protocol. **C.** is incorrect there are two proper IOS commands, SHOW BRIDGE and SHOW SPAN, but no IOS command allows you to do both in a single command.

57. ☑   **C.** is the correct answer because an NBMA network is a nonbroadcast, multi-access Frame Relay network. The NBMA model applies when every router is connected to all other routers via a dedicated DLCI. The key to remember is that all peers reside in the same IP network.

    ☒   **A.** is incorrect because a hub-and-spoke Frame Relay model is the other common Frame Relay model and does not require the Frame Relay cloud be on the same IP network. **B.** is incorrect because Multilink PPP is an ISDN technology, not a Frame Relay technology. A question to ask yourself is whether ISDN is packet switched or circuit switched. ISDN is circuit switched. **D.** is incorrect because "meshed-node" is an invalid term.

58. ☑ **D.** APPLETALK ZIP-REPLY-FILTER 605 is the appropriate command to apply a ZIP reply filter to the interface. Once routers learn about a network address, they send out ZIP queries to determine associated zone information. AppleTalk ZIP replay filters let an administrator confine routers from learning about certain zones dynamically. The command syntax for applying a ZIP reply filter to an interface is the following:

```
appletalk zip-reply-filter access-list-number
```

☒ **A.** The command ZIP-FILTER 605 is an illegal command since it is invalid. **B.** The interface configuration command APPLETALK ACCESS-GROUP 605 IN is incorrect because this applies the access list filter as a data filter. **C.** The interface configuration command APPLETALK GETZONELIST-FILTER 605 is incorrect because this will apply the filter as a GETZONELIST filter, which is used for client-to-router denial of zone information, not router-to-router.

59. ☑ **A.** INTERFACE ETHERNET0 and APPLETALK DISTRIBUTE-LIST 610 IN filter the 100–104 network route from being propagated to any upstream routers. Notice that all AppleTalk filters for protocol covered within this section have been filtered by applying access lists at the interface. If EIGRP is used for routing AppleTalk, networks can be filtered by applying an access list to its router configuration commands. For this example we are applying the routing filter as incoming on the interface. Thus, we used the ACCESS-LIST CABLE-RANGE configuration command. For outgoing RTMP filters, the access list can only be specified by using Zone, so we use the ACCESS-LIST ZONES configuration command.

☒ **B.** These configuration commands are incorrect for the reason stated in the proceeding paragraph. Outgoing RTMP filters can only be specified by zones and not by cable ranges. **C.** The configuration commands on Router3 are incorrect because this will only deny communication to network 200–205, leaving network 110–114 unaccounted for within the Development zone.

60. ☑ **A.** 110 represents the internal OSPF process identifier for this example. The process identifier is used internally by the router to distinguish between separate OSPF processes running on the same router. The process identifier will never be exchanged with external routers. It is recommended, however, to keep the process identifier consistent for ease of management among routers which are participating within the same routing domain. If your organization has an autonomous system number and is running one OSPF process as the interior gateway protocol, it is a good idea to use this number instead of picking an arbitrary number.
☒ **B.** The OSPF area, is incorrect because ROUTER OSPF 110 will change your configuration mode into *router configuration mode*, this is where areas are defined. **C.** The autonomous system number is incorrect; however, the process identifier could be selected to reflect the AS number.

61. ☑ **A, D.** are the correct answers because packet switched networks include X.25, Frame Relay, SMDS, and ATM, although ATM is actually cell switched. LAPB is Layer 2 of the X.25 protocol stack. IETF is defined in RFC 1490 as an encapsulation type for Frame Relay. Note that Cisco also has its own proprietary Frame Relay encapsulation type. You would need to use IETF when connecting to another vendor's equipment.
☒ **B.** is incorrect because LAPD is a circuit-switched encapsulation for ISDN D channel. **C.** is incorrect since HDLC is an encapsulation protocol for dedicated point-to-point serial links. **E.** is incorrect because CSLIP is an outdated encapsulation protocol for dial-up access.

62. ☑ **B, C.** AppleTalk needs to add the broadcast parameter to allow AppleTalk broadcast and multicasts to be forwarded over the NBMA network. NBMA networks are designed to be fully meshed.
☒ **A.** is incorrect because a Frame Relay network can be configured using map statements, Inverse ARP, and subinterfaces. **D.** is incorrect because with multipoint NBMA configurations, you do need to use the LOCAL ROUTING command to assure that all AppleTalk interfaces on the multipoint subnet can access each other.

63. ☑ **B, C.** are the correct answers because the Route Descriptor (RD) field portion of the RIF consists of both ring numbers and bridge numbers. A point worth noting is the difference between IBM Token Ring and 802.5 Token Ring. IBM Token Ring defines a maximum of eight rings and seven bridges. 802.5 Token Ring defines a maximum of 14 rings and 13 bridges.
☒ **A.** is incorrect because the type field is part of the Routing Control (RC) field rather than the RD field. A RIF consists of two parts—RC and RD. **D, E, F.** are incorrect because they are also part of the RC field rather than the RD field.

64. ☑ **D.** When the traffic load becomes greater than the transmission capacity best describes the conditions when a queuing strategy can improve critical traffic performance. When conditions are reversed, the overhead added by sophisticated data classification queuing techniques will only increase the latency by adding unnecessary CPU cycles to the router. However, when there is more traffic than bandwidth, this bottleneck could be causing transaction packets or other critical application packets to be drowned out by larger, batch-oriented, packets. This is when alternative queuing strategies should be investigated, according to your network's specific requirements.
☒ **A.** When you have low bandwidth or transmission capacity is incorrect because, although this potentially becomes a bottleneck, it does not necessarily mean it is currently one. **B.** When transmission capacity is greater than the traffic load is incorrect because this is the opposite of the necessary conditions for considering alternative queuing strategies. **C.** While you are configuring a serial interface is incorrect. Although most alternate queuing techniques are performed on serial interfaces, this happens only when their link becomes a bottleneck.

65. ☑ **C.** Router 2 as DR and Router 1 as BDR. Routers 1 and 2 should be assumed to contain the default router priority value of 1, since they are not specified otherwise within the scenario. Highest-router priority is the first precedence in deciding the DR and BDR election process, with the highest router ID being the tiebreaker. Router priorities set to 0 mean that the router will never be elected DR or BDR. This excludes Router 3 of our scenario from becoming the DR or BDR. Since Router 1 and 2 have the same router priority, Router 2 will become the DR, due to its higher router ID of 10.1.1.1, and Router 1 will be selected the BDR.

☒ **A.** Router 1 as DR and Router 2 as BDR is incorrect because Router 1 has a lower router ID than Router 2. **B.** Router 3 as DR and Router 2 as BDR is incorrect because Router 3 has a router priority configured as 0, excluding it from becoming the DR election process.

66. ☑ **D.** O IA 172.16.32.0/19 is the correct answer because a summarized route is advertised to all areas except for the one it is defining. This means that it will always be deciphered as an inter-area (IA) route to all other routers participating within the same OSPF routing domain. The O indicates that this is a route discovered by OSPF. E1 stands for External Type 1 routes, which represent routes that are imported for external routing domain and that accumulate additional costs as they are propagated within OSPF. E2 stands for External Type 2 routes. This is the default metric for which external routes are redistributed into OSPF. External Type 2 routes are similar to E1 routes except that they maintain the same cost throughout the OSPF network.

☒ **A.** O 172.16.32.0/19 is incorrect because this would indicate that this route is an intra-area OSPF route, which it is not. **B.** O E1 172.16.32.0/19 is incorrect because 172.16.32.0/19 is not an external route. **C.** O E2 172.16.32.0/19 is incorrect because 172.16.32.0/19 is not an external route.

67. ☑ **C.** AREA 2 RANGE 172.16.32.0 255.255.224.0 is the correct command syntax for summarizing Area 2 with the network address 172.16.32.0/19. This command will enable only one route, Area 0, to be advertised out to the backbone while allowing it to be further subnetted within Area 2 itself. All routers configured to be within Area 2 will exchange the explicitly subnetted network addresses.

☒ **A.** NETWORK 172.16.32.0 255.255.224.0 AREA 2 is incorrect because this is an illegal command. **B.** NETWORK 172.16.32.0 0.0.31.255 AREA 2 is incorrect because this command enables OSPF on interfaces that are within the specified range. It also sets these interfaces to Area 2 and allows their network addresses to be advertised within this area. **D.** AREA 2 RANGE 172.16.32.0 0.0.31.255 is incorrect because the wildcard mask is illegal within this command.

68. ☑ **D.** Point-to-point serial links. Only a full time dedicated (leased) line provides this type of connectivity.

☒ **A.** is incorrect because dial-on-demand routing (DDR) by definition is not available full time. **B.** is also incorrect because ISDN is a typical circuit-switched service and cannot guarantee the same full-time connectivity that a serial line does. **C.** PPP is incorrect because it is an encapsulation protocol, not a WAN service.

69. ☑ **B.** SHOW DIALER shows general information on the configuration and current status of the dial interface.

☒ **A.** is incorrect because SHOW SNAPSHOT *interface* is used to show the current status of a snapshot interface, line status, and timer configuration. **C.** is incorrect because, while SHOW PPP MULTILINK shows current information during the Multilink operation, Multilink is not necessary since you can use a single channel. **D.** is incorrect because, while SHOW DIALER INTERFACE is a legal command, it is used to show information on a specific serial interface rather than general information on the configuration and current status of the dial interface.

70. ☑ **D.** The syntax to specify the local bridge connection is:

```
Router(config-if)#source-bridge local-ring bridge-number target-ring
```

In the illustration (shown next), the local ring is the 500 ring, the bridge number is 1, and the target ring is the 501 ring.

☒ **A.** is incorrect because the target ring 501 is listed as the local ring. **B.** is incorrect because the bridge number is placed before either of the rings. The correct placement for the bridge number is between the rings. **C.** is incorrect because the bridge number follows the two rings instead of being between the two rings.

71. ☑ **C.** DLSw Lite is the transport used for a point-to-point network and uses the LLC2 encapsulation as defined in RFC 1490.

☒ **A.** is incorrect because DLSw Lite specifically uses just LLC2 encapsulation. **B.** is incorrect because PPP is not allowed as one of the four DLSw encapsulations. **D.** is incorrect because the four allowable encapsulation methods are TCP/IP, FST/IP, Direct, and LLC2.

72. ☑ **A, B, C.** The SHOW SOURCE-BRIDGE command displays information about the explorer packets that the router has transmitted and received, as well as information about the ring groups and ring and bridge number of the ring. SHOW RIF displays how the RIF was learned, the number of minutes since the last response was received directly from this node, and the RIF. SHOW INTERFACES TOKENRING displays information about the Token Ring interfaces and the state of source-route bridging.

☒ **D.** is incorrect because you cannot use this abbreviation for source-route. **E.** is incorrect because SHOW SOURCE-BRIDGE and SHOW RIF are two separate commands.

CISCO CERTIFIED NETWORK PROFESSIONAL

Test Yourself:
ACRC Practice
Exam 2 Questions

Q

&

A

B
efore you register for the actual exam, take the following test and see how you make out. Set a timer for 90 minutes—the time you'll have to take the live CCNP Advanced Cisco Router Configuration certification exam—and answer the following 72 questions in the time allotted. Once you've finished, turn to the ACRC Practice Exam 2 Answers section and check your score to see if you passed. Good luck!

ACRC Practice Exam 2 Questions

1. What are the three tiers of the hierarchical design model?

A. Core, intermediate, and access

B. Core, distribution, and access

C. Backbone, intermediate, and Internet

D. Backbone, distribution, and access

Refer to the Following Illustration to Answer Question 2

If a specification is not listed for a router, assume it is the default.

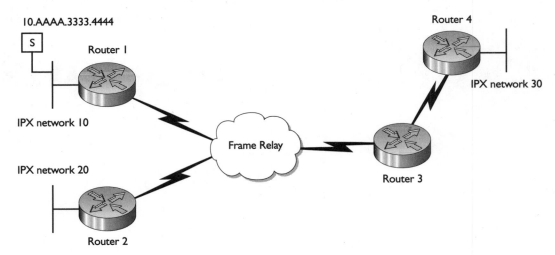

2. Which IPX interface configuration command would allow an RIP-IPX output filter to be applied to an interface? Assume the access list to be applied is numbered 999.

A. IPX OUTPUT-RIP-FILTER 999

B. IPX ACCESS-GROUP 999 OUT

C. IPX OUTPUT-NETWORK-FILTER 999

D. None of the above

3. What is the decision making process for selecting routes within EIGRP?

A. DUAL

B. Dijkstra's algorithm

C. RIP

D. None of the above

Refer to the Following Illustration and Scenario to Answer Question 4

Network 50 is another IPX RIP network. The EIGRP autonomous system number is 1. Here is a part of the configuration on Router A:

```
ipx routing
!
ipx router eigrp 1
network 20
network 50
!
ipx router rip
no network 20
no network 50
!
interface fddi0
ipx network 20
ipx sap-incremental eigrp 1
!
interface serial 0
ipx network 50
```

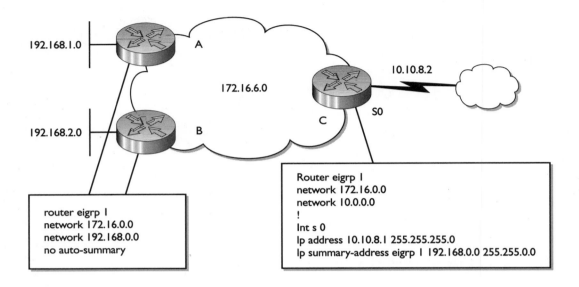

192.168.1.0

192.168.2.0

A

B

172.16.6.0

C

S0

10.10.8.2

router eigrp 1
network 172.16.0.0
network 192.168.0.0
no auto-summary

Router eigrp 1
network 172.16.0.0
network 10.0.0.0
!
Int s 0
Ip address 10.10.8.1 255.255.255.0
Ip summary-address eigrp 1 192.168.0.0 255.255.0.0

4. Which command specifies the format of the route summary and the autonomous system of the network being summarized?

A. ROUTER EIGRP 1
B. NO AUTO-SUMMARY
C. NETWORK 192.168.0.0
D. IP SUMMARY-ADDRESS EIGRP 1 192.168.0.0 255.255.0.0

Refer to the Following Illustration and Scenario to Answer Question 5

The following illustration represents an ISDN backup solution for a serial link. The corresponding configuration for Router A reads as follows:

```
INT S 0
BACKUP INTERFACE SERIAL 1
BACKUP DELAY 40 NEVER
```

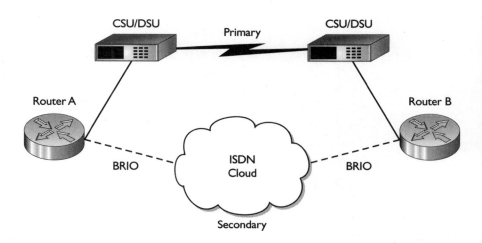

5. What is the meaning of delay 40 in the final line of the given configuration?

A. Delay for 40 seconds after the primary link is available before disconnecting the backup link

B. Delay for 40 seconds after the secondary link is established before transmitting data

C. Delay for 40 seconds after the primary link failed before bringing up the ISDN line

D. Never delay after the primary link fails, connect immediately

6. What is the Routing Information Indicator (RII)?

A. The first bit in the destination address of an 802.5 MAC frame

B. The first bit in the RIF's RC field and the first bit in the destination address of an 802.5 MAC frame

C. The first bit in the source address of an 802.5 MAC frame

D. The first bit in the RIF's RD field

7. As a general rule, what percentage of end-user traffic should remain local to the access layer?

A. 60 percent

B. 40 percent

C. 99.9 percent

D. 80 percent

8. What is the main purpose of routing protocols?

A. To summarize as much as possible in order to reduce routing tables

B. To create a routing table containing a network address with complete path-to-destination addresses

C. To dynamically determine the best-path-next-port interface to send a data packet

D. To statically determine the network topology

Refer to the Following Scenario to Answer Question 9

If a specification is not listed for a router, assume it is the default.

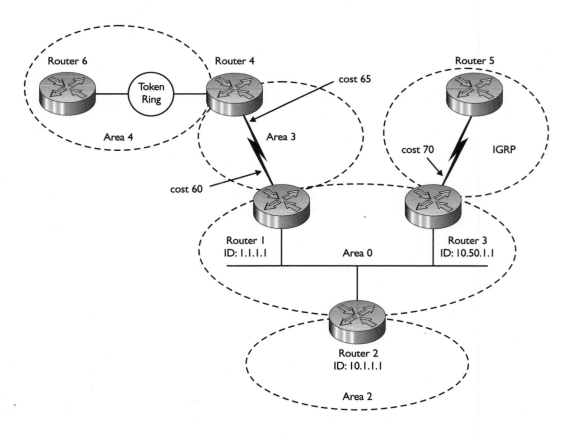

9. Assuming that there is no route summarization being performed, what should Router 4's cumulative OSPF cost be for reaching the IP network address defined on the T-1 circuit between Routers 2 and 5?

A. 75

B. 145

C. 135

D. 70

10. For what type of WAN connection is SMDS designed?

A. Point-to-point over serial lines

B. Access servers

C. Dial-on-demand routing and circuit-switched services

D. Packet-switched services

Refer to the Following Illustration to Answer Question 11

Bridge Group 10

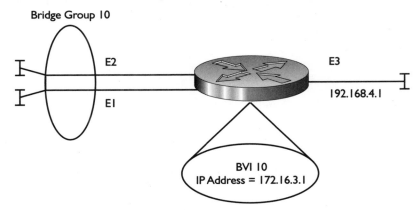

11. Which command enables IRB?

A. BRIDGE IRB

B. INTERFACE BVI 10

C. BRIDGE 10 ROUTE IP

D. INTERFACE BVI 10
   IP ADDRESS 172.16.3.1 255.255.255.0

12. How does an SRT bridge determine when a frame is using SRB and when a frame is using transparent bridging? Choose two.

A. If the RIF bit is 1, then the bridge performs source routing

B. If the RII bit is 1, then the bridge performs source routing

C. If the RIF bit is 0, then the bridge performs transparent bridging

D. If the RII bit is 0, then the bridge performs transparent bridging

13. Which of the following primary design goals describe the core layer of a corporate network?

A. Symmetry, filtering, and access lists

B. Redundancy, security, and encryption

C. Complexity, scalability, and bandwidth

D. Redundancy, scalability, and throughput

14. Which generic term is used for all routing protocols to determine the best path when more than one exists?

A. Cost

B. Metric

C. Hops

D. The fastest outgoing interface

15. Which SHOW command will display the router IDs of a router's OSPF neighbors?

A. SHOW IP PROTOCOLS

B. SHOW IP OSPF NEIGHBOR

C. SHOW IP OSPF

D. SHOW IP OSPF INTERFACE

16. The ACME Rocket Science Company is searching for a WAN solution to connect its corporate headquarters with 20 branch offices. What are some of the connection considerations for making an optimum service selection using Cisco equipment? Choose three.

A. Limited service

B. Bandwidth

C. Routing protocol characteristics

D. Cost

E. Application traffic

17. In which situation would you use IRB? Choose two.

A. To conserve IP, IPX, or AppleTalk addresses

B. To bridge more than one protocol

C. When you want to add VLANs to your network

D. When you need serial interfaces for X.25

18. What does a peer connection between two Cisco routers consist of?

A. A single data-link connection

B. Two data-link connections

C. A single TCP connection

D. Two TCP connections

19. Of the following connection strategies, which would *not* be considered ideal within a good hierarchical network design?

A. Redundant connections between core and distribution-layer routers

B. Connections between distribution-layer routers

C. Connections between access-layer routers

D. Connections between core-layer routers

20. Which of the following is a type of dial-up authentication?

A. PPP

B. CHAP

C. DES

D. DDR

21. What is the term for the amount of time that it takes routers within a group, running the same routing protocol, to agree on the network topology once a change has occurred within that topology?

A. Synchronization

B. Convergence

C. Consolidation time

D. Initialization time

22. On what OSI routing protocol is NLSP based?

A. OSPF

B. IS-IS

C. IGRP

D. BGP

23. Which WAN encapsulation types can be used for point-to-point links between Cisco routers? Choose all that apply.

A. PPP

B. LAPD

C. LAPB

D. HDLC

E. IETF

Refer to the Following Illustration to Answer Question 24

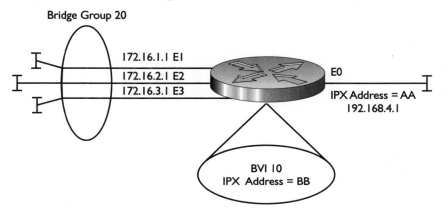

24. Without IRB enabled on an Ethernet network, a given routable protocol can be which of the following? Choose all that apply.

A. Routed on all interfaces

B. Bridged on all interfaces

C. Simultaneously routed and bridged on all interfaces

D. None of the above

25. Which is NOT a use for access lists?

A. Filtering data traffic and routing updates

B. Defining traffic for initiating DDR connections

C. Defining traffic-destination interface

D. Defining queuing strategies

26. In addition to VLSM, what concept that was introduced by RFC 1918 has contributed to survival of IPv4's diminishing number of network addresses?

A. Supernetting

B. Virtual private networking

C. Private addressing

D. Network address translation

Refer to the Following Illustration to Answer Questions 27–28

If a specification is not listed for a router, assume it is the default.

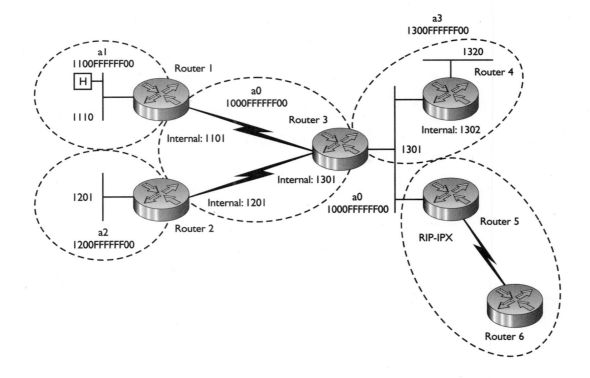

27. Which additional router configuration command would Router 3 use to summarize the routes from NLSP Level A3?

    A. ROUTER3(config)# IPX ROUTER NLSP A3
       ROUTER3(router)# ROUTE-AGGREGATION

    B. ROUTER3(config)# IPX ROUTER NLSP A0
       ROUTER3(router)# ROUTE-SUMMARIZATION

    C. ROUTER3(config)# IPX ROUTER NLSP A3
       ROUTER3(router)# ROUTE-SUMMARIZATION

    D. ROUTER3(config)# IPX ROUTER NLSP A0
       ROUTER3(router)# ROUTE-AGGREGATION

28. What type of NLSP routers are Routers 1, 2, and 3?

    A. Level 1

    B. Level 2

    C. Level 3

    D. ABRs

29. Cisco uses which three types of compression in an Internet-working environment?

    A. Van Jacobson header

    B. Encapsulated

    C. Link

    D. Packet

    E. Payload

30. Which of the following non-routable protocols must be bridged? Choose three.

    A. LAT

    B. IP

    C. DECnet

    D. MOP

    E. NetBIOS

    F. IPX

31. If an access list is defined as an incoming traffic filter on an interface and a match is not found within the list for a specific packet, what happens to the packet?

   A. The packet is denied and dropped

   B. The packet is forwarded according to the routing table

   C. The packet is routed to the Null 0 interface

   D. The packet retransmits back to the original sender

32. Which layer of the OSI model is not filterable by an extended IP access list?

   A. Layer 2

   B. Layer 3

   C. Layer 4

   D. Layer 5

33. Which of the following is not a characteristic of Cisco's IGRP?

   A. Support for VLSM

   B. Supports poison reverse, split-horizons, and holddowns

   C. Supports multi-paths

   D. Supports a vector metric that combines delay, bandwidth, reliability, and load

34. You want to configure channelized E1 for an MIP card in Slot 1 Port 1 using CRC4 as the E1 frame type. Enter the appropriate command to define CRC4 framing at the following prompt:

```
Router(config-controller)#
```

   A. FRAMING NO-CRC4

   B. FRAMING CRC4

   C. FRAME CRC4

   D. LINECODE FRAMING CRC4

35. Which command would you enter to verify transparent bridging?

A. SHOW SPAN

B. SHOW BRIDGE

C. VERIFY BRIDGE

D. SHOW TRANSPARENT-BRIDGE

36. What is the default IPX encapsulation type (or IPX frame type) for an Ethernet?

A. ARPA or Ethernet_II

B. Novell-Ether or Ethernet_802.3

C. SAP or Ethernet_802.2

D. SNAP or Ethernet_Snap

37. EIGRP supports routing for which of the following protocol types?

A. IP, DECNet, and Banyan VINES

B. IP, IPX, and DECNet

C. IP, IPX, and AppleTalk

D. IP, IPX, and Banyan VINES

38. Which of the following are features of EIGRP? Choose four.

A. Route tagging

B. Formal neighbor relationships

C. Classful routing

D. Configurable metrics

E. Equal-cost load balancing

F. Infrequent route updates

Refer to the Following Illustration to Answer Question 39

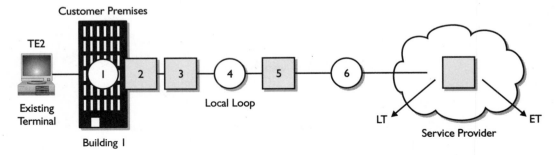

39. What is the proper location for the Terminal Adapter (TA)?

A. 1

B. 2

C. 3

D. 4

E. 5

F. 6

40. Suppose you have a loop in your network topology. Which of the following best describes what the Spanning-Tree algorithm would do?

A. Determines a point of redundancy, then blocks all packets until the loop is removed

B. Determines a point of redundancy, then disables the interface until it is needed

C. Determines a point of redundancy, then load balances

D. Determines a point of redundancy, then changes the path-cost for that interface

41. Which of the following is NOT an AppleTalk protocol?

A. DDP

B. UDP

C. NBP

D. ZIP

Refer to the Following Illustration to Answer Question 42

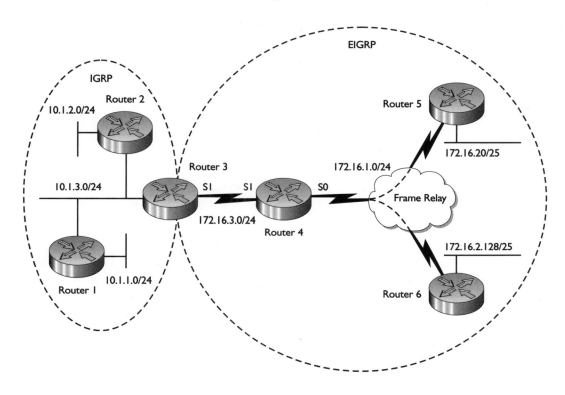

42. Which of the following commands would change the hello interval to two
minutes over the point-to-point serial link on Routers 3 and 4?

A. INTERFACE SERIAL1
   IP HELLO-INTERVAL EIGRP 5 120

B. ROUTER EIGRP 5
   IP HELLO-INTERVAL 120

C. IP HELLO-INTERVAL EIGRP 10 120

D. INTERFACE SERIAL0
   IP HELLO-INTERVAL EIGRP 10 120

43. You can filter routing update traffic for any protocol. Which steps are necessary to configure a filter? Choose three.

    A. Create an access list for the addresses you want to filter

    B. Determine which interface to filter them on

    C. Configure redistribution filtering of that interface

    D. Assign the access list to filter routing updates

Refer to the Following Illustration to Answer Question 44

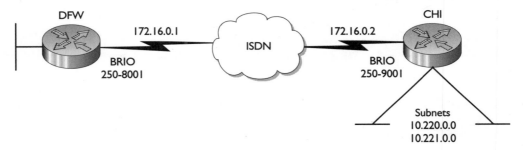

44. The DIALER MAP statement must be defined to initiate dialing. If you want to reach network 10.220.0.0 from router DFW, which command is the proper implementation of the DIALER MAP command? Assume the ISDN link speed is 56Kbps.

    A. DIALER-MAP IP 172.16.0.1 NAME DFW SPEED 56 250-9001

    B. DIALER-MAP IP 172.16.0.2 NAME DFW SPEED 56 250-9001

    C. DIALER-MAP IP 172.16.0.1 NAME CHI SPEED 56 250-9001

    D. DIALER-MAP IP 172.16.0.2 NAME CHI SPEED 56 250-9001

45. What limitation of Token Ring does the SOURCE-BRIDGE RING-GROUP command fix?

    A. That IBM Token Ring chips can only process two ring numbers

    B. That IBM Token Ring chips can only process seven ring numbers

    C. That IBM Token Ring chips can only process eight ring numbers

    D. That IBM Token Ring chips can only process fourteen ring numbers

Refer to the Following Illustration
to Answer Questions 46–47

If a specification is not listed for a router, assume it is the default.

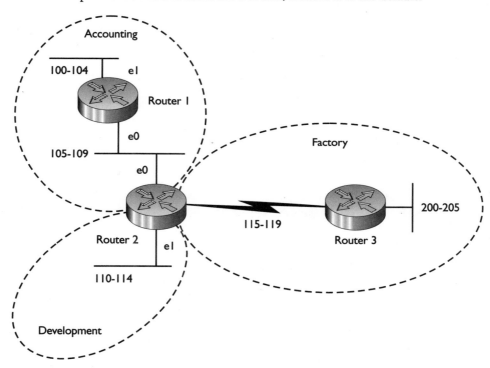

46. What is the correct command to create an access list that can be applied as a GetZoneList filter, so that the host on extended network 105–109 cannot discover the *Development* zone?

A. ACCESS-LIST 601 DENY ZONE DEVELOPMENT and
   ACCESS-LIST 601 PERMIT ADDITIONAL-ZONES

B. ACCESS-LIST 601 DENY ZONE DEVELOPMENT

C. ACCESS-LIST 601 DENY ZONE DEVELOPMENT and
   ACCESS-LIST 602 PERMIT ADDITIONAL-ZONES

D. ACCESS-LIST 601 PERMIT ZONE ACCOUNTING FACTORY

47. Which configuration commands below will appropriately apply the access list from the previous question as a GetZoneList filter so those hosts on network 105–109 cannot discover the Development zone?

A. ROUTER1(config)# INTERFACE ETHERNET0
ROUTER1(config-if)# APPLETALK GETZONELIST-FILTER 601

B. ROUTER1(config)# INTERFACE ETHERNET0
ROUTER1(config-if)# APPLETALK ACCESS-GROUP 601

C. ROUTER1(config)# INTERFACE ETHERNET0
ROUTER1(config-if)# APPLETALK GETZONELIST-FILTER 601
ROUTER2(config)# INTERFACE ETHERNET0
ROUTER2(config-if)# APPLETALK GETZONELIST-FILTER 601

D. ROUTER2(config)# INTERFACE ETHERNET0
ROUTER2(config-if)# APPLETALK GETZONELIST-FILTER 601

48. What is the default administrative distance for EIGRP and IGRP?

A. 100 for both

B. 90 and 120, respectively

C. 90 for both

D. 90 and 100, respectively

49. How many Frame Relay encapsulation methods does the Cisco IOS support for Frame Relay?

A. One

B. Two

C. Three

D. Four

50. To enable AppleTalk EIGRP routing, you must first initialize AppleTalk routing on the router. This is done by using the command APPLETALK ROUTING EIGRP 1, where 1 is the process-ID number. You notice that once this command is entered, AppleTalk route redistribution is turned on as well. Which commands can you use to fine-tune AT-EIGRP? Choose three.

   A. EIGRP-BANDWIDTH-PERCENT
   B. REDISTRIBUTE EIGRP APPLETALK
   C. EIGRP-TIMERS
   D. APPLETALK SAP-INCREMENTAL EIGRP *autonomous-system-number*
   E. EIGRP-SPLITHORIZON

51. Which of the following commands enables the BGP routing protocol for Autonomous System 100?

   A. ROUTER(config)# BGP ROUTING 100
   B. ROUTER(config)#ROUTER BGP
   C. ROUTER(config)#ROUTER BGP AS 100
   D. ROUTER(config)# ROUTER BGP 100

52. Which of the following can only be addressed with SR/TLB?

   A. IP to SNA communication
   B. IP to NetBIOS communication
   C. IPX to SNA communication
   D. Token Ring to Ethernet bridging

53. What is the default queuing technique for a LAN interface?

    A. WFQ

    B. FIFO

    C. Priority

    D. Custom

54. For what purpose is Inverse ARP used?

    A. To map ATM addresses to DLCIs

    B. To map DLCIs to q933a LMIs

    C. To parse the map statements

    D. To map the next-hop protocol address dynamically

55. Which of the following commands are used to troubleshoot legacy DDR? Choose two.

    A. DEBUG IP

    B. CLEAR LINE X

    C. DEBUG DIALER

    D. DEBUG Q931

56. Which of the following are features of DLSw+? Choose three.

    A. Multiple encapsulation types

    B. No requirement for reachability caching

    C. Border-peer groups

    D. Load balancing

57. If data traffic is not explicitly assigned to a queue type within the queuing technique that contains the queues listed below, to what does it default?

    A. High

    B. Medium

    C. Normal

    D. Low

58. Which global configuration command below successfully sets the priority level to medium for AppleTalk access-list number 601?

A. PRIORITY-LIST 5 PROTOCOL APPLETALK MEDIUM LIST 601
B. PRIORITY-LIST 1 APPLETALK MEDIUM APPLETALK 601
C. QUEUE-LIST 1 PROTOCOL APPLETALK MEDIUM 601
D. QUEUE-LIST 5 PROTOCOL MEDIUM LIST 601

59. Which of the following is NOT a benefit of OSPF as an interior gateway protocol?

A. Periodic broadcasts
B. Support for VLSM
C. Fast convergence
D. Scalability

60. BGP routes can be redistributed into which of the following interior gateway protocols?

A. EIGRP
B. RIP
C. IS-IS
D. Static

61. What are the two parts of Frame Relay?

A. Frame Relay DTE switch
B. Frame Relay DCE switch
C. Frame Relay DTE router
D. Frame Relay DCE router

62. Joe has an IPX network and wants to configure dial backup, in case his main serial link goes down. He decides to bring up a backup link if the serial link has been down for more than 40 seconds. Furthermore, he decides, that once the main serial link has been restored, to disconnect the DDR link after the serial link has been reestablished for 60 seconds. What commands does Joe use?

A. BACKUP-INTERFACE SERIAL 0
   BACKUP-DELAY 40 60
B. BACKUP-INTERFACE SERIAL 0
   BACKUP DELAY 40 60
C. BACKUP INTERFACE SERIAL 0
   BACKUP-DELAY 40 60
D. BACKUP INTERFACE SERIAL 0
   BACKUP DELAY 40 60

63. Which DLSw+ operation modes are supported by Cisco? Choose three.

A. DUAL mode
B. Single mode
C. Standards compliance mode
D. Enhanced mode
E. Combined mode

64. Which of the following is a configuration command that applies a priority list number to an interface, for the preceding question?

A. PRIORITY-GROUP 1
B. QUEUE-GROUP 5
C. PRIORITY-LIST 1
D. PRIORITY-GROUP 5

65. Which of following OSPF parameters is NOT exchanged between neighbors?

A. Area identifier

B. Authentication information

C. Router priority

D. Hello and keepalive intervals

66. Which command shows the BGP route table?

A. SHOW IP BGP

B. SHOW IP ROUTE

C. SHOW IP BGP ROUTE

D. SHOW IP BGP PATHS

67. Which protocol does snapshot routing NOT support?

A. RIP

B. IGRP

C. RTMP

D. OSPF

68. Integrated Routing and Bridging (IRB) is used most on which of the following?

A. Token Ring networks

B. FDDI Networks

C. Ethernet Networks

D. All of the above

69. With which commands can you verify SRB operation? Choose three.

A. ROUTER#SHOW SOURCE-BRIDGE

B. ROUTER#SHOW RIF

C. ROUTER#SHOW INTERFACES TOKENRING

D. ROUTER#SHOW SRB

E. ROUTER#SHOW SOURCE-BRIDGE RIF

70. You need to configure compression. Which of the following types of interface would provide the best solution?

A. Slow-speed serial interface

B. High-speed serial interface

C. ATM interface

D. Ethernet interface

71. Susan needs to set the priority within priority queuing on inbound traffic through an interface to a medium type queue. Which global configuration command should she use?

A. PRIORITY-LIST PROTOCOL

B. PRIORITY-LIST INTERFACE

C. PRIORITY-LIST DEFAULT

D. PRIORITY-GROUP LIST

72. Joe has an IPX network and decides to configure DDR on his remote site. Joe wants to configure a dialer profile. What are the minimum requirements for Joe's configuration?

A. Cisco 2501 with IOS version 11.2

B. Cisco 2501 with IOS version 11.1

C. He cannot configure a dialer profile with an IPX network

D. Cisco 2501 with IOS version 11.3

Test Yourself:
ACRC Practice
Exam 2 Answers

Q

$\&$

A

The answers to the questions are in boldface, followed by a brief explanation. Some of the explanations detail the logic you should use to choose the correct answer, while others give factual reasons why the answer is correct. If you miss several questions on a similar topic, you should review the corresponding section in the *CCNP ACRC Advanced Cisco Router Configuration Study Guide* before taking the test.

ACRC Practice Exam 2 Answers

1. ☑   **B.** Core, distribution, and access are the three tiers that make up the hierarchical network design model. The core layer's primary function is to provide optimal connectivity and high-speed switching to ensure constant, efficient, and seamless communication throughout the internetwork. The distribution layer defines distinct routing policies for each geographical or logical region of the corporate Internetwork. Finally, the Access layer routers reside on the LAN segments and provide local and remote users with connectivity or access to the internetwork.

    ☒   **A.** Core, intermediate, and access, is incorrect because *intermediate* is not used to describe this network design model. **C.** Backbone, intermediate, and Internet, is incorrect because all of these terms are inappropriate within the network design model. **D.** Backbone, distribution, and access is incorrect, because, although *backbone* is often used interchangeably with *core* when describing the top layer of a hierarchical network, the traditional topological network design model defines this layer as the core.

2. ☑   **C.** IPX OUTPUT-NETWORK-FILTER 999 is the appropriate command to apply a filter to the RIP-IPX routing protocol. Unlike most routing protocols, which use the distribution list command in router configuration mode for filtering, RIP-IPX follows the configuration approach for filtering SAP. This approach allows for more control on a per-interface basis, since it has to be applied to individual interfaces and not to the routing protocol as a whole.

    ☒   **A.** IPX OUTPUT-RIP-FILTER 999 is an illegal command due to the invalid keyword OUTPUT-RIP-FILTER. **B.** IPX ACCESS-GROUP 999 OUT is incorrect because this command would apply access list 999 as a data filter and not a routing filter.

3. ☑ **A.** Diffusing Update Algorithm (DUAL) is EIGRP's decision-making process for route selection. DUAL maintains all routes advertised by all neighbors and selects routes for insertion into the routing table, based on feasible successors. A *feasible successor* is the neighboring router used for packet forwarding that is a least-cost path to a destination.
☒ **B.** Dijkstra's algorithm is incorrect because it is the algorithm used by the OSPF protocol to determine the short path to a destination. C. RIP is incorrect, since this is a routing protocol, that uses the Bellman-Ford algorithm to determine the best path selection.

4. ☑ **D.** IP SUMMARY-ADDRESS EIGRP *as-number address mask* is used to specify the format of the route summary and the autonomous system into which it needs to be injected. In this case, the AS number is 1 and the 192.168.0.0 address is being advertised as the summary address. Note that for manual summarization, the summary is only advertised if a component of the summary is present in the routing table.
☒ **A.** is incorrect because the ROUTER EIGRP 1 command activates EIGRP routing and assigns an autonomous system number of 1. **B.** is incorrect because the NO AUTO-SUMMARY command turns off automatic summarization. Although EIGRP automatically summarizes routes at the classful boundary, you may need to turn off automatic summarization if you have discontiguous networks as in the present case. **C.** is incorrect because although the 192.168.0.0 network is the address of the network being advertised as the summary address, in this case, 192.168.0.0, is simply being used to enable EIGRP routing on this network, as seen in the configuration excerpt on the left hand side.

5. ☑ **C.** is the correct answer because correct syntax for the backup delay command is as follows:

```
Router(config-if)#backup delay {enable-delay | never} {disable-delay | never}
```

This means that the delay 40 portion is the number of seconds to wait after the primary link has failed before bringing up the ISDN backup line.
☒ **A.** is incorrect because the time to wait before disconnecting once the primary link is back up in this case is *never*. **B.** is incorrect because there are no provisions for waiting to transmit data once the proper links are established. **D.** is incorrect because *never* is the number of seconds to wait after a primary link is available before the backup ISDN link is disconnected.

6. ☑ **C.** The RII is the most significant bit of the source address and is set by the source to indicate routing information is contained in the frame. An easy way to tell is that if the first bit is a 1, indicating a RIF is present, the first hex digit will be in the range 8-f as shown in the following table.

1000	8
1001	9
1010	a
1011	b
1100	c
1101	d
1110	e
1111	f

☒ **A.** is incorrect because the destination address is the destination address and the first bit has no special meaning other than it is simply the first bit of the address. **B.** is incorrect because the first three bits in an RC field are used to indicate the type of explorer frame. **D.** is incorrect because the first bit in an RD field would indicate a unique ring number within the network.

7. ☑ **D.** The 80/20 rule of the access layer states that 80 percent of the data traffic of end users should remain local to the access layer, while 20 percent is permitted to be routed to remote corporate locations. This rule's purpose is to ensure minimal traffic aggregation to the core layer. Specifically, positioning servers near end users, and filtering routers to reduce unnecessary protocol distribution, are examples of maintaining this rule.
☒ **A.** 60 percent is incorrect; this would lead to the saturation of the distribution and core layers of the network. **B.** 40 percent is incorrect for the same reason that A is. **C.** 99.9 percent is incorrect; this percentage is unrealistic for any organization that requires a network to support network applications.

8. ☑ **C.** To dynamically determine the best-path-next-port interface to send a data packet is the purpose of routing protocols. Routing protocols allow routers to share routing information with one another in order to create a network topology. They then run an algorithm, based on many parameters that were exchanged via other routers, to calculate the best path to a particular destination that it knows about. The result of this calculation is a routing table, which provides the best next-hop address to forward data packets to for a destination network.

☒ **A.** To summarize as much as possible to reduce routing tables is incorrect because this is not the primary objective of a routing protocol. It is a welcome feature of sophisticated protocols, however. **B.** To create routing tables containing network addresses with complete path-to-destination addresses is incorrect because routers only calculate for best-next-hop addresses. It would be entirely too cumbersome to try to maintain a complete path through a large Internetwork. **D.** To statically determine the network topology is incorrect since routing protocols are dynamic due to constant communication with other routers.

9. ☑ **B.** 145 is the cumulative cost for Router 4 reaching the network address defined on the T-1 between Routers 2 and 5. Remember that the total OSPF cost to a particular network is the sum of the costs assigned to each of the outgoing router interfaces, which defines the shortest cost path to that network. In this example there is only one available path to reach the T-1 segment. This path transverses three outgoing interfaces, Router 4's serial interface, Router 1's Ethernet interface, and Router 2's serial interface. Therefore, the cumulative OSPF cost is 65 + 10 + 70, or 145. Although the cost for the Ethernet segment is not shown, its default cost is 10. Directly connected networks are an exception to this rule in that they are always assigned a cost of 0.

☒ **A.** 75 is incorrect because this cost only accounts for the first two outgoing interfaces. **C.** 135 is incorrect because it does not include the cost of the Ethernet segment. **D.** 70 is incorrect because it only represents the cost on the last interface of the actual cumulative cost.

10. ☑ **D.** Packet-switched services. Cisco offerings in the Packet-switched service realm include X.25, Frame Relay, and SMDS/ATM.
☒ **A.** is incorrect because dedicated (leased) lines are point-to-point over serial lines. **B.** is incorrect because access servers provide asynchronous dial-in, using modems. **C.** is incorrect because circuit-switched and dial-on-demand services correspond to dial-up connections using a router.

11. ☑ **A.** This command enables IRB and provides capability to route routable traffic from the bridged interfaces.
☒ **B.** is incorrect because this command configures the BVI by assigning the corresponding bridge group's number to the BVI. Each bridge group can have only one corresponding BVI. **C.** is incorrect because this command enables the BVI to accept and route routable packets received from its corresponding bridge group. **D.** is incorrect because these commands enable routing on the BVI for those protocols that you want to route from the bridge group. Note that the IP address is the address of the BVI.

12. ☑ **B, D.** The RII is the first bit of the source address in the frame, and this bit determines whether to use source routing or transparent bridging.
☒ **A.** is incorrect because it should specify the RII bit, which is not a part of the RIF. **C.** is incorrect for the same reason. You should note that SRT bridges do not add or remove RIFs to frames they are bridging. This means that these bridges do not integrate source-route bridging with transparent bridging. A host that does not understand RIFs cannot communicate with a host that expects RIFs.

13. ☑ **D.** Redundancy, scalability, and throughput are all primary goals to maintain when building the core layer of a corporate network infrastructure. Redundancy is important in maintaining high network availability. The core should be easily scaleable to accommodate future growth of the network.

Throughput is the amount of traffic or information that can be passed through a point of the network. Since the core layer
is the aggregate point for data traffic between dispersed distribution locations, it is important that the core provides adequate throughput to handle this requirement.

☒ **A.** is incorrect because filtering and access lists are part of defining routing policies, which are a function of the distribution layer. **B.** is incorrect because security and encryption are features that will require evaluation at the distribution and access layers. **C.** is incorrect because simplicity, not complexity, is a goal within the core layer to diminish troubleshooting and downtime.

14. ☑ **B.** The metric is the generic term for routing protocols, maintaining parameters to prefer one route to another.

☒ **A.** The cost associated with the path is incorrect because cost is a specific metric used by OSPF. **C.** The number of hops is incorrect because it is a specific metric usually used by distance vector protocols. **D.** The fastest outgoing interface is incorrect because, although it is the determining factor in some load balancing techniques, it is not used as a path metric.

15. ☑ **B.** The command SHOW IP OSPF NEIGHBOR is correct because this command displays information about its neighbors, such as router ID priority, adjacency status, DR status if on a multi-access segment, dead time, link IP address, and local forwarding interface.

☒ **A.** SHOW IP PROTOCOLS is incorrect because this command provides global information about all routing protocols that are configured for IP. **C.** The command SHOW IP OSPF is incorrect because this command displays global and area information pertaining to the local router's OSPF operation. **D.** The command SHOW IP OSPF INTERFACE is incorrect because it only provides local OSPF information and status as appropriate to respective interfaces.

16. ☑ **B, C, E.** WAN bandwidth is expensive, typically making up 80 percent of the entire IS budget, so one must carefully consider the amount of traffic that will cross the WAN, as well as how often a WAN connection is necessary. One also needs to categorize the type of traffic crossing the wan. Is the traffic small packets or large files? Lastly, different routing protocols have different overhead traffic in the form of routing updates and broadcasts. Low bandwidth lines may not be able to handle this traffic and still support user applications.

    ☒ **A.** is incorrect because what you really need to consider is the availability of services. Not all services are available in all parts of the world. For example, in some Third World countries, X.25 or Frame Relay may be your only option. **D.** is not the best choice because, although cost is certainly important, the question asks specifically for connections considerations and does not address cost.

17. ☑ **A, C.** Connecting network segments with bridges and assigning each bridge group one network address conserves network addresses and also allows you to add VLANs to your network.

    ☒ **B.** is incorrect because IRB must be set up for each individual protocol. There are no commands to enable the bridging of multiple protocols. **D.** is incorrect because IRB is not supported on either X.25 or ISDN bridged interfaces.

18. ☑ **C.** The question specifies two Cisco routers. The standard published by the AIW calls for initially establishing two connections, but then allows one to be torn down. Cisco routers will always tear down one of the connections unless connected to a router from another vendor.

    ☒ **A, and B.** are incorrect because a peer connection requires a TCP connection, not a data-link connection. **D.** is incorrect because two TCP connections are only required in the case of a Cisco router connecting to another vendor's router that requires two TCP connections. A peer connection between two Cisco routers will tear down one of the TCP connections.

19. ☑ **C.** Connections between access-layer routers is not an ideal connectivity strategy within hierarchical network design. Interconnections at this layer restrict load balancing between it and the distribution layer, as well as between the distribution and core layers. These connections would also increase complexity within the implementation of routing protocols, and could possibly result in routing loops and slow convergence times.
☒ **A.** is incorrect because this is a good strategy within hierarchical network design. **B.** is incorrect because this is also ideal in the event that connections to core layer routers are down. **D** is incorrect because these connections create the backbone links of the network.

20. ☑ **B.** Challenge Handshaking Authentication Protocol (CHAP) is the only answer from this list that is a type of dial-up authentication. It is used with the Point-To-Point Protocol (PPP) for negotiating an authorized connection. CHAP challenges the requesting device for an encrypted password before allowing PPP to bring up the connection. Password Authentication Protocol (PAP) is another type of dial-up authentication; however, it sends clear-text passwords across the wire.
☒ **A.** PPP is incorrect because it is the open standard used for dial-up connections that allows for the negotiation of authentication; however, PAP and CHAP are the protocols that provide this feature. **B.** Digital Encryption Standard (DES) is incorrect because it is part of the standards that allow for encrypted communications between peer routers. **C.** Dial-on-demand routing (DDR) is incorrect because it is Cisco's set of configuration commands that allow for network applications to initiate non-dedicated or dial-up services, such as ISDN.

21. ☑ **B.** Convergence times are faster on link state because they can immediately update neighboring routers when the network topology changes. Most distance vector protocols are set to send updates at a pre-configured time, regardless of topology changes. This results in distance vector protocols being more susceptible to creating routing loops.
☒ **A.** Synchronization is incorrect because this term does not exist within our topic. **C.** Consolidation time is also incorrect for this reason. **D.** Initialization time, too, is incorrect for this reason.

22. ☑ **B.** Intermediate System-to-Intermediate System (IS-IS). NLSP is based on IS-IS because it is an open standard and constitutes a hierarchical link-state routing protocol that has been proven in large internetworks.
☒ **A.** OSPF is incorrect although it is also an open standard and a proven link-state routing protocol. **C.** IGRP is incorrect because it is a Cisco proprietary protocol. **D.** BGP is incorrect because it is a routing protocol for use between autonomous systems.

23. ☑ **A, C, and D.** Dedicated point-to-point links between Cisco devices can use the HDLC, PPP, and LAPB protocols.
☒ **B.** is incorrect because LAPD is an encapsulation for the D channel in ISDN. **E.** is incorrect because IETF is a Frame Relay encapsulation type.

24. ☑ **A and B.** Without IRB, a protocol can never be routed and bridged on the same interface. It can only be either routed or bridged.
☒ **C.** is incorrect because IRB must be enabled before a given protocol can be simultaneously routed and bridged on all interfaces.

25. ☑ **C.** Defining traffic-destination interface is correct because access lists cannot be used to manipulate the routing process. Deciding which port to forward or route data packets is determined by the routing table. Although access lists can be applied as traffic filters and even route filters, these features only affect whether or not the packet will be able to be forwarded, not to which destination port they will be forwarded if permitted. Access lists can be associated with DDR commands to define allowable traffic types for initiating a dial-up connection. Certain queuing strategies also require traffic type definitions, which are established by access lists.

☒ **A.** Filtering data traffic and routing updates is incorrect because this is an applicable use for access lists. **B.** Defining traffic for initiating DDR connections is also incorrect for this reason. **D.** Defining queuing strategies is also incorrect for this reason.

26. ☑ **C.** Private addressing was introduced to allow organizations that do not require publicly routable addresses to freely implement any of the private network addresses provided within RFC 1918 without having to get authorization from the InterNIC. These address ranges are listed in the following table.

Class	Network Address Range
Class A	10.0.0.0–10.255.255.255
Class B	172.16.0.0–172.31.255.255
Class C	192.168.0.0–192.168.255.255

☒ **A.** Supernetting is incorrect because it describes that a network address has aggregated and now contains a shorter subnet mask then its default classful subnet mask. **B.** Virtual private networking (VPN) is incorrect because this is the concept of providing secure communication between two or more routers spanning a public network, such as the Internet. **D.** Network address translation (NAT) is incorrect because NAT is a router process that translates IP packet addressing such that an internal network can appear to external networks as having a different network address.

27. ☑ **D. IPX ROUTER NLSP A0 and router configuration command ROUTE-AGGREGATION.** The route-aggregation commands enable network interface within the specified NLSP tag (in this case, A0) to check for a possible aggregate route before using explicit routes. The command syntax to perform this is simply, ROUTE-AGGREGATION.
☒ **A.** is incorrect because this will not enable route-aggregation to be performed on the serial interface, therefore, not meeting the specifications of the question. **B.** is incorrect because the keyword ROUTE-SUMMARIZATION is incorrect. **C.** These configuration commands are incorrect for the reasons stated in **A** and **B**.

28. ☑ **B. Level 2.** Within the NLSP standard, routers that connect multiple areas are defined as Level 2 routers. Level 1 routers are defined as those that reside within a single NLSP area. Level 3 routers are autonomous systems; they connect two or more ASs. Level 3-router communication has yet to become an official standard.
☒ **A.** Level 1 is incorrect because these routers reside in more than one area. Router 4 is an example of a Level 1 router. **C.** Level 3 is incorrect because these routers do not join ASs. **D.** ABRs is incorrect because Area Border Router is really an OSPF term with the same meaning as Level 2 routers in NLSP.

29. ☑ **A, C, E.** The Van Jacobson algorithm compresses the header of an IP packet while leaving the data intact. Payload compression works in the opposite way and leaves the header intact, but compresses the data. Finally, link compression combines both header and payload compression, but to use it, the data must be encapsulated in either PPP or LAPB.
☒ **B.** is a bogus answer since encapsulated compression doesn't exist. Compressed packets can be encapsulated in another protocol, not the other way around. **D.** is incorrect because packet impression implies that both the header and data are compressed, which is *link compression.*

30. ☑ **A, D, E.** LAT, MOP, and NetBIOS do not have a network-layer address associated with them. In order for a protocol to be routable, it must have both a MAC and a network-layer address.
☒ **B, C, F** are incorrect because these protocols have both Layer 2 and Layer 3 addresses, making them routable.

31. ☑ **A.** The packet is denied and dropped. Regarding filters, Cisco's maintains that what is not explicitly permitted will be denied. Therefore, once an access list has been applied to an interface, whether incoming or outgoing, there is an explicit DENY at the end of the list. Any packets that do not match any commands within the list will therefore be dropped.
☒ **B.** The packet will be forwarded according to the routing table is incorrect since access lists have an explicit DENY at the end of the list. **C.** the packet will be routed to the Null 0 interface, is incorrect because this is an alternate technique for access lists that uses the routing table to drop packets. **D.** the packet retransmits back to the original sender is incorrect because packets never retransmit back to the sender.

32. ☑ **A.** Layer 2 is correct because it has already been striped off by the interface before processing of an access list begins. Switches, such as Cisco's Catalyst 5000 series, can typically perform Layer 2 filtering. Cisco's extended access lists have the ability to evaluate packets starting at Layer 3, the network layer, and continuing through the Transport and Session layers, Layers 4 and 5 of the OSI model, respectively.
Specifically, within Layer 3 the source and destination IP addresses or range of addresses must be specified. Within Layer 4, the protocol type must be specified. Optionally, within Layer 5 the source-and-destination port can be specified.
☒ **B.** Layer 3 is incorrect because this layer of the OSI model is investigated by an extended IP access list. **C.** Layer 4 is incorrect for the same reason. **D.** Layer 5 is incorrect for the same reason.

33. ☑ **A.** Support for VLSM is correct because IGRP does not support VLSM. IGRP was created by Cisco in the mid-1980s, which was before VLSM became popular. Poison reverse, split-horizons, and holddown timers are all techniques used by distance vector routing protocols to prevent routing loops. Hold-downs tell routers to not change routing information until this timer has expired. The holddown timer is usually set to a time greater than the amount of time that it would take the entire network to receive the routing change. Split-horizons prevents local routing loops by not advertising routes via the interface on which it was received, while poison reverse attempts to prevent large routing loops by removing routes for which the metric has increased. Support for multi-path and a combined-vector metric are benefits over the RIP routing protocol, which was the most popular routing protocol at the time IGRP was developed. ☒ **B.** Supports poison reverse, split-horizons, and holddowns is incorrect because it is a characteristic of IGRP. **C.** Supports multi-paths is incorrect because this is also a characteristic of IGRP. **D.** Supports a vector metric that combines delay, bandwidth, reliability, and load is incorrect for the same reason.

34. ☑ **B.** FRAMING CRC4. The correct command syntax uses the key word FRAMING followed by the desired type of framing. The only allowable types of framing for a channelized E1 are CRC4, the default; NO-CRC4, which specifies that CRC checking is disabled in the E1 fame type, and AUSTRALIA, which specifies the frame type for E1 lines in Australia. ☒ **A.** is incorrect because it specifies NO-CRC4, yet the instructions clearly specify CRC4 framing. **C.** is incorrect because this choice does not use the proper syntax. It uses the word *frame* instead *framing*. **D.** is incorrect because the word LINECODE is not used with the framing command. LINECODE is used in another command to specify AMI or HDB3 as the line-code type.

35. ☑ **B.** SHOW BRIDGE verifies transparent bridging. ☒ **A.** is incorrect because the SHOW SPAN command is used to verify which type of Spanning-Tree Protocol (IEEE or DEC) the bridge group is executing. **C.** is incorrect because the Cisco IOS uses SHOW commands to verify equipment status and settings. **D.** is incorrect because the Cisco IOS does not allow you to specify the type of bridging in use with a SHOW command. The correct command is to simply use SHOW BRIDGE.

36. ☑ **B.** Novell-Ether or Ethernet_802.3 is the correct answer. Novell IPX defines four encapsulation types for an Ethernet segment. These are the four listed above as possible answers. IPX Cisco router interfaces can support multiple encapsulation types per interface as long as each type has a unique IPX network address associated with it. Configuring simply an IPX network number will currently default to encapsulation type of Novell-Ether. A troubleshooting point to remember, however, is that Novell's latest software

defaults to IPX frame-type Ethernet_802.2. Both IPX network addresses and encapsulation types have to be configured to match before communication between routers and servers will work.

☒   **A.** ARPA, or Ethernet_II, is incorrect because Novell-Ether is the default encapsulation type for a Cisco router's Ethernet IPX interface. **C.** SAP, or Ethernet_802.2, is incorrect for the same reason. **D.** SNAP, or Ethernet_Snap, is incorrect for the same reasons.

37. ☑   **C.** IP, IPX, and AppleTalk. EIGRP's main advantages is its support for the three most-utilized protocols and its ease of integration. AppleTalk's implementation of EIGRP automatically redistributes with RTMP. Novell IPX's implementation defaults to redistribute with RIP-IPX and SAP advertisements. IP's implementation will automatically redistribute with IGRP if the autonomous system number is the same. EIGRP supports redistribution to most other routing protocols including OSPF, RIP, IS-IS, EGP, and BGP; however, they must be manually configured.

☒   **A.** IP, DECNet, and Banyan VINES is incorrect because EIGRP does not support DECNet or Banyan VINES. **B.** IP, IPX, and DECNet is incorrect because DECNet is not supported. **D.** IP, IPX, and Banyan VINES is incorrect because Banyan VINES is not supported.

38. ☑   **A, B, D, E.** EIGRP uses route tagging to differentiate routes learned via different EIGRP sessions. EIGRP also uses the Hello protocol to establish peering relationships. As with IGRP, EIGRP supports five different metrics, but the default metrics are bandwidth and delay. EIGRP also supports sending traffic across multiple connections equally for load balancing.

☒   **C.** is incorrect because EIGRP supports classless routing, not classful routing, while the default setting is for classful routing. **F.** is incorrect because EIGRP updates based on changes in the network. There are no timed complete route table updates as with RIP.

39. ☑   **B.** 2 is the correct location for the terminal adapter in this scenario because it converts EIA/TIA-232, V.35, and other signals into BRI signals.

☒ **A.** 1, is incorrect because location 1 represents the connection point that is between a non-SDN compatible device and a terminal adapter. **C.** 3, is incorrect because this is the NT2 or point at which all ISDN lines at a customer site are aggregated and switched using a customer switch. **D.** 4, is incorrect because this is the point referenced by S/T that connects into the NT2, or customer-switching device. **E.** 5, is incorrect because this is the location for the NT1, which converts BRI signals into a form used by the ISDN digital line. **F.** 6, is incorrect because this point is the U reference point connection between the NT1 and the ISDN network owned by the phone company.

40. ☑ **B.** The Spanning-Tree Protocol ensures a loop-free topology by blocking duplicate paths between network segments, and automatically activates backup paths if a link segment or bridge fails.

☒ **A** is incorrect because the interface will only block packets for that particular interface, not all interfaces. **C** is incorrect because the spanning-tree algorithm does not load balance across both possible links. Instead, it shuts one of the links down to avoid a topology loop. **D** is incorrect because the path-cost parameter must be changed manually. Path cost is a number from 0–65535, with higher values indicating higher costs. The spanning-tree algorithm will use the path cost to decide which interface to block.

41. ☑ **B.** UDP is the only protocol within the list that is not an AppleTalk protocol. User Datagram Protocol (UDP) is a connectionless TCP/IP protocol. Data Delivery Protocol (DDP) is very similar in function to UDP. It is a connectionless protocol on which other AppleTalk protocols run. AppleTalk Name Binding Protocol (NBP) is the protocol responsible for name-to-address translation, similar to DNS within TCP/IP. Zone Information Protocol (ZIP) defines how zone names-to-networks are mapped and exchanged over the network.

☒ **A.** DDP is incorrect because this is a fundamental protocol within the AppleTalk suite of protocols. **C.** NBP is incorrect because, as described above, it is instrumental in providing name-to-address conversion within AppleTalk networks. **D.** ZIP is also incorrect because it is also an AppleTalk protocol, as described above.

42. ☑ **A.** INTERFACE SERIAL1 and IP HELLO-INTERVAL EIGRP 5 120 successfully change the hello interval for a slow WAN link from one minute to two minutes. The default interval for LAN interfaces is five seconds. Hello intervals are configured on a per-interface basis; however, they should be the same for all router interfaces on a shared segment. The interface command for setting the hello interval rate is:

```
ip hello-interval eigrp autonomous-system-number seconds
```

☒ **B.** ROUTER EIGRP 5 and IP HELLO-INTERVAL 120 is incorrect because hello intervals are not set within router configuration mode, nor is the second command's syntax correct . **C.** The command IP HELLO-INTERVAL EIGRP 10 120 is incorrect because the format implies that it is configured within global configuration mode, which is incorrect, and also because the AS number of 10 is incorrect. **D.** INTERFACE SERIAL0 and IP HELLO-INTERVAL EIGRP 10 120 is incorrect because Serial 0 is not the interface connected to Router 3, nor is the AS number correct.

43. ☑ **A, B, and D.** are correct because you cannot configure a distribution list without an access list to go with it. To enter the DISTRIBUTE-LIST command, you need to know whether to apply it on the inbound or outbound interface. Finally, you need to know which access list to use for the DISTRIBUTE-LIST command. The number specified in the command must match an access list number.

☒ **C.** is incorrect because, although redistribution may be occurring, it doesn't necessarily have to. You might just be using only a single routing protocol.

44. ☑ **D.** DIALER-MAP IP 172.16.0.2 NAME CHI SPEED 56 250-9001 is correct in this case because the syntax for the DIALER MAP command is as follows:

```
dialer map protocol next-hop-address [name hostname] [speed 56 | 64]
[broadcast] dialer-string
```

Protocol refers to IP, IPX, AppleTalk, DECnet, VINES, and others, and in this case is IP. The next-hop-address in this case is 172.16.0.2 and the host name of the remote device is CHI. Note that this is used for PPP authentication or ISDN calls supporting caller ID. Speed 56 indicates the link speed in Kbps to use and the dialer string is the telephone number sent to the DCE device when packets with the specified next-hop-address are received.

☒ **A.** is incorrect because 172.16.0.1 is not the address of the next-hop router. **B.** is incorrect because, although 172.16.0.2 is the correct address for the next-hop router, DFW is not the correct host name of that router. **C.** is incorrect because, although CHI is the correct host name for the next-hop router, 172.16.0.1 is not the correct address for that router.

45. ☑ **A.** A ring group is a collection of Token Ring interfaces in one or more routers that share the same target ring number. As a result, each ring can bridge traffic to the other interfaces. A feature of the Cisco IOS is capability to support virtual rings, also known as ring groups. This IOS feature helps overcome the limitation that all IBM Token Ring chips can only process two ring numbers.

☒ **B.** is incorrect because IBM chips can only support two ring numbers. The likely source of confusion is that specifications for IBM Token Ring define a maximum of eight rings and seven bridges. This fact leads to the reason choice **C.** is incorrect, as well. Although the RIF supports encoding of up to eight rings, IBM Token Ring chips can still only support two ring numbers. **D.** is also incorrect because a RIF field supports a maximum of 14 rings, but the actual IBM Token Ring chip still only supports two ring numbers.

46. ☑ **A.** ACCESS-LIST 601 DENY ZONE DEVELOPMENT and ACCESS-LIST 601 PERMIT ADDITIONAL-ZONES is the correct answer because both meet the correct command syntax and specification requirement in the question. This list will successfully deny GETZONELIST requests for the zone *Development*, and permit all other zones. The command syntax for creating an AppleTalk zone access list is the following:

```
access-list access-list-number {deny | permit} zone zone-name
```

The command syntax for default zone actions is the following:

```
access-list access-list-number {deny | permit} additional-zone
```

☒ **B.** The configuration command ACCESS-LIST 601 DENY ZONE DEVELOPMENT is incorrect because it will deny all zones since it does not have an explicit permit at the end of the access list. **C.** ACCESS-LIST 601 DENY ZONE DEVELOPMENT and ACCESS-LIST 602 PERMIT ADDITIONAL-ZONES is incorrect because these commands actually define two filters, 601 and 602. List 601 denies all zones and 602 permits all zones. **D.** ACCESS-LIST 601 PERMIT ZONE ACCOUNTING FACTORY is an illegal command. Only one zone specification can be defined per access-list command.

47. ☑ **C.** The configuration command INTERFACE ETHERNET0 and interface configuration command APPLETALK GETZONELIST-FILTER 601 on both Router's 1 and 2 successfully filter GETZONELIST requests for the Development zone. It is applied to both Router 1 and 2 because both routers reside on the 105–109 network and inconsistent client services can be a result of only one router containing the filter. The command syntax for applying a GetZoneList filter is the following:

```
appletalk getzonelist-filter access-list-number
```

☒ **A.** These configuration commands are incorrect because they only apply the filter to one of the routers on network 105–109. **D.** The configuration commands are incorrect for the same reason as A.. **B.** The configuration command APPLETALK ACCESS-GROUP 601 is incorrect because the keyword ACCESS-GROUP applies this command as a data filter.

48. ☑ **D.** 90 and 100, respectively, because the administrative distance for EIGRP is 90 and for IGRP is 100. Administrative distance is assigned by Cisco to each type of routing protocol in the event that two routing protocols are running for one routed protocol, such as IP. In this event, if the same route is learned by both routing protocols, the protocol with the lowest administrative distance will be the one selected for entry within the routing table (lower distance value means a higher precedence). The other will become a floating route that will only be seen in the routing table if the higher-precedent protocol has lost its route to that destination. The default administrative distance is configured for most routing protocols.

☒ **A.** 100 for both is incorrect because EIGRP's default administrative distance is 90. **B.** 90 and 120, respectively, is incorrect because IGRP's administrative distance is 100; **C,** 90 for both is incorrect for the same reason.

49. ☑ **B.** Cisco IOS supports both Cisco's own Frame Relay encapsulation and Internet Engineering Task Force (IETF) encapsulation. You will need to use IETF encapsulation when connecting to another vendor's router.

☒ **A, C, and D.** are incorrect because Cisco only supports the two encapsulation methods discussed above.

50. ☑ **A, C, and E.** EIGRP-BANDWIDTH-PERCENT allows a user to set a bandwidth limit for EIGRP. EIGRP-TIMERS sets AT-EIGRP hello and holdtime timers. EIGRP-SPLITHORIZON enables split-horizon processing, generating AT-EIGRP updates. Note that you must also use the command **appletalk protocol eigrp** on every directly connected interface participating in the AppleTalk EIGRP routing process.

☒ **B.** REDISTRIBUTE EIGRP APPLETALK, is wrong because redistribution occurs automatically, and it is not necessary to explicitly enable redistribution unless you have an older version of IOS. **D.** APPLETALK SAP-INCREMENTAL EIGRP *autonomous-system-number,* is wrong because SAPs are used with IPX, not AppleTalk.

51. ☑ **D.** The correct syntax to enable BGP routing is ROUTER(config)#ROUTER BGP *autonomous-system.*

☒ **A, B, and C.** are incorrect because of improper syntax. **A.** does not begin with the key word ROUTER. **B.** does not include the AS number, and **C** is incorrect because of a bogus keyword, AS.

52. ☑ **D.** Token Ring to Ethernet bridging. In this case we need to cross bridging domains. Ethernet generally uses transparent bridging and Token Ring generally uses SRB bridging. It is also worth noting that S/TLB is a specific Cisco IOS feature rather than an industry standard. There are also a number of issues that need to be considered in SR/TLB, including MTU size, lack of support for RIF in Ethernet frames, and different systems of MAC addressing.

☒ **A.** is incorrect because the underlying protocols such as IP, IPX, and AppleTalk cannot be directly converted from one to another. **B and C are incorrect for the same reason. SR/TLB is a technology for communicating between Ethernet networks and Token Ring networks.**

53. ☑ **B.** First-in-first-out (FIFO) queuing. Because of the high-speed nature of LAN interfaces, they are less likely to constitute a bottleneck, especially in WANs. As the name indicates, this queuing technique forwards packets out the interface in the order that they were received from incoming interfaces.

☒ **A.** Weighted fair queuing (WFQ) is incorrect because this technique is most often found on slower-speed interfaces such as serial interfaces, for which it is the default. **C.** Priority queuing is incorrect for the same reason. **D.** Custom queuing is also incorrect for the same reason.

54. ☑ **D.** Inverse ARP resolves a remote network-layer address with a local DLCI, even if the remote network address does not belong to the local subnet. One key point to note is that Inverse ARP only resolves network addresses of remote Frame Relay connections that are directly connected. This causes problems in a partial mesh topology.

☒ **A.** is incorrect because Inverse ARP is used with Frame Relay, not ATM. **B.** is incorrect because an LMI is a DLCI enhancement and Inverse ARP maps network addresses to local DLCIs. **C.** is incorrect because inverse ARP dynamically maps remote network-layer addresses to local DLCIs, but map statements statically map remote network-layer addresses to local DLCIs.

55. ☑ **C and D.** are the correct answers because DEBUG DIALER is used to show all DDR calling statistics and DEBUG Q931 shows the call setup, monitoring, and teardown of an ISDN connection.
☒ **A.** is incorrect because the DEBUG IP is only the first part of the DEBUG IP command. You would most likely check DEBUG IP PACKET to observe more detailed information when troubleshooting an IP network. **B.** is incorrect because CLEAR LINE X resets asynchronous interfaces and terminates current connections.

56. ☑ **A, C and D.** While DLSw+ conforms to the DLSw specification in RFC 1795, DLSw+ also adds many enhanced features, including four encapsulation types instead of just TCP/IP, reachability caching, border-peer groups and on-demand peers, and additional back-up, security, and load balancing features, all of which are not defined in the original DLSw standard.
☒ **B.** is incorrect because, although the DLSw specification mentions the use of reachability caching, it does not say that it is required. A Cisco DLSw+ peer maintains both a local and remote-reachability cache.

57. ☑ **C.** Normal is correct since data types that do not meet the criteria for classifying traffic defined by the priority-list commands are directed to the normal queue. The list-queue types are for priority queuing and the order in which they are listed reflects their level of priority.
☒ **A.** High is incorrect since data types will have to be explicitly configured to be directed to this queue. The only exception here would be a keepalive packet, if used. These are assigned to the high queue by default. **B.** Medium is incorrect because, for packets to be directed to this queue, they must be specifically configured. **D.** Low is incorrect for the same reason.

58. ☑ **A.** PRIORITY-LIST 5 PROTOCOL APPLETALK MEDIUM LIST 601 is the appropriate command to apply a filter to the AppleTalk routing protocol in a priority cue. The correct syntax is router(config)#**priority-list** *list-number* **protocol** *protocol-name* {**high|medium|normal|low**}

queue-keyword keyword-value. In this case, the keyword is list, which specifies the use of an AppleTalk access list.

☒ **B.** PRIORITY-LIST 1 APPLETALK MEDIUM APPLETALK 601, is wrong because in order to use an access list, you must use the keyword list. **C.** QUEUE-LIST 1 PROTOCOL APPLETALK MEDIUM 601, is wrong because the **queue-list** command is used for custom queuing, not priority queuing. **D.**, QUEUE-LIST 5 PROTOCOL MEDIUM LIST 601, **is wrong because not only is the queue-list** command used for custom queuing rather than priority queuing, but custom queuing specifies queues by number, not by high, medium, normal, or low. Custom queuing has a total of 16 queues, not just the 4 that priority queuing has.

59. ☑ **A.** Periodic broadcasts are not a benefit of an interior gateway protocol or a characteristic of OSPF. Periodic broadcasts of routing information are typical of distance vector routing protocols, such as RIP, because they do not learn information pertaining to their neighboring routers nor do they have a mechanism for sending only changed information. OSPF more efficiently uses network bandwidth once routers share a common topology database since only changes are sent to its neighbor routers.

☒ **B.** Support for VLSM is incorrect because it is a benefit of OSPF since OSPF sends subnet information within its routing updates. **C.** Fast convergence is incorrect because it is a benefit of OSPF and link-state protocols. **D.** Scalability is incorrect because it is a benefit of OSPF, due to its concept of areas.

60. ☑ **A, B, C and D.** Redistribution supports all protocols including BGP, EGP, EIGRP, IGRP, ISIS, ISO-IGRP, mobile routes, on-demand stub routes, OSPF, RIP, and static routes.

61. ☑ **C and D.** Frame Relay requires two routers. One must be the data circuit-terminating equipment (DCE) and the other, the data terminal equipment (DTE). Note that the provider is almost always the DCE end.

☒ **A and B.** are incorrect because Frame Relay requires routers, not switches. This is changing, however, since many high-end switches have routing cards. These are usually referred to as Layer 3 switches.

62. ☑ **D.** The syntax for this task is to first indicate the backup interface in case the primary link fails. The command syntax for this is BACKUP INTERFACE *interface-name*. Second, Joe defines the number of seconds to wait before enabling the backup link when the primary link fails, then defines the number of seconds to wait after a primary link is available that must be reached before the backup line is torn down. This is accomplished by the command BACKUP DELAY {*enable-delay* | **never**} {*disable-delay* | **never**}.

☒ **A.** is incorrect because of the hyphen between backup and interface, as well as the hyphen between backup and delay. **B.** is incorrect because of the hyphen between backup and interface; **C.** is incorrect because of the hyphen between backup and delay.

63. ☑ **A, C and D.** DUAL mode allows a router to communicate with peers using either RSRB or DLSw+. This provides an easy migration path from RSRB to DLSw+. Standards compliance mode allows a router running DLSw+ to dynamically detect another router using RFC standards during the capabilities exchange setup step. This mode is primarily used when connecting Cisco routers to other manufacturer's equipment. Enhanced mode allows Cisco routers running DLSw+ to dynamically detect other Cisco routers running DLSw+ and makes all DLSw+ features available to SNA and NetBIOS networks.

☒ **B and E.** are incorrect because they don't exist.

64. ☑ **D.** The interface configuration command "priority-group 5" is the correct answer because this is the command used to specify a priority list with an interface. Since the correct answer from the previous question defined priority list 5, answer D is correct over answer A, despite the same command syntax.

☒   **A.** The command syntax to specify a priority list to an interface is the following:

```
priority-group list
```

The interface configuration COMMAND PRIORITY-GROUP 1 is incorrect because it contains the incorrect priority list number. **B.** QUEUE-GROUP 5 is incorrect because the keyword QUEUE-GROUP makes this an illegal command. **C.** The command PRIORITY-LIST 1 is incorrect because this command syntax is also invalid.

65. ☑   **D.** Hello and keepalive intervals. There is no concept of keepalive intervals within the OSPF protocol. A *hello interval* represents the amount of time between hello packets. A *dead interval* represents the amount of time a router waits to receive another hello packet before it assumes the neighboring router is down. For Cisco routers, the hello interval is 10 seconds by default and the dead interval is four times the hello interval, or 40 seconds by default. ☒   **A.** Area identifier is incorrect because this 32-bit piece of information, indicating the OSPF area to which a router belongs, is contained within a hello packet. **B.** Authentication information is incorrect because it also is contained within the Hello protocol. Authentication type and a password string would be included if the optional authentication feature of OSPF were configured. **C.** Router priority is incorrect because this parameter is used to negotiate which router will become the DR and BDR within a multi-access segment.

66. ☑   **A.** The SHOW IP BGP command shows the BGP route information table. ☒   **B.** is incorrect because it shows the entire IP routing table. **C.** is incorrect because there is no such command as SHOW IP BGP ROUTE. **D.** is incorrect because it shows BGP paths.

67. ☑   **D.** OSPF is a link-state protocol and snapshot routing does not support link-state protocols.

    ☒   **A, B and C.** are incorrect because they are distance vector protocols and snapshot routing supports the common distance vector protocols, including RTMP, RTP, RIP, IGRP, and SAP.

68. ☑   **C.** IRB can only be used on Ethernet networks. IRB is the follow-on solution to concurrent routing and bridging, but is an improvement because IRB allows nonroutable or local packets to be bridged among the bridged interfaces in the same bridge group, while routable traffic is routed to other routed interfaces or bridge groups. Note that IRB supports IP, IPX, and AppleTalk.
    ☒   **A.** is incorrect because IRB does not support source-route bridging. **B.** is an incorrect choice because it is not Ethernet. Knowing the difference between CRB and IRB is important. CRB allows bridging and routing of the same protocol to coexist on the same router, but never mixes the two. IRB allows bridged and routed traffic of the same protocol to be interchanged.

69. ☑   **A, B and C.** The SHOW SOURCE-BRIDGE command displays information about the explorer packets that the router has transmitted and received, as well as information about the ring groups and ring and bridge number of the ring. SHOW RIF displays how the RIF was learned, the number of minutes since the last response was received directly from this node, and the RIF. SHOW INTERFACES TOKENRING displays information about the Token Ring interfaces and the state of source-route bridging.
    ☒   **D.** is incorrect because you cannot use this abbreviation for source-route. **E.** is incorrect because SHOW SOURCE-BRIDGE and SHOW RIF are two separate commands.

70. ☑   **A.** Slow-speed serial interfaces is correct because of the overhead that compression imposes on a router. The interface would have to constitute a bottleneck in order for this technique to increase efficiency in the overall packet-per-second (PPS) performance of the router. All of the other options represent high-speed interfaces for which the process routines that compression would impose may actually reduce overall data throughput.

☒ **B.** High-speed serial interfaces (HSSI), is incorrect because typically the high-speed links that these interfaces support are less likely to constitute a bottleneck, since the sheer bandwidth is unlikely. **C.** ATM interfaces is incorrect because it is a high-speed interface. **D.** Ethernet interfaces is incorrect because it's also a high-speed LAN interface.

71. ☑ **B.** PRIORITY-LIST INTERFACE is the correct answer because this command will allow incoming traffic for a particular interface to be set to a specific priority level, once forwarded to an outbound interface. Since the queue type was specified as medium, it should be obvious that Susan is using priority queuing.
☒ **A.** PRIORITY-LIST PROTOCOL is incorrect since it is used to establish queuing priorities based on protocol types. **C.** PRIORITY-LIST DEFAULT is incorrect because this command is used to change the default queue to be used for unspecified traffic. **D.** PRIORITY-GROUP LIST is incorrect because this command assigns a priority list to an interface for outbound packets.

72. ☑ **A.** Dialer profiles came into existence with the release of Cisco IOS 11.2.
☒ **B.** is incorrect because if Joe's router is only loaded with IOS version 11.1, then he will not be able to configure a dialer profile. **C.** is incorrect because he can configure a dialer profile on an IPX network with Cisco IOS version 11.2. **D.** is incorrect because Joe only needs Cisco IOS version 11.2, not 11.3.

Part 6

Test Yourself: CIT
Practice Exams
(Exam 640-406)

Test Yourself:
CIT Practice
Exam 1
Questions

Q
$_{\&}A$

Before you register for the actual exam, take the following test and see how you make out. Set a timer for 105 minutes—the time you'll have to take the live CCNP Cisco Internetwork Troubleshooting 4.0 certification exam—and answer the following 77 questions in the time allotted. Once you've finished, turn to the CIT Practice Exam 1 Answers section and check your score to see if you passed. Good luck!

CIT Practice Exam 1 Questions

1. In a large-scale, meshed RIP routing network with 14 routers in the longest path, how long will it take routing in the network to stabilize?

    A. Eight minutes, since this is the maximum route stabilization time defined in the protocol

    B. Eight minutes, since it takes 90 seconds for the invalid timer period to expire and the route to no longer be advertised, followed by an additional seven minutes and 30 seconds for the route to be flushed through the entire network

    C. Seven minutes and 30 seconds for the route to be flushed through the entire network

    D. 12 minutes and 30 seconds, since it takes 90 seconds for the invalid timer period to expire and the route to no longer be advertised, followed by 270 seconds for the flush timer to expire, and an additional seven minutes and 30 seconds for the route to be flushed through the entire network.

2. Which output from SHOW IPX INTERFACE ONLY is not displayed in SHOW IPX INTERFACE BRIEF?

    A. Assigned network address

    B. Encapsulation

    C. Interface status

    D. Filters

3. Which one of the following is a correct command for setting a trunk on a port?

A. SET TRUNK NONNEGOTIATE

B. SET TRUNK NEGOTIATE

C. SET TRUNK ENABLE

D. SET TRUNK DISABLE

4. The DIALER MAP command on the BRI interface is used to define whom to call. We are at the console of a router in Annapolis, Maryland with an IP of 10.10.2.1 and a MASK of 255.255.255.0. Which of the following is the correct command to call to the next-hop address 10.10.2.2 at 202-555-1212 in Washington, D.C.?

A. AMD(config-if)#DIALER MAP 10.10.2.2 255.255.255.0 555-1212

B. WDC(config-if)# DIALER MAP 10.10.2.1 255.255.255.0 5551212

C. AMD(config-if)# DIALER MAP IP 10.10.2.2 12025551212

D. None of the above

5. How are external routes to an IGRP autonomous system learned?

A. Border Gateway Protocol/Exterior Gateway Protocol

B. Redistribution from another routing protocol or a static route

C. Forwarded from another IGRP router

D. From a directly connected interface

6. Which of the following is the complete output from the command SHOW ATM VC?

A. VCD used for local VCC identification on the router

B. VPI/VCI, peak rates, average rates, burst cells and interface status

C. AAL5 encapsulation method as AAL5sanp, AAL5nlpid or AAL5mux

D. All of the above

7. You have a Catalyst 5000 with port 1/1 trunked to a 4700 router. There are four VLANs on the 48 Fast Ethernet ports of the switch. You need to capture traffic from the VLANs to the router for analysis and you found port 5/12 is unused. To achieve your goal without interruption to the network, what must you do?

A. Plug a sniffer to supervisor port 1/2, connect a terminal to console port, log into ENABLE mode and send SET SPAN ENABLE

B. Plug a sniffer to port 5/12, connect a terminal to console port, log in to ENABLE mode and send SET SPAN ENABLE

C. Plug a sniffer to port 5/12, connect a terminal to console port, log in to ENABLE mode, send SET SPAN 1/1 5/12 BOTH then SET SPAN ENABLE

D. Plug a sniffer to port 5/12, connect a terminal to console port, log in to ENABLE mode, send SET SPAN ENABLE, then SET SPAN 5/12 1/1 RX/TX

8. If you enter DEBUG DIALER for diagnostic purposes and perform a PIN, what type of problems can you diagnose?

A. Traffic has passed the dialer list and if the correct phone number is associated with the IP address

B. DHCP is correctly associating phone numbers with IP addresses

C. Analog phone lines, such as a *busy*, or a speed mismatch

D. Errors or dropped packets due to a noisy analog line or packet collisions

9. Which of the following is NOT an OSPF link-state update?

A. Link-state acknowledge

B. AS external advertisement

C. Summary link advertisement

D. Network link advertisement

10. Which of the following is a quality of Internal Flash Memory?

A. Allows additional memory for alternative IOS images of configuration

B. Is where start-up configurations are usually saved

C. Can be used to store IOS software images or backup

D. None of the above

11. When there is a mismatch of the speed settings between the NIC and the port on the Catalyst, what is likely to happen?

A. The Catalyst switch will shut down automatically

B. The NIC card will crash the computer instantly

C. Both A and B

D. Excessive collisions will be showing on the corresponding router system log and the switched port will be shut down automatically

12. Which of the following is NOT an issue when enabling CHAP on a PPP encapsulated connection?

A. CHAP must be configured on both the source and remote router

B. Implementing CHAP to increase security requires additional changes in the dialer map

C. CHAP requires that a user name and password be specified for the remote Cisco router

D. None of the above

13. What are the three types of routes contained in the IGRP?

A. Interior, system, exterior

B. Load, delay, system

C. Flag, system, exterior

D. None of the above

14. To view individual PID for excessive CPU usage, which Cisco IOS command is used?

A. SHOW CPU PID

B. SHOW PID CPU

C. SHOW CPU PROCESSES

D. SHOW PROCESSES CPU

15. The collision rate of an Interface on a CISCO 4500 router can be obtained with which statement?

A. SHOW COLLISIONS INTERFACES ETHERNET 0
B. SHOW INTERFACE SERIAL 0 COLLISIONS RATE
C. SHOW INTERFACES SERIAL 0 COLLISIONS
D. SHOW INT E 1

16. A router that has multiple interfaces in various areas is called an *area border* router. This router will maintain a separate link-state network topology for each attached area. Which answer shows the main OSPF features?

A. Supporting cost metric
B. Allows multi-path/equal path
C. Stub areas
D. Database description

17. Which of the following services cannot be used with the Cisco DEBUG command?

A. AAA
B. ATM
C. RIP
D. Modem

18. Which of the following shows parts of an Ethernet frame?

A. Preamble, destination address, source address, and data field
B. Data address, preamble, destination address, and frame check sequence
C. Preamble, destination address, protocol, and data type
D. Destination address, preamble, source address, and data address

19. Which command would be used to review route maps associated with community routing tags?

    A. SHOW ROUTE MAP
    B. SHOW ROUTE-MAP
    C. SHOW MAP-ROUTE
    D. SHOW MAP ROUTE

20. Which one of the following is NOT valid Cisco SNMP commands?

    A. SNMP-SERVER COMMUNITY <name> RO
    B. SNMP-SERVER COMMUNITY RO
    C. SNMP-SERVER COMMUNITY RW
    D. SNMP-SERVER COMMUNITY <name> RW

21. What is the cause of an Open Lobe Fault message at the console?

    A. Relay open in the multistation access unit (MAU)
    B. Station is waiting for data frame
    C. Station is waiting for token frame
    D. None of the above

22. Which of the following is NOT an extended IP ping option?

    A. TTL
    B. Type of service
    C. DF bit option
    D. Data pattern

23. What is the command to view a list of micro code on a Cisco router?

    A. LIST MICROCODE
    B. CHECK MICROCODE
    C. SHOW MICROCODE
    D. FIND MICROCODE

24. On an IP network, users can access some remote hosts but not others on remote networks. What could most likely be the problem?

A. The DNS configuration

B. Misconfigured subnet masks or addresses on hosts

C. Not having a default gateway

D. None of the above

25. Which of the following is not a Cisco-supported protocol for the accounting feature?

A. AppleTalk

B. DecNet

C. IP

D. IPX

Refer to the Following Scenario to Answer Questions 26–27

The following is a sample output from the SHOW BUFFERS command.

```
Router# show buffers

Buffer elements:
 500 in free list (500 max allowed)
 1840000 hits, 20 misses, 0 created

Public buffer pools:
Small buffers, 104 bytes (total 50, permanent 50):
     50 in free list (20 min, 150 max allowed)
     124000 hits, 22100 misses, 0 trims, 0 created
     0 failures (0 no memory)
Middle buffers, 600 bytes (total 25, permanent 25):
     25 in free list (10 min, 150 max allowed)
     1231270 hits, 1220 misses, 0 trims, 0 created
     0 failures (0 no memory)
Big buffers, 1524 bytes (total 50, permanent 50):
     50 in free list (5 min, 150 max allowed)
     312320 hits, 1222 misses, 0 trims, 12 created
     0 failures (0 no memory)
VeryBig buffers, 4520 bytes (total 10, permanent 10):
```

```
         10 in free list (0 min, 100 max allowed)
         13200 hits, 90 misses, 0 trims, 0 created
         0 failures (0 no memory)

   Large buffers, 5024 bytes (total 0, permanent 0):
         0 in free list (0 min, 10 max allowed)
         0 hits, 0 misses, 0 trims, 0 created
         0 failures (0 no memory)
   Huge buffers, 18024 bytes (total 0, permanent 0):
         0 in free list (0 min, 4 max allowed)
         0 hits, 0 misses, 0 trims, 0 created
         0 failures (0 no memory)
```

26. Which statement is true regarding network traffic on this sample?

A. A majority of the traffic is classified in the range of 105–600 bytes long

B. A majority of the traffic is classified in the range of 601–1524 bytes long

C. A majority of the traffic is classified in the range of 1525–5024 bytes long

D. A majority of the traffic is classified in the range of 5025–18024 bytes long

27. What conclusion can be drawn regarding the traffic in this scenario?

A. Small buffers require adjustments because of missed packets

B. Middle buffers require adjustments because of missed packets

C. Big buffers require adjustments because of created buffers

D. The existing overall buffer allocations are sufficient to handle the traffic. No adjustments are required on any of the system buffers.

28. To get a quick listing of the interfaces carrying IPX traffic on a router which command(s) would you issue?

A. SHOW IPX ROUTE

B. SHOW IPX TRAFFIC

C. SHOW IPX INTERFACE

D. Both SHOW IPX ROUTE and SHOW IPX INTERFACE

29. Which of the following is used for statistics gathering via SNMP?

   A. CiscoView
   B. Resource Manager
   C. TrafficDirector
   D. UserTracker

Refer to the Following Scenario to Answer Question 30

Consider the following SHOW VERSION output sample:

```
Router>show  version
Cisco Internetwork Operating System Software
IOS (tm) 2500 Software (C2500-I-L), Version 11.2(10a)P,
RELEASE SOFTWARE (fc1)
Copyright (c) 1986-1997 by cisco Systems, Inc.
Compiled Tue 02-Dec-97 23:28 by ccai
Image text-base: 0x030239EC, data-base: 0x00001000

ROM: System Bootstrap, Version 11.0(10c)XA, PLATFORM
SPECIFIC RELEASE SOFTWARE (fc1)
BOOTFLASH: 3000 Bootstrap Software (IGS-BOOT-R), Version
11.0(10c)XA, PLATFORM SPECIFIC RELEASE SOFTWARE (fc1)

Router uptime is 123 day, 1 hour, 8 minutes
System restarted by power-on
System image file is "flash:c2500-i-l.112-10a.P", booted
via flash

cisco AS2509-RJ (68030) processor (revision I) with
2048K/2048K bytes of memory.
Processor board ID 06174808, with hardware revision
00000000
Bridging software.
X.25 software, Version 2.0, NET2, BFE and GOSIP
compliant.
1 Ethernet/IEEE 802.3 interface(s)
1 Serial network interface(s)
8 terminal line(s)
32K bytes of non-volatile configuration memory.
8192K bytes of processor board System flash (Read ONLY)

Configuration register is 0x2102
```

30. Which statement is false?

A. This router has the IOS Version of 11.2(10a)P
B. The router was restarted by RELOAD
C. This is an access server router
D. It has a total of 4MB DRAM

31. To perform informational lookups of Name Binding Protocol (NBP) entities on a router that carries AppleTalk protocol, which command would you use?

A. TEST APPLETALK
B. SHOW APPLETALK TRAFFIC
C. SHOW APPLETALK ZONE
D. None of the above

32. You are a Cisco Engineer for a major telecom company. You have been asked to work with the E-mail administrator to test the E-mail service's availability for Internet users, which must go through a Cisco router interface. The extended access list for users to connect to the E-mail server is already set up. What command do you use to verify that the Email server is listening to the SMTP port without using an E-mail account?

A. PING
B. EXTENDED PING
C. TRACEROUTE
D. TELNET

33. What is the first default port on a CISCO 4000 router and a Catalyst 5500 switch?

A. Port 0/0 for the router and port 1/1 for the Catalyst
B. Port 0/0 for the router and port 0/0 for the Catalyst
C. Port 1/1 for the router and port 0/0 for the Catalyst
D. Port 1/1 for the router and port 1/1 for the Catalyst

34. At which layer does SPID verification occur?

    A. Interface BRI

    B. Q.921

    C. Q.931

    D. LCP

35. You are the Cisco engineer for a large bank. You need to manage the network's Cisco routers and switches using network management software. You must manage VLAN on Catalyst switches, router configuration, inventory, and individual devices, and gather statistics via SNMP & RMON. Which one of the following network management software tools will be the most helpful?

    A. CiscoWorks 2000

    B. HP Open View

    C. CiscoView

    D. None of the above

36. Which one of the following is NOT a valid command for setting the duplex on a Fast Ethernet port of a CISCO Catalyst 5000?

    A. SET PORT DUPLEX 2/4 <half>

    B. SET PORT DUPLEX 2/2 <full>

    C. SET PORT DUPLEX 2/8 <half>

    D. SET PORT DUPLEX 1/8 <full>

37. Which of following ISDN switch types is not supported by the Cisco IOS?

    A. Basic net

    B. Basic-ts013

    C. Basic-1tr6

    D. Basic dms-100

38. Using the SHOW IPX INTERFACE command, which of the following would be used to verify whether the data-link layer is up?

A. CORRECT IP ADDRESS

B. LINE PROTOCOL IS UP

C. APPLIED ACCESS-LIST IS CORRECT

D. APPROPRIATE SWITCHING MODE IS SET

39. Multiple ports can be grouped into a VLAN on a Catalyst with one SET VLAN command. Which one of the following commands is correct?

A. SET VLAN 10 5/1-12

B. SET VLAN 10 5/1-5/12

C. SET VLAN 10 2-4/1-12

D. All of the above

40. Which one of the following commands can be used for checking SPID status?

A. SHOW SPID STATUS

B. SHOW ISDN STATUS

C. SHOW RUNNING CONFIG

D. DEBUG ISDN STATUS

41. When determining reasonable utilization levels, which one of the following should you consider?

A. Time of day

B. Applications behavior

C. Traffic patterns

D. Network equipment

42. What is the best definition of a late collision?

   A. One station starts transmitting before another station stops transmitting

   B. Two stations start transmitting 64-byte packets at the same time

   C. One station continues transmitting after it should have stopped and another station begins transmitting

   D. One station transmits more than 513 bits when another station starts transmitting

43. At which layer of the OSI model does a packet become a frame?

   A. Layer 1

   B. Layer 2

   C. Layer 3

   D. Layer 4

44. To troubleshoot incorrect routes for AppleTalk with multiple Cisco routers in your network, you need to gather information such as AppleTalk addresses of the directly connected routers. Which of the following is the IOS command used to do this?

   A. SHOW CDP NEIGHBORS DETAIL

   B. SHOW VERSION

   C. SHOW APPLETALK ARP

   D. SHOW IP ARP

45. How does a good problem solving model help you?

   A. It identifies problems

   B. It isolates problems

   C. It resolves problems

   D. None of the above

46. Which of the following is NOT a function of the Token Ring active monitor?

A. Initiates the neighbor notification process

B. Purges the ring

C. Maintains the master clock

D. Mediates collisions

47. Port numbers are divided into three ranges. What are the range names and port numbers?

A. Well Known (0–1024), Registered (1025–49150), Dynamic/Private (49151–65535)

B. Dynamic/Private (0–1024), Well Known (1025–49150), and Registered (49151–65535)

C. Well Known (0–1023), Registered (1024-49151), and Dynamic/Private (49152–65535)

D. Registered (0–1024), Dynamic/Private (1025–49150), Well Known (49151–65535)

48. You are the network engineer for a Major International Bank and have been told that TCP/IP users cannot communicate with a group of servers. Which application would you use to send packets of information to a specific address and receive host and timing information about each hop?

A. Ping

B. Traceroute

C. SNMP

D. Netstat

49. What is the most probable cause of an alarm indicating a duplicate hardware address?

A. A LEC has multiple entries in an ELAN

B. Two Ethernet cards have the same MAC address

C. The two rings of a dual attached FDDI ring accidentally get cross connected

D. The locally administered router MAC addresses get duplicated

50. What is the purpose of a sliding window?

A. It allows TCP to adjust the size of the packet to maximize transmission time

B. It allows TCP to send an acknowledgement prior to completely receiving the frame

C. It allows TCP to send all the packets prior to acknowledging the transmission

D. It allows TCP to adjust the number of packets it sends at one time prior to an acknowledgement

51. What is the function of connection-oriented protocols?

A. They acknowledge each frame or packet of data received

B. They do not acknowledge each frame or packet of data received

C. They acknowledge only high-priority frames or packets of data received

D. None of the above

52. What are the two authentication methods that PPP uses?

A. Logon and reverse calling

B. User ID and privilege authentication

C. Protocol authentication and Port ID

D. Password Authentication Protocol and Challenge Handshake Authentication Protocol

53. Internet Control Message Protocol (ICMP) is a Layer 3 protocol only. Is this true or false? Why?

A. True, ICMP only functions at Layer 3

B. True, ICMP performs out of band management but only at Layer 3

C. False, ICMP performs out of band management at Layer 3 and above

D. False, ICMP performs out of band management at Layer 2 and Layer 3

54. Which protocol provides alternate paths, dynamic flow though the network, and potential for non-sequential delivery of packets and frames?

A. Connection-oriented protocol

B. Connectionless protocol

C. Private virtual circuit

D. SNMP

55. What does Cisco use to ensure connectivity for its serial line?

A. Ping

B. Keepalive protocol

C. Watchdog

D. Non-Broadcast MultiAccess Service (NBMA)

56. You are the Network Engineer of a major international bank. Your users can communicate with other users on their own TCP/IP network. After their workstation was relocated to another department on a different network segment, a user cannot communicate with users that reside on another TCP/IP network within the company's enterprise network. What is most likely the problem?

A. The server address has changed and users were not notified to change their workstations

B. A printer was added to the segment using an unassigned IP address

C. The gateway was never changed after the workstation was moved

D. The loss of communications on segments is normal from time to time, so there is no problem

57. What does Token Ring technology allow?

A. That stations may transmit whenever they are ready to transmit

B. That two stations may transmit whenever they are ready to transmit

C. That stations may transmit whenever there is a free token available to transmit

D. That multiple stations may transmit whenever there is one free token available

58. Which Cisco router command is least likely to be used when determining problems with your PVC link state?

A. SH CDP NE

B. SH INT

C. SH FR LMI

D. SH FR PVC

59. What is the correct Cisco IPX addressing format for a workstation on network 123 with Media Access Control (MAC) address of 0080C712202D?

A. 00000123.0080.C712.202D

B. 00000123:0080:C712:202D

C. 0080.C712.202D.00000123

D. 0080:C712:202D:00000123

60. DARPA designed TCP/IP with how many layers in its reference model?

A. Four

B. Five

C. Six

D. Seven

61. The Cisco router command, DEBUG LAPD, provides what type of information?

    A. Physical connection between local and remote

    B. Call setup and cause/diagnostic

    C. Level 2 X.25 information

    D. Level 3 X.25 information

62. Which statement about NetWare Link Service Protocol (NLSP) is accurate?

    A. NLSP is more commonly deployed than RIP in small-sized and medium-sized network environments

    B. NLSP is a link-state protocol

    C. NLSP updates its routing table every 60 seconds

    D. It uses a metric calculation to determine link cost

63. Which TCP/IP Internet address format class is used for experimenting?

    A. Class B

    B. Class C

    C. Class D

    D. Class E

64. Identify, in order, the format of a User-to-Network Interface (UNI) header structure for an ATM cell.

    A. Virtual path identifier, virtual circuit identifier, payload type, cell loss priority, header error check

    B. Virtual path identifier, virtual circuit identifier, payload type, cell loss priority

    C. Header error check, virtual path identifier, virtual circuit identifier, payload type, cell loss priority, generic flow control

    D. Generic flow control, virtual path identifier, virtual circuit identifier, payload type, cell loss priority, header error check

65. What are the most important criteria for a workstation to select its initial Novell server on a bindery connection?

A. Based on the highest IPX external network number

B. Based on the highest IPX internal network number

C. Based on the first GNS response it receives

D. Based on the first RIP response it receives

66. Which of the following defines an IPX node number and network?

A. (32-bit)network; (48-bit)node

B. (48-bit)network; (32-bit)node

C. (48-bit)node; (32-bit)network

D. (32-bit)node; (48-bit)network

67. The ISDN Basic Rate Interface is made up of how many channels?

A. One

B. Two

C. Three

D. Four

68. Which one of the following numbering schemes does AppleTalk use to differentiate nodes?

A. Hard address

B. Automatically assigned according to MAC

C. Dynamic addressing scheme

D. None of the above

69. An extended AppleTalk network allows which of the following?

A. 127 hosts

B. 127 servers

C. 253 hosts/servers

D. Both A and B

70. Which test pattern is normally used to test network devices that are dropping bits?

A. All ones

B. All zeros

C. Framed ones

D. Quasi

71. AppleTalk uses source socket numbers to differentiate among multiple processes running on various nodes. Source socket numbers are defined at which layer of the OSI model?

A. Layer 2

B. Layer 3

C. Layer 4

D. Layer 5

72. Which of the following is NOT a task performed by the MAC layer?

A. It performs calculations on CRC and places information in the FCS field

B. It presents a serial bit stream to the physical layer for transmission

C. It monitors broadcast traffic

D. It provides congestion control

73. Which layer of the OSI model most closely corresponds to users working with E-mail on a workstation?

A. Physical

B. Network

C. Session

D. Application

74. Which Cisco IOS command do you use to display the Zone Information Table?

A. SHOW APPLE ARP

B. SHOW APPLETALK NBP

C. SHOW APPLE ZONE

D. SHOW ROUTING TABLE

75. Which one of the following statements is true?

A. LLC type 1 Ethernet SNAP sets the DSAP to AA, the SSAP to AA, and the control field to AA

B. LLC type 1 Ethernet SNAP sets the DSAP to AA, the SSAP to 55, and the control field to 03

C. LLC type 1 Ethernet SNAP has a 5-byte protocol discriminator field after the 802.2 header

D. LLC type 1 Ethernet SNAP sets the DSAP to the destination address, the SSAP to the source address, and the control field to 03

76. What are the two primary IP protocols that are used at the transport layer of the OSI model?

A. Transmission Control Protocol (TCP)

B. Internet Control Message Protocol (ICMP)

C. User Datagram Protocol (UDP)

D. Simple Network Management Protocol (SNMP)

77. Which one of the following is the AppleTalk common routing protocol?

A. PAP

B. AFP

C. RTMP

D. DDP

Test Yourself:
CIT Practice
Exam 1 Answers

Q & A

The answers to the questions are in boldface, followed by a brief explanation. Some of the explanations detail the logic you should use to choose the correct answer, while others give factual reasons why the answer is correct. If you miss several questions on a similar topic, you should review the corresponding section in the CCNP Cisco Internetwork Troubleshooting 4.0 Study Guide before taking the test.

CIT Practice Exam I Answers

1. ☑ **B.** Eight minutes, since it takes 90 seconds for the invalid timer period to expire and the route to no longer be advertised, followed by an additional seven minutes and 30 seconds for the route to be flushed through the entire network. In a 14-hop network it would take 30 seconds for a route to be updated. It would then take an additional 30 seconds per hop for this routing information to be promulgated through to the other routers in the network. This takes a total of seven minutes and 30 seconds.
   ☒ **A.** is incorrect since the maximum parameters of the protocol definition are not applicable to this question. **B.** is false, since the invalid timer period has expired before the reconvergence process begins. **D.** is incorrect since the flush timer is not applicable to this question.

2. ☑ **D.** Filters will show in the command SHOW IPX INTERFACE ONLY, but not in SHOW IPX INTERFACE BRIEF.
   ☒ **A.** ASSIGNED NETWORK ADDRESS, is incorrect. It is displayed by the commands SHOW IPX INTERFACE and SHOW IPX INTERFACE BRIEF. **B.** Encapsulation, is incorrect. Encapsulation is displayed by both SHOW IPX INTERFACE and SHOW IPX INTERFACE BRIEF commands. **C.** Interface status is incorrect. Interface status is displayed by both SHOW IPX INTERFACE and SHOW IPX INTERFACE BRIEF commands.

3. ☑ **A.** The SET TRUNK NONNEGOTIATE performs the same function as SET TRUNK ON, but does not send trunk negotiation frames. To disable trunking on a port, use SET TRUNK OFF. To set a port back to its default, use SET TRUNK AUTO.

☒ **B.** SET TRUNK NEGOTIATE, is not a valid command. **C.** SET TRUNK ENABLE, **D.** SET TRUNK DISABLE, are also not valid commands. Keep in mind that not all commands are known as ENABLE or DISABLE.

4. ☑ **C.** AMD(config-if)# DIALER MAP IP 10.10.2.2 12025551212.
☒ **A.** AMD(config-if)# DIALER MAP 10.10.2.2 255.255.255.0 555-1212 is incorrect. The router AMD is trying to map to WDC but the keyword IP is missing. **B.** WDC(config-if)# DIALER MAP 10.10.2.1 255.255.255.0 5551212 is incorrect because the mapping is from the router WDC in Washington, D.C., trying to map to AMD without the IP keyword. **D.** None of the above is incorrect.

5. ☑ **B.** Redistribution from another routing protocol or a static route, since routes into an IGRP autonomous system can be redistributed into the system from another routing protocol. In addition, a static route can be created linking the IGRP autonomous system with other routes. This is the most complete of the answer choices.
☒ **A.** Border Gateway Protocol/Exterior Gateway Protocol is incorrect since, in addition to BGP and other EGPs, external routes can be learned through route redistribution from another routing protocol. **C.** Forwarded from another IGRP router is incorrect since forwarding into an autonomous system does not occur with IGRP. **D.** From a directly connected interface is incorrect since a directly connected interface is located within an autonomous system.

6. ☑ **D.** All of the above. SHOW ATM VC will output all of the above statements. VCD used for local VCC identification on the router is part of the output from SHOW ATM VC. VPI/VCI, peak rates, average rates; burst cells and interface status are part of the output from SHOW ATM VC. AAL5 encapsulation method as AAL5sanp, AAL5nlpid, or AAL5mux, is part of the output from SHOW ATM VC.
☒ **A, B,** and **C.** All are incorrect independent of each other.

7. ☑ **C.** By default, port 1/1 is the monitoring source and port for VLAN1. To monitor activities from port 5/12, the user needs to execute the command SET SPAN 1/1 5/12 BOTH. Then, when the command SET SPAN ENABLE is executed, port 5/12 will become the monitoring port for the sniffer.

☒ **A, B,** and **D** would have brought the network down and would have produced incorrect results because of the improper sequence of the commands.

8. ☑ **A.** Traffic has passed the dialer list and the correct phone number is associated with the IP address. This is correct since the DEBUG DIALER command will show information concerning how the dialer list is interpreted by the router. In addition, it will show if the correct IP address has been associated with the correct telephone number.

☒ **B.** DHCP is correctly associating phone numbers with IP addresses is incorrect. There would be no way of determining if there is a DHCP-related issue from entering DEBUG DIALER mode. **C.** Analog phone lines, such as a *busy*, or a speed mismatch, and **D.** Errors or dropped packets due to a noisy analog line or packet collisions are incorrect, since the DEBUG provides you with a problem symptom at the Q.931 layer, not at the physical layer.

9. ☑ **A.** Link-state acknowledge. A link-state acknowledgement is not a type of link-state update packet. A link-state acknowledgement packet replies to information concerning entries in the link-state database. Consequently, this is not an update packet.

☒ **B.** AS external advertisement is incorrect. It is a valid type of link-state update packet. **C.** Summary-link advertisement is incorrect since it is a valid type of link state update packet. **D.** Network-link advertisement is incorrect since it is a valid type of link-state update packet.

10. ☑ C. Internal Flash Memory can be used to store IOS software images or backup.

☒ A. is incorrect, since PCMCIA flash allows additional memory for alternative IOS images of configuration. B. is incorrect, since nonvolatile memory is where start-up configurations are usually saved. D. None of the above is incorrect.

11. ☑ D. There will be excessive collisions showing up on the router and the switched port will be shut down automatically by the Catalyst.

☒ A. The Catalyst switch will shut down automatically, and B. The NIC card will crash the computer instantly, are incorrect because they are not likely to happen. Therefore, C is incorrect.

12. ☑ D. None of the above. All of the other items are issues that must be considered in successfully configuring CHAP in a Cisco routing environment.

☒ A. CHAP must be configured on both the source and remote router, is incorrect. CHAP must be configured on both sides of the connection to work correctly. B. Implementing CHAP to increase security requires additional changes in the dialer map, is incorrect. Implementing CHAP to increase security requires additional changes, such as the name of the remote router to be specified in the dialer map. C. CHAP requires that a user name and password be specified for the remote Cisco router is incorrect. CHAP requires that a username and password be specified for the remote Cisco router at the global level or that AAA be configured on the router.

13. ☑ A. Interior, system, exterior. Interior routes are part of a router's directly connected interface. System routes are routes within the IGRP's autonomous system; Exterior routes are outside IGRP's autonomous system.

☒ B. Load, delay, system, and C. flag, system, exterior, are incorrect. Both answers contain incorrect route types.

14. ☑ **D.** SHOW PROCESSES CPU is used to view individual PID for excessive CPU usage and also to view five-second, one-minute, and five-minute CPU utilization.

☒ **A.** SHOW CPU PID is incorrect. It is not a Cisco IOS command. **B.** SHOW PID CPU is incorrect. It is also not a Cisco IOS command. **C.** SHOW CPU PROCESSES is incorrect. It is not a Cisco IOS command, either.

15. ☑ **D.** SHOW INT E 1. SHOW INTERFACES Ethernet <port#> provide statistics of the Ethernet port. The list includes the number of output packets, output errors, collisions, interface resets and restarts. From these numbers the collision rate of a Ethernet port can be calculated and should be kept under 10 percent.

☒ **A.** SHOW COLLISIONS INTERFACES ETHERNET 0, **B.** SHOW INTERFACE SERIAL 0 COLLISIONS RATE, and **C.** SHOW INTERFACES SERIAL 0 collisions, have the keyword COLLISIONS, which is not a valid command option.

16. ☑ **A, B,** and **C.** Supporting cost metric allows multi-path/equal path, type-of-service routing, variable-length subnet mask, route summarization, and stub areas, which are the main features of OSPF.

☒ **D.** Database description is incorrect since it is a packet type OSPF supports.

17. ☑ **C.** RIP. There is no DEBUG RIP command. However, one can use DEBUG IP RIP for viewing the state of information on RIP routing transactions.

☒ **A.** AAA is incorrect. It is a valid DEBUG command to view AAA Authentication, Authorization, and Accounting events as they occur. **B.** ATM is incorrect. DEBUG ATM is used to review ATM information such as (Asynchronous Transfer Mode) ATM Signaling and ATM interface information. **D.** Modem, is incorrect. DEBUG Modem is used to check on modem control/process activation activities.

18. ☑ **A.** An Ethernet frame consists of a preamble, destination address, source address, type field, data field, and the frame check sequence (FCS).
☒ **B.** Data address, preamble, destination address, and frame check sequence; and **D.** destination address, preamble, source address, and data address, are incorrect because data address is not part of an Ethernet frame. **C.** Preamble, destination address, protocol, and data type is incorrect because protocol and data type are not part of an Ethernet frame.

19. ☑ **B.** SHOW ROUTE-MAP is the correct Cisco IOS command.
☒ **A.** SHOW ROUTE MAP, **C.** SHOW MAP-ROUTE, and **D.** SHOW MAP ROUTE, are incorrect. They are not considered to be correct Cisco IOS commands.

20. ☑ **B.** SNMP-SERVER COMMUNITY RO and **C.** SNMP-SERVER COMMUNITY RW are not valid Cisco SNMP commands.
☒ **A.** SNMP-SERVER COMMUNITY <name> RO, and **D.** SNMP-SERVER COMMUNITY <name> RW, are incorrect since they are both valid Cisco SNMP commands. The SNMP community string is represented by <name>, RO is read-only access with this community string, and RW is read-write access with this community string.

21. ☑ **A.** Relay open in multistation access unit (MAU). The Open Lobe Fault message indicates that there is a relay open in MAU. The interface or MAU appears to no longer be available to the station. Disconnect the interface or MAU and/or verify the cabling.
☒ **B.** Station is waiting for data frame and **C.** Station is waiting for the token frame, are incorrect because the problem is with the physical layer, not the frame.

22. ☑ **A.** Time to Live (TTL) is a method used to identify packets caught in a routing loop. Once the TTL threshold is reached, the packet is discarded. TTL is used by the TRACEROUTE command. It is not an advanced ping option.

☒ **B.** Type of service is an extended IP ping option and is incorrect. The default type is [0], which is echo request. **C.** DF bit option is incorrect because it is an extended IP PING option. DF stands for don't fragment. **D.** Data pattern is incorrect since it specifies the string of bytes to be repeated to fill the datagram size.

23. ☑ **C.** SHOW MICROCODE is the correct command for viewing a list of micro code on a Cisco router.

☒ **A.** LIST MICROCODE, **B.** CHECK MICROCODE, and **D.** FIND MICROCODE, are incorrect. They are not valid commands.

24. ☑ **B.** Misconfigured subnet masks or addresses on hosts. When users can access some hosts but not others, the problem is often misconfigured subnet masks or addresses on hosts. First check the subnet and IP information on hosts and router to be sure it is configured correctly. Another possible cause is not having a default gateway specified on the local host. If a default gateway has not been configured, the host will be unable to reach any remote networks. Also, be sure to check the router to see if restrictions are set using access lists. Access lists work as filters and will not allow access to specified networks or hosts.

☒ **A.** The DNS configuration is incorrect since the host address may be contained in a HOST file. **C.** Not having a default gateway would preclude remote servers being accessed unless their route was cached by a device on the subnet. **D.** None of the above is incorrect.

25. ☑ **A.** AppleTalk is not a Cisco-supported protocol for the accounting features available on Cisco routers.

☒ **B.** DecNet, **C.** IP, and **D.** IPX, are incorrect. They are all Cisco-supported protocols for the accounting features available on Cisco routers.

26. ☑ **A.** The majority of the traffic is classified in the range of 105–600 bytes long. Middle buffers (600-bytes long) are experiencing the most hits from the sample above.

☒ **B.** The majority of the traffic is classified in the range of 601–1524 bytes long, **C.** The majority of the traffic is classified in the range of 1525–5024 bytes long, and **D.** The majority of the traffic is classified in the range of 5025–18024 bytes long are all incorrect. The following table shows the relationship of the frame size to the buffer categories.

Buffers Category	Bytes Size
Small buffers	0–104 bytes
Middle buffers	105–600 bytes
Big buffers	601–1524 bytes
Very Big buffers	1525–4520 bytes
Large buffers	4521–5024 bytes
Huge buffers	5025–18024 bytes

27. ☑ **A.** Small buffers require adjustments because of missed packets. The ratio of misses to hits is high (about 18 percent), reflecting the total number of times a request for a system buffer is missed by the existing buffer allocation on the small buffers.

☒ **B.** Middle buffers require adjustments because of missed packets and **C.** Big buffers require adjustments because of created buffers are incorrect. The ratio of misses to hits is not significant enough to require any buffer adjustments on these categories. **D.** The existing overall buffer allocations are sufficient to handle the traffic and no adjustments are required on any of the system buffers is incorrect, since adjustment of system buffers is required on the small buffers.

28. ☑ **D.** SHOW IPX ROUTE displays entries in the IPX routing table, including all interfaces carrying IPX traffic. SHOW IPX INTERFACE displays the IPX status of all IPX interfaces on the router.
☒ **B.** SHOW IPX TRAFFIC is incorrect. SHOW IPX TRAFFIC displays IPX info about packets but does not show which interface carries IPX. **A.** SHOW IPX ROUTE, and **C.** SHOW IPX INTERFACE, are both used, so D is the only correct answer.

29. ☑ **C.** TrafficDirector is used for statistics gathering via SNMP. It is also used to gather statistics via RMON.
☒ **A.** CiscoView is incorrect. It displays and manages individual devices. **B.** Resource Manager is incorrect because it is used for managing configuration and inventory information. **D.** UserTracker is incorrect, as it displays end-station information retrieved from switches and routers.

30. ☑ **B.** The router was restarted by RELOAD. The router was restarted by POWER ON, instead of by RELOAD.
☒ **A.** This router has the IOS Version of 11.2(10a)P, **C.** This is an access-server router, and **D.** It has a total of 4MB DRAM, are incorrect. They are all true statements regarding this output.

31. ☑ **A.** The command TEST APPLETALK is used to enter test mode, through which you can test the NBP protocol. This command is useful when you find that AppleTalk zones are listed in the Chooser but services in these zones are unavailable.
☒ **B.** SHOW APPLETALK TRAFFIC is incorrect. This command displays statistics about AppleTalk traffic and describes only NBP packets. **C.** SHOW APPLETALK ZONE is incorrect. This command displays all entries in the zone information table. **D.** None of the above, is incorrect.

32. ☑ **D.** TELNET. Remember that Telnet allows you to verify connectivity to TCP services. e-mail uses the Simple Mail Transport Protocol (SMTP), so if you can connect successfully to the SMTP port using Telnet, you know the port is listening and e-mail service is available. The correct Telnet command for this test is TELNET HOST SMTP. An E-mail account is not needed for this test.

☒ **A, B,** and **C.** PING, EXTENDED PING, and Traceroute are incorrect. They are not capable of conducting port listing tests.

33. ☑ **A.** Port 0/0 for the router and port 1/1 for the Catalyst.
☒ **B.** Port 0/0 for the router and port 0/0 for the Catalyst is incorrect because the Catalyst switch's first port is listed as port 1/1. **C.** Port 1/1 for the router and port 0/0 for the Catalyst is incorrect because the router port is listed as port 1/1 on the Catalyst switch's port is listed as port 0/0. **D.** Port 1/1 for the router and port 1/1 for the Catalyst is incorrect because the port is not listed as port 0/0.

34. ☑ **C.** SPID verification occurs in a Q.931 INFO message. This occurs after the BRI interface is up and after the Q.921 interface is up. Then Q.931 passes SPID verification information in a Q.931 INFO message.
☒ **A.** Interface BRI is incorrect since SPID information is not exchanged at the BRI layer. **B.** Q.921 is incorrect since the verification occurs in a Q.931 frame and not a Q.921 frame. **D.** LCP is incorrect. The PPP/LCP protocol occurs after SPIDs verification has been completed.

35. ☑ **A.** CiscoWorks 2000 is Cisco's latest version in its collection of SNMP management products. The components included in CiscoWorks 2000 can satisfy all of the requirements described in this scenario. These components include a graphical map, TrafficDirector, ATMDirector, VLANDirector, UserTracker, Resource Manager, and CiscoView.
☒ **B.** HP Open View is incorrect. It is a third-party resource manager. Older versions of CiscoWorks ran on top of this and similar third-party products. CiscoWorks 2000 contains its own resource manager, while it is still possible to run CiscoWorks 2000 on top of a third party product, it is no longer required. **C.** CiscoView is incorrect. It is only one of the SNMP management products included in CiscoWorks. CiscoView is designed to manage individual network devices. It is not capable of managing other aspects of the network, such as VLAN management or statistical reporting. Therefore, it is an incomplete solution and does not satisfy all of the requirements described in this scenario. **D.** None of the above, is incorrect.

36. ☑ **D.** SET PORT DUPLEX 1/8 <full>. Valid syntax for setting the duplex mode on a Fast Ethernet port is SET PORT DUPLEX <mod#/port#> <full | half>. 1/8 is not a valid port number on a Catalyst 5000, since only port 1/1 and 1/2 exist on module 1 (the Supervisor module).

☒ **A.** SET PORT DUPLEX 2/4 <half>; **B.** SET PORT DUPLEX 2/2 <full>, and **C.** SET PORT DUPLEX 2/8 <half>; are incorrect because each of these is a valid catalyst command.

37. ☑ **A.** Basic net. Cisco IOS does not support this switch type.

☒ **B.** Basic-ts013, **C.** Basic-1tr6, and **D.** Basic dms-100, are incorrect because Cisco does support these ISDN switch types.

38. ☑ **B.** LINE PROTOCOL IS UP means the data-link layer is working.

☒ **A.** CORRECT IP ADDRESS is incorrect. CORRECT IP ADDRESS is for Layer 3 verification. **C.** APPLIED ACCESS-LIST IS CORRECT is part of Layer 3 verification, so is incorrect. **D.** APPROPRIATE SWITCHING MODE IS SET is incorrect, as it is part of Layer 3 verification.

39. ☑ **A.** SET VLAN 10 5/1-12. The correct command is SET VLAN <mod#/port# | port-range>.

☒ **B.** SET VLAN 10 5/1-5/12, and **C.** SET VLAN 10 2-4/1-12, are incorrect. They display an incorrect port range selection for a valid command. **D.** All of the above is incorrect.

40. ☑ **B.** SHOW ISDN STATUS. Under the SPID status heading, we can see that our SPIDs have been sent and are considered valid by the ISDN switch.

☒ **A.** SHOW SPID STATUS, and **D.** DEBUG ISDN STATUS, are incorrect. They are not valid IOS commands. **C.** SHOW RUNNING CONFIG, is incorrect; it cannot be used to show SPID status.

41. ☑ **A, B,** and **C.** Time of day, applications behavior, traffic patterns. To determine what constitutes reasonable utilization levels, you should consider the following: number of stations on a LAN segment, applications behavior, frame-length distribution, traffic patterns, and time of day.

☒ **D.** Network Equipment, is incorrect. Network equipment is not really considered in determining reasonable utilization levels because the equipment is usually capable of reasonable performance. If two computers are simultaneously communicating at 100 Mbps to a 100- Mbps Internet connection, you have overloaded the capabilities of the communications link. If the same two computers were alternating, or only one computer was communicating at 100 Mbps to a 100- Mbps Internet connection, the capabilities of this link to the Internet would not be overloaded.

42. ☑ **D.** One station transmits more than 513 bits when another station starts transmitting. A late collision occurs when two stations transmit at the same time. However, for the collision to be late, the first station must have completed the transmission of 64 bytes, or 512 bits, of data before the second station starts transmitting.

☒ **A.** One station starts transmitting before another station stops transmitting, is incorrect since this is just the general definition of a collision. **B.** Two stations start transmitting 64-byte packets at the same time, is incorrect. This is a general definition for a collision and not for a late collision. **C.** One station continues transmitting after it should have stopped and another station begins transmitting, is incorrect. This refers to a collision and is not necessarily the definition of a *late* collision.

43. ☑ **B.** Layer 2. A packet is a collection of bytes that represents the Layer 3 and higher portions of a network communication. When a packet is put into an actual network, Layer 2 headers and possibly trailers are placed around the packet, and it becomes a frame. Frames contain packets, and packets contain connections.

☒ **A.** Layer 1, is incorrect. This is the layer that defines the physical topology and bit synchronization. **C.** Layer 3, is incorrect. This is the layer that is mostly responsible for routing but is also responsible for addressing devices. **D.** Layer 4, is incorrect. This is the layer that is responsible for flow control, acknowledgments and coordinating communications between systems.

44. ☑ **A. SHOW CDP NEIGHBORS DETAIL.** This will display AppleTalk and the IP addresses. Cisco Discovery Protocol (CDP) is a proprietary Cisco protocol. Its purpose is to help various pieces of Cisco equipment to find one another. This can be a valuable network management aid.
    ☒ **B. SHOW VERSION,** is incorrect. It will display the configuration of the system hardware, the software version, and the names and sources of configuration files and boot images. **C. SHOW APPLETALK ARP,** is incorrect. It displays AppleTalk and hardware addresses. **D. SHOW IP ARP,** is incorrect. It will display IP and hardware addresses.

45. ☑ **A, B,** and **C.** Identifies, isolates, and resolves problems. In a network environment, it is imperative for you to use a systematic approach to troubleshoot any problem that is affecting your network. A good start would be to devise a generic problem-solving model to aid your efforts, in order to identify, isolate, and resolve the problem. Having a good systematic model will allow you to eliminate specific pieces of equipment or areas of the network in order to narrow down the possibilities of what is causing the problem. Once you can determine what the problem is, you can take the appropriate steps to resolve it.
    ☒ **D.** None of the above, is incorrect because **A, B,** and **C** are all steps in a generic problem solving model.

46. ☑ **D. Mediates collisions.** You cannot have a collision on a Token Ring.
    ☒ **A.** Initiates the neighbor notification process, is incorrect, because it's a function of the Token Ring active monitor. The active monitor initiates the neighbor notification process. **B.** Purges the ring, is a function of the Token Ring active monitor. The active monitor purges the ring. **C.** Maintains the master clock, is also a function of the Token Ring active monitor, so this is incorrect. It is one of the functions of the active monitor to maintain the master clock.

47. ☑ **C.** Well Known (0–1023), Registered (1024–49151), and Dynamic/Private (49152–65535). The port numbers are divided into three ranges: The Well-Known Ports, the Registered Ports, and the Dynamic and/or Private Ports. The Well Known Ports are those from 0–1023, the Registered ports are those from 1024–49,151, and the Registered Ports are those from 49,152–65,535.

☒ **A.** Well known (0–1024), Registered (1025–49,150), Dynamic/Private (49,151–65,535), is incorrect. It is showing the ranges defined in the proper order, but the port numbers are incorrect for each of the ranges. It should be 0–1023, 1024–49,151, and 49,152–65,535 respectively. **B.** Dynamic/Private (0–1024), Well known (1025–49,150), and Registered (49,151–65,535), is incorrect. This is showing the ranges in the incorrect order and the port numbers are incorrect for each of the ranges. This should be 0–1023, 1024–49,151, and 49,152–65,535, respectively. **D.** Registered (0–1024), Dynamic/Private (1025–49,150), Well known (49,151–65,535), is incorrect. This is showing the ranges in the incorrect order and the port numbers are incorrect for each of the ranges. This should be 0–1023, 1024–49,151, and 49,152–65,535, respectively.

48. ☑ **B.** Traceroute. Initiating a traceroute will provide you with the host and timing information about each hop that a data packet takes to get to a specific address. Traceroutes are helpful when used to determine where packets are being discarded or slowed down.

☒ **A.** Ping, is incorrect. It does not reply with host and timing information about each hop. The ping utility does provide you with the host information only and will give you enough information to determine if the host is reachable or not. **C.** SNMP, is incorrect. It will collect information, once it is set up, to provide you with statistics and it can be presented in a format which will allow you to manage and track performance parameters. SNMP will not allow you to send packets of information to a specific address and receive host and timing information about each hop. **D.** Netstat, is incorrect. It provides protocol statistics and current TCP/IP network connection information on windows clients.

49. ☑ **D.** The locally administered router MAC addresses get duplicated. This can happen even with correct protocol operation. Duplicate MAC addresses can happen if, on locally administered addresses (LAAs), the same MAC address is entered twice.

☒ **A.** A LEC has multiple entries in an ELAN, is incorrect since a LEC should not generate duplicate MAC addresses and the LES should be capable of resolving any conflict. **B.** Two Ethernet cards have the same MAC address, is incorrect since most Ethernet card MAC addresses are factory assigned in order to be different. **C.** The two rings of a dual attached FDDI ring accidentally get cross connected, is incorrect, since on a typical FDDI ring, only one of the two dual attachments should be active at any given time.

50. ☑ **D.** Allows TCP to adjust the number of packets it sends at one time prior to an acknowledgement. Having large files to transmit, the sender would start out sending only one or two packets at time. The number of packets sent before an ACK is required is the *window size*. A window size is increased if things are going well, all packets being ACKed, and the sender isn't having to retransmit. If the sender is having to resend often, the Window Size will be decreased. As the Window Size increases and decreases, it is known as a Sliding Window.

☒ **A.** Allows TCP to adjust the size of the packet to maximize transmission time, is incorrect. This adjusts the size of the packet which will require the transmission of fewer packets. **B.** Allows TCP to send an acknowledgement prior to completely receiving the frame, is incorrect. It does not allow the receiving station to verify the completeness of the packet that it is receiving prior to acknowledging it. **C.** Allows TCP to send all the packets prior to acknowledging the transmission, does not allow for the adjusting that needs to be done in order for the packets to be more efficiently acknowledged and retransmitted when necessary.

51. ☑ **A.** Protocols that acknowledge each frame or packet of data received. Connection-oriented protocols do several things. A request for service establishes the circuit, provides sequential and guaranteed delivery of packets and frames. Connection-oriented protocols also require end nodes to acknowledge each frame or packet of data received. If the frame or packet is not acknowledged, it will be retransmitted.

☒ **B.** Protocols that do not acknowledge each frame or packet of data received, is incorrect. It shows a characteristic of a connectionless protocol. Connectionless protocols do not acknowledge each frame or packet of data that is received by the destination device. **C.** Protocols that acknowledge only high-priority frames or packets of data received, is incorrect. This is neither a characteristic of a connection-oriented protocol or a connectionless protocol. **D.** None of the above, is incorrect.

52. ☑ **D.** Password Authentication Protocol (PAP) and Challenge Handshake Authentication Protocol (CHAP). PAP is used to establish an initial link and CHAP is used to verify the credibility of a connection using a three-way handshake.

☒ **A.** Logon and reverse calling, is incorrect because PPP operates at Layer 2 and it does not initiate a callback session. **B.** User ID and privilege authentication, is incorrect because is normally authenticates by the host and not PPP. **C.** Protocol authentication and Port ID, is incorrect because PPP operates at Layer 2, whereas Port ID (in the sense of TCP/IP) is at Layer 4, the transport layer.

53. ☑ **C.** False, ICMP performs out-of-band management at Layer 3 and above. ICMP is not properly a transport protocol like TCP or UDP, and it doesn't fit neatly into the OSI layers. ICMP is a better mechanism for informing hosts and routers about status and errors. ICMP is a Layer 3 protocol, but you'll see that it has some of the characteristics and functionality of higher-layer protocols, as well.

☒ **A.** True, ICMP only functions at Layer 3, is incorrect. This states that ICMP is only a Layer 3 protocol which is incorrect. **B.** True, ICMP performs out-of-band management but only at Layer 3, is incorrect. This states that it performs out-of-band management, which it does, but only at Layer 3, which is incorrect. **D.** False, ICMP performs out-of-band management at Layer 2 and Layer 3, is incorrect. This states that it performs out of band management at Layers 2 and 3, while it actually 3performs out of band management at Layers 3 and above.

54. ☑ **B. Connectionless protocol.** Connectionless protocols provide dynamic flow through the network, provide alternative paths, require receiving nodes to manage non-sequential delivery of packets and frames. If a frame or packet is lost it will not be retransmitted.

☒ **A.** Connection-oriented protocol, is incorrect. It provides for sequential delivery of packets and frames. **C.** Private virtual circuit, is incorrect. It is not a protocol that provides alternate paths or dynamic flow though the network. **D.** SNMP, is incorrect. It is not a protocol that has characteristics of a virtual circuit, switched virtual circuit, or even a single path through the network for all packets and frames.

55. ☑ **B. Keepalive protocol.** Cisco uses a keepalive protocol to ensure connectivity of its point-to-point serial lines. Each end of the link periodically sends two 32-bit sequence numbers to the other side. These numbers are the identifiers of each side. If the numbers are not correct, or if no keepalive is sent, the link is considered to be down.

☒ **A.** Ping, is incorrect because ping is a command, offered in the Cisco router and switch that send ICMP requests to the specified IP address. The command is normally executed in a manual mode. If a response is received, the connection is considered up. Otherwise, there may be any of several problems occurring, ranging from host failure to firewall issues. **C.** Watchdog, is incorrect because watchdog is a process of monitoring, not connectivity. **D.** Non-Broadcast MultiAccess Service, is incorrect because NBMA provides access to multiple devices that do not broadcast. However, without keepalive, the link is considered down.

56. ☑ **C. The gateway was never changed after the workstation was moved.** Most of what can go wrong with default gateways on hosts has to do with misconfiguration. The gateway address may be wrong; it may not be on the same subnet as the host, or the gateway may not be functional in some way.

☒ **A.** The server address has changed and the users were not notified to change their workstations, is incorrect. This would not affect a user who cannot communicate with anybody outside of their own network segment.

B. A printer was added to your segment using an unassigned IP address, is incorrect. Unless the printer was added to your network segment and inadvertently used the IP address of the workstation or gateway, this would not be correct. **D.** The loss of communications on segments is normal from time to time, so there is no problem, is incorrect. The loss of communications on any segment of the network is not normal from time to time. Anytime a segment loses the ability to communicate there is a problem.

57. ☑ **C.** Stations may transmit whenever there is a free token available to transmit. Token Ring is a LAN technology in which all stations are connected in a ring topology. Token Ring grants every station equal access to the network unless configured otherwise. Token passing allows only the station with the token to have access to the ring for data transmission. When a station wants to transmit, it waits upon the arrival of the token. Essentially, you need to possess the token in order to transmit.
☒ **A,** Stations may transmit whenever they are ready to transmit, is incorrect. This is giving the impression that any station can transmit whenever they are ready, regardless of whether or not somebody else is already transmitting. **B.** Two stations may transmit whenever they are ready to transmit, is incorrect. This also gives the impression that either of the two stations can transmit whenever they are ready, regardless of whether anybody is already transmitting. **D.** Multiple stations may transmit whenever there is one free token available, is incorrect. This suggests that if only one token is free it will only allow one station to communicate and not multiple stations.

58. ☑ **A.** SH CDP NE. This command displays information about Cisco devices' immediate neighbors and nothing relating to PVC status.
☒ **B.** SH INT, is incorrect because the SH INT command shows the status of both the physical and line-protocol interface. It also identifies LMI connectivity. **C.** SH FR LMI, is incorrect because this command expands upon the LMI information. **D.** SH FR PVC, is incorrect because this command identifies the DLCI and PVC status. It also shows the create and status-change times on the PVC.

59. ☑ **A.** 00000123.0080.C712.202D. Cisco designates an IPX network format with network address followed by a period. The node address follows; there is a period between each of the four hex digits on its 12 bytes node address.

☒ **B.** 00000123:0080:C712:202D, is incorrect because it uses colons instead of periods. **C.** 0080.C712.202D.00000123, is incorrect because it begins with the node address instead of the network number. **D.** 0080:C712:202D:00000123, is incorrect. It has two errors. First, it uses colons instead of periods. Second, it begins with the MAC address instead of the network address.

60. ☑ **A.** Four. Defense Advanced Research Projects Agency (DARPA) presented a reference model for this new development, which separates the functions performed by communications protocols into manageable, stackable layers. Each layer controls a certain aspect for data transmission from source to destination. This model is not only designed for protocols to communicate across the network, but can also be used as a platform to develop protocols. Four layers form this model: the application layer, transportation layer, Internetwork layer, and the network interface layer.

☒ **B.** Five, is incorrect. **C.** Six, is incorrect. **D.** Seven, is incorrect. Given the four layer model for the DARPA TCP/IP model, all remaining answers are incorrect.

61. ☑ **C.** Level 2 X.25 information. The LAPD standard provides methods to setup, maintain, and tear down communications circuits at Level 2 of the OSI data-link layer. The DEBUG LAPD command displays any Level 2 X.25 information.

☒ **A.** Physical connection between local and remote, is incorrect because the physical connection between the local and the remote device is provided by the common carrier and is normally presented as an electrical signaling or interface, also known as Level 1 of the OSI model. **B.** Call setup and cause/diagnostic, is incorrect because the call setup and cause/diagnostic is presented at Level 3 of the OSI network layer and will not show in Level 2 diagnostic information. The DEBUG X25 EVENTS will provide information regarding call setup and cause and diagnostic information. **D.** Level 3 X.25 information, is incorrect because LAPD is a Level 2 and not a Level 3 protocol. Therefore, executing DEBUG LAPD will not show any Level 3 X.25 information.

62. ☑ **B.** NLSP is a link-state protocol; and **D.** It uses a metric calculation to determine link cost. NLSP is a link-state protocol that uses a metric calculation to determine its link cost. Link-state protocol was developed to address the distance-state protocol issues such as convergence and hop count limitations. NLSP uses a more efficient and faster metric calculation instead of the ticks and hops count method to determine link cost. This results in a faster convergence time for determining the best route. The convergence time feature is most advantageous when utilized in large network environments.

☒ **A.** NLSP is more commonly deployed than RIP in small-sized and medium-sized network environments, is incorrect. NLSP is more commonly deployed in large network environments because it is not constrained by the 16-hop limitation of the RIP protocol. Also, it can adapt more quickly to network topology changes than the RIP protocol because it only updates its routing table to its directly connected neighbors instead of all neighbors on the network. **C.** NLSP updates its routing table every 60 seconds, is incorrect. NLSP updates its routing table only when there is a network topology change. It does not update according to a fixed time interval.

63. ☑ **D.** Class E. Class E addresses are reserved for experimental purposes.Multicasting and experimental address ranges are not used frequently. Although they have special uses, it is important to understand that they do exist and have their purposes.

☒ **A.** Class B; and **B.** Class C, are incorrect. These classes are reserved for personal and business Internet addressing purposes. **C.** Class D, is incorrect because these addresses have been reserved for Multicasting purposes.

64. ☑ **D.** Generic flow control, virtual path identifier, virtual circuit identifier, payload type, cell loss priority, header error check. An ATM cell header structure is made up in one of two formats, either UNI (User-to-Network Interface) or NNI (Network-Node Interface). Both of these contain an 8-to-12 bit virtual path identifier (VPI), a 16-bit virtual circuit identifier (VCI), a 3-bit payload type (PT), a 1-bit cell loss priority (CLP), and an 8-bit header error check (HEC). However, the UNI cell contains a generic flow control (GFC) field, which steals four bits from the VPI field. These fixed fields allow for greater speeds because active devices can be configured for set lengths, permitting hardware switching versus accessing software routing tables.

☒ **A.** Virtual path identifier, virtual circuit identifier, payload type, cell loss priority, header error check, is incorrect because the cell header structure does not contain the generic flow control at the beginning of the header. **B.** Virtual path identifier, virtual circuit identifier, payload type, cell loss priority, is incorrect because the cell header structure did not contain the generic flow control at the beginning of the header and did not contain the header error check at the end of the header structure. **C.** Header error check, virtual path identifier, virtual circuit identifier, payload type, cell loss priority, generic flow control, is incorrect because the header error check should be at the end of the header not at the beginning. In addition, the generic flow control should be at the beginning of the header structure, not at the end.

65. ☑ **C.** Based on the first GNS response it receives. The workstation will use the first GNS response it receives to select its initial server. That SAP packet contains the necessary server information such as the server name and the IPX internal address of the first server that responded. Normally, the first server that responded to a workstation's "get nearest request" is the fastest server.

☒ **A.** Based on the highest IPX external network number; **B.** Based on the highest IPX internal network number; and **D.** Based on the first RIP response it receives, are incorrect. They are not relevant for a workstation to select its initial server.

66. ☑ **A.** (32-bit)network.(48 Bit)node. In the IPX world, the node number and the network number define the network address, as expressed in the NETWORK.NODE format. The network number is a 4-byte (32-bit) number that identifies a physical network. Each physical chunk of wire is required to have a single network number, which is the same number that you bind when a file server is configured. The node number identifies a node on the network. The node number is a 48-bit MAC layer address of the physical interface. Given this information the address is as follows: (32-bit)network.(48-bit)node.

☒ **B.** (48-bit) network.(32-bit)node, is incorrect. It shows the network number being 48 bit and the node number being 32-bit which is incorrect for the size of each. **C.** (48-bit)node.(32-bit)network, is incorrect. **D.** (32-bit)node.(48-bit)network, is incorrect. It shows the node number being displayed before the network number, which is also incorrect.

67. ☑ **C.** Three. The ISDN BRI (Basic Rate Interface), often called 2B+D or bonded ISDN, uses two bearer channels with 64 Kbps for data and one signalling channel with a 16-Kbps bandwidth totaling three channels. The data channels do exactly what they promise: pass traffic such as data, voice, or video. The signaling channel communicates with the switch by passing any connection-related traffic.

☒ **A.** One, is incorrect because ISDN BRI needs two additional channels for data. **B.** Two, is incorrect because ISDN BRI needs an additional channel for signaling. **D.** Four, is incorrect because this answer provided has one extra channel.

68. ☑ **C.** Dynamic addressing scheme. The dynamic addressing scheme is used to differentiate nodes.

☒ **A.** Hard-address, is incorrect. The hard-address scheme is used for IP or DECNet nodes. **B.** Automatically assigned according to MAC, is incorrect. Automatic assignments according to the MAC address are used for IPX. **D.** None of the above, is incorrect because it is eliminated by the presence of the correct answer, C.

69. ☑ **C.** 253 hosts/servers. An extended AppleTalk network allows 253 hosts and/or servers per network. A range of network numbers, called a *cable range*, is allowed per wire.

☒ **A.** 127 hosts, and **B.** 127 servers, are incorrect because there are non-extended AppleTalk network specifications. Using a non-extended AppleTalk network, your network will be divided into a maximum of 127 hosts and 127 servers per network. **D.** Both **A** and **B**, are correct for a non-extended AppleTalk network, but not for an extended AppleTalk network.

70. ☑ **A.** All ones. All-ones test patterns send out an unframed pattern of continuous 1s in an attempt to see if any network devices are dropping bits.

☒ **B.** All zeros, is incorrect because all zeros test patterns send out a pattern of all 0s. It is meant to test active network devices in an ESF environment by forcing B8ZS. Any device that does not substitute the 0s pattern with the intentional BPVs would be identified as mis-optioned. **C.** Framed ones, is incorrect because the framed ones test pattern is a low-stress test that inserts 1s into all bits except those reserved for framing. It has a low functionality in the grand scheme and is rarely used to identify less than obvious problems. **D.** Quasi, is incorrect because the Quasi test pattern is often referred to as a stress test. It's a type of testing that randomly changes the bit pattern (using the pulses –1s) around in an attempt to create a signal that physically stresses the circuit past the level that normal data transmissions would cause. Often this is an unframed signal. This pattern is meant to test the actual physical media, but it can also show equipment failures.

71. ☑ **B.** Layer 3. AppleTalk uses Layer 3 for source socket numbers.

☒ **C.** Layer 4, is incorrect. Layer 4 is used by IP, not by AppleTalk, for source socket numbers. **A.** Layer 2, and **D.** Layer 5, are incorrect since Layer 2 (data link) and Layer 5 (session) of the OSI model do not directly participate in packet addressing or routing.

72. ☑ **D.** Provides congestion control. Congestion control is more appropriately performed at the LLC layers specifically by LLC2-type protocols.

☒ **A.** Performs calculation on CRC and places information in the FCS field, is incorrect since the MAC layer does perform CRC calculations. **B.** Presents a serial bit stream to the physical layer for transmission, is incorrect since one important role of the MAC layer is to parse the data stream serially to the physical layer for transmission. **C.** Monitors broadcast traffic, is incorrect, since one role of the MAC layer is to monitor broadcast traffic.

73. ☑ **D.** Application. The application layer of the OSI model is closest to the user working on a workstation. The user working on the workstation is typically running an application to accomplish a certain task. That application is written in such a manner as to pass the pertinent instructions to the lower layers of the OSI model.

☒ **A.** Physical, is incorrect. This refers to the physical media on which the workstation is communicating, typically, the network card and cabling. **B.** Network, is incorrect. This refers to the layer of the OSI that is addressing devices and routing frames and packets through an Internetwork. **C.** Session, is incorrect. This refers to the layer of the OSI that is responsible for coordinating communications between systems.

74. ☑ **C.** SHOW APPLE ZONE. This is the correct command to display the Zone Information Table. The table contains a list of zone names and their corresponding cable ranges.

☒ **A.** SHOW APPLE ARP, is incorrect. This displays the Address Mapping Table (AMT), also known as the ARP table. **B.** SHOW APPLETALK NBP, and **D.** SHOW ROUTING TABLE, are incorrect because they do not use the proper command format. Therefore, they are not valid Cisco IOS commands to display the Zone Information Table.

75. ☑ **C.** LLC type 1 Ethernet SNAP has a 5-byte protocol discriminator field immediately following the 802.2 header.

☒ **A.** LLC type 1 Ethernet SNAP sets the DSAP to AA, the SSAP to AA, and the control field to AA, is incorrect since LLC type 1 Ethernet SNAP sets the DSAP to AA, the SSAP to AA, and the control field to 03. **B.** LLC type 1 Ethernet SNAP sets the DSAP to AA, the SSAP to 55, and the control field to 03, is incorrect for the same reason. **D.** LLC type 1 Ethernet SNAP sets the DSAP to the destination address, the SSAP to the source address, and the control field to 03, is incorrect since LLC type 1 Ethernet SNAP sets the DSAP to AA, the SSAP to AA, and the SNAP header includes the data-link encapsulation headers.

76. ☑ **A.** Transmission Control and **C.** User Datagram Protocol (UDP). TCP and UDP are the two primary transport-layer (Layer 4) protocols. These two transport protocols provide nearly all the functionality a protocol designer could want for a transport protocol. TCP is a connection-oriented protocol and UDP is a connectionless protocol.

☒ **B.** Internet Control Message Protocol (ICMP), is incorrect. It is a transport-layer protocol but it is not one of the primary protocols. The ICMP is not as widely used as the TCP or UDP. **D.** Simple Network Management Protocol (SNMP), is incorrect. It is a management-based protocol. SNMP is widely used to do a lot of network management. The SNMP protocol is also not as widely used as the TCP or UDP.

77. ☑ **C.** RTMP. The Routing Table Maintenance Protocol (RTMP) is the default AppleTalk common routing protocol. EIGRP is another AppleTalk common routing protocol, but it is not the default protocol.

☒ **A.** PAP, is incorrect. Printer Access Protocol (PAP) is used for print sharing. **B.** AFP, is incorrect. AppleTalk Filing Protocol (AFP) is used for file sharing. **D.** DDP, is incorrect. Datagram Delivery Protocol (DDP) manages the sequencing and delivery of data packets.

CCNP™
CISCO CERTIFIED NETWORK PROFESSIONAL

Test Yourself:
CIT Practice
Exam 2 Questions

Q & *A*

Before you register for the actual exam, take the following test and see how you make out. Set a timer for 105 minutes—the time you'll have to take the live CCNP Cisco Internetwork Troubleshooting 4.0 certification exam—and answer the following 77 questions in the time allotted. Once you've finished, turn to the CIT Practice Exam 2 Answers section and check your score to see if you passed. Good luck!

CIT Practice Exam 2 Questions

1. Which of the following statements are true?

I. In a RIP network only one subnet mask can be used for the entire address space

II. In a RIP classful subnetting environment, subnet mask information is transmitted along with the destination network information

III. When a RIP router receives an advertisement from a network number not belonging to the same major network number, as on the receiving interface with the host portion of the route being all zeros, this is a classful summary

IV. RIP will route packets from Ethernet subnet 10.1.1.0/24 connected on the same router to the Frame Relay subnet 10.1.2.0/30

A. I and II
B. II and IV
C. II and III
D. I and III

2. The five minute input/output rate shows the load on the circuits for an interface. This interval can be changed for a trouble shooting purpose. What IOS command is used?

A. LOAD INTERVAL
B. LOAD-INTERVAL
C. LOAD-INTERFACE
D. LOAD INTERFACE

3. The SHOW command is useful in troubleshooting a switched network of Catalysts. Which of the following commands is invalid?

A. SHOW VLAN

B. SHOW CAM DYNAMIC

C. SHOW PORT

D. SHOW MODULE

4. As a LAN administrator, you are receiving complaints from the telecommunications department about excessive telephone charges associated with the LAN department's outbound calls to remote sales offices. In reviewing server outbound traffic logs, the servers do not appear to be sending a lot of traffic out to the remote sales offices. Which of the following commands would you consider implement to help alleviate this situation?

A. HEADQUARTERS# CONFIGURE TERMINAL
HEADQUARTERS(config)# DIALER-ISDN IDLE-TIMEOUT 120

B. HEADQUARTERS# CONFIGURE TERMINAL
HEADQUARTERS(config)# INTERFACE DIALER 1
HEADQUARTERS(config-if)# DIALER IDLE-TIMEOUT 2

C. HEADQUARTERS# CONFIGURE TERMINAL
HEADQUARTERS(config)# INTERFACE BRI 0/0
HEADQUARTERS(config-if)# DIALER IDLE-TIMEOUT 2

D. HEADQUARTERS# CONFIGURE TERMINAL
HEADQUARTERS(config)# INTERFACE BRI 0/0
HEADQUARTERS(config-if)# DIALER IDLE-TIMEOUT 300

5. Which command verifies whether the Novell host AAAA.0060.8394.e940 is available?

A. PING IPX AAAA.0060.8394.E940

B. TRACEROUTE IPX AAAA.0060.8394.E940

C. SHOW IPX SERVER AAAA.0060.8394.E940

D. SHOW IPX ROUTE

6. What do the Frame Relay results of the SHOW INTERFACE SERIAL command output verify?

A. LMI Type is Cisco, ANSI, or Q933a

B. LMI is established via LMI packets sent and received and DTE LMI up

C. Packet counters are increasing

D. All of the above

7. What will most likely cause alignment errors on a port of a Catalyst switch?

A. A chatty protocol, such as NetBIOS or NetBEUI

B. Traffic saturation on the switched port

C. A mismatch of duplex modes between the switched port and the NIC

D. Too many protocols loaded on the NIC

8. When troubleshooting an ISDN call teardown, what is the correct cause code for a call rejection?

A. 0x890

B. 0x8290

C. 0x8291

D. 0x8095

9. Which of the following has RIP NOT implemented to reduce looping effects that can occur within certain network topologies?

A. Holddown

B. Split-horizon

C. Poison reverse

D. Round robin

10. Which of the following is NOT output of SHOW VERSION?

A. Boot ROM version

B. Router serial number

C. Processor type

D. NVRAM size

11. Which of the following is NOT likely to cause CRC errors and collision rates?

    A. Noise on wire

    B. Damaged cabling

    C. Incorrect cabling

    D. Intermittent system crashes

12. In what ways is IGRP similar to RIP?

    A. IGRP is a periodic broadcast-based routing protocol

    B. IGRP and RIP are incapable of routing

    C. IGRP is also a classful IP routing protocol. It follows the same IP subnetting rules as RIP.

    D. IGRP and RIP are both associated with autonomous systems

13. What describes many buffer creations?

    A. CPU-intensive

    B. Memory-intensive

    C. Routing-intensive

    D. None of the above

14. What causes runt frames?

    A. Not using appropriate cabling

    B. Bad software on a network interface card

    C. Bad taps spacing

    D. Damaged cable

15. Which of the following are added features of EIGRP?

    A. Variable-Length Subnet Masking (VLSM)

    B. Partial event-driven updates

    C. Multiple network layer support

    D. All of the above

16. What is the command to disable all Cisco debugging activities?

    A. NO DEBUG ALL

    B. LOGOFF DEBUG ALL

    C. CANCEL DEBUG ALL

    D. DISABLE DEBUG ALL

17. One of the common problems in ISDN is that the router does not dial. Which of the following items needs to be checked?

    A. Router configuration

    B. Misconfiguration in dialer map or dialer list

    C. Status of interface

    D. All of the above

18. To whom does BGP advertise by default?

    A. All neighbors

    B. No neighbors

    C. Nearest neighbors

    D. None of the above

19. Which of the following characteristics most accurately reflects the definition of a core dump?

    A. A dump of hardware information to a file

    B. A dump of routing information to a file

    C. A dump of memory registers to a file

    D. A dump of CPU information to a file

20. To have the router forward Novell NetBIOS packets across a WAN interface, which two statements should be included with the interface after you have enabled IPX routing?

    A. IPX NETBIOS ENABLE and SPX PROPAGATION-TYPE-IPX

    B. IPX NETBIOS ENABLE and TYPE IPX-PROPAGATION

C. IPX NETWORK NOVELL and IPX TYPE-20-PROPAGATION
D. IPX NETWORK BABE20 and IPX TYPE-20-PROPAGATION

21. Which of the following statements is true?

A. Ping is limited to TCP
B. Ping is not limited to TCP
C. Ping is limited to IP
D. Ping is not limited to IP

22. Which of the following commands is not a valid Cisco test command?

A. TEST VINES
B. TEST INTERFACES
C. TEST IP
D. TEST MEMORY

23. On an IPX network, servers advertise services using Service Advertisement Protocols (SAPs). One type of SAP is Get Nearest Server (GNS) which allows a client to locate the nearest login server when it first powers up. To locate all the Novell servers on the network, which command can you use at the router console?

A. SHOW IPX ROUTER
B. SHOW IPX TRAFFIC
C. SHOW IPX SERVERS
D. Both B and C

24. With the SNMP protocol, what is the host doing the querying called?

A. SNMP agent
B. SNMP manager
C. Agent
D. Manager

25. Which of the following is NOT a useful Cisco IOS command for troubleshooting problems with physical and data-link protocols?

    A. SHOW INTERFACE

    B. SHOW DEBUG

    C. SHOW CONTROLLER

    D. CLEAR COUNTERS

26. The AppleTalk zone appears in the Chooser list, but no devices appear in the device list when a service is selected. What is the likely cause?

    A. A misconfigured access list

    B. A problem with noise on the wire

    C. An invalid zone name specified

    D. Excessive magnetic interference near the computer

27. Which of the following is a CMU-SNMP command-line program?

    A. SNMPGET

    B. SNMPGETNEXT

    C. SNMPSET

    D. All of the above

28. What is the range of valid VLAN numbers on a Catalyst switch?

    A. 1–1000

    B. 1–1005

    C. 0–999

    D. 0–1024

29. What is the function of the D channel?

    A. Call setup

    B. Carry user data

    C. Handle in-band signaling

    D. Control signaling for the B channels

30. You are the network manager for a large bank. You have been asked to monitor the users' IP address and WAN link usage on a router interface. No commercial network-monitoring tool is available to you. Which of the following IOS diagnostic tools would be helpful?

A. Accounting

B. Telnet

C. Both A and B

D. Neither A nor B

31. The network administrator wants to dedicate a mail server to the first port of the second module of the Catalyst 5000 on the campus backbone. The mail server has one NIC with MAC address 00-A0-C9-8F-19-18. Which of the following commands is correct?

A. SET PORT 1/2 TO 00-A0-C9-8F-19-18

B. SET PORT SECURITY 2/1 ENABLE

C. SET SECURITY PORT 1/2 TO 00-A0-C9-8F-19-18 ENABLE

D. SET PORT 2/1 SECURE 00-A0-C9-8F-19-18

32. Which of the following is true?

A. The change of ISDN switch type takes effect right after entering the ISDN SWITCH-TYPE {switch type} command

B. All versions of Cisco IOS support one switch type at a time

C. ISDN switch-type commands can only be specified in global configuration mode

D. The switch-type parameter should be supplied by the ISDN service provider

33. One of your tasks in the CCIE lab exam is troubleshooting bad frames or protocol errors. Which IOS command enables a Cisco router's packet-analyzing feature?

A. SNIFFER PRO

B. DEBUG LIST

C. ETHERPEEK

D. All of the above

34. When using the SET VLAN command in a Token Ring environment, what range can be used for assigning the ring number?

A. 0–1000
B. 1–1005
C. 0x1–0xfff
D. 0x1–0xffff

35. The following code is a result of issuing the IOS command, DEBUG ISDN Q921. What is the current status of the router?

```
Router#DEBUG ISDN Q921
2256.712TX -> IDREQ ri=12613 ai=127
2256.748RX <- IDASSN ri=12613 ai=64
```

A. TE is attempting to establish multiple-frame communication with ISDN switch
B. TE is sending SABME message
C. TE is requesting TEI from the switch
D. TE is exchanging keepalives with the switch

36. Which of the following commands is used to view all the default IP settings that are enabled or disabled on the interface?

A. SHOW IP INTERFACE BRIEF ETHERNET 0
B. SHOW IP INTERFACE ETHERNET 0
C. SHOW INTERFACE EHTERNET 0
D. SHOW INTERFACE ETHERNET

37. When setting trunk on a port, a VLAN range, that is, multiple VLANs, may be specified. If no option is given, what is the default VLAN range to be trunked?

A. VLANs 1–1000
B. VLANs 1–1005
C. VLANs 0–999
D. VLANs 0–1000

38. Which of the following access-list combinations will allow Telnet and FTP traffic to bring up an ISDN link while denying other traffic?

A. DIALER-LIST 8 PROTOCOL IP LIST 101
   ACCESS-LIST 101 PERMIT TCP ANY ANY EQ 20
   ACCESS-LIST 101 PERMIT TCP ANY ANY EQ 21
   ACCESS-LIST 101 PERMIT TCP ANY ANY EQ 23
   ACCESS-LIST 101 PERMIT TCP ANY ANY EQ 25

B. DIALER-LIST 8 PROTOCOL IP LIST 101
   ACCESS-LIST 101 PERMIT TCP ANY ANY EQ 20
   ACCESS-LIST 101 PERMIT TCP ANY ANY EQ 21
   ACCESS-LIST 101 PERMIT TCP ANY ANY EQ 23

C. DIALER-LIST 8 PROTOCOL IP LIST 101
   ACCESS-LIST 101 DENY TCP ANY ANY
   ACCESS-LIST 101 PERMIT TCP ANY ANY EQ 20
   ACCESS-LIST 101 PERMIT TCP ANY ANY EQ 21
   ACCESS-LIST 101 PERMIT TCP ANY ANY EQ 23
   ACCESS-LIST 101 PERMIT TCP ANY ANY EQ 25

D. None of the above

39. Which utilization levels can be helpful in determining excessive load conditions?

A. Utilization exceeds 10–20 percent, averaged over an 8-hour work day
B. Utilization exceeds 20–30 percent, averaged over the heaviest-load hours of the day
C. Utilization exceeds 50 percent, averaged over the heaviest-load 15 minutes of the day
D. All of the above

40. Which statement is false?

A. A bridge splits a network into two or more physical segments
B. A router links multiple logical networks together
C. A bridge only forwards packets when necessary
D. A router links logical networks to one physical segment

41. In a Three-Way TCP Handshake, the client sends a SYN (synchronize) packet to the server. The server responds with a SYN+ACK (acknowledgment) packet. The client then sends what back to the server?

A. Nothing

B. SYN

C. ACK

D. SYN+ACK

42. When all zones are missing, it means that either the local router or the workstation is not working properly. If a single workstation is having trouble, the most likely cause is a connectivity problem at which layer of the OSI model?

A. Layer 1

B. Layer 2

C. Layer3

D. Layer4

43. The help desk tells you that some users in the finance department are having problems getting onto the Internet. Where in the problem-solving model does the help desk begin?

A. Define and state the problem

B. Gather facts and analyze the problem

C. Review and evaluate alternatives and possibilities

D. Design a plan of action (POA)

44. How is a frame removed from circulation on an FDDI ring?

A. When the frame reaches the destination hub

B. When the transmitting station receives its own frame back from the FDDI ring

C. When the Frame Copied indicator gets set

D. When new data is inserted into the frame token

45. In what way can a TCP connection be closed?

A. The server or client sends a stop packet

B. The server or client initiates a FIN (finished) packet

C. Either the server or client initiates a RST (Reset) packet

D. Session times out

46. What would you consider in the process of isolating and eliminating a problem?

A. Are there any common symptoms?

B. Is the problem only a single device?

C. Are several, but not all, devices experiencing the same problem?

D. What services are being affected?

E. All of the above

47. Which command verifies that HDLC keepalive packets are being passed?

A. DEBUG PPP NEGOTIATION

B. DEBUG PPP PACKET

C. DEBUG SERIAL INTERFACE

D. DEBUG PPP ERRORS

48. What is the Address Resolution Protocol (ARP) used for?

A. To map IP addresses to Layer 2 addresses

B. To map Layer 2 addresses to IP addresses

C. To maintain a listing of only the routers interfaces and the address of the interface connected to them in memory

D. To maintain a list of all frequently accessed interfaces in memory

49. What are connectionless protocols?

    A. Protocols that acknowledge each frame or packet of data received

    B. Protocols that do not acknowledge each frame or packet of data received

    C. Protocols that acknowledge only high priority frames or packets of data received

    D. None of the above

50. Which of the following commands is NOT used to troubleshoot serial line outages?

    A. SHOW CONTROLLERS

    B. SHOW SERIALS

    C. SHOW BUFFERS

    D. PING

51. You are the network engineer of a major international bank. You are using Dynamic Host Configuration Protocol (DHCP) to supply all of the addresses for your network. You have a new network segment that you are initializing for use in your enterprise. You want the users to get their addresses from a DHCP server and you don't want to install a DHCP server on that segment. What is your best option?

    A. Use an IP helper-address on the router interface of that network

    B. Give your workstation a static IP address

    C. Set the workstation to use a DHCP server to provide the IP address

    D. No network configuration is necessary. The workstation will get the IP address from any DHCP server that has been configured to service that network segment.

52. Using the Ethernet protocol, when a Jam Signal is sent, it is an indicator of what event?

    A. A workstation has an urgent priority transmission that needs to interrupt a current active transmission

    B. A workstation has tried to start the transmission of its pending communications and caused a collision on the network

C. A workstation has tried to retransmit a packet that has not been acknowledged by the receiving machine

D. A server is waiting for a missing packet that has not been received by its default time

53. In a Frame Relay network, a frame may experience latency due to congestion. Which two bits are normally used to notify a subscriber device of congestion on the network?

A. FECN and BECN

B. M-Bit a H-Bit

C. Xon and Xoff

D. None of the above

54. Which statement is true about the nature of Novell IPX Routing Information Protocol (RIP)?

A. RIP is a link-state protocol

B. RIP broadcasts its entire routing table to all neighbors, even if they are not directly connected

C. RIP is a distance-vector protocol

D. RIP is not a routable protocol

55. Media Access Units are often used with which type of technology?

A. Ethernet

B. X.25

C. Token Ring

D. Frame Relay

56. What bandwidth is available with the Subscriber Network Interface (SNI) for interconnection with the Switched Multi-megabit Data Service (SMDS) network?

A. T1 and T3

B. 56K to T1

C. 56K to T3

D. 56K to OC-3

57. How many bytes are the standard lengths in an IPX header format?

A. 16
B. 30
C. 32
D. 48

58. Which layer on the DARPA TCP/IP model has the same layer name and function as the OSI model?

A. Application
B. Transport
C. Internet
D. Network interface

59. Which Cisco router command is not normally used for troubleshooting an ATM-specific problem?

A. SH ATM TRAFFIC
B. SH ATM MAP
C. SH ATM ROUTE
D. DEBUG SIGNALING

60. When a workstation attempts to lookup its preferred server on an initial Novell connection, what must it first issue?

A. NCP Destroy Connection request
B. TCP Create Service Connection request
C. NCP Create Service Connection request
D. NETBIOS Create Service Connection request

Refer to the Following Illustration to Answer Questions 61–64

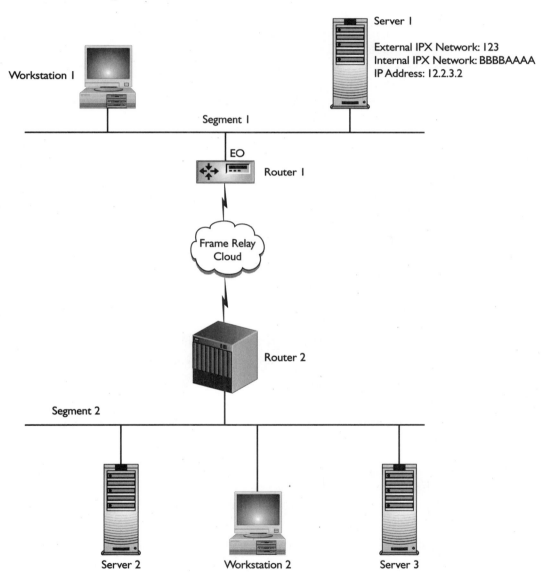

Workstation 1

Server 1

External IPX Network: 123
Internal IPX Network: BBBBAAAA
IP Address: 12.2.3.2

Segment 1

EO
Router 1

Frame Relay
Cloud

Router 2

Segment 2

Server 2   Workstation 2   Server 3

61. The console on Server 2 has the following message: WARNING! ROUTER CONFIGURATION ERROR! Router claims 122 should be 12. What is the cause of the problem?

   A. External IPX Network Number of Server 2 has been configuration as 12 and should be 122

   B. External IPX Network Number of Server 3 has been configuration as 12 and should be 122

   C. External IPX Network Number of Server 3 has been configuration as 122 and should be 12

   D. External IPX Network Number of Server 2 has been configuration as 122 and should be 12

62. In the illustration, what is the correct IPX configuration on the Router 2 interface Ethernet 0 (E0)? Choose all that apply.

   A. IPX NETWORK 00000012

   B. IPX Network 12

   C. IPX Network BBBBAAAA

   D. IPX Network 2

63. Workstation 2 has been experiencing intermittent connection problems to Server 2. What could have caused this problem?

   A. Mismatched Network number between Server 2 and Router 2

   B. Not enough user licenses on Server 2

   C. Mismatched Ethernet frame type between Server 2 and Workstation 2

   D. Cabling problem on Segment 2

64. The user of Workstation 1 has complained that he can not connect to Server 3. However, he can connect to Servers 1 and 2. Which of the following statement(s) are true?

   A. There is no frame relay network connectivity problem

   B. There are no router hardware and software problems on both Router 1 and Router 2

C. There are no configuration problems on the routers and file servers

D. There is a mismatched network number between workstation 1 and Server 3

65. Which TCP/IP Internet address format class is used for conventional purposes?

A. Class A

B. Class B

C. Class C

D. All of the above

66. In North America, ISDN PRI normally multiplexes up to how many bearer channels?

A. 23

B. 24

C. 31

D. None of the above

67. Which Cisco IOS command is used to display the Apple ARP table?

A. SHOW APPLE ARP

B. SHOW APPLE-TALK ARP

C. SHOW APT ARP

D. SHOW APT ARP CACHE

68. What is the native routing protocol for an AppleTalk network?

A. Open Shortest Path First (OSPF)

B. Routing Information Protocol (RIP)

C. Routing Table Maintenance Protocol (RTMP)

D. Point-to-Point Protocol (PPP)

69. An IPv4 Address consists of has how many bits?

A. 4

B. 8

C. 16

D. 32

70. The primary purpose of the startup range is for communication with an AppleTalk router to determine the correct network number(s) to use. How is this communicated?

A. Via NBP

B. Via ZIT

C. Via ZIP

D. Via AARP

71. Which IEEE standard defines LLC?

A. IEEE 802.2

B. IEEE 802.3

C. IEEE 802.5

D. IEEE 802.x

72. The concepts of sequencing and checksumming were designed to resolve which of the following?

A. Corrupt packets or frames

B. Delayed packets or frames

C. Dropped packets or frames

D. Packets arriving out of order

73. What is an AppleTalk router that is not in discovery mode called?

A. Non-discovery router

B. Passive router

C. Active router

D. Seed router

74. What is the maximum number of stations that can have simultaneously colliding transmissions?

A. One

B. Two

C. Three

D. Unlimited

75. At which layer of the OSI model are TCP/IP port numbers specified?

A. Layer 1

B. Layer 2

C. Layer 3

D. Layer 4

76. Which of the following is the correct order for a MAC workstation to obtain an NBP name service?

A. Forward request, broadcast request packet, lookup request packet

B. Forward request, lookup request packet, broadcast request packet

C. Broadcast request packet, lookup request packet, forward request

D. Broadcast request packet, forward request, lookup request packet

77. Assume EIGRP is being used to route AppleTalk. EIGRP will occasionally fail to update a neighboring router. Which of the following is not the way to force EIGRP to send an update?

A. SHUTDOWN INTERFACE/NO SHUTDOWN INTERFACE, then CLEAR APPLETALK ROUTE

B. SHUTDOWN INTERFACE/NO SHUTDOWN INTERFACE then CLEAR EIGRP NEIGHBORS

C. CLEAR COUNTERS

D. Reboot the router

Test Yourself:
CIT Practice
Exam 2 Answers

Q

&

A

The answers to the questions are in boldface, followed by a brief explanation. Some of the explanations detail the logic you should use to choose the correct answer, while others give factual reasons why the answer is correct. If you miss several questions on a similar topic, you should review the corresponding section in the *CCNP Cisco Internetwork Troubleshooting 4.0 Study Guide* before taking the test.

CIT Practice Exam 2 Answers

1. ☑ **D. I and III.** A RIP network does not support VLSM, so the subnet mask must be consistent within the entire address space. In addition, an advertisement from another major network with zeros in the host portion is considered to be a classful summary.

   ☒ **A. I and II**, is incorrect since it is redundant to transmit the subnet mask in a network where the same subnet mask is used for the entire address space. Consequently, statement II is false. **B. II and IV**, is incorrect because not only is statement II false, but in IV, packets cannot be forwarded between networks with different subnet masks in a RIP network. **C. II and III**, is incorrect because statement II is false, even though statement III is true.

2. ☑ **A. LOAD-INTERVAL** is used to change the length of time for which data is used to compute load statistics.

   ☒ **B. LOAD-INTERVAL; C. LOAD-INTERFACE;** and **D. LOAD INTERFACE**, are incorrect because they are not Cisco IOS commands.

3. ☑ **D. SHOW MODULE.**

   ☒ **A. SHOW VLAN** is incorrect, as it would show all active ports assigned to VLANS. **B. SHOW CAM DYNAMIC** is incorrect. This command would show MAC-to-port association. **C. SHOW PORT** displays port status of all ports.

4. ☑ **D.** HEADQUARTERS# CONFIGURE TERMINAL/HEADQUARTERS(config)# INTERFACE BRI 0/0/HEADQUARTERS(config-if)#DIALER IDLE-TIMEOUT 120. This sequence of commands will configure the INTERFACE BRI 0/0 with a dialer idle-timeout of 300 seconds. Five minutes is a suitable timeout period to drop idle connections.

☒ **A.** HEADQUARTERS# CONFIGURE TERMINAL/ HEADQUARTERS(config)# DIALER-ISDN IDLE-TIMEOUT 120 is incorrect. DIALER-ISDN IDLE-TIMEOUT 120 is not a valid interface configuration command. **B.** HEADQUARTERS# CONFIGURE TERMINAL/HEADQUARTERS(config)# INTERFACE DIALER 1/HEADQUARTERS(config-if)# DIALER IDLE-TIMEOUT 2 is incorrect because setting the DIALER IDLE-TIMEOUT 2 to two seconds will drop the connection very quickly, and very likely, during a valid session. **C.** HEADQUARTERS# CONFIGURE TERMINAL/HEADQUARTERS(config)# INTERFACE BRI 0/0/HEADQUARTERS(config-if)# DIALER IDLE-TIMEOUT 2 is incorrect for the same reason. Setting the DIALER IDLE-TIMEOUT 2 to two seconds will drop the connection very quickly, and, very likely, during a valid session.

5. ☑ **A.** PING IPX AAAA.0060.8394.E940. This command sends, by default, 5 IPX ping packets to the Novell IPX host AAAA.0060.8394.e940. Success responses indicated by !!!!! communicate that the Novell IPX host is responding to the IPX ping packets. Consequently, this response from the host indicates that the Novell host is available.

☒ **B.** TRACEROUTE IPX AAAA.0060.8394.E940 is incorrect since there is no IPX TRACEROUTE command. **C.** SHOW IPX SERVER AAAA.0060.8394.E940 is incorrect since this command will only show Novell IPX servers in table order based upon route and server information and it is possible that the server may be in the table even though the Novell server is not available. **D.** SHOW IPX ROUTE is incorrect since this command will only show the IPX routing table; not the actual availability of the IPX server.

6. ☑ **D.** All of the above. The SHOW INTERFACE SERIAL command for a Frame Relay interface verifies all of the above. **A.** LMI Type is Cisco, ANSI, or Q933a is a partial output of SHOW INTERFACE SERIAL from the Frame Relay interface. **B.** LMI is established via LMI packets sent and received and DTE LMI up display partial output of the command. **C.** Packet counters are increasing display partial output, also.

7. ☑ **C.** Problems caused by duplex mismatches can be difficult to diagnose and most often show up as alignment errors on the switched port.
☒ **A.** a chatty protocol, such as NetBIOS or NetBEUI, would not show alignment errors simply because of a protocol being chatty. **B.** a traffic saturation on the switched port, is incorrect and would cause collisions, not alignment errors. **D.** too many protocols loaded on the NIC, would not produce alignment errors.

8. ☑ **D.** 0x8095. This is the cause code associated with a rejected call.
☒ **A.** 0x890 is incorrect since this is a cause code for a normal call clear. **B.** 0x8290 is incorrect since this is also a cause code for a normal call clear. **C.** 0x8291 is incorrect since this indicates that the user is busy.

9. ☑ **D.** Round robin, a concept used in load sharing, which therefore has no relationship to reduce routing loops.
☒ **A.** Holddown is incorrect because it is a concept of instructing the router to wait a period of time before reinstating a route that may have been invalid. This prevents downstream routers, which may not yet be aware of invalid routes, from making them valid again. **B.** Split-horizon is incorrect because it prevents a router from advertising a route back to its source. Split-horizons prevent two-node routing loops, which can cause a "count to infinity" hop-count problem. **C.** Poison reverse is incorrect because it prevents larger, multi-hop routing loops by using holddowns for routes that have increasing metrics.

10. ☑ **B.** Router Serial number must be obtain from the router physically; it is not part of the output from SHOW VERSION.

☒ **A.** Boot ROM version is incorrect; it is part of the output of SHOW VERSION. **C.** Processor type is incorrect; it is part of the output of SHOW VERSION. **D.** NVRAM size is incorrect; it is also part of the output of SHOW VERSION.

11. ☑ **D.** Intermittent system crashes are due to a fault with the software. CRC errors and collision are normally caused by physical or electrical interference.

☒ **A.** Noise on wire; **B.** damaged cabling; and **C.** incorrect cabling; are not correct. On serial links, CRC works by building a mathematical equation and transmitting it across the control bits in an ESF frame. The result of the calculation is then transmitted in the next frame. The distant end performs the calculation and compares answers. If the resulting answers do not match, a CRC is incremented. As a result, if there is noise or interference on the wire, calculation will not match on each end of the data frame, causing a CRC error. Damaged cabling would also cause noise and interruption in the transmission of data. Incorrect cabling, such as using CAT3 for 100BaseT links, will also cause loss of signal and synchronization to the data frame, resulting in the miscalculation of the frame and causing CRC errors.

12. ☑ **A and C.** Interior Gateway Routing Protocol (IGRP) is a periodic, broadcast-based routing protocol. It is also a classful IP routing protocol. It follows the same IP subnetting rules as RIP. Both answers show IGRP to be a periodical, broadcast-based routing protocol and a classful IP routing protocol. IGRP follows the same IP subnetting rules as RIP.

☒ **B.** IGRP and RIP are incapable of routing, is incorrect since IGRP and RIP are routing protocols. **D.** IGRP and RIP are both associated with autonomous systems, is incorrect. IGRP support links with the autonomous system ; RIP does not support links with autonomous systems.

13. ☑ **A.** Many buffer creations are CPU-intensive.
    ☒ **B.** Memory-intensive is incorrect. This has nothing to do with buffer creation. **C.** Routing-intensive is incorrect; it has nothing to do with buffer creation. **D.** None of the above is, of course, also incorrect.

14. ☑ **B.** Bad software on a network interface card. There is a limit to the size of frames an Ethernet segment can transmit. The maximum is 1518 bytes and the minimum is 64 bytes. Runt frames are a violation of the minimum 64-byte frame size. Runt frames are a result of bad software on a network interface card (NIC), if the frame occurs with a low collision rate or in a switched network. It's necessary to find the source address of the bad frame with a protocol analyzer. Runt frames may also result from late collisions when shared media networks exceed maximum length.
    ☒ **A.** Not using appropriate cabling (that is, Category 5 cabling); **C.** bad taps spacing; and **D.** cable is damaged; are incorrect because they all are caused by noise on the wire, not the runt frames.

15. ☑ **D.** All of the above. These features are fully compatible with IGRP and more robust and are all event-driven Cisco enterprise routing EIGRP protocols.

16. ☑ **A.** NO DEBUG ALL is the command used to disable all current Cisco debug activities.
    ☒ **B.** LOGOFF DEBUG ALL; **C.** CANCEL DEBUG ALL; and **D.** DISABLE DEBUG ALL; are incorrect. They are not valid Cisco debug commands.

17. ☑ **D.** All of the above. There are numerous possible causes for the ISDN router not to dial. All of the above items need to be checked. First check your router configuration for ISDN to ensure it is correct. Then check the router for a misconfiguration in the dialer map command, dialer list, and access list. Finally, check the status of the interface to be sure it is not in shutdown mode.

18. ☑ **A.** All neighbors. BGP advertises to all configured neighbors.

☒ **B.** No neighbors; **C.** Nearest neighbors; and **D.** None of the above; are incorrect due to BGP advertising to all neighbors.

19. ☑ **C.** A core dump is a dump of memory registers to a file when a Cisco router encounters a set of conditions that have not been programmed or coded to be handled in the router (during a hardware or software failure, for example.)

☒ **A, B** and **D.** A dump of hardware, routing, or CPU information to a file is incorrect since these characteristics do not accurately reflect the definition for core dump. However, the dump file might have contained some of the hardware, routing, or CPU information.

20. ☑ **D.** IPX NETWORK BABE20 and IPX TYPE-20-PROPAGATION. To allow Novell IPX/SPX on the WAN, you need to specify IPX NETWORK <network-number-in-hex> to be part of a network and IPX TYPE-20-PROPAGATION to allow the router to forward announcements of Novell services.

☒ **A.** IPX NETBIOS ENABLE and SPX PROPAGATION-TYPE-IPX, and **B.** IPX NETBIOS ENABLE and TYPE IPX-PROPAGATION, are incorrect commands. **C.** IPX NETWORK NOVELL and IPX TYPE-20-PROPAGATION is incorrect. This has an invalid network address.

21. ☑ **D.** Ping is not limited to IP. The IOS implements a ping client to support various other protocols such as IPX, VINES, XNS, CLNS, AppleTalk, and Apollo.

☒ **A.** Ping is limited to TCP is incorrect. There is no such thing as ping being limited to TCP. **B.** Ping is not limited to TCP is incorrect. There is no such thing as ping being limited to TCP. **C.** Ping is limited to IP is incorrect, since ping clients exist to support several protocols.

22. ☑ **C.** TEST IP is not a valid Cisco TEST command.
☒ **A.** TEST VINES is incorrect, since it performs VINES diagnostic validation tests. **B.** TEST INTERFACES is incorrect since it performs a network interfaces diagnostic test. **D.** TEST MEMORY is incorrect, since it performs hardware non-volatile and/or multibus memory tests.

23. ☑ **C.** SHOW IPX SERVERS. This command displays all the IPX servers available on the network.
☒ **A.** SHOW IPX ROUTER is incorrect. This command is an invalid command. **B.** SHOW IPX TRAFFIC, is incorrect. This command displays info about IPX packets going through the router. **D.** Either B or C, is incorrect.

24. ☑ **B.** SNMP manager. By definition, the host doing the querying is called the SNMP manager.
☒ **A.** SNMP agent is incorrect, since it is the host being queried by the SNMP manager. **C** and **D**, Agent and manager, are incorrect. These labels are incomplete, thus invalid.

25. ☑ **B.** SHOW DEBUG. This command shows the state of each debugging option. It is different than DEBUG, which allows the setup of various debugging functions to diagnose network problems, including physical and data-link protocol problems.
☒ **A.** SHOW INTERFACE is incorrect. It displays valuable information on interface status and configurations. **C.** SHOW CONTROLLER is incorrect, since it displays interface controller information. **D.** CLEAR COUNTERS is incorrect, since it resets the counters of one or more interfaces to zero. All these commands are good Cisco IOS commands for troubleshooting physical and data-link problems.

26. ☑ **A.** A misconfigured access list. Disable the access list, and then check to see if devices appear. If a device appears, that means that the access list needs to be reconfigured to filter appropriately.

    ☒ **B.** A problem with noise on the wire is incorrect. This most likely is the cause of CRC errors. **C.** An invalid zone name specified, and **D.** a sign of excessive magnetic interference near the computer, are incorrect. They have no effect on the problem.

27. ☑ **D.** All of the above. SNMPGET, SNMPGETNEXT, and SNMPSET are all command-line programs. The CMU SNMP library is a command-line SNMP manager.

    ☒ **A.** SNMPGET, **B.** SNMPGETNEXT, and **C.** SNMPSET, are incorrect independently. Since all of these items are valid CMU SNMP command-line programs, selecting just one of them would result in an incomplete command-line program.

28. ☑ **B.** 1–1005. Current versions of the software for the Catalysts permit VLAN numbers in this range.

    ☒ **A.** 1–1000, **C.** 0–999, and **D.** 0–1024, are incorrect because the ranges are invalid.

29. ☑ **A** and **D.** Call setup and Control signaling for the B channels.

    ☒ **B.** Carry user data is incorrect since it is done by B channel. **C.** Handle in-band signaling is incorrect since this method of signaling is what we refer to as *out-of-band* signaling. The B channels carry actual user data.

30. ☑ **A.** The accounting features available on Cisco routers will track the number of bytes and packets sent between each pair of network addresses. You can also use it to determine what percentage of the bandwidth is being used by a particular address at a given moment in time.

    ☒ **B.** Telnet is incorrect. The main purpose of Telnet is to verify connectivity to TCP services. Telnet does not have the capability to analyze network activity according to the IP addresses, nor can it provide statistics on bandwidth usage. **C.** both A and B; and **D.** neither A nor B; are incorrect.

31. ☑ **B.** SET PORT SECURITY 2/1 ENABLE. The command is SET PORT SECURITY <mod#/port#> <enable|disable> [mac-addr]. If the optional MAC address is omitted, the first MAC address transmitted will be the one that has the port secured. Since this is a dedicated connection, the MAC address is automatically picked up.

☒ **A.** SET PORT 1/2 TO 00-A0-C9-8F-19-18; **C.** SET SECURITY PORT 1/2 TO 00-A0-C9-8F-19-18 ENABLE; and **D.** SET PORT 2/1 SECURE 00-A0-C9-8F-19-18; are incorrect, considering the syntax of the scenario.

32. ☑ **D.** The switch-type parameter should be supplied by the ISDN service provider. Switch-type parameters have to match with the service provider. This information is typically provided for compatibility purposes.

☒ **A.** The change of ISDN switch types takes effect right after entering the ISDN SWITCH-TYPE {switch type} command is incorrect since, if you change your switch type after initial configuration, you need to reload the router for it to take effect. **B.** All versions of Cisco IOS support one switch type at a time is incorrect since, starting with IOS 11.3T or higher, Cisco IOS supports multiple ISDN switch types. **C.** ISDN switch-type commands can only be specified in global configuration mode is incorrect since switch types can be configured on a per-interface basis when configuring multiple switch types on the same router.

33. ☑ **B.** DEBUG LIST. This command is the IOS command that allows a Cisco router to function as a rudimentary packet analyzer.

☒ **A.** SNIFFER PRO is incorrect, since it is a commercial packet analysis product by Network Associates. **C.** ETHERPEEK is a commercial packet analysis product by AG Group. **D.** All of the above is incorrect because only answer B is an IOS command; Sniffer Pro and Etherpeek are names of third-party software products.

34. ☑ **C.** To set VLAN for FDDI or Token Ring, the valid range for ring assignment is 0x–0xfff in hexadecimal values.

☒ **A** and **B.** These values cannot be listed in a decimal form. They must be listed in hexidecimal value. **D.** is showing an incorrect value of 0xffff. This value should be 0xfff, not 0xffff.

35. ☑ **C.** TE is requesting TEI from the switch. TE is sending a TEI=127, which indicates a broadcast to the ISDN switch to request a TEI assignment, and ISDN assigns TEI=64 back to the router.

☒ **A.** TE is attempting to establish multiple-frame communication with ISDN switch; **B.** TE is sending SABME message; and **D.** TE is exchanging keepalives with the switch; are incorrect. Multiple-frame communication happens after TEI has been assigned and TE sends a SABME message in order to move to multiple-frame communication state. The switch and TE will exchange keepalives after the layer 2 connection is established.

36. ☑ **B.** SHOW IP INTERFACE ETHERNET 0. This will display the default IP settings that are enabled or disabled on the interface.

☒ **A.** SHOW IP INTERFACE BRIEF ETHERNET 0 is not correct because it will display IP address, administrative and physical status on the interface and Protocol signaling on the interface. **C.** SHOW INTERFACE ETHERNET 0 is incorrect. It will display statistics for Ethernet interface configured on a router. **D.** SHOW INTERFACE ETHERNET, is incorrect. It will display statistics for all Ethernet interfaces configured on a router.

37. ☑ **A.** By default, if no VLANs are specified, VLANs 1–1000 will be trunked.

☒ **B.** is incorrect because you can specify individual VLANs 1–1005. **C.** and **D.** have invalid VLAN range values.

38. ☑ **B.** DIALER-LIST 8 PROTOCOL IP LIST 101/ACCESS-LIST 101 PERMIT TCP ANY ANY EQ 20/ACCESS-LIST 101 PERMIT TCP ANY ANY EQ 21/ACCESS-LIST 101 PERMIT TCP ANY ANY EQ 23/ACCESS-LIST 101 DENY TCP ANY ANY. This access list explicitly permits ports 20, 21, and 23, then implicitly denies all other IP traffic.
    ☒ **A.** DIALER-LIST 8 PROTOCOL IP LIST 101/ACCESS-LIST 101 PERMIT TCP ANY ANY EQ 20/ACCESS-LIST 101 PERMIT TCP ANY ANY EQ 21/ACCESS-LIST 101 PERMIT TCP ANY ANY EQ 23/ACCESS-LIST 101 PERMIT TCP ANY ANY EQ 25 is incorrect since ACCESS-LIST 101 PERMIT TCP ANY ANY EQ 25 will also permit SMTP. **C.** DIALER-LIST 8 PROTOCOL IP LIST 101/ACCESS-LIST 101 DENY TCP ANY ANY/ACCESS-LIST 101 PERMIT TCP ANY ANY EQ 20/ACCESS-LIST 101 PERMIT TCP ANY ANY EQ 21/ACCESS-LIST 101 PERMIT TCP ANY ANY EQ 23/ACCESS-LIST 101 PERMIT TCP ANY ANY EQ 25 is incorrect since the DENY TCP ANY ANY is processed first, denying any TCP traffic to bring up the interface. **D.** None of the above, is incorrect.

39. ☑ **D.** All of the above. Each answer gives situations that can occur during the same time frame for short periods of time. It is not uncommon for some networks to experience short term spiking. Each of the utilization time frames should be considered separately within their own time frame. Over an eight-hour workday, does your utilization continually exceed 10–20 percent? During your heaviest-load portions of the workday, does your utilization continually exceed 20–30 percent? During your heaviest-load portion of the day for any 15-minute period, does your utilization continually exceed 50 percent? If you can say *yes* to any of these questions, you need to look at your network to determine if something is wrong or if you need to eliminate a possible bottleneck.

40. ☑ **D.** A router links logical networks to one physical segment, since a router performs physical segmentation. A router also performs logical segmentation. Consequently, a router routes multiple logical networks to multiple physical networks.
    ☒ **A,** A bridge splits a network into two or more physical segments, is incorrect, since it's true that a bridge splits a network into two or more

physical segments. **B,** A router links multiple logical networks together, is incorrect, since it is true that a router links multiple logical networks together. **C,** A bridge only forwards packets when necessary, is incorrect, since it's true that a bridge only forwards packets when necessary.

41. ☑ **C.** ACK. The client sends a special type of packet called a SYN packet. The server responds with a SYN+ACK packet. Finally, the client sends an ACK packet to acknowledge the SYN+ACK. This is called the Three-Way TCP Handshake. At this point, the client and server are said to have a TCP connection and can exchange data.

☒ **A.** Nothing, is incorrect due to the serve waiting for an ACK from the client before completing the process. **B.** SYN, is incorrect. It would start another Three-Way TCP Handshake process. The initial process would be dropped by the server as being incomplete. **D.** SYN+ACK, is incorrect since it is not a valid sequence for the client. The client does not send a SYN+ACK.

42. ☑ **B.** Layer 2. Layer 2 is the most likely cause of connectivity problems for the workstation.

☒ **A.** Layer 1; **C.** Layer 2; **D.** Layer 4; are all incorrect. The cause for workstation connectivity problems does not occur in Layers 1, 3, or 4 of the OSI model.

43. ☑ **A.** Define and state the problem. As a network engineer, you typically have a help desk or a centralized group that notifies you of any problem that it is aware of in the network. With a well-defined problem-solving model, you will be able to determine what you need to do to start looking at the problem. The first step is figuring out if there is a problem.

☒ **B.** Gather facts and analyze the problem, is incorrect. It is not where you need to start, as you must first figure out what the problem is before you can start to gather facts or even know where to start looking. **C.** Review and evaluate alternatives and possibilities, is incorrect. This is ahead of the process, you need to gather facts on what is actually happening with the network before you review and evaluate alternatives and possibilities. **D.** Design a plan of action (POA), is incorrect. This is what you do once you have figured out exactly what is causing the problem.

44. ☑ **B.** When the transmitting station receives its own frame back from the FDDI ring. FDDI removes the frame from the ring when the originating station receives the frame back.

☒ **A.** When the frame reaches the destination hub, is incorrect since FDDI removes the frame from the ring when the originating station receives the frame back. **C.** When the Frame Copied indicator gets set, is incorrect because the this gets set when the receiving station receives the frame. **D.** When new data is inserted into the frame token, is incorrect since FDDI removes the frame from the ring when the originating station receives the frame back.

45. ☑ **B.** The server or client initiates a FIN (finished) packet; and **C.**, Either the server or client initiates a RST (Reset) packet. TCP's graceful close method has a sequence similar to the three-way handshake. The host decides that the conversation should be terminated and sends a FIN packet. The FIN packet is then ACKed by the client, and half of the connection is closed. The client will also send a FIN packet, which is ACKed by the host. Now both sides have closed the connection. TCP's ungraceful close method terminates the connection abruptly. This party sends out a RST packet. Once the RST packet is sent, the connection is terminated immediately with no further packet exchange.

☒ **A.** The server or client sends a stop packet, is incorrect due to the type of packet being sent. **D.** Session times out, indicates that a session has timed out. This would then be followed by the FIN method of closing a connection or the RST method of closing a connection.

46. ☑ **E.** All of the above. When isolating and eliminating a problem you should consider all the above questions. They help you get a good idea of what could be causing the problem. Answering all of these questions will narrow down the areas of your network that you need to look at. This will also reduce the time it will take to resolve the problem.

47. ☑ **C.** DEBUG SERIAL INTERFACE, verifies that HDLC keepalive packets are being passed.

☒ **A.** DEBUG PPP NEGOTIATION, is incorrect because the command will show PPP packets being transferred during startup. **B.** DEBUG PPP PACKET, is incorrect because the command will identifies low-level PPP packet dumps. **D.** DEBUG PPP ERRORS, is incorrect because the command identifies LCP errors during connection and link operation.

48. ☑ **A.** To map IP addresses to Layer 2 addresses. Address Resolution Protocol (ARP) is used for mapping IP addresses to Layer 2 addresses. For an IP stack to deliver an IP packet to the IP stack of another host, it has to determine the other host's Layer 2 address so that delivery can happen at Layer 2.

☒ **B.** To map Layer 2 addresses to IP addresses, is incorrect. It is better known as Reverse Address Resolution Protocol (RARP). **C.** To maintain a listing of only the routers interfaces and the address of the interface connected to them in memory, is incorrect. Although the routers do maintain a list of all the network interfaces that it can communicate with, it does not only maintain a list of the addresses of the interfaces that it connects to. **D.** To maintain a list of all frequently accessed interfaces in memory, is incorrect. It is a cache table that a router sets up and uses to increase the speed of delivering packets and frames to the proper router interface.

49. ☑ **B.** Protocols that do not acknowledge each frame or packet of data received. Connectionless protocols provide no guarantee that the packet will be delivered. It is better known as a best effort delivery method. Connectionless protocols will send the packet or frame to its destination but there is no monitoring done to determine if it makes it to the destination. The destination device will not reply with an acknowledgment stating that the frame or packet was received.

☒ **A.** Protocols that acknowledge each frame or packet of data received, is incorrect. This shows a characteristic of a connection-oriented protocol. Connection-oriented protocols acknowledge each frame or packet of data received by the destination device. **C.** Protocols that acknowledge only high priority frames or packets of data received, is incorrect. This is neither a characteristic of a connection-oriented protocol or of a connectionless protocol. Frames are not prioritized, server processes are at the server, and routers can be set up to assign a cost value for communicating on certain links. **D.** None of the above, does not answer to this question.

50. ☑ **B.** SHOW SERIALS. This command does not exist, thus it is an invalid command.

☒ **A.** SHOW CONTROLLERS, is incorrect because this command determines which cable is connected to the interface. **C.** SHOW BUFFERS, is incorrect because this command displays statistics for the router's buffer pools on the entire router or a specific interface. **D.** PING, is incorrect because this command sends ICMP requests to the specified IP address. If a response is received, the connection is up.

51. ☑ **A.** Use an IP helper-address on the router interface of that network. Many routers will include a broadcast forwarding mechanism, often for the purpose of forwarding DHCP packets. On a Cisco router, this is called IP HELPER. It is an interface command that is applied to the interface where the IP address to which you want to broadcast packets is forwarded, usually a DHCP server. This command not only causes the broadcasts to be forwarded; it also re-addresses the packet so the DHCP server knows from which subnet it forwarded the broadcast.

☒ **B.** Give your workstation a static IP address, is incorrect. This will not allow the DHCP server to track the static IP that is assigned and it has not met the requirement of using the DHCP server for issuing the address. **C.** Set the workstation to use a DHCP server to provide the IP address, is incorrect. This sets the workstation up for DHCP, but if the broadcast cannot make it out of the new network and into the network that contains the DHCP server, the DHCP server can't reply to the address request. **D.** No network configuration is necessary, the workstation will get the IP address from any DHCP server that has been configured to service that network segment, is incorrect. The IP Helper command must be added on the required interface.

52. ☑ **B.** A workstation has tried to start the transmission of its pending communications and caused a collision on the network. Once a collision is detected, a special bit pattern called a Jam Signal may be sent by other stations to ensure that all stations recognize the collision and defer any pending transmission. All stations then stop transmitting for a randomly selected time frame before they are permitted to retransmit.

☒ **A.** A workstation has an urgent priority transmission that needs to interrupt a current active transmission, is incorrect. This does not correctly represent a characteristic of what happens to cause a Jam Signal. **C.** A workstation has tried to retransmit a packet that has not been acknowledged by the receiving machine, is incorrect. This is describing what happens during the normal operation of a connection-oriented protocol. **D.** A server is waiting for a missing packet that has not been received by its default time, is incorrect. This also describes what happens during the normal operation of a connection-oriented protocol.

53. ☑ **A.** FECN and BECN, also known as Forward/Backward Explicit Congestion Notification bits. In a Frame Relay network, a frame may experience latency due to congestion. This is where the FECNs and BECNs can be useful. These bits explicitly notify a subscriber's device of congestion on the network; they help that device determine whether to withhold traffic or reduce its transmission rate until the congestion has cleared. Also, by identifying possible problematic spots in the cloud, some circuits may be repositioned to ease connectivity.

    ☒ **B.** M-Bit and H-Bit, is incorrect because More Data Bit (M-Bit) is used in X.25 network. **C.** X-on and X-off, is incorrect because it is used as flow control in an asynchronous protocol. **D.** None of the above, is incorrect because FECN and BECN bits are used to notify of congestion.

54. ☑ **C.** RIP is a distance-vector protocol. This is correct because IPX RIP is based on the Bellman-Ford algorithm. This algorithm uses a hop count to determine the shortest route. It declares the route as unreachable once the count reaches 16 hops.

    ☒ **A.** RIP is a link-state protocol, is incorrect because RIP uses "ticks" mechanics, which by definition is a distance-state protocol. **B.** RIP broadcasts its entire routing table to all neighbors, even if they are not directly connected, is incorrect because RIP only broadcasts its entire routing table to its directly connected neighbors. It then depends on its neighbors to forward the routing table to the next neighbors. **D.** RIP is not a routing protocol, is incorrect. RIP is a routing protocol.

55. ☑ **C.** Token Ring. In a Token Ring environment, stations on the ring are connected through a central hub: Media Access Unit (MAU).
☒ **A.**, Ethernet, is incorrect. Ethernet networks are connected to hubs but these hubs are not considered MAUs. **B.** X.25, is incorrect. X.25 networks are connected via ITU-TSS standard interfaces. **D.** Frame Relay, is incorrect. The Frame Relay circuit is connected via CSU/DSU device.

56. ☑ **C.** 56K to T3. One advantage in using SMDS is that it's scaleable. The networks can connect to an SMDS cloud via SNI using T1 and T3 circuits. The latest technology, however, allows for bandwidth including 56K–64K. This gives SMDS connectivity to networks in a range from 56 Kbps to 45 Mbps (T3).
☒ **A.** T1 and T3, is incorrect because T1 and T3 are the traditional connectivity, but the technology is not limited to these two bandwidths. **B.** 56K to T1, is incorrect because recent technology has expanded the SNI to support up to T3 bandwidth. **D.** 56K to OC-3, is incorrect because OC-3 (155Mbps) bandwidth is available, but only for the Synchronous Optical Network (SONET).

57. ☑ **B.** 30. An IPX header consists of the following fields with its associated length.
☒ **A.** 16; **C.** 32; **D.** 48;are incorrect. See the following table for details.

Field	Length (bytes)
Checksum	2
Length	2
Transport Control (TC)	1
Packet type	1
Destination Network Address	4
Destination Node Address	6
Destination Socket	2

Field	Length (bytes)
Source Network Address	4
Source Node Address	6
Source Socket	2
Total	**30**

58. ☑ **B.** Transport. DARPA TCP/IP model has four layers: the Application layer, Transportation layer, Internetwork layer, and the Network interface layer. The OSI TCP/IP model has seven layers: the application layer, the presentation layer, the session layer, the transport layer, the network layer, the data-link layer, and the Physical layer. Given the responsibilities of each layer of each model, the Transport layer on both models perform the same function and maintains the same positioning in their respective models, not to mention having the same layer name.

    ☒ **A.** Application, is incorrect in the DARPA TCP/IP model due to the application layer performing the same functions as the OSI TCP/IP models application layer, presentation layer, and session layer. **C.** Internet, is incorrect. The DARPA TCP/IP model Internet layer and the OSI TCP/IP model network layer perform the same function as each other but they are not known by the same name. **D.** Network interface, is incorrect in the DARPA TCP/IP model due to the network interface layer performing the same functions as the OSI TCP/IP models data-link layer and physical layer.

59. ☑ **C.** SH ATM ROUTE. This is an invalid command. ATM does not use the conventional routing, but instead uses the switching and multiplexing technologies.

    ☒ **A.** SH ATM TRAFFIC is incorrect because this displays the current global ATM traffic information connected to the router. **B.** SH ATM MAP, is incorrect because this displays all of the configured ATM static maps to their remote hosts. **D.** DEBUG SIGNALING, is incorrect because this shows all signaling to the router.

60. ☑ **C.** NCP Create Service Connection request. A NetWare Core Protocol (NCP) Create Service Connection request frame is the first frame that a workstation issues to establish a connection with a server. Once the workstation has established the connection with the server, it can then issue requests for additional information such as finding the route to its preferred server.

☒ **A.** NCP Destroy Connection request, is incorrect. The workstation generates a NCP Destroy Connection request to terminate a connection previously established by the NCP Create Service request. **B.** TCP Create Service Connection request; and **D.** NETBIOS Create Service Connection request, are incorrect. They are not relevant to this question.

61. ☑ **C.** External IPX Network Number of Server 3 has been configuration as 122 and should be 12. All servers physically attached on the same LAN must have the same external network number. Packets will not be forwarded correctly if the network numbers are mismatched.

☒ **A.** External IPX Network Number of Server 2 has been configuration as 12 and should be 122, is incorrect. Server 2 already has the correct External Network number of 12 and it should not be changed to 122. Router 2 has the external network number of 12 as well. **B.** External IPX Network Number of Server 3 has been configuration as 12 and should be 122, is incorrect. If Server 3 had been configured as 12, then Server 2 would not have received the error message. **D.** External IPX Network Number of Server 2 has bee configuration as 122 and should be 12, is incorrect. Server 2 has been configured as 12 instead of 122.

62. ☑ **A.** IPX NETWORK 00000012, and **B.** IPX NETWORK 12. The Cisco router is using the External IPX Network number on its configuration. Answer B is more commonly used than Answer A, because it is not necessary to place zeroes before the number.

☒ **C.** IPX NETWORK BBBBAAAA, is incorrect. IPX Network BBBBAAAA is an internal network number. The Cisco router is using an External Network Number instead of an Internal Network Number. **D.** IPX NETWORK 2, is incorrect. IPX Network 2 does not exist.

63. ☑ **A, B, D.** Mismatched network number between Server 2 and Router 2; not enough user licenses on Server 2; and cabling problems on Segment 2. If there is a mismatched network number between Server 2 and Router 2, then there will be connecting problems between Server and Workstation 2, and between Workstation 2 and other devices. Insufficient user licenses on Server 2 can cause intermittent connection problems between a workstation and file server, especially during peak hours. One can verify this by using the Monitor utility on the server console to check the connections parameter. Faulty cables can also cause intermittent connection problems. Check all cabling and connectors. Use "show interface E0" on Router 2 to check the input or output errors.

☒ **C.** is incorrect because a mismatched Ethernet frame type between Server 2 and Workstation 2 will result in no connection, instead of intermittent connections.9

64. ☑ **A.** There is no frame relay network connectivity problem; and **B.**, There are no router hardware and software problems on both Router 1 and Router 2. There is no frame relay network connectivity problem on the network because Workstation 1 can connect to Server 2, which is on the remote side of the LAN. If there had been any hardware and software problems on either Router 1 or Router 2, then Workstation 1 could not connect to Server 2. Both routers are required to make the connection between these two LANs.

☒ **C.** There are no configuration problems on all routers and file servers, is incorrect because we do not know if Server 3 has been correctly configured. **D.** There is a mismatched network number between workstation 1 and Server 2, is incorrect because there is no configuration option for the network number on Workstation 1.

65. ☑ **D.** All of the above. Class A, B, and C address spaces have been reserved for personal and business Internet addressing purposes. These addresses identify devices connected to the network. The Internet and higher layers use the IP address for routing functionality.

66. ☑ **A.** 23, In North America and Japan, ISDN PRI connection multiplexes 23 bearer channels for actual data, often called the B channels, and one signaling channel called a D (or data) channel.

☒ **B.** 24, is incorrect because ISDN PRI needs 1 signaling channel for data. **C.** 31, is incorrect because the 31 B channels is only offered in Europe. **D.** None of the above, is incorrect because A is the correct answer.

67. ☑ **A.** SHOW APPLE ARP. This is the correct Cisco IOS command to display the Apple ARP table.

☒ **B.** SHOW APPLE-TALK ARP; **C.** SHOW APT ARP; and **D.** SHOW APT ARP CACHE, are incorrect because they do not use the proper command format. Therefore, they are not valid Cisco IOS commands.

68. ☑ **C.** Routing Table Maintenance Protocol (RTMP). The native routing protocol for an AppleTalk network is the Routing Table Maintenance Protocol (RTMP). Routers on the network use this protocol to exchange and update routing information. RTMP calculates the shortest path to each destination.

☒ **A.** Open Shortest Path First (OSPF), is incorrect. **B.** Routing Information Protocol (RIP), is incorrect. **D.** Point to Point Protocol (PPP), is incorrect. These are not native protocols for an AppleTalk network. AppleTalk's native routing protocol is RTMP.

69. ☑ **D.** 32. An IP (version 4) Address consists of four bytes. As you may know, one byte is equal to eight bits. Since there are four bytes at eight bits-per-byte, this would equal 32 bits. The address is usually represented in dotted decimal notation, for example: 192.168.1.1.

☒ **A.** Four, is incorrect. An IP address does have four bytes but not four bits. **B.** Eight, is not correct. Eight bits would only equal one byte. **C.** 16, is not correct since 16 bits would equal two bytes.

70. ☑ **C.** Via ZIP. The Zone Information Protocol (ZIP) uses a startup address to the local AppleTalk router to get the correct network number(s).
☒ **A.** Via NBP, is incorrect. The Name Binding Protocol (NBP) maps a named service to its network number, its node ID, and socket number. **B.** Via ZIT, is incorrect. The Zone Information Table (ZIT) maintains a list of zone names and their associated cable ranges. **D.** Via AARP, is incorrect. The AppleTalk Address Resolution Protocol (AARP) manages node ID assignments to prevent the conflicting (duplicate) node IDs.

71. ☑ **A.** IEEE 802.2. The IEEE standard 802.2 defines the Logical Link Control field that is used by 802.3 and 802.5.
☒ **B.** IEEE 802.3, is incorrect since IEEE 802.3 defines an Ethernet frame format. **C.** IEEE 802.5, is incorrect since IEEE 802.5 defines a Token-Ring frame format. **D.** IEEE 802.x, is incorrect since IEEE 802.x refers generically to the group of IEEE 802 standards.

72. ☑ **A, B, C and D.** Corrupt packets or frames, Delayed packets or frames, Dropped packets or frames, and Packets arriving out of order. Sequencing means that a number is attached to each packet. If the packets arrive out of order, or not at all, the other end can tell because it keeps track of the sequence numbers. Checksumming refers to an algorithm called a checksum that is applied to a set of bytes. This checksum is applied to a certain portion of the packet and another number is produced. This number is sent along with the packet so that the receiving end can perform the same calculation and compare the numbers. Any discrepancy indicates that the packet was somehow modified or corrupted in transit and is considered to have not been received.

73. ☑ **D.** Seed router. A seed router is not in discovery mode once it has obtained network and node addresses.
☒ **A.** Non-discovery router; **B.** Passive router; and **C.** Active router, are incorrect. Non-discovery router, passive router, and active router are not the proper terms for describing an AppleTalk router that is not in discovery mode.

74. ☑ **D.** Unlimited. The maximum number of stations that can transmit packets simultaneously is only limited by the size of the Ethernet collision domain. Theoretically, a very large number could initiate transmission simultaneously within a particular collision domain.
☒ **A.** One, is incorrect since you cannot have a collision with only a single station. **B.** Two, is incorrect since more than two stations could be colliding within a collision domain at one time, due to the effects of propagation delay. **C.** Three, is incorrect because more than three stations could be attempting to communicate at the same time on the same Ethernet collision domain.

75. ☑ **D.** Layer 4. Port numbers are specified in the Layer 4 header inside a packet. For the current version of TCP/IP, port numbers are 16 bits long and unsigned, which gives them a decimal range of 0 through 65535.
☒ **A.** Layer 1; **B.** Layer 2; and **C.** Layer 3, are incorrect due to the port number being assigned at Layer 4.

76. ☑ **D.** Broadcast request packet, forward request, lookup request packet. This is the correct order.
☒ **A.** Forward request, broadcast request packet, lookup request packet; **B.** Forward request, lookup request packet, broadcast request packet; and **C.** Broadcast request packet, lookup request packet, forward request, are all incorrect. Compare these answers to the proper sequence in choice **D.**.

77. ☑ **C.** CLEAR COUNTERS. Clearing counters will not force AppleTalk EIGRP to update a neighboring router. It is used to reset the interface counters to zero to help diagnose problems for the interface. It can't force AppleTalk EIGRP to send an update.
☒ **A.** SHUTDOWN INTERFACE/NO SHUTDOWN INTERFACE, then CLEAR APPLETALK ROUTE, is incorrect. This will force EIGRP to send an update to a neighboring router. **B.** SHUTDOWN INTERFACE/ NO SHUTDOWN INTERFACE, then CLEAR EIGRP NEIGHBORS, is incorrect. This will also force EIGRP to send an update to a neighboring router. **D.** Reboot the router, is incorrect. Rebooting the router will force EIGRP to send an update to a neighboring router. It is recommended that you reboot during off-peak hours.

Part 7

Test Yourself:
CLSC Practice Exams
(Exam 640-404)

Test Yourself:
CLSC Practice
Exam 1 Questions

Q & A

Before you register for the actual exam, take the following test and see how you make out. Set a timer for 60 minutes—the time you'll have to take the live CCNP Cisco LAN Switch Configuration certification exam—and answer the following 70 questions in the time allotted. Once you've finished, turn to the CLSC Practice Exam I Answers section and check your score to see if you passed. Good luck!

CLSC Practice Exam I Questions

1. Which of the following statements is correct?

   A. Repeater ports all reside in a collision domain but not a broadcast domain

   B. Hub ports all reside in a broadcast domain but not collision domain

   C. Bridge ports all reside in a collision and broadcast domain

   D. Router ports each create a collision domain and broadcast domain

2. Choose two priority levels that the Catalyst incorporates to handle oversubscribed interfaces.

   A. Back-plane base

   B. High priority

   C. Normal priority

   D. Switch cache

3. What is the light source for a fiber module with single-mode fiber?

   A. LED

   B. Bright light

   C. Laser

   D. Blue light

4. Port VLAN membership based on MAC address was originally released on what software version?

   A. Software release 4.2

   B. Software release 2.2

   C. Software release 4.3

   D. Software release 2.3

5. What is the theoretical maximum number of SAIDs that can be in use?

   A. 1024
   B. 255
   C. 4 million
   D. 4.29 billion

6. How does the Catalyst 3000 Series switch determine whether it is connected to a matrix, and also see what other switches are connected to the stack?

   A. By means of a broadcast
   B. By using a 9th pin on an RJ45 cable
   C. By broadcasting heartbeats
   D. By sending a packet destined for the MAC address of the management PC

7. Which statement best describes a LAN segment?

   A. A group of LANs
   B. A group of routers
   C. A group of departments
   D. A group of defined ports on a switch

8. Which of the following functions does the console port allow?
Choose all that apply.

   A. Configure the switch from a web-based application
   B. Configure the switch from the CLI
   C. Monitor RMON parameters
   D. Monitor network statistics

9. Which command will copy a software image from a module to a specified host?

   A. COPY TFTP FLASH
   B. DOWNLOAD *host file-name*
   C. UPLOAD *host file-name*
   D. CONFIGURE NETWORK

10. Which one of the following statements about the difference between in-band and out-of-band connections is true?

  A. A Telnet server is needed for in-band connections, while nothing except a modem is needed for out-of-band connections

  B. Out-of-band connections require a modem, while in-band connections do not

  C. Out-of-band requires external access to the network, while in-band is internal to the network

  D. Access can be denied via out-of-band services, while there is no real control over in-band connections

  E. None of the above

11. Which of the following is NOT an option that a LEC has to contact the LECS?

  A. ILMI

  B. Broadcast

  C. Pre-configured address

  D. Well-known LECS ATM address

12. What is the maximum number of outbound Telnet sessions allowed on a Catalyst 3000 Series switch?

  A. 0

  B. 1

  C. 5

  D. 8

  E. 10

13. Which of the following forms of switching is best for high levels of data integrity?

  A. Cut-through switching

  B. Store-and-forward

  C. Both work equally well

  D. None

14. In the scenario, which Catalyst product is required to support redundancy with a supervisor II module installed?

A. 5000

B. 5002

C. 5300

D. 5500

15. Below is the output from a SHOW NTP command.

```
C5k> (enable) show ntp
Current time: Mon Jun 14 1999, 14:34:36 bst
Timezone: '', offset from UTC is 0 hours
Summertime: 'bst', enabled
Last NTP update: Mon Jun 14 1999, 14:34:11
Broadcast client mode: disabled
Broadcast delay: 3000 microseconds
Client mode: enabled
NTP-Server
----------------------------------------
ntp-server.intranet.xyzco.com
```

Which of the following are true?

A. Both DNS and NTP are enabled

B. NTP is enabled but not updating

C. The NTP client is a Stratum 2 server

D. The NTP broadcasts are sent every 3000 microseconds by the switch

E. The time zone has not been set

16. What is an imperative for using in-band management?

A. The need to be on the same subnet as the device you are trying to manage

B. The need to be running TCP/IP

C. The need for CWSI to be running

D. The need to have a Telnet client

17. Which of the following is true about the ATM multi-mode fiber module?

    A. Can be used to a maximum distance of 2km

    B. The light source used to transmit on an ATM module is an LED

    C. Supports up to 4096 virtual circuits.

    D. Does not support AAL5

    E. Uses an MIC-type connector

18. What devices propagate collided frames? Choose all that apply.

    A. Catalyst switches running store-and-forward switching

    B. Routers

    C. Bridges

    D. Hubs

19. When a switch does not have the destination address in its forwarding table, how do packets get forwarded?

    A. Packets don't get forwarded—they get dropped

    B. An unreachable error message gets sent back to the source

    C. The packet is flooded to all ports except the source port within the VLAN

    D. The packet is automatically forwarded to another VLAN

20. Which supervisory modules can have multiple boot images residing in Flash? Choose all that apply.

    A. Supervisor engine II

    B. Supervisor engine III

    C. Supervisor engine III FSX

    D. Supervisor engine III FLX

21. The CDP information detailed below allows you to make what assumptions about the network?

```
C5k> (enable) show cdp neighbors
Capability Codes: R - Router, T - Trans Bridge, B - Source Route Bridge
S - Switch, H - Host, I - IGMP, r - Repeater
Port    Device-ID            Port-ID           Platform          Capability
------- -------------------- ----------------- ----------------- ------
1/1     123456789(C5k_F1)    6/5               WS-C5509          T B S
2/1     987654321(C5k_F2)    4/1               WS-C5509          T B S
```

  A. Port 1/1 of Switch C5k connects to Port 6/5 of Switch C5k and Port 2/1 of Switch C5k connects to Port 4/1 of Switch C5k
  B. Port 1/1 of Switch C5k connects to Port 6/5 of Switch C5k_F1 and Port 2/1 of Switch C5k connects to Port 4/1 of Switch C5k_F2
  C. Both the remote and local systems are Catalyst 5509s
  D. Both C5k_F1 & C5k_F2 are Catalyst 5509s
  E. The local Switch is capable of source-route bridging

22. Which of the following is characteristic of Simple Server Redundancy Protocol?

  A. Operates on all platforms
  B. Always enabled when LANE is in use
  C. Allows multiple LECS and LES/BUS pairs
  D. Supported since IOS version 11.1

23. How is a LAN segmented? Choose all that apply.

  A. By function
  B. By project
  C. By application
  D. By department
  E. All of the above

24. On which of the switches in the following illustration could you create a new VLAN, assuming they are all running VTP version 2, and are all in the same VTP domain?

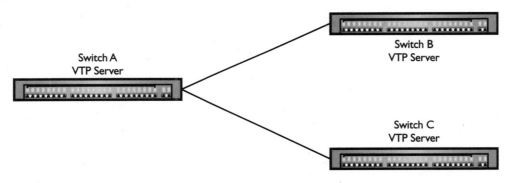

Switch A
VTP Server

Switch B
VTP Server

Switch C
VTP Server

A. A and B

B. B

C. C

D. A and C

E. A, B and C

Use the Following Scenario to Answer Questions 25–26

AP Manufacturing has three campus-like facilities across the country. Each campus consists of three buildings supporting around 300–500 users per campus. The company runs in such a way that working at home is greatly encouraged. The company policy is, "do not come to the office unless required," and is highly encouraged. Also, there are no specified seating assignments, thereby providing a great deal of flexibility for interdepartmental corroboration. For example, if finance has a meeting with manufacturing, the meeting is facilitated by users simply plugging laptops into network jacks and logging in from wherever they are.

25. What is the difference between dynamic VLAN and static VLAN configuration?

A. Static VLANs do not require special configuration on each port and dynamic VLANs do

B. Configuring static VLANs is only done when more than one VLAN is set up

    C. Proper configuration of dynamic VLANs allows a user to log in to any VLAN

    D. Dynamic VLANs require a server to support the configuration and static VLANs do not

26. What configuration values does VTP NOT distribute?

    A. Emulated LAN names

    B. 802.10 SAID values

    C. MTU

    D. RTMP

27. What is the purpose of the spanning-tree algorithm?

    A. To provide two active paths to a destination

    B. To provide loop detection and backup of data paths

    C. To send out explorer packets so that the source host knows the paths to a destination host

    D. To allow IP and IPX to work together

28. What must the default ELAN in an ATM LANE be?

    A. Restricted membership

    B. Unrestricted membership

    C. A member of both the VLAN and ELAN

    D. Does not require anything

29. How many VLANs can be active on a Catalyst switch?

    A. 100

    B. 200

    C. 250

    D. 1024

30. When trying to disable an Ethernet port on a switch, which of the following applications could you use?

    A. CDP

    B. RMON

    C. Telnet

    D. CiscoView

    E. VLAN Director

31. When configuring LANE, which of the following is NOT correct?

    A. A LEC and LES from two or more different ELANs cannot be configured on the same subinterface

    B. You cannot set up a LEC, LES and BUS on the same subinterface

    C. A BUS can be on a different ELAN to the LES for the ELAN

    D. LECs from different ELANs cannot be configured on the same subinterface

32. With cut-through switching, when does frame forwarding start?

    A. When the CRC is checked

    B. When the whole packet is read

    C. When the destination address is read

    D. The switch cuts the packet up into smaller pieces before it forwards

33. What type of packet does a Token Ring station broadcast when the host does not know a path to the desired destination?

    A. MAC

    B. Routing

    C. Explorer

    D. NWC

34. Which of the following is the correct statement regarding the RSM module?

    A. Uses the same operating system as the Catalyst switch

    B. Is menu driven, as is the 3000 series switch

    C. Uses the Cisco IOS independently of the Catalyst operating system

    D. Stores its operating system with the Catalyst supervisor module

35. Which two answers would best describe the effect of the following two Catalyst commands on an Ethernet 5224 card (24 port 10/100 card)?

    A. C5K> (ENABLE) SET PORT BROADCAST 4/12 50%

    B. C5K> (ENABLE) SET PORT BROADCAST 4/19 50

    C. Allow the broadcasts on port 4/12 to be 50 percent of the total traffic

    D. Allow the broadcasts on port 4/12 to be 50 percent of the total bandwidth of the port

36. On a 10/100 Ethernet module, you notice that the 100M is green and the link light is amber. What could this mean?

    A. The port has detected that another switch is connected

    B. The port has security on it and has seen a different MAC address to the one with which it was configured

    C. The port has been disabled

    D. The port is working correctly

    E. The port is inserted at an incorrect speed

37. Which of the following are characteristics of TACACS+?

    A. Uses TCP Port 49

    B. Uses a UDP high port

    C. Requires that the Catalyst has a valid IP address configured

    D. The server is only supported on NT

    E. Only one TACACS+ server can be configured per VLAN

38. How can VLANs improve security? Choose all that apply.

A. Filtering by source address

B. Filtering by destination address

C. Filtering by network layer protocol types

D. Allowing broadcast traffic defined by the router only

39. Which two of the answers below are NOT true when comparing a Cisco 2820 Series switch to a Cisco 1900 Series switch?

A. The 2820 can have stored 2048 or 8096 MAC addresses; the 1900 can only store 1024

B. The 2820 has two expansion slots; the 1900 has none

C. The 2820 supports cut-through or store-and-forward; the 1900 only supports cut-through

D. The 2820 can be field upgraded to a higher MAC address count; the 1900 cannot

40. How many switch modules does the Catalyst 5002 support?

A. One

B. Two

C. Three

D. None

41. What differences would you see by using CGMP on the switches in the following illustration?

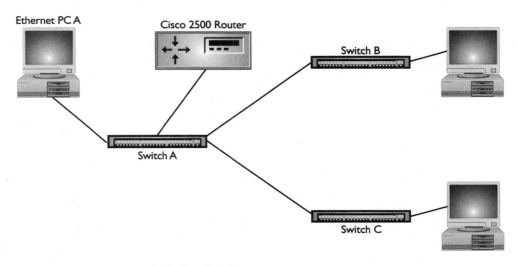

A. Less available bandwidth

B. A saving on network bandwidth

C. Reconfigured workstations to work with CGMP

D. Less CPU usage

E. A slowing of network speed

42. Of the following commands, which could be used on the switches to only troubleshoot the problem of why a client on switch A (on VLAN100) cannot see a client on switch B (on VLAN 200), assuming there were RSMs in both switches?

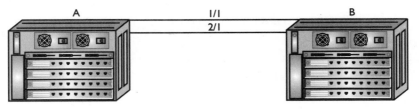

A. SHOW PORT

B. SHOW TRUNK

C. SHOW CAM

D. SHOW MAC

E. SHOW ARP

43. At the core of the Cisco 1900/2820 Series Switches ClearChannel architecture is the forwarding engine. Which of the following answers is NOT a function of the forwarding engine?

     A. It is implemented in an ASIC

     B. Examining packets from incoming ports and sending packets to the correct port for transmission

     C. Has a feature very similar to the Catalyst 5000 CAM

     D. Makes the routing decisions

     E. Maintains statistics for the switch

44. Which protocol is used to connect with the registration of multicast services?

     A. IGMP

     B. ICMP

     C. ASDL

     D. CGMP

     E. SNMP

     F. VMPS

45. Choose the best description for port-centric VLANs.

     A. All VLANs plugged into the port are flooded to every port on the switch

     B. Token Ring information is flooded to other rings

     C. All end stations connected to ports belonging to the same VLAN are assigned to the same VLAN number

     D. The routing of VLAN information from one VLAN port to another

46. Which command will allow you to overwrite or erase switch settings? Choose all that apply.

     A. SET

     B. SHOW

     C. CLEAR

     D. ERASE

47. AP manufacturing, in the scenario, wishes to employ TACACS+ for security. TACACS+ supports authentication, authorization, and accounting. On the Catalyst 5000 series switches that AP Manufacturing currently has in place, which of the following functions does the Catalyst switch support?

A. Authentication

B. Authorization

C. Accounting

D. None of the above

48. A workstation is connected to a switch, but there is no link light on a 10/100 port. What could be the possible reason?

A. The cable is a crossover

B. The device is switched off

C. The device is running at 10 Mbps, instead of 100 Mbps

D. The distance of the cable is 87 meters

49. When a packet is received by the Cisco 1900/2820 Series switch, which two processes take place simultaneously?

A. Destination address check

B. Forwarding decision

C. Broadcast control

D. Address learning

E. Inter-VLAN routing

50. Which of the following trunking protocols and physical layer pairs are NOT supported on the Catalyst 5500?

A. Ethernet and 802.1q

B. Token Ring and ISL

C. Ethernet and ISL

D. FDDI and 802.10

E. Token Ring and 802.1q

Refer to the Following Illustration to Answer Questions 51–53

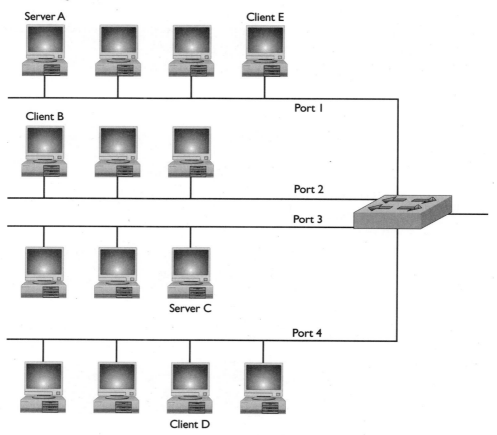

51. Which statement best describes a broadcast domain?

A. A special address reserved for sending messages to all stations

B. The set of devices that receive broadcast frames originating from any device within the set

C. An area where hosts are allowed to send broadcasts

D. None of the above

52. If ports 1–4 are single VLANs, and Client E on port 1 sends out packets to client D on port 4, who will see the packets?

A. All stations on all switch ports

B. Client B

C. All stations on port 4

D. All stations on port 3

53. If ports 1–4 are individual VLANs, how will client D communicate with server C?

A. The same way communication would take place if ports 1-4 were set up as a single VLAN

B. Through a router

C. Through a bridge

D. By sneaker net

54. Which of the following protocols map 802.10, LAN Emulation, and ISL together to create integrated VLAN implementation?

A. 802.1q

B. VTP

C. SAID

D. LANE

55. How do you display the VLANs that are configured on a Cisco Switch? Choose all that apply.

A. SHOW CONFIGURATION

B. SHOW VLAN

C. SHOW INTERFACE

D. SHOW ACTIVE

56. In the scenario, Building1 campus1 has DNS configured at the backbone Catalyst 5000 switch. A user pings ApmfgServer1 which is in another building and receives a reply back. In pinging the server using the server's name, why does an echo reply return to that workstation?

A. The user was already logged in

B. DNS maps IP addresses to device names

C. The PING command really takes place on the DNS server

D. The network administrator forwards the request

57. Which of the following does NOT characterize FDDI/CDDI?

A. It can use STP & UTP for distances up to 100m

B. It can use single mode fiber

C. It can run at speeds of 100 Mbps

D. It is a LAN standard as specified by the IEEE 802.10 committee

E. It is a dual token passing ring

58. Given the output below, what is NOT true?

```
Catalyst 2820 - System Configuration
System Revision:  0              Address Capacity:     8192
System Last Reset:      Sunday  June 27  15:45:45 1999
[N]    Name of system
[C]    Contact name
[L]    Location
[D]    Date/time                           Sun June 27  17:55:55  1999
[S]    Switching mode                      FastForward
[U]    Use of store-and-forward for multicast    Enabled
[A]    Action upon address violation       Disable
[G]    Generate alert on address violation       Disabled
[M]    Management Console inactivity timeout     600 second (s)
[I]    Address aging time                  300 second (s)
[P]    Network Port                        None
----------------------------------Actions----------------------------------
[R]    Reset system                  [F]   Reset to factory defaults
---------------------------------Related Menus------------------------------
[B]    Broadcast storm control       [X]   Exit to Main Menu
```

A. This is a Cisco 2822 switch

B. The system was reset earlier today

C. The system has been reset to factory defaults

D. The CAM aging timer is five minutes

E. The switching type is established on a per port basis

59. Which of the following is NOT a LAN emulation service?

A. LECS
B. LEC
C. LES
D. BUS
E. LE-ARP

60. What does Token Ring CRF provide? Choose all that apply.

A. A logical grouping of Token Ring numbers
B. A logical grouping of Token Ring ports on a switch
C. A logical grouping of Token Ring network numbers
D. A proven backup mechanism

61. Which port on the Catalyst 5000 supports SLIP?

A. Serial port
B. Console port
C. Auxiliary port
D. Any LAN interface

62. Why is routing required between different VLANs on the same switch?

A. To control broadcast traffic to other VLANs
B. VLANs do not communicate with each other at the transport layer
C. VLANs do not communicate with each other at the data-link layer
D. VLANs do not communicate with each other at the network layer

63. Which of the following is true about FDDI check?

A. It checks to make sure that the FDDI ring is up and running
B. It normally needs to be enabled when there are older FDDI devices on the ring
C. It stops possible useless frames from endlessly circling the ring
D. It is a health check on the ring to make sure that all stations are sending and receiving as should be

64. Which one of the following specifications regarding the Cisco Catalyst 3000 features is incorrect?

A. 16 switched 10 Mbps ports as standard

B. Can support up to 1700 addresses per port

C. Can support up to 8096 addresses in the system address table

D. Has a forwarding rate of 714kbps

E. Has two high-speed expansion slots

F. The Cisco Catalyst 3000 can have up to 10,000 addresses in the system address table

65. As which of the following can the Cisco ATM LAN emulation module be configured?

A. LEC

B. LECS

C. LES

D. BUS

66. What is considered a cardinal rule for segmented network configuration with regards to demand and resource nodes?

A. Design so that demands equal resources

B. Design so that demands exceed resources

C. Design so that demands never exceed resources

D. Demands to matter to resources

67. At what layer of the OSI model does RMON work?

A. Data link

B. Network

C. Session

D. Application

68. On certain Fast Ethernet and Gigabit Ethernet ports you can specify three different trunking protocols. What three are they?

A. ISL

B. DTP

C. 802.1Q

D. VMPS

69. Which of the following is NOT true?

A. The maximum distance of Multimode FDDI SAS is 2km

B. The maximum distance of a UTP SAS is 100m

C. If all card tests pass OK, the status light on an FDDI/CDDI module turn green when completed

D. FDDI can either be single or multi-mode fiber

E. There is an optical bypass switch port on both the FDDI and CDDI modules

70. Which of the following statements regarding VLANs is NOT true?

A. A Catalyst 3000 Series switch supports VTP

B. The Catalyst 3000 can recognize and use up to 1024 VLANs

C. The Catalyst 3000 Stack can only support up to 64 active VLANs

D. The Catalyst 3000 supports ISL and ATM LANE trunking protocols

CCNP

CISCO CERTIFIED NETWORK PROFESSIONAL

Test Yourself:
CLSC Practice
Exam 1 Answers

Q

&

A

The answers to the questions are in boldface, followed by a brief explanation. Some of the explanations detail the logic you should use to choose the correct answer, while others give factual reasons why the answer is correct. If you miss several questions on a similar topic, you should review the corresponding section in the *Cisco LAN Switch Configuration Study Guide* before taking the CLSC test.

CLSC Practice Exam 1 Answers

1. ☑ **D. Each interface of a router creates a collision domain and a broadcast domain.**
   ☒ **A.** is incorrect. Repeater ports reside in both a collision domain and broadcast domain. Repeaters forward traffic to all ports, regardless of other ports supporting devices on a different network. An example of a multiport repeater is a 10BaseT hub. All traffic is forwarded to all ports, except the port on which traffic is received. **B.** Hub ports, is incorrect, since they are like repeater ports. The device supports a higher concentration of ports, but still forwards all traffic to all ports, except to the port on which traffic is received. **C.** is incorrect because on bridges the ports break up collision domains. So if a single device were attached to each bridge port, there would be no collisions. Broadcast traffic would still be forwarded.

2. ☑ **B and C. High priority and normal priority.** Each port can be set to a desired priority level. The two options available per port are high priority or normal priority. To assign a high priority to a port, you must configure the port for that priority level. Following is an example of configuring a port for high priority:

   ```
   Console> (enable) set port level 1/1 high
   ```

   ☒ **A.** Back-plane base, is incorrect as there is no such priority on the Catalyst. **D.** Switch cache, is incorrect because there is no such priority on the Catalyst.

3. ☑ **C.** In order for single mode fiber to achieve the distance requirements with minimal signal loss, the light source must be powerful enough to drive the signal. LED is okay for short distance requirements, but there is smearing and signal degradation. With Laser as the source, distances of up to 10KM can be achieved.

☒ **A.** is incorrect. LED is used in multimode fiber, which provides a maximum distance of 2KM or 1.2 miles. **B.** bright light, and **C.** laser, are not valid sources of light for fiber optic.

4. ☑ **D.** Software release 2.3. This feature enables dynamic assignment of a port's VLAN membership based on the source MAC address of the incoming packet. The MAC address should be configured with the VLAN. If the source MAC address changes, the VLAN will change. Furthermore, if the user moves to a different port on the switch the VLAN port assignment will move as well. This feature was made available on software release 2.3.

☒ **A.** Software release 4.2, and **B.** software release 2.2, are incorrect. They are much newer releases of Catalyst software, and they do contain this feature, but this is not the revision of the software in which this feature was originally presented. **C.** Software release 4.3, is incorrect. This release came out before the feature stated was available.

5. ☑ **D.** The four-byte SAID allows for 2^{32} distinct VLANs, which equals 4.29 billion. The SAID is a value which is used to map Ethernet VLANs when trunking over 802.10 links. When a frame is transmitted over an 802.10 link, the SAID is used in the frame header. This value will then map to a specific Ethernet VLAN.

☒ **A.** 1024; **B.** 255; and **C.** 4 million; are all incorrect values.

6. ☑ **C.** The Catalyst 3000 Series switch sends heartbeats to its neighbors, these consist of the stack ID, source MAC address, and the box number.

☒ **A.** is incomplete because a heartbeat broadcast is required. **B.** is incorrect because the method isn't limited to the type of cable or pin number. **D.** is incorrect, because the switch sends a broadcast, not a packet destined to one address.

7. ☑ **D.** A group of defined ports on a switch is what defines a LAN segment on a switch device. Switch devices offer the flexibility to divide a network in many different ways. Security, along with other controls, may also be a factor in defining a LAN segment; grouping switch ports to provide the desired LAN segment offers those flexibilities.
☒ **A.** A group of LANs, is incorrect because each LAN is a segment. **B.** A group of routes, is incorrect because it hosts multiple segments and even networks. If you should try to configure two ports on a router with the same network address, the router will alert you with an error. **C.** A group of departments, is incorrect because a group of departments does not define anything on a LAN. A group of departments can be combined on a LAN segment, but the statement does not provide that option.

8. ☑ **B and D.** The console port is used for the initial configuration of the switch, the IP address of the switch, and the SNMP read/write strings. The console port can also be configured to monitor network statistics with SNMP.
☒ **A.** is incorrect. It is not possible to configure the switch from a Web-based GUI. However, some of the 2900 Series switches can be configured via a Web-based GUI. **C.** To monitor the RMON parameters, a program such as CiscoWorks for Switched Internetworks is needed (CWSI).

9. ☑ **C.** The upload command will enable you to copy a software image (switch operating system) from a module to a specified host. If you should try to load the incorrect image into a module it will be rejected.
☒ **A,** COPY TFTP FLASH, is an incorrect direction. This command will copy a software image from a specified host to a module. **B.** DOWNLOAD *host file-name* does the same thing as copy TFTP flash. This is the true form of the command. **D.** CONFIGURE NETWORK download a configuration file form a specified host to a switch.

10. ☑ **E.** None of the above.
☒ **A.** is false. If you Telnet to the Admin Interface then a Telnet server is needed on the interface; however, in-band could also be used via SNMP. Also, a modem can be used for SLIP access, but a direct terminal

connection does not require a modem to be connected. **B.** Out-of-band management does not always require a modem; however, the second part of the statement is true—in-band connections do not require a modem to connect. **C.** This statement is false, since a person external to the network could possibly Telnet to a switch within the network. This would in turn allow an external accessor to use an in-band management option. **D.** is false. In-band connections could be managed by means of access lists on routers or MAC-based access lists on each port of the switch, only allowing certain hosts access to either the admin port or to the SNMP information.

11. ☑ **B.** Broadcast. This option is not valid, as it is not possible to find out the address of the LECS via a broadcast packet. ATM does not even allow native broadcast packets. When a station needs to send a broadcast packet, it actually uses the BUS as a resolution for broadcasts.
    ☒ **A,** Interim Local Management Interface (ILMI) uses a type of SNMP to enable communication between two ATM devices. **C.** A LEC can be configured to look for a pre-configured LECS address. **D.** There is also a well-known ATM address that is used specifically for the LECS service.

12. ☑ **C.** Five. The Cisco 3000 Series switch allows up to five outbound Telnet sessions, the maximum allowed (a value between 1–5). This can be configured from the Telnet configuration menu.
    ☒ **A.** 0; **B.** 1; **D.** 8; and **E.** 10; are all incorrect values.

13. ☑ **B.** In store-and-forward mode, the port adapter reads the entire frame into memory and then determines if the frame should be forwarded. At this point, the frame is examined for any errors and frames with errors are not forwarded. If the frame contains no errors, it is sent to the destination port for forwarding. While store-and-forward reduces errors on the LAN, this form of switching increases latency, and that latency is dependent on the length of the frame.
    ☒ **A.** Cut-through mode, does not provide any error checking algorithms. **C.** Both work equally well, is incorrect, since cut-through mode does not provide error checking. **D.** none, is incorrect.

14. ☑ **A** and **D.** The Catalyst 5500 supports redundant supervisor modules. The redundant supervisor-engine operation feature allows you to install a second supervisor-engine module in a Catalyst 5505, 5509, or 5500 switch. The second supervisor engine takes over if the active supervisor engine fails. No software commands are needed to enable this functionality.

    ☒ **B.** Catalyst 5002, is incorrect. It does not support the supervisor II engine. The Catalyst 5002 uses the supervisor I. **C.** 5300, is incorrect. This is not a Catalyst product, but an access server.

15. ☑ **A** and **E.** Both NTP and DNS are enabled and seem to be working correctly due to two facts. First, according to the information given, the last NTP update was received roughly 25 seconds since the current time, this would mean that the NTP is working correctly. Secondly, the NTP-server is NOT an IP Address, but has been resolved from an IP address onto a DNS Name. When entering the list of NTP servers, you can either enter the NTP server as an IP address (and when it gets resolved, you know that DNS is working), or as a DNS name. If entering a DNS name, the switch will not allow you to enter a name that is not in the DNS. That the time zone has not been set can be observed, since time has been set for BST (British Summer Time); however, the offset from UTC is 0 hours.

    ☒ **B.** NTP is enabled but not updating, is incorrect. According to the output, the NTP client has received its last update from the NTP server 25 seconds ago, which means that the NTP server is updating the NTP client. There is the possibility that the NTP server may have gone down in the last 25 seconds and we do not know about it. However, with the information, we could not come to that conclusion. **C.** The switch is set up to be an NTP client and, therefore, announces itself as being able to be synchronized, and cannot synchronize other clients. A Stratum 1 server has a direct connection to a reliable clock source such as a GPS. A Stratum 2 server gets its NTP information from a Stratum 1 server. **D.** NTP broadcast packets are not being sent out by the switch, the broadcast delay of 3000 microseconds is an adjustment made by the switch to the actual time for any possible latency between the NTP server and the client.

16. ☑ **B.** The need to be running TCP/IP. Whether you are going to use Telnet to access the management console or use an SNMP-capable device to change parameters via SNMP, you need to have IP running on the device you want to use.

☒ **A.** A need to be on the same subnet as the device you are trying to manage, is incorrect. It is not necessary for you to be on the same subnet as the device you are trying to manage, as long as you have a route to the device (this could involve several routers on the way). **C.** Although CWSI can be used in part to do in-band management, it is not the sole way in which in-band management can be accomplished on a Catalyst switch. **D.** The need to have a Telnet client, is incorrect. To have the capability to Telnet to a switch is one way in which to use in-band management; however, it is not the sole way, as CiscoView or CWSI could be used.

17. ☑ **A, B** and **C.** The multi-mode fiber ATM card has a maximum distance of 2km, and its source is an LED. The ATM multi-mode module also supports up to 4096 virtual circuits.

☒ **D.** Does not support AAL5, is incorrect. The module does support the ATM adaptation Layer 5 (AAL5). **E.** Uses a MIC-type connector, is incorrect. The multi-mode fiber module actually uses an SC connector, and not a MIC connector.

18. ☑ **C** and **D.** Hubs are not much more than concentrated repeaters. Hubs have no intelligence in terms of looking at packets to decipher source and destination, the condition of the packet that is being propagated, or which LAN segment the packet is being sent from or going to. All that a hub knows is that data is being transmitted into it, and its job is to forward the information, without determining condition, source, or destination of the packets. Bridges will look at the source address and build a table to determine which devices reside on which segment. But, like hubs, switches don't analyze the packets being received.

☒ **A.** is incorrect. A Catalyst switch running the store-and-forward switching method will do a CRC check on every packet. Any packets that do not pass the CRC check are discarded. **B.** is incorrect because routers also do a CRC check on packets received. Forwarding packets that do not pass CRC checks add traffic to the network, and routers as well as the store-and-forward switching method provide means to make the network more efficient.

19. ☑ **C.** The packet is flooded to all ports except the source port within the VLAN. As a switch is powered up, the device begins to read in MAC addresses of the host that is transmitting data from switch ports. Those MAC addresses are placed in a table. Thus when a frame needs to get to a destination, the switch looks at its switching table and forwards the packet based on the information in that table. If the switch does not have the destination MAC address in its switching table, the switch floods the packet to all ports in its corresponding VLAN. When a reply comes back from the destination-end system, the MAC address from the reply is placed in the switching table.

☒ **A.** Packets don't get forwarded—they get dropped, is incorrect. Packets do not get forwarded if the packet was destined for a different network or VLAN. **B.** An unreachable error message gets sent back to the source, is incorrect. An unreachable message does not get sent back, at least not from the switch. The packet is either forwarded to a switch port or flooded to all ports in that VLAN. **D.** The packet is automatically forwarded to another VLAN, is incorrect. Forwarding the packet to another VLAN would require a Layer 3 or network layer device to facilitate the forwarding of the frame to another VLAN.

20. ☑ **B, C and D.** Since you can store multiple boot images on the supervisor engines III, III FSX, and III FLX modules, the modules need to know the name of the boot-file image and the location of the image file in the Flash file system in order to boot and synchronize properly.

☒ **A.** is incorrect. The supervisor II engine does not support multiple boot images.

21. ☑ **B and D.** From the information given in the question, the following can be deduced. The local Port 1/1 goes to the remote switch C5k_F1 Port 6/5, and local port 2/1 goes to remote Switch C5k_F2 Port 4/1. From the heading platform, you can see WS-C5509, which indicates that the remote device is a Catalyst 5500 (You should be able to look up the part number on the CCO.)

☒ **A.** is incorrect. From the output in the question, the local ports connect to remote ports, and not local ports as indicated above. **C.** is incorrect. Unfortunately, with the information provided, we do not know what platform the local Catalyst is on. **E.** is incorrect. Although you can see from the Capability column that both of the remote switches are capable of being a Transparent Bridge, Source Route Bridge, and Switch, we are given no information about the local switch.

22. ☑ **B** and **C.** By default, when LANE is enabled, SSRP is automatically enabled as well. SSRP gives you the ability to have backup LECS and LES/BUS servers in case the primary servers fail.

☒ **A.** Operates on all platforms, is incorrect. Unfortunately, SSRP is only supported on Cisco LECS and LES/BUSs. No support has been provided for any other vendors. **D.** Supported since IOS version 11.1, is incorrect. SSRP was a new implementation in IOS Version 11.2.

23. ☑ **E.** All of the above. LANs can be segmented in many different ways. Depending on the policies in place, the network administrator's design, along with other factors such as security and control, all can dictate how a LAN is segmented.

24. ☑ **D.** A and C. Only in VTP server mode can you add or delete VLANs. There are other features that can be accessed in server mode, such as the VTP version number, which can be either version 1 or version 2. Please note that version 1 and version 2 are NOT compatible. If you are suing Token Ring on the Catalyst Switches, then version 2 must be used. There is also an option to enable VTP pruning.

☒ **A, B, C,** and **E.** are all incorrect. These combinations are both VTP server and clients. Unfortunately, in VTP client mode, you cannot add or delete VLAN information. However, the functionality of VTP is the same, with the same options as in VTP server mode.

25. ☑ **D.** Dynamic VLANs require a server to support the configuration; static VLANs do not. To properly configure dynamic VLAN memberships, a VMPS must be set up so that the MAC address-to-VLAN mapping database is downloaded from the TFTP server and VMPS can begin to accept client requests. Dynamic VLAN membership allows hosts to log into a VLAN based on the host MAC address. Static VLAN assignment is a per-port configuration where a port is mapped to a specific VLAN, regardless of the host MAC address. The port can be configured so that only a specific host MAC address is authorized to access a specific port on a switch.

☒ **A.** Dynamic VLANs require a server to support the configuration and static VLANs do not, is incorrect. Static VLANs do no require specific configuration if the desired VLAN for all the ports is going to be the default (VLAN 1), otherwise the ports do need to be configured for the desired VLAN. **B.** Configuring static VLANs is only when more than one VLAN is set up, is incorrect. If the switch is to have more than one VLAN, the switch will need to be configured to assign the desired VLAN to a specific port. **C.** Proper configuration of dynamic VLANs allows a user to log in to any VLAN, is incorrect. With proper configuration of dynamic VLAN membership, the host is required to log into a designated VLAN and will not be able to access other VLANs without the aid of a router.

26. ☑ **D.** RTMP is an AppleTalk distance-vector routing protocol that functions at the network layer. Switches do not affect routing protocols in terms of adding to the hop count.

☒ **A.** Emulated LAN names, is incorrect. It is an ATM function that is distributed to other switches using VTP. Emulated LAN names are distributed across the ATM networks. **B.** 802.10 SAID values, is incorrect. They are distributed across the switched network. The 802.10 field is used as the VLAN ID in FDDI. **C.** Maximum Transmission Unit (MTU), is incorrect. These sizes are distributed across the network. MTUs define the maximum size of data packets. Different protocols have different maximums: Ethernet has 1518 bytes, and Token Ring or FDDI, 4096 bytes, for example. If FDDI is translated into Ethernet without placing the FDDI information into a format that Ethernet can understand (packet size of 1518 bytes), the packet is dropped on the Ethernet segment.

27. ☑ **B.** Spanning-Tree Protocol is a link management protocol that provides path redundancy while preventing loops in the network. For an Ethernet network to function properly, only one active path can exist between two stations. Multiple active paths between hosts cause loops in networks. These loops provide the potential for the duplication of messages. When loops occur, switches can see hosts on both sides of the switch. This condition confuses the forwarding algorithm and allows a duplicate frame to be forwarded. Spanning tree forces certain redundant paths into standby mode. So, if the primary path fails, the backup path is activated and frames are forwarded through the secondary path.

　　 ☒ **A.** To provide two active paths to a destination, is incorrect. The spanning tree does exactly the opposite. The spanning tree does not allow two active paths, but recognizes that there are two and places one of the paths in standby mode. **C.** To send out explorer packets so that the source host knows the paths to a destination host, is incorrect. The explorer packet technology is not used to disable the possibility of loops, but uses special frames to decipher the best route to a destination. **D.** To allow IP and IPX to work together, is incorrect. IP and IPX are two different frame types, and although both encapsulations can run on the same wire, IP does not communicate with IPS transparently.

28. ☑ **B.** Unrestricted membership. On an ATM network, ELANs are designated by a name. You can configure some ELANs from a router and some from a Catalyst 5000 series switch. You can configure some ELANs with unrestricted membership and some with restricted membership. You can also configure a default ELAN, which must have unrestricted membership.

　　 ☒ **A.** Restricted ELAN membership, is incorrect. It must be configured. **C.** The default ELAN does not need to be mapped to a VLAN. **D.** the default ELAN does need some configuration and the configuration needs to have unrestricted membership.

29. ☑ **C.** A maximum of 250 VLANs are supported by any single Catalyst switch; however, this it would mean that almost every port on the switch (even if it was an almost fully laden 5500) would be in a different VLAN. This would most probably lead to routing issues as each VLAN is essentially it's own broadcast domain which would mean that to route between VLANs you would need at least a couple of routers processing a single port at a time.

    ☒ **A.** 100; **B.** 200; and **D.** 1024; are all incorrect values. The maximum number of VLANs supported by a 5500 is 250, but as the correct answer suggests, this would lead to each port being in its own VLAN.

30. ☑ **C** and **D.** Telnet and CiscoView. The easiest and quickest way to disable an Ethernet port is to Telnet to the management IP address and use the command-line editor. The second way is to use CiscoView, which brings a graphical picture of the Catalyst onto the screen. On the condition that you have SNMP read/write capability, you should be able to disable the offending port.

    ☒ **A.** CDP, is incorrect. This is a data-link protocol that allows you to view other Cisco devices connected to the device you are on. **B.** RMON, does not have this capability. **E.** VLAN Director, is part of CWSI that manages VLANs. It has nothing to do with the actual physical port layer.

31. ☑ **B.** LEC, LES, and BUS can all be set up on the same subinterface.

    ☒ **A, C** and **D.** All of these statements are incorrect.

32. ☑ **C.** When the destination address is read. Cut-through switching does not read the entire packet into the switch cache, but only reads the destination address before the forwarding decision is made and begins. This improves throughput of packets within a LAN segment by enabling a packet to be forwarded even before the entire packet is read into memory. On high performance networks, latency is always of great concern; cut-through switching directly addresses performance issues.

☒   **A.** When the CRC is checked, is incorrect because the leading edge of the packet is read on, and forwarding decisions are based on, the data in the leading edge. Also, this is where the forwarding information is located. **B,** When the whole packet is read, is incorrect because the whole packet is not read into memory, just the leading edge of the packet. **D.** is incorrect because the packet in any of the two forms of switching is not broken up into smaller pieces.

33. ☑   **C.** The explorer packet is the tool used to find the destination host. An explorer reply is what gets sent back to the source host to determine the best path to the destination.
☒   **A.** MAC, is the acronym for Media Access Control and is usually the hardware address given to a device by the manufacturer. **B.** Routing, is a Layer 3 operation, which makes the best path decision based on IP addressing and network-layer data. **D.** NWC, is a bogus acronym.

34. ☑   **C.** Uses the Cisco IOS independently of the Catalyst operating system. The Catalyst switch does not use Cisco's IOS. Some of the commands are initiated similarly, such as the SHOW command. But the commands for setting up interfaces, addressing, and other functions are designed with different syntax than that of the traditional IOS. The RSM stores a complete IOS within itself on a FLASH memory module. The IOS that is stored on the RSM is the same IOS that is used in Cisco's routers.
☒   **A.** The Catalyst Switch has its own operating system, which the RSM (although physically part of the switch), does not use. It instead uses a version of IOS, with the same command style as the conventional Cisco Router IOS. **B.** The RSM is not menu-driven, like the Catalyst 3000, but rather has its own operating system. **D.** The RSM module has its own Internal Flash (as well as the option for an External PCMCIA Flash), as well as its own RAM, and NVRAM (for configuration files), and is basically a self-contained router. This means that the RSM does not store any operating system on the supervisor module.

35. ☑   C. This is known as hardware broadcast and multicast suppression. The percentage is achieved by the switch monitoring the first bit of the destination address. This bit is commonly known as the I/G, which is the individual or group bit. If the packet is destined for a unicast address, this bit is set to 0 (unicast), and if destined for a multicast / broadcast address, the bit is set to 1 (group). On most of the Ethernet line cards, it is only possible to set the hardware broadcast / multicast suppression on a per-card basis, not on a per port basis.

☒   A. This answer is incorrect, as the command bases port 4/12 on a basis of 50 percent of the total band. B. While this command is partly correct, the hardware broadcast/multicast suppression is actually placed on a per-card method, not on a per-port. D. This type of command is known as software broadcast and multicast suppression, and is based on a per-packet per-second basis. The command would only effectively allow 50 broadcasts per second on the above port. In a real world switched environment, you would most probably find this value very low.

36. ☑   B and C. If the port has security enabled and sees a MAC address on the port that is different than one with which it is configured, the port will send a trap and disable itself. If a port has been manually disabled by using the command SET PORT DISABLE X/XX and a device is connected to the port, then the link light will be amber, and the speed light will be green (if 100 Mbps).

☒   A. The port has detected that another switch is connected, is incorrect, as the port would not be able to tell if it has another switch connected to it. D. If the port is working correctly, then there would be a green-link light, not an amber one. E. If the port was inserted at the incorrect speed, the switches autosensed its running speed, and change it.

37. ☑   A and C. TACACS+ is a TCP-based security protocol, which works by providing restricted access to network services. The TACACS+ server works by exchanging network access server information between the TACACS+

server and client (The Catalyst). This information is encrypted. If it is being used on a Catalyst switch, the switch needs to be configured with a valid IP address on either the Sl0 or the Sc0 interface. The IP addresses of the TACACS+ servers should also be entered at the switch command line.

☒ **B.** Uses a UDP high port, is incorrect because TACACS+ is TCP based, and a session is established between the TACACS+ Server and the Catalyst switch. **D.** The server is only supported on NT, is incorrect because TACACS+ is supported on several platforms including NT and UNIX. **E.** Only one TACACS+ server can be configured per VLAN, is incorrect because multiple TACACS+ servers can be specified on a switch. When multiple servers are configured, the switch will first look for the primary TACACS server, which is configured with the keyword *primary* at the end. If the primary server is not available, then the Catalyst will attempt to establish a TCP session with any other servers configured.

```
C5k> (enable) set tacacs server 10.64.0.3 primary
```

38. ☑ **A and C.** Filtering by source address and filtering by network layer protocol types. Catalyst switches can be configured to filter or allow traffic from a specific source, and also to authenticate users. Catalyst switches allow for great flexibility in security. Filtering can be set up by source address so that only specific host MAC addresses are allowed to use a port. So, for example, if an unauthorized user decided to gain access to the network by plugging in a laptop, the laptop NIC would have a different MAC address than assigned to the user, and the switch would not allow traffic to go through. Filtering can also be set up by the network layer protocol. Table entries are compared with the filter, and the switch takes action based on the entries.

☒ **B.** Filtering by destination address, is incorrect—this would filter all incoming traffic, not just unauthorized traffic. **D.** Allowing broadcast traffic defined by the router only, is incorrect. Routers do not forward broadcast traffic. When configured to do so, they change broadcast traffic into uni-cast or multi-cast traffic.

39. ☑ C and D. Both the Cisco 2820 Series switch and the Cisco 1900 Series switch support both store-and-forward as well as cut-through switching methods. D. Although the second part of the answer is correct, inasmuch as the Cisco 1900 Series switch cannot be upgraded to a larger number of MAC addresses, it is not true that the 2820 can be field upgraded. The Cisco 2820 Series switch must be pre-ordered with the correct amount of MAC address cache.

☒ A. It is correct that the 2820 can support either a 2048 or an 8096 MAC address cache; however, the 2820 Switch must come pre-installed with the correct amount of MAC address cache space. The 1900 on the other hand cannot be upgraded, and comes standard with a 1024 MAC address cache. B. The 2820 has two expansion slots that can fit a mixture of 100BaseT, FDDI and ATM modules. These modules can be added when the need arises, as they are just plugged in boards.

40. ☑ A. The Catalyst 5002 is a two-slot chassis that supports one supervisory module, and one switch module. The switching modules that are supported are:
Ethernet
Fast Ethernet
Gigabit Ethernet
FDDI
Token Ring
ATM
RSM
A supervisor module is required. It is the switch fabric that runs the switch. Since there are only two slots, and one of the slots is reserved for the supervisory engine, there are not enough slots to support an RSM.

☒ B. Although the switch chassis does have two slots, one of the slots must be occupied by a supervisor engine, thereby leaving one slot for a switch module. C and D are wrong because the Catalyst 5002 chassis is a two-slot chassis.

41. ☑ **B** and **D.** A saving on network bandwidth and Less CPU usage. Precious network bandwidth would be saved by implementing CGMP, due to multicast traffic only sending to the ports that are part of a particular multicast group. As this minimizes the network traffic, it also decreases the load on the CPU.

☒ **A.** Less available bandwidth, is incorrect. Since network traffic is contained from certain multicast groups to certain clients, this will increase the available bandwidth of links. **C.** Reconfigured workstations to work with CGMP, is incorrect. CGMP is very easy to install, as no reconfiguration is required on any workstations, and only a few commands are needed on routers and switches. **E.** A slowing of network speed, is incorrect. There will be more network bandwidth available, and more available CPU cycles, so by using CGMP, it should cause an increase in available bandwidth (as opposed to without CGMP).

42. ☑ **A.** It is possible that either one of the ports or one of the trunk ports may be down.

☒ **B.** SHOW TRUNK, is incorrect. If all the ports seem to be up and running, you could check the trunks to make sure that they are trunking the correct VLANs. **C.** If the ports seem to be up, and the witch seems to be trunking, you could check to see if the MAC address of the PC on switch A can be seen by switch B, and vice versa. **D.** SHOW MAC, is incorrect. This would issue the MAC counters for each individual port. The argument could be made that this answer is correct; however, the MAC counters are only cleared when a CLEAR COUNTERS command is issued, so it would be very difficult to determine if a device was connected to the port. **E.** SHOW ARP, is incorrect. This command would only show ARPs that are on the management VLAN.

43. ☑ **D.** The forwarding engine actually makes forwarding decisions based on MAC address destination address (Layer 2 of the OSI model), as opposed to a destination protocol address (such as the IP address of a host), which is at Layer 3 of the OSI model.

☒ **A.** The entire forwarding engine is based in ASIC, to speed up the processing features. **B.** The forwarding engine, among many other packet-type responsibilities examines all packets going to incoming ports, and makes sure that the packet is queued for the correct destination port. **C.** The forwarding engine also has the responsibility of maintaining a CAM-type table, with destination MAC addresses, and to which port they are attached. The forwarding engine also looks at each incoming packet to see if the source address is in its address table or not. If not, then the station address is added to the table. **E.** The forwarding table also maintains statistics for the switch by listening to all packets on the X-BUS. By doing so, the forwarding engine can change the relevant information when packets are seen.

44. ☑ **A.** IGMP, and **D.** CGMP. Cisco Group Management Protocol (CGMP) is a process for managing multicast traffic on a Catalyst 5000, or any routers running version 11.3 or later software. CGMP works alongside IGMP, from which CGMP generates its packets. When a Cisco receives an IGMP packet, the router/switch creates a CGMP packet with the relevant information, and forwards this on a per-port basis to the destination MAC Address

☒ **B.** ICMP, is incorrect. Internet Control Message Protocol is most commonly used in commands such as PING and TRACEROUTE. **C.** ADSL is a modem type, which has nothing to do with multicast registration. **E.** SNMP, is incorrect. Simple Network Management Protocol can be used to make modifications to a router via SNMP sets and is also used by most network management tools to get useful (and sometimes not so useful) information from an IP-enabled, SNMP-aware device. F. VMPS, is incorrect. VLAN Management Policy Server is used to allow you to dynamically map a VLAN to a MAC address by means of a VMPS server.

45. ☑ **C.** All end stations connected to ports belonging to the same VLAN are assigned to the same VLAN number. Port-centric VLANs are assigned to the switch port. This method of assigning VLANs gives Catalyst switches great flexibility in that modules, or whole boxes, do not have to be dedicated to a desired VLAN, but the administrator can tailor the environment to his or her requirements.

So, if an administrator needed four ports on Ethernet module 3, and four more on Ethernet module 4, he or she can configure the switch accordingly.

☒ **A.** All VLANs plugged into the port are flooded to every port on the switch, is incorrect. Only one VLAN can be attached to a port. If multiple VLANs could be assigned to a port, then all security, and broadcast features would be lost. **B.** If Token-Ring ports are assigned different VLAN IDs, traffic will not be flooded. Token-Ring is still bound by the OSI model rules, and will not propagate network-layer traffic without a router in place. **D,** The routing of VLAN information from one VLAN port to another, is incorrect. Routing VLAN information form one VLAN port to another will not take place without a router in place.

46. ☑ **A and C.** When a command has been input to specify parameters of a configuration, and a change needs to be made, it can be typed in using the SET command. The previous command will be overwritten to the desired parameter. If you wish to clear the parameter applied, the CLEAR command will delete the function that was applied.

☒ **B.** The SHOW command will show status and/or configuration of a designated switch or port. **D.** ERASE is not a valid command on the Catalyst switch.

47. ☑ **A.** A TACACS+ server can provides authentication, authorization, and accounting functions. These are all independent services of TACACS+. This allows for the flexibility of using all, some, or one of the services. On the Catalyst 5000 series switches, only the authentication feature is supported. When a TACACS+ server receives a packet it does the following: Authenticates the user and lets the user know that the authentication passed or failed. Then, notifies the client that authentication will continue and that the client must provide additional information.

    ☒ **B.** Authorization, is incorrect. It is part of the TACACS+ functions, but is not supported on the Catalyst 5000 series products. **C.** Accounting, is incorrect. It is part of the TACACS+ functions, but is not supported on the Catalyst 5000 series products. **D.** None of the above, is incorrect.

48. ☑ **A and B.** If the cable is a crossover, the port will not connect to a workstation. Also, if the device is switched off, then no link light will be shown on the switch.

    ☒ **C.** Even if a device is running at 10 Mbps, the switch should still auto-sense to whatever speed the device is set. **D.** If the device is running on Cat 5 cable, the distance limitation is 100 meters and the 87 meters specified is well within the limitations.

49. ☑ **B.** The forwarding decision is made up of several parts including buffer allocation, matching the destination address with an entry in the CAM. If there is no entry, then flood the packet out of either all ports, or send it to the network port. The packet is then queued to be sent. **D.** The address-learning process is made up of several different steps, including checking the source address to make sure that it complies with any security enabled on the port. It also learns the source address if it is not already in the CAM (on the condition that the security process has been passed).

⊠ **A.** Although a destination address check is part of the forwarding decision, it is only a part of a bigger process that is going on. **C.** The broadcast control is not part of either the forwarding decision or the address learning phase. **E.** Inter-VLAN routing takes place on a router, not on a switch.

50. ☑ **E.** Token Ring & 802.1q. Token Ring is currently only supported over ISL. No provision has been made for Token Ring over 802.1q

⊠ **A.** Ethernet & 802.1q and **C.** Ethernet & ISL, are incorrect. Ethernet is supported on both Cisco's proprietary ISL trunking and the new IEEE standard of 802.1q. **B.** Currently, Token Ring is only supported over ISL. **D.** VLANs can be extended by using 802.10 over FDDI. 802.10 using a VLAN Identifier called a SAID (Security Association Identifier).

51. ☑ **B.** Devices that receive broadcast frames originating from any device within the set. This defines a broadcast domain. Broadcast domains are created to prevent the broadcasting from propagating throughout the network. Broadcast domains can be defined by aggregating ports on a switch, as shown in the illustration. Ports 1, 2, 3, and 4 can be configured as independent broadcast domains, by configuring the switch so that the ports are individual VLANs. This will limit the broadcast to that VLAN or domain. For traffic to traverse the switch to other VLANs, a router will have to be implemented.

⊠ **A.** A special address reserved for sending messages to all stations, is incorrect. A broadcast domain is not defined by addressing. For example, when running two networks over a shared hub, all ports on the hub see all the data from both networks. **C.** An area where hosts are allowed to send broadcasts, is incorrect. If a host is required to send a broadcast frame, it will do so regardless of whether or not a broadcast domain is defined. **D.** None of the above, is incorrect.

52. ☑ **C. All stations on port 4.** A switch operates so that once source and destination MAC addresses are learned, the switch will forward packets from the source port to the destination port on the switch, with no other ports on the switch seeing any traffic, thereby, greatly reducing bandwidth usage, especially in Ethernet environments. The nature of Ethernet is a broadcast environment, in that, when a host has information to send to a destination, all nodes on the network will see the data. This has two major negative performance effects. First, more of the bandwidth on the wire will be used unnecessarily because all stations are essentially broadcasting the information being sent out. Second, each station on that broadcast domain has to process every frame that comes across the wire, thus consuming more CPU cycles on every device in that broadcast domain.

☒ **A.** All stations on all switch ports, is incorrect, since they will not see the packets. The packets will be directly forwarded to the destination port in a way where no other ports see the traffic. **B.** Client B, is incorrect. It is on port 2, and the traffic being forwarded is for port 4, so Client B will not see any traffic. **D.** All stations on port 3, is incorrect. The traffic being sent from the host on port 1 is destined for port 4, so port 3 will not see any traffic.

53. ☑ **B. Through a router.** If each port on a switch is designated as a separate VLAN, each port is essentially a broadcast domain, it does not forward any broadcast to any other port on the switch. Forward traffic to another port on the switch is the same as forwarding traffic to another network. This requires a router. Switches forward frames based on MAC addresses that reside at the data-link layer. Forwarding traffic between networks, regardless of the network being of different VLANs on the same switch or geographically differentiated networks, is the same. This is network-layer forwarding of traffic, and a router is the instrument that provides Layer 3 capability.

☒ **A.** The same way communication would take place if ports 1-4 were set up as a single VLAN, is incorrect. Since each port is a LAN, the switch will not forward packets unless a routing device is in place. **C.** Through a bridge, is incorrect. A bridge basically functions the same as a switch, so implementing a switch to support forwarding of traffic from one VLAN to the other will do nothing. **D.** Although sneaker net would work, it discounts all the advancements of technology.

54. ☑ **B.** VTP. This allows you to map the trunking protocols together to create an integrated VLAN implementation across a user-defined management domain. The following configuration information is distributed in VTP advertisements:

- VLAN IDs (ISL and 802.1Q)
- Emulated LAN names (for ATM LANE)
- 802.10 SAID values (FDDI)
- VTP domain name
- VTP configuration revision number
- VLAN configuration, including (MTU) size for each VLAN
- Frame format

☒ **A.** 802.1Q, is incorrect. Its information is included in the VTP update. **C.** SAID, is incorrect. Its information is included in the VTP update. **D.** LANE, is also incorrect. Its information is included in the VTP update.

55. ☑ **A** and **B.** The SHOW CONFIGURATION command displays the configuration of the switch. A configuration parameter will be displayed for each module installed, the port configuration, and the VLAN information that the port belongs to. Another useful command for viewing VLAN information is SHOW VLAN. This command, without a specific VLAN designator, shows VLAN information for a specifically configured VLAN. ☒ **C.** SHOW INTERFACE, is incorrect. It is an IOS command. On Catalyst switches that use the IOS, viewing VLAN information through the CLI will have to be accomplished with the SHOW INTERFACE command. On Catalyst switches, this command does not work. **D.** SHOW ACTIVE, is an invalid command.

56. ☑   **B.** Domain Name System (DNS) is a distributed database that maps host names to IP addresses through the DNS protocol. When you configure DNS on a Catalyst 5000 series switch, you can substitute the host name for that hosts IP address. This method can be used for commands, such as PING, TELNET, UPLOAD and DOWNLOAD. To use DNS, a DNS name server must be present on the network.

☒   **A.** The user was already logged in, is incorrect. The user being logged in will not resolve names to IP addresses. DNS being configured is the method to do so. **C.** The PING command really takes place on the DNS server, is incorrect. It does not take place on the DNS server; rather, the DNS server maps the IP address to the host name. If the desired host is not configured, the host name will not be resolved in such commands as PING. **D.** The network administrator forwards the request, is incorrect. It would put such a high load on an administrator that that is all that person would have time to do, so this is an unrealistic option.

57. ☑   **D.** FDDI is a LAN standard as defined by ANSI X3T9.5 and not by the 802.10 committee. 802.10 is a trunking protocol for extending FDDI VLANs.

☒   **A, B, C,** and **E.** FDDI is a dual token passing ring, which runs at 100 Mbps, and can use STP & UTP for distances up to 100 Meters and either single mode, or multimode fiber for longer distances.

58. ☑   **A** and **E. A.** The switch is actually a 2828, not a 2822, and this can be seen by the fact that there is an 8192 address capacity. **C.** From the information above, it is not possible to ascertain whether the switch has been reset to factory defaults or not. **E.** The switching type is actually set for the entire switch and it is not possible to have each port running its own switching type.

☒   **B.** By comparing the date/time on the switch to the *System Last* reset, you see that the difference is a couple of hours, which would indicate that the switch was reset earlier in the day. **D.** The CAM aging timer is set to 300 seconds, which is 5 minutes. This would indicate that if the switch did not hear from a specific MAC address with the 5-minute period, it would age out of the CAM.

59. ☑ **E.** The LE-ARP is not a LAN emulation service, it is however used by the LEC, LES, and BUS for ATM to MAC address mappings.

☒ **A.** LECS (LAN-emulation configuration server), is incorrect. It has configuration information for all ELANs on a network. When a LEC first boots up, it sends a request to the LECS to provide it with the address of the LES, and also to find out to which ELAN it belongs. **B.** LEC, the LAN emulation client, which is part of the LAN emulation service. **C.** A LES (LAN emulation server) manages stations on a specific ELAN. The LES maintains a database of ATM to MAC addresses of the LAN emulation client. It stores this information when the LEC first registers itself with the LES. **D.** The broadcast and unknown server (BUS) does exactly what it is called. The BUS handles all the broadcast/multicast and unknown traffic, by establishing a VPI/VCI to each individual station within an ELAN. When, for example, a broadcast packet is received, the BUS will forward the packet to all stations to which it has a connection.

60. ☑ **B** and **D.** A logical grouping of Token Ring ports on a switch and a proven backup mechanism. Token Ring Concentrator Relay Function VLANs define port groups with the same logical ring number. Two types of TrCRF can be configured, namely, undistributed and backup. Undistributed TrCRF VLANs are limited by the ports on a single Catalyst 5000 series switch. Multiple TrCRFs on the same or different switches can be associated with a single parent TrBRF. Note that in order for TrCRF to function, TrBRF must be configured. The backup TrCRF allows an alternate path to be configured between undistributed TrCRFs, but must be connected by a TrBRF. This system allows one backup, and only one port per switch may be configured as a backup.

☒ **A.** A logical grouping of Token Ring numbers, is incorrect. This assumes multiple ring numbers can belong to a TrCRF, when only one ring number is allowed. **C.** Although a logical grouping of networks can be configured, it would take the implementation of a router to allow communication between the networks.

61. ☑ **B.** The SLIP interface is used for point-to-point connections between the switch and an IP host. The SLIP interface is the s10 interface on a Catalyst Switch. SLIP uses the console port for a SLIP connection. When SLIP is enabled and attached to the console port, an EIA/TIA-232 terminal attached to the console port cannot establish a CLI connection.

If you are connected to the switch in CLI through the console port and the command SLIP ATTACH is entered, you will lose the console port connection. At that point you will need to use Telnet to access the switch. Following is an example of the activating SLIP on the console port.

```
Console> (enable) set interface s10 10.1.1.1 10.1.1.2
Interface s10 slip and destination address set.
Console> (enable) slip attach
Console Port now running SLIP.
Console> (enable) show interface
s10: flags=51<UP,POINTOPOINT,RUNNING>
slip 10.1.1.1 dest 10.1.1.2
```

☒ **A, C,** and **D.** These answer choices are incorrect because they do not support SLIP.

62. ☑ **C.** VLANs do not communicate with one another at the data-link layer. VLANs separate networks at the network layer, and so, require a router between VLANs for VLANs to communicate. VLANs or broadcast domains can be related to IP subnets or an IPX network. A router is needed to facilitate communication between the IP and/or IPX networks. Switches are able to forward traffic at the data-link layer, but the information from source to destination must be on the same network. For example, VLAN 1 is defined with IP address 10.1.1.3 255.255.255.0, and VLAN 2 is defined with IP address 10.1.2.3 255.255.255.0. If a host on VLAN 1 wishes to send information to a host on VLAN 2, because the requirements for forwarding the information is no longer at data-link layer capability, it now becomes a network layer responsibility, and so requires a router.

☒ **A,** To control broadcast traffic to other VLANs, is incorrect. Broadcast traffic is more than controlled–it is not distributed. Broadcasts stay on that VLAN, and are not propagated to other networks. **B,** VLANs do not communicate with each other at the transport layer, is incorrect. VLANs do communicate with each other at the transport layer. The transport layer hosts TCP and UDP, which allow reliable, and unreliable, communication between the host, but to define the reliability (or lack thereof), the packet must first be processed by the network layer. And the network layer defines networks. **D.** The network layer is the layer responsible for networks communicating with one another.

63. ☑ **B and C.** FDDI check is a method used by the Catalyst 5000s to stop some older FDDI devices from sending spurious void frames onto the ring, wreaking havoc with the frames. It basically stops the FDDI ring from updating its CAM with the MAC addresses of devices that are actually on Ethernet, but seem to be on the FDDI ring.

☒ **A, D.** These options are invalid and are fictitious.

64. ☑ **C.** The Cisco Catalyst 3000 cannot support up to 8096 addresses in the system address table, but rather can support up to 1700 Address per port, or 6000 per system (10000 as an option on the Catalyst 3000, and as standard on Catalyst 3100 and 3200).

☒ **A.** The Cisco Catalyst 3000 has 16 switched 10BaseT RJ-45 ports, and 1 AUI Port as standard. **B.** Each port on the Cisco Catalyst 3000 can support up to 1700 addresses. **D.** The Cisco Catalyst 3000 has a forwarding rate of 714 Kbps. **E.** The Catalyst 3000 has two expansion slots, the Catalyst 3100 has one flexislot, and the catalyst 3200 has room for seven expansion slots. **F.** The Catalyst 3000 supports 6000 addresses per system, however if specified when ordering it is possible for the Catalyst 3000 to have an address table of up to 10000 addresses.

65. ☑ **A, B, C, and D.** The Cisco ATM LAN emulation module can be configured as a LAN emulation configuration server (LECS), LAN emulation client (LEC), LAN emulation server (LES), or broadcast unknown server (BUS), with up to 255 LANE clients supported.

66. ☑ **C.** Design so that demands never exceed resources. In designing networks, demand nodes should never exceed the requirements that resource nodes may fill. Allowing demand to exceed resources serves no purpose regardless of whether one designs a switched network or not. For example, the result of configuring a network with four demand segments and one resource segment would give the effect that all nodes are on the same segment.

67. ☑ **A.** RMON monitors network traffic at the data-link layer of the OSI model. The RMON feature does not require a dedicated monitoring probe or network analyzer. RMON allows you to analyze network traffic, set up alarms for proactive detection of problems that may affect users, do trend analysis for long-term planning, and even identify power users as candidates to be moved to faster ports. RMON is disabled by default and must be activated. The embedded RMON agent allows Catalyst 5000 Series switches to monitor traffic from all ports simultaneously. The following command enables RMON:

```
Console> (enable) set snmp rmon enable
```

☒ **B.** Network; **C.** session; and **D.** application; are incorrect because they are all layers of the OSI model that are above the data-link layer, which is where RMON works.

68. ☑ **A, B,** and **C.** Inter-Switch Link (ISL) is a Cisco proprietary trunking protocol used for Fast Ethernet and Gigabit Ethernet. IEEE 802.1Q is an industry standard for Fast Ethernet and Gigabit Ethernet. You can configure a single port or bundle Fast or Gigabit Ethernet Channel bundle. ISL is usually used when connecting Cisco equipment together, although you can set the switch trunks to communicate via 802.1Q. If you are connecting dissimilar equipment, you must use 802.1Q. Non-Cisco products do not understand the ISL encapsulation and errors will occur. DTP is an auto-negotiation Dynamic Trunking Protocol in Catalyst 5000 Series software release 4.2 and later. This allows the negotiation of the trunking protocol between switches automatically.
☒ **D.** VMPS is a dynamic VLAN feature, not a trunking protocol.

69. ☑ **E.** There is an optical bypass switch port on both the FDDI and CDDI modules. Unfortunately, there is only an optical bypass port on the FDDI modules—there are no optical bypass ports on the CDDI modules.

☒ **A, B, C,** and **D** are all true statements.

70. ☑ **B.** Although the Catalyst 3000 Series switch can recognize up to 1024 VLANs, it is only capable of supporting up to 64 active VLANs.

☒ **A.** The Catalyst 3000 Series switch supports VTP in server, client or transparent mode. When the Catalyst 3000 boots up, it sends out packet on all ports, requesting information regarding VTP. When it receives this information, it makes a decision as to whether its stored information is obsolete and, if so, sends out requests for full VTP information. **C.** Although the Catalyst can recognize up to 1024 VLANs, the 3000 stack only supports up to 64 active VLANs. The way that the switch decides which VLANs are active is by seeing if any ports are configured for that VLAN. If ports are configured, then the VLAN is active. If the switch has less than 64 active VLANs, it fills up its quota by adding any VLANs that it has learned about via VTP information. These VLANs are known as transit VLANs, as the switch (or stack) has no ports configured for the VLAN. **D.** The Cisco 3000 Series switch supports ISL and ATM LANE trunking protocols.

CISCO CERTIFIED NETWORK PROFESSIONAL

Test Yourself: CLSC Practice Exam 2 Questions

Q&A

Before you register for the actual exam, take the following test and see how you make out. Set a timer for 60 minutes—the time you'll have to take the live CCNP Cisco LAN Switch Configuration certification exam—and answer the following 70 questions in the time allotted. Once you've finished, turn to the CLSC Practice Exam 2 Answers section and check your score to see if you passed. Good luck!

CLSC Practice Exam 2 Questions

1. Which devices function at the data-link layer? Choose all that apply.

   A. Switches
   B. Routers
   C. Bridges
   D. Hubs

2. What is the speed of the ATM switch fabric in a Catalyst 5500 switch?

   A. 3.6 Gbps
   B. 5.0 Gbps
   C. 1.2 Gbps
   D. 13.2 Gbps

3. In the illustration below, what do the following two commands do to Switch A?

   ```
   SET SPANTREE PORTVLANPRI 1/1 4 99-100

   SET SPANTREE PORTVLANPRI 2/1 4 101-102
   ```

   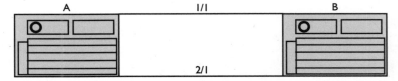

   A. Allows 4 VLANs including 99 and 100 to be allowed on Port 1/1
   B. Allows 4 VLANs including 101 & 102 to be allowed on Port 2/1
   C. Forces VLANs 99 & 100 to use Port 1/1 as a primary path
   D. Forces VLANs 101 & 102 to use Port 2/1 as a primary path

4. Which commands could you use to solve a hardware failure on a Catalyst 5000?

    A. SHOW HARDWARE

    B. SHOW TEST

    C. SHOW DEBUG

    D. SHOW CONFIG

    E. SHOW LOG

5. Which of the following best describes a network port on a Cisco 1900/2820 Series switch?

    A. It's secure port that has access to the network

    B. It's port that learns unknown MAC addresses and then passes this information to the forwarding engine

    C. It's port that is the destination port for all unknown unicast packets

    D. It's port to which an analyzer could be attached to monitor the network

    E. It's a port that connects to another switch

6. Which form of switching is fastest, and why? Choose the best answer.

    A. Store-and-forward is faster because it uses a faster processor

    B. Cut-through is faster because only part of the frame is read before a packet is forwarded

    C. Cut-through is faster because the whole packet is read into memory

    D. Both methods function at equal speeds

7. Which supervisory module becomes the active module when two supervisory modules are installed?

    A. The unit with the highest MAC address

    B. The unit with the lowest MAC address

    C. The first unit to come online

    D. The redundant supervisory modules load share tasks

8. Where could an ISL tag be added to a frame, assuming all devices could be ISL-aware devices?

A. As a frame exits the workstation's NIC card

B. As a frame exits the switch port

C. When a frame leaves a port configured as a trunk

D. When a frame leaves a server port

E. When a frame leaves a port configured as a non-trunk port.

9. You cannot connect to a switch via SLIP. From the output below, what assumptions can be made?

```
C5k> (enable) show int

sl0: flags=51<UP,POINTOPOINT,RUNNING>

slip 0.0.0.0 dest 192.168.1.1

sc0: flags=63<UP,BROADCAST,RUNNING>

VLAN 1 inet 10.0.0.1 netmask 255.255.255.0 broadcast 10.0.0.255
```

A. The modem connected to sc0: is not working correctly

B. Everything seems to be working correctly

C. PPP is working correctly

D. The port is assigned to the wrong VLAN

10. Which of the following answers are incorrect when talking about the status of a port on the Cisco 1900/2820 Series switch? Choose all that apply.

A. A port can be enabled, forwarding, suspended, and disabled

B. The enabled port is active

C. The forwarding port is enabled and forwarding packets

D. The suspended port has a problem that has temporarily shut the port down

E. A port is disabled and must be enabled by using the management software

11. Which switching method calculates the CRC before forwarding packets?

A. Tag

B. Network

C. Store-and-forward

D. Netflow

12. What is the default VLAN for Ethernet on the Catalyst switch?

A. VLAN 1

B. VLAN 1000

C. VLAN 1002

D. VLAN 1005

13. To which well-known address do Cisco routers send CGMP packets?

A. 0100.0000.0000

B. 224.0.0.10

C. 224.0.0.1

D. 0100.000d.dddd

E. 0100.0100.0100

14. The output from the SHOW PORT command is shown below. What information can be learned about the port?

```
C5k> (enable) show port 3/11

Port  Name               Status      Vlan       Level   Duplex Speed Type

----- ------------------ ----------- ---------- ------- ------ ----- ---------

3/11                     connected   12         normal  a-full a-100 10/100BaseTX

Port  Security Secure-Src-Addr    Last-Src-Addr      Shutdown Trap     IfIndex

----- -------- ------------------ ------------------ -------- -------- -------

3/11 disabled                                        No       enabled  17
```

```
Port      Broadcast-Limit Broadcast-Drop

--------  --------------- --------------

3/11             -               0

Port  Align-Err FCS-Err   Xmit-Err  Rcv-Err    UnderSize

----- --------- --------- --------- --------- ---------

3/11       0         0         0         0         0

Port  Single-Col Multi-Coll Late-Coll Excess-Col Carri-Sen Runts      Giants

----- ---------- ---------- ---------- ---------- --------- --------- ---------

3/11       0         0         0         0         0         0         0
```

A. The port is not functioning correctly

B. The port has been set to accept only 100 Mbps full-duplex connections

C. The port seems to be functioning correctly

D. The port has had errors that have been reset

15. Of the following FDDI bridge types, which are not valid FDDI-to-Ethernet bridging types?

A. Ethernet 802.2 to FDDI 802.2

B. Ethernet 802.2 LLC to FDDI SNAP

C. Ethernet 802.3 RAW to FDDI SNAP

D. Ethernet 802.3 RAW to FDDI 802.3

E. Ethernet SNAP to FDDI SNAP

F. Ethernet II to FDDI SNAP

16. What is the term for the trend toward fewer users per segment?

A. VLAN

B. Microsegmentation

C. Multi-layer LAN switch

D. Routing

17. What does the LE ARP do?

    A. Maps IP addresses to hardware addresses

    B. Maps VCs to VP

    C. Maps MAC addresses to ATM addresses

    D. Maps an NNI address to UNI address

18. In the illustration below, PC A is on VLAN 100, PC B is on VLAN 200, and PC C is on VLAN 300. What is the only method that CANNOT be used to restrict access so that PC B can only see PC C, assuming there is an RSM Switch A?

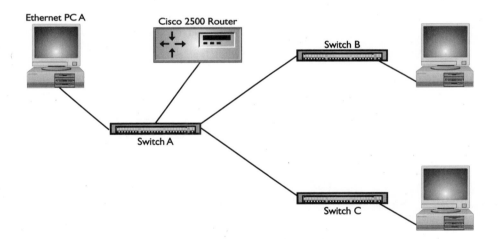

    A. Access lists on Switch A

    B. VTP pruning on Switch A

    C. Access lists on Switches B and C

    D. VTP pruning on Switches B and C

19. Which of the following best describes APaRT?

A. Automatic Packet ReTransmission

B. Automated Packet Recognition and Translation

C. Available Partial Routing Table

D. Uses an FDDI Address and matches a Layer 3 address to allow greater throughput

E. Uses FDDI/CDDI CAM entries to match Layer 2 Ethernet frame types with MAC addresses

20. Which two of the following is used by the Catalyst 3000 to transfer between 10-Mbps ports, and for high-speed ports?

A. SAMBA

B. SAINT

C. LMA

D. PFPA

21. Which device in source-route-bridging is responsible for determining the route to the destination host?

A. The bridge or switch

B. The router

C. The sending station

D. The receiving station

22. AP Manufacturing has three campus-like facilities across the country. Each campus consists of three buildings supporting between 300 and 500 users per campus. The company runs in such a way that working at home is greatly encouraged. The company policy is "do not come to the office unless required" and is highly encouraged. Also, there are no specified seating assignments, thereby providing a great deal of flexibility for interdepartmental corroboration. For example, if finance has a meeting with manufacturing, the meeting is facilitated by users simply plugging laptops into network jacks and logging in from wherever they are.

If engineering is located on network 10.2.3.0, and manufacturing is located on network 10.3.3.0 with 255.255.255.0 subnet mask, how can the two networks communicate with each other?

A. The networks will communicate using the RIF table

B. The networks will communicate using the CAM table

C. The networks will communicate using SRB

D. The networks will communicate using RSM

23. Which of the following is NOT a TACACS+ feature?

A. Supports authorization

B. Supports MD5 encryption of TACACS+ packet to TACACS+ server

C. Local login available

D. Supports NAT

24. In the following illustration, Client A has problems maintaining conversations with the server. What may be the problem?

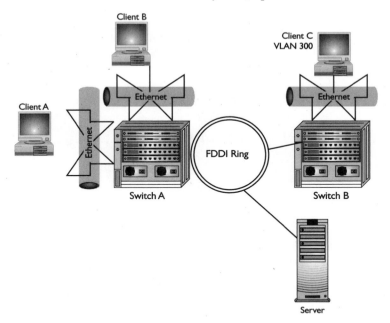

A. The LAN is being overloaded

B. Fddicheck needs to be enabled

C. The server has a problem with its memory

D. The Ethernet port is faulty

25. How many slots does the Cisco 3200 have?

A. 1

B. 5

C. 7

D. 9

E. 13

26. Which sub-layer in the OSI model can be configured on the Catalyst switches for basic security?

A. LLC

B. DLCI

C. MAC

D. Network

27. After replacing an Ethernet module in slot 2 of a Catalyst 5000 switch, what command do you type to verify that the switch recognizes the module?

A. SHOW INTERFACE 2

B. SET ETHERNET

C. SHOW MODULE

D. INT ETHERNET 2

28. Which command enables DNS on a Catalyst switch?

A. INT 3/2, DNS ENABLE

B. SET DNS SLOT/PORT ENABLE

C. SET IP DNS ENABLE

D. DNS ENABLE

29. What is the maximum distance of an FDDI SMF module?

A. 2km

B. 5km

C. 10km

D. 32km

E. 100km

30. What happens when a switch sees that a switch has left the stack, and it sends and receives a loopback?

A. The switch assumes that the matrix has gone down

B. The switch assumes that its port is faulty and disables the matrix port

C. The switch realizes that the matrix is fine and that a neighbor has left the stack and carries on as normal

D. The switch sees the loopback and realizes that is has left the stack, and loops the matrix port back to itself

Use the Following Scenario to Answer Questions 31-34

AP Manufacturing has three campus-like facilities across the country. Each campus consists of three buildings supporting 300 to 500 users per campus. The company runs in such a way that work at home is greatly encouraged. The company policy is "do not come to the office unless required" and is highly encouraged. Also, there are no specified seating assignments, thereby providing a great deal of flexibility for interdepartmental corroboration. For example, if finance has a meeting with manufacturing, the meeting is facilitated by users simply plugging laptops into network jacks and logging in from wherever they are.

31. What method of VLAN allows for the environment at AP Manufacturing?

A. A very robust firewall application

B. Dynamic VLAN membership configuration

C. A Cisco 7000 VLAN configuration

D. Static VLAN configuration

32. What type of Cisco product is required for the scenario to work?

A. Cisco Catalyst 5xxx

B. Cisco 7000 router

C. Cisco Catalyst 29xxXL

D. Cisco Catalyst 3xxx

33. In the scenario, what protocol is used so that switches in each building can communicate configuration and multiple-trunking protocol information to each other?

A. RIP

B. CSMA/CD

C. VTP

D. NLSP

34. In the scenario, the Catalyst 5000 Series switches are configured for multiple VLANs at each campus. For example, manufacturing is on network 10.2.x.x, and engineering is on 10.3.x.x. What module can be used within the Catalyst switch instead of implementing an external router?

A. Supervisor II module

B. Redundant supervisor II module

C. Router switch module

D. VLAN membership policy server

35. What command sets the name of a port on a Catalyst 5000 Series switch?

A. SET NAME PORT/MOD_NUM [name_string]

B. SET PORT NAME MOD_NUM/PORT_NUM [name_string]

C. INT SLOT_NUM/PORT_NUM NAME

D. WRITE NAME PORT//MOD_NUM NAME

36. Which of the following is NOT a default value when configuring an FDDI module?

A. All the FDDI ports on a module are enabled

B. IP fragmentation is disabled

C. FDDI 802.2 to Ethernet 802.3 IPX protocol translation

D. Ethernet 802.3 RAW to FDDI SNAP

37. What is the maximum number of EtherChannels that can be configured on a Catalyst 3000 Series switch?

A. 0

B. 1

C. 2

D. 4

E. 7

F. 16

38. Which VLAN is NOT removed from a VLAN trunk?

A. VLAN 1

B. VLAN 1001

C. VLAN 1006

D. None of the above

39. At what layer of the OSI model does SNMP work?

A. Data-link

B. Network

C. Session

D. Application

40. Which of the following is a Cisco proprietary protocol?

A. ISL

B. 802.1Q

C. 802.10

D. ELAN

41. To what would a Client send an LE-ARP?

A. LECS

B. LES

C. LEC

D. BUS

42. What does the acronym TrCRF stand for?

    A. Token Ring Concentrated Redundancy Frame
    B. Token Ring Concentrator Relay Function
    C. Token Ring Confirming Redundant Frame
    D. Token Ring Catalyst Repeater Function

43. Select the two true statements about embedded RMON on the Catalyst Series switches.

    A. Consists of four groups: stats, history, alarm, events
    B. Must use third-party management software to monitor
    C. Will not work with SNMP
    D. Can be directed to monitor traffic of any port

44. What type of cable connectors is used to connect to the console port on a Supervisor I card?

    A. RJ45
    B. EIA/TIA 232 9 pin D-type connector
    C. EIA/TIA 232 25 pin D-type connector
    D. RJ11

45. If the status light on an ATM module is amber, what does it mean?

    A. All tests have passed, and everything is OK
    B. The system could be booting
    C. One or possibly more tests have failed
    D. The module has been disabled for some reason or another

46. What function do Token Ring BRF VLANs perform?

    A. TrBRF VLANs interconnect TrCRF VLANs
    B. A logical grouping of Token Ring ports on a switch

C. A logical grouping of Token Ring network numbers

D. A proven backup mechanism

47. Which of the following commands will enable you to determine the switch MAC address?

A. SHOW MAC

B. SHOW MODULE

C. SHOW MEMORY

D. SHOW CONFIG

48. Which of the following is true about the Telnet capability of the Catalyst 5000?

A. Allows connections to two other devices

B. Allows connections to four other device

C. Allows connections to eight other devices

D. Allows connections to 16 other devices

49. How many MAC addresses are assigned to each Cisco LANE interface?

A. 4

B. 8

C. 16

D. 32

E. 64

50. Choose the correct statement regarding remote resources.

A. Remote conversations take place between a demand node and a resource node

B. Remote conversations take place between a demand node and a resource node in a different collision domain

C. A remote resource contains demand-node routing information

D. Multiple segments in a switch domain enable multiple conversations in respective collision domains

51. Which command sets the port duplex in configuring a fast Ethernet port:

   A. SET DUPLEX [half | full] SLOT/PORT

   B. SET PORT DUPLEX [half | full] SLOT/PORT

   C. SET PORT DUPLEX SLOT/PORT [half | full]

   D. PORT/SLOT [half | full]

52. Which three applications are included in CWSI Solutions?

   A. CiscoWorks, LANView, Traffic Generator

   B. CiscoView, VlanView, TrafficView

   C. CiscoView, TrafficDirector, VlanDirector

   D. HP OpenView, CiscoView, LANView

53. Given the configuration commands below, what is missing?

```
C5K> INTERFACE ATM 0.20

C5K> LANE SERVER-BUS ETHERNET ACCOUNTING

C5K> LANE CLIENT ETHERNET 20 ACCOUNTING
```

   A. There is no LES configured

   B. There is no LECS configured

   C. The interface ATM0.20 is not valid

   D. The LES/BUS pair is not configured

   E. The LEC is not configured

54. How many bits wide is the Catalyst 5000 switching bus?

   A. 1.2 gigabits

   B. 48 bits

   C. 3.6 gigabits

   D. 25 bits

55. Which commands could be used to create an Ethernet VLAN in the marketing department assuming that you are on a Catalyst switch that is set up to be a VTP server? Choose a name that will associate the VLAN with the department.

A. SET VLAN marketing department type ETHERNET
B. SET VLAN 100 *marketing department type* ETHERNET
C. SET VLAN 100 NAME *marketing department type* ETHERNET
D. SET VLAN 100 *type* ETHERNET *name marketing department*
E. SET VLAN 100
F. SET VLAN 100 *name marketing_department type* ETHERNET

56. Should we wish to get data regarding the use of a specific port, which of the four embedded RMON groups would we use?

A. Alarm
B. Event
C. History
D. Statistics

57. Which of the following is not a component of the Cisco 2820/1900 Series switch ClearChannel architecture?

A. 1-Gbps packet exchange BUS
B. Embedded control unit
C. SAGE
D. Forwarding engine
E. 3MB shared buffer memory

Refer to the Following Scenario to Answer Questions 58–60

AP Manufacturing has three campus-like facilities across the country. Each campus consists of three buildings supporting 300 to 500 users per campus. The company runs in such a way that work at home is greatly encouraged. The company policy is "do not come to the office unless required" and is highly encouraged. Also, there are no specified seating assignments, thereby providing a great deal of flexibility for interdepartmental corroboration. For example, if finance has a meeting with manufacturing, the meeting is facilitated by users simply plugging laptops into network jacks and logging in from wherever they are.

58. What piece of equipment is required for dynamic VLAN membership to function properly?

    A. Firewall

    B. DNS server

    C. VMPS

    D. DHCP server

59. Trunks allow a switch to define multiple ports to communicate VLAN information between switches when multiple paths are defined. What protocol is required to protect against network loops? Choose all that apply.

    A. ISL

    B. VTP

    C. STP

    D. 802.1d

60. Which of the following inter-switch protocols would be used in the scenario if AP Manufacturing required existing Ethernet protocols to communicate between switches?

    A. VTP

    B. ISL

    C. LANE

    D. 802.10

61. From the output below, please choose the LEAST correct answer.

```
C5k> (enable) show spantree 4/12

Port      Vlan  Port-State     Cost    Priority  Fast-Start  Group-Method
--------- ----  -------------  -----   --------  ----------  ------------
4/12       9    forwarding      100      32       enabled
```

A. Port 4/12 has something attached
B. Certain characteristics of STP are being bypassed
C. The priority has not been modified
D. Port 4/12 is an 802.1q trunk. The cost of the port is low.

62. Which of the following are out-of-band management options?

A. SLIP, PPP
B. SLIP, Telnet, SNMP
C. SLIP, Terminal
D. Telnet, SNMP
E. VTY

63. Which of the following most directly gets a SLIP connection to a switch?

A. Connect a Cisco 2501 router to the console interface
B. Use RAS to obtain an IP address, then use SLIP to dial into the switch
C. Connect a terminal with a modem attached to the terminal
D. Connect a modem to the console port, and configure sl0

64. Which four RMON groups are embedded in the supervisor engine software?

A. Alarm, history, statistics, traffic
B. Accessibility, alarm, event, statistics
C. Alarm, event, history, statistics
D. Event, scalability, statistics, traffic
E. Alarm, accessibility, events, history

65. Which of the following is NOT a Catalyst 5000 management option?

A. PPP connection through the console port
B. Telnet
C. RMON
D. CWSI
E. Terminal
F. SLIP connection through the console port

66. Which type of FDDI/CDDI media connectors is used on the Catalyst switch?

A. Category 5 UTP RJ45

B. ST connector for single mode fiber

C. RJ11

D. MIC connector for multimode fiber

E. MIC connector for single mode fiber

67. In the following illustration, what could cause Client B to be unable to receive from the server?

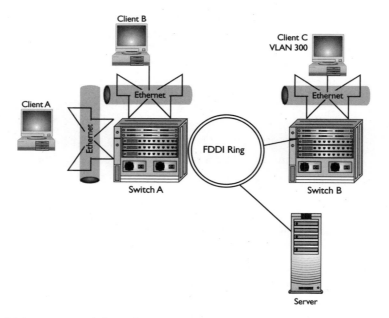

A. This is not a valid configuration.

B. The server cannot resolve ARPs.

C. IP fragmentation is disabled.

D. The FDDI ring does not know about Ethernet.

E. The ratio of three Ethernet to FDDI loads up the FDDI, so the server cannot have any conversations with clients.

68. While trying to troubleshoot a problem, you notice the lights on the CDDI module appear as in the following list. What do they tell you?

Status=Green

RingOp=Green

Thru=Off

Wrap A=Green

Wrap B=Off

A. The CDDI port looks OK

B. The A port is connected and wrapped, but the B port is isolated

C. The B port is connected, but the A port is wrapped

D. The system is down

69. How many expansion slots does the Cisco 1900 have?

A. 0

B. 1

C. 2

D. 3

E. 4

70. On the Cisco 1900/2820 Series switches, which port has the lowest priority?

A. Port 0

B. Port 1

C. Port 24

D. Port 25

E. Port 27

Test Yourself:
CLSC Practice
Exam 2 Answers

Q & A

Threedfff

The answers to the questions are in boldface, followed by a brief explanation. Some of the explanations detail the logic you should use to choose the correct answer, while others give factual reasons why the answer is correct. If you miss several questions on a similar topic, you should review the corresponding section in the *Cisco LAN Switch Configuration Study Guide* before taking the CLSC test.

CLSC Practice Exam 2 Answers

1. ☑ **A and C.** Both switches and bridges function up to the data-link layer. When a bridge or switch is powered on the devices, examine MAC (Media Access Control) to determine what host is on which port. Bridges usually only have two ports, where switches have multiple ports. Also, bridges typically have limited intelligence, in terms of port configuration, while today's switches offer great flexibility and control. LAN segmentation, filtering, authentication, and different switching algorithms are just a few features that today''s switches offer.

   ☒ **B.** Routers, can operate at the data-link layer, but usually are implemented for network layer routing functions. Cost and port concentration are two inhibiting factors for using a router in a bridge or switches place. **D.** Hubs, operate primarily at the physical layer, working as repeaters/concentrators. With no segmenting functions, a hub is usually passive and has no intelligence or capabilities to decipher source or destination of packets being taken in or sent out. Once again, all packets are sent to every port.

2. ☑ **B. 5.0Gbps Gbps.** The Catalyst 5002 and Catalyst 5000 switches have a single, integrated 1.2-Gbps switching backplane; the Catalyst 5505, 5509, and 5500 switches have three 1.2Gbps Gbps switching backplanes. All Catalyst 5000 series switches support switched 10/100-Mbps Ethernet/Fast Ethernet, Token Ring, and Ethernet repeater connections, with backbone connections to Fast Ethernet, Gigabit Ethernet, FDDI, and CDDI, but only the 5500 series Catalyst switches can support ATM.

☒   **A.** 3.6 Gbps, is incorrect. This is the figure for the 5500 switching bus without the consideration of ATM. In other words, if ATM is NOT implemented, 3.6 Gbps would be the combined capabilities of the three 1.2-Gbps switching buses. **C.** 1.2 Gbps, is the data transfer rate of the data switching bus on the 500x series switches. The 5500 has three 1.2-Gbps switching buses. **D.** 13.2 Gbps, is incorrect. Cisco has not manufactured a switching bus that operates at this rate in the Catalyst series switches.

3. ☑   **C and D.** Setting the spanning-tree port priority for a particular VLAN or set of VLANs effectively forces the port to the primary link for a particular VLAN. The possible port priorities are from 0–63 (the lower the number, the higher the priority.) If two or more ports have the same value, the port with the lowest port number will be chosen.
☒   **A and B.** These choices are invalid because by default, trunking all VLANs are enabled on ports. If specific VLANs need to be stopped (filtered or pruned) from propagating throughout the network, then VTP pruning needs to be enabled and configured.

4. ☑   **B and E.** The SHOW TEST module number command would give you output about the diagnostics tests performed on a particular module. The SHOW LOG command will show you information about the reset counts, and the last exception that has happened.
☒   **A.** show hardware, is normally used on routers to show the current hardware, and the reason for the last reboot. **C.** SHOW DEBUG is not a valid command. **D.** SHOW CONFIG shows the current configuration file on a Catalyst switch.

5. ☑   **C.** The network port is a port to which all unknown unicast packets are sent instead of the switch sending out a broadcast. Only one port-per-switch can be defined as a network port, and this port cannot have security enabled on the port.

☒ **A.** A secure port that has access to the network, is incorrect. Although a network port is used to access unknown MAC addresses, the port cannot be a secure port because if it were, it would only learn the addresses for which it is configured. If the switch does not know the MAC address, there is a good chance that you would not have configured that specific MAC address on the secure port. **B.** The network port does NOT learn MAC addresses; instead, it assumes that it knows about every other address that the switch does not know about. **D.** An analyzer can be attached to any port on the switch, and not just a network port (although you would not want to put an analyzer on a network port because then all the unknown unicast MAC addresses packets would be sent to the analyzer). **E.** Although in theory you probably would have connected the network port to another switch, you can also connect it into a hub, and a router as well (as long as you have the correct cabling).

6. ☑ **B.** In cut-through mode the switch checks the destination address and immediately begins forwarding frames, thereby greatly decreasing latency of the packet as it traverses the LAN segment to its destination. The latency that cut-through switching does present is not only much less than store-and forward, but it is constant, regardless of frame size.
   ☒ **A.** is incorrect because, although a faster processor will improve switch performance, multiple methods of switching can be implemented on that faster processor, and cut-through will still be more efficient. **C.** is incorrect because in cut-through switching, the whole packet is not read into the switching memory before it is forwarded. **D.** is incorrect because store-and-forward reads the whole packet into the switching cache before making a forwarding decision, as opposed to cut-through which only reads the first few frames.

7. ☑ **C.** When two supervisory engine modules are installed in the Catalyst 550X series switch, the first supervisor module to come online is the active module. The second supervisor module goes into standby mode. All

administrative and network management functions, such as SNMP, CLI console, Telnet, Spanning-Tree Protocol, Cisco Discovery Protocol (CDP), and VLAN Trunk Protocol (VTP) are processed on the active supervisor engine module.

☒ **A.** the unit with the highest MAC address, and **B.** the unit with the lowest MAC address, are invalid answers. The election process has nothing to do with MAC addresses. As the first supervisor to come online, it assumes the role of active supervisor, while the other supervisor goes into standby mode. **D.** the redundant supervisory modules load share tasks, is incorrect, as all administrative and network management functions are processed on the active supervisor engine module, and are not load-shared between the two supervisor modules.

8. ☑ **A and D.** Both a workstation and a server could be configured to be ISL aware. A workstation's NIC could be an ISL-aware card (Compaq and Intel make ISL aware NIC cards), although generally the ISL-aware cards are used for servers, rather than workstations.

☒ **B.** If a Catalyst line card is ISL aware, it will automatically trunk should it see an ISL-aware station at the remote end. On cards such as the 5225-R (24 port 10/100 line card), each individual port can be configured as a trunk. **C.** When a frame leaves a port configured as a trunk, is incorrect. If a port is configured as a trunk, it will automatically add a VLAN tag when moving frames through its ports. **E.** If a port is configured as a non-trunk port, or is not capable of being a trunk, then no VLAN tag is added to a frame when it leaves or enters the port.

9. ☑ **B.** From the output from the switch, it seems as if everything is up and running and configured well. Both the sc0 and sl0 seem to be functioning correctly. The sl0 interface has been configured for SLIP and has been assigned an IP Address. The sc0 interface (for Telnet connections), is also configured with an IP address, and subnet mask, and has been assigned to a VLAN.

☒ **A.** The modem connected to sc0: is not working correctly, is incorrect. From the information given, the status of the modem cannot be determined. To do this, you have to look at the lights on the front of the modem to determine the status. **C.** PPP is working correctly, is incorrect. When working over the console port, or more precisely, the sl0 port, it is important to understand that PPP is not supported. The only protocol supported over the sl0 interface is SLIP, and according to the output above, this seems to be functioning correctly. **D.** From the information given in the output, it is not possible to determine which VLAN the SLIP port is connected to. If you look at the output of the sc0 interface, the VLAN is specified.

10. ☑ **A and C.** A Cisco 1900/2820 Series switch port can only be in one of three states. The port is enabled, which means that the port is in use and is forwarding packets, as it should. The suspended port has a problem (possibly such as spanning tree or a security violation), that is causing the port to be suspended. The last state is disabled—either manually or automatically—after the port has received a packet from a non-secure source. The forwarding state is not a valid port state. "The forwarding port is enabled and forwarding packets" is also not a valid 1900/2820 port state, however, if you were talking about a spanning-tree port state, then this answer would be correct.

☒ **B.** The enabled state means that the port is active and passing packets as it should. **D.** The suspended port has received a packet that has caused a condition, and put the port into a suspended state. This could be due to spanning tree, or possibly something to do with the security enabled on a port. **E.** If the port is in a disabled state, this will most probably be due to either one of two things: First, it could have been disabled via the management console. Second, the port has received a packet on the port that was not from the secure address configured on the port and this will cause the port to disable.

11. ☑ **C.** In store-and-forward mode, the port adapter reads the entire frame into memory and then determines if the frame should be forwarded. At this point, the frame is examined for errors and frames with errors are not forwarded. If the frame contains no errors, it is sent to the destination port for forwarding.

☒ **A.** Tag switching, provides both Layer 2 and Layer 3 with support. It is primarily used in ATM environments. **B.** Network switching, is an industry term used in both voice and data communities with the general understanding of moving information from source to destination. **D.** Netflow switching, is a Layer 3 switch algorithm that is supported on 7200 and 7500 series routers and is primarily used for accounting and for billing to customers.

12. ☑ **A.** VLAN1 is the default VLAN configuration on Ethernet modules. If more that 1 VLAN is required, the VLAN must be configured.

☒ **B.** VLAN 1000 is a pruning-eligble VLAN. **C.** VLAN 1002, is the default VLAN for FDDI. **D.** VLAN 1005, is the default Token Ring TrBRF VLAN.

13. ☑ **C** and **D.** 224.0.0.1 and 0100.000d.dddd. A Cisco router will always sends CGMP packets to the same multicast MAC address which is 0100.000d.dddd and is equivalent to multicast IP address 224.0.0.1

☒ **A.** 0100.0000.0000, is incorrect, since this value does not exist. **B.** 224.0.0.10, is also incorrect. The multicast address of 224.0.0.10 is used by EIGRP to send out multicast updates. **E.** 0100.0100.0100, is incorrect. This value does not exist in multicast packets.

14. ☑ **C.** From the information given in the output, the port seems to be working correctly—the port is connected and looking at the statistics provided, and there have been no errors on the port.

☒ **A.** is incorrect because there is no information provided to suggest that the port is not working correctly. **B.** If you look at the speed and duplex, you will notice that both of the values have *a-* in front of them, which indicates that the ports are auto-sensing and so will accept either 10 or 100Mbps Mbps. **D.** Although there are no errors on the port, there is no evidence that the port statistics have been reset.

15. ☑ **B and D.** Ethernet 802.2 LLC to FDDI SNAP and Ethernet 802.3 RAW to FDDI 802.3. Both of these encapsulation types are not valid FDDI-to-Ethernet bridging types.
    ☒ **A.** Ethernet 802.2 to FDDI 802.2; **C.** Ethernet 802.3 RAW to FDDI SNAP; **E.** Ethernet SNAP to FDDI SNAP; and **F.** Ethernet II to FDDI SNAP. All of the above are all valid FDDI bridging types.

16. ☑ **B.** Microsegmentation is a term that describes the trend toward fewer users per segment in today's LAN environments. This term is used to describe fewer users per collision domain. This is important because Ethernet is a contention-based network; the more hosts that reside in a broadcast domain, the smaller the amount of available bandwidth per host. This results in more collisions, greater latency, and an overall network that is not efficient. With microsegmentation, LAN administrators can trim the amount of host-per-broadcast domain and, in essence, provide more bandwidth per user within that broadcast domain. Depending on an organization's budget, using switches can be taken to a level where only one host resides on a broadcast domain, thereby enabling that host the full available bandwidth.
    ☒ **A.** VLAN, is incorrect. Although there is a trend to create VLAN for specific functions, groups, or security reasons, VLANs imply fewer users per segment. **C.** Multi-layer LAN switching, is incorrect. It is also a growing trend, but it does not address the trend toward fewer users per segment. Rather, it implies a switch that goes beyond the Layer 2 boundaries, and possibly provides Layer 3 capabilities. **D.** Routing, is incorrect. Routing does not address the trend toward fewer users per segment. Routers are used to forward information from one network to another, be they different

VLANs located in the same facility, or networks located in different geographical areas.

17. ☑   **C.** The LE ARP table maps MAC addresses to ATM addresses. As communications occur over the ELAN, each LEC dynamically builds a local LE ARP table. The local LE ARP table can also be statically configured. LE ARP is not the same as IP ARP. IP ARP maps a Layer 3 IP address to a Layer 2 Ethernet MAC address. LE ARP maps ELAN Layer 2 MAC addresses to ATM Layer 2 addresses.
    ☒   **A.** Maps IP addresses to hardware addresses, is incorrect. It describes the function of IP ARP. **B.** A VC is part of a VP. Although these are parts of ATM communication, these functions are not part of the LE ARP process. **D.** Maps an NNI address to a UNI address, is incorrect. NNI and UNI do not map to one another. NNI is network related and UNI is user-communication related.

18. ☑   **C.** It is impossible to put access lists on a switch unless it has an RSM installed. If there is an RSM installed, even though it is physically part of the switch, it has nothing to do logically with the switch.
    ☒   **A.** Access lists on Switch A, is an incorrect choice. By using access-lists on the RSM, it is possible to stop access between PC A & and PC B, and PC A & and PC C. **B.** VTP pruning on Switch A, is incorrect. If you were to use VTP pruning on the trunks from Switch A, it is possible to exclude the VTP information for Switch A and pass this information onto Switches B and C. **D.** By using VTP pruning, you can achieve the same end as if you were doing the pruning on Switch A, but it takes twice as much work.

19. ☑   **B** and **E.** Automated Packet Recognition and Translation matches a specific Layer 2 frame type with a MAC address.
    ☒   **A.** Automatic Packet ReTransmission, and **C.** Automatic Packet ReTransmission and Available Partial Routing Table, are incorrect. They are fictitious names. **D.** APaRT actually maps layer 2 addresses to FDDI CAM entries, not Layer 3.

20. ☑ C and D. C. The LAN module ASIC (LMA) is used to transfer packets between 10-Mbps dedicated ports. D. The Proprietary Fat Pipe ASIC (PFPA) is used to transfer files between ports that are bigger than 10Mbps Mbps.

☒ A. The SAMBA has nothing to do with the Catalyst 3000 system, it is actually the BUS arbiter for the Catalyst 5000 Series switch. B. The SAINT chip is not part of the Catalyst 3000 Series switch, but is part of the Catalyst 5000 Series switch. It is used with all Ethernet ports.

21. ☑ C. SRBs are so named because they assume that the complete source-to-destination route is placed in all inter-LAN frames sent by the source. To determine the location of the destination host, the source host sends out an explorer frame. Each bridge that receives the frame copies the frame to all ports. Route information is added to the explorer frames as they travel through the network. When the explorer frame reaches the destination host, the destination host replies to each explorer frame individually. Upon receipt of all response frames, the host chooses the best path to the destination. SRB is a Token Ring-based algorithm. The logic required in Token Ring network equipment makes the equipment more costly than Ethernet. Token Ring is an IEEE 802.5 standard.

☒ A. The bridge and the switch, is incorrect. They both play a part in the Token Ring path determination, but bridges and switches are the devices responsible for initiating or determining, not merely adding route information to the explorer frame and forwarding the frame. B. The router, is incorrect. If configured for SRB, the router works in the same way that bridges or switches work. D. is incorrect, since the receiving station is not responsible for route determination; it only has the task of responding to all explorer packets.

22. ☑ D. The networks will communicate using RSM. Engineering and manufacturing are on separate subnets, separated at the Layer 3 network layer. For networks to communicate with one another at Layer 3 requires a routing function. The RSM is a Catalyst module that is a router on a

module that fits in the Catalyst 5000 series switch to facilitate communications between subnetworks. Without the RSM, the two subnetworks or VLANs would not be able to communicate. The RSM is a full-fledged router, specifically designed to route subnetworks or VLANs to communicate with each other. The RSM does have a full Cisco IOS in it. The RSM does not have serial connections or network connections, but communicates via the Catalyst 5000 backplane. A console port is available so that configuration can be done without requiring the administrator to set up the RSM by traversing the Catalyst backplane.

☒ **A.** RIF table; **B.** CAM table; and **C.** SRB, are all incorrect as the networks cannot communicate in this situation without RSM.

23. ☑ **D.** Supports NAT. NAT is not a part of TACACS+. TACACS+ is a security system made up of a server, router, and TACACS server. The three components are: authentication, authorization, and accounting. Of the three, the Catalyst 5000 Series switch only supports authorization.

☒ **A.** Supports authorization; **B.** supports MD5 encryption of TACACS+ packet to TACACS+ server; and **C.** local login available, are incorrect. These choices are all features of the TACACS+ system.

24. ☑ **A** and **B.** While the LAN may be overloaded, this may not always be the cause. It is possible that the FDDI server has an old adapter type, and is sending spurious traffic onto the FDDI ring, it may also be that this traffic is hogging the ring. The solution would be to enable FDDI check to help resolve the problem.

☒ **C.** From the information given, it is not possible to ascertain if the Server has a memory problem, and from a network perspective, you should not need to know this. **D.** Although there may be a slight chance that the port may be faulty, it seems too intermittent for the problem to be the port. If the port is generating an excessive amount of errors, this may be a way to check the physical port.

25. ☑ **C.** The Catalyst 3200 has seven slots that can house a variety of expansion modules. The 3200 comes with no 10BaseT ports. Any ports must be added by way of an expansion module. One of the slots can accommodate either a standard width, or an extra-wide module. This slot can accommodate a Cisco 3011 WAN router module, which comes with standard Cisco IOS. By default, the 3200 switch arrives with the enhanced feature set.

☒ **A.** The Cisco 3200 comes with seven slots; the Cisco 3100 comes with one expansion slot. **B.** The Cisco 3200 comes with seven slots, not five; however, the Cisco 5500 and 5505 have five slots. **D.** The Cisco 3200 comes with seven slots, not nine; however, the Cisco 5509 has nine slots. **E.** The Cisco 3200 has seven slots, not 13; however, the Cisco 5500 and 7513 have 13 slots.

26. ☑ **C.** The MAC address is the data-link layer sub-layer with which Catalyst switches can manipulate port settings to configure different security requirements.

☒ **A.** The LLC sub-layer of the data-link layer, is incorrect. It is not used by the Catalyst switches to manipulate security requirements. **B.** DLCI, is incorrect. It is a data link connection identifier used in Frame Relay. **D.** Network, is incorrect. It is a standard term that enables devices to share resources.

27. ☑ **C.** The SHOW MODULE command will the display status of all the modules installed on the switch. It also lists the ports and the port status of each module on the switch. When a new module is placed in a Catalyst 5000 series switch, make sure to verify the switch recognizes the modules just installed with the SHOW MODULE command. Another command (not listed here) that is more specific can also be used. This is SHOW PORT *mod_num/port-num*. This command is more tailored to looking at a specific module and port.

☒ **A.** SHOW INTERFACE is an IOS-based command that will show all interfaces on a router or other IOS-based product and the state of that interface, along with other detailed status. **B.** SET, does not verify that the module has been recognized. It activates a desired parameter on the switch. **D.** INT ETHERNET 2, is an IOS-based command that will switch to command prompt to the Ethernet 2 interface only after the router is placed in configuration mode.

28. ☑ **C.** Domain Name System is enabled on the Catalyst 5000 series switch with the COMMAND SET IP DNS ENABLE. Enabling DNS on a Catalyst switch allows for the resolution of names to IP addresses from the switch. For DNS to work, there must be a DNS name server on the network. DNS allows searching for servers, routers, and other devices on a network much more intuitively, especially if the organization has a device-naming policy. Having an IP address list on your person is not always convenient. With DNS enabled and network devices, and a consistent naming policy, administrators do not need to worry about having to search a list for a network device.
☒ **A.** INT 3/2, DNS ENABLE, is incorrect. The SET command on Catalyst switches is almost always used to configure features. **B.** SET DNS SLOT/PORT ENABLE, is incorrect. DNS is a global configuration. The whole switch is DNS capable. A defined port cannot be enabled on the switch alone. **D.** DNS ENABLE, is incorrect. The SET command on Catalyst switches is almost always used to configure features.

29. ☑ **D.** 32km. The maximum distance for single-mode fiber is 32km, although most implementations are less than this. Single-mode fiber differs from multi-mode fiber in that multi-mode fiber is an LED, whereas single-mode fiber is a laser.
☒ **A.** 2km, is incorrect. The maximum distance is 32km. The 2km may refer to the maximum distance for multi-modes fiber. **B.** 5km; **C.** 10km; and **E.** 100km, are all incorrect distances.

30. ☑ **C.** After a switch has not received five heartbeats from a neighbor, it assumes that there is a problem. When this occurs, the switch sends out a loopback; if it receives its loopback back, then it presumes that a switch has left the stack. If it does not receive its loopback back, then it assumes that the matrix is faulty.

    ☒ **A.** is incorrect because the switch only assumes the matrix is faulty if it does not receive its loopback back. **B.** is incorrect because the switch doesn't assume the port is faulty; it realizes instead that the neighbor has left the matrix. **D.** is incorrect because the switch carries on as normal once it receives the loopback and acknowledges that the neighbor has left the matrix.

31. ☑ **B.** Dynamic Port VLAN membership allows a user to attach to any data jack and the switch will apply the proper VLAN membership in accordance to the MAC address of the station that is attached to that specific port on the Catalyst switch. This is done using the VLAN management policy server (VMPS). VMPS is based on two components, the switch and a TFTP server that hosts the MAC address-to-VLAN mapping database. When the VMPS is enabled, the database is downloaded from the TFTP server and VMPS begins to accept client requests. VMPS opens a User Datagram Protocol (UDP) socket to communicate and listen to client requests. When the VMPS server receives a valid request from a client, it searches its database for a MAC address-to-VLAN mapping.

    ☒ **A.** A very robust firewall, is incorrect. It is a good tool to implement to help secure an enterprise network from external threats. Firewalls are not usually configured to protect vital resources from the inside of the LAN. **C.** A Cisco 7000 VLAN configuration, is incorrect. Configuring VLANs on a Cisco 7000 series router does not provide the flexibility or functionality of the Dynamic Port VLAN membership. **D.** Static VLAN configuration, is incorrect. When a static VLAN is configured on an interface, either the host is committed to the VLAN and it''s limitations, or the host has tried to log into a switch port that has been configured for a specific MAC address, which would not really provide the best solution for the scenario presented.

32. ☑   **A.** The Dynamic VLAN membership function is only available on the Cisco Catalyst 5000 series switches.
☒   **B.** Cisco 7000 route;, **C.** Cisco Catalyst 29xxXL; and **D.** Cisco Catalyst 3xxx, are all incorrect because only the Cisco Catalyst 5000 series switches will work.

33. ☑   **C.** VLAN Trunk Protocol (VTP). This is a software feature on the Catalyst 5000 series that allows you to map these trunking protocols together to create an integrated VLAN implementation across a user-defined management domain.
☒   **A.** RIP, is incorrect. It is a Layer 3 distance-vector routing protocol that makes routing decisions based on hop count. **B.** Carrier Sense, Multiple Access / Collision Detection (CSMA/CD), is incorrect. It is the algorithm on which Ethernet is based. **D.** Novell link-state protocol (NLSP), is incorrect. It allows Novell IPX packets a link-state routing mechanism, instead of the IPX RIP hop-count-based routing mechanism. This routing protocol is used to decrease SAP updates over the WAN.

34. ☑   **C.** Router switch module (RSM) is a module that fits in a Catalyst 5000 or 5500 slot. A Catalyst 5002 can host the module but the two slots would be occupied by a supervisor module and a router module only. The RSM allows different VLANs on the same switch to communicate. The RSM uses a full IOS, and must be configured in order for the VLANs to communicate with one another. The setup is not different than connecting two LAN networks into a router. Instead of physically connecting cables, the backplane of the switch is the connection.
☒   **A.** A supervisor II module is the module where the switching fabric resides. All switching functions and features reside in the supervisory module. **B.** A redundant supervisory module is insurance for the switch incase the primary switching module fails. The supervisory engine, although redundant, will still provide only Layer 2 functionality. In order to communicate between networks, a router is required. **D.** A VLAN membership policy server is a component that is required when dynamic VLANs are setup. This is not a piece of hardware, but a Catalyst switch feature.

35. ☑ **B.** To name a port on the Catalyst 5000 Series switch, the SET PORT NAME MOD_NUM/PORT_NUM [name_string]" command is used. The following is an example of the proper syntax:

```
Console> (enable) set port name 1/1 APEngineering
```

The command assigns the name APEngineering to module 1, port 1 on a Catalyst 5000 Series switch. This command, although not a requirement, helps administrators identify connections. If the administrator should leave the organization, features like port naming would help the new administrator learn the layout of the network without the tedious task of tracing wires.
☒ **A.** SET NAME PORT/MOD_NUM [name_string], is incorrect. The command syntax places the port designator in front of the module designator. **C.** INT SLOT_NUM/PORT_NUM NAME, is incorrect. The interface command is an IOS command, and the syntax in incorrect to specify a port name. **D.** WRITE NAME PORT//MOD_NUM NAME, is incorrect. WRITE is an incorrect method for designating a port feature. The set command must be used on the Catalyst switches to apply a parameter to a module and/or port.

36. ☑ **B.** IP fragmentation is disabled. By default, IP fragmentation is enabled, this is due to the fact that most of the time, FDDI networks are attached to Ethernet network, which have a maximum packet size of between 1500 and 1518.
☒ **A.** All the FDDI ports on a module are enabled; **C.** FDDI 802.2 to Ethernet 802.3 IPX protocol translation; and **D.** Ethernet 802.3 RAW to FDDI SNAP, are all incorrect. All of these options are enabled by default when a module is switched on.

37. ☑ **E.** The maximum number of EtherChannels Etherchannels that can be configured on the Catalyst 3000 Series Switch is 7 (Seven). These Etherchannels can be configured via the EtherChannel menu on the Switch.
☒ **A.** 0; **B.** 1; **C.** 2; **D.** 4; and **F.** 16, are all incorrect values.

38. ☑ **A.** VLAN 1. When you configure a trunk port, all VLANs are added to the allowed VLANs list for that trunk port. You can remove VLANs from the allowed VLANs list to prevent traffic from those designated VLANs passing over the trunk. However, you cannot remove VLAN 1, as this is the default VLAN. The default VLAN 1 is a permanently configured Ethernet VLAN. This allows a switch to be plugged and played right out of the box, with no configuration. All Ethernet modules and ports are assigned to VLAN 1 by default. There are other default VLAN assignments. For example, default FDDI VLAN and VLAN 1002.

☒ **B.** VLAN 1001, is incorrect. It is not a default VLAN number. **C**, VLAN 1006, is incorrect. It is not a default VLAN number. VLANs 1001 and 1006 are also illegal VLAN numbers and don't exist. **D.** none of the above, is incorrect.

39. ☑ **D.** Application. Simple Network Management Protocol (SNMP) is an application layer protocol that facilitates the exchange of management information between devices on a network. SNMP is part of the TCP/IP protocol suite. SNMP allow administrators to manage network devices, monitor performance, find and remedy network problems, and plan for network growth.

☒ **A.** The data-link layer, is incorrect. It does have some monitoring functionality, but is too low a layer in the OSI model to be part of the TCP/IP protocol suite. **B.** Network layer, is incorrect. It hosts IP, which is where the TCP/IP protocol suite starts. The network layer is responsible for routing decisions based on IP addressing. **C.** Session layer, is incorrect. It manages sessions between device applications, so the session layer does play a part in ensuring reliable communications take place between devices, though the SNMP functions don't reside at this layer.

40. ☑ **A.** ISL is a Cisco-proprietary trunking protocol for Fast and Gigabit Ethernet. ISL does not support any other LAN protocol. ISL allows for multiple VLANs to be carried over the trunk. Later versions of switch software also allowed 802.1Q to do the same.

☒ **B.** 802.1Q, is incorrect. It is an IEEE standard, not proprietary. **C.** 802.10, is incorrect. It is an FDDI trunking protocol and is also an IEEE standard, not proprietary. **D.** ELAN, is incorrect. ELAN stands for Emulated LAN, and is an ATM characteristic.

41. ☑ **B.** The client will send a LE-ARP to the LES. It then sends out messages to all of the LECs that have a VCC to it.
☒ **A.** LECS; **C.** LEC; and **D.** BUS, are all incorrect, as a LEC sends out LE-ARP requests first of all to the LES.

42. ☑ **B.** Token-Ring Concentrator Relay Function VLANs defines port groups with the same logical ring number. Two types of TrCRF can be configured in a network, namely, undistributed and backup. TrCRF VLANs are typically undistributed, which means each TrCRF is limited to ports on a single switch. TrCRFs can be associated on the same or different switches by a single parent TrBRF. The TrBRF forwards traffic among the undistributed TrCRFs. The default VLAN ID for TrCRFs is 1003, and the default TrBRF VLAN ID is 1005.
☒ **A.** Token Ring Concentrated Redundancy Frame; **C.** Token Ring Confirming Redundant Frame; and **D.** Token Ring Catalyst Repeater Function, are made-up options that don't have any significance.

43. ☑ **A and B.** RMON does consist of four groups defined by RFC 1757 for Ethernet. Although there are four groups supported without additional probes, there are a total of nine RMON groups, with five requiring additional network probes to monitor. They are:

- Statistics is group 1 and is part of the four that do not require a probe
- History is group 2 and is part of the four that do not require a probe
- Alarm is group 3 and is part of the four that do not require a probe
- Event is group 9 and is the Last of the four that do not require a probe
- Accessing RMON embedded data must be done through an NMS like Cisco Works 2000

The NMS must provide support to RFC 1757 for Ethernet or RFC 1513 for Token Ring. You cannot access RMON data via the Catalyst 5000 series CLI, but when in CLI, SHOW commands provide information that is similar.

☒ **C.** will not work with SNMP, is incorrect. For SNMP management stations to work, RMON data must be forwarded to using SNMP. **D.** can be directed to monitor traffic of any port, is incorrect. The traffic is directed to all ports, and is not specifically directed to a single, or a group of ports.

44. ☑ **C.** EIA/TIA 232 25 pin D-type connector. This is the correct type of cable to connect to a Supervisor I card.

☒ **A,** RJ45, is incorrect. This type of cable is actually used on the latest Supervisor III Cards, but isn't used on the Supervisor I card. **B,** EIA/TIA 232 9 pin D-type connector, and **D,** RJ11, are not valid types of connectors for this purpose.

45. ☑ **B** and **D.** The amber light on the module signals that the ATM module is either in a state of booting up, or has been disabled for one reason or another.

☒ **A.** If the system has passed all tests, the module light should be red. **C.** If one or more of the power-on tests have failed, then the status light on the module will be red.

46. ☑ **A** and **D.** TrBRF VLANs interconnect TrCRF VLANs and a proven backup mechanism. Token Ring Bridge Relay Function VLANs interconnect multiple Token Ring Concentrator Relay Function VLANs in a switched Token Ring network. The TrBRF can extend across multiple switches that are interconnected via trunk links. The backup TrCRF allows an alternate path to be configured between undistributed TrCRFs, but must be connected by a TrBRF. This system allows one backup, and only one port per switch may be configured as a backup.

☒ **C.** A logical grouping of Token Ring network numbers, is incorrect. Although a logical grouping of networks can be configured, it would take the implementation of a router to allow communication between the networks. **B.** A logical grouping of Token-Ring ports on a switch, is incorrect. It is a TrCRF function.

47. ☑ **B.** SHOW MODULE. To determine the MAC address of the switch, the SHOW MODULE command is used. Following is a sample output from this command:

```
console> show module

Mod Module-Name Ports Module-Type Model Serial-Num Status
-------------------- ---- ------------------- -------- -------- -------
1 Supervisor 2 100BaseTX Supervisor WS-X5009 002650014 ok
2 Management 24 10BaseT Ethernet WS-X5010 002475046 ok
4 Marketing 48 4 Segment 10BaseT Eth WS-X5020 002135955 ok
Mod MAC-Address(es) Hw Fw Sw
----------------------------------------- ------ ------ ----------------
1 00-40-0b-ac-80-00 thru 00-40-0b-ac-83-ff 1.6 1.4 2.113(Eng)
2 00-40-0b-4c-92-58 thru 00-40-0b-4c-92-6f 1.0 1.4 2.106
4 00-40-0b-14-00-20 thru 00-40-0b-14-00-23 0.1 1.4369 2.106
Mod SMT User-Data T-Notify CF-St ECM-St Bypass
--- -------------------------- -------- -------- --------- -------
4 Catalyst-5000 16 c-Wrap-B in absent
Console>
```

The MAC address of each module is shown. Module 1 is generally the MAC address used.
☒ **A.** SHOW MAC, is not a valid command. **C.** SHOW MEMORY, is incorrect. It will not show the MAC address of the switch, but will show the memory statistics of the switch. **D.** SHOW CONFIG is an IOS command and will not work on the Catalyst 5000 series switch.

48. ☑ **C.** When using Telnet to get to the management port of a Catalyst, it allows you to have up to eight outbound connections to other devices.

☒ **A.** allows connections to two other devices; **B.** allows connections to four other devices; and **D.** allows connections to 16 other devices, are all incorrect. These answers are not valid with regard to the Telnet capability of the Catalyst 5000.

49. ☑ **C.** Each LANE interface gets allocated 16 MAC addresses, and certain addresses within that range are assigned. Each LEC is allocated the 1st address within the range, each LES is assigned the 2nd, each BUS is assigned the 3rd, and last but not least, each LECS is assigned the 4th address.
☒ **A.** 4; **B.** 8; **D.** 32; and **E.** 64, are all incorrect answers, as there are 16 MAC addresses assigned per port.

50. ☑ **B.** Remote conversations are defined as conversations that take place between nodes located in different collision domains.
☒ **A.** Remote conversations take place between a demand node and a resource node, is incorrect. If the conversation takes place in the same domain, then the conversation is not taking place between a remote resource and that demand node. **C.** A remote resource contains demand-node routing information, is incorrect. A remote resource does not contain routing information. **D.** Multiple segments in a switch domain enable multiple conversations in respective collision domains, is incorrect. Multiple segments in a switch domain have nothing to do with remote resources, other than facilitating the conversation between the remote resource and the demand nodes.

51. ☑ **C.** SET PORT DUPLEX SLOT/PORT [half | full]. The correct command sets the port mode to full or half duplex. This option is available to relieve NICs on host machines that may sometimes have trouble with the auto-negotiation function that is one by default. Also, remember that you may not change the mode settings when auto-negotiation is configured on the port. Auto-negotiation must be turned off for the mode to be set.

When the mode of a Fast Ethernet port is set for duplex, the host with a 100Mbps-Mbps Network Interface Card that supports full duplex, can realize a throughput of 200Mbps Mbps. This is a very useful tool for servers, database processing hosts, and anything that requires fast throughput over the LAN.

☒ **A.** SET DUPLEX [half | full] SLOT/PORT, does not explain that the command is to specify the speed of the port, which is incorrect syntax. **B.** SET PORT DUPLEX [half | full] SLOT/PORT, is incorrect. This choice is incorrect because the mode is specified before telling the switch what slot/port is to be specified. **D.** PORT/SLOT [half | full], is incorrect.

52. ☑ **C.** CiscoView, TrafficDirector and VLANDirector are a standard part of CWSI Solutions. There is also an optional ATMDirector. CiscoView allows you to graphically view Cisco products that have an IP Address. TrafficDirector allows you to graphically view the embedded RMON. VLANDirector allows you to manage your VLANs via a GUI interface.

☒ **A.** CiscoWorks is a valid package, but isn't part of the CWSI acronym, LANview is not used in CWSI, and Traffic Generator is part of the Network Associates Sniffer. **B.** CiscoView is a valid option, but the other two names are either fictional, or non-Cisco. **D.** Although all the applications are valid, they are not part of CWSI.

53. ☑ **B.** In the configuration given, there is no LECS configured.

☒ **A.** There is no LES configured, is incorrect. The LEC is configured with the LANE SERVER-BUS command which enables both a LES and a BUS on the ELAN accounting. **C.** The interface ATM0.20 is not valid, is incorrect. The INTERFACE command is a valid command. **D.** The LES and BUS pair are configured with the command. **E.** The LEC is not configured, is incorrect. The LEC is configured with the LANE CLIENT ETHERNET 20 ACCOUNTING, which enables a LEC for the ELAN Accounting.

54. ☑ **B.** The Catalyst 5000 has a switching bus that is 48-bits wide and operates at 25MHz. When you multiply 48 bits by 25MHz you get a product of 1.2Gbps Gbps. This is how the computation for data rate is calculated for the switching bus. In looking at the Catalyst 5500 which has three 1.2-Gbps switching buses, you can easily see how the figure of 3.6 Gbps data rate is calculated.

☒ **A.** 1.2 gigabits, is incorrect. This options specifies the data rate, but does not explain how many bits wide the data bus is. **C.** 3.6 gigabits, provides the figure of the combined three 1.2-Gbps data buses that reside on the 5500. **D.** 25 bits, is the speed at which the 48-bit wide data bus processes information, but the answer is displayed in bits, so it is an incorrect figure.

55. **F.** SET VLAN 100 *name marketing_department type* ETHERNET. This command creates an Ethernet VLAN 100 with a VLAN name of marketing_department. This command will successfully create the VLAN according to the information given.

☒ **A.** SET VLAN marketing department type ETHERNET, does not specify a VLAN number, which should be added directly after the set VLAN part of the command. **B.** Although this command appears to be correct, the Catalyst switch does not allow any spaces in the VLAN name. If there are spaces, then the switch treats the second part of the VLAN name as the next part of the SET VLAN. The SET VLAN command also requires the keyword *name* in front of the specified VLAN name to identify the VLAN. **C.** SET VLAN 100 NAME *marketing department type* ETHERNET, is incorrect. The only problem with this command is the fact that there is a space in the VLAN name, which means that the switch will interpret the word *department* as the next part of the SET VLAN command. **D.** SET VLAN 100 *type* ETHERNET *name marketing department*, creates the same problem. **E.** SET VLAN 100, is incorrect. While this would create a VLAN, because there was no name specified, the VLAN will use the default VLAN name, which is VLAN0010.

56. ☑ **C and D.** The statistics RMON group holds, among other things, the utilization statistics for the port monitored. The history RMON group can hold snapshots of the utilization until the statistics are needed.

☒ **A.** The Alarm RMON Group allows you to set thresholds for any item that can be recorded by the other RMON groups. **B.** The Events RMON Group sends out SNMP Traps.

57. **C.** The SAGE is an ASIC used on the Catalysts 5000 Series switches for non-Ethernet ports (an Ethernet port uses a SAINT).

☒ **A.** The switches use a 1-Gbps packet exchange BUS (53-bits wide x 20MHz), which sees all packets that cross the switch. In theory, this bus should never be fully utilized, as there are 25 10-Mbps ports, and a possible 2 x 100-Mbps ports. This equates to (25x10)+(2x100)=450 Mbps. **B.** The ECU is responsible for the configuration of the switch as well as may other responsibilities, such as the embedded RMON and diagnostics and error handling. **D.** is implemented in an ASIC to ensure fast response. The forwarding engine does exactly what it says by taking over the major role when it comes to making forwarding decisions. **E.** The shared-memory buffer, is exactly what it says—a place to park packets while the way is being paved for the packet to be routed towards its destination.

58. ☑ **C.** VMPS is a VLAN management policy server. When you enable VMPS, a MAC address-to-VLAN mapping database downloads from a Trivial File Transfer Protocol (TFTP) server and VMPS begins to accept client requests. If you reset to power cycle the Catalyst 5000 series switch, the VMPS database downloads from the TFTP server automatically, and VMPS is re-enabled. VMPS opens a UDP socket to communicate and listen to clientsclients'' requests.

☒ **A.** Firewall, is incorrect. Firewalls are intended to provide protection from external threats, and will not usually be implemented on the LAN side. Firewalls usually reside in what is known as a DMZ, where the firewall protects from the outside. **B.** DNS server, is incorrect. It provides domain-naming services, which maps IP addresses to domain addresses.

This function has no impact on the requirements of dynamic VLAN membership. **D.** DHCP server, is incorrect. A DHCP server provides hosting services for IP addresses. A host requests an IP address, and the DHCP server provides an IP address to that host.

59. ☑ C and D. STP and 802.1d. When VLAN trunks are defined on more than one port on a switch, there is the possibility for a loop between the two switches, which could have a negative affect on network performance. The Spanning Tree Protocol is an algorithm that disables one port to a network, placing the other ports on standby. If the primary port or connection should fail, the secondary port will be activated. The IEEE 802.1d defines STP.

A, ISL, is incorrect. It is a proprietary FasterEthernet faster Ethernet trunking protocol, and requires the Spanning Tree Protocol to prevent loops when multiple ports are destined to a particular switch. **B.** VTP, is incorrect. It is a software feature on the Catalyst 5000 series switches that allows the mapping of trunking protocols together to create an integrated VLAN.

60. ☑ B. ISL. Fast Ethernet and Gigabit Ethernet VLAN trunks use Cisco's ISL or industry-standard IEEE 802.1Q encapsulation to carry traffic for multiple VLANs over a single link. You can configure a trunk on a single Fast or Gigabit Ethernet port or on a Fast or Gigabit EtherChannel bundle. ISL is a Cisco proprietary trunking protocol that functions with Fast and GigbitGigabit Ethernet only. Fast Ethernet and Gigabit Ethernet trunk ports support five different trunking modes. These trunk ports can be configured to a specific mode, or can be set to *autonegotiate*.

☒ **A.** VTP, is incorrect. It encapsulates the trunking protocol in use. **C.** LANE, is incorrect. It is ATM's LAN emulation and will allow for legacy products to be integrated into the ATM infrastructure. **D.** 802.10, is incorrect. It is the IEEE standard for VLAN trunks on FDDI.

61. ☑ **D.** The priority has not been modified. From the information given, we do not have enough evidence to suggest that the port is a trunk, never mind an 802.1q trunk.

☒ **A.** Port 4/12 has something attached, is incorrect. Due to the fact that the port is in a forwarding state, this means that something is attached to the end of the port. A port has several different phases when initializing and can be summarized as initialization, blocking, listening, learning and finally, a forwarding state. **B.** Certain characteristics of STP are being bypassed, is incorrect. Under the heading of Fast-Start, you can see that the port is enabled. This means that this port has had the command SPANTREE PORTFAST 4/12 ENABLE added to the Catalyst. This will allow the port to bypass most of the STP and move almost directly from an initializing state to a forwarding state. This command should only really be applied to workstations as it bypasses the STP. If attached to a hub, this may cause problems should another port on the hub be connected to the switch. **C.** The priority has not been modified, is incorrect. By default, the switch assigns a standard priority of 32. The valid value of the port can be between 0–63. **E.** The cost of the port is normally 1000/LAN speed in Mbps. If we look at the example, this would equate to a 100Mbps-Mbps Port (1000/10=100). This answer is true for ports connected at 10Mbps Mbps half duplex.

62. ☑ **C.** SLIP can be used to get an IP session running to the CLI, if you connect a 100-percent Hayes Compatible modem to the console port, and configure the interface sl0 with an IP address. A terminal session means that you can plug a terminal or a device with terminal emulation software directly into the active supervisor card of the Catalyst 5000.

☒ **A.** SLIP, PPP, is incorrect. Although SLIP can be used to connect via IP to the Catalyst 5000, PPP (Point-to-Point Protocol) is not supported. **B**, SLIP, Telnet, SNMP, is incorrect. It is supported via out-of-band; both Telnet and SNMP are in-band options. **D.** VTY, is incorrect. Virtual Terminal (VTY) ports are considered identical to Telnet, and are thus in-band.

63. ☑ **D.** Once a 100 percent-Hayes-compatible modem is connected to the console port via a 25-pin straight-through cable it is possible to dial in via SLIP. The sl0 port also needs to be configured with an IP address and a subnet mask.

☒ **A,** Connect a Cisco 2501 router to the console interface, is incorrect. The modem is expecting SLIP, rather than a router. Of course, you could always put a router on one of the VLANs and use this router to get to the management router via Telnet etc. **B.** It could be possible to use RAS to dial into the network, but you would have to use either Telnet or SNMP to gain access to the switch. **C.** If a modem were connected to a terminal connected to the switch, it may be possible to dial into the terminal and connect via the console port; however, this is not the most direct way to connect to a switch via SLIP.

64. ☑ **C.** The four RMON groups embedded into the Supervisor module are alarm, event, history, and statistics. This is remembered by the phrase, *All Elves Help Santa.*

☒ **A.** Alarm, history, statistics, traffic; **B.** Accessibility, alarm, event, statistics; **D.** Event, scalability, statistics, traffic; and **E.** Alarm, accessibility, events, history, are incorrect. These options only contain one or two of the embedded RMON groups, and the rest of the names are fictitious.

65. ☑ **A.** PPP connection through the console port, is correct. PPP is not a Catalyst 5000 management option. The only connection type valid on the console port is via SLIP or a terminal connection to the console. In a round about way, it is possible to get PPP running to the console, but it would have to be connected to a router, which could then have an async connection to the switch.

☒ **B.** Telnet, is incorrect. It is possible to Telnet to the sc0 interface on a

Catalyst switch on the condition that it configured with an IP Address and a subnet mask, along with single, or possibly multiple, routes to the rest of the network. Once connected via Telnet, it is possible to make up to eight outbound Telnet connections. **C.** RMON, is incorrect. You can manage the network via RMON, to get data about objects on the network. **D.** CWSI, is incorrect. It is possible to configure the Switch via CWSI, or more precisely, CiscoView, which gives you a graphical interface to the switch. CiscoView then uses SNMP to make the appropriate changes to the switch. **E.** A terminal can be connected to the console port and the switch can be configured via the command line. A PC with terminal emulation software could also be used to connect to the console port. **F.** If interface sl0 is configured correctly with an IP address subnet mask and the relevant routes on the switch, it is possible to connect a modem to the console port and for a remote PC to dial in and connect via SLIP.

66. ☑ **A, B,** and **D. A.** The Category 5 UTP RJ45 connector is supported on the Catalyst 5000 by means of the WS-X5103 Catalyst 5000 CDDI Switching Module (UTP, RJ-45). **B.** The ST Connector for Single Mode Fiber is supported by means of the WS-X5104 Catalyst 5000 FDDI Switching Module (Single-mode, ST). **D.** The MIC Connector for Multimode Fiber is supported by means of the WS-X5101 Catalyst 5000 FDDI Switching Module (Multimode, MIC).

    ☒ **C.** RJ11, and **E.** MIC connector for single mode fiber, are both incorrect. Neither of these cable types is supported by the FDDI/CDDI module. The only models for the Catalyst 5000 are supported.

67. ☑ **C.** FDDI can use a larger frame size than Ethernet, so if the server was sending out packets larger than the Ethernet maximum and the switch had IP fragmentation disabled, the switch would drop the packets, and NO clients would be able to connect to the FDDI server.

    ☒ **A.** This is not a valid configuration, is incorrect. From the output given, this looks like a valid configuration. **B.** The server cannot resolve

ARPs, is incorrect. The answer is a bit ambiguous, as the server will be able to resolve ARP"s on the local FDDI Ring. **D.** The FDDI ring does not know about Ethernet, is incorrect. From the output, it looks as if the FDDI ring does know about the Ethernet segments. **E.** is invalid, and most probably incorrect if the Ethernet segments were 10Mbps Mbps.

68. ☑ **B.** The A port is connected and wrapped, but the B port is isolated. The problem seems to be that the B port is isolated for some reason. This will cause the A port to wrap back to itself. Although the Ring is still working, the problem needs to be rectified.

☒ **A.** The CDDI port looks OK, is incorrect. From the output, the A port is wrapped, so, although the port is functioning, it is not functioning correctly. **C.** The B port is connected, but the A port is wrapped, is incorrect. The problem is actually the other way around, port A is connected, and port B is isolated. **D.** The system is down, is incorrect. As can be seen from the output, at least one of the rings is functioning, which would mean that the system is not actually down.

69. ☑ **A.** Zero. The Cisco 1900 has no expansion slots; however, it comes in a couple of different configurations. All 1900s have 25 10Mbps-Mbps ports (The exception to this is the 1912 which has 13 ports, 12 RJ45 and a 13th AUI port on the back), 24 of which are on the front, and are based on RJ45 connectors, with another port at the back. The port at the back has an AUI connector. The 1900 comes with a choice of either one 100BaseTX, two 100BaseTX ports, or one 100BaseTX, and one 100BaseFX port.

☒ **B.** 1; **C.,** 2; **D.** 3; and **E.** 4, are all incorrect, as the 1900 Series switch has no expansion slots.

70. ☑ **B.** Port 1 has the lowest priority, and port 27 has the highest. This port priority is used when sending packets onto the X-BUS. The user should not notice any difference, as the BUS runs fast enough for the speed difference to not be evident.

☒   **A** is incorrect because there is no port 0 on the Cisco 1900.2820 Series switch. **C.** Port 24; **D.** Port 25; and **E.** Port 27, are all wrong, as the correct answer is Port 1.

Part 8

Test Yourself:
BCRAN
Practice Exams
(Exam 640-505)

CCNP™
CISCO CERTIFIED NETWORK PROFESSIONAL

Test Yourself:
BCRAN
Practice Exam 1
Questions

Q & *A*

efore you register for the actual exam, take the following test and see how you make out. Once you've finished, turn to the BCRAN Practice Exam 1 Answers and check your score to see if you passed. Good luck!

BCRAN Practice Exam 1 Questions

1. With which command string is weighted fair queuing activated on the initial configuration of a router with line connections at speeds of T1 or less?

   A. FAIR-QUEUE
   B. WEIGHTED FAIR-QUEUE
   C. QUEUE
   D. None of the above

2. Which two statements are true about V.90 modems?

   A. The highest-line speed is achieved on the transmit side of the user's modem
   B. The highest-line speed is achieved on the receive side of the user's modem
   C. Multiple analog links in the transmission path between source and destination do not impact the modem's speed
   D. Only one analog link can be in the transmission path between sender and receiver

3. The AAA accounting feature can audit all commands at a specified privilege level. How many privilege levels are there?

   A. 15
   B. 16
   C. 18
   D. An unlimited number

4. The rotary dialer group is a logical interface that must be mapped to a physical interface. Which of the following commands is proper for mapping dialer group 1 to a physical interface?

   A. ROUTER(config) #DIALER ROTARY-GROUP 1
   B. ROUTER #DIALER GROUP 1
   C. ROUTER (config-if) #DIALER GROUP 1
   D. ROUTER (config-if) #DIALER ROTARY-GROUP 1

5. You have been asked to verify the type of encapsulation on your S1 interface. Which command would you use to do this?

   A. SHOW ENCAPSULATION S1
   B. SHOW ENCAPSULATION TYPE S1
   C. SHOW INTERFACE S1
   D. SHOW IP INTERFACE S1

6. What type of DCEs are used to terminate point-to-point dedicated digital lines?

   A. Modem
   B. Digital modem
   C. DSU/CSU
   D. NT1

7. You have just issued the SHOW INTERFACE S0 command on a new router. What is the default bandwidth displayed under the BW statement for S0?

   A. 154.4 Kbps
   B. 1544 Kbps
   C. 1.544 Kbps
   D. 15.54 Kbps

8. What is the default auxiliary port speed for a Cisco 2500 router?

A. 9600 Kbps

B. 9600 bps

C. 38,400 bps

D. 38,400 Kbps

9. What is the default mode of operation for a DUAL mode synchronous/asynchronous WAN interface card?

A. Asynchronous

B. Synchronous

C. Synchronous/synchronous

D. Asynchronous/asynchronous

10. What is the maximum speed setting for an asynchronous interface?

A. 9600 bps

B. 38,400 bps

C. 57,600 bps

D. 115,200 bps

11. You have been asked to recommend a Cisco access router to use for your company's very small offices and telecommuters. Choose the best solution.

A. Cisco 1600

B. Cisco 1700

C. Cisco 3600

D. Cisco 700

12. What type of connector is used to connect to the console port of a Cisco 1600 series router?

A. RJ-45

B. RJ-11C

C. DB-9

D. RS 232

13. Your organization has just ordered a number of Cisco 1600 series routers with ISDN WAN interface cards. The WAN cards are 1-Port ISDN BRI U cards. What does this mean?

A. They will require an external NT1

B. They will require an external TA

C. They will not require an external NT1

D. They will support an ISDN PRI line

14. A WIC 1DSU-T1 card has been ordered for one of your Cisco 3600 series routers. Which statements are true? Choose all that apply.

A. This card will terminate a T1 line

B. This card does not require an external DSU/CSU

C. This card will not terminate a T1 line

D. This card will require an external DSU/CSU

15. With which Cisco series routers can the Cisco 2600 series share modular interfaces? Choose all that apply.

A. Cisco 3600

B. Cisco 3810

C. Cisco 2500

D. Cisco 1600

16. Which router can be partially configured via a DTMF telephone?

    A. 3600 series

    B. 2600 series

    C. 1000 series

    D. 700 series

17. Assume that you have placed a POTS telephone call through the nationwide telephone network. What is the proper order of steps to transmit this analog voice channel (VC) through the telephone network?
1. The digitized channel is transmitted over the digital telephone network between central offices
2. The channel is reconstructed into an analog signal
3. The channel is converted into a 64 Kbps digital signal
4. The call is routed to/from the end user

    A. 4, 1, 3, 2, 4

    B. 4, 3, 2, 1, 4

    C. 4, 3, 1, 2, 4

    D. 4, 1, 2, 3, 4

18. Which of the following is true for V.90 modems?

    A. Asymmetrical transmit and receive speeds up to 33.6 Kbps and 64 Kbps, respectively

    B. Asymmetrical transmit and receive speeds up to 33.6 Kbps and 56 Kbps, respectively

    C. Symmetrical transmit and receive speeds of 56 Kbps

    D. Symmetrical transmit and receive speeds of 64 Kbps

19. Which Cisco IOS runs on the 700 series routers?

    A. None

    B. Cisco IOS 12.0

    C. Cisco IOS-700

    D. Cisco IOS-7000

20. You have been asked to manually change the modem command strings in six modems connected to a Cisco 2500 series access router. You need to access the connected modems in order to make the changes.

```
CONFIGURATION ONE
ROUTER(config)IP HOST TACOMA1 2001 10.1.1.1
ROUTER(config)IP HOST TACOMA2 2002 10.1.1.1
ROUTER(config)IP HOST TACOMA3 2003 10.1.1.1
ROUTER(config)IP HOST TACOMA4 2004 10.1.1.1
ROUTER(config)IP HOST TACOMA5 2005 10.1.1.1
ROUTER(config)IP HOST TACOMA6 2006 10.1.1.1
ROUTER(config)END
```

What type of session did you establish with the router in order to change its command string?

A. TELNET

B. Reverse TELNET

C. Double reverse TELNET

D. Reverse double TELNET

21. Which command below defines a line as an asynchronous line?

A. ROUTER(config) PHYSICAL-LAYER ASYNC

B. ROUTER(config-if) PHYSICAL-LAYER ASYNC

C. ROUTER(config) ASYNCHRONOUS-ENABLE

D. ROUTER(config-if) ENABLE ASYNCH

22. You have established a TELNET session to a remote router with an external modem problem. The modem is not responding. You decided to check the status of the DTE-DCE interface leads. Which of the following commands gives the status of the DTE-DCE interface leads? Choose all that apply.

A. DEBUG MODEM

B. DEBUG ASYNC STATUS

C. SHOW INTERFACE

D. SHOW ASYNCH STATUS

23. Which are the following are NOT WAN link layer protocols? Choose all that apply.

A. HDLC

B. HSSI

C. IEEE 802.3

D. Frame Relay

24. How does the start-up of a PPP CHAP authentication begin?

A. With a two-way handshake

B. With a three-way handshake

C. With no handshake

D. With a handshake request

25. You have been asked to configure your router for PPP. In what mode must the router be and what command would you issue?

A. Global mode; ENCAPSULATION PPP

B. Interface mode; PPP ENCAPSULATION

C. Global mode; PPP ENCAPSULATION

D. Interface mode; ENCAPSULATION PPP

26. What does multilink multichassis (MMP) PPP provide?

A. It provides the bundling of multiple links from a single client using MLP to terminate across multiple-access servers and routers transparently

B. It provides the same functions as MLP

C. There are no common functions between MMP and MLP

D. MMP as an IOS feature begins with IOS 10.3

27. Four of the commands for configuring a router as a PPP call-back client for DDR are listed below. Which one of these commands is optional?

A. ENCAPSULATION PPP

B. PPP AUTHENTICATION CHAP

C. PPP CALLBACK REQUEST

D. DIALER HOLD-QUEUE

28. What type of protocol-level authentication is offered with SLIP?

A. CHAP

B. PAP

C. PAP and CHAP

D. None of the above

29. What is the speed of the D-channel associated with BRI service?

A. 64 Kbps

B. 128 Kbps

C. 144 Kbps

D. 16 Kbps

30. Which one of the PPP session establishment phases listed below is optional?

A. Authentication phase

B. Link establishment phase

C. Physical layer establishment phase

D. Network layer protocol phase

31. Please identify all the scenarios in which a dialer rotary group may be used.

A. Multiple lines to a single destination

B. Single line to multiple destinations

C. Multiple lines to multiple destinations mapped one to one

D. Single line to a single destination

32. If a connected ISDN or analog line remains connected, but in an idle state, and other traffic needs to bring up a line, how can the interface be configured so that the router can bring down the idle line to initiate the required call?

A. By decreasing the idle timeout period

B. By increasing the idle timeout period

C. By decreasing the fast-idle period

D. By configuring a WAIT FOR CARRIER time

Refer to the Following SHOW DIALER Output to Answer Questions 33–34

```
Router show dialer interface bri 0
BRI0 - dialer type = ISDN
Dial String       Successes    Failures     Last called
Last status
5551212      3              0          24secs
successful
0 incoming call(s) have been screened.
BRI0: B-Channel 1
Idle timer (120 secs), Fast idle timer (20 secs)
Wait for carrier (30 secs), Re-enable (15 secs)
Dialer state is data link layer up
Dial reason: ip (s=6.1.1.8, d=6.1.1.1)
Interface bound to profile Dialer0
Time until disconnect 102 secs
Current call connected 00:00:19
Connected to 5773872 (Router1)
BRI0: B-Channel 2
Idle timer (120 secs), Fast idle timer (20 secs)
Wait for carrier (30 secs), Re-enable (15 secs)
Dialer state is idle
```

33. Which statement defines NCP as being active?

A. BRI0: B-CHANNEL 1

B. CONNECTED TO 5773872 (Router1)

C. CURRENT CALL CONNECTED 00:00:19

D. DIALER STATE IS DATA-LINK LAYER UP

34. The IDLE TIMEOUT command is set to default. How much time has the idle timeout counter counted down?

A. 120 seconds

B. 20 seconds

C. 18 seconds

D. 102 seconds

35. The dialer profile consists of the following elements. Which one is optional when configuring dialer profiles?

A. A dialer interface

B. A dialer map class

C. A dialer pool

D. A physical interface

36. The following access list permits what type of traffic?

```
ACCESS-LIST 102 PERMIT TCP ANY HOST 172.18.21.2 EQ 23
```

A. FTP

B. WWW

C. TCP

D. Telnet

37. Referring to the access list below, select the statement that describes the type of traffic that will be allowed.

```
access-list 101 deny eigrp any any
access-list 101 deny ip any 224.0.0.10 0.0.0.0
```

A. All IP traffic except EIGRP

B. All IP traffic except EIGRP and traffic from 224.0.0.10

C. All IP traffic except EIGRP and traffic to 224.0.0.10

D. None of the above

38. If a Cisco 700 series router has a single B-channel up and running, but requires additional bandwidth to the same location, what method is used so that both B-channels function as a single link?

A. PPP

B. MLP

C. DNS

D. SNMP

39. Which of the following North American switch standards do the Cisco 700 series routers support? Choose all that apply.

A. AT&T 5ESS

B. Northern Telecom DMS 100

C. NI-1 ISDN standards

D. TPH

40. How are configurations saved in NVRAM on a Cisco 700 series router?

A. COPY RUN START

B. WRITE MEM

C. SET command automatically saves configuration

D. SAVE command

41. On a Cisco 700 series router, what does the following configuration define?

```
Set DHCP address 192.168.5.2 252
```

A. The network and subnet mask address of the DHCP server

B. The starting addresses and the number of addresses in the pool

C. A and B

D. None of the above

42. Which of the following features are provided by profile configurations on a Cisco 700 series router?

A. A method for defining DNS services

B. A method for DHCP services

C. Both A and B

D. None of the above

43. What's the best way to view the status and statistics for X.25?

A. SHOW X25

B. SHOW X25 STATISTICS

C. SHOW INTERFACE

D. SHOW LINE

44. A company wishes to install a new router and remotely install the configuration with the help of an existing router. Which resolution protocol can be used to facilitate the remote configuration?

A. AARP

B. IARP

C. SLARP

D. RARP

45. Using the DEBUG FRAME RELAY LMI command allows you to verify and troubleshoot a Frame Relay connection. In the output of the DEBUG command, a field entitled Status, followed by a number, is displayed. What does it mean when the value of 0x2 is displayed in the field?

A. The switch has the DLCI programmed, but is not useable

B. The Frame Relay switch does not have the DLCI programmed for the router; however, it was programmed at some point

C. The Frame Relay switch has the DLCI programmed and everything is operational

D. None of the above

46. Which of the following is a method of NAT that maps a virtual host to several real hosts?

A. TCP load distribution

B. Virtual NAT

C. NAT spoofing

D. None of the above

47. WAN links with certain types of traffic benefit most from prioritization. What type of traffic benefits most?

A. WAN links with continuous traffic

B. WAN links with bursty traffic

C. WAN links with multiple protocols

D. WAN links with a single protocol

48. When is the application or implementation of priority queuing best?

A. When the timeliness of packet transmission does not affect the application

B. When the timeliness of packet transmission does affect the application

C. When the size of the link is greater than T1 (1.54 Mbps)

D. When the link has no congestion

49. Which command applies a priority list to an interface?

A. ROUTERA(config) PRIORITY-GROUP list

B. ROUTERA (Config) PRIORITY GROUP list

C. ROUTERA (Config-if) PRIORITY GROUP *list*

D. ROUTERA (config-if) PRIORITY-GROUP *list*

50. What is the default byte count that is allocated to custom queuing when no modifications are made?

A. 64

B. 256

C. 1024

D. 1500

E. 1518

51. Which form of compression is also know as *per-virtual circuit* compression?

A. Link

B. Payload

C. Header

D. MPPC

52. Compression places a burden on the processor of a router. Which of the following compression methods places the highest burden on a router?

A. Link

B. Payload

C. Header

D. MPPC

53. At which layer of the OSI reference model does header compression function? (Choose all that apply.)

A. Application

B. Presentation

C. Session

D. Transport

E. Network

F. Data-link

54. What is stated by IP NAT INSIDE SOURCE STATIC 10.3.4.54 192.168.10.20?

A. The inside global address 10.3.4.54 will be translated to 192.168.10.20, the inside local address

B. The address 192.168.10.20 will be translate to 10.3.4.54 for use outside in the public network

C. The inside local address 10.3.4.54 will be translated to 192.168.10.20, an inside global address, when the packet is bound outside to the private global network

D. The inside local address 192.168.10.20 will be translated to 10.3.4.54, an inside global address, when the packet is bound outside to the private network

55. How many PAT addresses are allocated to a LAN on a Cisco 700 series router?

A. One

B. Two

C. Eight

D. An unlimited number

56. If a 20-user LAN needs to be connected to an ISP via ISDN using a Cisco 700 series router, how many IP addresses would be required to support the LAN?

A. Twenty

B. Two

C. One

D. None

57. The configuration command to enable AAA on a router is:

A. AAA ENABLE

B. AAA

C. AAA NEW-MODEL

D. AAA START

58. Which of the following is defined by the AAA authorization example configuration AAA AUTHORIZATION EXEC TACACS+ LOCAL?

    A. The user has access to the ENABLE shell through a TACACS+ server or through the local database if the TACACS+ server does not respond

    B. The user has access to the EXEC shell, and is authorized by the local database

    C. The user has access to certain shell attributes, authorized by a local TACACS+ database

    D. The user is allowed access to an EXEC session and the attributes in that session

59. Which are the best applications for the Cisco 700 series routers?

    A. Small office

    B. Home office

    C. Enterprise networks

    D. Telecommuting

60. Backup interfaces can be configured for multiple backup tasks. What are two of the tasks?

    A. When a primary link reaches or exceeds a set threshold

    B. When a primary link fails

    C. To connect to a different remote location

    D. There is only one use

61. The two WAN communications methods that complement or extend X.25 are:

    A. ATM

    B. ISDN

    C. Frame Relay

    D. Analog

62. You have been asked to configure X.25 address 211555222 on your router's serial 0 interface. Which command would you use to accomplish this?

A. INT S0
   ENCAPSULATION X25
   X25 ADDRESS 211555222

B. INT S 0
   ENCAPSULATION X25
   X121 ADDRESS 211555222

C. INT S 0
   ENCAPSULATION X121
   X25 ADDRESS 211555222

D. INT S 0
   ENCAPSULATION X121
   X121 ADDRESS 211555222

63. What is the maximum console speed for a Cisco 3600 series router?

A. 9600 bps

B. 38,400 bps

C. 57,600 bps

D. 115,200 bps

CCNP

CISCO CERTIFIED NETWORK PROFESSIONAL

Test Yourself: BCRAN Practice Exam 1 Answers

Q & A

The answers to the questions are in boldface, followed by a brief explanation. Some of the explanations detail the logic you should use to choose the correct answer, while others give factual reasons why the answer is correct.

BCRAN Practice Exam I Answers

1. ☑ **D.** Weighted fair queuing is on by default so that on an initial router configuration, it does not need to be activated.
   ☒ **A.** FAIR-QUEUE; **B.** WEIGHTED FAIR-QUEUE; and **C.** QUEUE; are all incorrect for the same reason: weighted fair queuing does not need to be activated upon initial configuration; it is on by default.

2. ☑ **B** and **D.** The V.90 modem technology assumes that one end of the modem connection has an all-digital connection to the phone network (e.g. ISPs) and takes advantage of the high-speed digital connection. The user's connection to the phone network is assumed to be analog. So, the lowest speed is on the transmit side of the modem (keystrokes, mouse clicks) and the highest speeds, on the receive side of the modem (file and image transfers).
   ☒ **A.** The highest-line speed is achieved on the transmit side of the user's modem, is wrong because the transmit path is usually over an analog facility with higher noise and consequently, lower transmission speeds. **C.** Multiple analog links in the transmission path between source and destination do not impact the modem's speed, is wrong because multiple analog/digital conversions is the assumption of other modem standards.

3. ☑ **B.** 16. There can be 16 privilege levels defined. The privilege levels range from 0–15. The privilege commands must be applied at an authentication or authorization level in order to be able to audit the level through accounting.
   ☒ All other answers are incorrect, since there are a total of 16 privilege levels that may be defined ranging from 0–15. 0 is the common user exec mode and 15 is the common privileged exec mode. All other levels are defined by the administrator via configuration commands.
   A. 15, **C.** 18, and **D.** an unlimited number, are all incorrect, since there are a total of 16 privilege levels that may be defined ranging from 0–15. 0 is the

common user exec mode and 15 is the common privileged exec mode. All other levels are defined by the administrator via configuration commands.

4. ☑   **D.** ROUTER (config-if) # DIALER ROTARY-GROUP 1. The dialer rotary group must be mapped to a physical interface. With the proper syntax of the raw command being DIALER ROTARY-GROUP 1, the user configuring the router must be sure that the router is in the interface to which the dialer rotary group is to be applied. ROUTER (config-if) # DIALER ROTARY-GROUP 1 is at a router prompt that indicates a physical interface with the proper syntax.

☒   **A.** ROUTER(config) # DIALER ROTARY-GROUP 1, is incorrect because the router is enabled in global configuration mode. **B.** ROUTER # DIALER GROUP 1, is incorrect because the router is not in configuration mode at the interface level, but is in privileged exec mode, where configuration command input will return an error. Also, the syntax is incorrect. **C.** ROUTER (config-if) # DIALER GROUP 1, is incorrect because the syntax is incorrect, although the prompt indicates that the router is at an interface.

5. ☑   **C.** SHOW INTERFACE S1, is the correct command. This command displays the encapsulation type used on the interface. Also displayed are a number of other parameters associated with the interface, such as real time statistics related to the interface operation.

☒   **A** and **B** are incorrect because these commands do not exist. **D.** SHOW IP INTERFACE S1, is incorrect because it only shows IP protocol-related information and not the type of encapsulation used on the interface.

6. ☑   **C.** Data Service Unit/Channel Service Unit (DSU/CSU). This device provides the physical layer signaling and interface to the DTE. It also provides the interface to the digital access line from the common carrier.

☒   **A. Modem, is incorrect because it operates on an analog line. B.** Digital modem, is incorrect as it is used in conjunction with dial-up service provided over a digital access line. **D.** NT1, is incorrect because an NT1 terminates an ISDN line.

7. ☑ **B.** 1544 Kbps. The default bandwidth for a serial interface on a Cisco router is 1544 Kbps. This is the speed of a T-1 line. 1544 Kbps is 1.544 Mbps. This bandwidth may not relate to the actual operational bandwidth of the interface.

☒ **A.** 154.4 Kbps; **C.** 1.544 Kbps; and **D.** 15.54 Kbps; are incorrect because they all are bandwidth values that are less than the correct speed of 1.544 Mbps.

8. ☑ **B.** The default speed of the aux port is 9600 bps. The port speed may be set up to 38,400 bps or, on newer models, 115,200 bps. The router can be remotely configured by dialing into this interface.

☒ **A.** 9600 Kbps, and **D.** 38,400 Kbps, are incorrect because the port will not accept either of these speeds. **C.** is an acceptable speed, but is not the default.

9. ☑ **B.** Cisco routers such as the 3600, 2600, and 1700 routers support multi-service WICs. Other routers, such as the 2522 have fixed configurations of these interfaces. The default mode of operation is synchronous. If you want asynchronous operation on the serial, you must configure it.

☒ **A.** Asynchronous, is incorrect because it has to be selected by configuration; **C.** Synchronous/synchronous; and **D.** Asynchronous/asynchronous, are incorrect because there is no such mode of operation in either case.

10. ☑ **D.** 115,200 bps. The maximum speed setting for an asynchronous interface is 115,200 bps. This represents the speed between the router and the modem, not the speed across the phone line.

☒ **A.** 9600 bps; **B.** 38,400 bps; and **C.** 57,600 bps, are incorrect because these are not the maximum speed settings.

11. ☑ **D.** The Cisco 700 series routers are designed for a very small office of five people or less. Its feature set is also designed to support telecommuters' remote access to the enterprise network.

☒ **A.** Cisco 1600; **B.** Cisco 1700; and **D.** Cisco 700, are incorrect because they were designed to serve a larger enterprise's remote-access needs.

12. ☑   **A.** RJ-45. The console port connection requires a cable with a RJ-45 connector to connect to the console port. Most Cisco routers use this type of connector for the console port connection.

☒   **B.** RJ-11C; **C.** DB-9; and **D.** RS 232; are incorrect because they are the wrong type of connectors for any of the ports on the Cisco 1600 series.

13. ☑   **C.** The 1-Port ISDN BRI U card indicates that the card has a built-in NT1. The ISDN U interface allows direct connection of an BRI line to the card.

☒   **A.** is wrong because the card contains in internal NT1. **B.** is wrong because the card already contains a built in NT1. **D.** is incorrect because the BRI card does not support an ISDN PRI interface.

14. ☑   **A and B.** The WIC 1DSU/CSU-T1 is a WAN interface card that has a built-in DSU/CSU and will terminate a T1 line. The built-in DSU/CSU eliminates the need for an external DSU/CSU to terminate the T1 line. The built in DSU/CSU also makes diagnosing problems easier.

☒   **C and D** are incorrect because the card will terminate a T1 line and it has a built-in DSU/CSU, not requiring an external one.

15. ☑   **A and D.** The routers that can share WAN interface cards (WICs) are the Cisco 1600, 2600 and 3600 series routers. These routers were designed as modular-access routers to provide flexibility and growth.

☒   **B.** Cisco 3810, and **C.** Cisco 2500, are wrong because neither the 3810 nor the 2500 series have modules that are interchangeable with the Cisco 2600 series.

16. ☑   **D.** 700 series. The Cisco 765M, 766M, 775M, and 776M routers support this feature. A basic network configuration can be created with a DTMF (dual-tone multi-frequency) push-button telephone. A network administrator can dial into the Cisco 700 router later and complete the configuration.

☒   **A.** 3600 series; **B.** 2600 series; and **C.** 1000 series, are wrong because these routers do not support this feature.

17. ☑   **C.** The steps are: 4. The call is routed from the end user to the local central office (CO). The CO equipment performs an analog-to-digital (A/D) conversion to convert the channel to a 64-Kbps digital signal. This 64-Kbps signal is transmitted over the digital network between COs. The 64-Kbps signal is converted from a digital signal back into an analog signal (D/A conversion). The call is then routed to the destination as an analog signal.

☒   **A, B,** and **D** are wrong because each has one or more steps in the incorrect sequence.

18. ☑   **B.** Asymmetrical transmit and receive speeds up to 33.6 Kbps and 56 Kbps, respectively. The V.90 standard supports a transmission speed of 33.6 Kbps and a receive speed of 56 Kbps. Due to FCC transmit power restrictions the actual receive speed will be about 53.33 Kbps.

☒   **A.** Asymmetrical transmit and receive speeds up to 33.6 Kbps and 64 Kbps, respectively, is incorrect because of an incorrect receive speed of 64 Kbps. **C.** Symmetrical transmit and receive speeds of 56 Kbps, and **D.** symmetrical transmit and receive speeds of 64 Kbps, are wrong because the V.90 standard was not written to support symmetrical speeds.

19. ☑   **A.** The 700 series does not run IOS. This is a family of routers made by Combinet and primarily used for remote ISDN access from small offices or home offices. The images differ by country and feature set. This is different from the traditional Cisco IOS images, so the command structure is different.

☒   **B.** Cisco IOS 12.0, is incorrect because it is traditional IOSs that cannot be loaded in the 700 series routers. **C.** Cisco IOS-700, and **D.** Cisco IOS-7000, do not exist.

20. ☑   **B.** Reverse TELNET. The session opened with the modem was a reverse TELNET session. A reverse TELNET means that a TELNET session is being initiated out the asynchronous line instead of into the router from an outside source.

☒   **A.** TELNET, is wrong because this would be a session initiated out of a VTY port. **C.** Double reverse TELNET, and **D.** reverse double TELNET, are wrong because there are no sessions of this type.

21. ☑ **B.** ROUTER(config-if)# PHYSICAL-LAYER ASYNC. The PHYSICAL-LAYER ASYNC is the proper command format to set a dual synchronous/asynchronous interface to asynchronous operation.

☒ **A, C,** and **D** are incorrect because of improper command syntax.

22. ☑ **A** and **C.** The SHOW INTERFACE command gives the status and statistics on the hardware interface. Five of the interface lead statuses, namely DCD, DSR, DTR, RTS, and CTS, are given. This would show whether the modem was electrically communicating with the router. The DEBUG MODEM command would show interface lead activity as a call was processed.

☒ **B.** DEBUG ASYNC STATUS, is wrong because there is no such command. **D.** SHOW ASYNCH STATUS, is wrong because it shows packet statistics.

23. ☑ **B** and **C.** High Speed Serial Interface (HSSI) is a WAN physical layer DTE-DCE interface specification. It defines the mechanical and electrical interaction between a DTE and a DCE. IEEE 802.3 is a LAN protocol specification. It defines the link-layer frame format and physical layer specification for a 10 Mbps-bus topology LAN.

☒ **A.** HDLC, is a WAN link layer protocol used over serial point-to-point and multipoint lines. **D.** Frame Relay, is also a WAN link layer protocol that is used over permanent virtual circuits (PVCs).

24. ☑ **B.** CHAP authentication begins with a three-way handshake. A challenge (encryption key) is sent to the remote router after the link-establishment phase is complete. The remote router uses the key to encrypt its username and password, then sends it to the central router. The central router decrypts the information and accepts or rejects it.

☒ **A.** A two-way handshake; **C.** no handshake; and **D.** a handshake request, are incorrect because of the description above.

25. ☑ **D.** The router must be in the interface configuration mode before you can correctly enter the command, ENCAPSULATION PPP. The encapsulation goes on the chosen WAN interface.

☒ **A.** Global mode; ENCAPSULATION PPP, is wrong because the global configuration mode was chosen. **B.** Interface mode; PPP ENCAPSULATION, is wrong because of the improper syntax for PPP encapsulation. **C.** Global mode; PPP ENCAPSULATION, is incorrect because the configuration mode and command syntax is wrong.

26. ☑ **A.** MMP allows an organization to maximize the use of access-server equipment and lines. The lines (Asynch, BRI or PRI) are organized into rotary hunt groups. Users dial a single number, which may terminate on any server or router transparently. Stack Group Bidding Protocol (SGBP) is used to communicate among the organization's servers and routers for call handling.

☒ **B.** It provides the same functions as MLP, is wrong because MLP only works on one router and MMP works across multiple equipment chassis. **C.** There are no common functions between MMP and MLP, is wrong because there are common functions. MMP is an extension of MLP features. **D.** MMP as an IOS feature begins with IOS 10.3, is wrong because MMP is a feature of the IOS beginning at IOS 11.2.

27. ☑ **D.** DIALER HOLD-QUEUE is optional. This command sets up a queue for packets that are to be sent out over the call-back connection. The packets are moving from a high-speed LAN to a lower-speed WAN link and need to be queued or they will be dropped.

☒ **A.** ENCAPSULATION PPP; **B.** PPP AUTHENTICATION CHAP; and **C.** PPP CALLBACK REQUEST are incorrect because they are required configuration parameters.

28. ☑ **D.** There is no protocol-level authentication offered with SLIP encapsulation. SLIP only supports the TCP/IP protocol suite.

☒ **A, B,** and **C** are incorrect, as neither PAP nor CHAP is offered with SLIP.

29. ☑ **D.** The speed of the D signaling channel associated with ISDN BRI service is 16 Kbps. This channel carries all of the signaling information for B-channel usage.

☒ **A.** 64 Kbps, is incorrect because it is the speed of a single B channel. **B.** 128 Kbps, is wrong because it is the combined speed of both BRI, B channels. **C.** 144 Kbps, is wrong because it is the combined speed of all BRI channels.

30. ☑ **A.** Authentication phase. This is an optional phase in establishing a PPP connection. The proper order of session establishment is **B**, **A**, and **D**, with **D** being optional.

☒ **C.** Physical layer establishment phase, is not correct because it is not formally a part of the PPP session establishment phase. It is assumed that the physical layer connectivity is handled by devices like modems.

31. ☑ **A and C.** Multiple lines can be set up to dial to a single destination or to multiple destinations. This application can be used for facilities that have burst traffic scenarios where a small bandwidth link is brought up and, as requirements for more bandwidth arise, additional links come up to facilitate the bandwidth requirements. A single physical interface or line may be programmed so that multiple logical interfaces are mapped to each, with each logical interface set up to connect to different sites. This is effective when links are established for short periods of time.

☒ **B.** Single line to multiple destinations, is incorrect because in rotary groups the logical configuration can be used in a one to one with a physical and also many physicals can be mapped to a single logical. A physical interface may only be mapped to a single logical. **D.** Single line to a single destination, is incorrect because, in the case of a single line going to a single facility, a rotary group is not required, and a single profile mapped to a single interface is not a group, but a mapping of a single logical interface to a single physical interface.

32. ☑ **C. By decreasing the fast-idle period.** The fast-idle timer enables the router to bring down an idle connection in order to make a connection to a different destination over the same line. The line is considered idle when no interesting traffic is sent across it. If the line becomes idle for the configured period of time (in seconds), the connection is immediately brought down and is made available for other calls. The proper syntax for configuring the fast-idle function is:
    ROUTER (config-if) # DIALER FAST-IDLE *seconds*
    This command string is applied to an interface, and the default time is 20 seconds.
    ☒ **A. By decreasing the idle timeout period**, and **B. by increasing the idle timeout period**, are incorrect because the timeout period defines the time in seconds before the line is disconnected, regardless of whether or not interesting traffic is passing over the connection. These command strings are used on a line for which there is no contention and are specified as inactivity timers. The default time is 120 seconds. **D. By configuring a WAIT FOR CARRIER time**, is incorrect because the WAIT FOR CARRIER time is a command string that specifies how long to wait for carrier time. On asynchronous interfaces, this command sets the total time allowed for the chat script to run.

33. ☑ **D. Dialer state is data-link layer up.** This command is a bit deceiving, but when you see the DIALER STATE IS DATA-LINK LAYER UP message, it suggests that the dialer came up properly. If you see a line in its place that states PHYSICAL LAYER UP the line protocol came up, but the network control protocol did not.
    ☒ **A. BRI0: B-CHANNEL 1**, is incorrect. It identifies the BRI channel that is in use, and could have a physical connection, but does not properly display status of the NCP. **B. CONNECTED TO 5773872 (Router1)**, is incorrect. It identifies the router to which it is connected, but again, does not state status of NCP. **C. CURRENT CALL CONNECTED 00:00:19**, is incorrect because the timer starts when the physical connection is made and the status of the NCP cannot be determined by the timer.

34. ☑ **C.** 18 seconds. The IDLE TIMEOUT default is 120 seconds. In analyzing the output, you can determine the amount of time that the counter has counted down by subtracting the IDLE TIMEOUT default allocation from the output that states time until disconnect.

☒ **A.** 120 seconds, is incorrect because it is the idle-timer default time, not the amount of time that has counted down. **B.** 20 seconds, is incorrect because this is the fast-idle timer default. **D.** 102 seconds, is incorrect because 102 seconds is the time until disconnect, not the amount of time that the counter has counted down.

35. ☑ **B.** A dialer map class defines specific characteristics for a call to a specified dial string. The map class can specify items such as ISDN line speeds for a particular profile while establishing different parameters altogether for another profile. A map class is an optional element for a dialer profile and can be referenced by multiple dialer interfaces.

☒ **A.** A dialer interface, is incorrect. It is a logical entity that establishes a per-destination dialer profile. **C.** The dialer pool, is incorrect. It is referenced by dialer interfaces. A dialer pool is a group of one or more physical interfaces that is associated to dialer profiles. **D.** The physical interface, is incorrect. It is the hardware entity that establishes connectivity within the parameters configured in the dialer profile.

36. ☑ **D.** The extended IP access list defines permitting TCP traffic of a particular type. Port 23 is an IP port that maps to Telnet traffic. So, if this access list is applied to a dialer list, the type of traffic that initiates the call is Telnet. A sample configuration is shown here:

```
access-list 102 permit tcp any host 172.18.21.2 eq 23
dialer-list 1 list 102
```

The access list will initiate a call from any host on the network that is destined for the specific host 172.18.21.2, if the traffic is Telnet traffic. The dialer list will then have to be applied to a physical interface.

☒ **A.** FTP; **B.** WWW; and **C.** TCP; are not port 23 protocols, and will not be permitted if this is the only access list configured.

37. ☑ **D.** None of the above. The access list will not allow any IP traffic to pass on the interface on which the access list is implemented. Access lists have implicit DENY statements that are not displayed in the configuration. So, at the end of the access list displayed, there will be a non-displayed statement as follows:

```
access-list 101 deny ip any any
```

One must be sure to implement a PERMIT statement that will allow all traffic except the traffic in the statement list prior to the general PERMIT statement. The PERMIT statement would look like this:

```
Access-list 101 permit ip any any
```

☒ **A.** All IP traffic except EIGRP; **B.** All IP traffic except EIGRP and traffic from 224.0.0.10; and **C.** All IP traffic except EIGRP and traffic to 224.0.0.10, are incorrect because the implicit DENY statement is not taken into consideration.

38. ☑ **B.** MLP is the acronym for Multilink PPP. MLP is an industry standard protocol that allows multiple links to the same location to function as a single link. All Cisco 700 series routers support MLP, which aggregates both B-channels to provide up to 128 Kbps of ISDN bandwidth.
☒ **A.** PPP, is incorrect because PPP supports a single link. **C.** DNS, is incorrect because Domain Name Service (DNS) is a method of mapping IP addresses to names. **D.** SNMP, is incorrect because it is the Simple Network Management Protocol.

39. ☑ **A, B,** and **C.** ATT 5ESS, Northern Telecom DMS 100, and NI-1 ISDN standards are all North American switch standards that the Cisco 700 series routers support. The Cisco 700 series routers include a built-in Network Termination device (NT-1) via the ISDN U port to provide an all-in-one solution for ISDN users in North America.
☒ **D.** TPH, is incorrect because it is an Australian switch type.

40. ☑ **C.** The SET command saves the parameters defined in the command string. An example of the SET command is: > SET SYSTEM NAME *NAME.* When RETURN is pressed, the system name configured is saved. The configuration string defined is saved to NVRAM.
☒ **A.** COPY RUN START, and **B.** WRITE MEM, are command strings used in IOS routers to save configuration files to NVRAM and are incorrect here. **D.** SAVE command, is not a valid command for saving configurations.

41. ☑ **B.** The command specifies the starting address and the number of addresses in the pool. The address range is 192.168.5.2–192.168.5.253. When the DHCP server initializes, default addresses are used if no existing internal or LAN addresses are defined. If internal and LAN addresses are defined, the router defines the default gateway, net mask, and DHCP address pool based on the defined address. The default setting of 10.0.0.1 is used for the LAN IP address, with the DHCP client range starting at 10.0.0.2, and the LAN default address used as the gateway address.
☒ **A.** The network and subnet mask address of the DHCP server, is incorrect because the command string sets up the starting IP address and range of DHCP addresses available to clients.

42. ☑ **D.** None of the above. The profile configuration provides the capability to define individual user profiles to connect to specific remote locations.
☒ **A.** A method for defining DNS services, and **B.** a method for DHCP services, are both parameters that can be defined on the Cisco 700 series routers, but are not defined in user profiles and are incorrect here.

43. ☑ **C.** The following is a sample output from the SHOW INTERFACES command for a serial X.25 interface:

```
Router# show interfaces serial 1
Serial 1 is up, line protocol is up
Hardware is CD2034 in sync mode
Internet address is 10.10.5.5/24
```

```
      MTU 1500 bytes, BW 128Kbit, DLY 2000 usec, rely 255/255,
      load 1/255
      Encapsulation X25, loopback not set
      X.25 DTE, address 311903101918, state R1, modulo 8, timer
      0
      Defaults: idle vc timeout 0
      Cisco encapsulation
      Input/output window sized 2/2, packet sizes 128/128
      Timers: T20 180, T21 200, T22 180, T23 180
      Channels: Incoming-only none, Two-way 1-1024,
      Outgoing-only none
      RESTARTs 1/0 CALLs 0+0/0+0/0+0 DIAGs 0/0
      LAPB DTE, stae CONNECT, modulo 8, k 7, N1 12056, N2 20
      T1 3000, T2 0, interface outage (partial T3) 0, T4 0
      VS 5, VR 3, tx NR 3, Remote VR 5, Retransmissions 0
      Queues: U/S frames 0, I frames 0, unack. 0, reTX 0
      IFRAMEs 5/3 RNRs 0/0 REJs 0/0 SABM/Es 0/1 FRMRs 0/0 DISCs
      0/0
      Last input 00:00:35, output 00:00:36, output hang never
      Last clearing of "show interface" counters never
      Queuing strategy: fifo
      Output queue 0/40, 0 drops; input queue 0/75, 0 drops
      5 minute input rate 0 bits/sec, 0 packet/sec
      5 minute output rate 0 bits/sec, 0 packets/sec
```

As you can see, there is a lot of information in the SHOW INTERFACE output.

☒ **A.** SHOW X25, is incorrect because it provides much less information, more cryptically. The following is an example of the SHOW X25 output:

```
Router> show x25
X25 is running in DTE MODE. VC Ranges - current value
(new value after reboot): lic 0 (0), hic 0 (0), ltc 0
(0), htc 0 (0), loc 1024 (1024), hoc 1024 (1024)
```

B. SHOW X25 STATISTICS, is incorrect. This command provides easy-to-read information, but is not nearly as informative as the SHOW INTERFACE command. Following is an example of the SHOW X25 STATISTICS output:

```
Host> show x25 statistics
LSVC 1
Outbound Requests: 0
```

```
Outbound Failed: 0
SVC Errors: 0
Out Packets: 0
In Packets: 0
LSVC 2
Outbound Requests: 0
Outbound Failed: 0
SVC Errors: 0
Out Packets: 0
In Packets: 0
```

D. SHOW LINE, is incorrect. This command will not display information about status or statistics of X.25.

44. ☑ **C.** SLARP. Serial Line Address Resolution Protocol (SLARP) is used to automatically install a new router via an HDLC-encapsulated serial interface. The serial interface must be configured with an IP address whose host portion has a value of 1 or 2. SLARP is used with the Cisco IOS auto-install function. SLARP is used to acquire a new router's IP address from an existing router in order to facilitate the auto-install feature.

    ☒ **A.** AARP, is incorrect because AppleTalk node address resolution is the objective. **B.** IARP, is incorrect because this is used to resolve IP addresses to DLCI numbers for Frame Relay. **D.** RARP, is incorrect because communication between the routers has to be established and this initial conversation between routers must be established before RARP can be initiated.

45. ☑ **C.** The Frame Relay switch has the DLCI programmed and everything is operational. The 2 displayed after the word Status means that the Frame Relay switch has the DLCI programmed and everything is operational. The following table lists available status readings that may occupy the Status field.

Status	Status value
0x00	Added/inactive
0x02	Added/active
0x04	Deleted
0x08	New/inactive
0x0a	New/active

   ☒   **A.** The switch has the DLCI programmed, but is not useable, is incorrect because the definition representing the Status field has a value of 0. **B.** The Frame Relay switch does not have the DLCI programmed for the router; however, it was programmed at some point, is incorrect because the definition representing the Status field has a value of 4.

46. ☑   **A.** TCP load distribution works by mapping a virtual host to several real hosts. The router translating a virtual address to several real network addresses does this. When a remote host sends a request to the virtual address, the router intercepts the request and translates the address to a real address. When the receiving host responds, the router refers to the NAT table and translates that real host address back to the virtual address to send the response to the originating host.
   ☒   **B.** Virtual NAT, and **C.** NAT spoofing, are incorrect because there is no such thing as Virtual NAT or NAT spoofing.

47. ☑   **B.** Prioritization is most effective on WAN links with bursty traffic and links with relatively lower data rates where temporary congestion may occur. Prioritization is most effective when applied to links at T1/E1 or lower bandwidth speeds. Note: If a WAN link is consistently congested even after prioritization is applied, adding bandwidth may be the only viable solution.
   ☒   **A.** WAN links with continuous traffic, is incorrect because continuous traffic flow over the WAN link does not benefit from prioritizing traffic. **C.** WAN links with multiple protocols, is incorrect because most WAN links have multiple protocols traversing them. **D.** WAN links with a single protocol, is incorrect because having a single protocol traversing the WAN will not require prioritization.

48. ☑   **B.** When the timeliness of packet transmission does affect the application. Priority queuing is a method to employ strict control of what type of traffic gets and retains priority in the queue. This traffic is useful where traffic has a hierarchy of importance, translating into most-important traffic being delayed least and less-important traffic being delayed more. Time sensitive traffic like SNA or mainframe traffic can be prioritized over TCP or UDP traffic. Priority queuing is employed on WAN connections that are congested and have time-sensitive traffic or transaction processing traffic that must be serviced over the link to avoid sessions being dropped. With priority queuing, the high-priority queue is always emptied first, then the medium-priority queue, and so on. If traffic in the higher-priority queues is always present, traffic in the lower-priority queues may not be processed. The high queue must be completely empty before a single packet will be dispatched out of the medium queue. Upon dispatching, the router will immediately check the high queue. If it is still empty, the router will check the medium, normal, and finally, the low queue.

☒　**A.** When the timeliness of packet transmission does not affect the application, is incorrect because when employing priority traffic, the timeliness of the type of traffic in the higher queues is important. **C.** When the size of the link is greater than T1 (1.54Mbps), is incorrect because queuing is rarely employed on links larger than T1. **D.** When the link has no congestion, is incorrect because when a link has no congestion, there is no need to employ queuing.

49. ☑　**D.** The proper syntax to apply a priority list to an interface is ROUTERA (config-if) PRIORITY-GROUP *list#*. The router must be at an interface where the priority list is going to be applied, and the list number identified must also be applied.

☒　**A.** ROUTERA(config) PRIORITY-GROUP *list#* is incorrect because although the syntax is correct, the router prompt indicates global configuration mode, while the router must be at the interface configuration mode. **B.** ROUTERA (Config) PRIORITY GROUP *list #*, is incorrect because the command PRIORITY-LIST requires a hyphen so that the user doesn't receive an error message when configuring. Also, the router is in global configuration mode, not in interface configuration mode. **C.** ROUTERA (Config-if) PRIORITY GROUP *list#*, is incorrect because the command PRIORITY-LIST requires a hyphen so that the user doesn't receive an error message when configuring.

50. ☑ **D.** The default byte count given to a queue that has not been modified is 1500. This count can be modified to provide the best results for a given network.

    ☒ **A.** 64; **B.** 256; **C.** 1024; and **E.** 1518, are incorrect for the default byte count allotted to a custom queue.

51. ☑ **B.** Payload. Per-virtual circuit compression is the not-so-common name for payload compression. Payload compression only compresses the data portion of a packet. The packet header is left intact. This form of switching provides great advantages when designing networks, in that the method of transport, be it X.25, Frame Relay, or ATM, doesn't have a negative effect on the packet being compressed. This contrasts with link compression, where the whole packet is compressed and, through a switched network, the header may not be readable at a particular hop.

    ☒ **A.** Link, is incorrect because per-virtual compression is the uncommon name for payload compression. **C.** Header, and **D.** MPPC, are incorrect for the same reason. Also, payload compression compresses the payload, whereas header compression compresses the header. This form of compression is a Microsoft standard and only allows data exchange with Microsoft clients.

52. ☑ **A.** Link compression places the highest burden on the router's processor.

    ☒ **B.** Payload; **C.** Header; and **D.** MPPC, are all incorrect because they do not place as high a burden on the processor as link compression.

53. ☑ **D** and **E.** Transport and network. Header compression is specific to TCP/IP. TCP is a transport layer protocol. The TCP protocol is a connection-oriented protocol that requires confirmation of packets received. Because acknowledgments are expected, the structure of the TCP protocol packet is larger than that of a UDP protocol packet. Thus compression will benefit the TCP portion. The IP protocol resides at the network layer, and is responsible for routing. The IP addresses are all the same structure, so compressing and de-compressing the packet can be done quickly.

   ☒   **A.** Application; **B.** presentation; **C.** session; and **F.** data-link; are incorrect. The data-link layer of the header is left intact.

54. ☑   **C.** The statement indicates that the inside private local address 10.3.4.54 will be translated to 192.168.10.20, an inside global address, when a packet being routed from the inside to the outside interfaces.
   ☒   **A.** is incorrect because 192.168.10.20 is not the inside local address, but is the global private network address that 10.3.4.54 translates to. **B.** is incorrect because none of these addresses is allowed to be used outside in the public network. **D.** is incorrect because 192.168.10.20 is not the inside local address, but the inside global address.

55. ☑   **A.** One. A single IP address is assigned to an entire LAN. All WAN traffic is mapped to a single node address, the ISDN side of the 700 series router. This method of address translation greatly conserves network addresses.
   ☒   **B.** Two; **C.** eight; and **D.** an unlimited number; are all incorrect address numbers.

56. ☑   **C.** One. As in the previous question, the result is the same, only one outside address will support the LAN with 20 users on it.
   ☒   **A.** Twenty; **B.** two; and **D.** none; are incorrect because the Cisco 700 series router will only support a single IP address on its WAN port.

57. ☑   **C.** AAA NEW-MODEL. The proper configuration to enable AAA on a router is executed in global configuration mode.

```
Router(config)# AAA new-model
```

This command sequence enables AAA on a router.
   ☒   **A.** AAA ENABLE; **B.** AAA; and **D.** AAA START; do not use correct syntax, so they are incorrect.

58. ☑ **D.** The user is allowed access to an EXEC session and the attributes in that session. The authorization method is from a TACACS+ server, unless TACACS+ server times out. Authentication is then through the local database. The command AAA AUTHORIZATION EXEC TACACS+ LOCAL determines permission to access an EXEC shell, and the shell attributes that are permitted or denied. The method of authorization is TACACS+. If the server times out, the local username and password databases are used.

☒ **A.** The user has access to the ENABLE shell through a TACACS+ server or through the local database if the TACACS+ server does not respond, is incorrect because the user does not have access to the ENABLE shell in the command displayed, but only at the user exec level, after authorization. **B.** The user has access to the EXEC shell, and is authorized by the local database, is incorrect because the user has access to the EXEC shell by first passing authorization proceedings with a TACACS+ server. If the TACACS+ server times out, the local database is used. **C.** The user has access to certain shell attributes, authorized by a local TACACS+ database, is incorrect because the user does have access to certain shell attributes only at the user exec level, and the TACACS+ server is not the local authorization method but a separate server that the whole process is mapped to. Only after the TACACS+ server times out will the local database be used.

59. ☑ **A, B,** and **D.** Small office, home office, and telecommuting. The Cisco 700 series routers were designed to provide low-cost, high-performance ISDN connection capabilities to small offices, home offices, and telecommuters. The 700 series routers support two B-channels, providing a combined throughput of 128 Kbps before any compression algorithm is applied. The 700 series routers come with software that enables even users with no technical background to plug in, configure, test, and use the routers.

☒   C. Enterprise networks, is incorrect because the router does not have the processing capability—the capability to provide different connection types, such as Frame Relay, point-to-point leased lines, or ATM, or the flexibility in protocols that enterprise networks require.

60. ☑   A and B. When a primary link reaches or exceeds a set threshold and when a primary link fails. Backup interfaces can be used to expand bandwidth. When a threshold is reached, through configuration, the DIAL BACKUP can be activated. This is useful to organizations for analyzing the possible requirement for additional bandwidth. By knowing how often the dial backup is used to support additional bandwidth, a company can determine if the cost for additional bandwidth is needed, or if the dial-backup method of supporting additional bandwidth is sufficient. Dial backup can also be used to support a primary link in case of failure. When the primary link fails, the dial interface is activated to keep communication between the remote sites active. This is a key feature for organizations that require information from the home office on a continuous basis in order to conduct daily business.

☒   C. To connect to a different remote location, is incorrect because connecting to a different remote site does not back up the line to a primary remote site; it establishes connection with another site.

61. ☑   B and C. Modern desktop applications need LAN-to-WAN-to-LAN communications. Responding to this need, engineers designed newer forms of WAN communications technology. The two forms of WAN technology created were ISDN and Frame Relay. These newer technologies complement or extend, instead of replace, X.25. X.25 is still widely in use today.

☒   A. ATM, is incorrect because ATM is not a complement to X.25. **D.** Analog, is incorrect because analog was in existence before X.25, and does not provide the reliability or speed of which X.25 is capable.

62. ☑   **A.** INT S0
     ENCAPSULATION X25
     X25 ADDRESS 211555222
This configuration enables X.25 encapsulation on the interface and
establishes the X.121 address, 211555222. This configuration also
establishes the default encapsulation type as an X.25 DTE.
  ☒   **B, C,** and **D** are incorrect because each of them uses a non-existent
x121 character string.

63. ☑   **D.** 115,200 bps. The console port can be configured for speeds from
1200 bps–115,200 bps. The Cisco 3620 and 3640 have a jumper on the
motherboard that will allow setting the baud rate to 9600 bps if you cannot
use the regular methods to do so.
  ☒   **A.** 9600 bps; **B.** 38,400 bps; and **C.** 57,600 bps; are speeds that can be
set, but none of them are the maximum speed setting.

CISCO CERTIFIED NETWORK PROFESSIONAL

Test Yourself: BCRAN Practice Exam 2 Questions

Q&A

Before you register for the actual exam, take the following test and see how you make out. Once you've finished, turn to the BCRAN Practice Exam 2 Answers section and check your score to see if you passed. Good luck!

BCRAN Practice Exam 2 Questions

1. When is it best to use header compression instead of link compression?

   A. When using a point-to-point WAN connection
   B. When traversing a multiprotocol network
   C. When connecting to an ISP
   D. None of the above

2. Payload compression is a compression algorithm that only uses one compression method. Select the compression method used by payload compression.

   A. STAC
   B. Predictor
   C. MNP5
   D. LAPB

3. Frame Relay subinterfaces can be configured as multipoint or point-to-point. Select the feature that is NOT a multipoint.

   A. Subinterfaces act as default NBMA networks
   B. Subinterfaces act as leased lines
   C. Can save subnets because they use a single subnet
   D. Good for a full-mesh topology

4. In which of the following situations is FIFO preferred?

   A. Dedicated or Frame Relay links larger than T1
   B. On an analog DDR or dial backup
   C. Dedicated or Frame Relay links smaller than T1
   D. Both A and C

5. What are the available ports on the Cisco 700 series routers? Choose all that apply.

A. Ethernet

B. Token Ring

C. ISDN

D. Connection for POTS devices

6. What are the services provided by access layer routers? Choose all that apply.

A. They provide maximum availability and reliability

B. They address quality of service needs of different protocols

C. They provide secure access to workgroup resources

D. They localize broadcasts

7. Which features of the Cisco IOS assist in providing Internetwork reliability and availability? Choose all that apply.

A. Access lists

B. Dial backup

C. Weighted fair queuing

D. DDR

8. What are the first steps in configuring the network access server? Choose all that apply.

A. Enable AAA

B. Enable the AAA authentication process

C. Specify the TACACS+ or RADIUS server

D. Specify an encryption key

9. What is one of the Cisco IOS features used to reduce bandwidth?

A. Redistribution

B. Custom queuing

C. Dedicated access

D. Access lists

10. You have just configured your router for Frame Relay operation and want to apply the configuration to an interface. Which configuration statement should you use?

    A. INTERFACE E0
        IP ADDRESS 10.1.0.1 255.255.0.0
        ENCAPSULATION FRAME-RELAY

    B. INTERFACE S0
        IP ADDRESS 10.1.0.1 255.255.0.0
        ENCAPSULATION FRAME RELAY

    C. INTERFACE E 0
        IP ADDRESS 10.1.0.1 255.255.0.0
        ENCAPSULATION FRAME RELAY

    D. INTERFACE S 0
        IP ADDRESS 10.1.0.1 255.255.0.0
        ENCAPSULATION FRAME-RELAY

11. What is the maximum speed on an AUX port?

    A. 9600 bps
    B. 38,400 bps
    C. 57,600 bps
    D. 115,200 bps

12. What is the default type of encapsulation on an Ethernet interface for the Cisco 3600 series routers?

    A. SNAP
    B. 802.2
    C. ARPA
    D. IEEE 802.3

13. What type of connector does the WAN interface card on a Cisco 2600 series router support?

    A. RS 232
    B. V.35
    C. DB-9
    D. Cisco proprietary

14. What does an ISDN BRI S/T card indicate?

    A. An external NT1 is required

    B. An external NT1 is not required

    C. An external NT1 is only needed if your service provider requires it

    D. A DSU/CSU is required

15. If you are looking at a Cisco 3600 router from a rear view, how are the modules numbered?

    A. Left to right and top to bottom, starting at slot 0

    B. Right to left and bottom to top, starting at slot 0

    C. Left to right and top to bottom, starting at slot 1

    D. Right to left and bottom to top, starting at slot 1

16. Which statements about the Cisco 700 series routers are true? Choose all that apply.

    A. Some 700 series routers support POTS connections

    B. All 700 series support ISDN

    C. The 700 series uses regular IOS commands

    D. The 700 series do no support regular IOS commands

17. What does the acronym PCM stand for?

    A. Pulse-coded modulation

    B. Pulse code modulation

    C. Plus-coded modulation

    D. Plus code modulation

18. Which statements BEST describe the function of digital modems on a Cisco 3600 platform? Choose all that apply.

    A. They support V.90 and V.34 technologies

    B. They must operate in conjunction with T1/E1/PRI/BRI network modules

    C. They support V.90 technologies

    D. They may or may not operate in conjunction with T1/E1/PRI/BRI network modules

19. Digital modem module LEDs indicate which of the following conditions? Choose all that apply.

A. Flashing indicates that the module is initializing

B. Steady indicates that the module has passed power on self test

C. Off indicates a module has failed its diagnostics

D. Off indicates that the module has passed power-on self test

20. What is the default encapsulation on a Cisco router's asynchronous interface?

A. PPP

B. HDLC

C. LAP-A

D. SLIP

21. You have been asked to manually change the modem command strings in six modems connected to a Cisco 2500 series access router. You need to access the connected modems in order to make the changes.

```
ROUTER(config)#IP HOST TACOMA1 2001 10.1.1.1
ROUTER(config)#IP HOST TACOMA2 2002 10.1.1.1
ROUTER(config)#IP HOST TACOMA3 2003 10.1.1.1
ROUTER(config)#IP HOST TACOMA4 2004 10.1.1.1
ROUTER(config)#IP HOST TACOMA5 2005 10.1.1.1
ROUTER(config)#IP HOST TACOMA6 2006 10.1.1.1
ROUTER(config)# END
```

You have completed all of the necessary steps to access the external modem's command interface. What type of prompt does the modem provide?

A. It depends on the type of modem

B. The modem prompts you for a modem password

C. The prompt displayed is the AT> prompt

D. There is no prompt displayed

22. What command issued under the ROUTER(config-line)# prompt should you enter to enable processing of incoming and outgoing calls?

   A. MODEM-CALL IN-OUT

   B. MODEMCALL INOUT

   C. MODEM INOUT

   D. MODEM-INOUT

23. When a Frame Relay network is constructed with many virtual channels (VCs) to different locations on a single physical line into the network, the VCs send traffic as fast as the physical line speed allows. How does the rate enforcement feature aid in controlling VC bandwidth?

   A. By pre-allocating the bandwidth each VC receives

   B. By marking packets as discard eligible

   C. By throttling back the traffic when FECN messages are received

   D. By throttling back the traffic when BECN messages are received

24. What is the function of PPP LCP?

   A. PPP LCP is Layer Control Protocol and it negotiates layer optional functions

   B. PPP LCP is Link Control Protocol and it opens the connection and negotiates configuration parameters

   C. PPP LCP is Line Control Protocol and it opens the connection and negotiates configuration parameters

   D. PPP LCP is Lower Cisco Protocol and it opens the connection and negotiates configuration parameters

25. What is one advantage of CHAP over PAP?

   A. The password is encrypted before being sent over the line

   B. A user name is sent to the authenticating router

   C. A user name and password are sent to the authenticating router

   D. The authenticating router automatically assigns a user name

26. What command should you enter to configure CHAP on interface 1/1?

    A. ROUTER(config)# INT S 1/1
        PPP AUTHENTICATION CHAP

    B. ROUTER(config-if)# INT S 1/1
        AUTHENTICATION CHAP

    C. ROUTER(config)# INT S 1/1
        CHAP AUTHENTICATION

    D. ROUTER(config-if)# INT S 1/1
        AUTHENTICATION PPP CHAP

27. You are configuring the router that will authenticate other routers that are dialing in. Your organization has decided to use CHAP authentication. Which elements from the list below should be included in your configuration? Choose all that apply.

    A. Host name

    B. User name

    C. PPP authentication

    D. Sent user name

28. What does the following configuration line indicate?

```
ROUTER(config-if)#PPP MULTILINK
ROUTER(config-if)#DIALER LOAD-THRESHOLD 150 EITHER
```

    A. Limit the load on any bundle to 150/255

    B. Allow a load on any bundle to a value greater than 150/255

    C. Remove a link in the bundle when the load is less than 55 percent on either inbound or outbound calls

    D. Add another link to the bundle when the load exceeds 55 percent on inbound or outbound calls

29. Weighted fair queuing is supposed to prioritize traffic equally. Which choice best defines the operation of weighted fair queuing?

    A. Larger packets are automatically forwarded before smaller packets

B. Packet trains are prioritized over non-train packets

C. Smaller packets are given priority over large packets

D. Smaller packets are assembled into larger packets to ensure delivery

30. Which of the following are interface compression algorithms? Choose all that apply.

A. DES

B. MPPC

C. Stacker

D. Predictor

31. How many B channels can be derived from PRI service offered in Germany?

A. 24

B. 23

C. 30

D. 31

32. What is the command used to redistribute static routes?

A. ROUTER(config)#REDISTRIBUTE STATIC

B. ROUTER(config-router)REDISTRIBUTE STATIC

C. ROUTER(config-if)#DISTRIBUTE STATIC

D. ROUTER(config-if)REDISTRIBUTE STATIC

33. You have just finished installing an ISDN DDR configuration and wish to test it for proper call setup and tear down operation. Which commands would you use to test your configuration? Choose all that apply.

A. SHOW DIALER

B. SHOW IP ROUTE

C. DEBUG Q931

D. DEBUG DIALER

34. You are using DDR over ISDN and a call is currently connected over the configured interface. The idle reset timer is set for 180 seconds and the connection has been idle for 90 seconds. An interesting packet arrives at the interface. What happens at this point?

    A. The timer continues to count down

    B. The timer is reset to 180 seconds

    C. The timer remains at 90 seconds

    D. Nothing happens

35. You have configured a Cisco 2600 router for ISDN caller ID callback. The call back to the user does not take place. What condition below might prevent the callback? Choose all that apply.

    A. The incoming call number matches the numbers configured on the router

    B. The incoming number does not match the numbers configured on the router

    C. The DIALER WAIT-FOR-CARRIER command value is set for 15 seconds

    D. The router is configured for dialer callback security

36. Which organizations define WAN standards? Choose all that apply.

    A. ISO

    B. EIA

    C. IEEE

    D. ITU-T

37. What layers comprise the three-layer hierarchical model?

    A. LAN backbone, distribution, and access

    B. Distributed, WAN backbone, and access

    C. Core, distributed, and access

    D. Core, distribution, and access

38. What is the signaling standard that defines call control between the local ISDN switch and an ISDN TE?

A. Q.931

B. Q.921

C. I.400

D. E.163

39. You have been asked to verify the link status on one of the asynchronous interfaces on your router. Which of the following commands would you type to display this information?

A. SH INT ASYNC 1/0

B. SH ASYNC INT 1/0

C. SH INT 1/0

D. SH ASYNC INT 1/0

40. Which of the following statements are true regarding the use of Caller ID configuration on Cisco routers? Choose all that apply.

A. Caller ID screening can only be used to identify ISDN callers

B. Caller ID screening can only be used to identify POTS callers

C. POTS and ISDN callers can be identified by Cisco routers configured to use Caller ID screening

D. Caller ID requires that the local switch support caller ID service

41. When physical interfaces are assigned to a dialer rotary group, what profile does the physical interface inherit?

A. None. It retains the properties of the physical interface.

B. The physical interface inherits the profile of the dialer rotary group

C. This causes a conflict on that interface and shuts the interface down

D. None of the above

42. How is the logical interface *dialer group* properly created?

    A. ROUTER# config DIALER-GROUP *dialer-group* #

    B. ROUTER(config)# INTERFACE DIALER *dialer-group* #

    C. ROUTER(config)# DIALER-GROUP *dialer-group* #

    D. ROUTER(config)# DIALER ROTARY-GROUP *group-#*

43. Define the proper syntax to assign the following dialer list to the interface async 7.

```
interface async 7
async mode dedicatedip address 1172.30.45.2 255.255.255.0
encapsulation ppp
ppp authentication chap
dialer in-band
dialer map ip 172.30.45.1 name hub system-script hub 1234
dialer map ip 172.30.45.255 name hub system-script hub
1234
access-list 101 permit ip 0.0.0.0 255.255.255.255 0.0.0.0
255.255.255.255
dialer-list 1 protocol ip list 101
```

    A. ROUTER# GROUP 1

    B. ROUTER# DIALER-GROUP 1

    C. ROUTER(config)# DIALER-GROUP 1

    D. ROUTER(config-if)# DIALER-GROUP 1

44. Static IP addresses are not always good solutions for networks, whether large or small. If a small network has a Cisco 700 series router and a server is not in place, how can IP addresses be obtained?

    A. From the remote location to which the Cisco 700 router connects

    B. From the Cisco 700 router, itself

    C. From a desktop machine in a Windows peer-to-peer network

    D. From the network hub aggregating the workstations

45. How many IP node addresses does the Cisco 700 series router require in release 4.x when communicating with public networks?

A. One for every workstation being supported

B. Two

C. One

D. None

46. Select the correct commands on a Cisco 700 series router that define a new user profile by the name Corp and activate the profile.

A. INTERFACE CORP
   SET ACTIVE

B. PROFILE CORP
   SET ACTIVE-PROFILE CORP

C. SET PROFILE CORP
   SET ACTIVE CORP

D. SET USER CORP
   SET CORP ACTIVE

47. Which of the following statements are true in regard to the following configurations?

```
RouterA> set ppp callback request on 5551212
RouterB> set ppp callback reply on
```

A. Router A is the initiating router

B. Router B is the initiating router

C. Both routers can initiate the call

D. No router initiates the call

48. What does the following configuration define?

```
Router (config-if)# backup load 60 never
```

A. The backup interface never reaches 60 percent utilization

B. The backup interface is activated at 60 percent utilization

C. The NEVER statement defines that an average is not used to activate the line

D. The backup interface becomes active when the utilization is 60 percent, based on a scale of 1–255

49. What two challenges do queuing policies help network managers meet? Choose two.

A. Providing a specific group of users appropriate levels of service

B. Providing all users appropriate levels of service

C. Controlling WAN cost

D. Avoiding WAN cost because of the effective use of queuing

50. When overloading a NAT address, how does the router differentiate packets from one workstation to another workstation?

A. A time stamp is attached to each packet that is translated

B. A unique port address identifies the workstation that originated the packet

C. The computer name of the originating packet is identified within the packet

D. Both A and C

51. What are the two states of profiles on a Cisco 700 series router?

A. Set and not set

B. Active and inactive

C. On and off

D. There is only one state

52. You have been asked to verify PPP operation on one of your router's S1 interfaces. Which command would you use to verify this?

A. SHOW PPP INTERFACES

B. SHOW PPP INTERFACE S1

C. SHOW INTERFACE

D. SHOW INTERFACE S1

53. Where would static NAT best be implemented?

A. Networks with overlapping IP addresses

B. Large networks with few Internet IP addresses allocated

C. Simple NAT with a one-to-one translation that does not change

D. NAT implementation where the global inside addresses and local inside addresses are equal in number

54. If you use the NONE command in the configuration string AAA AUTHORIZATION NONE TACACS+ LOCAL, what authorization will be performed?

A. No authorization will be performed and the user will not have access to the router

B. No authorization will be performed and the user will have access to the router

C. Only local authorization will be performed

D. Only User Exec authorization will be granted

55. What requirements are characteristic of a scalable Internetwork?

A. Networks that are experiencing constant growth

B. Networks that contain over 100 routers

C. Networks that contain less than 100 routers

D. Networks that use Layer 2 switches

56. Which commands below display a summary of all asynchronous lines that have active connections? Choose all that apply.

A. SHOW USERS

B. SHOW SESSIONS

C. SHOW LINE

D. SHOW INTERFACE

57. Assume that you are already in interface configuration mode for serial 1, and you want to enable PPP. Which configuration command would you select?

A. PPP ENCAPSULATION

B. ENCAPSULATION PPP

C. PPP-ENCAPSULATION

D. ENCAPSULATION-PPP

58. What does the Cisco 700 release 4.x software support?

A. OSPF routing protocol features

B. Stacker compression with Cisco IOS routers

C. Analog dial backup

D. None of the above

59. Which of the following represents T1 line codes? Choose all that apply.

A. AMI

B. B8ZS

C. SF

D. ESF

60. Why are encapsulation types configured on the physical interfaces?

A. The encapsulation of the physical interface must match that of the logical

B. That is where the LCP is negotiated

C. The physical interfaces won't know what to choose if encapsulation is not configured

D. Physical interfaces will not work without defined encapsulation

61. You have been asked to finish the configuration of an ISDN PRI on a Cisco 3600 series router. Your colleague did not know what type of line code or framing to configure on the interface. What two choices would you make from the list below?

A. B8ZS and ESF

B. AMI and SF

C. B8ZS and AMI

D. SF and AMI

62. If packets are being sent to a dialer interface, and the connection has not yet been made, what is the Cisco IOS feature that will prevent packets from being dropped while the connection is being made?

A. The dialer will do that on its own

B. The router has enough intelligence to hold the packets until the connection is established

C. Packets are dropped, then retransmitted

D. The DIALER-HOLD QUEUE, when configured, will prevent packets from being dropped while the connection is made

63. X.25 is still in use today and serves as a viable mode of data transport. In what application is X.25 best suited?

A. In an area where digital or fiber-optic technologies are readily available

B. As an Internet gateway connection for large organizations

C. In areas of the world where reliability and quality of data circuits are low, and application data is critical

D. In areas of the world where only analog circuits are available

CISCO CERTIFIED NETWORK PROFESSIONAL

Test Yourself:
BCRAN Practice
Exam 2 Answers

Q&A

T

he answers to the questions are in boldface, followed by a brief explanation. Some of the explanations detail the logic you should use to choose the correct answer, while others give factual reasons why the answer is correct.

BCRAN Practice Exam 2 Answers

1. ☑ **C. When connecting to an ISP.** Header compression is the best choice when connecting to an ISP. ISP uses TCP/IP. Header compression specifically compresses TCP/IP headers, and the packets that traverse the Internet are usually smaller, so the large proportion of the data packet size is made up of the TCP/IP header. Link compression compresses the whole packet. If the packet is traversing a switched network, link compression should not be used.
    ☒ **A,** When using a point-to-point WAN connection, is incorrect because on point-to-point WAN connections the better of the two is link compression. Just be sure the load on the router is not too high, and that you have ample memory. **B.** When traversing a multiprotocol network, is incorrect because header compression does not benefit multiprotocol environments; link compression does. Header compression is specifically for TCP/IP. Link compression can be used with any protocol. **D.** None of the above, is incorrect.

2. ☑ **A. STAC.** The payload compression algorithm uses the STAC compression method. The STAC compression method works by searching the input data stream for redundant strings and replaces the strings with tokens. These tokens turn out to be smaller than the original data strings.
    ☒ **B.** Predictor, **C.** MNP5, and **D.** LAPB, are incorrect, since the payload compression algorithm uses the STAC compression method.

3. ☑ **B. Subinterfaces configured as multipoint do not act as leased lines.** A leased line is a point-to-point circuit that does not allow multiple-link communication. Multipoint subinterface configurations allow multiple destinations to be configured on a single subinterface. Multipoint requires that all connected routers be on the same IP subnet. Subinterfaces configured as leased lines are a point-to-point configuration option. This allows a pair of point-to-point routers to have their own subnet.
    ☒ **A.** Subinterfaces act as default NBMA networks, is incorrect. Sub-interfaces

that act as a default non-broadcast multi-access networks are a feature of multipoint subinterface configurations. **C.** Can save subnets because they use a single subnet, is not correct because the routers in the IP network need to be on the same subnet. **D.** is not correct because a router with a multipoint subinterface configuration is well suited for a full-mesh network.

4. ☑ **B.** On an analog DDR or dial backup. Analog connections should not have any queuing algorithm active. Packets should be forwarded as soon as they are received, with as little processing as possible. With FIFO, latency is decreased and, because analog lines are typically slower and less controllable in terms of maximum bandwidth, forwarding should occur with as little latency as possible. Furthermore, with dial-on-demand routing or dial backup, the traffic across the link is usually specific traffic that is filtered through an access list, so any undesirable traffic is not allowed to cross the link. Since WFQ makes sure that no one conversation uses all the available bandwidth, a dial-up link would not get optimum throughput. With FIFO, all bandwidth is available on a first come, first served basis.

☒ **A.** Dedicated or Frame Relay links larger than T1, is incorrect because when links larger than T1 are employed, FIFO is employed, but not because of the latency issue. The links are of larger bandwidth and queuing of any form is not required. **C.** Dedicated or Frame Relay links smaller than T1, is incorrect because, on links smaller than T1, weighted fair, priority or custom should be employed to provide the best performance. FIFO on smaller links could allow a certain type of traffic to consume the bandwidth, not allowing other traffic to cross a link in a timely manner.

5. ☑ **A, C and D.** Ethernet, ISDN, connection for POTS devices. The Cisco 700 series router is an Ethernet product that provides WAN connectivity via ISDN. The 700 series router also provides two basic telephone ports, or POTS ports, for connection of phones, fax machines or answering machines. This port feature provides a great cost savings by not requiring the user to invest in digital communications devices to replace their standard phone or fax machine.

☒ **B.** Token Ring, is incorrect because the 700 series router does not provide Token Ring support.

6. ☑   C and D. Addresses quality of service needs of different protocols and provides secure access to workgroup resources. These routers provide resource access to a workgroup on a network segment. Access routers keep broadcast for local media resources, such as servers, from leaving the local media. These routers also support DDR for access over low-speed serial links, and authenticate dial-in users requesting network resources.

   ☒   A. Provides maximum availability and reliability, is incorrect because this is a function performed by a core router. B. Addresses quality of service needs of different protocols, is incorrect because it describes a function of a distribution layer router.

7. ☑   B. Dial backup allows the router to automatically detect a link failure, dial a backup link, and reroute data from the failed link over the backup link. The dial backup feature provides for increased availability.

   ☒   A. Access lists, and D. DDR, are both incorrect. Access lists and DDR are both features of the Cisco IOS used to make the network more efficient. C. Weighted fair queuing, is not correct because it is a feature of the Cisco IOS that is used to make the network more responsive.

8. ☑   A, C, and D. Enable AAA, specify the TACACS+ or RADIUS server that will provide the AAA process, and specify an encryption key.

   ☒   B. Enable the AAA authentication process, is incorrect because the AAA authentication process is actually the next step after the three identified above.

9. ☑   D. Access lists can be used to selectively permit or deny specific types of network traffic. Access lists can filter broadcasts, protocol updates, and some data traffic.

   ☒   A. Redistribution, is incorrect because it is used to exchange routing updates between different routing protocols. B. Custom queuing, is incorrect because it is used to allocate the available bandwidth to different types of traffic. **C.** Dedicated access, is incorrect because it is a term used to describe router connectivity to basic telephone services, such as T1 lines.

10. ☑ **D.** INTERFACE S 0
    IP ADDRESS 10.1.0.1 255.255.0.0
    ENCAPSULATION FRAME-RELAY

This sequence of commands enables Frame Relay on S0 as well as an IP address. Frame Relay is a WAN protocol and is only installed on WAN links. The default Frame Relay in this configuration is Cisco, which assumes we are connecting to another Cisco router. The command ENCAPSULATION FRAME-RELAY IETF would allow for interoperability with other vendors.

☒ **A.** INTERFACE E0
    IP ADDRESS 10.1.0.1 255.255.0.0
    ENCAPSULATION FRAME-RELAY, is incorrect because Frame Relay is not a LAN protocol.

B. INTERFACE S0
    IP ADDRESS 10.1.0.1 255.255.0.0
    ENCAPSULATION FRAME RELAY, is incorrect because the format is incorrect.

C. INTERFACE E 0
    IP ADDRESS 10.1.0.1 255.255.0.0
    ENCAPSULATION FRAME RELAY, is incorrect because the format is incorrect and because you may not activate Frame Relay on a LAN interface.

11. ☑ **B** and **D.** 38,400 bps or 115,200 bps. The AUX port's maximum speed setting is 38,400 bps for most routers. Newer routers, such as the 3600 series, can support speeds up to 115,200 bps. The auxiliary port can also be configured as an asynchronous serial interface.

☒ **A.** 9600 bps, and **C.** 57,600 bps, are incorrect because neither represents the maximum speed setting. The port can, however, be configured to operate at 9600 bps if you choose.

12. ☑ **C.** ARPA is the default encapsulation on the Ethernet interfaces of all Cisco routers. This is Cisco's name for the original D.I.X. (DEC, Intel and Xerox) Ethernet frame encapsulation.

☒ **A.** SNAP, a special form of IEEE 802.2, is incorrect. **B.** IEEE 802.2, the upper sublayer of the OSI link layer, is incorrect. **D.** IEEE 802.3, is supported but is not the default encapsulation type.

13. ☑ **D.** A Cisco proprietary 60-pin D connector is used to connect a serial cable to a Cisco WAN interface. This connector requires less space than a standard WAN connector, such as V.35. However, a standard interface connector is used at the DCE end of the WAN cable.

☒ **A.** RS 232; **B.** V.35; and **C.** DB-9, are incorrect because these connector types are not supported as direct connects to the router.

14. ☑ **A.** An external NT1 is required. An ISDN BRI card with an ISDN S/T interface, requires an external NT1 to terminate the ISDN BRI line. An ISDN S/T interface indicates a need for an external NT1. If the card had an ISDN U interface, the external NT1 would not be required.

☒ **B.** An external NT1 is not required, is wrong because an S/T interface needs an external NT1 to terminate the BRI line. **C.** An external NT1 is only needed if your service provider requires it, is wrong because the electrical requirements of the interface have nothing to do with the service provider. However, in some countries the service provider does dictate the requirements for terminating ISDN service. **D.** An external NT1 is only needed if your service provider requires it, is wrong because a DSU/CSU is the wrong device to terminate a BRI line.

15. ☑ **B.** The numbering scheme for modules in the Cisco 3600 series router is numbered beginning with slot 0 for each interface type and continue from right to left and if necessary, from bottom to top.

☒ **A.** Left to right and top to bottom, starting at slot 0, is not correct because it starts the numbering scheme incorrectly from left to right and top to bottom. **C.** Left to right and top to bottom, starting at slot 1 and **D.** right to left and bottom to top, starting at slot 1, are incorrect because starting with slot 1 is incorrect.

16. ☑ **A, B,** and **D.** Some 700 series routers support POTS connections, All 700 series support ISDN, and The 700 series do no support regular IOS commands. Some of these routers feature POTS connections for standard telephone, fax, and modem connections. All of the 700 series support ISDN as the main means of connectivity. The 700 series features the proprietary Cisco 700 series IOS, which has its own command set.

☒ **C.** The 700 series uses regular IOS commands, is incorrect if the command set is different from the regular Cisco IOS.

17. ☑ **B.** Is the right answer. The acronym PCM stands for pulse code modulation. This is the standard technique used by carriers to convert analog to digital signals. The analog information is sampled at 8000 samples per second and the result is a series of coded pulses to represent the analog information.

☒ **A.** Pulse-coded modulation, **C.** plus-coded modulation, and **D.** plus code modulation, are incorrect because of the syntax used.

18. ☑ **A** and **B.** They support V.90 and V.34 technologies and they must operate in conjunction with T1/E1/PRI/BRI network modules. They support both V.34 and V.90 modem standards for maximum operating speeds of 33,600 bps and 56 Kbps respectively. These modems MUST operate over a digital facility such as T1/E1/PRI/BRI lines.

☒ **C.** They support V.90 technologies, is incorrect because V.34 is also supported. **D.** They may or may not operate in conjunction with T1/E1/PRI/BRI network modules, is incorrect because the digital modems MUST use a digital facility.

19. ☑ **A, B,** and **C.** Flashing indicates that the module is initializing; steady indicates that the module has passed power on self test; and off indicates a module has failed its diagnostics. A flashing light shows that the module is initializing, followed by a steady light that indicates that the module is diagnostically OK. If the diagnostics fail or no module is installed, the light is off.

☒ **D.** Off indicates that the module has passed power-on self test, is incorrect.

20. ☑ **D.** SLIP is the default encapsulation for asynchronous interfaces. Other encapsulation types must be configured.

☒ **A.** PPP, is incorrect because this has to be configured on an interface. **B.** HDLC, is wrong because it is the default encapsulation for a router's synchronous interface. **C.** LAP-A, does not exist.

21. ☑ **D.** There is no prompt displayed. The modem does not display a prompt because it is not capable of doing so. To insure that you are at the modem prompt you should type in the AT command and the modem should respond with OK.

☒ **A.** It depends on the type of modem, is incorrect because modems supporting the AT command set are universal in their response to these commands. **B.** The modem prompts you for a modem password, is incorrect because there is no modem password prompt. **C.** The prompt displayed is the AT> prompt, is wrong because there is no prompt at all.

22. ☑ **C.** MODEM INOUT is the command that would enable acceptance of incoming and outgoing calls on an asynchronous line.

☒ **A.** MODEM-CALL IN-OUT, and **B.** MODEMCALL INOUT, are incorrect because these commands do not exist. **D.** MODEM-INOUT, is incorrect because of incorrect syntax.

23. ☑ **A.** By pre-allocating the bandwidth each VC receives. The rate enforcement feature can pre-allocate the bandwidth each VC receives on the physical line into the network. This creates a virtual time-division multiplexing network. The following example may help you to visualize the rate enforcement feature. If router 1 has a physical line with 128Kbps and is connected to router B and router C, which have a 64Kbps physical link through a virtual link to each, router1 will automatically enforce the rate to router B and to router C to 64Kbps each.

☒ **B.** By marking packets as discard eligible, is incorrect because a packet is marked as discard eligible when the link becomes over subscribed. This is not a feature, but will happen regardless of which manufacturer router is used. **C.** By throttling back the traffic when FECN messages are received, is incorrect because FECN messages are received by the destination when the link becomes congested. **D.** By throttling back the traffic when BECN messages are received, is incorrect because BECN messages are received by the source when the link becomes congested. With both FECN and BECN, configurations to the router must be created to control traffic throughput on a VC.

24. ☑ **B.** PPP LCP establishes, configures, maintains, and terminates the PPP connection. It establishes the link, negotiates any configuration parameters which must be acknowledged by the remote end, determines link quality, brings up the network layer protocols, and finally, terminates when appropriate the link connection.
    ☒ **A, C,** and **D** are incorrect because these protocols do not exist.

25. ☑ **A.** The password is encrypted before being sent over the link. Encrypting this information protects against a modem playback attack, which PAP does not.
    ☒ **B.** A user name is sent to the authenticating router, and **C.** a user name and password are sent to the authenticating router, are incorrect because both PAP and CHAP have these items in common. **D.** The authenticating router automatically assigns a user name, is wrong because routers don't perform this function.

26. ☑ **A.** ROUTER(config)# INT S 1/1
        PPP AUTHENTICATION CHAP
    First, the router must be in the interface configuration mode. The first command INT S0/0 places the router in configuration mode for serial interface S 1/1. The command PPP AUTHENTICATION CHAP enables CHAP on interface S 1/1.
    ☒ **B, C,** and **D** are incorrect because of the wrong command syntax to enable PPP on the serial interface.

27. ☑ **A, B** and **C.** The elements that should be included are the case sensitive host name of the remote router, a user name and password for each remote router, and the type of PPP authentication, which, in this case, is CHAP.
    ☒ **D.** The sent user name is a part of PAP authentication configuration.

28. ☑ **D.** The PPP MULTILINK command enables multilink PPP on the interface. The DIALER-LOAD THRESHOLD command sets the threshold to reach before adding a link to the bundle on either inbound or outbound calls. In this case the load threshold is 150/255 or about 55 percent.

☒ **A.** Limit the load on any bundle to 150/255, and **B.** allow a load on any bundle to a value greater than 150/255, are incorrect because they indicate information about the bundle rather than links in the bundle. **C.** Remove a link in the bundle when the load is less than 55 percent on either inbound or outbound calls, is incorrect because this indicates removal of a link from the bundle rather than adding a link to the bundle.

29. **C.** Weighted fair queuing breaks up packet trains to assure that low-bandwidth traffic is transferred in a timely fashion. Weighted fair queuing gives low volume traffic, such as Telnet, priority over high-volume traffic. Packets are arranged into conversations in the fair queue before transmission. The last bit of each packet arriving at the queue determines the order of removal of the packet from the queue. Since a small packet will completely arrive into the queue before a large packet would, small, low-volume traffic is given priority over high-volume traffic. Weighted fair queuing ensures the proper amount of bandwidth for each message that is delivered. This translates into equal size file transmissions being allocated equal bandwidth.

☒ **A.** Larger packets are automatically forwarded before smaller packets, is incorrect because larger packets are not automatically forwarded through the queue in weighted fair queuing. **B.** Packet trains are prioritized over non-train packets, is incorrect because packet trains are not prioritized over packets that are not packet trains. Rather, they are broken up into conversations and processed through the queue with the last part of the packets' arrival determining the order of the queue process. **D.** Smaller packets are assembled into larger packets to ensure delivery, is untrue.

30. ☑ **B, C,** and **D.** MPPC, stacker and predictor are compression algorithms supported in both hardware and software on Cisco routers. Microsoft point-to-point compression (MPPC) can be used to compress data between Microsoft and Cisco devices using PPP. Stacker and Predictor are supported data compression algorithms.

☒ **A.** DES, is wrong because Data Encryption Standard is an encryption algorithm and not a compression algorithm.

31. ☑ **C.** 30. ISDN PRI (30B+D) service in Europe offers 30, 64-Kbps B channels. One D channel provides signaling services for the 30 D channels.

☒ **A.** 24, is wrong because it represents the combined B and D channels associated with ISDN in North America (23B+D). **B.** is wrong because it represents the number of B channels in a North American PRI. **D.** 31, is wrong because it represents the combined B and D channels in European ISDN PRI service.

32. ☑ **B.** ROUTER(config-router)REDISTRIBUTE STATIC. This command used under the config-router prompt provides for the advertising of static routes to other routers. First the static route is defined, then advertised by the configured routing protocol.

☒ **A.** ROUTER(config)#REDISTRIBUTE STATIC, is wrong because the command is configured under the global prompt. **C** and **D,** ROUTER(config-if)#DISTRIBUTE STATIC and ROUTER(config-if)REDISTRIBUTE STATIC, are wrong because they are the wrong command format for route redistribution.

33. ☑ **C** and **D,** DEBUG Q931 and DEBUG DIALER. DEBUG Q931 indicates communications with the switch and shows call setup and tear-down activity. DEBUG DIALER shows the number called along with call setup and tear-down activity.

☒ **A.** SHOW DIALER, is incorrect because it shows statistics about a connected call, such as timer information and called number. **B.** SHOW IP ROUTE, shows the current networks that are reachable.

34. ☑ **B.** The time is reset to 180 seconds. When a DDR call is connected and an interesting packet crosses the interface, the idle reset timer is reset to the configured value. Uninteresting packets may also use the interface during the call.

☒ **A.** The timer continues to count down, **C.** the timer is reset to 180 seconds, and **D.** nothing happens, are incorrect because the timer is reset.

35. ☑ **B and D.** If the incoming number has no match in the receiving router, the call is rejected. If dialer callback security is configured, it takes precedence over caller ID callback, which is ignored.

☒ **A.** The incoming call number matches the numbers configured on the router, is wrong because the matching numbers would cause the callback to take place. **C.** The DIALER WAIT-FOR-CARRIER command value is set for 15 seconds, is incorrect because this is the default timer setting for the dialer wait-for-carrier value, and preventing a callback with this setting is unlikely.

36. ☑ **A, B, and D.** The International Standards Organization, the Electronic Industries Association, and the International Telecommunications Union Standardization Sector. These organizations are all involved in defining and managing standards associated with WAN technologies and services.

☒ **C.** IEEE, is incorrect. The Institute of Electrical and Electronic Engineers is more widely known for defining standards for LANs.

37. ☑ **D.** Core, distribution, and access. These three layers of the hierarchical model are the core layer, which is the central intranet, the distribution layer, which contains the campus backbone, and the access layer, which provides access to workgroup resources.

☒ **A.** LAN backbone, distribution, and access; and **B.** distributed, WAN backbone, and access; are incorrect because the core layer includes both LAN and WAN backbones as part of its definition. **C.** Core, distributed, and access, is incorrect because a *distributed* layer does not exist.

38. ☑ **A.** Q.931 is the layer 3 specification for ISDN that uses packetized messages to initiate, monitor, and disconnect ISDN B channel connections. ☒ **B.** Q.921, is wrong because it is the ISDN layer 2 protocol that provides for framing of the messages between the ISDN switch and an ISDN TE. **C.** I.400, is wrong because it is the recommendation for ISDN network-to-user interfaces. **D.** E.163, is incorrect. It describes the international telephone numbering plan.

39. ☑ **A.** SH INT ASYNC 1/0. This will display the status of the physical and link layers of this interface, along with statistical information about the interface operation. The key words are asynchronous interface. Interfaces that are both synchronous and asynchronous would be monitored with the SHOW INTERFACE command.
☒ **B,** SH ASYNC INT 1/0; **C.** SH INT 1/0; and **D.** SH ASYNC INT 1/0, are incorrect answers because of incorrect command formats.

40. ☑ **C** and **D.** The local telephone switch must support Caller ID service. Both POTS and ISDN callers can be screened via the Caller ID information sent to the router.
☒ **A.** Caller ID screening can only be used to identify ISDN callers, and **B.** Caller ID screening can only be used to identify POTS callers, are incorrect because both are supported.

41. ☑ **B.** The physical interface inherits the profile of the dialer rotary group. When the physical interface is assigned to a rotary group, the physical interface inherits the profile of the dialer rotary group to which it is assigned. There are only a few parameters that need to be identified on the physical interface if dialer rotary groups are assigned to that interface. These are: Encapsulation (either PPP or HDLC), PPP multilink, and PAP or CHAP authentication methods. All the other parameters are configured within the dialer rotary group interfaces.

☒ **A.** None—it retains the properties of the physical interface, is incorrect because when a dialer rotary group is assigned to a physical interface, the attributes configured in the dialer rotary group are applied to the physical interface. **C.** This causes a conflict on that interface and shuts the interface down, is incorrect because there is not a conflict, the parameter of the dialer rotary group will take precedence over the configuration of the physical interface. In the case of what may cause problems, the router will notify the person entering the configuration at the time when the conflicting attributes are applied. **D.** None of the above, is incorrect.

42. ☑ **B.** ROUTER(config)# INTERFACE DIALER *dialer-group* #. The proper syntax for configuring the logical interface for a dialer rotary group is INTERFACE DIALER *dialer-group* #. As with any other interface or sub-interface creation, the INTERFACE command must be used to specify that it is an interface. Also the router prompt must be in global configuration mode to create the interface, which is denoted by (config), following the router host name.
☒ **A.** ROUTER# config DIALER-GROUP *dialer-group* #, is incorrect because the router is not in global configuration mode, and the command syntax does not designate the INTERFACE keyword within the command. **C.** ROUTER(config)# DIALER-GROUP *dialer-group* #, is incorrect because the command syntax does not designate the interface comment within the command. **D.** ROUTER(config)# DIALER ROTARY-GROUP *group-#*, is incorrect because the DIALER ROTARY-GROUP command is how the logical interface is mapped to the physical interface. This command would be placed on an ISDN or Async physical interface.

43. ☑ **D.** ROUTER(config-if)# DIALER-GROUP 1. The command must be entered with the router set in the configuration mode and at the interface level. If the router is not set at the interface, an error will be returned when the command string is entered.
☒ **A.** ROUTER# GROUP 1, is incorrect in two ways. First and most obvious is the command string syntax. The proper command string is: DIALER-GROUP 1. Second, the router must be in config mode on

an interface where the dialer list is to be applied. **B.** ROUTER#
DIALER-GROUP 1, is not in configuration mode on an interface. An
error will be returned when this command string is entered. **C.** ROUTER
(config)# DIALER-GROUP 1, is incorrect because the router, although
in global interface mode, is not at an interface. The dialer list must be
assigned to a physical interface.

44. ☑ **A and B.** The Cisco 700 series router has great flexibility and can
function both as a relay agent and also as a Dynamic Host Configuration
Protocol (DHCP) server. As a relay agent, the Cisco 700 series router will
relay a DHCP request to a DHCP server. The 700 series router will also
function as a stand-alone DHCP server that enables the host to obtain an IP
address. Additional features include Port Address Translation (PAT). This
enables a host on a private network to translate IP addresses to enable
communication on a public network.
☒ **C.** From a desktop machine in a Windows peer-to-peer network, is
incorrect because in a peer-to-peer network, IP addresses are either statically
assigned or not used, with workstations communicating on the data-link
layer. **D.** From the network hub aggregating the workstations, is incorrect
because hubs do not have that feature.

45. ☑ **C.** One. Port address translation (PAT) allows a remote LAN to be
configured using private network addresses that are invisible to the outside
world. The workstation's private port and IP address are translated to a
single IP address configured on the 700 series router. The IP address of the
Cisco 700 series router is the IP address that is seen by the public network.
This can be a cost savings when connecting to an ISP. The Cisco software
release required to provide this functionality to the 700 series router is 4.x.
☒ **A and B,** One for every workstation being supported and two, are
incorrect. The PAT feature available in Cisco version 4.x software for the
700 series routers provides the functionality where a single IP address is
used to communicate with public networks. **D.** None, is incorrect because
one address is required.

46. ☑ **C.** SET PROFILE CORP, SET ACTIVE CORP. The command string that defines the profile Corp is SET PROFILE CORP, then to set the profile active, the command string SET ACTIVE CORP is used. When a profile is created and set active, a virtual connection to the associated remote device is created. When a call is made to the associated remote device, the connection becomes active.

    ☒ **A.** INTERFACE CORP, SET ACTIVE, is incorrect because the syntax for the creating the profile is not correct, and the syntax to set the profile active is not correct because the profile name is not included in the profile. **B.** PROFILE CORP, SET ACTIVE-PROFILE CORP, is incorrect because the syntax that creates the profile is incorrect. **D.** SET USER CORP, SET CORP ACTIVE, is incorrect because the syntax that creates the profile is incorrect.

47. ☑ **A.** Router A is the initiating router. Router A is configured to initiate the call. Router B will be the router that calls back. Call back can be used to ensure that only authorized people are allowed to connect to a network. With the call-back option, authentication can be employed to ensure that when a call is made to the call-back router, the call-back router can authenticate and call back if the caller is authorized.

    ☒ **B.** Router B is the initiating router, is incorrect because Router A initiates the call and Router B will call back. **C.** Both routers can initiate the call, and **D.** No router initiates the call, are incorrect because Router A initiates the call.

48. ☑ **B.** The backup interface is activated at 60 percent utilization. The BACKUP LOAD 60 NEVER defines when the backup interface is activated in a percentage and when the interface is disabled. The word NEVER defines when the backup interface is deactivated (in this case, never). In place of the NEVER command, a percentage could be used. The number that defines when the backup interface should drop off should never be greater than the activation number.

    ☒ **A.** The backup interface never reaches 60 percent utilization, is incorrect because, in the backup load statement, the first number defines when the backup interface is activated and the second number defines when it is deactivated. **C.** The NEVER statement defines that an average is not used to activate the line, is incorrect because the backup load is calculated on a five-minute moving average and cannot be modified. The word NEVER communicates that, once the backup interface is activated, it will not be deactivated unless it is disabled manually. **D.** The backup interface becomes active when the utilization is 60 percent, based on a scale of 1–255, is incorrect because the load that activates the backup interface is a percentage. This can be confusing because, in the load of an interface expressed in the SHOW INTERFACE command, it is described as a ratio between 1 and 255.

49. ☑ **B, C.** Providing all users appropriate levels of service and controlling WAN cost. Queuing policies help network managers meet these two challenges. Corporations usually deploy one enterprise network that supports disparate applications, organizations, technologies, and user service levels. Network managers are concerned about providing all users with adequate levels of service while supporting mission-critical applications and maintaining the ability to integrate new technologies. WAN circuit cost forces managers to find a balance between cost and capacity of the WAN circuits, and maintain an adequate service level. Queuing allows network managers to manage network resources and ensure a seamless integration and migration of disparate technologies while maintaining control of cost. ☒ **A.** Providing a specific group of users appropriate levels of service, is incorrect because providing a one group of users with high service levels may provide unacceptable levels of service to other groups. **D.** Avoiding WAN cost because of the effective use of queuing, is incorrect because money is always an issue to every company, especially controlling cost.

50. ☑ **B.** When an IP address is overloaded, the router identifies each workstation originating the packet both by IP address and port number, so when the translation is made in an address overloading environment from

multiple originating workstations, the IP addresses are translated to the same IP address, but the port number translation is unique.

The following example may help you to understand the translation flow:

```
Inside local IP              Inside global IP
Address and port             Address and port
10.3.4.54: 1650              192.168.10.20: 165010.3.4.55:1650
                             192.168.10.20:1727
```

☒   **A.** A time stamp is attached to each packet that is translated, is incorrect because a time stamp is not used in NAT whether or not the translation is static or overloading. **C.** The computer name of the originating packet is identified within the packet, is incorrect because the computer name is not identified in the packet, other than by IP address.

51. ☑   **B.** Active and inactive are the two states of profiles. An active profile creates a virtual connection immediately to the associated remote device that the profile defines. A virtual connection is established and is followed by a call made to that profile's associated device. An inactive profile has no connections associated with it. On an inactive profile, no demand calls can be made.

☒   **A, C,** and **D,** Set and not set, on and off, and there is only one state, are incorrect because the two states are either active or inactive.

52. ☑   **D.** SHOW INTERFACE S1. This command will show if PPP encapsulation is configured on the interface. It will also show the states of link control protocol (LCP) and network control protocols (NCP).

☒   **A.** SHOW PPP INTERFACES, and **B.** SHOW PPP INTERFACES S1, are incorrect because these command formats do not exist. **C.** SHOW INTERFACE, is incorrect because it will display the status of all interfaces on the router and you are only interested in S1.

53. ☑   **C.** Static NAT is a one-to-one configuration where a designated address is translated to a specific designated address. For example, if a host on a remote network with address 192.168.12.2 needed to appear as a specific address 10.2.3.4, then the following configuration would be set up:

```
Ip nat inside source static 10.2.3.4 192.168.12.2
```

The interface commands would appear as follows:

```
Interface Ethernet 0
IP address 10.2.1.1 255.255.0.0
IP nat inside
Interface Serial 0
IP address 10.251.3.1 255.255.255.252
IP nat outside
```

This configuration would map the host address 192.168.12.2 to inside host address 10.2.3.4 permanently.

☒ **A.** Networks with overlapping IP addresses, is incorrect because networks with overlapping IP addresses that need to communicate need to employ dual or overlapping NAT. **B.** Large networks with few Internet IP addresses allocated, is incorrect because large networks with few Internet addresses allocated need to employ NAT overloading, where a few public addresses are shared with many internal host addresses. **D.** NAT implementation where the global inside addresses and local inside addresses are equal in number, is incorrect because dynamic NAT would be the best choice, since the router chooses the global private or public address to assign the host.

54. ☑ **B.** No authorization will be performed and the user will have access to the router. When NONE is used in the command string, the statement will not perform authorization.

☒ **A.** No authorization will be performed and the user will not have access to the router, is incorrect because access will be granted to the router. **C.** Only local authorization will be performed, is incorrect because no authorization will be performed when the NONE command is used. **D.** Only User Exec authorization will be granted, is incorrect because the user will be granted access to the router at all levels.

55. ☑ **A.** Networks that experience constant growth due to the need to support connectivity demands in business and the home are referred to as scaleable networks. Businesses have come to rely more and more on network connectivity to provide the means of achieving their business and organizational goals.

☒ **B.** Networks that contain over 100 routers, is incorrect because the number of routers is not the measurement of the scalability of a network. **C.** Networks that contain less than 100 routers, is incorrect for the same reason. **D.** Networks that use Layer 2 switches, is incorrect because they are used to segment a single LAN within an internetwork.

56. ☑ **A and C.** SHOW USERS and SHOW LINE. The SHOW USERS command displays a summary of all user addresses that have active connections open on the router at the time the command was entered. An "*" indicates the destination address or name of your present active connection. **C.** is also a correct answer since it will show all lines and the status of each. Should a "*" or the letter A be seen on the left-hand column, that line is active with a connection.

☒ **B.** SHOW SESSIONS, is incorrect because it only shows the outbound sessions that are currently open. **D,** SHOW INTERFACE, is wrong because it shows details of each of the routers interfaces.

57. ☑ **B.** ENCAPSULATION PPP activates PPP on the interface. This would allow the support of multiple Layer 3 protocols over the same physical interface.

☒ **A.** PPP ENCAPSULATION; **C.** PPP-ENCAPSULATION; and **D.** ENCAPSULATION-PPP; are incorrect. These formats would not be recognized by the Cisco IOS as the correct format to enable PPP on the interface.

58. ☑ **B.** Stacker compression with Cisco IOS routers. Stacker compression is a feature that can provide a compression ratio of 4:1 when both B channels are activated. The support of compression is realized when Cisco 700 series switches are communicating with one another via ISDN, or if a Cisco 700

series router is communicating with a Cisco IOS router.
☒ **A.** OSPF routing protocol features, is incorrect because the Cisco 700 series router with software release 4.x does not support OSPF. **C.** Analog dial backup, is incorrect because it is not supported. If the analog device needs to initiate a call, the 700 series router will drop one or both of the ISDN B-channels to allow the analog call. **D.** none of the above, is incorrect.

59. ☑ **A and B.** Alternate mark inversion (AMI) is a T1 line code that is usually used with channelized T1 service. B8ZS is a line code that provides timing for channelized and unchannelized T1 service as well as the required ones density.
☒ **C.** SF, and **D.** ESF, are wrong because superframe (SF) and extended superframe (ESF) are types of T1 framing formats.

60. ☑ **B.** The encapsulation type is configured on the physical interfaces because the router negotiates the Link Control Protocol (LCP) layer before an incoming call is bound to a dialer profile. This negotiation includes PPP, confirms authentication type and whether or not PPP Multilink will be used. The router authenticates the remote router with the configured method (PAP or CHAP). If the response to the challenge authenticates, then the router will try to bind the call to the correct dialer profile. Only after these progressions take place does the dialer profile take over.
☒ **A.** The encapsulation of the physical interface must match that of the logical, is incorrect because of the order the link is brought up. The physical interface is not required to match the encapsulation of the logical because the encapsulation method is defined before the logical profile is bound to the physical interface. **C and D.** The physical interfaces won't know what to choose if encapsulation is not configured and physical interfaces will not work without defined encapsulation, are incorrect because in both cases encapsulations are not defined. When encapsulations are not defined, the router reverts to the default HDLC.

61. ☑ **A.** B8ZS and ESF. This is the standard configuration selection for a PRI service. B8ZS supplies the required one's density for the signal. ESF provides the most bandwidth with 23 64-Kbps B channels and a 64-Kbps D channel. ESF provides better error-detection monitoring and frame synchronization.

☒ **B.** AMI and SF, is wrong because AMI and SF provide for 56-Kbps channels and rudimentary frame synchronization. **C.** B8ZS and AMI, is wrong because both are line codes. **D.** SF and AMI, is wrong because it only provides for 56-Kbps channels.

62. ☑ **D.** The DIALER-HOLD QUEUE command creates a buffer for interesting outgoing packets to be held in a queue while a modem connection is established. The number of packets that can be specified for the queue is 0–100. The following is proper syntax for the command: ROUTER(config-if)# DIALER HOLD-QUEUE *number* *Number* specifies the number of packets form 0–100.

☒ **A.** The dialer will do that on its own, and **B.** the router has enough intelligence to hold the packets until the connection is established, are incorrect because the dialer will not do it on its own, nor does the router have the intelligence to hold the packets. **C.** Packets are dropped, then retransmitted, is incorrect because there is an IOS feature that will prevent packets being dropped.

63. ☑ **C.** In areas of the world where reliability and quality of data circuits are low, and application data is critical. There are places where newer technologies such as digital or fiber-optic technologies have not yet been implemented in critical applications such as medical, banking, and government. Reliability and data integrity are extremely important, and X.25 provides that assurance. X.25 is an over-engineered Layer 3 protocol. Flow control and error checking are very strong in X.25, reducing the requirements for functions external to X.25.

☒ **A.** In an area where digital or fiber-optic technologies are readily available, is incorrect because in some parts of the world, digital and fiber-optic technologies are not available, and X.25 provides a link which is robust because of the error checking and sliding windows. Where digital and fiber-optic technologies are available, the reliability of the data circuits reduces the requirement for error checking and flow control services that X.25 provides. Those functions are now present on applications that reside on computers. **B.** As an Internet gateway connection for large organizations, is incorrect because at large organizations, Internet requirements are high in terms of the amount of data being accessed from the Internet. X.25 has a maximum bandwidth of 256 Kbps. Another consideration is large organizations residing in metropolitan areas where newer technologies have been implemented. The newer technologies are better suited to provide the bandwidth requirements for large corporation bandwidth requirements when accessing the Internet. **D.** In areas of the world where only analog circuits are available, is incorrect because, in areas where analog circuits are the only technology available, there are no other options.

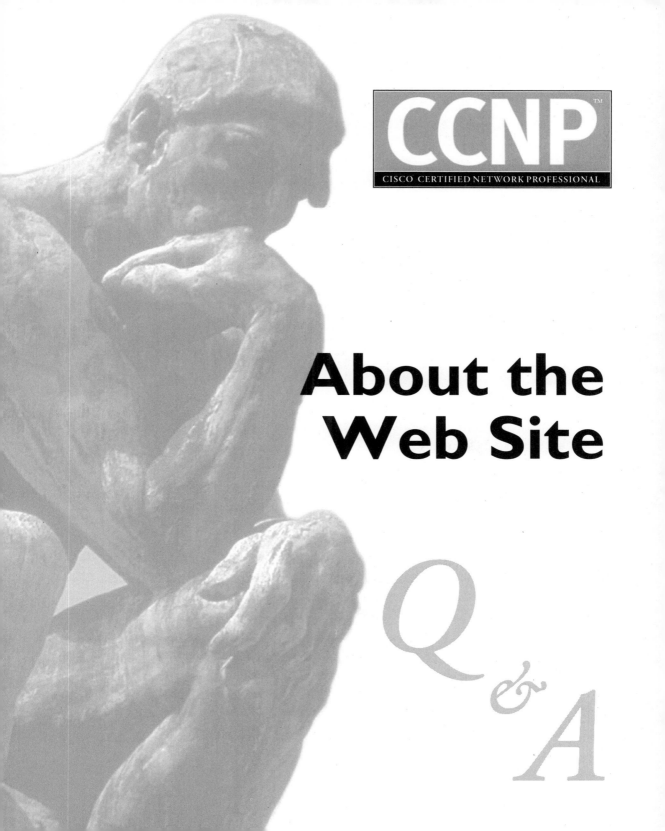

About the
Web Site

CCNP
CISCO CERTIFIED NETWORK PROFESSIONAL

Access Global Knowledge

As you know by now, Global Knowledge is the largest independent IT training company in the world. Just by purchasing this book, you have also secured a free subscription to the Global Knowledge Web site and its many resources. You can find it at: http://access.globalknowledge.com

You can log on directly at the Global Knowledge site, and you will be e-mailed a new, secure password immediately upon registering.

What You'll Find There. . .

The wealth of useful information at the Global Knowledge site falls into three categories:

Skills Gap Analysis

Global Knowledge offers several ways for you to analyze your networking skills and discover where they may be lacking. Using Global Knowledge's trademarked Competence Key Tool, you can do a skills gap analysis and get recommendations for where you may need to do some more studying. (Sorry, it just might not end with this book!)

Networking

You'll also gain valuable access to another asset: people. At the Access Global site, you'll find threaded discussions, as well as live discussions. Talk to other CCNP and CCIE candidates, get advice from folks who have already taken the exams, and get access to instructors and CCSIs.

Product Offerings

Of course, Global Knowledge also offers its products here, and you may find some valuable items for purchase—CBTs, books, or courses. Browse freely and see if there's something that could help you take that next step in career enhancement.

CCNP™

CISCO CERTIFIED NETWORK PROFESSIONAL

Glossary

Q&A

10Base2   Ethernet specification using 50-ohm thin coaxial cable and a signaling rate of 10-Mbps baseband.

10Base5   Ethernet specification using standard (thick) 50-ohm baseband coaxial cable and a signaling rate of 10-Mbps baseband.

10BaseFL   Ethernet specification using fiber-optic cabling and a signaling rate of 10-Mbps baseband, and FOIRL.

10BaseT   Ethernet specification using two pairs of twisted-pair cabling (Category 3, 4, or 5): one pair for transmitting data and the other for receiving data, and a signaling rate of 10-Mbps baseband.

10Broad36   Ethernet specification using broadband coaxial cable and a signaling rate of 10 Mbps.

100BaseFX   Fast Ethernet specification using two strands of multimode fiber-optic cable per link and a signaling rate of 100-Mbps baseband. A 100BaseFX link cannot exceed 400 meters in length.

100BaseT   Fast Ethernet specification using UTP wiring and a signaling rate of 100-Mbps baseband. 100BaseT sends link pulses out on the wire when there is no data traffic present.

100BaseT4   Fast Ethernet specification using four pairs of Category 3, 4, or 5 UTP wiring and a signaling rate of 100-Mbps baseband. The maximum length of a 100BaseT4 segment is 100 meters.

100BaseTX   Fast Ethernet specification using two pairs of UTP or STP wiring and 100-Mbps baseband signaling. One pair of wires is used to receive data; the other is used to transmit. A 100BaseTX segment cannot exceed 100 meters in length.

100BaseX   100-Mbps baseband Fast Ethernet specification based on the IEEE 802.3 standard. 100BaseX refers to the whole 100Base family of standards for Fast Ethernet.

80/20 rule   General network standard that 80 percent of traffic on a given network is local (destined for targets in the same workgroup); and not more than 20 percent of traffic requires internetworking.

AAL (ATM adaptation layer)   Service-dependent sublayer of the Data Link layer. The function of the AAL is to accept data from different applications and present it to the ATM layer in 48-byte ATM segments.

AARP (AppleTalk Address Resolution Protocol)   The protocol that maps a data-link address to an AppleTalk network address.

ABR (area border router)   Router located on the border of an OSPF area, which connects that area to the backbone network. An ABR would be a member of both the OSPF backbone and the attached area. It maintains routing tables describing both the backbone topology and the topology of the other area.

access list   A sequential list of statements in a router configuration that identify network traffic for various purposes, including traffic and route filtering.

accounting   Cisco command option that, when applied to an interface, makes the router keep track of the number of bytes and packets sent between each pair of network addresses.

acknowledgment   Notification sent from one network device to another to acknowledge that a message or group of messages has been received. Sometimes abbreviated ACK. Opposite of **NACK**.

active hub   A multiport device that repeats and amplifies LAN signals at the Physical layer.

active monitor   A network device on a Token Ring that is responsible for managing ring operations. The active monitor ensures that tokens are not lost, or that frames do not circulate indefinitely on the ring.

address   A numbering convention used to identify a unique entity or location on a network.

address mapping   Technique that allows different protocols to operate together by associating addresses from one format with those of another.

address mask   A string of bits, which, when combined with an address, describes which portion of an address refers to the network or subnet and which part refers to the host. *See also* **subnet mask**.

address resolution   A technique for resolving differences between computer addressing schemes. Address resolution most often specifies a method for mapping network layer addresses to Data Link layer addresses. *See also* **address mapping**.

Address Resolution Protocol   *See* ARP.

administrative distance   A rating of the preferability of a routing information source. Administrative distance is expressed as a value between 0 and 255. The higher the value, the lower the preference.

advertising   A process in which a router sends routing or service updates at frequent intervals so that other routers on the network can maintain lists of usable routes or services.

algorithm   A specific process for arriving at a solution to a problem.

AMI (alternate mark inversion)   The line-code type that is used on T1 and E1 circuits. In this code, zeros are represented by 01 during each bit cell, and ones are represented by 11 or 00, alternately, during each bit cell.

ANSI (American National Standards Institute)   An organization of representatives of corporate, government, and other entities that coordinates standards-related activities, approves U.S. national standards, and develops positions for the United States in international standards organizations.

APaRT *(automated packet recognition/translation)*   Technology that enables a server to be attached to CDDI or FDDI without necessitating the reconfiguration of applications or network protocols. APaRT recognizes specific data link layer encapsulation packet types; when these packet types are transferred to another medium, they are translated into the native format of the destination device.

AppleTalk   A suite of communications protocols developed by Apple Computer for allowing communication among their devices over a network.

Application layer   Layer 7 of the OSI reference model. This layer provides services to end-user application processes such as electronic mail, file transfer, and terminal emulation.

ARP (Address Resolution Protocol)   Internet protocol used to map an IP address to a MAC address.

ASBR (autonomous system boundary router)   An ASBR is an ABR connecting an OSPF autonomous system to a non-OSPF network. ASBRs run two protocols: OSPF and another routing protocol. ASBRs must be located in a nonstub OSPF area.

asynchronous transmission   Describes digital signals that are transmitted without precise clocking or synchronization.

ATM (Asynchronous Transfer Mode)   An international standard for cell relay suitable for carrying multiple service types (such as voice, video, or data) in fixed-length (53-byte) cells. Fixed-length cells allow cell processing to occur in hardware, thereby reducing latency.

ATM adaptation layer *See* AAL.

ATM Forum International organization founded in 1991 by Cisco Systems, NET/ADAPTIVE, Northern Telecom, and Sprint to develop and promote standards-based implementation agreements for ATM technology.

AUI (attachment unit interface) An interface between an MAU and a NIC (network interface card) described in the IEEE 802.3 specification. AUI often refers to the physical port to which an AUI cable attaches.

auto-discovery A mechanism used by many network management products, including CiscoWorks, to build a map of a network.

autonomous system A group of networks under a common administration that share in a common routing strategy. Sometimes abbreviated AS.

B channel (Bearer channel) An ISDN term meaning a full-duplex, 64-Kbps channel used to send user data.

B8ZS (binary 8-zero substitution) The line-code type that is used on T1 and E1 circuits. With B8ZS, a special code is substituted whenever eight consecutive zeros are sent over the link. This code is then interpreted at the remote end of the connection.

backoff The retransmission delay used by contention-based MAC protocols such as Ethernet, after a network node determines that the physical medium is already in use.

bandwidth The difference between the highest and lowest frequencies available for network signals. The term may also describe the throughput capacity of a network link or segment.

baseband A network technology in which a single carrier frequency is used. Ethernet is a common example of a baseband network technology.

baud   Unit of signaling speed equal to the number of separate signal elements transmitted in one second. Baud is synonymous with bits per second (bps), as long as each signal element represents exactly one bit.

bearer channel   *See* B channel.

BECN (backward explicit congestion notification)   A Frame Relay network facility that allows switches in the network to advise DTE devices of congestion. The BECN bit is set in frames traveling in the opposite direction of frames encountering a congested path.

best-effort delivery   Describes a network system that does not use a system of acknowledgment to guarantee reliable delivery of information.

BGP (Border Gateway Protocol)   An interdomain path-vector routing protocol. BGP exchanges reachability information with other BGP systems. It is defined by RFC 1163.

binary   A numbering system in which there are only two digits, ones and zeros.

bit stuffing   A 0 insertion and deletion process defined by HDLC. This technique ensures that actual data never appears as flag characters.

BNC connector   Standard connector used to connect coaxial cable to an MAU or line card.

BOOTP (Bootstrap Protocol)   Part of the TCP/IP suite of protocols, used by a network node to determine the IP address of its network interfaces, in order to boot from a network server.

BPDU (Bridge Protocol Data Unit)   A Layer 2 protocol used for communication among bridges.

bps   Bits per second.

BRI (Basic Rate Interface)   ISDN interface consisting of two B channels and one D channel for circuit-switched communication. ISDN BRI can carry voice, video, and data.

bridge   Device that connects and forwards packets between two network segments that use the same data-link communications protocol. Bridges operate at the Data Link layer of the OSI reference model. A bridge will filter, forward, or flood an incoming frame based on the MAC address of the frame.

broadband   A data transmission system that multiplexes multiple independent signals onto one cable. Also, in telecommunications, any channel with a bandwidth greater than 4 KHz. In LAN terminology, a coaxial cable using analog signaling.

broadcast   Data packet addressed to all nodes on a network. Broadcasts are identified by a broadcast address that matches all addresses on the network.

broadcast address   Special address reserved for sending a message to all stations. At the Data Link layer, a broadcast address is a MAC destination address of all 1s.

broadcast domain   The group of all devices that will receive the same broadcast frame originating from any device within the group. Because routers do not forward broadcast frames, broadcast domains are typically bounded by routers.

buffer   A memory storage area used for handling data in transit. Buffers are used in internetworking to compensate for differences in processing speed between network devices or signaling rates of segments. Bursts of packets can be stored in buffers until they can be handled by slower devices.

bus   Common physical path composed of wires or other media, across which signals are sent from one part of a computer to another.

bus topology   A topology used in LANs. Transmissions from network stations propagate the length of the medium and are then received by all other stations.

byte   A series of consecutive binary digits that are operated upon as a unit, usually eight bits.

cable   Transmission medium of copper wire or optical fiber wrapped in a protective cover.

cable range   A range of network numbers on an extended AppleTalk network. The cable range value can be a single network number or a contiguous sequence of several network numbers. Nodes assign addresses within the cable range values provided.

CAM   Content-addressable memory.

carrier   Electromagnetic wave or alternating current of a single frequency, suitable for modulation by another, data-bearing signal.

Carrier Detect   *See* CD.

carrier sense multiple access with collision detection   *See* CSMA/CD.

Category 5 cabling   One of five grades of UTP cabling described in the EIA/TIA-586 standard. Category 5 cabling can transmit data at speeds up to 100 Mbps.

CCITT (Consultative Committee for International Telegraphy and Telephony)   International organization responsible for the development of communications standards. Now called the ITU-T. *See also* ITU-T.

CCO (Cisco Connection Online)   Self-help resource for Cisco customers. Available 24 hours a day, seven days a week at http://www.cisco.com. The CCO family includes CCO Documentation, CCO Open Forum, CCO CD-ROM, and the TAC (Technical Assistance Center).

CD (Carrier Detect)   Signal that indicates whether an interface is active.

CDDI (Copper Distributed Data Interface)   The implementation of FDDI protocols over STP and UTP cabling. CDDI transmits over distances of approximately 100 meters, providing data rates of 100 Mbps. CDDI uses a dual-ring architecture to provide redundancy.

CDP (Cisco Discovery Protocol)   Used to discover neighboring Cisco devices, and used by network management software. The CiscoWorks network management software takes advantage of CDP.

cell   The basic data unit for ATM switching and multiplexing. A cell consists of a five-byte header and 48 bytes of payload. Cells contain fields in their headers that identify the data stream to which they belong.

CHAP (Challenge Handshake Authentication Protocol)   Security feature used with PPP encapsulation, which prevents unauthorized access by identifying the remote end. The router or access server determines whether that user is allowed access.

checksum   Method for checking the integrity of transmitted data. A checksum is an integer value computed from a sequence of octets taken through a series of arithmetic operations. The value is recomputed at the receiving end and compared for verification.

CIDR (classless interdomain routing)   Technique supported by BGP4 and based on route aggregation. CIDR allows routers to group routes together in order to cut down on the quantity of routing information carried by the core routers. With CIDR, several IP networks appear to networks outside the group as a single, larger entity. With CIDR, IP addresses and their subnet masks are written as four octets, separated by periods, followed by a forward slash and a two-digit number that represents the subnet mask.

CIR (committed information rate)   The rate at which a Frame Relay network agrees to transfer information under normal conditions, averaged over a minimum increment of time. CIR, measured in bits per second, is one of the key negotiated tariff metrics.

circuit switching   A system in which a dedicated physical path must exist between sender and receiver for the entire duration of a call. Used heavily in telephone networks.

CiscoWorks   Network management package that provides a graphical view of a network, collects statistical information about a network, and offers various network management components.

client   Node or software program, or front-end device, that requests services from a server.

CLNS (Connectionless Network Service)   An OSI network layer service, for which no circuit need be established before data can be transmitted. Routing of messages to their destinations is independent of other messages.

CMU SNMP   A free command-line SNMP management package that comes in source code form. Originally developed at the Carnegie Mellon University, and available at http://www.net.cmu.edu/projects/snmp/.

collision   In Ethernet, the result of two nodes transmitting simultaneously. The frames from each device cause an increase in voltage when they meet on the physical media, and are damaged.

collision domain   A group of nodes such that any two or more of the nodes transmitting simultaneously will result in a collision.

congestion   Traffic in excess of network capacity.

connectionless   Term used to describe data transfer without the prior existence of a circuit.

console   A DTE device, usually consisting of a keyboard and display unit, through which users interact with a host.

contention   Access method in which network devices compete for permission to access the physical medium. Compare with **circuit switching** and **token passing**.

cost   A value, typically based on media bandwidth or other measures, that is assigned by a network administrator and used by routing protocols to compare various paths through an internetwork environment. Cost values are used to determine the most favorable path to a particular destination—the lower the cost, the better the path.

count to infinity   A condition in which routers continuously increment the hop count to particular networks. Often occurs in routing algorithms that are slow to converge. Usually, some arbitrary hop count ceiling is imposed to limit the extent of this problem.

CPE (customer premises equipment)   Terminating equipment, such as terminals, telephones, and modems, installed at customer sites and connected to the telephone company network.

CRC (cyclic redundancy check)   An error-checking technique in which the receiving device performs a calculation on the frame contents and compares the calculated number to a value stored in the frame by the sending node.

CSMA/CD (carrier sense multiple access with collision detect)
Media-access mechanism used by Ethernet and IEEE 802.3. Devices use CSMA/CD to check the channel for a carrier before transmitting data. If no carrier is sensed, the device transmits. If two devices transmit at the same time, the collision is detected by all colliding devices. Collisions delay retransmissions from those devices for a randomly chosen length of time.

CSU (channel service unit)   Digital interface device that connects end-user equipment to the local digital telephone loop. Often referred to together with DSU, as CSU/DSU.

D channel   Data channel. Full-duplex, 16-Kbps (BRI) or 64-Kbps (PRI) ISDN channel.

DAS (dual attachment station)   Device that is attached to both the primary and the secondary FDDI rings. Provides redundancy for the FDDI ring. Also called a *Class A station. See also* SAS.

datagram   Logical unit of information sent as a network layer unit over a transmission medium without prior establishment of a circuit.

Data Link layer   Layer 2 of the OSI reference model. This layer provides reliable transit of data across a physical link. The Data Link layer is concerned with physical addressing, network topology, access to the network medium, error detection, sequential delivery of frames, and flow control. The Data Link layer is divided into two sublayers: the MAC sublayer and the LLC sublayer.

DCE (data circuit-terminating equipment)   The devices and connections of a communications network that represent the network end of the user-to-network interface. The DCE provides a physical connection to the network and provides a clocking signal used to synchronize transmission between DCE and DTE (data terminal equipment) devices. Modems and interface cards are examples of DCE devices.

DDR (dial-on-demand routing) Technique whereby a router can automatically initiate and close a circuit-switched session as transmitting stations demand. The router spoofs keepalives so that end-stations treat the session as active. DDR permits routing over ISDN or telephone lines using an external ISDN terminal adapter or modem.

de facto standard A standard that exists because of its widespread use.

de jure standard Standard that exists because of its development or approval by an official standards body.

DECNet Group of communications products (including a protocol suite) developed and supported by Digital Equipment Corporation. DECNet/OSI (also called DECNet Phase V) is the most recent iteration and supports both OSI protocols and proprietary Digital protocols. Phase IV Prime supports inherent MAC addresses that allow DECNet nodes to coexist with systems running other protocols that have MAC address restrictions. *See also* **DNA**.

dedicated line Communications line that is indefinitely reserved for transmissions, rather than switched as transmission is required. *See also* **leased line**.

default gateway Another term for default router. The router that a host will use to reach another network when it has no specific information about how to reach that network.

default route A routing table entry that is used to direct packets when there is no explicit route present in the routing table.

delay The time between the initiation of a transaction by a sender and the first response received by the sender. Also, the time required to move a packet from source to destination over a network path.

demarc The demarcation point between telephone carrier equipment and CPE.

demultiplexing   The separating of multiple streams of data that have been multiplexed into a common physical signal for transmission, back into multiple output streams. Opposite of **multiplexing**.

destination address   Address of a network device to receive data.

DHCP (Dynamic Host Configuration Protocol)   Provides a mechanism for allocating IP addresses dynamically so that addresses can be reassigned instead of belonging to only one host.

Dijkstra algorithm   Dijkstra's algorithm is a graph algorithm used to find the shortest path from one node on a graph to all others. Used in networking to determine the shortest path between routers.

discovery mode   Method by which an AppleTalk router acquires information about an attached network from an operational router and then uses this information to configure its own addressing information.

distance vector routing algorithm   Class of routing algorithms that use the number of hops in a route to find a shortest path to a destination network. Distance vector routing algorithms call for each router to send its entire routing table in each update to each of its neighbors. Also called Bellman-Ford routing algorithm.

DLCI (data-link connection identifier)   A value that specifies a virtual circuit in a Frame Relay network.

DNA (Digital Network Architecture)   Network architecture that was developed by Digital Equipment Corporation. DECNet is the collective term for the products that comprise DNA (including communications protocols).

DNIC (Data Network Identification Code)   Part of an X.121 address. DNICs are divided into two parts: the first specifying the country in which the addressed PSN is located and the second specifying the PSN itself. *See also* **X.121**.

DNS (Domain Name System) System used in the Internet for translating names of network nodes into addresses.

DSP (domain specific part) Part of an ATM address. A DSP is comprised of an area identifier, a station identifier, and a selector byte.

DTE (data terminal equipment) Device at the user end of a user-network interface that serves as a data source, destination, or both. DTE connects to a data network through a DCE device (for example, a modem) and typically uses clocking signals generated by the DCE. DTE includes such devices as computers, routers and multiplexers.

DUAL (Diffusing Update Algorithm) Convergence algorithm used in EIGRP. DUAL provides constant loop-free operation throughout a route computation by allowing routers involved in a topology change to synchronize at the same time, without involving routers that are unaffected by the change.

DVMRP (Distance Vector Multicast Routing Protocol) DVMRP is an internetwork gateway protocol that implements a typical dense mode IP multicast scheme. Using IGMP, DVMRP exchanges routing datagrams with its neighbors.

dynamic routing Routing that adjusts automatically to changes in network topology or traffic patterns.

E1 Wide-area digital transmission scheme used in Europe that carries data at a rate of 2.048 Mbps.

EIA/TIA-232 Common Physical layer interface standard, developed by EIA and TIA, that supports unbalanced circuits at signal speeds of up to 64 Kbps. Formerly known as RS-232.

EIGRP (Enhanced IGRP) A multiservice routing protocol supporting IPX, AppleTalk, and IP. BGP is used for interconnecting networks and defining strict routing policies.

encapsulation   The process of attaching a particular protocol header to a unit of data prior to transmission on the network. For example, a frame of Ethernet data is given a specific Ethernet header before network transit.

endpoint   Device at which a virtual circuit or virtual path begins or ends.

enterprise network   A privately maintained network connecting most major points in a company or other organization. Usually spans a large geographic area and supports multiple protocols and services.

entity   Generally, an individual, manageable network device. Sometimes called an alias.

error control   Technique for detecting and correcting errors in data transmissions.

Ethernet   Baseband LAN specification invented by Xerox Corporation and developed jointly by Xerox, Intel, and Digital Equipment Corporation. Ethernet networks use the CSMA/CD method of media access control and run over a variety of cable types at 10 Mbps. Ethernet is similar to the IEEE 802.3 series of standards.

EtherTalk   Apple Computer's data-link product that allows an AppleTalk network to be connected by Ethernet cable.

EtherWave   A product from Netopia (formerly Farallon) used to connect AppleTalk devices with LocalTalk connectors to Ethernet networks. They are an alternative to LocalTalk-to-EtherTalk routers.

explorer packet   Generated by an end-station trying to find its way through a SRB network. Gathers a hop-by-hop description of a path through the network by being marked (updated) by each bridge that it traverses, thereby creating a complete topological map.

Fast Ethernet   Any of a number of 100-Mbps Ethernet specifications. Fast Ethernet offers a speed increase ten times that of the 10BaseT Ethernet specification, while preserving such qualities as frame format, MAC mechanisms, and MTU. Such similarities allow the use of existing 10BaseT applications and network management tools on Fast Ethernet networks. Based on an extension to the IEEE 802.3 specification. Compare with **Ethernet**. *See also* **100BaseFX; 100BaseT; 100BaseT4; 100BaseTX; 100BaseX; IEEE 802.3.**

FDDI (Fiber Distributed Data Interface)   LAN standard, defined by ANSI X3T9.5, specifying a 100-Mbps token-passing network using fiber-optic cable, with transmission distances of up to 2 km. FDDI uses a dual-ring architecture to provide redundancy. Compare with **CDDI.**

FECN (forward explicit congestion notification)   A facility in a Frame Relay network to inform DTE receiving the frame that congestion was experienced in the path from source to destination. DTE receiving frames with the FECN bit set can request that higher-level protocols take flow-control action as appropriate.

file transfer   Category of popular network applications that features movement of files from one network device to another.

filter   Generally, a process or device that screens network traffic for certain characteristics, such as source address, destination address, or protocol, and determines whether to forward or discard that traffic or routes based on the established criteria.

firewall   Router or other computer designated as a buffer between public networks and a private network. A firewall router uses access lists and other methods to ensure the security of the private network.

Flash memory   Nonvolatile storage that can be electrically erased and reprogrammed as necessary.

flash update   Routing update sent asynchronously when a change in the network topology occurs.

flat addressing   A system of addressing that does not incorporate a hierarchy to determine location.

flooding   Traffic-passing technique used by switches and bridges in which traffic received on an interface is sent out all of the interfaces of that device except the interface on which the information was originally received.

flow control   Technique for ensuring that a transmitting device, such as a modem, does not overwhelm a receiving device with data. When the buffers on the receiving device are full, a message is sent to the sending device to suspend transmission until it has processed the data in the buffers.

forwarding   The process of sending a frame or packet toward its destination.

fragment   Piece of a larger packet that has been broken down to smaller units.

fragmentation   Process of breaking a packet into smaller units when transmitting over a network medium that is unable to support a transmission unit the original size of the packet.

frame   Logical grouping of information sent as a Data Link layer unit over a transmission medium. Sometimes refers to the header and trailer, used for synchronization and error control, which surround the user data contained in the unit. The terms cell, datagram, message, packet, and segment are also used to describe logical information groupings at various layers of the OSI reference model and in various technology circles.

Frame Relay   Industry-standard, switched Data Link layer protocol that handles multiple virtual circuits over a single physical interface. Frame Relay is more efficient than X.25, for which it is generally considered a replacement.

Frame Relay Cloud   A generic term used to refer to a collective Frame Relay network. For Frame Relay carrier customers, it generally refers to the carrier's entire Frame Relay network. It's referred to as a "cloud" because the network layout is not visible to the customer.

frequency   Number of cycles, measured in hertz, of an alternating current signal per unit of time.

FTP (File Transfer Protocol)   An application protocol, part of the TCP/IP protocol stack, used for transferring files between hosts on a network.

full duplex   Capability for simultaneous data transmission and receipt of data between two devices.

full mesh   A network topology in which each network node has either a physical circuit or a virtual circuit connecting it to every other network node.

gateway   In the IP community, an older term referring to a routing device. Today, the term router is used to describe devices that perform this function, and gateway refers to a special-purpose device that performs an Application layer conversion of information from one protocol stack to another.

GB   Gigabyte. Approximately 1,000,000,000 bytes.

Gb   Gigabit. Approximately 1,000,000,000 bits.

GBps   Gigabytes per second.

Gbps   Gigabits per second.

giants   Ethernet frames over the maximum frame size.

GNS (Get Nearest Server)   Request packet sent by a client on an IPX network to locate the nearest active server of a particular type. An IPX network client issues a GNS request to solicit either a direct response from a connected server or a response from a router that tells it where on the internetwork the service can be located. GNS is part of the IPX SAP.

half-duplex   Capability for data transmission in only one direction at a time between a sending station and a receiving station.

handshake   Sequence of messages exchanged between two or more network devices to ensure transmission synchronization.

hardware address   *See* MAC address.

HDLC (High-level Data Link Control)   Bit-oriented synchronous Data Link layer protocol developed by ISO and derived from SDLC. HDLC specifies a data encapsulation method for synchronous serial links and includes frame characters and checksums in its headers.

header   Control information placed before data when encapsulating that data for network transmission.

Hello packet   Multicast packet that is used by routers for neighbor discovery and recovery. Hello packets also indicate that a client is still operating on the network.

Hello protocol   Protocol used by OSPF and other routing protocols for establishing and maintaining neighbor relationships.

hierarchical addressing   A scheme of addressing that uses a logical hierarchy to determine location. For example, IP addresses consist of network numbers, subnet numbers, and host numbers, which IP routing algorithms use to route the packet to the appropriate location.

holddown   State of a routing table entry in which routers will neither advertise the route nor accept advertisements about the route for a specific length of time (known as the holddown period).

hop   Term describing the passage of a data packet between two network nodes (for example, between two routers). *See also* **hop count.**

hop count   Routing metric used to measure the distance between a source and a destination. RIP uses hop count as its metric.

host   A computer system on a network. Similar to the term node except that host usually implies a computer system, whereas node can refer to any networked system, including routers.

host number   Part of an IP address that designates which node is being addressed. Also called a host address.

hub   A term used to describe a device that serves as the center of a star topology network; or, an Ethernet multiport repeater, sometimes referred to as a concentrator.

ICMP (Internet Control Message Protocol)   A network layer Internet protocol that provides reports of errors and other information about IP packet processing. ICMP is documented in RFC 792.

IEEE (Institute of Electrical and Electronics Engineers)   A professional organization among whose activities are the development of communications and networking standards. IEEE LAN standards are the most common LAN standards today.

IEEE 802.3   IEEE LAN protocol for the implementation of the Physical layer and the MAC sublayer of the Data Link layer. IEEE 802.3 uses CSMA/CD access at various speeds over various physical media.

IEEE 802.5   IEEE LAN protocol for the implementation of the Physical layer and MAC sublayer of the Data Link layer. Similar to Token Ring, IEEE 802.5 uses token-passing access over STP cabling.

IGP (Interior Gateway Protocol)   A generic term for an Internet routing protocol used to exchange routing information within an autonomous system. Examples of common Internet IGPs include IGRP, OSPF, and RIP.

InARP (Inverse Address Resolution Protocol)   A basic Frame Relay protocol that allows routers on the Frame network to learn the protocol addresses of other routers.

interface   A connection between two systems or devices; or in routing terminology, a network connection.

Internet   Term used to refer to the global internetwork that evolved from the ARPANET, that now connects tens of thousands of networks worldwide.

Internet protocol   Any protocol that is part of the TCP/IP protocol stack. *See* TCP/IP.

internetwork   Collection of networks interconnected by routers and other devices that functions (generally) as a single network.

internetworking   General term used to refer to the industry that has arisen around the problem of connecting networks together. The term may be used to refer to products, procedures, and technologies.

Inverse ARP (Inverse Address Resolution Protocol)   Method of building dynamic address mappings in a Frame Relay network. Allows a device to discover the network address of a device associated with a virtual circuit.

IP (Internet Protocol)   Network layer protocol in the TCP/IP stack offering a connectionless datagram service. IP provides features for addressing, type-of-service specification, fragmentation and reassembly, and security. Documented in RFC 791.

IP address A 32-bit address assigned to hosts using the TCP/IP suite of protocols. An IP address is written as four octets separated by dots (dotted decimal format). Each address consists of a network number, an optional subnetwork number, and a host number. The network and subnetwork numbers together are used for routing, while the host number is used to address an individual host within the network or subnetwork. A subnet mask is often used with the address to extract network and subnetwork information from the IP address.

IPX (Internetwork Packet Exchange) NetWare network layer (Layer 3) protocol used for transferring data from servers to workstations. IPX is similar to IP in that it is a connectionless datagram service.

IPXCP (IPX Control Protocol) The protocol that establishes and configures IPX over PPP.

IPXWAN A protocol that negotiates end-to-end options for new links on startup. When a link comes up, the first IPX packets sent across are IPXWAN packets negotiating the options for the link. When the IPXWAN options have been successfully determined, normal IPX transmission begins, and no more IPXWAN packets are sent. Defined by RFC 1362.

ISDN (Integrated Services Digital Network) Communication protocol, offered by telephone companies, that permits telephone networks to carry data, voice, and other source traffic.

ISL (Inter-Switch Link) Cisco's protocol for trunking VLANs over Fast Ethernet.

ITU-T (International Telecommunication Union Telecommunication Standardization Sector) International body dedicated to the development of worldwide standards for telecommunications technologies. ITU-T is the successor to CCITT.

jabbers   Long, continuous frames exceeding 1518 bytes that prevent all stations on the Ethernet network from transmitting data. Jabbering violates CSMA/CD implementation by prohibiting stations from transmitting data.

jam pattern   Initiated by Ethernet transmitting station when a collision is detected during transmission.

KB   Kilobyte. Approximately 1,000 bytes.

Kb   Kilobit. Approximately 1,000 bits.

KBps   Kilobytes per second.

Kbps   Kilobits per second.

keepalive interval   Period of time between keepalive messages sent by a network device.

keepalive message   Message sent by one network device to inform another network device that it is still active.

LAN (local area network)   High-speed, low-error data network covering a relatively small geographic area. LANs connect workstations, peripherals, terminals, and other devices in a single building or other geographically limited area. LAN standards specify cabling and signaling at the physical and Data Link layers of the OSI model. Ethernet, FDDI, and Token Ring are the most widely used LAN technologies.

LANE (LAN Emulation)   Technology that allows an ATM network to function as a LAN backbone. In this situation LANE provides multicast and broadcast support, address mapping (MAC-to-ATM), and virtual circuit management.

LAPB (Link Access Procedure, Balanced)   The Data Link layer protocol in the X.25 protocol stack. LAPB is a bit-oriented protocol derived from HDLC.

LAPD (Link Access Procedure on the D channel)   ISDN Data Link layer protocol for the D channel. LAPD was derived from the LAPB protocol and is designed to satisfy the signaling requirements of ISDN basic access. Defined by ITU-T Recommendations Q.920 and Q.921.

LAPF   Data link standard for Frame Relay.

late collision   Collision that is detected only after a station places a complete frame of the network.

latency   The amount of time elapsed between the time a device requests access to a network and the time it is allowed to transmit; or, amount of time between the point at which a device receives a frame and the time that frame is forwarded out the destination port.

LCP (Link Control Protocol)   A protocol used with PPP, which establishes, configures, and tests data-link connections.

leased line   Transmission line reserved by a communications carrier for the private use of a customer. A leased line is a type of dedicated line.

LEC (LAN Emulation Client)   Performs data forwarding, address resolution, and other control functions for a single end system within a single ELAN. Each LEC has a unique ATM address, and is associated with one or more MAC addresses reachable through that ATM address.

LECS (LAN Emulation Configuration Server)   Assigns LANE clients to ELANs by directing them to the LES that corresponds to the ELAN. There can be logically one LECS per administrative domain, which serves all ELANs within that domain.

LES (LAN Emulation Server)   Implements the control function for an ELAN. There can be only one logical LES per ELAN. It has a unique ATM address.

link   Network communications channel consisting of a circuit or transmission path and all related equipment between a sender and a receiver. Most often used to refer to a WAN connection. Sometimes called a line or a transmission link.

link-state routing algorithm   Routing algorithm in which each router broadcasts or multicasts information regarding the cost of reaching each of its neighbors to all nodes in the internetwork. Link state algorithms require that routers maintain a consistent view of the network and are therefore not prone to routing loops.

LLC (Logical Link Control)   Higher of two Data Link layer sublayers defined by the IEEE. The LLC sublayer handles error control, flow control, framing, and MAC-sublayer addressing. The most common LLC protocol is IEEE 802.2, which includes both connectionless and connection-oriented types.

LMI (Local Management Interface)   A set of enhancements to the basic Frame Relay specification. LMI includes support for keepalives, a multicast mechanism; global addressing, and a status mechanism.

load balancing   In routing, the ability of a router to distribute traffic over all its network ports that are the same distance from the destination address. Load balancing increases the utilization of network segments, thus increasing total effective network bandwidth.

local loop   A line from the premises of a telephone subscriber to the telephone company central office.

LocalTalk   Apple Computer's proprietary baseband protocol that operates at the Dat Link and Physical layers of the OSI reference model. LocalTalk uses CSMA/CA and supports transmissions at speeds of 230.4 Kbps.

loop   A situation in which packets never reach their destination, but are forwarded in a cycle repeatedly through a group of network nodes.

MAC (Media Access Control)   Lower of the two sublayers of the Data Link layer defined by the IEEE. The MAC sublayer handles access to shared media.

MAC address   Standardized Data Link layer address that is required for every port or device that connects to a LAN. Other devices in the network use these addresses to locate specific ports in the network and to create and update routing tables and data structures. MAC addresses are 48 bits long and are controlled by the IEEE. Also known as a hardware address, a MAC-layer address, or a physical address.

MAN (metropolitan-area network)   A network that spans a metropolitan area. Generally, a MAN spans a larger geographic area than a LAN, but a smaller geographic area than a WAN.

Mb   Megabit. Approximately 1,000,000 bits.

Mbps   Megabits per second.

media   The various physical environments through which transmission signals pass. Common network media include cable (twisted-pair, coaxial, and fiber optic) and the atmosphere (through which microwave, laser, and infrared transmission occurs). Sometimes referred to as physical media.

Media Access Control   *See* MAC.

mesh   Network topology in which devices are organized in a segmented manner with redundant interconnections strategically placed between network nodes.

message   Application layer logical grouping of information, often composed of a number of lower-layer logical groupings such as packets.

MIB (Management Information Base)   Database for network management information; it is used and maintained by a network management protocol such as SNMP.

MSAU (multistation access unit)   A wiring concentrator to which all end stations in a Token Ring network connect. Sometimes abbreviated MAU.

multiaccess network   A network that allows multiple devices to connect and communicate by sharing the same medium, such as a LAN.

multicast   A single packet copied by the network and sent to a specific subset of network addresses. These addresses are specified in the Destination Address field.

multicast address   A single address that refers to multiple network devices. Sometimes called a group address.

multiplexing   A technique that allows multiple logical signals to be transmitted simultaneously across a single physical channel.

mux   A multiplexing device. A mux combines multiple input signals for transmission over a single line. The signals are demultiplexed, or separated, before they are used at the receiving end.

NACK (negative acknowledgment)   A response sent from a receiving device to a sending device indicating that the information received contained errors.

name resolution   The process of associating a symbolic name with a network location or address.

NAT (Network Address Translation)   A technique for reducing the need for globally unique IP addresses. NAT allows an organization with addresses that may conflict with others in the IP address space, to connect to the Internet by translating those addresses into unique ones within the globally routable address space.

NBMA (nonbroadcast multiaccess) Term describing a multiaccess network that either does not support broadcasting (such as X.25) or in which broadcasting is not feasible.

NBP (Name Binding Protocol) AppleTalk transport level protocol that translates a character string name into the DDP address of the corresponding socket client.

NCP (Network Control Protocol) Protocols that establish and configure various network layer protocols. Used for AppleTalk over PPP.

NDS (NetWare Directory Services) A feature added in NetWare 4.0 as a replacement for individual bindaries. NDS allows NetWare and related resources to be grouped in a tree hierarchy to better provide central administration.

NetBIOS (Network Basic Input/Output System) An application programming interface used by applications on an IBM LAN to request services from lower-level network processes such as session establishment and termination, and information transfer.

netmask A number, usually used as a bit-mask, to separate an address into its network portion and host portion.

NetWare A network operating system developed by Novell, Inc. Provides remote file access, print services, and numerous other distributed network services.

network Collection of computers, printers, routers, switches, and other devices that are able to communicate with each other over some transmission medium.

network interface Border between a carrier network and a privately owned installation.

Network layer   Layer 3 of the OSI reference model. This layer provides connectivity and path selection between two end systems. The Network layer is the layer at which routing takes place.

NLSP (NetWare Link Services Protocol)   Link-state routing protocol for IPX based on IS-IS.

node   Endpoint of a network connection or a junction common to two or more lines in a network. Nodes can be processors, controllers, or workstations. Nodes, which vary in their functional capabilities, can be interconnected by links, and serve as control points in the network.

NVRAM (nonvolatile RAM)   RAM that retains its contents when a device is powered off.

ODI   Novell's Open Data-link Interface.

OSI reference model (Open System Interconnection reference model)   A network architectural framework developed by ISO and ITU-T. The model describes seven layers, each of which specifies a particular network. The lowest layer, called the Physical layer, is closest to the media technology. The highest layer, the Application layer, is closest to the user. The OSI reference model is widely used as a way of understanding network functionality.

OSPF (Open Shortest Path First)   A link-state, hierarchical IGP routing algorithm, which includes features such as least-cost routing, multipath routing, and load balancing. OSPF was based on an early version of the IS-IS protocol.

out-of-band signaling   Transmission using frequencies or channels outside the frequencies or channels used for transfer of normal data. Out-of-band signaling is often used for error reporting when normal channels are unusable for communicating with network devices.

packet   Logical grouping of information that includes a header containing control information and (usually) user data. Packets are most often used to refer to network layer units of data. The terms datagram, frame, message, and segment are also used to describe logical information groupings at various layers of the OSI reference model, and in various technology circles. *See also* **PDU.**

packet analyzer   A software package (also sometimes including specialized hardware) used to monitor network traffic. Most packet analyzer packages will also do packet decoding, making the packets easier for humans to read.

packet burst   Allows multiple packets to be transmitted between Novell clients and servers in response to a single read or write request. It also allows NCP connections to greatly improve throughput by reducing the number of acknowledgments.

packet starvation effect   On Ethernet, when packets experience latencies up to 100 times the average, or completely starve out due to 16 collisions. Occurs as a result of the CSMA/CD implementation.

PAP (Password Authentication Protocol)   Authentication protocol that allows PPP peers to authenticate one another. The remote router attempting to connect to the local router is required to send an authentication request. Unlike CHAP, PAP passes the password and host name or username in the clear (unencrypted). PAP does not itself prevent unauthorized access, but merely identifies the remote end. The router or access server then determines if that user is allowed access. PAP is supported only on PPP lines.

partial mesh   Term describing a network in which devices are organized in a mesh topology, with some network nodes organized in a full mesh, but with others that are only connected to one or two other nodes in the network. A partial mesh does not provide the level of redundancy of a full mesh topology, but is less expensive to implement. Partial mesh topologies are generally used in the peripheral networks that connect to a fully meshed backbone. *See also* **full mesh; mesh.**

PDU (protocol data unit)   The OSI term for a packet.

Physical layer   Layer 1 of the OSI reference model; it corresponds with the Physical control layer in the SNA model. The Physical layer defines the specifications for activating, maintaining, and deactivating the physical link between end systems.

ping (packet internet groper)   ICMP echo message and its reply. Often used in IP networks to test the reachability of a network device.

poison reverse updates   Routing updates that explicitly indicate that a network or subnet is unreachable, rather than implying that a network is unreachable by not including it in updates. Poison reverse updates are sent to defeat large routing loops.

port   1. Interface on an internetworking device (such as a router). 2. In IP terminology, an upper-layer process that receives information from lower layers. Ports are numbered, and each numbered port is associated with a specific process. For example, SMTP is associated with port 25. A port number is also known as a well-known address. 3. To rewrite software or microcode so that it will run on a different hardware platform or in a different software environment than that for which it was originally designed.

PPP (Point-to-Point Protocol)   A successor to SLIP that provides router-to-router and host-to-network connections over synchronous and asynchronous circuits. Whereas SLIP was designed to work with IP, PPP was designed to work with several network layer protocols, such as IP, IPX, and ARA. PPP also has built-in security mechanisms, such as CHAP and PAP. PPP relies on two protocols: LCP and NCP. *See also* **CHAP**; **LCP**; **NCP**; **PAP**; **SLIP**.

Presentation layer   Layer 6 of the OSI reference model. This layer ensures that information sent by the Application layer of one system will be readable by the Application layer of another. The Presentation layer is also concerned with the data structures used by programs and therefore negotiates data transfer syntax for the Application layer.

PRI (Primary Rate Interface)   ISDN interface to primary rate access. Primary rate access consists of a single 64-Kbps D channel plus 23 (T1) or 30 (E1) B channels for voice or data. Compare to **BRI**.

protocol   Formal description of a set of rules and conventions that govern how devices on a network exchange information.

protocol stack   Set of related communications protocols that operate together and, as a group, address communication at some or all of the seven layers of the OSI reference model. Not every protocol stack covers each layer of the model, and often a single protocol in the stack will address a number of layers at once. TCP/IP is a typical protocol stack.

proxy ARP (proxy Address Resolution Protocol)   Variation of the ARP protocol in which an intermediate device (for example, a router) sends an ARP response on behalf of an end node to the requesting host. Proxy ARP can lessen bandwidth use on slow-speed WAN links. *See also* **ARP**.

PVC (permanent virtual circuit)   Permanently established virtual circuits save bandwidth in situations where certain virtual circuits must exist all the time, such as during circuit establishment and tear down.

Q.921   ITU (International Telecommunication Union) standard document for ISDN Layer 2 (Data Link layer).

Q.931   ITU (International Telecommunication Union) standard document for ISDN Layer 3.

query   Message used to inquire about the value of some variable or set of variables.

queue   A backlog of packets stored in buffers and waiting to be forwarded over a router interface.

RAM (random-access memory)   Volatile memory that can be read and written by a computer.

reassembly   The putting back together of an IP datagram at the destination after it has been fragmented either at the source or at an intermediate node. *See also* **fragmentation**.

reload   The event of a Cisco router rebooting, or the command that causes the router to reboot.

reverse path forwarding   If a packet server receives a packet through different interfaces from the same source, the server drops all packets after the first.

reverse Telnet   Using a router to connect to a serial device, frequently a modem, in order to connect out. For example, telnetting to a special port on an access router in order to access a modem to dial out. Called "reverse" because it's the opposite of the router's usual function, to accept calls into the modem.

RFC (Request For Comments)   Document series used as the primary means for communicating information about the Internet. Some RFCs are designated by the IAB as Internet standards.

ring   Connection of two or more stations in a logically circular topology. Information is passed sequentially between active stations. Token Ring, FDDI, and CDDI are based on this topology.

ring topology   Network topology that consists of a series of repeaters connected to one another by unidirectional transmission links to form a single closed loop. Each station on the network connects to the network at a repeater.

RIP (ROUTING INFORMATION PROTOCOL)   A routing protocol for TCP/IP networks. The most common routing protocol in the Internet. RIP uses hop count as a routing metric.

RMON (Remote monitor)   A set of SNMP standards used to collect statistical network information. RMON is divided into groups, with each additional group providing more statistical information.

ROM (read-only memory)   Nonvolatile memory that can be read, but not written, by the computer.

routed protocol   Protocol that carries user data so it can be routed by a router. A router must be able to interpret the logical internetwork as specified by that routed protocol. Examples of routed protocols include AppleTalk, DECNet, and IP.

router   Network layer device that uses one or more metrics to determine the optimal path along which network traffic should be forwarded. Routers forward packets from one network to another based on network layer information.

routing   Process of finding a path to a destination host.

routing metric   Method by which a routing algorithm determines preferability of one route over another. This information is stored in routing tables. Metrics include bandwidth, communication cost, delay, hop count, load, MTU, path cost, and reliability. Sometimes referred to simply as a metric.

routing protocol   Protocol that accomplishes routing through the implementation of a specific routing algorithm. Examples of routing protocols include IGRP, OSPF, and RIP.

routing table   Table stored in a router or some other internetworking device that keeps track of routes to particular network destinations and, in some cases, metrics associated with those routes.

routing update   Message sent from a router to indicate network reachability and associated cost information. Routing updates are typically sent at regular intervals and after a change in network topology. Compare with **flash update**.

RSRB (remote source-route bridging)   Equivalent to an SRB over WAN links.

RTMP (Routing Table Maintenance Protocol)   The protocol used by AppleTalk devices to communicate routing information. Structurally similar to RIP.

runts   Ethernet frames that are smaller than 64 bytes.

SAP (service access point)   1. Field defined by the IEEE 802.2 specification that is part of an address specification. Thus, the destination plus the DSAP define the recipient of a packet. The same applies to the SSAP. 2. Service Advertising Protocol. IPX protocol that provides a means of informing network routers and servers of the location of available network resources and services.

SAS (single attachment station)   Device attached to the primary ring of an FDDI ring. Also known as a Class B station. *See also* **DAS.**

segment   1. Section of a network that is bounded by bridges, routers, or switches. 2. In a LAN using a bus topology, a segment is a continuous electrical circuit that is often connected to other such segments with repeaters. 3. Term used in the TCP specification to describe a single Transport layer unit of information.

serial transmission   Method of data transmission in which the bits of a data character are transmitted sequentially over a single channel.

session   1. Related set of communications transactions between two or more network devices. 2. In SNA, a logical connection that enables two NAUs to communicate.

Session layer   Layer 5 of the OSI reference model. This layer establishes, manages, and terminates sessions between applications and manages data exchange between Presentation layer entities. Corresponds to the data flow control layer of the SNA model. *See also* **Application layer; Data Link layer; Network layer; Physical layer; Presentation layer; Transport layer.**

sliding window flow control   Method of flow control in which a receiver gives a transmitter permission to transmit data until a window is full. When the window is full, the transmitter must stop transmitting until the receiver acknowledges some of the data, or advertises a larger window. TCP, other transport protocols, and several Data Link layer protocols use this method of flow control.

SLIP (Serial Line Internet Protocol)   Uses a variation of TCP/IP to make point-to-point serial connections. Succeeded by PPP.

SNAP (Subnetwork Access Protocol)   Internet protocol that operates between a network entity in the subnetwork and a network entity in the end system. SNAP specifies a standard method of encapsulating IP datagrams and ARP messages on IEEE networks.

SNMP (Simple Network Management Protocol)   Network management protocol used almost exclusively in TCP/IP networks. SNMP provides a means to monitor and control network devices, and to manage configurations, statistics collection, performance, and security.

SNMP Manager   Software used to manage network devices via SNMP. Often includes graphical representation of the network and individual devices, and the ability to set and respond to SNMP traps.

SNMP Trap   A threshold of some sort which, when reached, causes the SNMP managed device to notify the SNMP Manager. This allows for immediate notification, instead of having to wait for the SNMP Manager to poll again.

socket   Software structure operating as a communications endpoint within a network device.

SONET (Synchronous Optical Network)   High-speed synchronous network specification developed by Bellcore and designed to run on optical fiber.

source address   Address of a network device that is sending data.

spanning tree   Loop-free subset of a network topology. *See also* **Spanning Tree Protocol.**

Spanning Tree Protocol   Developed to eliminate loops in the network. The Spanning Tree Protocol ensures a loop-free path by placing one of the bridge ports in "blocking mode," preventing the forwarding of packets.

SPF (shortest path first algorithm)   Routing algorithm that sorts routes by length of path to determine a shortest-path spanning tree. Commonly used in link-state routing algorithms. Sometimes called Dijkstra's algorithm.

SPIDs (Service Profile Identifiers)   These function as addresses for B channels on ISDN BRI circuits. When call information is passed over the D channel, the SPIDs are used to identify which channel is being referred to. SPIDs are usually some variant of the phone number for the channel.

split-horizon updates   Routing technique in which information about routes is prevented from being advertised out the router interface through which that information was received. Split-horizon updates are used to prevent routing loops.

SPX (Sequenced Packet Exchange)   Reliable, connection-oriented protocol at the Transport layer that supplements the datagram service provided by IPX.

SR/TLB (source-route translational bridging)   Method of bridging that allows source-route stations to communicate with transparent bridge stations, using an intermediate bridge that translates between the two bridge protocols.

SRB (source-route bridging)   Method of bridging in Token Ring networks. In an SRB network, before data is sent to a destination, the entire route to that destination is predetermined in real time.

SRT (source-route transparent bridging)   IBM's merging of SRB and transparent bridging into one bridging scheme, which requires no translation between bridging protocols.

standard   Set of rules or procedures that are either widely used or officially specified.

star topology   LAN topology in which endpoints on a network are connected to a common central switch by point-to-point links. A ring topology that is organized as a star implements a unidirectional closed-loop star, instead of point-to-point links. Compare with **bus topology**, **ring topology**, and **tree topology**.

static route   Route that is explicitly configured and entered into the routing table. Static routes take precedence over routes chosen by dynamic routing protocols.

subinterface   A virtual interface defined as a logical subdivision of a physical interface.

subnet address   Portion of an IP address that is specified as the subnetwork by the subnet mask. *See also* **IP address; subnet mask; subnetwork.**

subnet mask   32-bit address mask used in IP to indicate the bits of an IP address that are being used for the subnet address. Sometimes referred to simply as mask. *See also* **address mask; IP address.**

subnetwork   1. In IP networks, a network sharing a particular subnet address. 2. Subnetworks are networks arbitrarily segmented by a network administrator in order to provide a multilevel, hierarchical routing structure while shielding the subnetwork from the addressing complexity of attached networks. Sometimes called a subnet.

SVC (switched virtual circuit)   Virtual circuit that can be established dynamically on demand, and which is torn down after a transmission is complete. SVCs are used when data transmission is sporadic.

switch   1. Network device that filters, forwards, and floods frames based on the destination address of each frame. The switch operates at the Data Link layer of the OSI model. 2. General term applied to an electronic or mechanical device that allows a connection to be established as necessary and terminated when there is no longer a session to support.

T1   Digital WAN carrier facility. T1 transmits DS-1-formatted data at 1.544 Mbps through the telephone-switching network, using AMI or B8ZS coding. Compare with **E1**. *See also* **AMI**; **B8ZS**.

TCP (Transmission Control Protocol)   Connection-oriented Transport layer protocol that provides reliable full-duplex data transmission. TCP is part of the TCP/IP protocol stack.

TCP/IP (Transmission Control Protocol/Internet Protocol)   Common name for the suite of protocols developed by the U.S. DoD in the 1970s to support the construction of worldwide internetworks. TCP and IP are the two best-known protocols in the suite.

TDR (time-domain reflectometer)   A TDR test is used to measure the length of a cable, or the distance to a break. This is accomplished by sending a signal down a wire, and measuring how long it takes for an echo of the signal to bounce back.

TEI (Terminal Endpoint Identifier)   Field in the LAPD address that identifies a device on an ISDN interface.

TFTP (Trivial File Transfer Protocol)   Simplified version of FTP that allows files to be transferred from one computer to another over a network.

three-way handshake   The three required packets to set up a TCP connection. It consists of a SYN packet, acknowledged by a SYN+ACK packet, which is finally acknowledged by an ACK packet. During this handshake, sequence numbers are exchanged.

throughput   Rate of information arriving at, and possibly passing through, a particular point in a network system.

timeout   Event that occurs when one network device expects to hear from another network device within a specified period of time, but does not. A timeout usually results in a retransmission of information or the termination of the session between the two devices.

token   Frame that contains only control information. Possession of the token allows a network device to transmit data onto the network. *See also* **token passing**.

token passing   Method by which network devices access the physical medium based on possession of a small frame called a token. Compare this method to **circuit switching** and **contention**.

Token Ring   Token-passing LAN developed and supported by IBM. Token Ring runs at 4 or 16 Mbps over a ring topology. Similar to IEEE 802.5. *See also* **IEEE 802.5**; **ring topology**; **token passing**.

TokenTalk   Apple Computer's data-link product that allows an AppleTalk network to be connected by Token Ring cables.

transparent bridging   Bridging scheme used in Ethernet and IEEE 802.3 networks. Allows bridges to pass frames along one hop at a time, based on tables that associate end nodes with bridge ports. Bridges are transparent to network end nodes.

Transport layer   Layer 4 of the OSI reference model. This layer is responsible for reliable network communication between end nodes. The Transport layer provides mechanisms for the establishment, maintenance, and termination of virtual circuits, transport fault detection and recovery, and information flow control.

tree topology   A LAN topology that resembles a bus topology. Tree networks can contain branches with multiple nodes. In a tree topology, transmissions from a station propagate the length of the physical medium, and are received by all other stations.

twisted-pair   Relatively low-speed transmission medium consisting of two insulated wires arranged in a regular spiral pattern. The wires can be shielded or unshielded. Twisted-pair is common in telephony applications and is increasingly common in data networks.

UDP (User Datagram Protocol)   Connectionless Transport layer protocol in the TCP/IP protocol stack. UDP is a simple protocol that exchanges datagrams without acknowledgments or guaranteed delivery, requiring that error processing and retransmission be handled by other protocols. UDP is defined in RFC 768.

unicast   Regular IP packet sent from a single host to a single host.

UTP (unshielded twisted-pair)   Four-pair wire medium used in a variety of networks. UTP does not require the fixed spacing between connections that is necessary with coaxial-type connections.

VCC (virtual channel connection)   Logical circuit for carrying data between two end points in an ATM network.

virtual circuit   Logical circuit created to ensure reliable communication between two network devices. A virtual circuit is defined by a VPI/VCI pair, and can be either permanent or switched. Virtual circuits are used in Frame Relay and X.25. In ATM, a virtual circuit is called a virtual channel. Sometimes abbreviated VC.

VLAN (virtual LAN)   Group of devices on one or more LANs that are configured (using management software) so that they can communicate as if they were attached to the same wire, when in fact they are located on a number of different LAN segments. Because VLANs are based on logical instead of physical connections, they are extremely flexible.

VLSM (Variable-length Subnet Masking)   Ability to specify a different length subnet mask for the same network number at different locations in the network. VLSM can help optimize available address space.

VTY (Virtual Terminal)   VTYs work like physical terminal ports on routers so they can be managed across a network, usually via Telnet.

WAN (wide area network)   Data communications network that serves users across a broad geographic area and often uses transmission devices provided by common carriers. Frame Relay, SMDS, and X.25 are examples of WANs. Compare with **LAN** and **MAN**.

wildcard mask   32-bit quantity used in conjunction with an IP address to determine which bits in an IP address should be matched and ignored when comparing that address with another IP address. A wildcard mask is specified when defining access list statements.

X.121   ITU-T standard describing an addressing scheme used in X.25 networks. X.121 addresses are sometimes called IDNs (International Data Numbers).

X.21   ITU-T standard for serial communications over synchronous digital lines. The X.21 protocol is used primarily in Europe and Japan.

X.25   ITU-T standard that defines how connections between DTE and DCE are maintained for remote terminal access and computer communications in public data networks. X.25 specifies LAPB, a Data Link layer protocol, and PLP, a network layer protocol. Frame Relay has to some degree superseded X.25.

ZIP broadcast storm   Occurs when a route advertisement without a corresponding zone triggers the network with a flood of Zone Information Protocol requests.

zone   In AppleTalk, a logical group of network devices.

Zone Information Protocol (ZIP)   A protocol used in AppleTalk to communicate information about AppleTalk zone names and cable ranges.

Zone Information Table (ZIT)   A table of zone name to cable range mappings in AppleTalk. These tables are maintained in each AppleTalk router.

Custom Corporate Network Training

Train on Cutting Edge Technology   We can bring the best in skill-based training to your facility to create a real-world hands-on training experience. Global Knowledge has invested millions of dollars in network hardware and software to train our students on the same equipment they will work with on the job. Our relationships with vendors allow us to incorporate the latest equipment and platforms into your on-site labs.

Maximize Your Training Budget   Global Knowledge provides experienced instructors, comprehensive course materials, and all the networking equipment needed to deliver high quality training. You provide the students; we provide the knowledge.

Avoid Travel Expenses   On-site courses allow you to schedule technical training at your convenience, saving time, expense, and the opportunity cost of travel away from the workplace.

Discuss Confidential Topics   Private on-site training permits the open discussion of sensitive issues such as security, access, and network design. We can work with your existing network's proprietary files while demonstrating the latest technologies.

Customize Course Content   Global Knowledge can tailor your courses to include the technologies and the topics which have the greatest impact on your business. We can complement your internal training efforts or provide a total solution to your training needs.

Corporate Pass   The Corporate Pass Discount Program rewards our best network training customers with preferred pricing on public courses, discounts on multimedia training packages, and an array of career planning services.

Global Knowledge Training Lifecycle   Supporting the Dynamic and Specialized Training Requirements of Information Technology Professionals

- Define Profile
- Assess Skills
- Design Training
- Deliver Training
- Test Knowledge
- Update Profile
- Use New Skills

College Credit Recommendation Program   The American Council on Education's CREDIT program recommends 53 Global Knowledge courses for college credit. Now our network training can help you earn your college degree while you learn the technical skills needed for your job. When you attend an ACE-certified Global Knowledge course and pass the associated exam, you earn college credit recommendations for that course. Global Knowledge can establish a transcript record for you with ACE, which you can use to gain credit at a college or as a written record of your professional training that you can attach to your resume.

Registration Information

In the US:

CALL: 1 (888) 762-4442

FAX: 1 (919) 469-7070

VISIT OUR WEBSITE:

www.globalknowledge.com

MAIL CHECK AND THIS
FORM TO:

Global Knowledge

Suite 200

114 Edinburgh South

P.O. Box 1187

Cary, NC 27512

In Canada:

CALL: 1 (800) 465-2226

FAX: 1 (613) 567-3899

VISIT OUR WEBSITE:

www.globalknowledge.com.ca

MAIL CHECK AND THIS
FORM TO:

Global Knowledge

Suite 1601

393 University Ave.

Toronto, ON M5G 1E6

COURSE FEE: The fee covers course tuition, refreshments, and all course materials. Any parking expenses that may be incurred are not included. Payment or government training form must be received six business days prior to the course date. We will also accept Visa/MasterCard and American Express. For non-U.S. credit card users, charges will be in U.S. funds and will be converted by your credit card company. Checks drawn on Canadian banks in Canadian funds are acceptable.

COURSE SCHEDULE: Registration is at 8:00 a.m. on the first day. The program begins at 8:30 a.m. and concludes at 4:30 p.m. each day.

CANCELLATION POLICY: Cancellation and full refund will be allowed if written cancellation is received in our office at least six business days prior to the course start date. Registrants who do not attend the course or do not cancel more than six business days in advance are responsible for the full registration fee; you may transfer to a later date provided the course fee has been paid in full. Substitutions may be made at any time. If Global Knowledge must cancel a course for any reason, liability is limited to the registration fee only.

GLOBAL KNOWLEDGE: Global Knowledge programs are developed and presented by industry professionals with "real-world" experience. Designed to help professionals meet today's interconnectivity and interoperability challenges, most of our programs feature hands-on labs that incorporate state-of-the-art communication components and equipment.

ON-SITE TEAM TRAINING: Bring Global Knowledge's powerful training programs to your company. At Global Knowledge, we will custom design courses to meet your specific network requirements. Call 1 (919) 461-8686 for more information.

YOUR GUARANTEE: Global Knowledge believes its courses offer the best possible training in this field. If during the first day you are not satisfied and wish to withdraw from the course, simply notify the instructor, return all course materials, and receive a 100% refund.

REGISTRATION INFORMATION:

Course title ——————————————————————————————

Course location ————————————————— Course date ——————

Name/title ————————————————— Company ——————

Name/title ————————————————— Company ——————

Name/title ————————————————— Company ——————

Address ————————— Telephone ————— Fax —————

City ————— State/Province ————— Zip/Postal Code —————

Credit card ————— Card # ————————— Expiration date —————

Signature —————————————————————————————